MONEY, INTEREST, AND PRICES

MONEY, INTEREST, AND PRICES

An Integration of Monetary and Value Theory

by DON PATINKIN

The Eliezer Kaplan School of Economics and Social Sciences

The Hebrew University, Jerusalem

ROW, PETERSON AND COMPANY

Evanston, Illinois   White Plains, New York

Published by
Row, Peterson and Company
1956

Second Printing 1957

5205

Printed in Great Britain by
William Clowes and Sons, Limited, London and Beccles

To my Mother and Father

PREFACE

This work is the outgrowth of ideas first presented in a doctoral dissertation submitted to the University of Chicago in 1947 and then further developed in a series of articles published in various journals and anthologies through the years 1948 to 1954. The reader interested in consulting these articles will find them listed in the Bibliography at the end of the book. The book itself, however, makes but few explicit references to them. Correspondingly, it makes practically no attempt to show how its argument is specifically related to that of these earlier articles. It must also be emphasized that, with the exception of a few pages, the actual exposition of this book is entirely new. It represents an extensive reworking, elaboration, and refinement of the basic ideas of these articles within a much more systematic and comprehensive framework than was originally achieved.

Furthermore—and most gratifyingly—the text of the present book has been able to dispense with the apparently forbidding mathematical apparatus which marked the first of these articles. The argument is instead developed by the use of the more familiar literary and graphical techniques of modern economic analysis. There is an extensive Mathematical Appendix, which will, I hope, be of help and interest to the mathematically inclined reader. But this Appendix is not necessary for an understanding of the text. Indeed, the opposite is true: the text is necessary for a full understanding of the Appendix.

A similar statement holds for the Supplementary Notes and Studies in the Literature. These, too, are not necessary for the text, but the text is necessary for them. In particular, their full meaning can be understood only after reading Chapters VIII and XV, whereas these chapters can be understood without the Notes by the reader willing to accept their interpretations of doctrinal history without insisting upon detailed documentation from the literature.

The nature of the argument of this book has made it necessary to use numerous internal cross-references. These are of two types. First, there are those to the Mathematical Appendix and Supplementary Notes. Their purpose is to indicate to the reader the nature of the additional information that he can find in these places should he be interested in consulting them. Second, there are the cross-references to the text itself. Their main purpose is to remind the reader where—if need be—he can refresh his memory about an earlier conclusion which is being used as the basis for a further development in the argument. The reader who has no need for these reminders and who is interested only in the text itself can therefore ignore all cross-references and proceed with his reading undisturbed. On the other hand, anyone who wishes to follow up these references will find his task simplified by the fact that each page of this book carries the appropriate chapter-section number (in the case of the text), appendix-section number (in the case of the Mathematical Appendix), or note-section number (in the case of the Supplementary Notes).

In the process of working out the ideas of this book, I have been particularly fortunate in having had the opportunity of stimulating discussions—both oral and written, published and unpublished—with many individuals. I regret that it is impractical to name them all here. But I must make explicit my indebtedness to Kenneth J. Arrow, Leonid Hurwicz, and especially Trygve Haavelmo for the many illuminating informal discussions I enjoyed with each of them during the year (1946–47) I spent as a Social Science Research Council predoctoral fellow at the Cowles Commission for Research in Economics.

At a later stage I benefited greatly from the debate which developed in the journals as a consequence of the articles referred to above. With one or two minor exceptions, I have seen no point in returning in this book to these earlier polemics; the interested reader will, however, find the relevant critical articles and my replies to them listed in Supplementary Note M. Needless to say, the necessity for preparing these replies was an invaluable stimulus toward a constant reworking and improving of the argument and its exposition. I am particularly grateful in this respect to Herbert Stein, for clarifying the nature of open-market operations; to W. Braddock Hickman, for pointing out an incorrect usage of the concept "functional dependence" in one of the earlier articles; and to Frank H. Hahn, for showing the limitations of the one-period static model in terms of which the argument was initially developed.

I hope that without being presumptuous I may also indicate my general indebtedness to certain basic works in economic theory—an indebtedness which, by its very nature, cannot find adequate expression in mere footnote references. The analytical apparatus developed by J. R. Hicks in his *Value and Capital* is obviously fundamental to Part One. There is a correspondingly obvious dependence of Part Two on the macroeconomic concepts and techniques of J. M. Keynes'

General Theory and the later Keynesian literature. Crucial use has been made at various points in the book of the dynamic stability analysis developed by P. A. Samuelson in his *Foundations of Economic Analysis*. The influence of A. W. Marget's *Theory of Prices* on some of the Supplementary Notes and Studies in the Literature will also be evident. And from the text the reader will likewise see how much my thinking has been colored by Knut Wicksell's classic *Interest and Prices*.

I have more immediate debts to Professor Martin Bronfenbrenner, Mr. Nadav Halevi, and Professor William Jaffé, for providing valuable criticisms of earlier drafts of the text; to my colleague Professor Aryeh Dvoretzky, for writing the very interesting Mathematical Appendix to Chapter VII; and to many friends abroad for sending copies of materials that were not otherwise available.

It is a distinct pleasure also to express my deep gratitude and indebtedness to three successive classes of graduate students at the Hebrew University, Jerusalem. Stimulating contact with them—both in and out of seminars—has been a most valuable source of criticisms and suggestions. By their willingness to serve as critical "guinea pigs" for the earlier drafts of the text of this book, they have also helped repeatedly to indicate points of ambiguity and difficulty that needed further clarification. Once again, I regret that it is impractical to acknowledge all this help more explicitly. But I cannot let go unmentioned my special debts to Mr. Nissan Liviatan, whose valuable criticisms have been noted in Chapter XIII, and, in particular, to Mr. Tsvi Goldberger, whose fruitful suggestions and penetrating remarks have been indicated at various points in the text. I have also benefited from Mr. Goldberger's meticulous and conscientious assistance on various technical matters. Similarly, I am indebted to Mr. Azriel Levi, who has checked the computations of the Mathematical Appendix.

I wish finally to extend my thanks to Mrs. Aliza Argov, Mrs. Esther Copperman, and Mrs. Judith Schorr, for carefully seeing the typescript through its various drafts; to Miss Gila Abramowitz, for loyally providing technical assistance; and to the Eliezer Kaplan School of Economics and Social Sciences of the Hebrew University, for a research grant that made this technical and typing assistance possible

DON PATINKIN

Jerusalem
April 1955

ACKNOWLEDGMENTS

Appreciation is expressed to the following for permission to quote certain works in this book:

George Allen and Unwin Ltd. *and* Richard D. Irwin, Inc., *for*

L. Walras, *Elements of Pure Economics*, trans. and ed. W. Jaffé (London: George Allen and Unwin Ltd., 1954; Homewood, Illinois: Richard D. Irwin, Inc., 1954).

Ernest Benn Ltd. *and* Harcourt, Brace and Co., *for*

G. Cassel, *Fundamental Thoughts in Economics* (London: T. Fisher Unwin Ltd., 1925; New York: Harcourt, Brace and Co., 1925) *and* G. Cassel, *The Theory of Social Economy*, trans. S. L. Barron (new revised ed.; London: Ernest Benn Ltd., 1932; New York: Harcourt, Brace and Co., 1932).

Mr. Irving N. Fisher, *for*

I. Fisher, *The Purchasing Power of Money* (New York: The Macmillan Company, 1911).

Harcourt, Brace and Co. *and* Macmillan & Co. Ltd., *for*

J. M. Keynes, *General Theory of Employment, Interest and Money* (New York: Harcourt, Brace and Co., 1936; London: Macmillan & Co. Ltd., 1936).

Longmans, Green & Co. Ltd., *for*

J. S. Mill, *Principles of Political Economy*, ed. W. J. Ashley (London: Longmans, Green & Co. Ltd., 1909).

Macmillan & Co. Ltd., *for*

A. Marshall, *Money Credit and Commerce* (London: Macmillan & Co. Ltd., 1923).

Routledge & Kegan Paul Ltd. *and* The Macmillan Company, *for*

K. Wicksell, *Lectures on Political Economy*, trans. E. Classen (2 vols.; London: George Routledge and Sons Ltd., 1935; New York: The Macmillan Company, 1935).

The Royal Economic Society, *for*

D. Patinkin, "Wicksell's 'Cumulative Process,'" *Economic Journal*, LXII (1952),

K. Wicksell, *Interest and Prices*, trans. R. F. Kahn (Macmillan & Co. Ltd., 1936), *and*

Works and Correspondence of David Ricardo, ed. P. Sraffa (Cambridge: Cambridge University Press, 1951).

TABLE OF CONTENTS

PART ONE. MICROECONOMICS

1 The nature of an exchange economy. The excess-demand curve. 2. The excess-demand function. 3. The determination of the equilibrium price. 4. Individual-experiments and market-experiments.

1. Introduction. The role of money. 2. Types of moneys and prices. 3. The individual's excess-demand functions for commodities: substitution, income, and real-balance effects. 4. The concept of "money illusion." 5. The individual's excess-demand function for money. 6. The market excess-demand functions.

MATHEMATICAL APPENDIX

xvi

SUPPLEMENTARY NOTES AND STUDIES IN THE LITERATURE

INTRODUCTION

Money buys goods, and goods do not buy money. The natural place, then, to study the workings of monetary forces is directly in the markets for goods. This will be our central theme.

It cannot be claimed that the theme is a novel one. In a crude way it even appears in the transactions approach to the quantity theory of money. Specifically, the familiar $MV = PT$ can be looked upon as determining the equilibrium price level, P, as the resultant of forces represented by the aggregate demand for goods, MV, on the one hand, and their aggregate supply, T, on the other. This equation, however, does little to exploit the full potentialities of the theme: It restricts monetary theory to the case of an aggregate demand function for goods which, to outward appearances, is independent of the rate of interest and directly proportionate to the quantity of money. This is as misleading as it is unrealistic, for it gives the false impression that the results obtained by analyzing this equation are necessarily dependent upon these extreme assumptions.

For some time, however, the transactions approach has been out of fashion. It has largely been replaced by monetary theories which shift the center of emphasis from the markets for goods to the market for money. The basic analytical tool of these theories—whether of the neoclassical or of the Keynesian variety—is the demand function for money. Correspondingly, their main concern is to describe this function and to apply it to the problems of monetary theory.

There is nothing logically wrong with this procedure. There is no reason why we should not enjoy the semantic liberty of saying that goods buy money and of describing, accordingly, a demand function for money. For if such a function is correctly described, it cannot but be the obverse image of the aggregate demand function for goods; hence, as we shall always be at pains to show, the side of the transaction from which the analysis is conducted cannot affect the conclusions reached.

Our criticism of these contemporary monetary theories is instead the pragmatic one that they fail to provide this obverse image. True, the neoclassical cash-balance equation is developed with particular regard for the alternative of spending money in the commodity market, and the

1

Keynesian liquidity-preference equation with a corresponding regard for the bond market. Nevertheless, in neither case is there a systematic attempt to analyze the full implications of these markets for the respective monetary equation. Consequently, as we shall see, these theories have led to incorrect descriptions of the demand function for money.

The alternative approach developed in this book begins with a description of the demand functions for commodities and bonds, with particular emphasis on the relatively neglected influence of money balances. These functions are then used to carry out a static and dynamic analysis of the central problems of monetary theory—the effects of changes in the quantity of money and shifts in liquidity preference on interest, prices, and employment. In this way we achieve an integration of monetary theory and value theory: the propositions of both theories are derived by applying the same analytical techniques to the same demand functions of the same markets. Such an integration is desirable, not only for showing these two theories to be special cases of a general theory of price, but also for enabling a simple and direct treatment of otherwise complicated problems.

Of necessity, our viewpoint is that of general-equilibrium analysis. For since monetary changes are assumed to affect all markets of the economy, their effects can be fully appreciated only by a simultaneous study of all these markets. Indeed, it will be seen that in most cases where we reach conclusions at variance with the accepted ones, it is a direct result of taking into account the dynamic interactions between price-level variations in the commodity market and interest-rate variations in the bond market. This interdependence of markets is a fundamental and recurring element of the argument.

For convenience, this argument is divided into two parts, according to the analytical technique used. In Part One the technique is that of microeconomics in the broad sense. That is, the market demand functions of this part continue to reflect the idiosyncrasies of the individuals' demand functions from which they are constructed. In Part Two the technique becomes that of macroeconomics. Here the idiosyncrasies disappear, and the market demand functions assume the aggregative forms familiar from Keynesian models.

It is, however, more instructive to outline the argument from the viewpoint of content rather than technique. Specifically, there is a major theme—running through both Parts One and Two—which deals with the monetary theory of an economy with full employment. This theme is developed by Chapters I–IV and IX–XII, and can be followed independently of the intervening chapters. There is a second major theme which deals with the monetary theory of an economy with in-

2

voluntary unemployment. This is developed by Chapters XIII–XIV. Then there are minor themes, which the reader is free to follow or ignore in accordance with his interests. In particular, Chapters V–VI develop a marginal-utility theory of money and thus base the conclusions of the aforementioned chapters on the principle of utility maximization. Chapter VII offers a solution to a basic methodological problem of monetary theory. Finally, Chapters VIII and XV use the analytical results of this book as the background against which to develop a detailed critique of neoclassical and Keynesian monetary theory.

The more general conclusions of our argument can be summarized as follows: The propositions of the quantity theory of money hold under conditions much less restrictive than those usually considered necessary by its advocates and, *a fortiori*, its critics. Conversely, the propositions of Keynesian monetary theory are much less general than the *General Theory* and later expositions would lead us to believe. But this in no way diminishes the relevance of Keynesian unemployment theory for the formulation of a practicable full-employment policy.

PART ONE

MICROECONOMICS

CHAPTER I

The Theory of a Barter

Exchange Economy

1. *The nature of an exchange economy. The excess-demand curve.* 2. *The excess-demand function.* 3. *The determination of the equilibrium price.* 4. *Individual-experiments and market-experiments.*

1. The present part of this book is devoted to the rigorous development of the monetary theory of an exchange economy. By initially restricting ourselves to such a simple economy, we are able to concentrate on the essential features of the analysis with a minimum of distracting complications. The ultimate justification for this procedure will emerge from the argument of Part Two. This shows that the basic conclusions of the monetary theory here developed are equally valid for more complex, and more realistic, economies.

In order to review the analytical techniques of value theory that will be needed in the present part, we start with a practice-run over the familiar ground of an exchange economy which is also a barter economy. This is the ground covered by the Pareto-Slutzky-Hicks theory of consumer's behavior. Accordingly, this section and the two subsequent ones are devoted to summarizing Hicks' development of this theory.[1]

The distinguishing mark of an exchange economy is the absence of production. That is, the goods available in this economy are produced in fixed quantities by extraneous forces which then arbitrarily and gratuitously distribute them among the individuals of the economy. Correspondingly, the sole economic problem of an exchange economy

---

[1] J. R. Hicks, *Value and Capital* (Oxford, 1939), Chapters I, II, V, and IX.

is the optimal redistribution of these goods among the various individuals. This is not quite as restrictive as it first sounds; for included among these goods are the personal services of the individuals themselves, and —in view of the possibility of leisure—the amount of these services can vary.

For simplicity, it is assumed that time in this economy is divided into

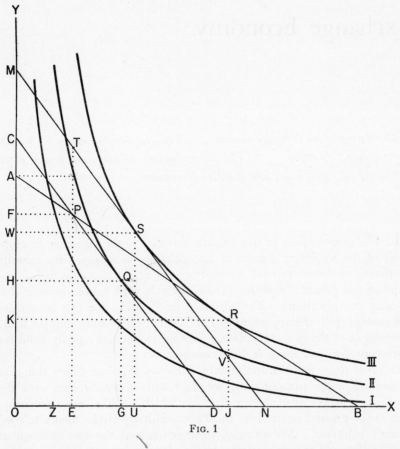

Fig. 1

discrete, uniform intervals called the "week." Each individual begins Monday morning of any given week with an initial collection of goods which, like the manna of the Children of Israel, has descended upon him "from the heavens" during the preceding night. On Monday afternoon he has the opportunity of bartering varying quantities of these initial goods for varying quantities of others which he prefers in their stead. The market in which these transactions take place is open only on Monday afternoon; no trading can take place at any other time during the week. It is assumed that the market is a perfectly competitive one.

The behavior of the individual in this market is now analyzed by use of an indifference map. In Figure 1, indifference curves *I*, *II*, and *III* correspond, respectively, to different, and ascending, levels of utility. As will be recalled, the slope of these curves has particular economic significance. Assume, for example, that the individual consumes the collection *Q*, consisting of *OG* units of *X* and *OH* units of *Y*. Assume now that we reduce his consumption of *X* by *EG* units and wish to determine the amount of *Y* with which we must compensate him in order to keep him just as well off as he was at the point *Q*; that is, the amount by which we must now vary his consumption of *Y* in order to enable him to remain at the same, fixed level of utility represented by the indifference curve *II*. From Figure 1 we see that this "compensating variation in *Y*" equals *HA*. The quotient *HA/EG* is thus the amount of *Y*, per unit of *X* taken away, with which we must compensate the individual. If we now take away smaller and smaller quantities of *X* from *OG*, this quotient approaches as a limit the slope of the line tangent to indifference curve *II* at *Q—HF/EG*. This slope measures "the marginal rate of substitution of *X* for *Y*" at the point *Q*. "It is the amount of *Y* which is needed by the individual in order to compensate him for the loss of a small unit of *X*."[2]

This slope also has meaning in terms of marginal utilities. Let the aforementioned "small unit" of *X* be the "marginal unit." Then, by definition, a decrease in the consumption of *X* by one such unit decreases the individual's total utility by an amount equal to the marginal utility of *X*. If, at the same time, his consumption of *Y* is increased by *HF/EG* units, there is an offsetting increase in total utility by an amount equal to the marginal utility of a unit of *Y times HF/EG* such units. By definition, the net effect of these compensating variations is to keep the individual's level of utility unchanged. That is, at the point *Q* the following relation must obtain:

$$\text{the marginal utility of } X = \frac{HF}{EG} \cdot \text{the marginal utility of } Y.$$

From this it follows that

$$\frac{\text{the marginal utility of } X}{\text{the marginal utility of } Y} = \frac{HF}{EG}$$

$$= \text{the marginal rate of substitution of } X \text{ for } Y.$$

---

2 *Ibid.*, pp. 14, 20.

This equality between the ratio of marginal utilities and the marginal rate of substitution will prove useful in Chapter VI.

Let us now turn from the individual's subjective calculations to the given objective conditions under which he must operate in the market. Assume that his initial collection of goods consists of *OE* units of *X* and *OF* of *Y*. This will be referred to alternatively as his "initial endowment." Assume further that the price of *X* in terms of *Y* with which the individual is confronted corresponds to the slope of the line *CD*. Then *CD* is his budget line, or budget restraint. It describes all the possible collections of goods into which the individual can—by bartering *X* for *Y* at the given market price—convert his initial collection *P*.

Under the conditions of Figure 1, the individual will obviously maximize his utility by bartering *HF* units of his initial endowment of *Y* in exchange for *EG* additional units of *X*. This brings him to the collection *Q*, for which the marginal rate of substitution of *X* for *Y* is equal to the price of *X* in terms of *Y*. The point *Q* thus denotes his "optimum collection" or "optimum position" under the given conditions. It describes the quantities of *X* and *Y* which the individual chooses to consume. Correspondingly, *OG* and *OH* are called the "amounts demanded" of *X* and *Y*, respectively, under the given conditions. They are to be contrasted with the "*excess* amounts demanded"—which are the respective differences between the amounts demanded and the amounts initially held of the various goods. A positive excess amount demanded means that the individual enters the market as a buyer; a negative one, as a seller. In our particular case the excess amounts demanded are, of course, *EG* of *X* and *minus HF* of *Y*. It will frequently be convenient to describe a *negative* amount of excess *demand* by the equivalent term "*positive* amount of excess *supply*." Thus we can in our case say that there is an excess supply of *HF* units of *Y*.[3]

Clearly, the optimum collection, hence the amounts demanded, and hence the excess amounts demanded, all depend on the given price ratio existing in the market. Thus if the individual's initial endowment remains *P* but he is now confronted with a lower price for *X*, his budget line becomes, say, *AB*. The corresponding optimum collection becomes *R*; the amounts demanded of *X* and *Y* become *OJ* and *OK*,

---

3 In order to avoid possible confusion it should be emphasized that our use of the term "amount demanded" does *not* correspond to its usual meaning, the amount an individual wishes to *buy* on the market at a given price. It is, instead, this amount *plus* the amount he wishes to retain out of his initial endowment. In other words, our "demand" is the ordinary demand *plus* Wicksteed's reservation demand.

respectively; and their excess amounts demanded become *EJ* and *minus* *KF*, respectively. Because of the cheapening of *X*, the individual is willing to barter a greater quantity of *Y* to acquire a corresponding greater quantity of *X*. This is represented in Figure 1 as the joint result of the substitution effect and a reinforcing positive income effect.

By varying the relative price of *X* once again we obtain yet another budget line passing through *P* and, correspondingly, yet another optimum collection. Indeed, we can consider the individual—with his

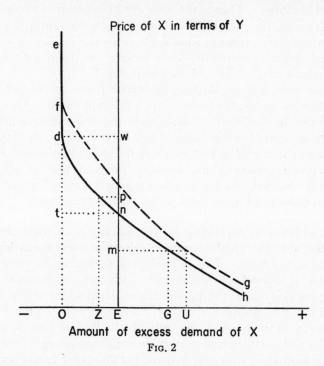

FIG. 2

given indifference map and initial endowment *P*—to be a "utility-computor" into whom we "feed" a sequence of market prices and from whom we obtain a corresponding sequence of "solutions" in the form of specified optimum positions. In this way we can conceptually generate the individual's excess-demand curve for, say, *X*; this shows the excess amounts of *X* he demands at the various prices. Such a curve—for our given individual with his initial endowment *P*—is represented by *edh* in Figure 2.

For reasons that will become evident in a moment, the origin of this diagram is designated as *E*. To its right are positive numbers, to its left, negative. The distances on the horizontal axis here represent the same quantities as in Figure 1. The curve *edh* shows that at any price below *En* the amount of excess demand is positive. For example, if we assume that the price *Em* is that represented by the slope of *CD* in Figure 1, then both diagrams yield (as they must) the same information: the individual will want to buy in the market the quantity *EG*. On the other hand, at the price *En* the individual's initial and optimum collections coincide; hence he does not enter the market at all   Finally, prices above *En* are sufficiently attractive to induce him to sell part of his initial holdings. Thus at the price *Ep* his amount of excess demand is negative—or, alternatively, his amount of excess supply is positive— to the extent *ZE*. Indeed, should the price rise to *Ew* or above, the individual deems it worth his while to offer on the market his entire initial amount of *X—OE*—in exchange for *Y*.

We now note that by shifting the vertical axis to the point *O*, we convert this excess-demand curve into a demand curve. This relation- ship reflects the fact that, by definition, the amount demanded of *X equals* the amount of excess demand *plus* the initial amount of *X*. Thus the demand curve tells us how much *X* the individual demands at each price—without distinguishing between demand that is satisfied by resort to the market and demand that is satisfied out of initial holdings. This dual nature of Figure 2 will subsequently prove useful.

2. In addition to depending on the market price with which he is confronted, the individual's optimum collection also clearly depends on his initial endowment. This is analogous to saying, in more familiar terms, that it depends on his income. Assume, for example, that for some unspecified reason the individual's initial quantity of *Y* is increased so that his initial position is now *T* instead of *P* in Figure 1. If the market price is unchanged, the individual's budget line is then *MN*, parallel to *CD*. His optimum position shifts accordingly from *Q* to *S*. Thus the individual uses only part of his increased initial endowment of *Y* to increase the amount demanded of *Y* itself (by *HW*, less than *PT*); part is also used to increase the amount demanded of *X* (by *GU*).

Once again, we can conceptually confront the individual with a sequence of different market prices; rotate, accordingly, his budget line through *T*; and determine his corresponding sequence of optimum positions. In this way we generate his excess-demand curve connected with the initial endowment *T*. This is depicted as the curve *efg* in Figure 2. Clearly, for *X* not an inferior good, this curve must lie to the right of *edh*. In particular, we see from this diagram—as we also see from Figure 1—that at the price *Em* the excess amount demanded has increased from *EG* to *EU*   Since the individual's initial amount of X is unchanged, the curve *efg* also becomes vertical at the point O. However, in view of the fact that the individual's income is now higher, it does so at a higher price than does *edh*.

Even for X not an inferior good, one should not conclude that an increase in the value of the initial endowment always causes a rightward shift of the *excess*-demand curve. This is true, as we have just seen, for the case in which the initial quantity of *another* good is increased while that of X remains unchanged. It is not necessarily true for the case in which the initial quantity of X itself also changes. Thus assume that the initial endowment is increased from P to V, instead of P to T. With the price ratio measured by the slope of MN, V and T clearly have the same value. It is also clear that the optimum collection remains S, so that the *amount* of X demanded remains OU. But now the *excess amount* demanded has changed from a *plus* EU to a *minus* UJ. It follows that at the price Em in Figure 2 the excess-demand curve corresponding to the initial endowment V lies to the left of the vertical axis.

So far we have tacitly restricted the analysis to the case of an economy with only two goods. If there are more goods, the amount of excess demand for X is also influenced by the given prices at which the individual can barter X for these other goods. Thus, should the individual be confronted with a rise in the price of one of these goods, the whole excess-demand curve of Figure 2 will shift: rightwards for a substitute good, leftwards for a complementary one.

We can summarize the discussion up to this point by saying that the individual's amount of excess demand for a given good is determined by the bartering ratios of all goods with which he is confronted on the market, the real value of his initial endowment, and his initial quantity of the good in question. Let us define the real value of his initial endowment of commodities as his real income. Then we can alternatively say that the individual's excess-demand function for a given good depends on the relative prices of all goods, his real income, and his initial quantity of the good in question. The excess-demand *curve* of Figure 2 is clearly a cross-section of this *function* taken at fixed values of the relative prices other than that of X, a fixed level of real income, and a fixed initial quantity of X.[4]

So much for the excess-demand curve of a single individual. By aggregating those of all the individuals in the economy, we can then obtain the excess-demand curve of the market as a whole. For

---

[4] The specialist in welfare economics is asked to forgive this cavalier treatment of the concept "real income" both here and in the rest of the book.

simplicity, assume that *edh* in Figure 2 now represents this latter curve. The quantity OE then measures the sum of all the individuals' initial endowments of X. From the curve we also see that at the price Em there may be some individuals who wish to buy X and others who wish to sell but that in the aggregate the individuals of the economy wish to augment their initial endowments of X by the net amount EG. Similarly, at the price Ep they wish on balance to sell the amount ZE, while at the price Ew there is no one who can afford to consume the commodity X.[5]

3. By continuing to consider *edh* as the market curve, we can also use Figure 2 to explain the determination of the equilibrium market price of X. At any price below En there is a positive amount of excess demand in the market, driving the price up. At any price above En there is a negative amount of excess demand—or a positive amount of excess supply—driving it down. Only at the price En—where the amount of excess demand is zero, where, that is, the amount people want to buy is equal to the amount others want to sell—can equilibrium prevail.

By shifting the origin of Figure 2 to O, this determination of the equilibrium price can alternatively be presented in terms of the more familiar supply-and-demand apparatus. The vertical line at E then becomes the supply curve, reflecting the fact that the total amount of X in the economy is absolutely fixed, and *edh* then becomes the demand curve. The equilibrium price is yielded in the usual manner by the intersection of these two curves at the quantity OE and price Ot.

This equilibrium price is assumed to be reached during the marketing period Monday afternoon. The details of this process are analyzed in Chapter III. For the moment it suffices to note that it presumes the existence of a recontracting arrangement. That is, individuals enter the market with offers to buy or sell varying quantities of X at the given price. If the market is not cleared, these offers are not binding. Instead, the price changes in response to the pressure of excess demand, and new offers are made accordingly. When the equilibrium price is finally reached, the marketing period is closed, contracts are made final, and arrangements are made for sellers to deliver the commodities to buyers during the ensuing week.

---

[5] The reader can readily verify that the same market excess-demand curve *edh* is also yielded as the difference between demand and supply in the ordinary sense of the term—that is, as the difference between what individuals wish to buy and sell on the market at given prices. See p. 10, footnote 3. For a simple numerical example, see G. J. Stigler, *Theory of Price* (revised ed.; New York, 1952), pp. 151–53.

4. There is a fundamental distinction between the analytical framework of the section just presented and of those that precede it. In the first two sections of this chapter, the economic unit under investigation is an individual or an aggregate of individuals. What we wish to explain—that is, the "dependent variables of the analysis"—are the amounts of excess demand of each individual. What we take as given and not subject to explanation—the "independent variables of the analysis"—are the individual's tastes and initial endowments, the prices with which he is confronted, and his desire to transform his initial endowment into an optimum one. The purpose of the analysis at this level is to conduct conceptual experiments with the individual—or group of individuals—in which arbitrary changes in one or more independent variables are made and the effects of these changes on the dependent variables observed. The results of one such "individual-experiment"—as we shall call them—are described by the excess-demand curve of Figure 2—understood as referring either to one individual or to the aggregate of all of them. This curve shows how the amount of excess demand varies with changes in the price of X—other independent variables being assumed constant.

In the preceding section, the unit of investigation is different, and so, accordingly, are the dependent and independent variables of the analysis. Specifically, this unit now becomes the organized market operating under conditions of perfect competition. What we now wish to explain is that price which establishes equilibrium in this market. What we take as given are the structure of this market and the tastes, endowments, and desire for maximum utility of those individuals who appear in it. Within this analytical framework it is meaningless to inquire as to the effects of an arbitrary change in price, for, by assumption, such a change can now occur only as the result of a prior change in one of the independent variables. Indeed, it is the purpose of the analysis at this level to conduct conceptual "market-experiments" in which the effects of changes in these independent variables on the equilibrium price of the market are investigated.

The force of this distinction—and the reason for elaborating at such length on what is probably well known—will become clear in the discussion which follows.[6]

---

6 For a precise description of this distinction, see Mathematical Appendix 1:*a*.

In "A Reconsideration of the General Equilibrium Theory of Money" [*Review of Economic Studies*, XVIII (1950–51), 55], I called individual-experiments "*ceteris paribus* experiments" and market-experiments "*mutatis mutandis* experiments." These terms have been replaced here because there are generally factors held in *ceteris paribus* even in market-experiments. Cf. equations (1.36)–(1.39) in Mathematical Appendix 1:*c*.

CHAPTER II

The Excess-Demand Functions

of a Money Economy

1. Introduction. The role of money. *2. Types of moneys and prices.*
3. The individual's excess-demand functions for commodities: substitution,
income, and real-balance effects. *4. The concept of "money illusion."*
5. The individual's excess-demand function for money. *6. The market*
excess-demand functions.

1. Let us now extend the foregoing analysis to the case of an exchange
economy with money. Our method of approach has already been
blocked out in the preceding chapter. We first describe the excess-
demand functions of the economy; this is the task that will absorb us in
the present chapter. We then use these functions to explain how
equilibrium prices are determined in the market and how these prices
are affected by changes in the amount of money; this is the task to which
we turn in the next chapter.

The individual's initial endowment of goods Monday morning is now
assumed to fall into two mutually exclusive and exhaustive categories:
commodities and money.[1] The former have reached him in the
miraculous way described in the preceding chapter; the latter has been
carried over from the preceding week. For the present we shall
assume that the individual makes no consumption plans for any week
beyond the current one. This enables us to postpone for later consideration the problems of borrowing, lending, and the rate of interest.

---

[1] The terms "goods," "commodities," and "money" will be used henceforth only in the
senses just indicated. This gives "goods" a different meaning than it has in the Introduction.

The individual's sole concern with the future is assumed to be his desire to start next Monday morning with adequate money balances—where the adequacy of these balances is judged in the light of his expectation that next week's prices will be the same as this week's. This desire necessarily influences the commitments which the individual makes during the marketing period this Monday afternoon, for these determine his initial money balances on next Monday. With this exception, we deal exclusively with one-week-horizon men in a one-week-horizon world.

One basic question immediately suggests itself: why does the individual of our economy plan to hold money balances? A rigorous answer to this question must await the discussion of Chapter VII. For the moment we merely assume—with full recognition that we have not yet provided the rigorous analytical framework which justifies such an assumption—that the individual finds it convenient to hold money as a reserve. In particular, we arbitrarily assume that payments on the final contracts of the Monday marketing period are made, not simultaneously at the close of this period, but at randomly determined hours of the ensuing week. It follows that the individual is uncertain both as to the hours he will receive payments for the commodities he has sold and as to the hours he will be called upon to make payments for the commodities he has bought. In other words, he is almost certain that these payments will not be perfectly synchronized during the week, and that there will therefore be generated discrepancies between the hourly inflows and outflows of money. Hence in order to have some means of meeting these discrepancies—and thereby to have some protection against the embarrassment of default—the individual will be interested in possessing at the beginning of each week reserves of money balances that will bear a certain relationship to the volume of his required payments. Clearly, the greater these reserves, the greater his security against financial embarrassment during the ensuing week. Thus the demand for money in our economy is explained in terms reminiscent of the familiar transactions and precautionary motives of the cash-balance approach to the quantity theory of money.[2]

2. Though we have spoken of "money" in the singular, we shall formally assume the presence of two distinct types of money in our

---

[2] Cf. K. Wicksell, *Interest and Prices* (London, 1936), p. 39; A. Marshall, *Money Credit and Commerce* (London, 1923), pp. 43–45; A. C. Pigou, "The Value of Money," *Quarterly Journal of Economics*, XXXII (1917–18), as reprinted in *Readings in Monetary Theory*, ed. F. A. Lutz and L. W. Mints (Philadelphia, 1951), pp. 164–65. For further references, see Chapter VIII:1 below.

economy.   First, there is an abstract unit of account, which serves only for purposes of computation and record keeping.   This unit has no physical existence; that is, it does not coincide with any of the goods which exist in the economy.   Examples of such money in various societies are well known.   Perhaps the most familiar is the guinea in present-day England.

Second, there is a fiat paper money, which serves as the actual, physical medium of exchange and store of value.   It is this money which was referred to in the preceding section.   It is only of this money that balances can be held.   We shall continue to denote it by the term "money," unmodified.   The first type of money, on the other hand, will be referred to explicitly as "the abstract unit of account."

Corresponding to these two types of money there are two types of prices.   Prices in terms of the abstract unit of account will be called "accounting prices."   Prices in terms of the medium of exchange will be called "money prices," or, alternatively, "absolute prices," or, simply, "prices."   In addition, there are "real" or, alternatively, "relative prices"; these represent the prices of commodities (as distinct from money) in terms of one another.   In a corresponding way we can distinguish between the accounting, money, and real values of a collection of goods.   These correspond, of course, to the aggregate value of these goods computed at their accounting, money, and real prices, respectively.   Once again, the term "value," unmodified, will be taken to denote money value.

The accounting price of a given good is distinctive in having no operational significance for the market.   The statement that "the money price of good X is 2" implies that the surrender of two pieces of paper money in the market procures in exchange one unit of X. Similarly, the statement that "the real price of X in terms of Y is 3" implies that X can be bartered for Y in this proportion, or that the money obtained by selling one unit of X suffices to purchase three units of Y.   But the statement that "the accounting price of X is 4"—in the absence of additional information on the accounting price of at least one other good—gives us no idea of what we must do to acquire a unit of X.   Stated otherwise, empirical observation alone could not detect the, say, doubling of the accounting prices of all goods.   In the market place we can observe only the manifestations of money, and hence real, prices.

It should be emphasized that paper money, like any other good, also has an accounting price.   Thus, for example, the accounting price of the paper sterling pound is 20/21 guineas.   Paper money also has a money price; but, unlike its accounting price, this, by definition, is always unity.   Thus one can conceive of a change in the *accounting* prices of all *goods*.   One can also conceive of a change in the *money* prices of all *commodities*.   But it is a contradiction in terms to conceive of a change in the *money* prices of all *goods*.   Similarly, it is a contradiction in terms to conceive of a change in the *relative* prices of all *commodities*.[3]

The reader may at this point feel that he has been unnecessarily encumbered with artificial distinctions.   And it is true that from the viewpoint of the analysis as such nothing would be lost—and simplicity would be gained—if we were to drop the assumption that the money which serves as the medium of exchange is distinct from the money which serves as the unit of account.   Nevertheless, we shall have to carry this distinction throughout the following argument, for only in this way will we be able to understand the nature of certain confusions which have become entrenched in the literature on monetary theory.[4]

3. Let us now consider the excess-demand functions.   The rigorous derivation of these functions from utility analysis is deferred to Chapters V–VI.   For the moment, we simply argue by analogy that in a money economy, as in a barter economy, the individual's excess demand for a given commodity depends on the relative prices with which he is confronted in the market and on the real value of his initial collection.[5] Now, however, this collection includes money as well as commodities. As in the preceding chapter, we denote the real value of the latter by "real income."   Correspondingly, we denote the real value of the initial money holdings—that is, the purchasing power over commodities

---

3 The following notation may help fix these distinctions in the reader's mind: Consider an economy with n goods, the nth good being paper money.   Let the respective prices of these goods in terms of an abstract unit of account be represented by

$$p_1, \ldots, p_{n-1}, p_n.$$

Then the respective money prices of the goods are

$$\frac{p_1}{p_n}, \ldots, \frac{p_{n-1}}{p_n}, 1.$$

Finally, the relative prices of the $n - 1$ commodities in terms of the first one are

$$1, \frac{p_2}{p_1}, \ldots, \frac{p_{n-1}}{p_1}.$$

We might, if we wish, also speak of the relative price of money, p_n/p_1; this represents the number of units of the first commodity that must be given up in order to acquire one unit of paper money.

4 These will be discussed in Chapter VIII:3–4.

5 See Chapter I:2.   The third factor mentioned there—the initial quantity of the given commodity—is assumed constant throughout the present discussion; hence this factor is ignored both here and in what follows.

The excess demand for money is discussed in the next section.

19

which these holdings represent—by the term "real balances." In this way we reach the following formulation: The individual's excess-demand function for any given commodity depends on the array of relative prices of all commodities, his real income, and his real balances.[6]

This dependence on real balances is the crucial element of the following analysis. Though consistently overlooked in the standard theory of consumer's demand,[7] it is simply the obverse side of the familiar demand for money described above. For to say that an individual adjusts his money balances so as to maintain a desired relationship between them and his planned expenditures on commodities is at the same time to say that he adjusts these expenditures so as to maintain a desired relationship between them and his money balances. The exact nature of this relationship depends both on objective factors—the precise character of the random payment process referred to in Section 1—and on subjective factors—the individual's attitude toward the risk that this process will generate discrepancies between money flows during the week, and his sensitivity to the social opprobrium which would fall upon him should inadequate money reserves force him to default. The more probable the lack of synchronization between payments and receipts, the weaker the individual's gambling spirit, and the more tender his sensibilities—the larger the reserves of money balances he will want to hold for a given volume of expenditures;[8] or, equivalently, the smaller the volume of expenditures he will be willing to undertake on the basis of a given level of money balances; or, to place our argument within a very familiar framework, the smaller the velocity of circulation of the money balances which he holds.[9]

It follows that if the individual's initial balances are for some reason increased above the level which he considers necessary, he will seek to

---

[6] See Mathematical Appendix 2:*a*.

[7] To be more specific—and to anticipate for a moment our future discussion—though the dependence on real balances has usually (if implicitly) been recognized in the analysis of the demand for *bonds*, it has not been so recognized in the analysis of the demand for *commodities*. This failure will be analyzed in detail in Chapter VIII:3.

[8] I.e., in terms of the Cambridge cash-balance approach, the larger his K; cf. Pigou, *op. cit.*, pp. 166–70.

[9] The reader will recognize that this paragraph has been deliberately patterned after the traditional discussions of the determinants of V—or of K. These discussions are, however, much more general than the one presented here because the implicit model on which they are based is a much more complicated one. Nevertheless, it is clear that our "objective factor" is a special case of what Fisher—in his classification of the causes which affect V—subsumes under the heading "systems of payments in the community," and our "subjective factors" a special case of his "habits of the individual" [*Purchasing Power of Money* (New York, 1911), p. 79; cf. also the reference to Pigou in the preceding footnote].

remedy this situation by increasing his amounts demanded of the various commodities, thereby increasing his planned expenditures, and thereby drawing down his balances.   On the other hand, should they be decreased below the level he considers necessary, he will seek to remedy the situation by decreasing his amounts demanded, thereby decreasing his planned expenditures, and thereby building up his balances.[10]

Clearly, in judging the adequacy of these money balances—and hence in determining their influence on his demand for commodities—the individual can be guided only by their real value.   For the magnitude of the discrepancies which these money reserves are designed to cover clearly depends on the prices which must be paid for commodities; hence the effective magnitude of these reserves can be determined only in relation to the level of prices.   In the language of the cash-balance theorists, it is with the extent of his liquid command over *real* resources that the individual is concerned.

Using the excess-demand function presented above, we can now extend the Hicksian theory of consumer's behavior to the case of a money economy.   Specifically, in analyzing the effect of a specified change on the amount demanded of a given commodity, we shall henceforth consider the "real-balance effect" of this change as well as the already familiar substitution and income effects.   As its name implies, this new effect measures the influence on demand of a change in real balances, other things being held constant.   For example, if the individual is confronted with a change in the price of a single commodity, the corresponding change in the amounts he demands of the various commodities is the resultant of all three effects: for there is a change in relative prices, and hence a substitution effect; there is a change in real income, and hence an income effect; finally, there is a change in the price level and therefore in the real value of his initial money holdings, and hence a real-balance effect.[11]

In general, as we have seen, the real-balance effect is positive; that is, an increase in real balances causes an increase in demand.   But this need not always be the case.   In particular, a commodity which is inferior with respect to income is also inferior with respect to real balances.   Even in the case of a positive effect nothing can be specified a priori as to the degree of the change in the amount of excess demand.

---

10 This paragraph paraphrases Wicksell, *op. cit.*, pp. 39–40.   This passage is cited in full in Supplementary Note E:1.   For similar references to other neoclassical advocates of the quantity theory, see Chapter VIII:1.

11 The "real-balance effect" is identical with what I first called in "Price Flexibility and Full Employment" [*American Economic Review*, XXXVIII (1948), 556] the "Pigou effect." This was clearly a bad terminological choice.

In particular, if the initial money balances of the individual are increased, prices constant, there is no reason to expect the amount of excess demand for any commodity to increase in the same proportion as the amount of money.

As will readily become evident, the real-balance effect in the commodity markets plays a central role in the analysis of this book. It is therefore worth emphasizing at the outset that the fulfillment of this role depends not on the *strength* of this effect but only on its *existence*. And of this existence there seems to be fairly persuasive evidence— particularly from the postwar experience of the inflationary pressures generated by accumulated liquid assets, and of the subsequent dissipation of these pressures in a rising price level.[12]

It must also be emphasized that, for the simple exchange economy with which we are now dealing, the assumption that there exists a real-balance effect in the commodity markets is the *sine qua non* of monetary theory. For, as we shall see below, in the absence of this effect the absolute level of money prices in such an economy is indeterminate. It follows that though approximations which neglect the real-balance effect may—because of the smallness of this effect—be useful in the theory of the determination of relative prices, such "approximations" ignore a basic analytical factor in the theory of the determination of the absolute price level. Thus, whatever the justification for neglecting the real-balance effect in value theory, there can be no justification for neglecting it in monetary theory.[13]

---

12 Cf. A. J. Brown, *The Great Inflation 1939-1951* (London, 1955), Chapter X, especially pp. 236–37. For an empirical study of the consumption function which has yielded statistically significant correlations with real balances, see C. Christ, "A Test of an Econometric Model for the United States, 1921–1947," *Conference on Business Cycles* (New York, 1951), p. 85. On the other hand, for a less affirmative view of the role of the real-balance effect in the commodity markets, see M. Cohen, "Liquid Assets and the Consumption Function," *Review of Economics and Statistics*, XXXVI (1954), 202–11. See also J. G. Gurley, "Excess Liquidity and European Monetary Reforms, 1944–1952," *American Economic Review*, XLIII (1953), 76–100.

13 In order to avoid any possible later misunderstanding—and in order to explain our hedging phrases "in the commodity markets" and "for the simple exchange economy"—it is worth while again anticipating our future discussion and pointing out that the determinacy of money prices depends on the existence of a real-balance effect *somewhere* in the economy; but once we extend our analysis to an economy with bonds, this "somewhere" may be the bond market, and not necessarily the commodity markets. However, I can see neither theoretical nor empirical justification for basing the analysis on the one-sided view that the real-balance effect manifests itself *only* in the bond market. On the other hand, it should be emphasized that all of the conclusions of this book can be shown to hold even under this extreme assumption. So though the real-balance effect in the commodity markets plays a "central role" in this book, this role—once bonds are introduced into the analysis—is *not* logically necessary for the validity of the argument.

I might also emphasize that the empirical evidence cited in the preceding footnote refers to

4. We now define a concept which is fundamental to the following argument—the concept of "money illusion." An individual will be said to be suffering from such an illusion if his excess-demand functions for commodities do *not* have the property specified in the preceding section—that is, if they do *not* depend solely on relative prices, real income, and real balances. Conversely, an individual will be said to be "free of money illusion" if his excess-demand functions *do* have this property. It follows that if an illusion-free individual were confronted with an equi-proportionate change in all *accounting* prices—including that of paper money—none of his amounts demanded of commodities would thereby be affected; for such a change would affect neither the array of relative prices confronting him, nor the level of his real income, nor the value of his real money balances. To revert to the example of the preceding section, all guinea prices would, say, be doubled; but this would in no wise reduce the purchasing power of his pound holdings, for the guinea value of each of these pounds would also have doubled.

Similarly, if the initial paper-money endowment of an illusion-free individual were suddenly increased and he were simultaneously confronted in the market by new money prices, all of which had increased in the same proportion, he would once again have no reason for changing the amount demanded of any commodity. In fact, this case differs from the preceding one only in the method of maintaining the real value of initial money holdings invariant in the face of an equi-proportionate change in the accounting prices of commodities: instead of accomplishing this by changing the accounting price of money too, holding its initial quantity constant, we do so by changing this quantity proportionately, holding its accounting price constant.

By way of contrast, consider the effects on the amounts of commodities demanded of simply confronting the individual with a proportionate change in all *money* prices. Once again, there is neither a substitution effect nor an income effect. But there is a real-balance effect. That is, a proportionate increase in all money prices decreases the real value of his fixed initial money balances and therefore causes the individual to decrease the amounts he demands of the various commodities. Thus an individual free of money illusion will definitely be affected by such a change.[14]

---

the existence of a real-balance effect in the *commodity* markets. As already noted, its existence in the *bond* market has usually—if implicitly—been taken for granted, particularly by Keynesian interest theory.

All these points will be discussed in further detail on pp. 109–10 and 163–64.

[14] For a demonstration—if it is necessary—that this and the preceding paragraphs use "substitution effect" in Hicks' sense of the term, see Mathematical Appendix 2:*b*.

We can summarize this discussion by saying that though the economic behavior of an individual free of money illusion depends solely on the *ratios* of the *accounting* prices, it does *not* depend solely on the *ratios* of the *money* prices. That is, such an individual does react to changes which affect only the *absolute level* of these *money* prices. On the other hand, an individual who *is* suffering from money illusion also reacts to changes which affect only the *absolute level* of *accounting* prices. That is, his economic behavior does *not* depend solely on the *ratios* of these prices.[15]

Alternatively, we can make use of the familiar concept of elasticity to state these results in the following way: Absence of money illusion is marked by uniform zero elasticity of the individual's commodity excess-demand functions with respect to an equi-proportionate change in all money prices and in initial money holdings. No such zero elasticity exists with reference to an equi-proportionate change in all money prices alone; in general, this elasticity is negative, though in some cases it may be positive. This is equivalent to saying that no such zero elasticity exists with reference to a change in his initial money holdings alone and that, in general, this elasticity is positive, though it may be negative. Even when positive, there is no special reason for it to equal unity.[16]

5. Just as there are excess-demand functions for commodities, so is there one for the money which serves as the medium of exchange in our economy. The opening section of this chapter makes some observations on the general nature of this demand. We must now provide an exact description of its properties.

By the term "amount of money demanded" we mean the amount of money which the individual plans during the marketing period this Monday afternoon to hold in his possession next Monday morning—after he has, in the course of the week, made and received all the payments on the contracts into which he plans to enter this afternoon. By

---

[15] The reader will recall that the ratios of accounting prices are money prices, and the ratios of money prices relative prices; cf. p. 19, footnote 3.

This paragraph makes it clear that our definition of "money illusion" differs fundamentally from the accepted one: the latter defines "money illusion" as sensitivity of the individual to changes in the absolute level of *money* prices. This will be discussed further in Chapter VIII:3–4.

[16] Absence of money illusion does, however, imply that the elasticity of Marshallian demand prices with respect to a change in initial money holdings is unity; see Mathematical Appendix 2:*a*.

From what has been said in Section 2, it should be clear that the phrase "all money prices" in the last three paragraphs is a shorthand expression for "all money prices that can change," i.e., "the money prices of all commodities."

"amount of excess demand for money" we mean the difference between this amount demanded and the amount of his initial money holdings this Monday morning. The excess-demand function for money shows how this difference varies with changes in the conditions with which the individual is confronted. As noted above, we assume that the individual expects prices next week to be the same as those this week.

Actually, there is nothing that can be said about the excess-demand function for money which is not already implicit in the discussion of the preceding section. This is a direct consequence of the fact that the individual must formulate his marketing decisions within the framework of his budget restraint. In simplest terms, this restraint expresses the condition that the individual neither beg nor steal: instead, every expenditure for commodities must be financed either by the sale of part of his initial endowment of commodities or by the drawing down of his initial endowment of money balances. It follows that the amount of the individual's *excess demand* for money—at a given set of relative prices, real income, and real balances—is necessarily equal to the aggregate money value of the amounts of his *excess supplies* of commodities—corresponding to this same set of prices, income, and balances.[17]

Some examples will help clarify this basic relationship. Consider the simple case in which, in the light of the conditions confronting him, the individual plans to retain the initial quantities of all commodities but one. That is, the excess amount demanded of every commodity but one is zero. Assume that this one amount of excess demand is positive. Clearly, the only way in which this additional quantity can be purchased is by drawing down initial cash balances to the extent of its money value. Thus when the individual formulates the preceding market plan for commodities, he is simultaneously formulating a plan

---

[17] Recognition of this relationship can be found far back in the literature. See, for example, J. S. Mill, *Principles of Political Economy*, ed. Ashley (London, 1909), Book III, Chapter VIII, Section 2, pp. 490–91.

For the meaning of "excess supply," see above, p. 10.

The word "excess" in the text should be emphasized, for it is *not* true that the amount of the individual's *demand* for money is equal to the aggregate money value of the amounts of his *supplies* of commodities. For one thing, the former refers to the *stock* of money which the individual plans to hold next Monday morning, whereas the latter refers to the *flow* of money receipts during the week; hence these two quantities do not even have the same time dimensions. In contrast, the *excess* demand for money also has the dimensions of a flow per week, for it is defined as the *difference* between the stock of money at the end and beginning of the week; hence it can properly be equated (as in the text) with the value of the excess supply of commodities, which, of course, also has the dimensions of a flow per week.

The reader interested in this "stock and flow" problem as related to the supply-and-demand analysis of money will find a more detailed discussion of it in my "Indeterminacy of Absolute Prices in Classical Economic Theory," *Econometrica*, XVII (1949), Section 8.

for reducing his initial holdings of money.   No additional independent decision on this score is involved.

More generally, assume that—at a given set of relative prices, real income, and real balances—the individual plans to increase the holdings of some commodities and to decrease those of others.   If the aggregate value of the increases is equal to the aggregate value of the decreases, the individual can carry out his plan without any change in his initial money balances.   There is, however, no reason why such an equality need exist.   If, instead, the value of the increases exceeds that of the decreases, the individual must of necessity be planning to draw on his initial money balances.   Or, in other words, the amount of excess demand for money balances must be negative to exactly the same extent that the aggregate value of the amounts of excess supplies of commodities is negative.   Conversely, if the value of the amounts of excess supplies of commodities is positive (i.e., the aggregate value of decreases exceeds that of increases), the individual must of necessity be planning an equal positive amount of excess demand for cash balances.

We should not conclude from this discussion that the excess-demand function for money is a purely passive ingredient of the individual's economic behavior, merely reflecting decisions initiated elsewhere.   All the individual's decisions are made simultaneously.   Hence we can just as well say that a decision for a positive amount of excess demand for money implies a decision for an equal positive aggregate value of excess supplies for commodities, or that the value of the amount of excess demand for any one commodity is equal to the aggregate value of the amounts of excess supplies of all other commodities, plus the amount of excess supply of money; or we can adopt the completely neutral statement that the aggregate money value of the amounts of the individual's excess demands for all goods must be zero.   All of these statements are equivalent expressions of the necessity for the individual's plans to be consistent with the restraint placed upon him by his budget.

Let us now examine some of the properties of the excess-demand function for money implied by this restraint.   Consider an individual free of money illusion who, at a certain set of relative prices and with a given real income and real balance, has a certain amount of excess demand for money.   Assume that this individual is now confronted with an equi-proportionate change in all money prices and in his initial endowment of money.   According to the assumption of the last section, the amount of excess supply of each commodity is unaffected by this change.   But the prices at which these amounts of excess supplies are valued have all changed in the same proportion.   There-

26

fore the money value of the amounts of excess supplies of commodities, and hence the amount of excess demand for money, are also changed in the same proportion.

An alternative statement of the preceding result is that the *real* value of the amount of excess demand for money is not affected by a proportionate change in all money prices and in the initial amount of money. It follows, then, that the excess-demand function for *real* money balances depends only on relative prices, real income, and the real value of initial money balances. Thus the assumed absence of money illusion in the excess-demand functions for commodities implies the corresponding absence of money illusion in the excess-demand function for real money balances.

This dependence of the excess demand for money on the initial amount of money should not arouse any fears that the argument is involved in circularity. The initial endowment of money is as much a datum of the problem as the initial endowment of any other good. There is no more circularity here than there is in the statement of Chapter I:2 that the excess demand for X depends on the initial amount of X. Again in analogy to Chapter I,[18] an increase in the initial amount of money can be assumed to be used partly to augment the demand for money itself—the individual makes use of his new riches to improve his liquidity position—and partly to augment the demand for commodities. These increases are the manifestation of the real-balance effect in the money and commodity markets, respectively.

The foregoing argument can be presented in somewhat more familiar terms if we speak of the demand for money, instead of the excess demand. By definition, the amount of money demanded is equal to the initial holdings of money *plus* the amount of excess demand for money. It then follows immediately from the preceding analysis that an individual confronted with a proportionate change in money prices and in initial money holdings will always change his amount of money demanded in the same proportion. Once again, an alternative statement of this result is that the demand function for *real* money holdings depends only on relative prices, real income, and the real value of initial money balances.

Graphically, we can present these conclusions in the following way. Define, first, the average price level, p. Since the present discussion is restricted to equi-proportionate changes in prices, the weighting system used for this average need not concern us. As already implied, the reciprocal of this price level, $1/p$, can be considered as the "real"

---

[18] See the first paragraph of Section 2.

or the "relative price" of money: it indicates the number of units of commodities-in-general which must be given up in order to acquire one unit of money.   Accordingly, we can conceive of a curve which describes the demand for money as a function of this relative price.   More specifically, let M_0 in Figure 3 represent the amount of money an

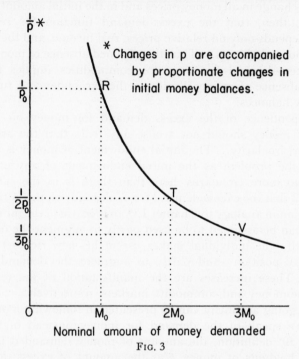

Changes in p are accompanied by proportionate changes in initial money balances.

Nominal amount of money demanded

FIG. 3

individual with fixed real income and initial real balances demands when the average of commodity prices is p_0.   Assume now that all prices and initial money balances are doubled.   Then, by the preceding paragraph, so will the amount of money demanded.   That is, the individual will move from the point R to the point T in Figure 3.   Similarly, a tripling of prices and initial money balances will cause him to move from T to V.   Continuing in this way, we obviously generate a demand curve for money which has the form of a rectangular hyperbola.   At any point on this curve the real value of the amount of money balances demanded—represented by the area of the subtended rectangle—is constant.   This is how absence of money illusion manifests itself in the money market.

In other words, absence of money illusion implies that the demand function for money has uniform unitary elasticity with respect to an equi-proportionate change in money prices *and* in initial money balances.   In general, no such elasticity exists—even at a single point, let alone uniformly—with respect to a proportionate change in prices unaccompanied by a change in initial money balances.   What distinguishes the latter case from the former is the presence of a real-balance effect, changing the amounts of the individual's excess supplies of commodities.   Consequently, it can no longer be argued, as it was above, that the amount of money demanded will increase in the same proportion as prices.

More specifically, if the good *real* money balances is not an inferior good, an equi-proportionate increase in money prices will cause a less-than-proportionate increase in the amount of *nominal* money balances demanded.   For, under this assumption, such a price increase creates a negative real-balance effect and hence a decrease in the amount of *real* money balances demanded; and this amount multiplied by the price level equals the amount of *nominal* balances demanded.   On the other hand, if commodities are also not inferior, this decrease in the amount of *real* money balances demanded cannot go so far as to cause a decrease in the amount of *nominal* balances demanded.   For the absence of inferiority implies that an equi-proportionate increase in prices causes a *decrease* in the amount of excess demand of each commodity, which means an *increase* in the amount of excess supply.   Since prices have risen, this implies an even greater increase in the aggregate value of the excess supply of commodities   Hence, by the budget restraint, the *excess amount* of money demanded increases by an equal amount.   But since the initial quantity of money is constant, this implies an equal increase in the *amount* of money demanded.[19]

---

[19] I am indebted to Mr. Yosef Yoran for catching an error in an earlier draft of this paragraph.

It may help to restate the argument symbolically.   Since for our present purposes all prices are assumed to change in the same proportion, we can represent the collection of all commodities by a single composite one (Hicks, *op. cit.*, pp. 33–34).   Denote the amount demanded of this composite commodity by G and its price by p.   Denote the amount of *nominal* money holdings demanded by M.   Let G_0 and M_0 be the respective given initial holdings of these goods.   Then the budget restraint is

(a) $$pG + M = pG_0 + M_0.$$

That is, the value of the optimum collection must equal the value of the initial collection. Transposing, this becomes

(b) $$M = p(G_0 - G) + M_0.$$

By the assumption of noninferiority, an increase in p decreases G and hence increases $G_0 - G$. Hence $p(G_0 - G)$ must increase *a fortiori*.   By (b), this implies that M must increase by the same amount.

If, now, the good real money balances is also not inferior, the increase in p decreases the amount of it demanded, M/p; hence M cannot increase in a greater proportion than p.

It is thus possible to conceive of a demand curve for nominal money holdings constructed along the lines of Figure 3, with the difference that changes in p are *not* accompanied by changes in the initial money balances of the individual. Such a curve is drawn in Figure 4 of Chapter III:5. As just emphasized, the real-balance effect prevents this curve from having the form of a rectangular hyperbola. More precisely, if neither commodities nor real money balances are inferior goods, this curve must be negatively sloped with a less-than-unitary elasticity. If, however, real money balances are inferior, this elasticity becomes greater than unity. On the other hand, if commodity inferiority is sufficiently pronounced, the slope of this curve can become positive. In what follows—and in Figure 4 below, in particular—both of these possibilities are ignored.[20]

6. So far we have examined the excess-demand functions of a single individual. Let us now extend the analysis to the excess-demand functions of the economy as a whole.

Consider, then, all the individuals of the economy, each free of money illusion, each with his given real income and real money balances, and each confronted with the same set of relative prices. These data enable us to determine the amount of excess demand of each individual for each commodity. By aggregating over all individuals, it is then possible to determine the amount of excess demand in the market as a whole. By changing the given prices, we can then conceptually generate a market excess-demand function for each commodity. Each of these functions clearly depends upon relative prices, the *array* of the real incomes of all the individuals in the economy, and the corresponding *array* of individual real balances. We can also define a market excess-demand function for money. For any given set of prices, this must yield an amount of excess demand for money equal to the value of the amounts of market excess supplies of commodities. This basic relationship thus holds for the market as a whole as well as for each individual.

There is, nevertheless, a clear lack of analogy between individual and market excess-demand functions. Specifically, the latter does not, in general, depend upon relative prices, *total* real income of the economy, and *total* real balances. This form of dependence would be valid only under the unrealistic assumption that the distribution of neither real incomes nor real balances affects the amounts of market excess demand.

---

[20] On the argument of this section—and of the last three paragraphs in particular—see Mathematical Appendix 2:*c*. This appendix also analyzes the respective shapes of the demand and excess-demand curves for *real* money balances. It also points out a certain ambiguity in Figure 3 above.

By contrast, the form specified in the preceding paragraph makes it clear that the effect of, say, an increase in the total real income of the economy on the amount of market excess demand for a good cannot be determined until the distribution of this increase among the members of the economy is first specified.

It follows that we cannot say that a proportionate change in all money prices and in the *total* initial amount of money in the economy leaves unaffected the amounts of market excess demands for commodities and for real money balances. Instead, we must be satisfied with the more restricted statement that this invariance will exist if the initial money holdings of each and every individual in the economy are changed in the same proportion as prices. Correspondingly, there exists a uniform unitary elasticity of the market demand function for money only with respect to an equi-proportionate change in all money prices and in the initial money holdings of each and every individual.[21]

---

21 See Mathematical Appendix 2:*d*.

CHAPTER III

Money and Prices

1. We now use the excess-demand functions developed in Chapter II to explain the determination of equilibrium prices in the market. Prices are thus no longer the given data of the analysis, subject to arbitrary change, but are instead the dependent variables, incapable of change without a prior shift in one of the independent variables. The latter now consist of the individuals' initial endowments, their tastes, and the structure of the market.[1] We shall be interested in presenting first a static analysis of our problem (the nature of the equilibrium position), then a dynamic analysis (the nature of the market forces which bring the economy to equilibrium from an initial position of disequilibrium), and finally a comparative-statics analysis (a comparison of equilibrium positions before and after a specified change in one or more of the independent variables).

The concept of equilibrium in the market for a single good has already been defined (Chapter I:3). The corresponding concept of equilibrium in the market as a whole—or, simply, in the market—is defined as the existence of equilibrium in the market for each and every good. A set of prices which brings the market as a whole into equilibrium will be called an equilibrium set.

---

[1] This paragraph makes the same distinction described at length in Chapter I:4.

In general, what is an equilibrium set of prices for one array of initial endowments will not be an equilibrium set for another. For assume that we begin with a market in equilibrium at a certain set of prices. Assume now that there occurs an arbitrary change in initial endowments, either in their distribution among individuals in the economy and/or in the sum total of initial endowments of one or more goods. From our discussion of the market excess-demand functions, we know that under these circumstances there will be changes in the amounts of excess demands. Hence, at the original set of prices, there will now exist positive or negative amounts of excess demands in at least some of the markets. Hence this original set is no longer an equilibrium one. Thus the term "equilibrium prices" must always be expressly or tacitly qualified by the phrase "at a given array of initial endowments." The same qualification must be made, *mutatis mutandis*, for the other independent variables of the analysis.

There is one fundamental property of equilibrium prices in our economy which must be noted at the outset. Assume that at a certain set of prices each of the commodity markets is in equilibrium. It follows that the money market must also be in equilibrium. For the amount of excess demand for money equals the aggregate value of the amounts of excess supplies of commodities. In equilibrium, the amount of excess supply in each commodity market is, by definition, zero. Hence the amount of excess demand for money must also be zero. Thus, in order to determine whether a certain set of prices is an equilibrium set for our economy, it is not necessary to examine the money market; instead, it suffices to show that this set of prices establishes equilibrium in each of the commodity markets alone. This relationship, which is a particular form of what is known as Walras' Law, is basic to the following analysis.[2]

It should be emphasized that there is no implication here that the equilibrating process in the money market is in any sense less significant than that in any other market. We could just as well have arbitrarily selected any one market and stated that equilibrium in all the other markets implies equilibrium in the chosen one too. This is the general form of Walras' Law, which follows from the general form of the budget restraint in our economy.[3] If we have chosen to work with the particular form of this law set out in the preceding paragraph, it is only out of considerations of symmetry and simplicity.

---

[2] See L. Walras, *Elements of Pure Economics*, trans. and ed. W. Jaffé (definitive ed.; London, 1954), pp. 162, 241, 281–82. This law was so named by O. Lange in "Say's Law: A Restatement and Criticism," *Studies in Mathematical Economics and Econometrics*, ed. O. Lange *et al.* (Chicago, 1942), p. 50.

[3] See p. 26 above.

It should also be emphasized that though they are logically connected in our economy, Walras' Law and the budget restraint are conceptually distinct relations. To anticipate the terminology of the next section, the former deals with excess-demand *equations*, the latter with excess-demand *functions*. Indeed, we can conceive of an economy in which the existence of the restraint does *not* imply the existence of the law. This special case also makes clear the impropriety of referring to Walras' Law as an "identity" which must always be true.[4]

2. Let us now examine the static meaning of the equilibrium set of prices. Define first the market excess-demand equation for a given good. This is a restriction which states that prices are such that the amount of market excess demand—that is, the value of the market excess-demand function for the good in question—is zero. By definition, this equation is satisfied if and only if the market for the good is in equilibrium.

Assume now that there are n goods in the economy: $n - 1$ commodities and paper money. As will be recalled, this money serves as the medium of exchange and store of value but not as the unit of account. To these n goods correspond, respectively, n market excess-demand equations. Actually, however, only $n - 1$ (at most) of these equations are independent. That is, only $n - 1$ of these equations place independent restrictions on the unknown equilibrium prices. For any set of prices which satisfies $n - 1$ market excess-demand equations must also necessarily satisfy the nth. This, of course, is an alternative statement of Walras' Law.

Thus the equilibrium set of money prices can be regarded as the solution to a set of $n - 1$ independent, simultaneous equations in these $n - 1$ unknown prices. Now, equality between the number of unknowns and the number of independent equations is neither a necessary nor a sufficient condition for the existence of a solution. Nor does it insure that solutions, if they do exist, will be only finite in number. For our purposes, however, these highly complicated issues can be ignored. Instead, we shall accept such equality as justifying the reasonableness of the assumption that one and the same set of money prices can simultaneously create equilibrium in each and every market. We shall also assume that only one such set exists.[5]

---

[4] This case is described in Note H, pp. 447–48.

[5] The discussion of this paragraph is obviously restricted to solutions in the real number system. On the second sentence, see the examples in my "Indeterminacy of Absolute Prices," *op. cit.*, p. 4. For discussions of the conditions under which the existence and uniqueness of a positive real solution can be assured, see the articles by Wald, Schlesinger, von Neumann, and Arrow and Debreu cited in Note B. p. 383 below.

Quite deliberately, we have omitted all discussion of the choice of the dependent equation to be "eliminated." Posing the question in this form might lead to misconceptions. It might be taken to imply that less is known about economic behavior in the "eliminated" market than in others or that the "eliminated" market is in some sense less significant. It might be taken to imply that there is a substantive choice involved and that different decisions as to which equation to "eliminate" will produce different results. Actually, of course, none of these statements is true. As can readily be deduced from the general form of the budget restraint,[6] the properties of the "eliminated" excess-demand equation are completely specified by those of the other $n - 1$ equations. The corresponding general form of Walras' Law then brings out the complete neutrality of the "elimination" process. It should also make clear that no matter what equation is eliminated, the solution for the equilibrium set of prices obtained from the remaining equations is always the same.

In order to avoid any such possible misconceptions, it is advisable not to "eliminate" explicitly any equation at all. Instead, the system is best considered as having n equations, equal in number to the n goods in the economy. But the excess-demand equation for money should be written in the form dictated by the budget restraint. This makes clear the nature of the equational dependence described by Walras' Law.

The discussion has until now been concerned with the $n - 1$ money prices. A unique solution for these implies, of course, a unique solution for the $n - 2$ relative prices. On the other hand, it does not imply a unique solution for the n accounting prices. For if one set of accounting prices yields (after dividing through by the accounting price of money) a given set of money prices, any multiple of that set will also yield this given set. Thus there is an infinite number of sets of accounting prices corresponding to the same set of money prices. We might also explain this indeterminacy of equilibrium accounting prices by noting that there are n such prices and only $n - 1$ independent excess-demand equations. An economic interpretation of this indeterminacy is presented in what immediately follows.[7]

3. Who solves the equations?

The fact that the number of independent excess-demand equations is equal to the number of unknown money prices and that the system can be formally solved might some day interest a Central Planning

---

6 P. 26.

7 See on this section Mathematical Appendix 3:*a*. Note that this proves the indeterminacy of accounting prices *without* resorting to the mere counting of equations and unknowns.

Bureau, duly equipped with electronic computors and charged with setting equilibrium prices by decree. But what is the relevance of this fact for a free market functioning under conditions of perfect competition ?

It was concern with this question which led Walras to formulate his celebrated theory of *tâtonnement*. This was a crucial element in his vision of the economy as reflecting the operations of a set of simultaneous equations. In simplest terms, this theory states that the free market itself acts like a vast computor. For start with any arbitrary set of prices—Walras' "*prix criés au hasard*." In general, it will not be an equilibrium one. That is, at this set of prices there will be some markets with positive amounts of excess demand and others with negative amounts. Prices will then rise in the former markets and fall in the latter, bringing us to a new set of prices. In general, this set, too, will not be an equilibrium one. Once again prices will change in accordance with the state of excess demand in the various markets, a third set of prices will thereby be reached, and so the process will go on. It is by this continuous groping—*tâtonnement*—that the economy ultimately finds its way to the equilibrium position.

The principle by which the market automatically generates these successive approximations is admittedly a primitive one. Actual computors operate according to much more efficient principles. But what our imaginary computor lacks in the elegance of its principle it makes up by its size. Indeed, this size enables it to deal with systems of equations far beyond the practical capacity of any existing computor. Thus, not only is there no need for a conscious mind to solve our excess-demand equations, but it is also doubtful if any mind—human or electronic—could today be depended upon for such a solution.

So far we have followed Walras in failing to deal adequately with one fundamental issue. It is one thing to say that the process of *tâtonnement* prevents the market from remaining at a nonequilibrium set of prices and even exerts some sort of pressure in the direction of equilibrium. It is quite another to say that this process must ultimately bring the market to the equilibrium prices themselves. In other words, Walras' theory of *tâtonnement* depends for its ultimate and rigorous validation on the modern economic theory of dynamics. Conversely, the significance of this latter theory can best be appreciated within the framework provided by Walras. From this viewpoint, a stable system is one in which the process of *tâtonnement* will succeed in establishing equilibrium prices; an unstable system is one in which it will not.[8]

---

[8] The implicit reference here is, of course, to the dynamic theory of Samuelson. See Mathematical Appendix 3:*b*.   [*Footnote* 8 *continued next page.*]

This whole process of successive approximation is assumed to take place during the marketing period, Monday afternoon. To give it concrete embodiment, we might think of a central registry where all offers to buy and sell at the proclaimed prices are recorded. The registry is presided over by a chairman whose function is to raise the price of any commodity for which the registry shows an excess of buyers and to lower the price of any commodity for which it shows an excess of sellers. As indicated above, none of the offers are binding unless the proclaimed set of prices at which they were made turns out to be the equilibrium set. If it does not, individuals are free to recontract at the new set of prices proclaimed accordingly by the chairman. This Edgeworthian assumption[9] serves its usual purpose of precluding the completion of any prior purchases which might otherwise affect the final equilibrium position itself. In other words, this assumption assures that no matter which of the infinite number of paths open to it a convergent sequence of approximations takes, it must always reach the same equilibrium set of prices.

The *tâtonnement* can be depicted as taking place in a less dramatic way, but the argument is accordingly less rigorous. Let us extend our view from one week to a whole series of weeks, while still restricting the economic horizon of the individuals themselves to one week. Let us also assume that on Monday morning of each of these weeks every individual of the economy is newly endowed with exactly the same collection of commodities that he received the preceding week. The marketing period is now reduced to a single instant, and the first price offered in that instant for any commodity becomes the price which prevails throughout the week. At this price individuals are free to buy or sell any quantities they desire—provided they can find a willing seller or buyer. Clearly, this price is not in general the equilibrium one. In the "marketing instant" of the next Monday, then, the price offered is raised or lowered in accordance with the state of excess demand which existed the week before. In this way the *tâtonnement* continues week after week until the equilibrium set of prices is finally reached.[10]

For a discussion of the role of the theory of *tâtonnement* in Walras' *Elements*, and of the neglect it suffered in the later literature, see Note B.

Some time after the above was written, I discovered that R. M. Goodwin had presented the same concept of dynamic analysis in his "Iteration, Automatic Computers, and Economic Dynamics," *Metroeconomica*, III (1951), 1–2. But Goodwin misinterprets Walras and fails to see that this is precisely the role that Walras assigned to his *tâtonnement*. See the detailed discussion in Note B below.

[9] For the specific references to Edgeworth and for the reason I have not followed the recent tendency to associate this assumption with Walras too, see Note B.

[10] See N. Kaldor, "A Classificatory Note on the Determinateness of Equilibrium," *Review of Economic Studies*, I (1933–34), 126–29.

Let us return to our assumption of recontract and show how the corresponding process of *tâtonnement* can be used to explain the two main results obtained in Section 2: the determinacy of equilibrium money prices and the indeterminacy of equilibrium accounting prices.[11]

Consider an economy during the marketing period. Assume first that the process of *tâtonnement* is at a stage where the average level of the presently proclaimed prices is the same as that in the ultimate equilibrium position but that the ratios between these proclaimed money prices differ from the corresponding equilibrium ratios. Then there are amounts of excess demand for those commodities whose relative prices are respectively lower than the corresponding equilibrium prices and amounts of excess supply for those commodities whose relative prices are respectively higher. Accordingly, in the next round of approximations, prices of the former goods will be raised and prices of the latter lowered. In brief, the existence of any discrepancy between the proclaimed relative prices and the equilibrium ones automatically generates market forces which themselves tend to eliminate the initial discrepancy. Clearly, these same corrective forces are also automatically called into being by any accidental departure from equilibrium values, should they once be reached.

Assume now that the process is at a stage where relative prices are the same as in the ultimate equilibrium position, but the average level of money prices is, say, lower. This implies that the real value of money balances is higher than in the equilibrium position. Correspondingly, there exist amounts of excess demand in the various markets pressing prices upwards. That is, any discrepancy between the proclaimed absolute level of money prices and the equilibrium level automatically generates market forces which tend to eliminate the discrepancy. Once again, these same forces will also automatically correct any accidental departure from the equilibrium level.

Assume, finally, that the process has reached equilibrium but that the chairman accidentally continues with the process of *tâtonnement*. In particular, assume that he proclaims a new set of accounting prices, each of which exceeds the corresponding price of the equilibrium set by a constant percentage. As we saw in Chapter II:4, this increase changes neither relative prices, nor real incomes, nor the real value of initial money balances. Hence none of the amounts of excess demand for commodities are thereby affected. Therefore, since the commodity

---

11 The approach of the following three paragraphs is adapted from that of Wicksell, *op. cit.*, pp. 23–24, 39–40; the latter passage is cited in full in Note E:1. The discussion here admittedly ignores many difficulties. For a more rigorous statement, the reader is referred to Mathematical Appendix 3:*b*.

markets were in equilibrium before this unnecessary *tâtonnement*, they must remain so afterwards too. By Walras' Law, the equilibrium of the money market must, therefore, also remain undisturbed. Thus the accidental proportionate departure of accounting prices from an initial equilibrium position creates no amounts of excess demand for any good—and hence generates no market forces anywhere in the economy —which might operate to force these prices back to their original levels. Therefore, if one set of accounting prices is an equilibrium set, every multiple of that set must also be one. Accounting prices are indeterminate.

Actually, the existence of this indeterminacy is almost self-evident. As pointed out in Chapter II:2, accounting prices are not even observable market phenomena. Hence it is certainly not surprising that their equilibrium values cannot be determined by market forces. Instead, these forces must be supplemented by an external decree arbitrarily fixing the accounting price of one—and only one—of the goods in the economy. If equilibrium money prices are already determined, this suffices to determine the equilibrium accounting prices of all other goods   Thus, for example, if we know the pound prices of goods and are told that the accounting price of a paper pound is arbitrarily set at 20/21 guineas, we can immediately determine the corresponding guinea prices of all other goods by simply multiplying their pound prices by 20/21. Similarly, if the accounting price of the pound were to be arbitrarily doubled and set instead at 40/21 guineas, this would immediately fix the guinea prices of all other goods at levels which were also double those of the original case. Clearly, the money and relative prices of these two cases are, respectively, identical. Equally clearly, in the absence of such an arbitrary specification, equilibrium guinea prices cannot possibly be determined.

Thus equilibrium money prices and equilibrium accounting prices are determined by two distinct processes: the former by internal market forces, the latter by the arbitrary decree of a *deus ex machina*. No such distinction exists between money prices and relative prices. Both of these are simultaneously determined by market forces alone. Only conceptually can we decompose these forces into two components, one which operates through the real-balance effect and thereby determines the absolute level of money prices, and one which operates through the substitution effects and thereby determines the ratios of these prices.

4. Let us now consider an economy in equilibrium and examine the effect of injecting into it an additional quantity of money. We continue with the assumption that to every set of given conditions there corresponds one and only one equilibrium position and that the process of successive approximation described in Section 3 always succeeds in reaching this position.

Assume that we stand at the close of the Monday marketing period with the set of equilibrium prices having just been reached. Let there now be some external force which, say, suddenly doubles the initial money holdings of each individual of the economy. The immediate implication of this increase is that the marketing period must be re-opened and the *tâtonnement* recommenced, for what constituted the equilibrium set of prices before the increase cannot constitute one afterwards. In particular, at these prices real balances are now higher than in the original equilibrium position, whereas relative prices and real incomes are the same. Hence at these prices a universal state of excess demand now replaces the original state of equilibrium.

In accordance with our accepted dynamic principle, these pressures of excess demand initiate a series of successive approximations which push proclaimed money prices upwards. For simplicity, let us assume that these prices rise simultaneously and equi-proportionately. It is then clear that a *tâtonnement* proceeding in this way will bring money prices to a level double that of the original equilibrium set. For should they rise less, real balances would still be greater than in the original position; hence a state of excess demand would continue to prevail, pressing prices further upwards. On the other hand, should prices more than double, real balances would become less than in the original position; hence a state of excess supply would be created, pressing prices downwards again.

Obviously, this doubled set of prices must be the equilibrium set corresponding to the doubled amount of money. For relative prices and real incomes corresponding to this new set are the same as they were in the original equilibrium position; similarly, the real values of the doubled money endowments are now once again the same as those of the original money endowments; hence the amount of market excess demand for each commodity and for real money holdings must be the same as in the original equilibrium position—that is, zero. In brief, an increase in the amount of money causes a proportionate increase in equilibrium money prices.[12]

---

[12] Note that the assumption that there exists an original equilibrium set implies that there also exists a new one; no separate existence assumption on this score is required. Note also that even if we permit several solutions, one of them must be a multiple of the original set. But in this case an increase in the amount of money need not increase prices proportionately; for prices may move to a new equilibrium set which is *not* this multiple. On these statements and the text in general, see Mathematical Appendix 2:*c*.

The validity of this conclusion clearly depends on the assumption that the individuals' initial money holdings are all increased in the same proportion. For consider a doubling of the total amount of money in the economy which does not take place in this way. In such a case the economy need not be restored to equilibrium by a doubling of all prices. For the real value of the increased money holdings of *each* individual will then not be the same as in the original equilibrium position. Hence the amounts of market excess demands will also not be the same. In general, the new equilibrium position in this case will involve higher relative prices for those goods favored by individuals whose money holdings have more than doubled and lower relative prices for those goods favored by individuals whose holdings have less than doubled. This fact was duly emphasized by the classical and neoclassical advocates of the quantity theory of money.[13]

On the other hand, the preceding argument does not presume any restriction on the nature of the dependence of the commodity excess demands on real balances. As a corollary, neither does it presume that all individuals in the economy must react in the same way to changes in these balances. For since real balances in the two equilibrium positions are identically the same, the question of what would happen to excess demands if these balances were changed can have no relevance for the comparative-statics analysis. But it is very much relevant to the dynamic analysis, for the path followed by the economy during the period of dynamic adjustment is clearly dependent upon the way in which individuals react to the temporarily increased real balances which mark this period. These observations hold even if we assume that some of the commodities are inferior. As just explained, this cannot affect the nature of the new equilibrium position itself, but it can and does affect the dynamic process by which this position is reached and in some cases might even prevent its being reached at all.

Nor, finally, does the argument depend on the simplifying assumption that the dynamic adjustment works itself out through simultaneous equi-proportionate increases in money prices. For if there always exists a unique equilibrium position, and if the system is stable, then—regardless of the nature of the dynamic price movements—the economy must ultimately reach the new equilibrium position in which each and every price has doubled.

5. Let us now approach the problem from the viewpoint of the money market. Clearly, we must reach the same conclusions as in the

---

[13] For the analytical background of this paragraph, see Chapter II:6. For references in support of the last sentence, see Chapter VIII:1, p. 98, footnote 11.

preceding analysis, where the approach is from that of the commodity markets. Nevertheless, it is interesting to show explicitly the obverse relationship that exists between these two approaches.

We continue to assume for simplicity that any change in money prices takes place in a simultaneous, equi-proportionate manner. Once again, p represents the average of these prices. Consider first the situation in which the aggregate initial endowment of money—that is, the amount supplied—is fixed at M_0. Assume this to be distributed in a

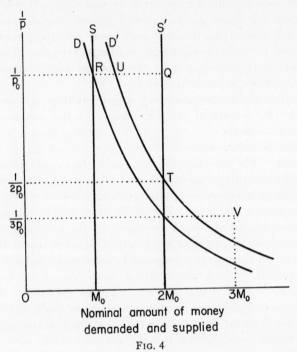

Nominal amount of money
demanded and supplied

Fig. 4

given way among the individuals of the economy. In Figure 4 let D and S represent, respectively, the demand and supply curves for *nominal* money holdings corresponding to this initial endowment.[14] In sharp distinction to Figure 3 (page 28), a movement of the price level along the vertical axis of Figure 4 is assumed to be unaccompanied by any change in the initial endowment of money. Hence, as will be recalled, not only is there no reason for the demand curve D to be a rectangular hyperbola, but it need not even have a negative slope.[15]

---

14 Figure 4 is patterned after the supply-and-demand interpretation of Figure 2 presented on p. 14.
15 See p. 30.

For simplicity, however, D is drawn with such a slope. The intersection of D with S at the point R then determines the equilibrium price level p_0.

Assume now that the initial money endowments are all doubled, so that the total amount of money in the economy rises to $2M_0$. This clearly causes a rightward shift of the supply curve to S' in Figure 4. Consider now the demand curve. As will be recalled,[16] not all of the increased endowment is expended in the commodity markets. That is, there is also a real-balance effect in the money market. This is reflected diagrammatically as a rightward shift from D to D': at the same level of absolute prices, individuals—because of their increased initial endowments—now feel themselves able to indulge in a higher level of liquidity.

With the exception of one point upon it, no restriction can be placed upon the form of the new demand curve D'. But, as it turns out, this one point is all that we need. We know from Figure 4 that when the total initial money endowment is M_0 and the price level p_0, the amount of money demanded is also M_0. It follows from the assumed absence of money illusion that when the total initial money endowment is $2M_0$ and the price level $2p_0$, the amount of money demanded is $2M_0$ (Chapter II:5). Thus the point T in Figure 4 must lie on D'—the demand curve corresponding to the initial money endowment $2M_0$. But the point T must obviously also lie on S'. Hence, whatever the form of D', it must intersect S' at the point T, corresponding to a price level of $2p_0$. Similarly, if the initial endowment of money were increased to $3M_0$, the new demand curve (not drawn in Figure 4) must intersect the new supply curve at the point V, corresponding to the price level $3p_0$.

It remains to describe the dynamic process by which the market actually moves from R to T. It is here that we can see the advantage of the approach of the preceding section over that of this one. For the essential nature of the market forces which activate this process are neither directly nor concretely pictured in Figure 4. Instead, we must resort to the reflection which this diagram casts on the state of demand in the commodity markets. Thus consider the price level p_0. After the amount of money has been doubled, there exists at this price an amount of excess supply equal to UQ. But an excess supply of money means an excess demand for commodities. Therefore, at this price level pressures exist in the commodity markets to drive p up and hence $1/p$ down. Figure 4 can thus be used only indirectly to explain the *tâtonnement* by which the point T is finally reached. Nevertheless, we do in this way ultimately reaffirm the conclusion of the preceding section:

---

[16] P. 27.

that an increase in the amount of money causes a proportionate increase in equilibrium money prices.

6. Let us now consider the points R, T, and V in Figure 4—and all other possible equilibrium points that can be generated by changing the amount of money. The locus of these points is traced out in Figure 5. It is obvious that the curve which emerges in this diagram is a

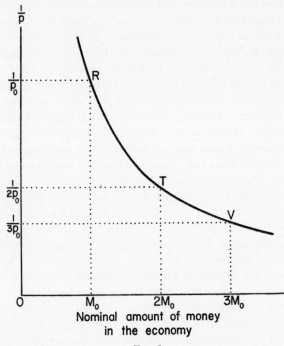

FIG. 5

rectangular hyperbola. It is equally obvious that it is *not* a demand curve. Indeed, by construction it is the locus of intersection points of demand curves and their corresponding supply curves.

To be more precise,[17] in back of Figure 5 there is a conceptual market-experiment in which we take an economy in equilibrium, introduce into it a disturbance in the form of an equi-proportionate change in initial money holdings, and then let this disturbance work itself out in all its manifestations until the economy returns again to an equilibrium position. The results of this experiment give us one point in Figure 5— a point which associates a quantity of money in the economy with its

---

[17] See Chapter I:4 for an explanation of the concepts now to be used.

corresponding equilibrium level of money prices. By continuing to change the quantity of money in this way we generate additional points. In accordance with the direct proportionate relationship that has been shown to hold between this quantity and the equilibrium price level, these points must trace out a rectangular hyperbola.

A curve generated in this way from market-experiments will be denoted henceforth by the term "market-equilibrium curve." It must be sharply distinguished conceptually from a demand curve—which, by definition, is generated by individual-experiments. In particular, it cannot be overemphasized that the market-equilibrium curve of Figure 5 will have the form of a rectangular hyperbola regardless of the form of the demand curves of Figure 4. This is evident from the graphical argument of the preceding section. In terms of our present terminology we can explain this independence by noting that these demand curves describe the outcome of an individual-experiment which is not at all relevant to the market-experiment under consideration. For at the close of this market-experiment, the individual finds himself confronted with an equi-proportionate change in prices *and* in his initial money holdings; whereas any *given* demand curve of Figure 4 describes the results of an individual-experiment in which prices are changed, but the individual's initial money holdings are kept constant.

This independence obviously disappears as soon as we consider a market-experiment and a *relevant* individual-experiment. Thus the market-equilibrium curve of Figure 5 implies that in an individual-experiment in which the individual is confronted with an equi-proportionate change in prices and initial money holdings, he increases the amount of money demanded proportionately. This information is clearly and consistently depicted either by Figure 4 in the movement from the point R on one demand curve to the point T on another; or by Figure 3 in the movement from R to T along a single demand curve which is itself a rectangular hyperbola. These are alternative descriptions of the same individual-experiment.[18]

---

[18] See Mathematical Appendix 3:*d*.

CHAPTER IV

Money and Interest

1. *Introduction. The meaning of time preference. The purpose and nature of bonds.* 2–3. *The excess-demand functions for commodities, bonds, and money.* 4. *The effects of an increase in the amount of money.* 5. *The argument extended to a production economy.*

1. The foregoing analysis is based on the simplifying assumption that the individual's sole concern with the future is to meet it with adequate money reserves. The present chapter moves one step closer to reality by permitting the individual's economic horizon to extend over a period of time—say a "month"—which includes several weeks. It follows that the optimum collection of goods which he chooses in the current Monday marketing period specifies the amounts to be consumed, not only during the current week, but during future weeks as well. This in turn implies that the individual plans *now* how much to buy or sell of each commodity in each of the marketing periods of the month. It should, however, be clear that when in the course of time the individual comes to the marketing period in question, he will not generally act in accordance with the plans he now makes. For by that time new information will be available which will cause him to modify them. Thus, for example, he will by that time have information on a week—or on weeks—which is now beyond his economic horizon. In brief, we assume that every Monday each individual reconsiders the whole situation that will confront him during the ensuing month and formulates or revises his plans accordingly.[1]

---

[1] The reader will recognize here the familiar technique of Hicks, *op. cit.*, Chapters IX–X, especially p. 124. But whereas Hicks' main purpose in devising this technique is to analyze the origin and significance of discrepancies between planned and actual behavior, we completely

An immediate implication of this extension of the economic horizon is that the money balances which the individual plans to hold at the end of, say, this week are intended to meet the transactions and precautionary needs of a clearly defined plan of expenditures for next week. Thus the demand for money in our present economy is a much more concrete concept than the one to which we were logically restricted in the one-week-horizon case of preceding chapters.

By analogy with the argument of Chapters I and II, these plans are assumed to be determined by the individual's tastes, his endowment of commodities, his initial money holdings, and the prices with which he is confronted. But now the term "tastes" refers to future consumption as well as present; "endowment of commodities" includes the endowments which will descend upon him during future Sunday nights as well as that received this Sunday; and "prices" includes those with which he will be confronted in future marketing periods as well as in the present one. For simplicity, it is assumed that these future prices are expected —with certainty—to be identical with current ones. It is, however, generally assumed that future endowments are expected—again, with certainty—to differ from the current one.

This last assumption can be restated in more familiar terms if we remember that the value of any week's endowment of commodities is analogous to the income of that week.[2] We can then say that each individual takes the time shape of his anticipated income stream as certain and unalterable but, in general, not uniform. Diagrammatically, we have the situation shown in Figure 6. The numbers on the abscissa represent the weeks of the one-month economic horizon. This is assumed to extend, say, four weeks beyond the current one— represented by the number zero. The curves *A*, *B*, and *C* describe various possible income streams. The uniform income stream *A* represents the special case of an individual who expects to continue to receive exactly the same endowment of commodities in each future week. On the other hand, income stream *B* is that of an individual who expects his weekly income to decrease steadily during the month, while stream *C* is that of an individual with opposite expectations. Clearly, we can also have more complicated cases in which the income

---

ignore this fundamental problem. Instead, we use this technique only in order to rationalize the holding of money and to make room for transactions which involve a rate of interest. See below.

2 This and the following paragraph are based on Irving Fisher, *The Rate of Interest* (New York, 1907), Chapters VI–VII; or, alternatively, his later *Theory of Interest* (New York, 1930), Chapters IV–V. Note, however, that our usage of "income" differs from Fisher's— though, for our present purposes, in an immaterial way.

stream is expected to rise during certain parts of the month and to fall during others. As already emphasized, the expectations in all these cases are held with certainty.

An immediate implication of these assumptions is that the individual will probably desire to redistribute his consumption over time; that is, he will in general not want to equate the value of his consumption for any week with the arbitrarily given income of that week. For example, the individual with income stream *B* may well prefer to consume less than his current income—that is, to save—in the early weeks of the month in order to be able to consume more than his income—that is, to dissave —in the later weeks. Conversely, the individual with income stream *C*

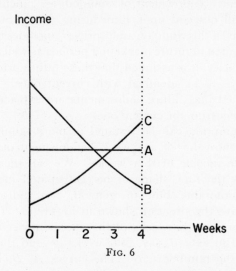

FIG. 6

will prefer to consume more than his income during the beginning of the month and less later. For the moment, it suffices to explain these desires to save and dissave with the common-sense observation that the individual cannot benefit by having weeks of gluttony alternate with weeks of starvation in accordance with arbitrary variations in income.[3]

It is assumed that the individual cannot effect this redistribution of consumption over time by hoarding commodities from one week to the next. Instead, he must resort either to changing the amount of money he carries over to the next week or to making the appropriate transactions with a new good that we shall introduce—the bond. This is a note obligating the issuer to redeem it from the bearer one week after issue

---

[3] A precise description of the optimum allocation of consumption over time will be given in Chapter VI:2, equation (9).

at the fixed price of one dollar.   An individual who wants to dissave in any given week can sell such bonds during the Monday marketing period of that week; that is, he can borrow.   An individual who wants to save can buy such bonds; that is, he can lend.   "Can," and not "must"; for, as just indicated, savings and dissavings may also express themselves in changes in money holdings.   We assume further that there is no risk of default; hence the identity of the borrower is a matter of indifference to the lender.   It follows that all bonds are economically indistinguishable from one another

Thus the bond is just another good which is bought and sold on the market.   Its price, like that of any other good, is also expected to be in the future exactly what it is today.   This price, denoted by q, is clearly related to the rate of interest, $100r$ per cent.   Specifically,

$$r = \frac{1-q}{q}.$$

As this relation shows, the higher the price of the bond, the lower the rate of interest, and conversely.   Note that a bond price of unity corresponds to a zero rate of interest, and a price greater than unity to a negative rate.

For simplicity, bonds are assumed to be just as illiquid as commodities.   That is, they cannot be sold except during the Monday marketing period and cannot be used to make any necessary payments.   Thus the individual in our simple exchange economy cannot regard bonds as even a partial substitute for money.   In brief, if he deals with bonds, he does so only as a means of modifying the time shape of his consumption stream.

The foregoing can be called a "time preference" theory of interest. If we have deliberately avoided doing so until now, it is because of the ambiguity which surrounds this term in the literature.   As originally used by Fisher it is merely a statement of the fact that individuals redistribute their consumption over time in an optimum way; it is not an explanation of the forces which bring them to feel that such a redistribution is desirable.[4]   For such an explanation Fisher depends primarily —and in this we have followed him—on the time shape of the income stream.   As a secondary explanation he brings in the possibility that, due to their lack of foresight and self-control, individuals may systematically prefer present over equivalent future consumption.[5] With or without awareness of their departure from Fisher's original

---

[4] See, e.g., *ibid.*, pp. 66–67.
[5] *Ibid.*, pp. 80 ff.

meaning, later economists seem to have used the term "time preference" to refer only to this possibility.[6] Clearly, the foregoing analysis of borrowing and lending operations does not presuppose the existence of "time preference" in this sense of the term. But such a "preference" may—in an exchange economy—be logically necessary to explain why these operations generate an equilibrium rate of interest greater than zero. We shall return to this question again.[7]

2. The extension of the individual's economic horizon to more than one week and the concomitant introduction of bonds obviously call for modifications in the demand theory of the preceding chapters. First of all, there are hitherto undefined goods whose excess-demand functions must now be described. Second, even the excess-demand functions for goods already defined are no longer the same as they were. For these functions must now reflect two new influences—one representing the past, the other the future.[8]

Let us begin with a discussion of the latter modifications. Consider the individual at the start of the Monday marketing period. The assets which he has carried over from the preceding week now comprise matured bonds as well as money. Unlike any other good of the initial collection, these bond holdings can be negative in magnitude. This is the case for anyone who sold bonds the preceding Monday, that is, for anyone who starts the current marketing period as a debtor. Conversely, these holdings are positive for anyone who starts the period as a creditor.

These initial bond holdings must clearly affect the individual's current excess-demand functions for commodities. A debtor tends—*ceteris paribus*—to decrease his amounts of excess demand in order to be able to redeem—with interest—the bonds he sold last Monday. Conversely, by virtue of the repayment he receives on the bonds bought last week, a creditor tends to increase his amounts demanded. Clearly, the degree of the decrease or increase in the amounts of commodities demanded can rationally depend only on the *real* value of these initial, matured bond holdings.

So much for the influence of the past. Consider now the influence of the future. This is reflected first of all in the dependence of the current excess-demand functions on the time path of the future income stream.

---

6 Cf., e.g., K. E. Boulding, *Economic Analysis* (revised ed.; New York, 1948), pp. 751–52; E. S. Shaw, *Money, Income, and Monetary Policy* (Chicago, 1950), pp. 322–23.

7 Section 4.

For further discussion of the distinction between the two senses of "time preference," see p. 79, footnote 5.

8 The rigorous development of what now follows is deferred to Chapter VI:1–2.

This has been sufficiently discussed in the preceding section. We need only add here that it is again the sequence of *real* values in this stream that is rationally significant for commodity demands.

The influence of the future is reflected, secondly, in the rate of interest. An increase in interest represents a cheapening of future commodities with respect to present ones. More specifically, it lowers the cost of the bonds necessary to provide purchasing power over a fixed quantity of future commodities. However, as is well known, it is impossible to specify a priori the effect of this change on the amount demanded of present commodities. If, for example, the demand for future commodities has only slight interest-elasticity, then the number of bonds which the individual demands in order to obtain purchasing power over them will increase only slightly; and in view of the lowered per-unit price of bonds, the individual's total expenditures on them will decrease. Hence funds will be released for additional expenditure on current commodities. If, however, the demand for future commodities is sufficiently interest-elastic, the total expenditure on bonds will increase, with a consequent decrease in the amount demanded of present commodities. We shall assume the latter possibility to hold. In other words, we shall assume that savings are positively related to the rate of interest.[9]

What is most significant for the following analysis is that the rate of interest is the analogue of a relative price. As we shall see in Chapter VI:2, just as the relative price measures the marginal rate of substitution between two different commodities consumed this week, so the rate of interest measures (though it is not equal to) the marginal rate of substitution between a commodity this week and the same commodity next week. Similarly, the formula of the preceding section shows that r is equal to a fraction whose denominator is q (the money price of a bond at time of issue) and whose numerator is $1 - q$ (the difference between this price and the money price of a bond at time of maturity —by definition, equal to unity). Thus the rate of interest, like a relative price, is the quotient of two amounts, each of which has the dimensions of a money price. Correspondingly, we argue by analogy that wherever the term "relative prices" appears in the demand theory of preceding chapters, we must now write "relative prices and rate of interest."

To summarize, the excess-demand functions for current commodities of an individual with given tastes (including whatever preferences for present as against equivalent future consumption that he may possess)

---

[9] For simplicity, this paragraph abstracts from the additional influence of interest changes on the demand for money; this will be taken account of in our more detailed discussion of Chapter IX.

51

are now assumed to depend upon relative prices, the rate of interest, present and future real incomes, the real value of initial bond holdings, and the real value of initial money holdings.[10]

3. Consider now the new goods introduced in this chapter. There are, first of all, those commodities which will come into existence only in the course of future weeks. Even though physically identical with the commodities now existing, they are more conveniently considered as analytically distinct.[11] Correspondingly, for each of these commodities there is a separate excess-demand function. This function describes the quantities which an individual decides this Monday to buy or sell of the commodity in question on some specified future Monday within his economic horizon. Now, by assumption, prices and interest in future weeks are expected—with certainty—to be identical with those currently prevailing. Hence the amount of excess demand for a future commodity depends on exactly the same relative prices, rate of interest, real income stream, and real value of initial bond and money holdings as does the amount of excess demand for a current commodity.

It should, however, be emphasized that the amounts of excess demand for a future commodity differ from those of a current one in *not* being registered on this Monday's market. That is, there is no futures market to provide a concrete manifestation of these plans. This "blackout" on the future lends somewhat more credibility to our assumption that the individual always expects prices and interest to continue unchanged. At the same time, we must remember that when the individual finally reaches the Monday in question, the prices which will then confront him will generally not be the same as those which he now envisages. But we shall have to abstract here from the complications generated by these discrepancies.[12]

The remaining new good is the bond. In order to prevent any possible confusion, it should be emphasized that we are now referring to the bonds currently issued and currently sold—or discounted—in the market. We are *not* referring to the bonds issued last week, which must now be redeemed at face value. From the viewpoint of the

---

[10] For simplicity, we continue to ignore the dependence on the initial endowment of the commodity in question; see p. 19, footnote 5.

On the argument of this section, see Mathematical Appendix 4:*a*.

[11] See Hicks, *op. cit.*, pp. 193–94.

[12] It should be clear that what we disregard here as a "complication" forms the basis of Hicks' dynamic analysis, *ibid.*, Chapters IX–X and Part IV. Conversely, what we—following Walras and Samuelson—have presented and shall continue to present under the caption "dynamic analysis" is more or less taken for granted by Hicks; see the Additional Note C which he appends to the second edition of *Value and Capital*. See also Note B below, especially pp. 383–84.

individual's behavior in the market this week, the latter are a datum; they are the initial holdings of matured bonds whose influence has already been discussed above. It is only with respect to currently issued bonds that different decisions can be made in accordance with the different given conditions of the market; hence it is only for these bonds that there can properly be said to exist a demand function.

By definition, the initial holdings of currently issued bonds are zero. Hence there is no difference between the *demand* for bonds and the *excess demand*. This amount demanded can be positive or negative— according to whether the individual decides, respectively, to lend or borrow during the current week. In the latter case we can say, alternatively, that the amount of bonds *supplied* is positive.

Before describing the properties of the demand function for bonds, we must first add restrictions which will keep it finite. In the absence of such restrictions, each individual would choose to borrow indefinitely large amounts each week and to provide for the payment of principal and interest on them by borrowing still larger amounts the following week. In this way he could continue interminably to refund his debt— no matter what its magnitude. This, in turn, would enable him to demand unlimited amounts of commodities each week.

The usual analysis bars this possibility by assuming that there is some type of "imperfection" in the capital market which prevents an individual from borrowing all he wants to at the going rate of interest. This is undoubtedly a realistic assumption. However, since it is desired to keep the analysis as simple as possible, we shall not employ it here. Instead, we shall accomplish the same result by arbitrarily assuming that the individual must formulate his present and future market plans under the additional restriction that on the final Monday of the month his planned holdings of bonds must be zero. Clearly, this Monday of reckoning recedes constantly into the future as time progresses. But as long as the individual acts on the assumption that it must ultimately come and that he must repay all his debts by the end of his economic horizon, he will curtail his planned borrowings accordingly.[13]

Like that for other goods, the demand function for bonds is assumed to depend upon prices, the rate of interest, present and future incomes, the value of initial bond holdings, and the value of initial money holdings. An increase in initial money holdings increases the amount of bonds demanded; this, of course, is the basic assumption implicit in Keynesian interest theory.[14] Similarly, an increase in the initial

---

[13] This point is discussed further in Mathematical Appendix 5:*b*, p. 319.
[14] See Note K:1; this will be discussed further in Chapter XI:1.

holdings of bonds also increases the amount demanded of new bonds. In particular, the more pronounced the individual's initial creditor position, the more inclined he will be to buy new bonds and thereby replenish his portfolio; the more pronounced his debtor position, the more pressed he will be to sell new bonds and thereby renew the credit previously extended to him.

Consider now the influence of the rate of interest. It has already been assumed in the preceding section that a decrease in it will decrease the amount of bonds demanded. It is also clear that if there are no costs of carrying over money balances from one week to the next, the amount of bonds demanded at any negative rate of interest must be zero or negative. For no individual will pay more than one dollar for the right to a dollar's worth of purchasing power next week if he can obtain this same power by merely adding one dollar to his planned money balances. Indeed, this line of reasoning implies that the amount of bonds demanded will become zero at some positive rate of interest which measures the satisfaction which the individual derives from being liquid. At any rate below this, the individual will always choose to carry purchasing power over to next week in the form of liquid money holdings rather than totally illiquid bond holdings. This is merely Keynes' familiar argument translated into a form appropriate for the bond market.[15]

One property of the bond demand function is fundamental to the following analysis. Assume the individual to be confronted with a doubling of all money prices (expected, of course, to be permanent), initial bond holdings, and initial money holdings, while the rate of interest is kept constant. By the assumptions made above as to the form of the excess-demand functions for commodities, there is no change in the amounts demanded of either present or future commodities. Thus there is no change in the extent to which the individual originally planned to re-allocate his consumption between this week and future weeks. Neither, then, is there any change in the total amount of real purchasing power which the individual plans to hold at the end of the week. Finally, in view of the constancy of the interest rate, there is no change in the relative amounts of this purchasing power which the individual desires to hold in the form of bonds and in the form of money. Thus the preceding change does not affect the extent of command over next week's commodities which the individual plans to hold in the form

---

15 *The General Theory of Employment, Interest and Money* (New York, 1936), p. 207. This argument will be presented more precisely in Chapters VI:1 and IX:4. In general, it has been considered advisable to defer a more detailed discussion of the bond market to this latter section.

of bonds. But the expected money prices of these future commodities have doubled. Hence, in order to maintain his originally planned level of future *real* purchasing power, the individual must also double his planned *nominal* holdings of bonds. That is, whatever he originally planned to lend or borrow, he must now plan to lend or borrow twice as much.

It remains to consider the excess-demand function for money. As in Chapter II:5, the form of this function is completely specified by the budget restraint. In particular, we can write

the amount of excess demand for current money holdings

= the (face) value of initial bond holdings

+ the aggregate value of the amounts of excess supplies of current commodities

− the (discounted) value of demand for current bond holdings.

From what has been said about the properties of the demand functions for commodities and bonds, we can immediately see from this formula that the change discussed in the immediately preceding paragraphs will also double the amount of money demanded.

More generally, an equi-proportionate change in money prices, initial bond holdings, and initial money holdings, the rate of interest being held constant, will cause a proportionate change in the amounts demanded of bonds and of money. It follows that the demand functions for *real* bond holdings and *real* money holdings, like those for commodities, depend only on relative prices, the rate of interest, present and future real incomes, the real value of initial bond holdings, and the real value of initial money holdings.[16]

So far we have discussed the excess-demand functions of the individual. The corresponding functions of the market are derived by aggregation, as in Chapter II:6. Once again, there is asymmetry in that the market functions depend on the *arrays* of initial real bond and money holdings of all individuals in the economy, and not generally on their respective *totals*. Another asymmetry appears in the form of the market excess-demand function for money. Since the economy is assumed to be closed, every existing debt must be owed by one of its members to another. Hence the value of *initial* bond holdings aggregated over all members of the economy must necessarily be zero: to every "positive" creditor there corresponds a "negative" debtor. On

---

[16] For a rigorous development, see Chapter VI:2.

the other hand, as emphasized in the next section, this is not generally true of the amount of aggregate *demand* for *new* bonds.   Thus we have

> the amount of market excess demand for current money holdings
>
> = the aggregate value of the amounts of market excess supplies of current commodities
>
> − the (discounted) value of the amount of market demand for current bond holdings.

An immediate implication of the foregoing discussion is that the definition of money illusion presented in Chapter II:4 is no longer appropriate.   For consider an individual confronted with an equiproportionate increase in money prices and initial money holdings. If he is a debtor, such a change reduces the real burden of his initial debts and hence tends to increase his demands for goods; while if a creditor, the change reduces the real value of his initial bond assets and hence tends to decrease his demands.   From the viewpoint of the self-interest of the individual, it is no more irrational for him to react to these changes in his real asset position than it is for debtor classes to support inflationary policies and creditor classes to oppose them.   In other words, though the specified change does not have a real-balance effect, it does have what we shall call a "real-indebtedness effect." Only if the terms of past indebtedness are adjusted to the new level of prices—or, what is equivalent, only if initial bond holdings are changed at the same time and in the same proportion as prices and initial money holdings—will this real-indebtedness effect disappear.

Accordingly, we must broaden the definition of money illusion in the following way: An individual is free of money illusion if the amount he demands of any real good (commodities, real bond holdings, and real money holdings) remains invariant under any change which does not affect relative prices, the rate of interest, real income, and the real value of initial bond and money holdings.   This definition clearly includes the earlier one as a special case.[17]

4. In accordance with our usual procedure, let us now pass from market excess-demand functions to excess-demand equations and the nature of the equilibrium position.

Since it is new to the analysis, it is advisable first to devote some particular attention to the bond market.   From the preceding section it is clear that the bond demand and excess-demand equations are

---

[17] On the argument of this section, see Mathematical Appendix 4:*a*.

identical. We can then say that at the equilibrium set of prices and interest, the aggregate amount demanded in this market is zero—that is, the total amount of desired borrowings in the economy is equal to the total amount of desired lendings. At any other set it can be either positive—indicating an excess of willing lenders over borrowers—or negative—indicating the opposite.

It is also clear from the preceding section that the equilibrium rate of interest cannot be negative, for at such a rate there would always exist an excess of borrowers over lenders. On the other hand, there is no assurance that it must be positive. For if the only reason people lend or borrow is because of the time shape of their future income streams, and if it is just as likely that these streams show an increase over time as a decrease, then it may well be that at the minimum rate of interest needed to compensate lenders for their loss of liquidity, no one desires to borrow. Thus the bond market might be in a vacuous equilibrium in which neither borrowing nor lending takes place.[18]

In order to preclude this possibility it is necessary to strengthen the supply side of the bond market—that is, the desire to borrow. This can be done, for example, by attributing to the income streams a systematic upward bias. In such a progressive economy the desire to anticipate future income may understandably predominate. Alternatively, we can achieve the same result by assuming the prevalence of a systematic preference for present as against equivalent future consumption.[19] Actually, however—for reasons which will become evident in the final section of this chapter—we need not concern ourselves overmuch with this problem.

Let us now turn to the overall equilibrium position of the market. As emphasized at the beginning of the preceding section, this market deals exclusively with current goods. Correspondingly, its equilibrium set of prices and interest must equate to zero the amounts of market excess demand for current goods only. It would be sheer accident if this same set could also equate to zero the aggregate amounts of excess demand for future goods. Conversely, these potential future disequilibria cannot even cast a shadow on current market developments. They manifest themselves only in the course of time, as the future becomes the present.

Nothing, then, is essentially different from the analysis of Chapter III:2. Once again there are $n - 1$ unknown equilibrium values—

---

[18] Were it not for the liquidity factor, we could replace this by the simpler—and more familiar—statement that it may well be that at a zero rate of interest there is no excess of borrowers over lenders.

[19] See the end of Section 1 above.

now consisting of the $n - 2$ respective money prices of current commodities and the rate of interest on current bonds. Once again there are n excess-demand equations: $n - 2$ for current commodities, one for current bond holdings, and one for current money holdings. And once again only $n - 1$ of these equations are independent; for, as can be seen from the form of the excess-demand function for money in the preceding section, any set of prices and interest that equilibrates the commodity and bond markets must also equilibrate the money market; that is, Walras' Law is still valid. In brief, the extension of the economic horizon to future weeks—under our simplified assumptions—does not make it necessary to take into account the excess-demand equations for future goods. In our present analytical framework these equations do not exist: they place no additional restrictions on the equilibrium set of prices and interest.

Let us assume for the present that the system is a stable one and investigate its comparative-statics properties. Let the economy be in equilibrium at a certain set of money prices and interest rate. Assume now that the initial money holdings of each individual are doubled. It is clear that the new equilibrium position corresponding to this increased amount of money is *not* in general one in which prices have doubled and the rate of interest has remained unchanged. For such a doubling of prices creates real-indebtedness effects which increase the amounts demanded by debtors and decrease the amounts demanded by creditors. Only by chance would these exactly offset each other in each and every market. This exceptional case will be described as one in which the price change has a "neutral distribution effect."

Thus a doubling of the amount of money can in general be expected to affect both equilibrium relative prices and the rate of interest. Specifically, the relative prices of those commodities favored by debtors will rise, while those favored by creditors will fall. Similarly, the interest rate will rise or fall, depending on which of two countervailing forces is stronger: the decrease in the demand for bonds, caused by the worsened real position of creditors; or the decrease in the supply of bonds, caused by the improved real position of debtors.[20]

Let us now assume that the equilibrium position of the economy is disturbed by a doubling of the initial money *and* bond holdings of each individual. In this case it is clear that equilibrium is reëstablished with doubled money prices and an unchanged rate of interest: for relative prices, the interest rate, the arrays of real incomes, initial real bond holdings, and initial real money holdings are then exactly the same as in

---

[20] Note the similarity between this discussion and that on p. 41 (top).

the original equilibrium position.   Hence the amounts of excess demand for commodities, real bond holdings, and real money holdings must also be the same as in that position : each of them must be zero.

Thus we conclude: If there is no money illusion and if outstanding debts are revalued (or, alternatively, if there is a neutral distribution effect), then a uniformly introduced increase in the amount of money causes a proportionate increase in the equilibrium prices of commodities and leaves the equilibrium rate of interest unaffected.[21]

This conclusion can be usefully restated in terms of the familiar concept of "neutral money." Strictly speaking, such neutrality obtains if the mere conversion of a barter economy to a money economy does not affect equilibrium relative prices and interest.[22] Now, because the systems of excess-demand equations of these two economies differ so fundamentally (in a barter economy there is obviously neither an excess-demand equation for money nor a dependence of commodity excess-demand equations on real balances), it is difficult, if not impossible, to make such a comparison in a general way. If, however, we conceive of a barter economy as the limiting position of a money economy whose quantity of money is made smaller and smaller, we can obviate this difficulty. For we can then remain within the system of excess-demand equations of a money economy and note what happens to its equilibrium values of relative prices and interest as the quantity of money approaches zero as a limit. Under the conditions specified in the preceding paragraph, we see that we can in this way get as "close" as we want to a barter economy without affecting the equilibrium values of these variables. In this sense, the foregoing conditions are all that are needed in order to assure the neutrality of money.[23]

5. So far we have only the sketch of a theory of interest. We have not yet adequately described the markets for bonds and money; we have not discussed the dynamic process by which the economy reaches its equilibrium position; nor have we really explained the full meaning of the invariance of the equilibrium rate of interest under a change in the amount of money. Furthermore, the theory itself is developed only for the case of a simple exchange economy. We must therefore extend it to the case of a production economy as well. At the same time, we must fill in the lacunae just listed. These are the tasks which await us in Part Two. The reader who is interested solely in these aspects of the argument can, then, continue directly with Chapter IX.

---

[21] See Mathematical Appendix 4:*b–c*.

[22] Cf. F. A. Hayek, *Prices and Production* (second ed.; London, 1935), pp. 129–30.

[23] See Mathematical Appendix 4:*c*.

Even without the details of this later development, we can intuitively see that the assumption of an exchange economy is nowhere near as restrictive as it first appears. To speak somewhat loosely, the conclusion reached above—the invariance of relative prices and the rate of interest under a change in the amount of money—flows from the assumption that there is no money illusion. Hence any change in the analytical framework which leaves this assumption intact must also leave this conclusion intact.

Consider, in particular, the case of a production economy. Its differentia is that the amount supplied of any commodity is not constant —as it is in an exchange economy—but variable. That is, there exists in this economy the possibility of production. This means that firms can transform varying inputs of factor services into varying outputs of commodities. But the essential point is that—according to the marginal-productivity theory—once the technical conditions of production are specified, the decisions of a firm with respect to these inputs and outputs are based entirely on relative prices. Its decision on the optimum quantitative relationship between any two factors depends on the relative price of these factors as compared with their marginal rate of technical substitution; its decision on the optimum quantitative relationship between a factor and a commodity depends on the price of the former relative to the latter, as compared with the marginal productivity of the former in terms of the latter; finally, its decision on the optimum relationship between two commodities depends on their relative price as compared with the marginal rate of technical substitution between them.[24] If, in addition, we admit the possibility of investment, these decisions will also depend on the relationship between the rate of interest and the marginal productivity of capital. Finally, if we follow recent developments in the theory of the firm and assume it to be concerned with its balance sheet as well as its profit-and-loss statement, it will again be the *real* value of its assets and liabilities that the firm will take into account in reaching its decisions.

In brief, firms, no less than individuals, can be assumed to be free of money illusion. That is, in an economy with given technical conditions of production, firms enter the market with supply functions for commodities and demand functions for factor services, each of which is dependent upon relative prices, the rate of interest, and the real value of assets. From the earlier sections of this chapter, we know that, at the same time, households enter the market from the other side with demand functions for commodities and supply functions for factor services

---

[24] Cf. Hicks, *op. cit.*, Chapter VI, especially p. 86.

dependent upon exactly the same variables.   Hence the market
excess-demand equations of a production economy have exactly the
same basic property—and reflect exactly the same absence of money
illusion—as do those of our simple exchange economy: they depend
solely on relative prices, the rate of interest, real income, and the real
value of assets.   It follows that the invariance of relative prices and
interest under a change in the amount of money holds with equal validity
for both types of economies.[25]

This generalization of the argument eliminates one basic difficulty in
the preceding interest theory.   For as soon as we take into account the
possibility of profitable investment in a production economy, we automatically provide that additional stimulus to the desire to borrow which
was shown above to be necessary for the assurance of a positive equilibrium rate of interest.   In fact, practically all of the borrowing in our
economy can now be assumed to originate from entrepreneurs who
require funds to finance investment and who are therefore willing to pay
interest in keeping with its marginal productivity.   Correspondingly,
the supply side of the bond market is dominated by these entrepreneurs.
In contrast, the consumption loans to which the analysis of this chapter
has hitherto been restricted now exert only a minor influence on this side
of the market.

We might finally note that the assumption that bonds are totally
illiquid instruments—made at the beginning of this chapter—is also
unnecessary for the validity of the argument.   This is intuitively clear.
For even if bond holdings are partial substitutes for money holdings,
it can only be the *real* value of these holdings that is of concern to the
individual.   Hence, once again, there is no change in the form of the
excess-demand equations on which the preceding analysis is based.[26]

---

[25] These paragraphs make clear the untenability of the position—recently endorsed by D. H.
Robertson—that there are, from the viewpoint of monetary theory, intrinsic differences between
an exchange and a production economy.   See Robertson's "More Notes on the Rate of
Interest," *Review of Economic Studies*, XXI (1953–54), 136–37.

[26] For a rigorous demonstration, see Chapter VI:3.

CHAPTER V

The Utility Theory of Money

1. *The nature of the utility of money.* 2. *The one-week-horizon case : the conditions for utility maximization ; the marginal utility of money and the marginal utility of expenditure.* 3. *The excess-demand functions of Chapter II derived alternatively from the foregoing conditions,* 4. *from indifference maps, and from revealed preferences.* 5. *The "circularity charge" refuted.*

1. The argument of the preceding chapters departs in one respect from the pattern set for it by Chapter I: instead of deriving the properties of the excess-demand functions from utility theory, it merely posits them by analogy. Actually, it is not at all clear that it is methodologically preferable to take utility functions—as against excess-demand functions—as the point of departure for the theory of demand. Furthermore, as will be shown below, the basic property of absence of money illusion can be derived even without recourse to utility analysis. It suffices, instead, to consider the revealed preferences of an individual assumed to be consistent in his choices. Nevertheless, in view of the fact that formal attempts to apply marginal-utility analysis to monetary theory are as old as the "subjective-value revolution" itself, it is worth while presenting a detailed description of how such an application can successfully be carried out.

Actually, the aforementioned attempts never achieved general acceptance. Indeed, their validity was for many years hotly debated among Continental followers of the marginal-utility school. Some of the deniers of this validity even went so far as to provide mathematical demonstrations that money could not have any "utility." Others merely stated that money did not have any "direct utility." In neither case was the meaning of these contentions made clear. What is worse, even those who took the opposite side of the argument rarely based their analyses on a proper definition of the utility of money. As a result they were drawn into protracted, confused, and indecisive debates on a sham "circularity" issue which never should have arisen in the first place.[1]

It is thus essential to make clear at the outset the sense in which "utility of money" will be used in the present discussion. In particular, it is not intended to denote the utility of the money commodity; indeed, we continue to assume a fiat paper money precisely in order to avoid any ambiguity on this score. Nor is it intended to denote "the marginal utility of the goods for which the money can be exchanged." Instead, our concern is with the utility of *holding* money, not with that of *spending* it. This is the concept implicit in all cash-balance approaches to the quantity theory of money; and it is the one that will be followed explicitly here.[2]

To be more precise, consider the role of money reserves as described in Chapter II:1. Were it not for them, the lack of synchronization between the inflow and outflow of money in the course of the week would almost certainly force the individual to default on some of the hourly payments he is called upon to make. The security that money reserves provide against financial embarrassment of this type is what invests them with utility. It cannot be overemphasized that there is no difference in kind between this utility and that of any other intangible service. Furthermore, it is clear that the larger these reserves are, the greater the degree of security they provide. As will also be seen in Chapter VII, constant additions to money balances yield—after a certain point— decreasing increments of such security. Hence, in a world of measurable utility, it is reasonable to assume that the marginal utility of money balances must eventually diminish with their size.

It is again noted that the efficacy of money balances in providing this security is dependent on their *real*—and not *nominal*—value.[3] Correspondingly, it is only the real value of money balances that is of relevance for the individual's utility calculus. This is the basic assumption of the following argument.

The organization of this argument parallels that of the preceding one. The present chapter first derives the excess-demand functions of the one-week-horizon case of Chapter II; the next chapter then

---

1 See below, Section 5.
2 The quotation in this paragraph is from L. von Mises, *The Theory of Money and Credit*, trans. H. E. Batson (New York, 1935), p. 109. On this and the preceding paragraphs, see the references to the literature in Note D below.
3 Cf. p. 21.

derives those of the multi-week-horizon case of Chapter IV. In each case the argument is presented first in terms of measurable utility, then in terms of indifference maps, and finally in terms of revealed preferences. As already indicated, for the rationalization of the aforementioned demand functions, a discussion of this last approach alone would suffice; the other approaches are described only in order to provide a basis for a critical appraisal of the literature which deals with them.[4]

2. In accordance with this plan of operation, let us first consider the case of the individual of Chapter II, who—with the exception of his desire to start next week with adequate money balances—limits his economic horizon to one week. Accordingly, the existence of borrowing and bonds is for the moment precluded. On the assumption of measurable utility, the analysis then proceeds along familiar lines. There is an obvious opportunity cost of holding money reserves. For the higher these reserves, the greater the quantity of commodities that must be given up in order to maintain them. This is nothing but a statement of the budget restraint.[5] Hence the individual confronted with a given endowment and a given set of market prices is faced with the classic economic problem of allocating his scarce resources among competing ends in such a way as to maximize his utility. This is achieved when he buys that collection of goods which equalizes the marginal utility of a dollar's expenditure on each good—where one of these goods is real money balances.

This conclusion can be described more precisely in the following terms. Let X, Y, ... represent commodities, and H, *real* money balances; while x, y, ... , and h represent the respective quantities of these goods. Let "the marginal utility of x units of X" be a shorthand expression for "the marginal utility of X when x units of it are consumed." Now, the reciprocal of the price of X equals the number of units of X that can be purchased for one dollar. Hence this reciprocal multiplied by the marginal utility of x units of X represents the marginal utility of a dollar's worth of X when x units of it are purchased *at the given set of market prices*. Similarly, the quantity of commodities-in-general that can be obtained for one dollar equals the reciprocal of the general price level. Hence this reciprocal multiplied by the marginal utility of h units of H represents the marginal utility of a dollar held in money balances when—*at the given set of market prices* —h units of real purchasing power are held in these balances.

---

[4] For this appraisal see the critique of Walras' marginal-utility theory of money in Note C:2–3 and the briefer discussions of other writers in Note D.

[5] Cf. p. 25.

It follows that an individual will maximize his utility when, at the given market prices with which he is confronted, he uses all—and just all—of his initial endowment to acquire the quantities x_0 of X, y_0 of $Y, \ldots$, and h_0 of H which satisfy the following conditions:

$$
\begin{aligned}
& \frac{\text{the marginal utility of } x_0 \text{ units of } X}{\text{the price of } X} \\[6pt]
(1) \qquad & = \frac{\text{the marginal utility of } y_0 \text{ units of } Y}{\text{the price of } Y} \\[6pt]
& = \cdots = \frac{\text{the marginal utility of } h_0 \text{ units of } H}{\text{the general price level}} = \lambda.
\end{aligned}
$$

This is, of course, equivalent to our original statement that the individual's optimum collection of goods is $x_0, y_0, \ldots, h_0$ if and only if this collection is consistent with his budget restraint and the following equations hold:

(2) the marginal utility of a dollar spent on X when x_0 units of X are purchased

= the marginal utility of a dollar spent on Y when y_0 units of Y are purchased

$= \cdots =$ the marginal utility of a dollar held in money balances when the total real purchasing power of such balances is $h_0 = \lambda$.

The variable λ in these relationships represents Marshall's "marginal utility of money." It is the uniform utility of a dollar on the margin of expenditure in all pursuits. It is the utility of the "last" dollar spent. In order to distinguish this concept from the "marginal utility of money" as used here, we shall refer to the former as the "marginal utility of expenditure."

The distinction between these two marginal utilities is quite clear. Consider, first, the marginal utility of money balances. This is measured by the following conceptual experiment: We take an individual with a given collection of goods (in general, *not* the optimum one) and increase his money balances by one dollar, while keeping constant his consumption of all other goods and the given prices which confront him. We then note the increase in his utility resulting from this increase in money balances. Clearly, there is no necessity for this increase to equal λ.

The marginal utility of expenditure is measured by a completely different experiment. We take an individual with a collection of goods which is the optimum one for the prices, income, and initial

65

money holdings with which he is confronted. We then increase his income by one dollar and permit him to spend it in the optimum way. Finally, we note the difference between the total utility from his new optimum collection of goods as compared with that from his original one. This difference must equal λ. For no matter how this additional dollar is spent, the optimum conditions (2) show that it generates λ additional units of utility.[6]

On the other hand, if the first experiment were performed for an individual with an *optimum* collection of goods, it too would yield the answer λ. But there is nothing special about this relationship. For, as equations (2) show, under these conditions the same result would obtain for a dollar's worth increase in the holdings of any good.

Similarly, there is no special connection between constancy of the marginal utility of expenditures and constancy of the marginal utility of money. From equations (1) it can readily be seen that in order for the former to hold—that is, for λ to be constant with respect to an increase in income—it is necessary that the marginal utility of at least one of the goods $X, Y, \ldots, H$ be so constant. The increase in income would then be spent entirely on that good, without any resulting change in any of the ratios in (1). Clearly, however, there is no necessity for the good with the constant marginal utility to be real balances, H.[7]

3. The foregoing utility-maximization conditions together with the budget restraint determine the individual's optimum holdings—or, alternatively, amounts demanded—of goods. In particular, since one of these goods is real money balances and since the price level is given, they also determine the amount demanded of nominal money balances. By varying the given data with which the individual is then confronted, we can conceptually use these optimum conditions to generate his demand—and, by implication, excess-demand—functions.[8] Let us now deduce some properties of the functions thus generated. Unless otherwise noted, the argument will be carried out on the assumption that the marginal utility of any good diminishes with its quantity and is independent of the quantity consumed of any other good.

Consider first the effects of a doubling of initial money holdings,

---

[6] In this and the following paragraph we ignore the fact that the increases in consumption change the marginal utilities of the goods concerned. Since the increases are small, this can be safely done.

[7] On all of the above, see Mathematical Appendix 5:*a*. On Marshall, see his *Principles of Economics* (eighth ed.; London, 1920), pp. 95–96. See also the discussion in his Mathematical Appendix, pp. 838–39. This makes it clear that our λ corresponds to Marshall's "marginal utility of money."

[8] For further details of this procedure, see above, Chapter I:1–2.

income and prices being kept constant.   For simplicity, assume that the individual at first uses all of this increment to increase his amount of money demanded.   From equations (1) we can then readily see that this will leave him with a collection of goods which is no longer an optimum one.   For, on the one hand, the marginal utility of a dollar spent on commodities X, Y, .. has not changed; while, on the other, by the assumption of diminishing utility, the marginal utility of a dollar held in cash balances has decreased.   Hence the individual will be able to increase his total utility by diverting part of the original cash increment to increasing his amounts demanded of commodities X, Y, ... In this way he will reach a new optimal collection in which he demands more than x_0 of X, more than y_0 of Y, ... , and more than h_0 of real balances.   Here is the rationale of the real-balance effect.

Assume now that instead of doubling his initial endowment of money, we halve all the prices with which the individual is confronted, keeping all endowments constant.   Assume that at first the individual changes neither the amounts of commodities nor the *nominal* amount of money demanded.[9]   Once again equations (1) show that this collection can no longer be an optimum one.   For as a result of the halving of prices, each dollar can now buy twice as many units of any commodity; hence the marginal utility of a dollar spent on any commodity of the original optimum collection has doubled.   On the other hand, the marginal utility of a dollar held in cash balances has less than doubled. For though each dollar now represents twice as much command over commodities-in-general, the halving of the price level has doubled the real value of the individual's originally demanded nominal balances and therefore reduced their marginal utility.   Hence once again the individual can increase his total utility by increasing his purchases of commodities.

Assume, finally, that we confront the individual with a doubling of prices *and* initial money holdings.   If now the individual doubles his amount of nominal balances demanded and maintains constant his amounts of commodities demanded, his resulting collection of goods will be an optimum one.   For his real balances are still h_0; hence the marginal utility of real balances has not changed.   On the other hand, the purchasing power of a dollar has halved; hence the marginal utility of a dollar held in cash balances has also halved.   But, by similar reasoning, so has the marginal utility of a dollar spent on any commodity.   Thus the marginal utility of a dollar is again everywhere the same.   It should

---

9 This actually violates the budget restraint; hence the argument of this paragraph is only heuristic.   It can be made more rigorous by assuming that the changes called for by the budget restraint are of a smaller magnitude than those now to be discussed.

be emphasized that the validity of this conclusion is *not* dependent either on the diminution or the independence of marginal utilities.

Thus by applying utility analysis to the assumptions of Chapter II we are able to deduce from prior premises those properties which we there had to posit. This is particularly true for the absence of money illusion. It should be emphasized that this derivation does not depend for its validity on any assumed special relationship between the magnitude of real money balances and their marginal utility. In particular, it does *not* depend on the assumption that the doubling of the nominal balances demanded, prices constant, is accompanied by the halving of the marginal utility of a dollar held in these balances.[10] All that is required is that this marginal utility decline; nothing need be specified about the extent of the decline.

On the other hand, as we have just seen, it is true that a doubling of nominal balances demanded *and* prices is accompanied by a halving of the marginal utility of a dollar held in cash balances. But this assumption is much less restrictive than the preceding one. It is simply an expression of the fact that the doubling of the price level has halved the amount of *real* liquid purchasing power that is acquired by adding a dollar to money balances. In other words, it is merely a reflection of the individual's freedom from money illusion.

4. Let us now abandon the assumption of measurable utility and show how the excess-demand functions of Chapter II can also be derived from indifference-curve analysis. To make the problem graphically manageable, we shall assume that all prices vary in the same proportion, so that we can consider the collection of all commodities as a single composite good.[11] Denote this good by G. Continue to denote real balances by H. Proceeding in the usual fashion, we can then construct an indifference map (Figure 7) showing equally desirable combinations of these two goods.[12]

Since both real balances and commodities are assumed to have positive marginal utilities, these indifference curves have the usual negative slope. We also assume a diminishing marginal rate of substitution: the greater his holdings of real balances, the less willing is the individual to give up units of commodities in order to obtain an additional unit of such balances. For the purposes of the following analysis, no further

---

10 This is emphasized here because of the allegation by Mises that the validity of the quantity theory depends on just this assumption; see Note D below, p. 414.

11 Hicks, *op. cit.*, pp. 33–34.

12 It is clear that the familiar indifference map of Hicks which represents "money" on one of the axes is completely different from the one of Figure 7. Indeed, Hicks' "money" corresponds more closely to our composite commodity (*ibid.*, pp. 33, 38 ff.).

assumptions need be made about the shapes of the indifference curves. However, for the sake of realism, these curves are drawn to reflect the additional assumption that real balances and commodities are poor substitutes. That is, the almost vertical slope of their initial portions shows that after the individual has satisfied a certain "minimum" need for real balances, he is not very anxious to surrender additional commodities in order to increase these balances further.

Consider now the nature of the budget line. Assume that at a given price level the individual uses all of his initial endowment to purchase commodities. Let the amount so purchased be a. Assume now that, instead, the individual devotes all of his initial endowment to the holding

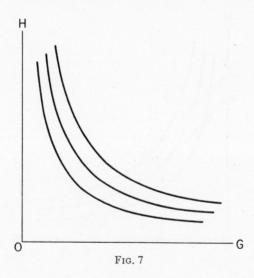

Fig. 7

of cash balances. Then the amount of real purchasing power represented by these balances must obviously also be a. Thus the budget restraint must be a 135° line intersecting both axes at a. The unitary negative slope of this line reflects the fact that, by definition, one unit of liquid command over commodities-in-general can always be exchanged for one unit of actual commodities-in-general.

Assume now that the individual's money income or initial holdings of money are increased, or that the price of the composite commodity is decreased. Each of these changes has the same effect of increasing the real value of the individual's initial endowment. Hence in each case the budget line will shift to the right. But in each case this line must clearly retain the same 135° slope. Thus our budget line has the special characteristic that its slope must remain invariant under any change.

We now combine indifference curves and budget line to determine the optimum position of the individual (Figure 8). Assume that the individual's given prices and initial endowment correspond to the budget line *aa*. Then the optimum position is at *P*. Here the individual will demand *c* units of commodities and *d* units of real balances. Clearly, in any such optimum position, the marginal rate of substitution between these two goods must equal unity.

Let us now return and examine in detail the effect of an increase in initial money balances. This shifts the budget line rightwards, say to *bb*. The new optimum position is then *Q*. As already implied, the marginal rate of substitution here must again be unity. Under the

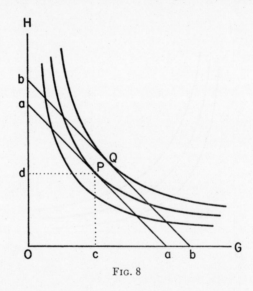

FIG. 8

simple assumptions of Figure 8, the quantities demanded of both real balances and commodities thus increase as a result of this change. Since prices are constant, this means that the amount demanded of nominal balances also increases. Thus the real-balance effect manifests itself in an increase in the amounts demanded of all goods.

Assume now that it is a proportionate decrease in commodity prices which pushes the budget line over to *bb*. Once again the point *Q* shows an increase in the quantities demanded of real balances and commodities. But this time the amount demanded of *nominal* balances must decrease. This is a direct implication of the budget restraint and the assumption that the composite commodity *G* is not inferior.[13]

---

[13] Cf. p. 29, footnote 19.

Assume finally that the individual is confronted with a proportionate increase in commodity prices and in his initial holdings of money. Then the real value of his initial endowment is not changed. Hence his budget line is unaffected, so that P remains his optimum point. Thus the amount demanded of neither commodities nor real balances is affected by this change. However, since prices have increased, this implies a proportionate increase in the amount demanded of nominal money balances. In brief, the individual is free of money illusion.

From the viewpoint of utility analysis, we have now proved too much! For the simplicity of Figure 8—together with the insight of Samuelson's method of revealed preferences—now discloses that our argument actually stands completely free of any utility underpinning. In particular, let Figure 8 be stripped clean of everything but the budget line *aa*. Assume that an individual endowed with the real income and initial real balances represented by this budget line chooses that combination of commodities and real balances represented by the point P. Now, this real endowment gives the individual the wherewithal to choose any point on *aa*—and *a fortiori* any point in the triangle cut off by *aa* and the axes. His choice of P thus reveals that he prefers this point to any of the others.

Consider now the effects of confronting the individual with an equiproportionate change in prices and initial money holdings. This does not change the real value of his initial endowment, and hence it does not change his budget line. Therefore, the individual faces now exactly the same real choices as he did before. Hence if before he chose the point P, he must do so again now. Thus the rationale of absence of money illusion—and, accordingly, of the special form of the excess-demand functions of Chapter II—depends on nothing more than the consistency of our individual's choices.[14]

5. It is now a simple matter to dispose of the "circularity charge" mentioned at the beginning of this chapter. According to this charge, the value of money—that is, the price level—cannot be said to be determined by its marginal utility. For the utility of a given nominal amount of money depends on its real value, and this cannot itself be known until the price level has first been determined. Hence in speaking of the marginal utility of money, we would already be implicitly assuming what we had undertaken to explain.[15]

---

[14] Samuelson has provided a lucid explanation of his method in "Consumption Theorems in Terms of Overcompensation rather than Indifference Comparisons," *Economica*, XX (1953), 1–9.

[15] This summarizes the argument of K. Helfferich, *Money*, trans. L. Infield (London, 1927), pp. 526–27. For further references to the literature, see Note D below.

The discussion of the preceding two sections makes it clear that this charge originates in a basic misunderstanding of the theory of price determination. It is, of course, true that money differs from other goods (making the usual reservations for "snob goods" and the like) in that its marginal utility cannot be determined unless prices are first specified. But, for the question at hand, this is a completely irrelevant distinction. For what interests us here is not the subjective utility calculus as such, but its implications for market behavior. And for information on this behavior, no more need be specified for the good money than for any other good.

Thus consider the exposition on page 64 above. It is clear that the italicized phrase *"at the given set of market prices"* is just as necessary for the determination of the amount of excess demand for commodity X as it is for the determination of the amount of excess demand for money. Or consider the indifference analysis of the preceding section. It is clear that the optimum quantity of neither commodities nor real balances can be determined in the absence of a budget line; but such a line, in turn, cannot be determined unless prices are first given.

In brief, here again is a confusion between types of experiments.[16] In a market-experiment, money prices are the variables whose values must be determined. Hence it would truly be a case of *petitio principii* to assume that prices are already determined. But in an individual-experiment, the amounts of excess demands are the variables to be determined, and money prices are the independent variables whose values *must* be given in order to conduct the experiment. Clearly, there is no circularity in stating that the market excess-demand equations derived from such individual-experiments are then used to determine the equilibrium money prices of the market-experiment.

In more familiar terms, we have here a confusion of "demand" with "amount demanded." It is true that the amount demanded of money —as well as of any other good—depends upon prices. Nevertheless, it is also true that the equilibrium prices depend upon the demand functions. The "circularity charge" is simply a denial of this elementary distinction.[17]

---

16 See Chapters I:4 and III:6.

17 So A. W. Marget, *The Theory of Prices* (New York, 1938), Vol. I, p. 445, footnote 86.

CHAPTER VI

The Utility Theory of Money (*Continued*)

1. *The multi-week-horizon case: the conditions for utility maximization.*
2. *The excess-demand functions of Chapter IV derived from these conditions translated into ordinal terms and, alternatively, from revealed preferences.*
3. *The case of liquid bonds.*   4. *The inadequacy of liquidity theories of interest.*

1. Having provided a rationale for the excess-demand functions of Chapter II, we must now do the same for those of Chapter IV. Reverting to the assumption of measurable utility, let us examine the properties of an optimum collection of present and future goods chosen by an individual who operates with a given budget within a multi-week horizon. In order to avoid possible confusion, we emphasize that the term "marginal utility of a good of a future week" in the following discussion means the marginal utility that the individual plans *now* to obtain in the future by buying the good in question then.

Consider first the commodities related to any given week. Clearly, the marginal utility of a dollar's expenditure on any one of these commodities must equal that on any other. But, in contrast to the situation described by equations (1), this marginal utility of expenditure does *not* also equal the marginal utility of a dollar held in cash balances at the end of that week.[1] The reason for this difference is not difficult to see. It is a direct consequence of the special nature of money reserves, which, alone of all goods, is not used up in the process of providing its utility service. Now, as long as we were dealing with the case of a one-week horizon, this could not affect the individual's utility calculus. For if he added a dollar to cash balances, he sacrificed a dollar's worth of

---

[1] In what follows, we restrict the term "marginal utility of expenditure" to expenditures on commodities, as distinct from money balances.

commodities for economic eternity. But as soon as the individual takes into account the consumption of more than one week, he must also take into account the fact that a dollar added now to cash balances will still exist at the beginning of next week and can still be used to purchase commodities then. Thus the *net* subjective cost of holding a dollar in cash balances at the end of this week is *not* the marginal utility of the dollar's worth of consumption foregone this week, but this utility *minus* the corresponding utility that can be recouped by spending the dollar next week.

Alternatively, we can argue in the following way. If the individual is in an optimum position, he cannot increase his utility by planning now to decrease his current expenditures by one dollar, add it to the cash balances held at the end of the week, and use this dollar to increase his expenditures next week. That is, a condition for maximum utility is

the marginal utility of a dollar's expenditure this week

(3)   = the marginal utility of a dollar held in real cash balances at the end of this week

     + the marginal utility of a dollar's expenditure next week.

Clearly, this equation holds for any two successive weeks within the individual's economic horizon. In the special case where this horizon extends for only one week, it obviously reduces to equation (2).

Of course, it is not necessary for the individual to spend this hoarded dollar next week. He can instead plan to keep it in his cash balances and spend it only in the last week of his economic horizon. It follows that for an optimum position the following relationship must obtain:

the marginal utility of a dollar's expenditure this week

     = the marginal utility of a dollar held in real cash balances at the end of this week

     + the marginal utility of a dollar held in real cash balances at the end of next week

(4)   + $\cdots$ + $\cdots$ + $\cdots$

     + the marginal utility of a dollar held in real cash balances at the end of the penultimate week

     + the marginal utility of a dollar's expenditure in the last week.

This equation is also obtainable by repeated application of equation (3).

74

This assumes that the individual has no concern whatsoever for what will happen after the close of his economic horizon and hence plans to spend the dollar in the last week, at the latest.   If, however, we assume that the individual considers the future after the last week in the same light that the one-week-horizon individual considers the future after the current week, we can obtain an interesting variant of the preceding equation.   For then the individual can plan to keep the additional dollar in his cash balances in every week of his economic horizon, including the last one.   Accordingly, the last term of equation (4) can be replaced by "the marginal utility of a dollar held in cash balances at the end of the last week," and the equation as a whole can be rewritten as

the marginal utility of a dollar's expenditure this week

(5)   = the marginal utility of a dollar held *permanently* in real cash balances,

where the right-hand term is the sum of the marginal utilities on the right-hand side of equation (4), modified as just indicated.   In this way we achieve a multi-week counterpart of equation (2).   Similarly, we could continue to carry out the analysis in terms of Figures 7 and 8— with H now interpreted as representing the real balances of future weeks as well as of the present one.

Let us now take account of the fact that the individual also has the alternative of redistributing his consumption over time through appropriate bond transactions.   This implies that an individual with an optimum collection of goods must be in such a position that he cannot increase his total utility by planning now to decrease current expenditures on commodities by one dollar, buy bonds with the savings, and use the principal and interest he receives for these bonds next week to buy commodities then.   That is, the following familiar relationship must hold for any two successive weeks:

the marginal utility of a dollar's expenditure this week

(6)   = the marginal utility of $(1 + r)$ dollars' expenditure next week,

where $100r$ per cent is the rate of interest.

By subtracting equation (6) from equation (3) we obtain

the marginal utility of a dollar held in real cash balances at the end of this week

(7)   = the marginal utility of r dollar's expenditure next week.

75

In other words, the subjective opportunity cost of carrying over a dollar's purchasing power from one week to the next in the form of liquid cash balances, instead of doing so in the form of illiquid bonds, is the utility of the commodities that could have been bought next week with the interest obtainable from the bonds. Hence, for an optimum collection, the marginal utility afforded by a dollar's worth of cash balances must be equal to this marginal subjective cost.

Thus the individual's optimum collection of goods must satisfy the conditions described by equations (1)—modified as indicated—(6), and (7). Any collection which does so must also satisfy equation (3)— which is subsumed under the last two equations. The same clearly holds true for equations (4) and (5) as well.

Equation (7) provides the rationale for Keynes' familiar statement that the existence of liquidity preference—that is, a marginal utility of cash balances greater than zero—implies a rate of interest greater than zero.[2] More precisely, if there are bond transactions, the rate of interest on them must be positive. But there may not be any such transactions. This will be the case if at the minimum rate called for by the marginal utility of cash balances there is also an absence of borrowers. Then the bond market would formally be in equilibrium, with neither borrowing nor lending taking place. The rate of interest in this case would not be defined, so that neither equation (6) nor, by implication, equation (7) would be operative. But the condition of equation (3) would continue to be operative and would now, in its own right, place a limitation on the size of cash balances demanded. It is interesting to note that equation (3) would also continue to imply that the planned marginal utility of expenditure for any given week must be greater than that of the following week. Thus the "discounting of future pleasures" would continue to take place even in the absence of a positive rate of interest.[3]

2. Let us now translate equations (1), (6), and (7) into terms of ordinal utility. For this purpose we consider them as defining the compensating variations that must be made in the individual's optimum collection of goods in order to keep his level of total utility unchanged. Read this way, equation (6), for example, states that, in his optimum position, an individual will be just as well off if one dollar's worth of this week's commodities is replaced by $(1 + r)$ dollars' worth of next week's. Similarly, equation (7) states that he will be just as well off if a dollar's worth of real balances is replaced by r dollar's worth of commodities

---

2 See Chapter IV:3–4.

3 On the argument of this section, see Mathematical Appendix 5:*b*.

next week.   In brief, these equations give us the individual's marginal rates of substitution in his optimum position.   More formally, these rates can be derived by dividing through the utility-maximization conditions by the appropriate marginal utility and then making use of the fact that the marginal rate of substitution is the ratio of the relevant marginal utilities.[4]

Applying this method to equations (1)—modified as indicated at the beginning of the preceding section—we obtain

(8) the marginal rate of substitution of any two commodities of the same week

= the ratio of their prices.

As might be expected, this familiar optimum condition thus carries over intact from the one-week-horizon case.

Consider now equation (6).   Remembering that λ in equations (1) is the marginal utility of a dollar's expenditure, let us replace the left-hand side of (6) by

$$\frac{\text{the marginal utility of } X \text{ this week}}{\text{the price of } X}$$

and the right-hand side by

$$\frac{(1 + r) \text{ marginal utility of } X \text{ next week}}{\text{the price of } X}.$$

Dividing through the resulting equation by "the marginal utility of X next week," we obtain

(9) the marginal rate of substitution of any commodity this week for the same one next week

$$= 1 + r.$$

Faced with a given rate of interest, the individual will adjust the quantitative pattern of his consumption over time—or, if we want, saving over time—so as to satisfy this optimum condition   The difference between the time shape of the resulting consumption stream and that of the given income stream is a primary source of the demand for, and supply of, bonds.   From equation (9) we also see that if the law of diminishing marginal rate of substitution obtains, and if the quantities of all other goods are held constant, then the substitution effect of an increase in interest causes a decrease in the amount demanded of current commodities and an increase in that of future ones.

---

4 For further description of this procedure, see Chapter I:1.

Let us turn now to equation (7).   Making use of equations (1) again, we rewrite this as

(10)
$$\frac{\text{the marginal utility of cash balances at the end of this week}}{\text{the general price level}}$$
$$= r \cdot \frac{\text{the marginal utility of a commodity next week}}{\text{the price of the commodity}},$$

from which we readily obtain

(11)
the marginal rate of substitution of real cash balances at the end of this week for a commodity next week
$$= r \cdot \frac{\text{the general price level}}{\text{the price of the commodity}}.$$

If instead of a specific commodity we consider the composite commodities-in-general, this becomes

(12)
the marginal rate of substitution of real cash balances at the end of this week for commodities-in-general next week
$$= r.$$

It should be emphasized—though it is clear from the ultimate derivation of this equation from equation (3)—that the foregoing rate of substitution takes into account only the utility of the liquidity afforded by money balances and not the utility of the commodities that can be bought with them next week.   It is also clear from equation (9) that if the law of diminishing marginal rate of substitution holds, and if the quantities of all other goods are held constant, then the substitution effect of an increase in interest causes a decrease in the amount of money demanded and an increase in that of future commodities.

Finally, we have the individual's budget restraint.   This we write as

the real value of the optimum collection of commodities, bonds, and money for any week

(13)   = the real value of the collection of commodities, matured bonds, and money held at the beginning of the week.

The equations which define the optimum position of the individual are thus (8), (9), (12), and (13).   The right-hand sides of these four equations are constants, reflecting the given conditions with which the individual is confronted; the left-hand sides of the first three are marginal rates of substitution, dependent on the collection of commodities and real money balances which the individual holds, while the left-hand side of the last equation is this collection itself, plus the real value of bond holdings. Thus these equations state that the individual who maximizes utility within a given budget adjusts the composition of his collection of real goods—including real bond holdings—until the left-hand sides of these equations are respectively equal to the given right-hand sides. It follows that the amounts demanded of commodities, real bond holdings, and real money holdings depend upon—reading the right-hand sides of these equations from top to bottom—relative prices, the rate of interest, real income, the real value of initial bond holdings, and the real value of initial money holdings. In this way we have deduced the excess-demand functions of Chapter IV—with their absence of money illusion—from the principle of utility maximization.[5]

The foregoing development is particularly helpful for the insight it provides into the role of the rate of interest. The analogy of this rate to a relative price—already employed in Chapter IV:2—is immediately apparent from a comparison of equations (8) and (9). Indeed, $1 + r$ is effectively the price of a present commodity relative to the same one in the future. From equations (9) and (12) we also see that this rate operates simultaneously on the individual's margin of choice between present and future consumption, that is, on his saving decisions; and on his margin of choice between holding money and holding bonds, that is, on his liquidity decisions. Were we to extend our theory from an exchange to a production economy, this twofold margin would become a threefold one; for the rate of interest would then operate on the margin of investment decisions as well. This triple role of the rate of interest was duly recognized by neoclassical monetary theorists.[6]

Having displayed all the paraphernalia of the utility analysis, we must now assure ourselves that it is dispensable. The basic money-illusion property of the excess-demand functions can instead be derived by simply considering the budget restraint (13) from the viewpoint of revealed preferences. Any change which affects the real value of the

---

[5] See Mathematical Appendix 5:*c*.

We can now distinguish more precisely between the two senses of "time preference" noted in Chapter IV:1. In Fisher's sense, this is a property of the excess-demand functions for present and future goods; in the sense of the later literature, it is a property of the utility function. Specifically, "time preference" in this sense exists if the value of this function is affected by changes in the time sequence in which the individual plans to consume given collections of goods. Thus these two senses correspond to two distinct levels of discourse. See the end of Mathematical Appendix 5:*b*.

[6] For emphasis on this fact, see D. H. Robertson, *Essays in Monetary Theory* (London, 1940), pp. 16–17; "threefold margin" is, of course, his term. Nevertheless, neoclassical economists—including Robertson—were guilty of some confusion on this matter; see Note D, especially p. 418.

individual's initial collection of goods or the terms on which he can exchange them for other goods—be it a change in relative prices, or interest, or the real value of his initial holdings—will affect this restraint and hence the nature of the optimum collection. Such a change is analogous to a shift of the budget line *aa* in the two-dimensional case of Figure 8. Clearly, however, an equi-proportionate change in prices and initial bond and money holdings, interest being kept constant, does not cause any such shift. Hence the array of collections of real goods from which it leaves the individual free and able to choose is exactly the same array that was open to him before. Hence, if he is consistent, he will again choose the same collection of real goods. Of such simple consistency is the absence of money illusion brewed.[7]

3. The foregoing argument has assumed throughout that bonds are completely illiquid instruments. This implies that no utility attaches to the holding of bonds per se. Accordingly, in none of the preceding equations is there a term referring to or dependent upon the marginal utility of bond holdings: by definition, this must be zero. Nevertheless, as we have seen, individuals may well choose to hold bonds. For by doing so they can both earn interest and improve the time shape of their consumption streams. Accordingly, they can increase the total utility they derive from commodities over the extent of their economic horizon. In this sense we might say that holding bonds generates "indirect utility."

Let us now relax this assumption and permit bonds to acquire some degree of liquidity, though not as much as that of money. For example, we might assume that if in the course of the week the individual should unexpectedly run out of money, he can—by undergoing certain unspecified inconveniences—make his required payments in bonds discounted at the going rate of interest. Thus, unlike commodities, bonds can—if necessary—be "bartered" during the week. It is the existence of this possibility which invests them with liquidity. Accordingly, the individual may now plan to hold bonds both for their "indirect utility" in redistributing consumption optimally over time and for their direct utility in providing a secondary liquid reserve.[8]

This calls for a corresponding modification of equation (6). For in

---

[7] See Mathematical Appendix 5:*d*.

[8] It should be emphasized that the discounted bonds referred to in this paragraph are those which the individual originally contracted to buy during the Monday marketing period and which he has already acquired in accordance with the random payment procedure described on pp. 17 and 49. We do *not* permit the individual to make *new* bond contracts in the course of the week. That is, we do *not* permit him suddenly to issue and discount new bonds in order to meet his liquidity needs.

considering whether to decrease current consumption by one dollar, buy a bond, and use the matured value of this bond next week to buy commodities, the individual must now also take into account the fact that the bond thus in his possession at the end of the current week will have afforded him, during the course of that week, the utility of a secondary reserve. Accordingly, equation (6) now becomes

the marginal utility of a dollar's expenditure this week

(14)   = the marginal utility of a dollar held in real bonds at the end of this week

+ the marginal utility of $(1 + r)$ dollars' expenditure next week.

Substituting from equation (3), we then obtain, instead of equation (7),

the marginal utility of a dollar held in real cash balances at the end of this week

(15)   − the marginal utility of a dollar held in real bonds at the end of this week

= the marginal utility of r dollar's expenditure next week.

Translating these, respectively, into terms of ordinal utility, we then obtain

the marginal rate of substitution of commodities-in-general this week for commodities-in-general next week

(16)   − the marginal rate of substitution of real bond holdings at the end of this week for commodities-in-general next week

$$= 1 + r$$

and

the marginal rate of substitution of real cash balances at the end of this week for commodities-in-general next week

(17)   − the marginal rate of substitution of real bond holdings at the end of this week for commodities-in-general next week

$$= r.$$

This last marginal rate of substitution has a meaning completely analogous to the marginal rate of substitution of real cash balances for commodities: it is the amount of commodities the individual must receive in order to compensate him for the loss of liquidity involved in reducing his bond reserves by one "small unit." From the derivation of the foregoing equations from equation (14), it is again clear—as it was in the case of equation (12)—that this rate does not and should not take into account the utility of the commodities that can be bought with the matured value of the bond next week. Hence, in the special case where bonds are assumed to be completely illiquid, this rate is identically zero. Accordingly, the foregoing equations then reduce to equations (9) and (12), respectively.

We can readily see that the investing of bonds with liquidity has not affected the validity of our basic argument. For once again the individual's optimum conditions—now described by equations (8), (16), (17), and (13)—require him to adjust the quantities of the real goods he consumes so as to bring their marginal rates of substitution into certain specified relationships with the given prices and interest prevailing on the market. Hence once again the resulting excess-demand functions have the same basic form as those of Chapter IV. The intuitive basis of this conclusion has already been noted at the end of that chapter. To repeat, attributing liquidity to bonds does not in the least change the fact that it is only the real value of bond and money holdings with which the individual can rationally be concerned.[9]

4. It was emphasized in the preceding section that some inconvenience is attached to the use of bonds as an emergency means of payment. It is this inconvenience, of course, which makes bonds less liquid than money and therefore makes individuals willing to hold the latter. The important point to note is that this liquidity differential is not a constant, but a variable dependent on the relative magnitudes of the individual's bond and money holdings. In particular—for a given collection of commodities, bonds, and money—it will be defined as the difference between the marginal rate of substitution of the money holdings for commodities *minus* the marginal rate of substitution of bond holdings for commodities. If the law of diminishing marginal rates of substitution continues to be valid, a movement out of money and into bonds— the amount of commodities being kept constant—will then increase the first of the foregoing rates and decrease the second; hence it will increase the liquidity differential. Conversely, an opposite movement will decrease the differential. Equation (17) thus tells us that in order to achieve an optimum position, the individual must adjust his relative holdings of money and bonds so as to bring their differential liquidity into equality with the given rate of interest.

Let us now use equation (17) to analyze the effect of, say, decreasing the inconvenience of making payments with bonds. The fundamental

---

[9] See on this section Mathematical Appendix 5:*e*.

point of departure of this analysis is the fact that the good "bond" is defined only as of a specified degree of inconvenience. Strictly speaking, then, a change in this degree introduces one new good into the individual's field of choice and eliminates one old one. For simplicity, however, we shall denote this new good by the unchanged term "bond" and treat this lessened inconvenience as a shift in the individual's tastes in favor of holding his liquid reserves in the form of bonds rather than money.

The immediate impact of this shift is to increase the marginal rate of substitution of bonds for commodities, relative to that of money for commodities. As a result, optimum condition (17) is no longer satisfied, for the liquidity differential between bonds and money is now less than the fixed rate of interest with which the individual is confronted. In order to rewiden this differential—and thereby move upwards along the new utility function which corresponds to his "changed tastes"— the individual will begin moving out of money and into bonds. He will continue doing this until the liquidity differential is once again optimally equal to the given and unchanged rate of interest.

Thus confronting the individual with a decrease in the inconvenience of using bonds as a means of payment generates a positive shift in his demand for bonds and a negative shift in his demand for money. In the limiting case where this inconvenience is completely eliminated, the demand for money is eliminated as well. For no one will voluntarily hold sterile money reserves when he can with equal convenience hold interest-bearing bond reserves. Accordingly, equation (17) in this case becomes inoperative; for it is pointless to describe the effect of the rate of interest on the margin of choice between holding bonds and holding money when—no matter what this rate—the individual does not choose to hold any money. On the other hand, the influence of the rate of interest continues undisturbed on the combined savings-and-liquidity margin described by equation (16); and, in a production economy, it would also continue undisturbed on the margin of capital investment.

So much for the individual-experiment; it remains to discuss the corresponding market-experiment. In more familiar terms, it remains to analyze the effect of the foregoing shifts in demand on equilibrium interest and prices. This must be deferred to Chapter X:4. There it will be shown that increasing the liquidity of bonds decreases the equilibrium rate of interest; but even in the case where bonds are completely monetized, there is no reason why this rate must fall to zero. To speak somewhat loosely, the primary manifestation of an increased liquidity for bonds is not a lowered rate of interest, but a decreased use of money as a medium of exchange. Correspondingly, the end result of making bonds completely liquid is to eliminate not the rate of interest, but the use of money. In this limiting case the medium of exchange would consist of bonds—whose rate of interest would continue to reflect the traditional forces of thrift and capital productivity.[10]

The foregoing discussion suffices to demonstrate the untenability of any theory which attempts to explain the rate of interest solely in terms of the imperfect liquidity of bonds. In particular, it shows that the basic proposition of Hicks' theory—namely, that in the absence of such imperfections the rate of interest would disappear—is involved in a *non sequitur*.[11] This is not to deny the contribution of liquidity theories in stressing the influence of the rate of interest on the demand for money and in emphasizing that a shift in liquidity preference can permanently affect the equilibrium rate of interest.[12] Nor is it to deny the valuable insight they give us into the relation between interest differentials and liquidity differentials in an economy with many types of bonds. But it is to deny that illiquidity is the *sine qua non* of interest. And it is to deny that the way to build a theory of interest is to base the long-run rate on a short-run rate predicated on such illiquidity.[13] Instead, it seems to me that a proper approach to interest differentials begins in the classical manner with the determination of the rate on long-term bonds by the basic forces of thrift and productivity, and goes down from this rate to the shorter-term ones.

From the viewpoint of our own analytical framework, these monetary theories make yet another fundamental contribution. In particular, we can use them to clarify the nature of the hitherto unspecified "inconvenience" which makes individuals willing to hold money when they can instead hold bonds. If we follow Hicks, we can now explain this in terms of the risk of default involved;[14] as we shall see in Chapter VII:4, this element can be introduced into the preceding argument without much difficulty. Alternatively, following Keynes, we can explain this "inconvenience" in terms of the risk of capital losses created by the uncertainty of future interest rates;[15] the introduction of such uncertainties would greatly complicate the microeconomic argu-

---

10 A detailed description of this limiting case is given in Mathematical Appendix 5:*f*.

11 Hicks, *op. cit.*, p. 165. This *non sequitur* has already been noted by F. Modigliani, "Liquidity Preference and the Theory of Interest and Money," *Econometrica*, XII (1944), as reprinted in *Readings in Monetary Theory*, pp. 233–35; and by P. A. Samuelson, *Foundations of Economic Analysis* (Cambridge, Mass., 1947), p. 123.

12 This will be discussed in Chapter X:4.

13 Cf. Hicks, *op. cit.*, p. 166.

14 *Ibid.*, p. 165.

15 *General Theory*, pp. 168–69.

ment and could demolish all the precision of the macroeconomic one.[16] In any event, it should again be emphasized that the logical problem solved by Keynes and Hicks is not—as they believed—the existence of interest, but rather the peaceful coexistence of money and interest-bearing bonds.[17]

---

[16] This imprecision will be discussed in Chapter XI:3.

[17] It might be noted that this coexistence cannot be explained by the mere bother of constantly converting bonds into money and vice versa. For, as Hicks has so aptly emphasized, this bother is the *result* of illiquidity, and not the *cause*: if bonds were perfectly liquid, they could themselves be used to make payments, so that there would be no need to convert them first into money (Hicks, *op. cit.*, pp. 164–65).

CHAPTER VII

The Nature of the Demand
for Money

1. *The problem stated.*   2. *The model of the random payment procedure.*
3. *The probability distribution and its implications.*   4. *Concluding observations.*

   1. Anyone who attempts a microeconomic theory of money is immediately confronted with a familiar methodological dilemma. If his model is simple enough to be developed without complicated mathematical analysis, it will be too simple to provide a motive for the holding of money. Our own model is no exception.

   Consider first the Monday marketing period. Since by assumption no transactions are completed until the *tâtonnement* reaches the equilibrium set of prices, the individual clearly has no need to hold money balances during this period. Nor does the closing of contracts at the end of the period necessarily change this situation. For there is no logical reason why the payments on these final contracts should not be effected by mere bookkeeping transfers in an economy-wide clearing center in which each and every individual would maintain an account. Such accounts would be debited for purchases and credited for sales—all in terms of an abstract unit of value. In the absence of a concrete medium-of-exchange money, the budget restraint would then assure that the total credit items of any individual account must exactly offset the total debit items. Hence the economy could work consistently on what is essentially a barter basis.[1]

---

   [1] This and the following paragraph should be read against the background of the payment procedure described on pp. 14, 17, and 49.

   The barter economy just described is Wicksell's "pure credit economy" (*Interest and Prices*, pp. 68 ff.). It will be discussed further in Chapter VIII:7.

The preceding argument precluded this "natural" emergence of a barter economy—and hence rationalized the demand for money balances—by arbitrarily removing the timing of payments from the control of individuals and tying it instead to an exogenous random process. It is the purpose of this chapter to spell out the details of this process. The reader uninterested in these details—and willing to accept their validity on faith—can therefore omit this chapter without loss of continuity.

Since the following discussion is based on highly unrealistic assumptions, it is advisable to preface it with a statement of its intended context. This is actually a double one. At a lower level of significance we are concerned with a problem in pure logic: with showing that the argument of this book is internally consistent; with demonstrating that its assumption of a positive demand for money need not contradict its assumption of static, certain expectations—or even of perfect foresight—with respect to future prices, interest, and income; with proving, therefore, that the existence of dynamic or uncertain price and interest expectations is not a *sine qua non* of a theory of money.[2]

If, however, we accept the methodological position that the realism of a set of assumptions can mean only the accuracy of its predictions for the real world, we can invest the following discussion with even greater significance.[3] In particular, we can then claim that it "explains" the role of money in a real economy. For the model now to be presented implies that individuals have a positive demand for money balances, that the extent of this demand is dependent upon the price level and rate of interest, that an increase in the individual's planned volume of expenditures need not cause a proportionate increase in his demand for money, and that the individual may well continue to hold money even when he is fully aware that its purchasing power is steadily decreasing. All of these implications are in accordance with our observations of the real world. Conversely, the extent to which the neglect of dynamic or uncertain expectations makes our model unrealistic can be determined only by the extent to which there are real phenomena which cannot be explained by our model but which can be explained by one which takes account of these speculative factors.

---

[2] The need for establishing these propositions can most conveniently be seen from the survey of the literature in J. C. Gilbert, "The Demand for Money: The Development of an Economic Concept," *Journal of Political Economy*, LXI (1953), 144–59.

An individual with "static expectations" expects the prices and interest of future weeks to be the same as present ones; an individual with "dynamic expectations" expects them to be different. These expectations can be held with or without certainty.

[3] For a persuasive development of this position, see Milton Friedman, *Essays in Positive Economics* (Chicago, 1953), pp. 3–43.

Actually, this methodological position is implicit in all of the preceding argument, for there is nothing more realistic about its assumptions of discrete weeks, recontracted *tâtonnements*, uniform monetary increases, and so forth.   It is only the unfamiliarity of the following assumptions that might create the impression that they are intrinsically different from the preceding ones.   In point of fact, however, the realism of the latter too can be tested only by the realism of their conclusions.

2. At the risk of some repetition, let us then describe in detail our model of the payment procedure.   Assume that at the close of the marketing period all the final contracts for commodities and newly issued bonds are placed in a common pool.   To these are added the now matured bonds issued the preceding week.   Random drawings are then made from this pool in groups, say, of ten.   Payments on the first ten contracts and/or matured bonds so drawn are then due at 8:00 A.M. Tuesday, payments on the second ten at 9:00 A.M., and so on for every business hour during the week.   These random drawings are continued until the pool has been exhausted and every contract and bond tied up with a specific payment hour during the week.

It is possible that an individual will be called upon to make both payments and receipts at a given hour.   To the extent that this happens he can offset one against the other.   Clearly, however, the random process by which the payment hours for the various contracts are determined makes it irrational for the individual to depend upon a perfect hourly synchronization of his required payments and receipts. Nor can he meet any discrepancy by an emergency selling or bartering of commodities or bonds, for, by assumption, transactions can take place only during the Monday marketing period.   That is, at this stage we are assuming bonds—whether new or matured—to be completely illiquid: their payment hours are no more subject to the individual's control than are those of commodities.   Hence the only way the individual can avoid almost certain default at one or more payment hours during the week is to hold money reserves at its beginning.

It is also emphasized that such default subjects the individual to a social opprobrium that he is anxious to avoid; hence he is definitely interested in maintaining these money reserves.   On the other hand, different individuals will clearly accord different weights both to the risk of default and to the embarrassment which accompanies it.   Hence the demand for money reserves in a given objective situation will vary from individual to individual in accordance with their subjective evaluations.

In order to preclude the individuals' circumventing this random process by colluding to set up informal clearing arrangements among themselves, we assume further that it is forbidden to make payments before the designated hours; similarly, it is forbidden to make them afterwards—except for the case in which an individual's money reserves are inadvertently exhausted. In such a case the payments due at one hour are necessarily deferred to the next one. Clearly, this delay will help only if the money inflow of that hour sufficiently exceeds the outflow so as to leave a surplus for covering the overdue payment. If it does not, this will have to be deferred to yet another hour.

The foregoing model not only rationalizes the demand for money, but also idealizes the traditional motives that have been associated with it. Thus the transactions motive is represented by the lack of synchronization between payments and receipts, and the precautionary motive by the uncertainty of the timing of these payments. Other aspects of the precautionary motive—say the desire to have a liquid reserve to be able to meet unexpected emergencies—can also be superimposed upon this model. Thus we might assume that there is a second random process which draws the names of individuals during the various payment hours, fines those individuals who are found with exhausted reserves, and distributes these fines as prizes to those found with positive reserves. This seemingly simple device actually introduces serious analytical complications, for it changes the individual budget restraints in the course of the week. In order to keep the argument as simple as possible, we shall not explore this possibility further here.

It should be clear that the monetary demand now being discussed is that for next week. The foreknowledge that the payments of that week will be randomly timed is assumed to make the individual adjust his commitments of the current marketing period so as to provide for the money reserves he will then need. True, temporary insolvency of some of his buyers may delay payment on their purchasing contracts with him. But since no one can obligate himself in excess of his budget restraint, our individual can be sure that such delays can at most be intra-week ones. Hence his money balances at the end of this week—or, equivalently, the beginning of next week—must be exactly at the level implied by his final current marketing decisions.

Correspondingly, these decisions cannot affect the absolute level of the money balances with which the individual meets his liquidity needs of the current week, for these balances were in turn determined by the decisions of the preceding one. On the other hand, current decisions can very clearly affect the *relative* adequacy of these balances. This is nothing but the obverse side of the real-balance effect. In brief, at any given set of prices, the individual can always adjust his amounts of excess demand so as to enable his given initial money balances to provide any desired degree of security against insolvency during the ensuing week. Indeed, in the limiting case, he can—by restricting the value of his purchases to the level of these given balances—assure their complete adequacy for any possible time pattern of payments that might be determined by the random process.[4]

3. We shall now sharpen the implications of our model by deriving the probability distribution which is implicit in it. Consider, then, an individual who at the given market prices—expected with certainty to continue unchanged—currently plans to buy or sell certain amounts of commodities and bonds in next Monday's marketing period. Let us now consider the situation with which the individual would be confronted in the course of this next week should he enter it without any initial money balances at all.

Let the "excess payment due" at any given hour be the difference between the payments and receipts randomly selected as falling due on that hour. In addition to these payments, the individual is also assumed to be liable at this hour for any payment on which he might previously have defaulted because of insolvency. To take account of this factor we define his "net payment due" at any hour as the excess payment due for that hour *plus* the sum of excess payments due at all preceding hours. Both the excess and net payments due at any given hour can, of course, be negative; this will be the case when receipts exceed payments. We note also that the individual's net payment due on the last hour of the week is the sum of all planned payments during the week minus the sum of all planned receipts; by the budget restraint, this must equal his planned decrement in money balances over the week.

Clearly, the number representing the net payment due at any given hour during the week is a random number, for it is determined by a time sequence of payments and receipts which is itself the outcome of a random process. Only the number representing the net payment due on the last hour of the week is an exception; as just noted, this is uniquely fixed by the decisions of the individual. Consider now the maximum of all these numbers; obviously, this too must be a random number. Let us denote it by w and see what we can say about its probability distribution.[5]

---

[4] These last two paragraphs should be read against the background of pp. 19–21 and 24.

[5] Some readers may be helped by a mathematical statement of these definitions. Assume that there are m payment hours during the week. Let y_i $(i = 1, \ldots, m)$ be the excess pay-

For simplicity, assume that the individual plans to end the week with the same zero money balances with which he begins it. This planned constancy of money balances over the week implies that—regardless of the outcome of the random process—the net payment due on the last hour must be zero. Hence, under this assumption, the minimum value of w is also zero. This minimum is attained if there is a perfect hourly synchronization of payments and receipts or if the early hours of the week are marked by negative excess payments which build up a reserve adequate to deal with the positive excess payments of later hours. Clearly, in either of these cases, the net payment due at each hour is either negative or zero.

At the other extreme, the maximum value of w is equal to the aggregate value of all the individual's *positive* amounts of excess demands. It is attained if chance should decree that the individual must first pay for all his purchases before he receives payment for any of his sales. Let the sum of all these purchases be represented by A. Probability distribution I in Figure 9 then reflects the fact that neither the minimum nor the maximum value of w is likely to occur.

The economic interpretation of this probability distribution is quite straightforward. Consider the point C. Assume that the total area underneath probability curve I from this point until A is, say, one-tenth of the total unit-area of the curve. This means that there is a probability of 90 per cent that the hourly net payments due during the week will not exceed C dollars. But this in turn means that if the individual had been equipped at the beginning of the week with money reserves of C dollars, there would have been a probability of 90 per cent that they would have sufficed to cover the timing discrepancies that might be generated by the random payment process. If these balances had been increased to D dollars, this probability would have been increased accordingly to, say, 95 per cent. And so on.

The sharp rightward skewness of the foregoing probability curve is perhaps its most significant property. Let us define the "volume of transactions" as the aggregate value of the individual's planned purchases—represented in the present case by A Then this skewness

---

ment due at the ith hour. Similarly, let w_i be the net payment due at this hour. Then

$$w_1 = y_1,$$
$$w_2 = y_1 + y_2 = w_1 + y_2,$$
$$w_3 = y_1 + y_2 + y_3 = w_2 + y_3,$$
$$\dots\dots\dots\dots\dots\dots\dots\dots\dots\dots\dots\dots$$
$$w_m = y_1 + y_2 + \cdots + y_m = w_{m-1} + y_m.$$

The variable w is the maximum of the w_i.

shows us that a small reserve ratio of money to volume of transactions suffices to provide the individual with a large degree of security against possible insolvency. The intuitive basis of this property can be seen in the fact that high values of w can be attained only by long initial sequences of consecutive hours in which the individual must pay out more than he receives. At the same time, the budget restraint implies that the longer any such sequence, the smaller the probability that the next hour will also have a positive excess payment; for over the week as a whole, payments and receipts must be equal. In other words, the law of averages works here even more effectively than in the case of independent

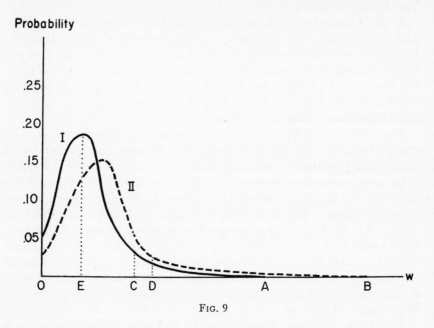

Fig. 9

events to quickly reduce the probability that the cumulative excess of payments over receipts will reach any high value.

Another interesting property revealed by probability curve I is that—after the point E—equal additions to cash balances are decreasingly effective in reducing the probability of default. This is an important consideration for an individual on the margin of devoting additional resources to cash balances. It should, however, be noted that the increasing marginal effectiveness of cash balances up to the point E does not imply—for a world of measurable utility—increasing marginal utility of cash balances up to this point. For this increased effectiveness may be more than offset by the decreased marginal satisfaction the individual can be assumed to derive from additional security against financial embarrassment.

Let us now explore the possible effects of changes in the volume of transactions. Assume that the individual suddenly changes his excess demands so as to increase his planned volume of transactions to *B*. Let curve *II* in Figure 9 represent the corresponding new probability distribution. We note first that the level of money reserves *A*—which previously provided complete security against any contingency—no longer does so. Conversely, if the individual had originally planned the volume of transactions *B* and had held money reserves equal to *A*, he could have assured the complete adequacy of these reserves by reducing his planned volume of transactions to *A*. This illustrates the fact already emphasized above that the individual can affect the relative adequacy of his money reserves, even when he cannot affect their absolute level.[6]

Assume that the individual's increased volume of transactions is generated by an increase, not in the *average value* of each of his contracts, but in their *number*. Then the increase in money reserves necessary to maintain a given level of financial security is less than proportionate to the increase in the volume of transactions. The intuitive basis for these "large-scale economies" in the relative size of money reserves is similar to that presented earlier for the skewness of the probability distribution. The existence of these economies is represented in Figure 9 by the fact that though *C* on probability curve *I* and *D* on curve *II* correspond to the same 90 per cent level of security, the ratio of *C* to *D* is less than that of *A* to *B*.[7]

The importance of the opening proviso of the preceding paragraph can be appreciated by considering the case in which the increase in the planned volume of transactions is the result of, say, a doubling of all prices and initial bond and money holdings. From Chapter IV we know that the amounts of the individual's excess demands are not thereby affected. He therefore continues to make the same number of

[6] See end of preceding section.
[7] The analogue of this conclusion for a bank's reserve ratio has a long history. See the references to Edgeworth and Wicksell (*op. cit.*, pp. 66–68) in the stimulating article by W. J. Baumol, "The Transactions Demand for Cash: An Inventory Theoretic Approach," *Quarterly Journal of Economics*, LXVI (1952), 556. Baumol also points out that Fisher applied Edgeworth's theory to an individual's cash balances (*Purchasing Power of Money*, p. 167). [Pigou, however (*op. cit.*, p. 179), at one time assumed large-scale *dis*economies!]
The reasoning of these writers differs, however, from that followed here. In particular, they based themselves on an apparently timeless stochastic model in which sampling from an infinite population generates a normal distribution. They also failed to bring out the distinction emphasized in the next two paragraphs of the text. See, however, the reference to Schlesinger in the next footnote.

contracts for the same amounts of commodities and real bonds. Hence the probability of drawing any particular time sequence of these contracts is also exactly the same as before. The only difference is that this same sequence will now call for payments and receipts twice as high as those it originally called for. It follows that the probability that the maximum net payment called for by this sequence will be, say, $2C$ is exactly the same as the original probability that it would have been C. Thus the new probability distribution is once again the solid curve of Figure 9, with $C, D, A, \ldots$ replaced by $2C, 2D, 2A, \ldots$, respectively.

In brief, the probability distribution corresponding to the individual's changed circumstances is obtained from the original one by merely changing the unit of measure of the abscissa. It follows that if the individual still wishes to maintain the same level of security against insolvency, he will have to hold twice the amount of money that he planned to before. Thus by another path we reach the already familiar conclusion that doubling prices and initial bond and money holdings doubles the amount of money demanded. But now this conclusion has the additional connotation that the resulting doubling of the individual's volume of transactions does not enable him to economize on the relative size of his cash balances.[8, 9]

---

8 These two paragraphs also explain why inflationary expansions of demand deposits do not create opportunities for "large-scale economies" which might permit banks to lower their reserve ratios; see the preceding footnote.

After this section was written, I discovered that Karl Schlesinger—in a little-known monograph entitled *Theorie der Geld- und Kreditwirtschaft* (Munich, 1914)—makes use of similar probability concepts in his analysis of the demand for money (*ibid.*, especially p. 88, footnote 1). Schlesinger, however, does not develop the full implications of his model and, in particular, does not attempt to describe any probability-distribution curve. On the other hand, he repeatedly emphasizes that, because of the "law of large numbers," an increase in the volume of payments causes a less-than-proportionate increase in the demand for money; but, in contrast to the writers mentioned in the preceding footnote, he also emphasizes that this holds only subject to the distinction just made in the text. Schlesinger also presents an interesting marginal-utility analysis of money. For further details, see Note D below.

9 I am happy to say that the conjectured probability distribution described in this section can be rigorously derived, and I am deeply grateful to my colleague Aryeh Dvoretzky for showing this in Mathematical Appendix 6. Indeed, as the reader can see from Figure 47 there (p. 331), the tail of the probability distribution is much longer and narrower than I even dared to imagine here in Figure 9.

The reader will also find it instructive to consult the table on p. 332, which shows that if during the week the individual makes and receives, say, 50 payments of one dollar each, he must hold a money reserve of approximately 21 per cent of his volume of payments to be 90 per cent secure against default, and approximately 30 per cent to be 99 per cent secure. The corresponding figures for 1000 one-dollar payments and receipts are 5 per cent and 7 per cent, respectively. Here we can clearly see the "large-scale economies" mentioned in the text. In general, if N represents the number of one-dollar payments and receipts that must be made during the week, the amount of money that must be held in order to maintain a given level of security increases in proportion to $\sqrt{2N}$.   [*Footnote* 9 *continued next page.*]

4. The preceding argument has been oversimplified in many respects. It assumes that the individual first decides on his excess demand for commodities and bonds, and then decides on his money reserves. A more adequate theory would show all these decisions being made simultaneously. It would also show that the individual must take account of the possibility that the temporary insolvency of others may prevent his receiving payments from them at the hours he is entitled to. This danger might be dealt with by adding an arbitrary "safety factor" allowance to the reserves that would otherwise be held.

We have also assumed throughout that bonds are completely illiquid instruments. This assumption can be relaxed in the manner indicated in Chapter VI:3. That is, the individual can be permitted to make payment in discounted bonds should he become insolvent. We could then follow Hicks in attributing the less-than-perfect liquidity of these bonds to their risk of default, and we could introduce this risk into our model by positing a supplementary random process which selects and cancels a fixed percentage of the newly discounted bonds. Once the illiquidity of bonds is thus assured, we could continue to follow Hicks in postulating a certain "bother" in using bonds as a means of payment. This would further strengthen the transactions motive for holding money.[10]

Once again we neglect dynamic or uncertain price and interest expectations and the speculative monetary demand they generate. This is not to say that the model should not—or cannot—be extended to provide for this demand. But, by its very nature, such an extension would carry us beyond the limited objective set out at the beginning of this chapter—that of providing microeconomic validation for the theory of money developed in this book, a theory independent of such expectations and based solely on the transactions and precautionary motives.

Professor Dvoretzky has also pointed out to me that my usage of "skewness" in the text does not accord with any of its accepted senses. The measure of skewness implicit here might instead be defined—in a variation upon the usual percentile measure—as $\dfrac{(U - M) - (M - L)}{U - L}$, where U is the highest value the variable can attain, L the lowest, and M the median. This measure gives much more weight to the tail of a distribution than do the standard ones. And for our purposes this highly attenuated tail is the most significant property of the distribution.

I might finally note that formulas (6.4) and (6.5) of Mathematical Appendix 6 were also conjectured by Mr. Tsvi Goldberger on the basis of some numerical examples which he worked out.

[10] Hicks, *op. cit.*, pp. 164–66; cf. pp. 84–85 above, especially footnote 17. The way in which such a "bother" can generate a demand for money is neatly shown by Baumol, *op. cit.*

The supplementary random process just described is completely analogous to that of p. 89 above: it "fines" the holders of the selected bonds and "rewards" the issuers. It thereby also creates the same budget-restraint complications noted there.

CHAPTER VIII

A Critique of Neoclassical

Monetary Theory[1]

1. *Introduction.* *The deficiencies of the traditional transactions and cash-balance approaches in analyzing the effects of a change in* M. *The failure to test the stability of the equilibrium absolute price level and the significance thereof.* 2. *The cash-balance equation and the "uniform unitary elasticity of demand for money."* 3. *Valid and invalid dichotomies of the pricing process.* *The proper relation between monetary theory and value theory. Conclusion: the failure of neoclassical monetary theory to fully understand the real-balance effect.* 4. *The etiology of the invalid dichotomy.* 5. *The effects of a change in* K. 6. *The effects of a change in* T. 7. *The implications of Say's Identity.*

1. Terminological disputes are rather sterile. Hence it is best to preclude them by making clear at the outset that "neoclassical" is being used here as a shorthand designation for the once widely-accepted body of thought which organized monetary theory around a transactions or cash-balance type of equation, and which then used these equations to validate the classical quantity theory of money. Subsidiary—though, as we shall see, persistently recurring—components of this body of thought were a certain description of the demand function for money and a certain conception of the role of monetary theory vis-à-vis value theory.

---

1 This chapter concentrates on the theory of money and prices. The discussion of neoclassical interest theory is best deferred to Chapter XV:1.

In its cash-balance version—associated primarily with the names of Walras,[2] Marshall,[3] Wicksell,[4] and Pigou[5]—neoclassical theory assumed that, for their convenience, individuals wish to hold a certain proportion, K, of the real volume of their planned transactions, T, in the form of real money balances. The demand for these balances thus equals KT. Correspondingly, the demand for nominal money balances is KPT, where P is the price level of the commodities transacted. The equating of this demand to the supply of money, M, then produced the famous Cambridge equation, $M = KPT$. In the transactions version —associated primarily with the names of Newcomb and Fisher[6]—the velocity of circulation, V, replaced its reciprocal, K, to produce the equally famous equation of exchange, $MV = PT$. These equations were the parade-grounds on which neoclassical economists then put the classical quantity theory of money through its paces.[7]

The most persuasive formulations of this theory were developments of the following tripartite thesis: an increase in the amount of money disturbs the optimum relation between the level of money balances and the individual's expenditures; this disturbance generates an increase in the planned volume of these expenditures (the real-balance effect); and this increase creates pressures on the price level which push it upwards until it has risen in the same proportion as the amount of money. Among the writers mentioned above, only Wicksell[8] and Fisher[9] provided complete, systematic statements of this thesis. Nevertheless, the other writers made sufficient—if unintegrated—use of its individual components to justify our identifying these components with the general analytic background of neoclassical monetary theory.

---

2 But it will be argued in Note C:2 that though Walras definitely presented a cash-balance *equation*, he did not present a cash-balance *theory*.

3 For references, see Note G:1.

4 For references, see Note E:1.

5 For references, see Note G:1.

6 For references, see Note F:1.

7 The reader will observe that $M = KPT$ and $MV = PT$ are treated here as *equations*, and not as *identities*. This interpretation is borne out by the works referred to in the preceding footnotes. It will also be observed that these two equations have been treated as analytically equivalent. Without committing ourselves on the attempts that have sometimes been made to distinguish substantively between them, we merely note that for our present purposes any such distinction can be disregarded. Cf. J. M. Keynes, *Treatise on Money* (London, 1930), Vol. I, pp. 237–39; Marget, *op. cit.*, Vol. I, pp. 424–33.

For good recent accounts of the two neoclassical equations and their respectively associated theories, see L. V. Chandler, *The Economics of Money and Banking* (revised ed.; New York, 1953), Chapters XXIII–XXV; A. G. Hart, *Money, Debt, and Economic Activity* (revised ed.; New York, 1953), Chapters X and XII.

8 *Op. cit.*, pp. 39–41. This is cited in full in Note E:1.

9 *Purchasing Power of Money*, pp. 153–54. This is cited in full in Note F:1.

Indeed, the basic fact underlined by the foregoing thesis—that the causal relationship between money and prices is not at all a mechanical one, but is instead the economic consequence of the prior effect of changes in the amount of money on the demand for commodities—was already a commonplace of the classical quantity-theory tradition of Cantillon, Thornton, Ricardo, and Mill,[10] and was particularly vivid in the expositions of those writers who emphasized that the effects of an increase in the amount of money on prices could not in general be said to be equi-proportionate, but depended instead on whose money holdings, and hence whose demands, were increased.[11] This, after all, was the consideration which brought both classical and neoclassical economists to the recognition that a change in the amount of money could generate "forced savings" and need not therefore always be neutral in its effects.[12]

On the other hand, it must be emphasized that, in contrast to the neoclassical ones, none of these earlier expositions of the quantity theory should be regarded as having recognized the real-balance effect in the fullest sense of the term; for none of them brought out the crucial intermediary stage of the foregoing thesis in which people increase their *flow* of expenditures because they feel that their *stock* of money is too large for their needs. Instead, in a Keynesian-like fashion, these expositions more or less directly connected the increased *outflow* of money expenditures with the increased *inflow* of money receipts: people spend more money because they receive more money, not because their real cash balances as such have been augmented beyond the amount "which their convenience had taught them to keep on hand."[13] But it is precisely this augmentation—and the real-balance effect which it

---

[10] For specific references, see Note A.

This is one of the central themes of Marget's study; see, in particular, *op. cit.*, Vol. I, pp. 307, 345 ff., and 500 ff. It also seems to me that a good part of H. Hegeland's recent monograph on the *Quantity Theory of Money* (Göteborg, 1951) suffers from the failure to recognize this fact; see *ibid.*, especially pp. 38–39, 57, 87–92.

[11] Cf., e.g., R. Cantillon, *Essay on the Nature of Trade* (1755), trans. and ed. H. Higgs (London, 1931), p. 179; Mill, *op. cit.*, pp. 491–92. Marget (*op. cit.*, Vol. I, p. 502) cites similar passages from Lubbock and Cairnes.

For this emphasis in later writers, see Walras, *Eléments d'économie politique pure* (first ed.; Lausanne, 1874), p. 181, who essentially repeats Mill; see also the definitive ed. of the *Elements*, ed. Jaffé, p. 328. See also Wicksell, *op. cit.*, p. 40, and Mises, *op. cit.*, pp. 139–40. But Mises carries himself away to an invalid extreme when he attempts to prove that even in the case of an equi-proportionate increase in initial individual money balances, prices will not rise equi-proportionately (*ibid.*, pp. 141–42). The nature of his error is best seen from the discussion on p. 41 above.

[12] This will be discussed further in Chapter XV:1.

[13] Fisher, *Purchasing Power of Money*, p. 153, with "his" changed to "their," and "him" to "them."

engenders—which helps explain why demand, and hence prices, remain at a higher level even in periods subsequent to the one in which the injection of new money into the economy takes place.[14]

Each part of the foregoing thesis clearly has its counterpart in the argument of Chapters II–IV. This parallelism not only brings out the traditional flavor of this argument—a flavor already accentuated by the suggestive footnotes referring to earlier writers with which it has been deliberately and justifiably seasoned—but it also shows that this argument provides the ultimate, rigorous validation of the classical quantity theory of money itself. Indeed—and this is the paradox—the only traditional elements missing from this demonstration are those very neoclassical equations which have become so strongly associated with the quantity theory as to become almost identified with it! But, as emphasized in the Introduction to this book, this omission, too, is deliberate; for the alternative approach followed here is at once more general, more rigorous, and less likely to mislead.

Thus, for example, the neoclassical equations suffer from the obvious disability that they assign no explicit role to the rate of interest and hence are automatically excluded from the whole body of theory which deals with this rate. In particular, they cannot serve to validate the classical proposition that a change in the amount of money leaves the rate of interest unaffected. Indeed, not only can they not help, they hinder. For the omission of the rate of interest from the cash-balance equation creates the misleading impression that the classical invariance of this rate holds only in the special case where it does not affect the demand for money. As we have seen in Chapter IV:4, no such restriction is necessary. This is not to deny that in other contexts neoclassical economists did recognize the influence of the rate of interest on the demand for money, and did make other significant extensions of classical interest theory. But it is to stress that these contributions found no place in those fundamental equations which, more than anything else, are the hallmarks of neoclassical monetary theory.[15]

Again, our approach does not depend on the use of the cumbersome and frequently criticized aggregates K, V, P, T, but instead builds only on individual demands for individual commodities with their individual prices. And even when presented in an aggregative form—as it will be in Part Two—it does not needlessly cripple the quantity theory by implying—as does the MV of the transactions equation—that the

---

[14] The distinction made in this sentence will become clearer from the detailed period analysis of Chapter X:3.

[15] As already noted, the full discussion of neoclassical interest theory is deferred to Chapter XV:1.

validity of this theory holds only in the obviously unrealistic case where the aggregate demand for commodities is directly proportionate to the amount of money. The preceding approach insists only that the demand functions be free of money illusion; otherwise it leaves them completely free to reflect the full range and variety of individual reactions to changes in the level of initial money balances.[16]

The cash-balance equation frequently replaced these unnecessary and vitiating restrictions on the commodity functions with equally un-necessary—and even invalid—restrictions on the money function. Since the details of these restrictions will be described in the next section, there is no need to discuss them further here. Aside from this substantive criticism, the neoclassical cash-balance approach is subject to the more general, pragmatic criticism that has already been voiced in the Introduction. In its neat description of the factors which lead individuals to hold money balances, this approach certainly accomplished its proclaimed objective of bringing these holdings "into relation with volition."[17] But all too often this humanizing of the demand for money led to an undue concentration on the money market, a corresponding neglect of the commodity markets, and a resulting dehumanizing of the analysis of the effects of monetary changes.

The force of this criticism can best be illustrated with the aid of Figure 4 (page 42) and its accompanying discussion—though, as will be emphasized in the next section, this figure differs fundamentally from the usual neoclassical one. What we are saying is that despite the already emphasized fact that adherents of the cash-balance approach recognized the real-balance effect, they frequently remained satisfied with the mechanical comparative-statics proposition that a doubling of the amount of money shifted the equilibrium position in the money market from R to T; they frequently failed to provide a systematic dynamic analysis of the way in which the monetary increase generated real-balance effects in the commodity markets which propelled the economy from its original equilibrium position to its new one. Now, as the incisive counterexample of Wicksell proves, such an omission is *not* a necessary consequence of this approach. Nevertheless, it cannot be mere coincidence that it is precisely this dynamic analysis which was *not* integrated into the Cambridge cash-balance tradition of Marshall, Pigou, Keynes, and Robertson, with its deliberate emphasis on the money market. It thus appears that, in its analysis of the inflationary impact of a monetary increase, the Cambridge theory was actually less

---

16 Cf. above, p. 41.
17 Pigou, " The Value of Money," *op. cit.*, p. 174.

illumed by the spark of "volition" and individual behavior than the Fisherine transactions theory whose "mechanicalism" it was designed to correct![18]

As emphasized sufficiently above, it is one of the specific objectives of the alternative approach developed in this book to avoid this pitfall by taking the analysis directly into the commodity markets. A corollary advantage of this approach is that it enables a precise economic explanation of why, say, a doubling of the amount of money causes a doubling—and just a doubling, neither more nor less—of the price level. It shows the essence of the quantity theory to lie in the automatic, corrective market forces which continue to operate through the real-balance effect until this doubled price level is attained. Once again, there is no logical reason why these forces could not have been developed as a standard component of neoclassical monetary theory. Nevertheless, the stubborn fact seems to be that only Wicksell bestirred himself to ask what would happen if prices deviated from the equilibrium level called for by the amount of money, and to describe how the dynamic forces thereby generated would return them to this level.[19]

The essence of the three preceding paragraphs can be summed up in one sentence: There is a basic chapter missing in practically all neoclassical monetary theory—the chapter which presents a precise dynamic analysis of the determination of the equilibrium absolute level of money prices through the workings of the real-balance effect. This is said, not for that aspect of dynamic analysis which describes the forces propelling the economy toward its new equilibrium position after an initial monetary increase—a problem adequately discussed by many neoclassical economists[20]—but for that aspect which describes the forces stabilizing the economy at this new position once it is reached—a problem separated by just a nuance from the preceding one, but nevertheless discussed only by Wicksell.

It would be a serious error to underestimate the significance of this nuance. The easiest way of convincing the reader of this is to bring

---

[18] It is for this reason that the foregoing Cambridge economists are not listed together with Wicksell and Fisher on p. 97 as having presented a full statement of the tripartite quantity-theory thesis. In order to evaluate the validity of this criticism, the reader must himself compare the expositions of the Cambridge school (as cited in Note G:1) with those of Wicksell and Fisher. It is similarly instructive to contrast the Cambridge expositions with those of such cash-balance theorists as Mises (*op. cit.*, pp. 132–35, 138–40, 147–49) and R. G. Hawtrey [*Currency and Credit* (third ed.; London, 1927), Chapters III–IV, especially pp. 35, 59–60; as can be seen from p. 35, Hawtrey's "unspent margin" is identical with what is usually referred to as a cash balance].

[19] Cf. Chapter III:3 and the reference to Wicksell's *Interest and Prices*, pp. 39–40, there cited. As already noted, this crucial reference is reproduced in full in Note E:1.

[20] Cf. the references to Fisher, Wicksell, Mises, and Hawtrey in footnote 18 above.

him up sharply against the following facts: Walras was a man who never tired of establishing the stability of his system by elaborating on the corrective forces of excess supply that would be called into play should the price lie above its equilibrium value, and the forces of excess demand that would be called into play should it lie below. He did it when he explained how the market determines the equilibrium prices of commodities; he did it again when he explained how the market determines the equilibrium prices of productive services; and he did it a third time when he explained how the market determines the equilibrium prices of capital goods. But he did not do it when he attempted to explain how the market determines the equilibrium "price" of paper money. And Walras is the rule, not the exception. Precisely the same asymmetry recurs among writers of the Cambridge tradition—with their standard supply-and-demand exercise of testing the stability of the equilibrium price in value theory and their standard omission of a corresponding exercise for testing the equilibrium absolute price level in monetary theory![21]

Thus in back of this nuance is the persistent failure of these economists to carry over to their monetary theory a simple, familiar technique of their value theory. What endows this failure with crucial significance is the contrast it provides with the obvious desire of these very same economists to integrate these two theories! It is this systematic contrast which prevents our dismissing this failure as the mere product of chance, accident of exposition, or neglect to make explicit what was taken for granted. Something much deeper must be involved. All the evidence indicates—and this evidence will be reinforced by the findings of the next two sections—that the recognition of the real-balance effect remained only a surface phenomenon, that neoclassical economists never did realize its full logical implications, and that, in particular—except for Wicksell—they never did become conscious of that first, vital step toward a dynamic theory of money which lies latent in it.

Perhaps it was the beguiling mechanical simplicity of the neoclassical equations which concealed the need for analyzing their dynamic workings. Perhaps the fault lay in the infrequency with which these equations were presented graphically and the resulting infrequency with which there was a visual challenge to trace out the dynamic path to equilibrium. Whatever its etiology, we seem to be confronted here with a most curious and most fascinating intellectual phenomenon.[22]

---

[21] On Walras, see Notes B and C:4, especially p. 404. On the Cambridge tradition, see Note G:2. See Note F:2 for a discussion of Fisher.

[22] That this inconsistent pattern has persisted down to the present can be seen by examining

2. Another familiar proposition of the neoclassical cash-balance approach—one already alluded to in the preceding section—is that the demand for paper money has "uniform unitary elasticity" and is accordingly represented by a rectangular hyperbola.   This theme recurs specifically in the writings of Walras, Marshall, and Pigou.   In the case of the latter it is clear that it was considered to be a necessary precondition for the validity of the quantity theory of money.   In Pigou's words, "an increase in the supply of legal tender ought always, since the elasticity of demand [for legal tender] is equal to unity, to raise prices in the proportion in which the supply has increased."   And there is the strong impression that this was also the intended context in which this proposition was advanced by other writers as well.   Indeed, it is probably this assumed causal relationship which explains the importance that was attached to it.[23]

This makes it all the more essential to recall that not only is this proposition not necessary for the quantity theory, it is not even valid! All this has been sufficiently explained in Chapters II:5 and III:5, with their demonstrations that the real-balance effect makes it impossible for the demand for money to be of uniform unitary elasticity but that nevertheless an increase in the amount of money causes a proportionate increase in prices.   It should, however, be clear that the foregoing invalid proposition is not inherent in the Cambridge function as such. Thus, if KPT is the demand for money and M its supply, the excess demand for money, $KPT - M$, correctly reflects the by-now familiar property that an equi-proportionate change in P *and* in M causes a proportionate change in the excess amount of money demanded.   On the other hand, a change in P alone generates a real-balance effect, hence a change in the planned volume of transactions, T, and hence a *non*-proportionate change in the amount of money demanded, KPT. Thus, if properly interpreted, the Cambridge function does *not* imply uniform unitary elasticity.

There are two possible explanations for the failure of neoclassical economists to see this.   First, they apparently never realized the need to pin down the meaning of T.   Only occasionally did they give it the volitional connotation on which the argument of the preceding

---

the more recent literature from the same viewpoint that has just been used for the neoclassical. On the other hand, there is not much point in trying to trace this inconsistency back to the classical literature: its value-theory discussions are of too different a nature.   See end of Note A.

[23] Pigou, *Essays in Applied Economics* (London, 1923), p. 195.   For references to the three writers mentioned here, see Note C (pp. 388–89 and 408–9) and Note G:3.   The latter contains references to other writers too.   For the existence of this assumption in the case of Cassel, see end of Note H.

paragraph depends. At other times they treated it as something beyond the will of individuals—as the fixed "total resources . . . enjoyed by the community." And at still other times they shifted unawares from one meaning to the next within the compass of a page or two.[24] Second, even when they used T in its volitional sense—which is, of course, the only one that is consonant with the *raison d'être* of the cash-balance approach—they never realized that the real-balance effect precludes T from remaining constant in the face of a change in P. Indeed, a standard lemma of the neoclassical proof of the quantity theory of money was that P and T were independent! Whether this lack of recognition should be taken as another manifestation of the mental block whose existence was strongly suggested in the preceding section or whether it has some more prosaic explanation, the basic fact remains that no writer ever pointed out that the real-balance effect implies that the demand curve for money could not have uniform unitary elasticity.

In all fairness, it should, however, be said that some exponents of the cash-balance approach merely used "unitary elasticity of demand" as a complicated way of stating that an increase in the amount of money causes a proportionate increase in prices. In other words, they had in mind—or should have had in mind—the elasticity of the market-equilibrium curve of Figure 5 (page 44), not that of the demand curves of Figure 4 (page 42). That is, despite their use of his term, they were not really referring to what Marshall denoted by "elasticity of demand." It would, however, be carrying fairness to the point of distortion if we were to create the impression that these writers in any way indicated awareness of the existence of the two distinct curves and of the difference between them. This should be clear from the last sentence of the preceding paragraph. It is even clearer from the fact that the writers in question shifted uninhibitedly (and, it might be added, unrebuked) from one meaning of elasticity to the other—sometimes even within the same sentence. This points up the general fuzziness from which neoclassical monetary theory suffered as a result of its failure to draw the fundamental distinction between individual-experiments, on the one hand, and market-experiments, on the other.[25]

---

24 The quotation is from Pigou, *Essays*, p. 176. But just on the preceding page Pigou gives T a volitional connotation by connecting it with the volume of an individual's "payments" in his "ordinary transactions of life."

The reader will find it instructive to examine from this viewpoint the other expositions of the Cambridge equation referred to in Note G.

25 For specific references to the literature, see Note G:3.

Once again Wicksell is an exception. For he makes it clear that the rectangular hyperbola he draws in his monetary theory is a market-equilibrium curve. On the other hand, he does not explicitly say that the demand curve for money is *not* such a hyperbola. See Note E:2.

3. Let us return to the analysis of the effects of a change in the quantity of money. Instead of carrying out this analysis in terms of the absolute level of money prices—which is, of course, the usual approach—we can do it equivalently in terms of the *real* quantity of money; for once the nominal quantity of money is fixed, its real value varies in inverse proportion to the absolute level of money prices—or, in short, to the absolute price level. Such an approach can then proceed as follows: In the initial equilibrium position of our economy, the real quantity of money is just at that level which satisfies its transactions and precautionary needs. A sudden increase in the nominal quantity of money then pushes the real quantity above this equilibrium value and thereby creates inflationary pressures in the various markets. The resulting price rise then reduces this real quantity and thereby lessens the disequilibrating inflationary pressures themselves. Now, by assumption, the initial monetary increase has not affected the economy's "taste" for real balances—that is, its desire to hold such balances in order to avoid the embarrassment of default. Hence the economy cannot achieve a new equilibrium position until the absolute price level has risen sufficiently to reduce the real quantity of money to its initial level once again.[26]

Let us now separate into two categories the given conditions (independent variables) which determine the nature of our exchange economy's equilibrium position. First, there are those which describe the economy's "real framework": namely, tastes (including those for *real* money balances) and initial holdings of commodities. Second, there are the conditions which describe its "monetary framework": namely, initial nominal holdings of money. Correspondingly, let us also separate the dependent variables of the analysis into two categories: "real variables," namely, the equilibrium values of relative prices, the rate of interest, and the real quantity of money; and the "monetary variable," namely, the equilibrium value of the absolute price level.[27]

Consider now the classical proposition that a change in the quantity of money merely causes an equi-proportionate change in equilibrium money prices. The opening paragraph of this section enables us to

---

[26] Compare this with the change in the equilibrium real quantity of money that characterizes a shift in liquidity preference; see below, Section 5.

[27] On the distinction between dependent and independent variables, see Chapters I:4 and III:1 above.

Throughout the following analysis we abstract from distribution effects. This enables us to consider the total of initial nominal—and hence real—bond holdings as identically zero. Accordingly, neither of these holdings appears in the preceding classificatory scheme.

replace this proposition by the equivalent one that such a change has no effect on the equilibrium values of relative prices, the rate of interest, and the real quantity of money. Now, to say that these values are independent of the nominal quantity of money is to say that they can be determined even without knowing this quantity. This permits us to conceive of the pricing process of our exchange economy as being divided into two successive stages: In the first one, specification of the real framework determines the equilibrium values of the real variables of the system. In the second, specification of the monetary framework then determines the equilibrium value of the monetary variable—for this value is simply the ratio between the specified nominal quantity of money and the equilibrium real quantity.[28]

It should be clear that this arbitrary and mechanical act of specifying the nominal amount of money has nothing whatsoever to do with monetary theory. For, as we shall argue below, this theory is concerned, at the individual level, with the relation between commodity demands and real balances and, at the market level, with the causes of changes in the equilibrium value of these balances. And both of these problems are fully analyzed in the first stage of the foregoing dichotomy. Thus this stage is coterminous with economic analysis: it comprises both value theory and monetary theory. Correspondingly, the second stage of this dichotomy is beyond the pale of economic analysis: it deals with a completely adventitious act.

It should also be clear that the foregoing dichotomy is purely a conceptual one. The real and monetary frameworks of the actual market place are obviously "specified" simultaneously. Similarly, there are only money prices in this market, and these are simultaneously determined. In brief, our dichotomy has no operational significance other than that of the basic quantity-theory proposition from which it is derived.[29]

This dichotomy between relative and money prices must be sharply distinguished from that of Chapter III:3 between money and accounting prices.[30] First of all, there is the obvious difference in the nature of the prices involved. Parallel to this difference is the one between the data respectively specified by the second stages of these dichotomies. In the earlier dichotomy this consists of the accounting price of one of the goods; in the present one it consists of the nominal amount of money.

---

28 See Mathematical Appendix 7:*a*(i).

29 For echoes of the foregoing dichotomy in the literature, see Note I:1.

30 Above, p. 39. For examples of this dichotomy in the writings of Wicksell, Fisher, Bowley, Cassel, and others, see Note I:2. For a mathematical statement, see Mathematical Appendix 7:*a*(ii).

Correspondingly, a change in the value of the supplementary datum in the present dichotomy affects money prices, whereas in the earlier one it does not. Finally, the earlier dichotomy can have direct operational significance: there can be actual economies in which first money prices and then accounting prices are determined. Clearly, this additional set of prices is of no economic significance; but, in the present context, this is irrelevant.

Both of these dichotomies must be even more sharply distinguished from yet a third one which, though it has neoclassical roots in the works of Walras, Fisher, Pigou, and Cassel, did not achieve its most explicit form until the later expositions of Divisia, Lange, Modigliani, Schneider, and others. In this form it became undisputedly accepted as a statement of the proper relation between monetary theory, on the one hand, and value theory, on the other.

The point of departure of this familiar dichotomy (in practically every case in which it appears in the literature) is an economy consisting of commodities and money, but not bonds. The dichotomy then begins by dividing the economy into two sectors: a real sector, described by the excess-demand functions for commodities, and a monetary sector, described by the excess-demand function for money. The former functions are assumed to depend only on relative prices; the latter, on these variables and the absolute price level as well. This assumed insensitivity of the demand functions of the real sector to changes in the absolute level of money prices is referred to as the "homogeneity postulate"[31] and is said to denote absence of "money illusion."[32]

In a corresponding way, the market excess-demand equations corresponding to these functions are also separated into two groups. The equations of the real sector taken by themselves are then able to determine the equilibrium values of the only variables which appear in them—relative prices. These equations and the variables they determine thus constitute the domain of value theory. The equation of the monetary sector then determines the equilibrium value of the remaining variable—the absolute price level. And this equation and

---

[31] This term was first used by W. Leontief, "The Fundamental Assumption of Mr. Keynes' Monetary Theory of Unemployment," *Quarterly Journal of Economics*, LI (1936–37), 193. It originates in the fact that, in mathematical terms, demand functions which depend only on relative prices are said to be "homogeneous of degree zero in the money prices."

[32] It should be clear to the reader that this does *not* correspond to our use of this term, which defines absence of money illusion as insensitivity to changes in the absolute level of *accounting*—and not *money*—prices; cf. p. 24.

In order to avoid any possible confusion, we might repeat that throughout this discussion "absolute price level" is a shorthand expression for "absolute level of *money* prices."

the variable it determines thus constitute the domain of monetary theory.[33]

As with the "unitary elasticity of demand," much of the attractiveness of this dichotomy lay in the belief that it was a necessary precondition for the validity of the quantity theory of money.[34]   It was felt that unless the demand functions were independent of the absolute price level, monetary increases—which necessarily affect this level—could not preserve their classical neutrality with respect to the real phenomena of the economy.   But once again the truth of the matter is that not only is this dichotomy not necessary, not only is it not valid, but its basic assumption is even a denial of the quantity theory itself!   For to say that the demand functions of the real sector are not affected by changes in the absolute price level—that is, to assert that they satisfy the "homogeneity postulate"—is to imply that they are not affected by changes in the real value of cash balances.   But it is precisely on this real-balance effect that the quantity theory depends for the inflationary impact of a monetary increase!   On the other hand, this dependence in no way violates the *final* neutrality of, say, a doubling of the amount of money.   For in the new equilibrium position the individual is confronted not only with a doubled price level, but also with a doubled initial holding of money.   Hence—as compared with the initial equilibrium position—there is no real-balance effect; hence there is no change in behavior; and hence the classical neutrality of money is reaffirmed.[35]

More generally, if the function of monetary theory is to explain the determination of the absolute price level, then the "homogeneity postulate"—or, equivalently, absence of "money illusion" in the sense of the foregoing dichotomy—is the antithesis of all monetary theory. For let the assumptions of the dichotomy obtain.   Assume now that an initial position of equilibrium is disturbed in such a way as to cause an equi-proportionate change in all money prices.   Since this does not change relative prices, the "homogeneity postulate" implies that none of the demand functions in the real sector are thereby affected.   Hence,

---

[33] For the highly probable presence of the foregoing dichotomy in the writings of Walras, Fisher, Pigou, and Cassel, see Notes C:4 (end), F:3, G:4, and H (end), respectively.   See also Note E:3 for a discussion of the ambiguities on this point in Wicksell.

For the explicit statement or endorsement of this dichotomy by Divisia, Lange, Modigliani, and Schneider—as well as by Marget, Rosenstein-Rodan, Myrdal, Hickman, and Hart—see Note I:3.   This also discusses the case of Hicks.

For examples of the usage of "homogeneity postulate" and/or "money illusion" in the sense cited here, see the references to Leontief, Haberler, Marschak, Samuelson, Tinbergen, and Boulding in Note I:3.

[34] This was explicitly claimed by, for example, Leontief, *op. cit.*, p. 193, and Modigliani, *op. cit.*, p. 217.   For further details, see Note I:3.

[35] Cf. Chapter III:4.   On the concept of neutrality, see p. 59.

since the commodity markets of this sector were initially in equilibrium, they must continue to be so. By Walras' Law, so must the money market. Thus the equi-proportionate departure of money prices from any given equilibrium level creates no market forces—that is, creates no amounts of excess demand anywhere in the system—which might cause money prices to return to their initial level. Hence if any set of money prices is an equilibrium set, any multiple of this set must also be an equilibrium set. The absolute price level is indeterminate.[36]

It follows that the foregoing dichotomy is involved in a basic internal contradiction. For if the demand functions of the real sector have the property it attributes to them, there cannot possibly be a "second stage" in which the absolute price level is determined.[37]

Actually, a much simpler way of dealing with this dichotomy is to note that it provides an operationally significant hypothesis—one capable of being tested by the facts of the real world. In particular, its basic "homogeneity postulate" implies that the behavior of consumers in commodity markets can never be affected by the real value of their money balances. But as noted above (page 22), there is fairly persuasive evidence from the postwar experience of inflationary pressures generated by accumulated liquid assets that this behavior has been so affected. Hence this evidence alone suffices to refute this dichotomy. In brief, reality shows that there cannot be a money economy without a "money illusion."[38]

This empirical approach enables us to dispose of a certain variation of the foregoing dichotomy which—though it has never been advanced as such in the literature—can pass the test of internal consistency. Specifically, we now consider an economy with bonds as well as commodities and money. We assume further that though the commodity equations continue to be independent of real balances, the bond equation is not. In such a Keynesian system, relative prices and the rate of interest can be determined in the commodity markets and the absolute price level in the bond or money market. In particular, the argument by which we previously established the indeterminacy of the absolute price level no longer holds. For an equi-proportionate departure of money prices from their equilibrium level now disturbs the equilibrium of the bond market, and the resulting excess demand then acts through the rate of interest to force prices back to their original level. Neverthe-

---

[36] Contrast this with the way determinacy is assured in the case where the real-balance effect does operate; above, p. 38.

[37] For a mathematical statement and critique of the foregoing dichotomy, see Mathematical Appendix 7:*a*(iii).

[38] Once again, the reader is warned that this is *not* being used here in our sense of the term.

less, this variation of the dichotomy is also unacceptable. For it implies that the real-balance effect manifests itself only in the bond market and never in the commodity markets. This implication, too, is refuted by the facts of the real world.[39]

It should also be noted that if the bond market, too, is assumed to be independent of real balances, then the resulting model is not even internally consistent. In particular, it is involved in exactly the same type of indeterminacy already shown to hold for the invalid dichotomy. For once again an equi-proportionate departure of money prices from an initial equilibrium position, the rate of interest being held constant, does not create any excess demands anywhere in the system. Hence no force is generated to bring prices back to their initial position.[40]

The conclusion to be drawn from the foregoing discussion is that, once the real and monetary data of the economy are specified, the equilibrium values of relative prices, the rate of interest, and the absolute price level are simultaneously determined by all the markets of the economy. It is generally impossible to isolate a subset of markets which can determine the equilibrium values of a subset of prices. In the true spirit of general-equilibrium economics, "everything depends on everything else."

In particular, as we have seen, it is fatal to succumb to the temptation to say that relative prices are determined in the commodity markets and absolute prices in the money market. This does not mean that value theory cannot be distinguished from monetary theory. Obviously, there is a distinction; but it is based on a dichotomization of *effects*, not on a dichotomization of *markets*. More specifically, both monetary theory and value theory consider *all* markets of the economy simultaneously. But, in each of these markets, value theory analyzes individual-experiments which measure the substitution and income effects; and monetary theory, those which measure the real-balance effect. Correspondingly, value theory analyzes market-experiments which do not (significantly) affect the absolute price level and hence do not generate real-balance effects; and monetary theory, those which do

---

[39] See Mathematical Appendix 7:*a*(iv). This "Keynesian case" will be discussed further on p. 163.

I might also add the conjecture that it is impossible to derive the excess-demand functions of this Keynesian case from the microeconomic analysis of Chapter VI—whether of the utility or revealed-preference type. For one of the characteristics of this analysis is the symmetrical dependence of *all* the excess-demand functions on *all* the given factors with which the individual is confronted. Hence it is difficult to see how this analysis could be made to yield a system in which only the bond function, and none of the commodity functions, would be dependent on the individual's given initial real balances.

[40] See Mathematical Appendix 7:*a*(iii). For an example of this model in the literature, see the discussion of Lange in Note I:3.

not (significantly) affect relative prices and real income and hence do not generate substitution and income effects. Thus shifts in tastes, changes in technology, and the like are in the domain of value theory. Changes in the amount of money and—as we shall see—shifts in liquidity preference are in the domain of monetary theory.[41]

If we now examine this classificatory scheme, we will discover the grain of truth in the intuitive feeling that in some sense value theory is connected with the determination of relative prices and monetary theory with the determination of absolute prices. In particular, assume that by a *tâtonnement* involving all prices and all markets the equilibrium values of money prices have been reached. We can now make use of this information to take a step backwards and approach the equilibrium position once again—but this time by a restricted *tâtonnement*. For example, holding the absolute price level constant at its already determined *equilibrium* value, we can arbitrarily shift relative prices from theirs, and then study the nature of the dynamic forces that—working simultaneously in *all* markets—return the economy to its original equilibrium position. By the very definition of this procedure, such a return can be accomplished without any change in the absolute price level. Hence the restricted *tâtonnement* by which equilibrium relative prices are thus redetermined need involve only these prices, need accordingly generate only substitution and income effects, and can therefore be studied entirely within the confines of value theory.

Similarly, we can define a restricted *tâtonnement* which—starting from a knowledge of the *equilibrium* values of relative prices and interest—works simultaneously through *all* the markets of the economy to redetermine the equilibrium value of the absolute price level. Such a *tâtonnement* can clearly succeed without requiring any changes in relative prices and interest; that is, it need generate only real-balance effects. Hence it can be studied entirely within the confines of monetary theory.

This decomposition of the overall *tâtonnement* into two components is a convenient expository device which has already been exploited in Chapter III:3. It can be used safely provided we are clear in our own minds that it separates out effects and not markets. In particular, we must guard against the apparent tendency to slip over from this valid device into the invalid proposition of the false dichotomy that, starting with an absolute price level held constant at an *arbitrary* level, a *tâtonnement* on relative prices in the *commodity markets alone* can

---

[41] In accordance with the plan of the chapter as set out in its first footnote, the classification of the rate of interest as a real or monetary variable is deferred until Chapter XV.

determine these prices; that, holding these relative prices constant at the values so determined, a *tâtonnement* on the absolute price level in the *money market alone* can then determine this level; and that the absolute price level so determined, together with the relative prices determined by the first *tâtonnement* in the commodity markets, must *necessarily* preserve the equilibrium initially achieved in these markets. Clearly, this last statement will generally *not* be true unless the excess-demand equations of the commodity markets are actually independent of the absolute price level.[42]

This is the crucial point. The dynamic groping of the absolute price level toward its equilibrium value will—through the real-balance effect —react back on the commodity markets and hence on relative prices. And it is precisely the constant failure to find this point explicitly recognized—and, indeed, the constant sensation of being just on the verge of having it explicitly contradicted—that is the basis of our original contention that the roots of the invalid dichotomy are to be found in the neoclassical analyses of Walras, Fisher, Pigou, and Cassel.[43]

As the reader has probably realized for himself, this extended discussion of the invalid dichotomy has uncovered yet another manifestation of the mental block that cut off the real-balance effect from complete understanding. First, and most revealing of all, the failure to present a stability analysis of the equilibrium absolute price level. Then the failure to describe correctly the demand curve for money. And now, finally, the failure to realize the direct and immediate contradiction between the real-balance effect, on the one hand, and the "homogeneity postulate" of the invalid dichotomy, on the other; or, from an alternative viewpoint, the failure to realize the complete inappropriateness of denoting sensitivity of the individual to a change in the absolute price level by the term "money illusion," when in fact it is precisely this sensitivity which demonstrates the existence of a rational

---

[42] The second half of this paragraph is an attempt—I hope not overelaborate—to give economic meaning to a simple mathematical proposition. For details, see Mathematical Appendix 7:*a*(v).

[43] The reader will find it particularly instructive to compare the last two paragraphs of the text with the passages from these analyses cited in full and discussed on pp. 402–4, 436, 443–44, and 451–52, respectively. See also the passage from Fisher cited at the end of the next section.

It should be clear that the criticism of these paragraphs is *not* directed against the frequent neoclassical practice of taking the absolute price level as given in the partial-equilibrium analysis of value theory. The same methodological considerations which permit this analysis to hold certain relative prices constant also permit it to do the same for the absolute price level. The purpose of this assumption is simply to enable the money price of a commodity to serve as a perfect index of its relative price. Cf. Marshall, *Principles* (eighth ed.), p. 62. This practice goes back at least to Mill, *op. cit.*, p. 439; cf. Marget, *op. cit.*, Vol. II, p. 281, footnote 128.

concern on the part of the individual with the concrete and surely non-illusory effects of such a change on the real value of his money holdings. Having seen this triple failure to carry through the real-balance effect to its own logical implications, can we be left with any doubt but that its full meaning was never really understood?[44, 45]

4. The preceding section not only analyzes the invalid dichotomy, it also shows the reassuring passwords which discouraged critical examination and thus made the dichotomy's continued acceptance possible. The password of being a friend of the quantity theory, the password of connecting value theory with relative prices and monetary theory with absolute prices. The password of demand depending only on the ratios of prices, the password of providing an additional bit of information and determining thereby an additional set of prices. The password of determining relative prices independently of the absolute price level. All of these are valid passwords—within a certain context. But this very multiplicity of respectable passwords dissuaded economists from looking more closely and seeing that in every single case the context was false! That in every single case there was a seemingly slight—but actually vital—difference.

Fortunately for our understanding of doctrinal history, there are certain places in the literature where we can catch this deception in the very act! Thus there is at least one explicit example of the way in which the valid insensitivity of demand to equi-proportionate changes in *accounting* prices shifts undetected into the invalid insensitivity to equi-proportionate changes in *money* prices. That is, the valid dependence of demand solely on the ratios of accounting prices is explicitly confused with the invalid dependence solely on the ratios of money prices. Indeed, this example considers this dependence to be a direct consequence of the "postulate . . . that the consumer's behaviour is independent of the units in which prices are expressed. . . ." But here again the same confusion is at work. For after a change in the monetary unit has worked itself out, the individual is confronted with an equi-proportionate change in money prices *and* in his money holdings. Thus if the dollar is replaced by the half dollar as the unit of measure,

---

[44] It might be noted that the approach of Keynesian economics—with its concentration on flows to the neglect of stocks—was hardly conducive to breaking down a mental block whose essence was the failure to see the significance of the effect of a change in the absolute price level on the real value of the *stock* of money. See Note K:1.

[45] The compartmentalization of thinking described in this paragraph should make clear the superficiality—and fallaciousness—of recent attempts to write the history of the invalid dichotomy in terms of an a priori ascription of consistency, and on this basis to assert that recognition of the real-balance effect is itself evidence of rejection of the invalid dichotomy.

all money prices will eventually double; but—as the very first result of this conversion itself—so will havê the initial money holdings of each and every individual.   Hence the proper analogue of a change in the monetary unit is an equi-proportionate change in *accounting* prices (which leaves the real value of initial money balances intact), not an equi-proportionate change in *money* prices (which does not).[46]

Similarly, there are instances in which the valid dichotomy between accounting and money prices is confused with the invalid dichotomy between money and relative prices.   Thus, in order to prove that *money* prices cannot be determined unless a special equation is added on, it is argued that: "There are always just one *too few equations* to determine the unknown quantities involved.   The equation of exchange [$MV = PT$] is needed in each case to supplement the equations of supply and demand"—and the first sentence is supported by an explicit reference to a mathematical development by the same author which, in order to determine *accounting* prices, adds an equation arbitrarily setting the accounting price of one of the goods equal to unity![47]

Examples in the literature of an alleged connection between the invalid dichotomy and the quantity theory of money have already been noted in the preceding section.[48]   As will be recalled, these allegations were based on a misunderstanding of the nature of the neutrality of money.   It remains now to suggest that in its more sophisticated form this may have expressed itself as a confusion between the invalid dichotomy and the first dichotomy described in the preceding section— the one which is essentially a restatement of the quantity theory and which shows the valid sense in which relative and absolute prices are independently determined.   In particular, we can find an example which states that "the proposition that the material set-up of our economic system determines only the *relative* and not the absolute prices of all commodities is so familiar that it hardly deserves further discussion"—and then justifies this statement with an implicit reference to the "homogeneity postulate" that demand remains unaffected by an equi-proportionate change in money prices.   Here we can almost see the exact point at which the line of reasoning slips off the correct path:

---

[46] Cf. above, p. 23.   The example referred to here is that of Samuelson; the quotation is also his.   For details, see Note I:3.

The line of reasoning in the second half of this paragraph is one that I have frequently heard—though I have not succeeded in finding any additional example of it in the literature. Cf., however, Boulding, *op. cit.*, p. 320.

[47] Cf. above, p. 106.

The passage cited is from Fisher, italics in original.   Precisely the same confusion can be found in Cassel.   For details, see Notes F:3 and H (pp. 450–51).

[48] See the references to Leontief and Modigliani above, p. 108, footnote 34.

Relative prices are determined independently of the absolute price level by the "material set-up of our economic system"—the valid dichotomy; "material set-up" means the conditions of demand in the commodity markets—the invalid dichotomy; but if these conditions alone determine relative prices, they can depend only on these prices—and the circle is closed.[49]

Finally, we can find an example which—though not as definitely clear as the preceding ones—seems to show how the valid intuitive feeling that different forces determine absolute and relative prices slips imperceptibly into the invalid identification of these forces with separate equations   How else can we interpret the train of thought revealed by the following passage: ". . . it is important to distinguish between the influences determining the general price level and the influences determining an individual price.   The price level is determined by a comparatively simple mechanism, that of the equation of exchange.   It is the result of the quantity of money and deposits, the velocities of their circulation, and the volume of trade.   The general price level then helps to fix individual prices, although not interfering with relative variations among them. . ."[50]

This is admittedly a small number of examples.   Nevertheless, the stature of the economists who provide them, the definitive aura of received doctrine that they all gave to the reasoning by which they justified their statements, and the fact that this reasoning was never challenged—all this endows these few examples with a weight far out of proportion to their number.   All this permits us to suggest that the explicit reasoning of these examples is representative of the general intellectual process that gave rise to the invalid dichotomy.

5. Let us now turn from these adventures of the mind to more mundane matters.   Until now, this chapter has essentially been concerned with the relation between the amount of money and the level of prices—that is, with the relation between M and P in the Cambridge equation $M = KPT$.   But neoclassical monetary theory also used this equation to analyze the relation between K and P, on the one hand, and T and P, on the other.   Since, unlike changes in M, the exact translation of changes in K and T into terms of our model is difficult to determine, the exact bearing of the following argument on the neoclassical one must also remain slightly unclear.   Nevertheless, as the

---

[49] The example referred to is that of Leontief, italics in original.   It is discussed in Note I:3.   As the reader will see from this discussion, I have interpreted Leontief's reference more specifically than he explicitly indicates.   But I think it is quite clear that this is what he had in mind.

[50] The example is that of Fisher.   It is discussed in Note F:3.

reader will see, the economic forces that appear in this argument have a distinctly neoclassical character.

We begin with the effects of a change in K. (Needless to say, whatever will be said for these effects holds in the inverse for those of a change in the V of $MV = PT$.) Consider, in particular, an economy whose equilibrium is disturbed by a sudden increase in K. This is represented in our model by an increased fear of insolvency on the part of each and every individual, that is, by a suddenly increased desire for liquidity. More specifically, this "change in tastes" reflects itself as an increase in the amount of money individuals demand at a given set of prices, interest, and initial endowments. By the budget restraint, this upward shift in the demand for money implies a simultaneous downward shift in the demand for commodities and real bond holdings. That is, because of their given incomes, individuals cannot demand more of one good unless they give up something of another. As a result of this latter shift, equilibrium prices will fall. The interesting question which now confronts us is whether the equilibrium rate of interest must also change.

As already noted, a full analysis of this question must await Chapter X:4. Nevertheless, there is a simple, intuitive answer that can be given at this point To say that there has been an increase in the individuals' liquidity preferences is analytically equivalent to saying that the liquidity satisfaction they each derive from one dollar of cash balances is now less than it was before. And this, in turn, is equivalent to saying that the "subjective quantity" of money in the hands of individuals has decreased. Hence it seems only natural to argue that the conditions under which the rate of interest remains constant after an increase in liquidity preference are precisely those under which it remains constant after a decrease in the quantity of money.

Let us state this somewhat more exactly. As in the case of a decrease in the amount of money, we abstract from distribution effects. We also assume the increase in liquidity preferences to be "uniformly distributed"; that is, the liquidity preference of each and every individual is assumed to change with the same "intensity." As explained above, this increase causes downward shifts in the demands of all markets and hence replaces their original state of equilibrium by one of excess supply. Consider now any one market. Clearly, the excess supply in this market can now be removed by an equi-proportionate decline in prices, while the rate of interest remains constant. Specifically, this decline will continue until the real value of cash balances has increased sufficiently to satisfy the individuals' increased liquidity preferences and hence restore their demand in this market to its original level. Thus,

116

in some subjective sense, the real quantity of money that influences this market is the same as it originally was. Now, by assumption, the initial shift in liquidity preferences is a "neutral" one: it changes only the relative desirability of money vis-à-vis all other goods, not the relative desirabilities of these other goods amongst themselves. Hence if this subjective quantity of money is "the same" with respect to the market for one of these goods, it must be "the same" with respect to that for any other. That is, the equi-proportionate price decline needed to equilibrate one market must be equal to that needed to equilibrate any other. Hence equilibrium can be restored to the economy as a whole at a lowered price level and an unchanged rate of interest.[51]

Thus under these assumptions we obtain a reaffirmation of the classical position: An increase in K causes a decrease in P but leaves T and the rate of interest unaffected. By resorting to the device of carrying out the analysis in terms of changes in the real quantity of money instead of changes in P,[52] we can bring out the deeper connotation that neoclassical economists ascribed to this proposition: An increase in K creates automatic market forces which themselves generate the increased equilibrium amount of real balances desired by the community. The wonders of the "invisible hand" never cease.

6. Consider now an economy whose equilibrium is disturbed by a sudden increase in T. Let this be represented in our model by an exogenous doubling, say, of the individuals' initial commodity endowments. Such a change creates two opposing forces. On the one hand, there is, of course, an increase in the fixed supply of every commodity. On the other hand, there is an increase in income and a consequent increase in demand. If it should so happen that the increased demand for each and every commodity exactly offsets its increased supply, no further changes will occur, and the economy will remain in equilibrium at its original set of prices and interest rate. Clearly, this latter case implies a unitary marginal propensity to spend out of money income. In general, however, this marginal propensity can be assumed to be less than unity. Hence it can be expected that the increases in the amounts demanded will be less, respectively, than in those supplied. Thus amounts of excess supplies will be created in the commodity markets and a downward pressure on prices thereby generated.

Let us now see if an equi-proportionate decline in these prices can

---

[51] For details—and for explanation of all the phrases set off in quotation marks—see Mathematical Appendix 7:*b*.

[52] Above, beginning of Section 3.

return the economy as a whole to a position of equilibrium. Consider first the market for one particular commodity. Clearly, it is possible to conceive of the price decline continuing until the resulting positive real-balance effect together with the original positive-income effect suffice to increase the amount demanded to the same extent that the amount supplied was originally increased. That is, it is possible that by an equi-proportionate decline in prices, the rate of interest being held constant, the market for *any one* particular commodity can be brought back into equilibrium.

But the economy consists of many commodity markets, and each of them has been disturbed by the original increase in endowments. The income and real-balance effects of these markets are certainly not uniform. Hence, in contrast with the preceding section, there is no reason why the equi-proportionate decline in prices needed to bring one of these markets into equilibrium should be the same as that needed for any other one. That is, there is no reason why a given equi-proportionate decline in prices should succeed in equilibrating all markets simultaneously. Hence, in order for such an overall equilibrium to be restored, relative prices and interest will, in general, also have to change.[53]

Assume now that the exceptional occurs and that an equi-proportionate decline in prices—interest constant—does succeed in restoring the economy as a whole to equilibrium. Clearly, even in this case there is no reason why this decline should be in inverse proportion to the original increase in commodity endowments. For the necessary magnitude of this decline depends on the strengths of the income and real-balance effects, as well as on the size of the increase in endowments.

Thus we can confirm the neoclassical position that an increase in T decreases P. Furthermore, we also confirm the neoclassical contention that (even when there is no change in the rate of interest) this decrease will, in general, *not* be an inversely proportionate one. In terms of the Cambridge equation, this contention rests on the assumption that K and T are *not* independent; that a change in the latter will affect the former. In particular, it assumes that an increase in the volume of transactions creates the possibility of economies in the relative magni-

---

[53] The reason this argument is not relevant to the case of a decrease in M—and, by analogy, to the case of an increase in K as analyzed in the preceding section—can be seen from p. 41. In particular, the (subjective) quantity of real balances in these two cases is the same in the new equilibrium position as in the original one; hence no account need be taken of the fact that different demand functions show different sensitivities to changes in real balances. But in the present case the quantity of real balances is different in the two equilibrium positions; hence these different sensitivities now become significant.

tude of money balances necessary for a given level of security against insolvency. That is, it implies that an increase in T decreases K Hence, $M=KPT$ can continue to be satisfied even though P does not change in inverse proportion to T.[54]

7. We conclude this chapter with a discussion of Say's Identity. My own sympathies are with those who deny that this identity is a basic component of the classical and neoclassical position. Nevertheless, there are certain passages which can be cited in support of the opposite contention. Furthermore, whatever the proper interpretation, the attention that has been given to the identity since Keynes makes it desirable to analyze it in detail—particularly since some of its logical implications have not been correctly understood.[55]

Following Lange, we define Say's Identity as stating that—regardless of the prices and interest with which they are confronted—individuals always plan to use all of their proceeds from the sale of commodities and bonds for the purpose of purchasing other commodities and bonds. In other words, they never plan to change the amount of money they hold: its amount of excess demand is identically zero. In still other words—and as a direct consequence of the budget restraint—the aggregate value of the amounts of excess *supply* of commodities must always equal the value of the amount of *demand* for bonds: people divert any reduced expenditures on commodities to the purchase of bonds, never to the building up of money balances.[56]

It can readily be seen that this assumption implies that equilibrium money prices are indeterminate. For consider an economy with n goods: $n - 2$ commodities, bonds, and money. Assume that this economy is in equilibrium at a certain set of values for the rate of interest and for the $n - 2$ money prices. Let us now arbitrarily change

---

[54] On these economies, cf. Chapter VII:3, and particularly the reference to Fisher, *Purchasing Power of Money*, pp. 165–69. On this section as a whole, see Mathematical Appendix 7:*c*.

[55] On the literature—classical and Keynesian—see Note L.
"Say's Identity" is the useful term suggested by G. S. Becker and W. J. Baumol in order to emphasize that it may not really represent "Say's Law" in its classical and neoclassical meaning. But Becker and Baumol's attempt to give a classical connotation to the concept they call "Say's Equality" can only mislead. Cf. the discussion in Note L.

[56] The reader will recall that the budget restraint on p. 56 is
  the amount of market excess demand for current money holdings
    = the aggregate value of the amounts of market excess supplies of current commodities
    − the (discounted) value of the amount of market demand for current bond holdings.
By Say's Identity, the left-hand side of this equation is identically zero, so that this yields the conclusion just stated in the text.

one of these prices. Consider first the $n - 2$ commodity markets. In general, it will be possible to find another set of $n - 2$ values for the rate of interest and for the remaining $n - 3$ money prices which will again equilibrate these $n - 2$ markets. But, by Say's Identity, any set of prices and interest which equilibrates these markets must also equilibrate the bond market, for, under this assumption, if the excess supplies of commodities are zero, so is the demand for bonds.[57] Finally, since the excess demand for money is identically zero, this market too is obviously in equilibrium. Thus the economy as a whole can be in equilibrium at an infinite number of sets of money prices. In mathematical terms, Say's Identity reduces the number of independent market excess-demand equations to $n - 2$, and these do not suffice to determine the equilibrium values of the $n - 1$ price and interest variables.[58]

Thus Say's Identity is inconsistent with the existence of a money economy with determinate prices. But this is the only type of money economy that has any economic meaning. Hence we can say that the existence of Say's Identity implies the existence of a barter economy. Conversely, the existence of a barter economy implies the existence of Say's Identity. For in such an economy it is physically impossible to "sell" one commodity or bond without "buying" another; thus Say's Identity in this economy is nothing but a statement of the budget restraint. In other words, people never plan to change their level of money balances in a barter economy, because, by definition, such balances are always zero.

Let us now return for a moment to the "homogeneity postulate." As was demonstrated above,[59] this postulate implies the absence of a real-balance effect and the consequent indeterminacy of money prices. By the same argument as the preceding paragraph, we can then say that the existence of the "homogeneity postulate" implies the existence of a barter economy. Conversely, the existence of a barter economy

---

[57] The reader will recall that the demand and *excess* demand for bonds are identical, so that equilibrium exists in this market when either is zero; cf. p. 53.

[58] These two paragraphs essentially present Lange's analysis of Say's Identity, *op. cit.*, pp. 52–53. This analysis is also summarized in Mathematical Appendix 7:*d*. For generality, however, I have extended Lange's analysis to the case of an economy with bonds.

[59] P. 110. Note that the extension of the present argument to an economy with bonds has caused us to make a corresponding extension of the "homogeneity postulate" to include the bond market. However, the reader who prefers to retain the original sense of this term as applying only to the commodity markets can simply ignore all references here to the bond market and the rate of interest and follow the analysis as if it applied to an economy with only commodities and money. This does not change the argument in any significant way. At the same time, this modification brings us back to the framework actually considered by Lange and Modigliani; cf. the preceding and following footnotes.

implies the existence of the "homogeneity postulate." For in such an economy there are no money holdings, the "absolute price level" has no meaning, and hence there can be no real-balance effect.

Thus, contrary to the accepted opinion,[60] Say's Identity and the "homogeneity postulate" are logically equivalent properties: both are necessarily present in a barter economy; both are necessarily absent from a money economy. Thus the existence of the one implies the coexistence of the other.

With this we have also said all that need be said for our purpose about a barter economy. Such an economy is the home—the necessary and only home—of the "homogeneity postulate" and Say's Identity. Prices in this economy can be measured either in terms of one of the commodities or—as in a Wicksellian "pure credit economy"—in terms of an abstract unit of account. Thus, at most, only relative and accounting prices are defined. The former are determined by the workings of market forces, the latter—as always[61]—by arbitrary decree. Money prices not even being defined, their determinacy or indeterminacy cannot even be meaningfully discussed.[62]

---

[60] Cf. Modigliani, *op. cit.*, p. 217, noting also the reference to Lange.

[61] Cf. p. 39.

[62] As the reader has undoubtedly realized, to the deceptive "passwords" of the false dichotomy described in Section 4 above, we can now add that of the "homogeneity postulate" —valid only in a barter economy.

On Wicksell, see *Interest and Prices*, p. 68. Such a "pure credit economy" is described in detail in our discussion of Cassel's system in Note H.

On the general argument of this section, see Mathematical Appendix 7:*d*. This also points out a *non sequitur* that invalidates the accepted Lange proof of the proposition that Say's Identity implies the "homogeneity postulate." But, as the proof presented here in the text shows, the proposition itself is true.

PART TWO

MACROECONOMICS

CHAPTER IX

The Model

1. *Introduction.*   2. *The markets for labor services,*   3. *commodities,*
4. *bonds, and*   5. *money.*

1. We go back now to pick up the thread of the argument interrupted
at the end of Chapter IV.   The task that awaits us has already been set
out there.   It is, in brief, to present both a static and a dynamic monetary theory of a production economy under conditions of perfect competition.

We gain information in this direction by giving up information in
another.   In particular, we forego microeconomic detail and work
instead with an aggregative model which divides all the goods of the
economy into four composite categories: labor services, commodities,
bonds, and money.   To each of these categories there corresponds a
market, a price, an aggregate demand function, and an aggregate
supply function.   Conceptually, each of these functions is built up from
the individual demand and supply functions of the relevant individual
goods.   Thus, for example, the demand function for commodities is
the aggregate of all the individual demand functions for each and every
commodity.   There is, however, no pretense of showing how this
process of aggregation is actually carried out.   As before, it is also
assumed, unless otherwise noted, that the price of each good is expected
with certainty to be the same in the future as it is in the present.

Each of the foregoing aggregate functions is assumed to reflect
absence of money illusion.   Each is also assumed to remain unaffected
by any change in the distribution of real income, real bond holdings, or
real money balances which leaves constant the sum total of the respective
item.   Thus each of these functions can be represented as dependent
upon—among other things—the real values of the *total* income, bond

125

holdings, and money balances of the individuals or firms whose collective behavior it describes. In brief, the assumed absence of distribution effects makes it unnecessary to consider the *arrays* of the individual incomes, holdings, and balances in the economy.[1]

In principle, having left behind the confines of an exchange economy, we should also take account of the fact that, in addition to assets in the forms of money and bonds, economic units now hold physical assets and that variations in the real value of these assets also affect the demand and supply for the various goods. This necessity to supplement the already familiar real-balance and real-indebtedness effects with an analogous "physical-asset" effect is obviated by restricting our analysis of a production economy to a period of time during which net investment is small relative to the existing stock of physical assets. Hence, as a convenient approximation, this stock can be considered as remaining constant during the discussion, and the physical-asset effect can accordingly be ignored.[2] If, however, we were to extend the analysis to a longer period of time, the effects of an increase in physical-asset holdings in increasing the wealth of individuals, and hence their propensity to consume, and the more problematic effects of this increase on the firms' propensity to invest would assume crucial significance. But these are problems of the theory of business cycles and, more so, of the theory of secular development into which we cannot venture here.[3]

Our economy is inhabited by households, firms, and a government. Households sell their productive services to firms and use the proceeds to buy consumer commodities and bonds, to add to their cash balances, and to pay taxes. Firms sell consumer commodities to households and government, investment commodities to other firms, and bonds to households. They use the proceeds to pay for the productive services of households, to pay interest, to buy investment commodities, to repurchase the bonds they have issued, and to add to their cash balances. Any profit is appropriated by the entrepreneurs. Thus bonds are the sole item on the liability side of the firms' balance sheets.

The government receives taxes from households and uses the proceeds entirely for the purchase of consumer commodities from firms. These

---

[1] This distinction between totals and arrays has already been made on pp. 30 and 55.

[2] This also requires us to assume that the prices of these assets always change in the same proportion as the general price level.

[3] For further discussion of some of these points, see James Tobin, "Asset Holdings and Spending Decisions," "Papers and Proceedings," *American Economic Review*, XLII (1952), 109–23, and the papers and discussions by James S. Duesenberry, James Morgan, and James Tobin in *Savings in the Modern Economy*, ed. W. W. Heller *et al.* (Minneapolis, 1953), pp. 195–200, 213–17, 220–23.

are then provided to the economy free of charge. For simplicity, it is assumed that the *real* value of these government expenditures is fixed at a constant level. It is also assumed that the government never holds cash balances and that it has no bonds outstanding. That is, it has always exactly balanced its budget with tax receipts.

These assumptions can be schematically summarized in the following "input-output" table, where, as usual, the rows represent sales or money inflows, and the columns represent purchases or money outflows. The difference between the sum of a row and the sum of its corresponding column is, of course, equal to the change in the cash balances of the economic unit in question.

PURCHASES FROM	SALES TO		
	Households	Firms	Government
Households	———	Productive services Profits and interest Bonds (retirement)	———
Firms	Consumer commodities Bonds (new issues)	Investment commodities	Consumer commodities
Government	Taxes	———	———

The rest of this chapter is devoted to a detailed examination of each of our four composite markets. Subsequent chapters study the interrelationships among these markets and explain the workings of the system as a whole under varying conditions. All this will be done from the same general analytical viewpoint developed in Part One.

2. It is most convenient to start with the market for labor services. Despite the heterogeneous nature of these services, they are considered as one composite good with a single price. By assumption, the demand for these services originates entirely in the firms of the economy.

Consider first the behavior of a single firm operating, as assumed, under conditions of perfect competition. It is confronted with a production function which specifies the given technological relationship between its inputs of factor services and the resulting outputs of commodities. For simplicity, it is assumed that the capital equipment of the firm is fixed, so that its sole problem is to choose its optimum input of labor services. For any real wage rate, this input will be that which yields a marginal product equal to the given rate. Thus the firm's demand curve for labor is the marginal-productivity curve derived from its production function.

If we transfer these concepts to the economy as a whole, we can conceive of an aggregate production function relating real gross national product, Y, to the total input of labor services in the economy, N, and to the total fixed capital equipment of the economy, K_0:

$$(1) \qquad Y = \phi(N, K_0).$$

Let w represent the money wage rate and p the general price level of commodities. Then at any real wage rate, w/p, the total amount of labor demanded in the economy must satisfy the relationship

$$(2) \qquad \frac{w}{p} = \phi_N(N, K_0),$$

where $\phi_N(N, K_0)$ is the marginal productivity of labor.[4]   Our aggregate demand curve for labor can then be obtained by inverting the preceding function and writing it as

$$(3) \qquad N^d = Q\!\left(\frac{w}{p}, K_0\right),$$

where N^d is the amount of labor demanded. Clearly, if the law of diminishing marginal productivity holds, this demand curve will be negatively sloped with respect to increases in the real wage rate.

Consider now the supply curve of labor. To the extent that an individual operates on the principle of utility maximization, the amount of labor he supplies will depend on the real wage rate. Therefore, we assume that the aggregate supply curve for labor also depends on this rate. Thus we write

$$(4) \qquad N^s = R\!\left(\frac{w}{p}\right),$$

where N^s is the aggregate amount of labor supplied. For simplicity, it is also assumed that this supply is an increasing function of the real wage rate, though there are well-known reservations on this score.

Finally, we have the condition that must be satisfied in order that this market be in equilibrium:

$$(5) \qquad N^d = N^s.$$

That is, the wage rate will not be an equilibrium one unless it equates the amounts demanded and supplied of labor. A graphical description

---

4 As usual, $\phi_N(\ )$ denotes the partial derivative of $\phi(\ )$ with respect to N.

of this market is presented in Figure 10. The equilibrium real wage rate is $(w/p)_0$, and to it corresponds the amount of labor, N_0. If the wage rate were above this equilibrium level, there would be an excess supply of labor and the money wage rate would fall; if it were below, there would be an excess demand and money wages would rise.

It will immediately be recognized that we have greatly oversimplified the analysis of this market. Both the demand and supply functions for labor should actually be presented as dependent on the real value

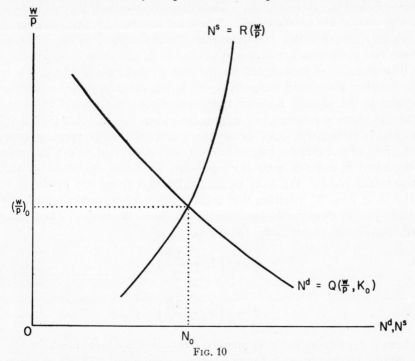

FIG. 10

of bond and money holdings as well as on the real wage rate. Furthermore, if we were to permit the firm to vary its input of capital, its demand for labor would depend also on the rate of interest. Finally, a full utility analysis of individual behavior would show the supply of labor also to depend on this rate.

If we have cavalierly ignored these additional influences, it is because the labor market as such does not interest us in the following analysis; its sole function is to provide the bench mark of full employment. Hence it has been considered desirable to introduce this market in as simple a manner as possible. The full meaning of these remarks will become clear in Chapter XIII:1. For the moment, we merely note that—as the reader will be able to confirm for himself in the next chapter—the introduction of these additional influences would not affect the comparative-statics analysis, but it would greatly complicate the dynamic analysis and would preclude the use of the helpful graphical device by which this analysis will be carried out.

3. Consider now the market for commodities. It is assumed that vertical integration of firms exists to such an extent that every firm is self-sufficient in raw materials. Thus the only commodities that appear in this market are finished ones. These are divided into two categories: consumer commodities and investment commodities. The prices of these two categories are assumed to change in the same proportion.

The demand of households for the first of these composite goods is the familiar consumption function, while the demand of firms for the second is the equally familiar marginal-efficiency-of-capital function. Each of these is conceptually aggregated from individual-experiments in which households and firms are confronted with varying combinations of real income, rate of interest, and initial real money balances and asked to indicate their corresponding optimum consumption and investment plans. We note in particular that firms are assumed to take their liquidity position into consideration when formulating their plans, just as households are assumed to do so in theirs. Thus these functions have, respectively, the forms

$$(6) \qquad\qquad C = g\left(Y, r, \frac{M_0^H}{p}\right)$$

and

$$(7) \qquad\qquad I = h\left(Y, r, \frac{M_0^F}{p}\right),$$

where C represents the real amount demanded by households of consumption commodities; I, the real amount demanded by firms of investment commodities; r, the rate of interest; M_0^H, the initial nominal money holdings of households; M_0^F, the initial money holdings of firms; and p, the general price level of both investment and consumption commodities. The variable Y here represents gross real national income, necessarily equal, of course, to gross real national product. To these demands we add the constant demand of government for consumption commodities,

$$(8) \qquad\qquad G = G_0,$$

where G is the real level of government expenditures, and G_0 is a constant not affected by any of the economic variables of our system.

For our purposes, it is only the total real demand for commodities, E, which is of interest. Thus we combine the preceding three functions into an aggregate demand function for commodities:

(9)
$$E = F\left(Y, r, \frac{M_0}{p}\right),$$

where

(10)
$$F\left(Y, r, \frac{M_0}{p}\right) \equiv g\left(Y, r, \frac{M_0^H}{p}\right) + h\left(Y, r, \frac{M_0^F}{p}\right) + G_0$$

and M_0 is the fixed total amount of money in the economy, equal to

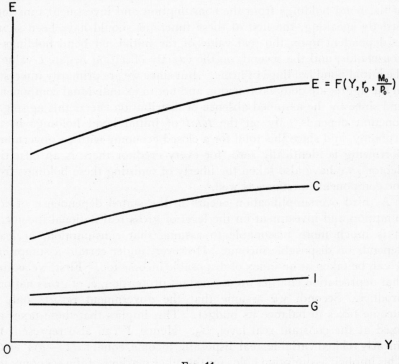

FIG. 11

the sum of M_0^H and M_0^F. For a given value of $r = r_0$ and $p = p_0$, this function has the familiar form indicated in Figure 11.

The curves labeled C, I, and G represent the consumption, investment, and government functions, respectively. As stated in equation (10), the aggregate demand curve, E, is the vertical sum of these three component curves. It shows the total amount demanded of com-

131

modities at varying levels of real income, assuming the rate of interest and price level to remain constant.   It reflects the assumption that, *ceteris paribus*, an increase in income increases the amounts demanded of both consumption and investment commodities but that this joint increase is less than the increase in income.   That is, the marginal propensity to demand commodities out of real income is assumed positive, but less than unity.

Before continuing with the description of this aggregate demand curve, let us note some oversimplifications already made.   There is first the exclusion of the holdings of physical assets from the demand function; the justification for this has already been explained in the first section of this chapter.   A second oversimplification is the exclusion of the bond holdings from the consumption and investment functions. Strictly speaking, the first of these functions should have been shown as dependent upon the real value of the initial net bond holdings of households, and the second, on the exactly offsetting negative value of the initial bond holdings of firms.   But since we are primarily interested in the aggregate demand function and not in its individual components, and since by the assumed absence of distribution effects this aggregate function depends only on the *total* of initial bond holdings in the economy, and since this total for a closed economy with no government borrowing is identically zero (for every creditor there is an offsetting debtor), we have also taken the liberty of omitting these holdings from the component functions as well.[5]

A third oversimplification occurs in the stated dependence of consumption and investment on the level of gross real national income, Y. It is much more reasonable to assume that consumption, at least, depends on disposable income.   However, under certain assumptions, Y can be taken as an index of disposable income too.   First, we assume that depreciation charges are a constant proportion, b, of gross national product.   Second, we assume that the government resorts only to income taxes to balance its budget.   This implies that these taxes are fixed at the constant real level, G_0.   Hence Y can also represent the linearly related variable, real disposable income, equal to $(1 - b)Y - G_0$. This implicit assumption holds for the other markets of the economy too.

Let us now return to our aggregate demand function and examine the effects of an increase in the rate of interest.   By assumption, the creditors' capital losses from such an increase exactly offset the debtors' capital gains.   Hence the increase in interest cannot affect aggregate demand in this way.   Instead, it exerts its influence through more

---

[5] This is the same type of argument already used on p. 55.

traditional channels. In particular, by its influence on the margin of a household's choice between consuming and saving, it is assumed to decrease the amount of current commodities demanded. This has been sufficiently discussed above.[6] To this we now add its influence on the margin of a firm's choice between expanding its investment program and retiring one of its outstanding bonds. Let us adopt the usual assumption of a declining marginal efficiency of capital. Then, the higher the rate of interest, the fewer the investment projects the firm can undertake which yield (after taking into account risk factors) a rate of return greater than or equal to the rate it could earn in interest-savings by simply repurchasing its bonds. Hence the higher the interest rate, the smaller the amount demanded of investment commodities and the greater the tendency toward debt retirement. Conversely, the lower this rate, the greater the number of projects for which it pays the firm to borrow and invest. Thus, in graphical terms, an increase in the rate of interest above r_0 causes a downward shift in the whole aggregate demand curve of Figure 11: at the same level of national income, the total amount of commodities demanded is decreased. Conversely, a decrease in interest below r_0 causes an upward shift in this curve.

It remains only to refer briefly to the by-now familiar real-balance effect. The greater these balances, the greater the amounts demanded of both consumption and investment commodities. More specifically, the marginal propensity to spend out of real balances is assumed to be positive, but less than unity. It follows that, *ceteris paribus*, an increase in the price level above p_0 causes a decrease in the real value of cash balances, M_0/p, and a consequent downward shift in the aggregate demand curve of Figure 11: at each level of national income, the amount of commodities demanded is decreased. Conversely, a decrease in the price level below p_0 causes an upward shift in this curve.

This last result can be presented in a more familiar framework by drawing the aggregate demand curve for commodities on a diagram whose vertical axis represents the price level, p, and whose horizontal axis represents the amount demanded of the composite commodity, E. Then, for a constant level of real income and interest, the resulting curve will show the traditional negative slope of a demand curve with respect to an increase in the price of its commodity. This negative slope follows, of course, from our assumption that the real-balance effect is positive: that, in other words, the composite commodity is not an inferior good with respect to changes in real balances—an inferiority

---

[6] Pp. 51 and 79.

which, in view of the comprehensive nature of the commodity, is hardly likely to exist.

Obviously, each of the foregoing components of the aggregate demand function, and, consequently, the aggregate demand function itself, reflects the absence of money illusion: each shows that any change which affects neither real income, the rate of interest, nor real balances does not affect economic behavior. The significance of this property for the consumption function is clear from Part One. Its significance for the government function is simply that there is a concern only with the real content of the budget. Its significance for the investment function can be made equally clear. Consider, for example, a doubling of prices and wages accompanied by a doubling of the firms' initial money and bond holdings, the rate of interest being held constant. This does, indeed, double the costs of any given investment project. But, by assumption, there is a simultaneous doubling of the money returns anticipated from this project. Hence, by definition, the marginal efficiency of capital—its marginal rate of return—is not affected by the combined wage and price increase. At the same time, the real asset position of firms is unchanged. Hence any project which firms found worth while to undertake before will still be found worth while. That is, the real demand for investment commodities is not affected by the specified change. And this is precisely what investment function (7) shows.

Let us now turn to the supply side of the market. Consider first the supply function of a given firm under conditions of perfect competition. This function describes the outcome of a conceptual individual-experiment in which the firm is confronted (in an unlimited market) with varying prices and costs and asked to specify the respective amounts of commodities it would like to supply in order to maximize its profits. It follows, under the simple assumptions of the preceding section, that the firm's supply function depends only on the technical conditions of production, its fixed amount of capital equipment, and the real wage rate. For, given the latter two, the firm's optimum input of labor is determined by its marginal productivity. And given this input and the firm's fixed capital equipment, the production function then determines the corresponding optimum output of commodities.

In a similar way we can conceive of an aggregate supply function for the economy as a whole which is dependent upon the real wage rate prevailing in the economy and on its fixed amount of capital. Write this function as

(11) $$Y = S\left(\frac{w}{p}, K_0\right),$$

where, in contrast to our description of the demand side of the market —but in accordance once again with our description of production function (1)—Y represents gross real national *product*, and not *income*. From the explanation of the preceding paragraph, it is clear that the output corresponding to a given real wage rate as given by this supply function must correspond to the output we would obtain by determining from the aggregate demand function for labor, (3), the optimum amount of labor firms would employ at this given rate and then determining from the production function, (1), the output corresponding to this input of labor. In other words, the supply function for commodities can be derived by substituting function (3) into function (1) to obtain

$$(12) \qquad \phi\left[Q\left(\frac{w}{p}, K_0\right), K_0\right] \equiv S\left(\frac{w}{p}, K_0\right).$$

Thus supply function (11)—like the more familiar one described in the preceding paragraph—indicates the amounts of commodities the firms of the economy would like to supply in order to maximize their profits at the given real wage rate with which they are confronted in the market.[7]

It follows that, for any given real wage rate, the aggregate commodity supply function must appear in Figure 11—or 12—as a vertical line drawn at the level of gross national product yielded by equation (11) for that specified wage rate. As long as this rate remains unchanged, so, too, must this vertical line. If, however, the real wage rate should rise, then the optimum input of labor, and hence the optimum output of commodities, will decrease. Hence the aggregate supply curve— though still represented by a vertical line—will shift to the left in Figure 12 until it reaches the level of gross national output yielded by (11) for the increased real wage rate. In the opposite case of a decrease in the real wage, the vertical supply curve will shift to the right. But we shall for the most part not be interested in such shifts until we reach the analysis of involuntary unemployment in Chapter XIII; until then the aggregate commodity supply function will play a rather passive role in the argument.

We might, however, note that a somewhat less strange representation of the supply function can be obtained by drawing it on a diagram whose vertical axis represents the price level, p, and whose horizontal axis represents the amount supplied of the composite commodity, Y. This

---

[7] It is obvious from equation (12) that if we were to abandon our oversimplified form of the labor demand function and, instead, represent it as dependent also on real balances and the rate of interest, the commodity supply function would also be so dependent.

curve will have the traditional positive slope of a supply curve. For the higher the price level, the lower the real wage rate, the greater the input of labor, and the greater, therefore, the aggregate amount of commodities supplied.

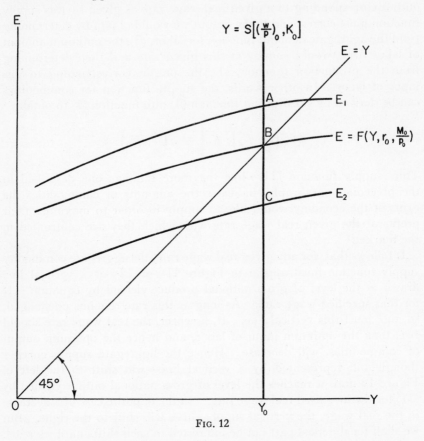

FIG. 12

The equilibrium condition for the commodity market is the usual one: the amount demanded must equal the amount supplied. That is,

(13) $$E = Y.$$

Graphically, we have the situation represented in Figure 12, where $w_0/p_0 = (w/p)_0$ and where Y_0 is, of course, the commodity output resulting from the input of N_0 units of labor in Figure 10. Equilibrium exists when the demand and supply curves intersect on the 45° radius vector.

The meaning of this equilibrium condition can be seen as follows.

Assume, for example, that the rate of interest remains r_0 but that the price and wage levels fall in the same proportion below w_0 and p_0, respectively. The real wage rate being unchanged, the supply curve in Figure 12 is unaffected. But, due to the real-balance effect, the demand function now rises above the solid curve of this diagram—say to E_1. Hence, at the unchanged real income Y_0, there exists an excess of commodities demanded over supplied equal to AB, inventories are drawn down, and an upward pressure on prices is created. In the opposite case, with a price level greater than p_0, the demand curve lies below that of Figure 12—say at E_2. There then exists an excess of commodities supplied over demanded equal to BC, inventories accumulate, and a downward pressure on prices is created. Equilibrium in the commodity market can therefore exist only when the demand curve intersects the supply curve at the point B.

4. Let us now examine the market for bonds. In the real world there are many kinds of bonds, of varying risks and maturities. We shall represent all of these by a composite perpetuity of representative risk paying one dollar per period. Thus the technical nature of this bond differs from that of Part One. For the purposes of the present analysis, however, this difference is unimportant; we can always consider the redemption of the one-period bond of Part One as being equivalent to the repurchase of a perpetuity.[8] The price of this perpetuity must obviously equal the reciprocal of the rate of interest.

It is assumed that the only demanders of bonds are households, whereas the primary suppliers are firms. Households can also supply bonds, but their relative importance on this side of the market is quite small. That is, the large majority of loans in our model are for production, and not consumption, purposes.

It should be noted that we are now using "demand for bonds" in a somewhat different sense than in Chapter IV. Specifically, this term now represents the demand for *positive* bond holdings; that is, it represents only the behavior of lenders. The behavior of borrowers, formerly described as a *demand* for *negative* bond holdings, is now represented separately as the "supply of bonds." Both the demand and the supply are for a *stock* of bonds. Households decide on the total stock of bonds they wish to hold; changes in these stocks represent their net lending during the period. Firms decide on the total stock they wish to have outstanding; changes in this stock represent their net borrowing during the period.

---

8 Cf. Hicks, *Value and Capital*, pp. 144–45.

The demand side of the market has been sufficiently discussed in Chapters IV:3 and VI:2. Letting B^d represent the number of bonds demanded and $1/r$ their per-unit price in dollars, we can summarize this discussion by writing

$$(14) \qquad \frac{B^d}{rp} = H\left(Y, \frac{1}{r}, \frac{M_0^H}{p}\right).$$

That is, the real value of bond holdings demanded depends only on real income, the rate of interest, and the real value of cash balances held by households. The form of the foregoing function makes explicit the assumed absence of money illusion: a doubling of prices and initial household money holdings, real income and the rate of interest being held constant, does not affect the amount demanded of *real* bond holdings, B^d/rp; that is, it causes a doubling of the amount demanded of *nominal* bond holdings, B^d.

The demand curve for bonds, as of a fixed level of real income and prices, is represented by the curve B^d in Figure 13. As can be seen from equation (14), this curve abstracts from the influence of the initial bond holdings of households. Under this oversimplification, the internal consistency of our model then requires that the elasticity of this curve be both negative and greater than unity in absolute value. For it has already been assumed that an increase in interest—that is, a decrease in the price of bonds—decreases the amount demanded of consumption commodities; it will also be assumed below that it decreases the amount demanded of money balances; hence, by the households' budget restraint, their total expenditure on bond holdings must increase.

The demand curve B^d also depicts Keynes' basic proposition that there is a minimum positive rate of interest on which individuals insist in order to compensate themselves for the loss of liquidity involved in holding bonds instead of money.[9] Figure 13 shows that—for the given real income Y_0, initial money balances M_0^H, and price level p_0—this rate at which the desired amount of bond holdings becomes zero is r_1. This is the economic meaning of the fact that above the price $1/r_1$ the demand curve for bonds is identical with the vertical axis.

Let us now examine the influence of changes in variables other than the rate of interest. Consider first an increase in real income or real balances. This is assumed to shift the whole demand curve to the right: at the same rate of interest individuals are willing to hold more

---

[9] This has already been mentioned on pp. 54 and 76.

bonds. As can be seen from the form of the demand function, an increase in the price level has no such clear-cut effect. *If* the real command over future commodities which the individual desires to hold in the form of bonds were to remain constant, then, clearly, the demand for bonds would increase in the same proportion that the anticipated costs of these future commodities had increased. But, under our assumptions, this desire cannot have remained constant, for the

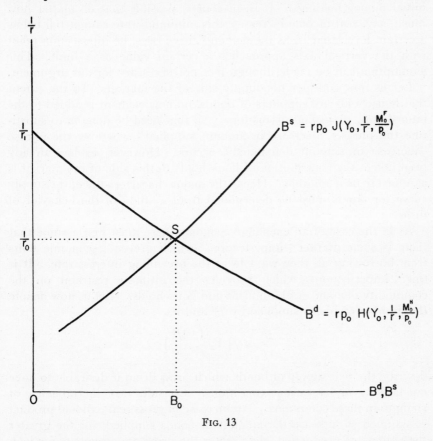

FIG. 13

decrease in real cash balances occasioned by the price increase must exert a downward influence on this desire as well as on the demand for current commodities. Indeed, this real-balance effect may even be so strong as to cause a decrease in the demand for bonds. Disregarding this possibility, we conclude that, say, a doubling of the price level causes a less-than-proportionate rightward shift of the demand curve for bonds; that is, at a given interest rate, the amount of bonds demanded is increased, but not doubled.[10]   Conversely, a decrease in prices causes a less-than-proportionate leftward shift in the demand curve.

It should be emphasized that the shifts described in the preceding paragraph will, in general, also change the intersection point of the demand curve with the vertical axis.   That is, the minimum rate of interest on which the individual insists is not generally an absolute constant of his behavior, but is itself influenced by his income and initial money holdings.   It is, of course, possible that no matter how much, say, real income increases, this minimum rate cannot fall below a certain level; that is, as the demand curve rises, its intersection point with the vertical axis approaches a certain value as a limit.   This assumption can be made, though it is not necessary for our argument.

Let us now consider the supply side of the market.   To the extent that households are suppliers of bonds, no new element is added to the immediately preceding discussion.   All that need be done is to substitute the phrase "decrease in amount supplied" wherever the phrase "increase in amount demanded" occurs.   However, as has already been noted, the contribution of households to this side of the market is assumed to be negligible.   Hence the major characteristics of the supply curve for bonds must be determined from a study of the behavior of firms.

As in the case of an exchange economy,[11] we must first assume that there is some market "imperfection" which prevents economic units from borrowing all they want to at the prevailing interest rate.   It is this "imperfection" which provides the ultimate restraint on the commodity demands of both firms and households.   Let us now denote the number of bonds supplied by B^s and let

$$(15) \qquad \frac{B^s}{rp} = J\left(Y, \frac{1}{r}, \frac{M_0^F}{p}\right)$$

describe the real supply of bonds which firms deem it desirable to have outstanding under various conditions.   Consider now the influence of changes in these conditions.   An increase in gross real national product is assumed to increase the amount of bonds supplied; for the greater the volume of production, the greater the firms' requirements for loan capital with which to finance the necessary plant, equipment, and inventories.   On the other hand, an increase in real balances decreases the amount supplied; for the decreased marginal value of the security

---

[10] The reader will find it instructive to compare this case with that in which the initial holdings of bonds and money are also doubled, so that—by the absence of money illusion—the whole demand curve shifts over exactly twice as far to the right; cf. pp. 54–55.

[11] Cf. p. 53.

against financial embarrassment provided by these increased balances will no longer compensate the firms for the interest-savings that can be achieved by using these balances for debt retirement.[12]

Let us now abstract from the influence of the firms' initially outstanding bonds and consider the effect of an increase in the rate of interest. The internal consistency of our model requires that this decrease the amount of *real* bonds supplied. For the higher the interest rate, the more firms will find it worth while to decrease their money balances and use the proceeds to retire debt. Similarly, the higher this rate, the smaller the demand for investment goods and the fewer, therefore, the number of projects that have to be financed. Hence the *real value* of bonds outstanding, B^s/rp, must decrease. But this does not mean that the *number* of bonds outstanding, B^s, must also decrease. For the rise in interest has lowered the price received for bonds and so may *increase* the number of bonds necessary to finance the firms' expenditures on investment commodities, even though these expenditures have *decreased*. We shall, however, assume that this latter tendency is outweighed by the first two, so that an increase in interest can be assumed to decrease both the real value and the number of bonds supplied.

The form of the foregoing supply function reflects the assumption that firms, too, are free of money illusion. A doubling of prices, wages, and initial money holdings, real income and interest held constant, does not change the firms' real positions and hence does not affect the real volume of their planned activities. Hence there is no change in the real value of bonds, B^s/rp, which firms deem it desirable to have outstanding. But, due to the increase in costs and prices, these same activities now require twice the nominal volume of bond financing as before. Hence B^s doubles.[13]

The curve B^s in Figure 13 depicts the foregoing supply function of bonds as of a fixed level of real national product and prices. In accordance with the foregoing discussion, this curve is drawn with a positive slope. Again in accordance with this discussion, it is assumed that an increase in real national income or a decrease in firms' real

---

12 Cf. pp. 63 and 88.

13 There is an implicit assumption here that all the firms' capital equipment must be replaced during the period in question. Alternatively, we can assume that firms immediately write up their capital equipment in accordance with its increased market value, sell additional bonds to the extent of this increased value, and pass on the implicit capital gains to their respective entrepreneurs. Conversely, in the event of a decrease in prices, entrepreneurs must make good the implicit capital loss, and firms then use these funds to retire bonds. In this way the nominal amount of bonds outstanding can always be kept equal to the current value of the firms' assets.

balances shifts the whole curve to the right: at the same rate of interest, firms wish to have more bonds outstanding. As can be seen from the supply function (15), an increase in the price level also shifts the curve to the right. But, in contrast to the demand side of the picture, this shift is more than proportionate to the increase in prices. For here the real-balance effect reinforces the "cost effect." That is, firms have to increase their borrowing, not only to finance the increased costs of operations, but also to replenish their real balances. Conversely, a decrease in prices causes a more-than-proportionate leftward shift of the supply curve.

The condition for equilibrium in the bond market is, of course,

$$(16) \hspace{3cm} B^d = B^s.$$

At the level of real national income Y_0 and prices p_0, such an equilibrium exists in Figure 13 at the rate of interest r_0. If, *ceteris paribus*, the rate of interest were less than this, there would be an excess supply of bonds, driving the price of bonds down (and, *ipso facto*, the rate of interest up). If it were greater, there would be an excess demand for bonds, driving the rate down again.

Throughout this section we have followed the practice of the preceding one and have disregarded the influence of the initial holdings of bonds. Let us now examine the significance of this omission. Strictly speaking, the demand for bonds should have been shown as depending also on the initial *positive* bond holdings of households, and the supply of bonds on the initial *negative* bond holdings of firms. If we were to take these additional influences into account in Figure 13, both the demand and supply curves would shift to the right: the former shift reflecting the fact that the stock of bonds demanded depends not only on the current income of households but also on the size of their initial bond portfolios; the latter shift reflecting the fact that the stock of bonds supplied depends not only on the need of firms to finance current activities but also on their need to keep on financing their initially outstanding debt. But if the assumption of neutral distribution effects holds, these two shifts would be exactly equal, so that the equilibrium rate of interest would not be affected. Thus, from the narrow viewpoint of the equilibrium interest rate, this omission is of no importance. On the other hand, this discussion makes it clear that no meaning can be attached to the amount, B_0, at which the curves intersect in Figure 13; for the true intersection point—representing the equilibrium number of bonds outstanding—must be to the right of B_0.

This complication—as well as others that have beset us in the course of this section—can be avoided by conducting the analysis in terms of the demand for *real* bond holdings—where "demand" is now used in the sense of Chapter IV to refer to both positive and negative holdings.[14] This demand function for these real holdings is the difference between the real demand and supply functions of this section and can therefore be represented by

$$(17) \qquad D = B\left(Y, \frac{1}{r}, \frac{M_0}{p}\right),$$

where

$$(18) \qquad B\left(Y, \frac{1}{r}, \frac{M_0}{p}\right) \equiv H\left(Y, \frac{1}{r}, \frac{M_0^H}{p}\right) - J\left(Y, \frac{1}{r}, \frac{M_0^F}{p}\right).$$

As illustrated in Figure 14, at a rate of interest below r_0 the net demand

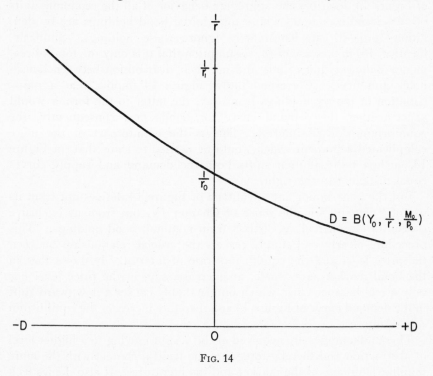

FIG. 14

for real bond holdings, D, is negative; that is, there is an excess of potential borrowers over lenders, and this drives the rate up. At a rate above r_0 the net demand is positive; there is an excess of potential

14 See third paragraph of this section.

lenders over borrowers, and this drives the rate down. Equilibrium exists in this market when

$$(19) \qquad B\left(Y, \frac{1}{r}, \frac{M_0}{p}\right) = 0,$$

that is, when the total amount of desired borrowings is equal to the total amount of desired lendings. Figure 14 shows that—for real income Y_0, price level p_0, and initial money holdings M_0—this condition is satisfied at the rate of interest r_0, at the price corresponding to which the demand curve for real bond holdings intersects the vertical axis.[15]

This alternative description of the bond market exploits to the full our simplifying assumption that what matters is only the total of any item and not its distribution. In particular, since the demand curve of Figure 14 describes the aggregate behavior of all the economic units of our closed economy—whose total initial bond holdings are by definition zero—it can legitimately ignore these holdings. Similarly, identity (18) makes use of the assumption that it is only the total of real money balances that counts and not their distribution between households and firms. Correspondingly, Figure 14 implies that a redistribution of money holdings from, say, the latter to the former would affect neither the demand curve for bonds nor, consequently, the equilibrium rate of interest. This is the counterpart of the more complicated argument which would be needed to show that, in Figure 13, such a redistribution shifts both the demand and supply curves equal distances to the right.

But the most important advantage of Figure 14 derives not from its use of "demand" in the sense of Chapter IV, but from its exclusive concentration on real, as distinct from nominal, bond holdings. This procedure clearly and simply reveals the crucial relationship between the price level and the equilibrium rate of interest. It shows that in the bond market as a whole, an increase, say, in the price level has only a real-balance effect which unmistakably causes a downward shift in the demand curve of Figure 14 and therefore increases the equilibrium rate of interest.

These advantages are achieved at the cost of moving to a higher level of abstraction and thereby foregoing the fruitful contact with the more familiar language of the market and the literature. It also denies us a graphical representation of the meaning of Keynes' minimum rate of interest. For the purposes of the text, this price is too high to pay. Hence in what follows we shall work mainly with the more clumsy

---

[15] This is the same argument presented at the beginning of Chapter IV:4.

description of Figure 13, though we shall always indicate to the reader
how he can simplify the argument by working instead with Figure 14.

5. Let us turn finally to the market for money. We continue to
restrict the discussion to a fiat paper money issued by the government.
As in the case of bonds, the demand and supply in this market are for a
stock and not a flow. We shall also continue to consider only the
transactions and precautionary demands, though we no longer restrict
ourselves to the rigorous framework specified by Chapter VII.

Actually, of course, the preceding discussion of the other three
markets, together with the budget restraint, has already completely
specified the form of the excess-demand function for money. If we
have assumed that an increase in real income or initial money balances
is devoted partly to increasing the demands for commodities and bonds,
then we have also assumed that the remainder of this increase—and
exactly the remainder—is devoted to increasing the demand for money.
If we have assumed that the demand functions for labor, commodities,
and real bond holdings are free of money illusion and are independent
of the distribution of initial bond and money holdings, then we have
also assumed this for the demand function for real money holdings
The function which reflects these assumptions can be written as

$$(20) \qquad M^d = p\, L\!\left(Y, r, \frac{M_0}{p}\right),$$

where M^d represents the amount of nominal money holdings demanded
by households and firms taken together—the governmental demand
being assumed zero.

By assuming the rate of interest and real income to remain constant,
we can obtain from function (20) a demand curve for money which
depends on the absolute price level. This has already been presented
in Figure 4 (page 42). However, in order to make our analysis
graphically comparable to that of Keynesian interest theory, we choose
instead to hold the price level and real income constant and to obtain
accordingly a demand curve which depends on the rate of interest.
Such a curve is presented in Figure 15. It should be clear that the
choice between Figures 4 and 15 is not a substantive one; the same
analysis can be carried out in terms of either diagram. In each case,
the choice depends only on what happens to serve best the purposes
of the exposition.

The negative slope of the following demand curve reflects the
assumption that money holdings are not an inferior good. Hence a
decrease in the price that must be paid for such holdings—in terms of

interest foregone—causes an increase in the amount demanded. On
the other hand, an increase in either real income or initial money
balances causes a rightward shift in the curve as a whole: at the same
rate of interest, the amount of money demanded is greater than it was
before. Finally, an increase in the price level is assumed to cause a
less-than-proportionate rightward shift in the curve as a whole. This,
of course, is implicit in what has already been said about the shapes of
the demand curves in Figure 4 (page 30).

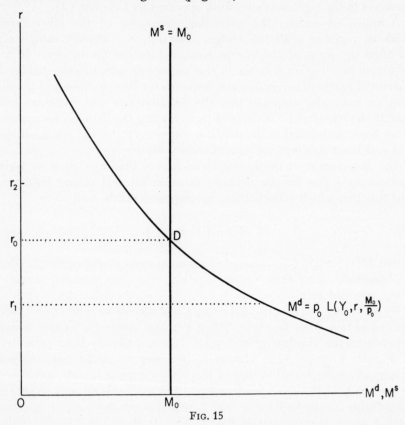

FIG. 15

As the reader can immediately see, the demand curve of Figure 15
differs in one significant respect from that curve which has become the
standard equipment of monetary theory since Keynes. Specifically, it
does not become indefinitely horizontal at the rate of interest r_1 at which,
by Figure 13, no one is any longer willing to hold bonds. This conclusion emerges directly from the budget restraint after feeding into it
the assumptions already made as to the effects of, say, a decrease in

146

interest on the other markets of the economy. It is a conclusion which again illustrates the pitfalls created by the failure to approach monetary theory from the mutual interdependence viewpoint of general-equilibrium analysis.

In particular, a decrease in the rate of interest has been assumed to affect the planned inflow and outflow of money by causing an

increase in the total planned expenditures of households on consumer commodities, an

increase in the total planned expenditures of firms on investment commodities, a

decrease in the total planned holdings by households of the bonds of firms and other households (i.e., total planned lendings of households), an

increase in the total planned issuance by households of their own bonds (i.e., total planned borrowings of households), and an

increase in the total planned issuance by firms of their own bonds (i.e., total planned borrowings of firms).

Let us designate a money inflow as a positive amount and a money outflow as a negative one. Then to say that a decrease in the rate of interest increases the amount of money demanded is to say that the algebraic sum of the above five items is positive. That is, the planned inflow of money exceeds the planned outflow, so that—by the budget restraint—there is a planned increase in the stock of money holdings.[16]

---

[16] It may help the reader to see this if we write the budget restraint for the economy as a whole in the following form:

> the amount of money demanded (that is, the stock of money planned for the end of the period)

> = the given holdings (stock) of money at the beginning of the period

> + the planned money inflow from the sale of labor services, commodities, and bonds during the period

> — the planned money outflow on the purchase of labor services, commodities, and bonds during the period.

Since this restraint views the economy as a whole, it does not include a term representing the interest payments made and received each period on bonds: by assumption, the net aggregate amount of these payments is zero. [Cf. my "Reconsideration of the General Equilibrium Theory of Money," *op. cit.*, equations (2.1), (2.2), and (5.3).] Note also that in the text we have ignored the influence of labor services; this follows from our assumption that the demand and supply for these services are independent of the rate of interest.

It should finally be emphasized that by transposing the term "given holdings (stock) of money at the beginning of the period" to the left-hand side of the preceding restraint, we obtain a statement that a *change in the stock* of money over a period of time is equal to a net *flow* during that same period. Thus the "stock and flow" dimensions of the foregoing restraint are seen to be properly related; cf. above, p. 25, footnote 17.

Assume now that the rate of interest has been reduced to r_1 and consider the effects of a still further reduction. The only significance of having reached this minimum rate of interest is that the third item in the preceding list becomes zero: individuals no longer plan to convert bond holdings into money holdings for the simple reason that they no longer have any such bonds to sell. But if money is still a noninferior good, the planned inflows of the last two items continue to overbalance

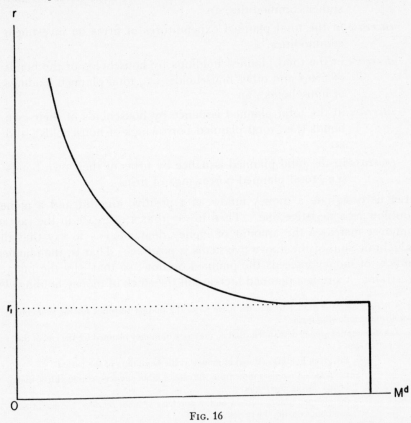

Fig. 16

the outflows of the first two, so that planned money holdings continue to grow. Thus, in general, the rate of interest r_1 does not manifest itself in any particular way in the demand curve for money.[17]

Only in very special instances would this demand curve become horizontal at the rate r_1. This would be the case, for example, if the demand curve for bonds in Figure 13 happened to have a horizontal

---

17 This is the counterpart of its failure to manifest itself in any particular way in Figure 14.

segment at the price $1/r_1$ and if, at this rate of interest, the first two of the above five items happened exactly to offset the last two. Then the demand for money would also be horizontal at the rate of interest r_1 for an extent equal to the money value of the maximum number of bonds held at this rate of interest. But a properly defined constellation of forces could produce this horizontality at any rate of interest, and not necessarily at r_1. Furthermore, even in the special case just described, the horizontality extends only until all bonds have been converted into money. Once this is done, and provided that the first two items continue to offset the last two, the demand curve becomes a vertical line, as in Figure 16.

The only case in which the demand curve could become indefinitely horizontal at r_1 is the one in which the supply of bonds in Figure 13 becomes infinite at this rate. But an individual who plans an infinite supply of bonds is for some reason unconcerned with his obligation to make interest payments on these bonds. Hence if the amount supplied is infinite at any positive rate of interest, it must be so at all rates. Under this assumption, it follows that the demand for money would also be infinite at all positive rates. Indeed, the same must hold true for the demand for commodities. These unrealistic implications explain why we ignore this possibility and retain our original assumption that the institutional framework of the economy keeps the supply of bonds finite.[18]

Nevertheless, as we have had ample opportunity to see from our critique of neoclassical theory in Chapter VIII, every shibboleth starts from a grain of truth. And there is such a grain at the root of the Keynesian demand curve too. But we shall have to wait until Chapter XIV:3 to understand the nature of this original grain and of the later process by which it was falsely mutated.

Let us turn finally to the supply side of the market. We have assumed throughout our analysis that the amount of money in circulation is constant. Thus our supply function is simply

$$(21) \qquad\qquad M^s = M_0,$$

where M^s is the nominal amount of money supplied and M_0 is a constant. The equilibrium condition is

$$(22) \qquad\qquad M^d = M^s,$$

and this is shown to obtain in Figure 15 at the rate of interest r_0 Alternatively, in Figure 4 (page 42), equilibrium could have been

---

[18] See p. 140.

shown to obtain at $1/p_0$ for a demand curve drawn for constant real income Y_0 and interest r_0. In either diagram we can see that if the rate of interest were below r_0 or the price level above p_0, then there would be an excess demand for money; by the budget restraint, this implies the existence of an excess supply of bonds and/or commodities. Hence the rate of interest would rise and the price level fall. Conversely, if the rate of interest were above r_0 and the price level below p_0, automatic market forces would be generated to lower the former and raise the latter.

CHAPTER X

The Workings of the Model:

Full Employment

1. The equality of the number of equations and variables. 2. The stability of the system: the method of successive approximation. 3. The effects of an increase in the amount of money. 4. The effects of a shift in liquidity preference.

1. The preceding chapter provides a description of each market of the economy. This chapter and the next one integrate these separate descriptions into an overall one of the functioning of the economy as a whole on the assumption of full employment. The meaning of this assumption and the implications of dropping it will be discussed at length in Chapter XIII. For the moment we shall simply understand it as implying that the level of real national product remains fixed at Y_0 throughout the analysis. Correspondingly, the level of employment remains fixed at N_0, the labor input necessary to produce Y_0.

Let us now describe our model in formal mathematical terms. There are four markets. For each market there are three equations: a demand equation, a supply equation, and an equilibrium equation. For each market there are also three variables: the amount demanded, the amount supplied, and the price of the good in question. The price of money is, by definition, unity. Hence there is a total of only eleven variables to be determined. On the other hand, if any three equilibrium equations are satisfied, the remaining one must—by Walras' Law—also be satisfied. Hence there is also a total of only eleven independent equations with which to determine these variables.

151

By substituting these demand and supply equations into their respective equilibrium equations, we can reduce the foregoing system of equations to the following one:

	Condition for Equilibrium	Market
(1)	$$Q\left(\frac{w}{p}, K_0\right) = R\left(\frac{w}{p}\right)$$	Labor services
(2)	$$F\left(Y_0, r, \frac{M_0}{p}\right) = Y_0$$	Commodities
(3)	$$rp \cdot H\left(Y_0, \frac{1}{r}, \frac{M_0^H}{p}\right) = rp \cdot J\left(Y_0, \frac{1}{r}, \frac{M_0^F}{p}\right)$$	Bonds
(4)	$$p \cdot L\left(Y_0, r, \frac{M_0}{p}\right) = M_0$$	Money

Here we have made use of the assumption that the level of output is fixed at Y_0. By Walras' Law, only three of these equations are independent. Correspondingly, there are only three unknown variables to be determined: the money wage rate, the price level, and the rate of interest. As in Chapters III:2 and IV:4, we then take this equality between the number of equations and unknowns as justifying the reasonableness of the assumption that this system of equations does have a solution. Indeed, this assumption is already implicit in the diagrams of the preceding chapter. For these posit the existence of a single set of values for our variables—w_0, p_0, and r_0—which can simultaneously equilibrate each and every one of the four markets of the economy.[1]

2. As emphasized in Chapter III:3, it is not enough to argue that a system of excess-demand equations has a solution; it must also be shown that the market, by its normal functioning, will itself reach this solution —that, in other words, the market is stable. Let us then examine the dynamic process of successive approximation—Walras' *tâtonnement*— by which the market "solves" the system of equations just set out. Taking advantage of Walras' Law, we need only trace this process for the first three markets. We further simplify our task by assuming that there is an instantaneous reaction to the pressure of excess demand or supply in the labor market. Specifically, any increase in the price level lowers the real wage rate, thereby creates an excess demand for labor,

---

[1] See above, Figures 10, 12, 13, and 15.

Note that the foregoing system can be simplified by replacing equation (3) by equation (19) on p. 144: $B\left(Y_0, \frac{1}{r}, \frac{M_0}{p}\right) = 0$.

thereby generates an immediate proportionate increase in the money wage rate, and thus uninterruptedly maintains the equilibrium of the labor market. Hence we can restrict our dynamic analysis to the commodity and bond markets.

The nature of the dynamic forces in these two markets has already been described in the preceding chapter. There it was shown that if there were an equilibrium rate of interest but a less-than-equilibrium price level, then there would exist a state of excess demand in the commodity market driving prices up. Similarly, if there were an equilibrium price level but a less-than-equilibrium rate of interest, then there would exist a state of excess supply in the bond market driving the rate of interest up.

In each of these cases it was assumed that initially only one variable differed from its equilibrium value. Let us now consider a case in which both do. Assume, for example, that we start from a position in which the price level is at p_2, less than p_0. Other things equal, this implies that the aggregate demand curve for commodities is at a position like that of E_1 in Figure 12 (page 136). There would then exist upward pressures on the price level. But assume that the rate of interest happens to lie at r_2, greater than r_0 just to the extent necessary to bring the aggregate demand curve down to an equilibrium level once again. This situation is depicted in Figure 17, which, for the sake of comparison, also reproduces the demand curve of Figure 12. By assumption, both of these demand curves intersect the supply curve on the 45° radius vector. This is the only necessary relation between them.

Clearly, under these circumstances, no corrective force emanates from the commodity market. But consider now the bond market as described by Figure 13 (page 139). By assumption, the lowering of the price level below p_0 has—at the price $1/r_0$—shifted the supply curve further to the left than the demand curve. Hence, even if the rate of interest were to remain r_0, a state of excess demand would now replace the former state of equilibrium. And this is *a fortiori* the case for r_2, a rate of interest greater than r_0. Alternatively, in terms of Figure 14 (page 143), the lowered price level has raised the excess-demand curve and thereby increased the excess demand existing at any rate of interest greater than r_0.

As a result of this excess demand, the rate of interest begins to fall. But this fall causes an upward shift in the commodity demand curve and so disturbs the assumed initial equilibrium described by Figure 17. In particular, there is now an excess demand for commodities which causes a rise in prices. This, in turn, reacts back on the bond market. At this higher price the demand curve for bonds will have shifted to the right proportionately less than the supply curve, so that this, together with the downward movement of the rate of interest, will reduce the excess demand in this market.   In this way market forces are created which tend to bring the economy back to the price level p_0 and the rate of interest r_0.

It is possible to generalize this analysis and to show that, under our simple assumptions, this convergence to the equilibrium position must

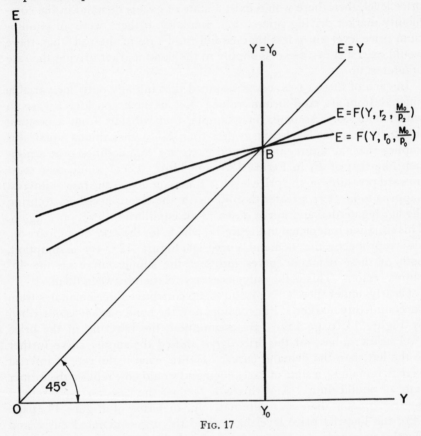

Fig. 17

always take place; that, in other words, the system must be dynamically stable.   A rigorous demonstration of this stability must be deferred to Mathematical Appendix 8:*a*.   Fortunately, however, an intuitive understanding of this proof can be obtained from a simple graphical device.[2]

---

[2] Adapted from the ingenious graph of Lloyd A. Metzler, "Wealth, Saving, and the Rate of Interest," *Journal of Political Economy*, LIX (1951), 104.

Consider first the equilibrium condition of the commodity market. From Figure 12 (page 136) we see that equilibrium exists for the price level p_0 and rate of interest r_0. However, as we have just seen in Figure 17, this market can be in equilibrium for other values of these variables as well. Indeed, we assume that for every rate of interest there exists a price level with a corresponding real-balance effect just exactly large

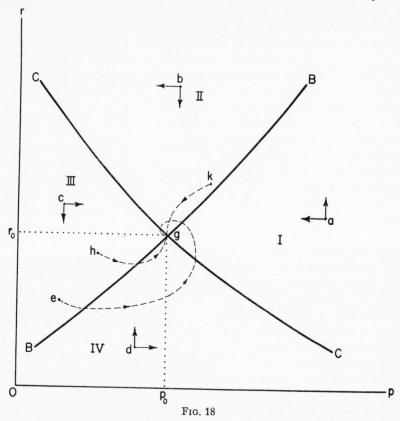

FIG. 18

enough to maintain the state of equilibrium in the commodity market. Clearly, the higher the given interest rate, the greater the real-balance effect necessary to offset its depressing effect on demand, and the lower, therefore, the price level necessary to generate this effect. Let the curve CC in Figure 18 be the locus of all such pairs of equilibrium values of the rate of interest and price level. It follows from what has just been said that this curve must have a negative slope throughout. It also follows that whenever the joint values of the price level and interest rate that happen to prevail in the commodity market correspond to a point to the right of CC, there will exist a state of excess supply in this market driving the price level downwards. Conversely, at any point to its left there will exist a state of excess demand driving it upwards.

In a similar way it is possible to construct a curve BB which is the locus of all pairs of values of the rate of interest and price level for which the bond market is in equilibrium. Clearly, this curve passes through the point (p_0, r_0) and has a positive slope. For consider a rate of interest higher than r_0. From Figure 13 (page 139) we see that at such a rate there will be an excess demand for bonds. But this excess demand can be eliminated and equilibrium restored by a sufficient increase in the price level. For such an increase causes a greater rightward shift of the supply curve than of the demand curve. Alternatively, in terms of Figure 14 (page 143), a rise in the price level shifts the excess-demand curve downwards, hence lowers its intersection point with the vertical axis, and thus causes the equilibrium rate of interest to rise too. It follows from the construction of BB that at any point below it there will be a state of excess supply in the bond market driving the rate of interest up; at any point above it, an excess demand driving it down.[3]

The two intersecting curves divide Figure 18 into four sectors, designated by roman numerals. Consider any point, a, in the first sector. The arrows attached to it indicate the directions of the dynamic forces operating on the rate of interest and the price level when the market is at a position corresponding to this point. These arrows show that should the economy be at any point in sector I, automatic market forces are generated which drive the rate of interest upwards and the price level downwards. Similarly, the directions of the dynamic market forces operating in sectors II, III, and IV are indicated by the arrows attached to the points b, c, and d, respectively.

Thus, no matter what the levels of prices and interest at which the market happens to be, there always exist forces which push at least one of the variables in the direction of the equilibrium position, g. As can be seen from Figure 18, the path generated by these forces moves in a counterclockwise direction. Sometimes it reaches the equilibrium position directly, as illustrated by the paths originating at the points h and k, respectively; sometimes it does so only after first spiraling about the equilibrium position, as illustrated by the path originating at the point e. Whatever the exact nature of the path, Figure 18 illustrates the fundamental fact that the very existence of disequilibrium anywhere

---

3 Mathematically, CC and BB are the graphs of equations (2) and (3), respectively, considered as implicit functions of r and p. Clearly, $B\left(Y_0, \dfrac{1}{r}, \dfrac{M_0}{p}\right) = 0$ is equivalent to (3) for this purpose.

in the economy automatically calls into operation corrective forces which ultimately eliminate it. Conversely, once the equilibrium position is reached, the generation of market forces making for further changes ceases. This is the process of *tâtonnement* by which the market successfully gropes its way toward the solution of the system of equations of the preceding section.

We must now bring to the fore one tacit assumption on which the foregoing proof of stability is conditioned. It is that excess demand in one market affects only the price of that market. For the most part, this assumption is uncritically taken for granted in the contemporary theory of economic dynamics.[4] Nevertheless, a moment's reflection shows that it is really an atavistic vestige of partial-equilibrium analysis which cannot be justified in a general-equilibrium framework. For just as this framework emphasizes that a change in the price of one good affects the amounts demanded of all other goods, so does it suggest that the pressure of excess demand in one market affects the price movements of all other markets. Thus, for example, an individual who does not succeed in buying all he wants of a given good will not only bid up its price but will also divert part of the money he was originally planning to spend on that good to bidding up the prices of other goods as well. Such interrelated market pressures are particularly noticeable during periods of suppressed inflation. Here the pent-up excess demand in the controlled markets spills over into the uncontrolled ones and pushes their prices upwards. Our contention is simply that this familiar characteristic of periods of "permanent disequilibrium" also manifests itself—even if in a milder form—during the periods of temporary disequilibrium which are necessarily inherent in the dynamic process of *tâtonnement*.

Let us then assume that households which do not succeed in buying all the commodities they want at the existing price level use part of their resulting excess purchasing power to bid up the price of bonds as well as of commodities. Similarly, firms which do not succeed in selling all the bonds they wish to at the current rate of interest attempt to alleviate their resulting shortage of funds by offering commodities as well as bonds at a lower price. These assumptions do not change the nature of the market forces at work in the first and third sectors of Figure 18. Indeed, in these sectors the forces emanating from one market reinforce those from the other. But they do cause a basic change in the forces at work in the two remaining sectors.

---

[4] Its inappropriateness was first pointed out to me by Milton Friedman. See also Samuelson, *Foundations*, p. 274.

Consider, for example, the fourth sector. Here there is an excess demand for commodities, exerting an upward pressure on both commodity and bond prices. At the same time, there is an excess supply of bonds, exerting a downward pressure on both these prices. Hence the movement of a point in this sector depends on the relative strengths of these two opposing sets of pressures. If we assume that the forces generated in one market always predominate in determining the price movement of the other market, then the direction of the arrows attached to point *d* must be reversed. A similar statement holds for point *b*. Thus, under this assumption, the automatic market forces of sectors *II* and *IV* propel both the price level and the rate of interest away from their equilibrium values. It follows that the *tâtonnement* will not necessarily succeed in reaching the equilibrium values of the economy; that, in other words, the system is not necessarily stable.[5]

In what follows we shall disregard this possibility. Though recognizing the interrelationships just emphasized, we shall always assume that they are never strong enough to change the directions of the market forces described by Figure 18. Hence the system remains stable. But this stability is now a matter of assumption—not a matter of proof.

3. Let us now investigate the effects of, say, a doubling of the quantity of money. Essentially, our present model can be considered to be a special case of the more general one developed in Chapter IV; hence the conclusions of that chapter carry over immediately to the present one. Even without this, equations (1)–(4) readily show that *if* for the amount of money M_0 the system is in equilibrium at the wage rate w_0, price level p_0, and rate of interest r_0, *then* for the amount $2M_0$ it is in equilibrium at $2w_0$, $2p_0$, and r_0. The reader can confirm this by substituting these values directly into these equations. It might also be noted that this conclusion holds even if the demand and supply functions for labor are assumed to depend on the rate of interest and real balances as well as on the real wage rate.[6]

So much for the comparative-statics analysis. Let us turn now to the dynamic analysis. The basic elements of this analysis have already been presented in the preceding section. It remains only to apply them specifically to the case at hand. In order to avoid repetition, we shall carry out this application in a somewhat mechanical way. The reader can breathe more economic life into it by referring back to the relevant discussions of the preceding chapter.

---

[5] See Mathematical Appendix 8:*a*.

[6] This was already mentioned at the end of our discussion of the labor market in Chapter IX:2.

The dynamic impact of an increase in the amount of money depends on the way in which it is introduced into the economy. Consider first the case in which the government suddenly decides to increase its purchases of commodities during a certain period and to finance these purchases by printing new money. It is also assumed that in subsequent periods the government reverts to its usual level of purchases and to its policy of balancing the budget, so that no further additions to the money supply take place.

In the first period, then, there are two forces exerting an upward pressure on the aggregate demand curve for commodities. First, the government component of this curve has increased. Second, the total real value of cash balances has increased, with resulting increases in the consumption and investment components (see page 131, Figure 11). As a result, the aggregate demand curve is pushed above its equilibrium level in Figure 12 (page 136) to, say, the position represented by E_1. Since real output remains fixed at the full-employment level Y_0, an inflationary gap equal to AB is accordingly created; but, for simplicity, we assume that this does not yet express itself in a rise in prices.

In the next period, and in all subsequent ones, only the second of these forces can—at most—be at work; for, by assumption, government expenditures now return to their original level. Hence the aggregate demand curve drops back somewhat toward its original position— though, because of the continued presence of the second force, not possibly all the way. Thus it is only the real-balance effect which prolongs the inflationary pressure in the commodity market in periods subsequent to the one in which the new money is injected into the economy. It might also be noted that the aggregate demand curve is now at the level to which it would have initially been pushed up if the original injection of money had taken place through government transfer payments instead of commodity purchases. For under this alternative assumption, the first force described in the preceding paragraph would clearly never have existed. Correspondingly, under this assumption, no inflationary pressure would ever have existed in the commodity market were it not for the real-balance effect.[7]

In any event, at this stage an inflationary gap continues to prevail in the commodity market. We now take account of the fact that this gap drives the price level upwards, thereby reduces the real value of cash balances, and thus causes the demand curve to shift downwards. Clearly, this process must continue until, and just until, prices have also

---

[7] As will be noted in a moment, we are at this point of the argument abstracting from the bond market and hence assuming that the rate of interest is as yet unchanged.

doubled. For, to repeat the argument of Chapter III:4, at any lower price level the real value of the doubled cash balances will still be greater than the real value of the original balances; correspondingly, the aggregate demand curve will still be higher than it originally was; and therefore an inflationary gap will continue to prevail in the commodity market driving prices further upwards. Conversely, should prices more than double, the real value of the doubled cash balances will be less than the real value of the original ones, so that a deflationary gap will be created to push prices downwards again. Only when the price level has exactly doubled will the real value of the doubled cash balances have been exactly reduced to the real value of the original ones. Hence only then will the aggregate demand curve have returned exactly to its original position, so that the inflationary gap will finally have been closed and equilibrium reëstablished in the commodity market. In this way we see how the inflationary process itself sets into operation an equilibrating force—the price rise—which ultimately brings it to an end.

So far we have tacitly assumed that during this dynamic process the rate of interest remains constant. Actually, of course, this is not to be expected. The initial doubling of the quantity of money shifts the bond demand curve to the right and the supply curve to the left, so that the rate of interest initially falls. This situation is represented by the dashed curves in Figure 19, where the unlabeled dot-dash curves are those of the original equilibrium position. Alternatively, in terms of Figure 14 (page 143), the monetary increase raises the bond excess-demand curve and, consequently, its intersection point with the vertical axis. In terms of either diagram, the basic fact is the increase in the *real* quantity of money in the economy and its consequent real-balance effect in the bond market. This causes an increase in the supply of loans and a decrease in the demand, with a consequent decline in the rate of interest.

What must now be emphasized—and what classical and neoclassical economists did emphasize—is that this fall in interest is temporary and, at the same time, an integral part of the dynamic mechanism by which the economy eventually returns to a new equilibrium position at an unchanged rate of interest, r_0, and a doubled price level, $2p_0$. In Wicksell's familiar terms, this initial decline in interest creates a discrepancy between the market rate and the natural rate; for in view of the unchanged marginal productivity of capital to which it is equal, the natural rate is still r_0. Hence the investment component of the aggregate demand curve rises, further strengthening the inflationary pressures of the commodity market. But as these pressures push the price level upwards, there is a reaction back on the bond market. Specifically, the price rise causes the dashed demand curve in Figure 19 to shift to the right less than the corresponding supply curve.   (In terms of Figure 14, the price rise causes a real-balance effect which pushes the excess-demand function down again.)   Hence the downward movement of the interest rate must eventually be reversed.   In particular, when the price level has finally doubled, this rate will have necessarily climbed

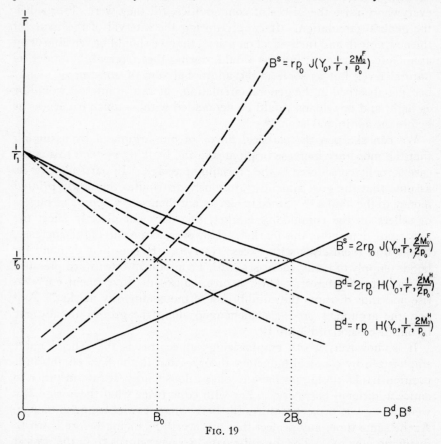

$$B^s = rp_0 \ J(Y_0, \tfrac{1}{r}, \tfrac{2M_0^F}{P_0})$$

$$B^s = 2rp_0 \ J(Y_0, \tfrac{1}{r}, \tfrac{2M_0^F}{2P_0})$$

$$B^d = 2rp_0 \ H(Y_0, \tfrac{1}{r}, \tfrac{2M_0^H}{2P_0})$$

$$B^d = rp_0 \ H(Y_0, \tfrac{1}{r}, \tfrac{2M_0^H}{P_0})$$

Fig. 19

back again to its original value, r_0. For, as shown by the dot-dash curves of Figure 19, at this rate individuals originally demanded B_0 units of bonds and supplied the same amount; hence, now, at a doubled price level and quantity of money, they must—by the absence of money illusion—demand $2B_0$ units of bonds and again supply the same amount. Therefore, the demand and supply curves must again intersect at the price corresponding to the rate of interest r_0—as is represented by the solid curves in Figure 19   In brief, as the rising price level eliminates the

161

initial increase in the *real* quantity of money in the economy, it also eliminates the excess demand for bonds (excess supply of loans) which temporarily depressed the rate of interest.[8]

Here is the essence of the classical and neoclassical view. If, for any reason, there is an increase in the quantity of legal-tender notes in the economy, these "notes would be sent into every market, and would everywhere raise the prices of commodities, till they were absorbed in the general circulation. It is only during the interval of the issue [of the new notes], and their effect on prices, that we should be sensible of an abundance of money; interest would, during that interval, be under its natural level; but as soon as the additional sum of notes or of money became absorbed in the general circulation, the rate of interest would be as high, and new loans would be demanded with as much eagerness as before the additional issue."[9]

We can sharpen the classical flavor of our argument by assuming that the monetary increase originates in the banking system; this is the case actually considered in the preceding passage. In particular, let us assume that the government gratuitously distributes the newly printed money to the banks.[10] Since banks do not themselves appear as buyers or sellers on the commodity market, this does not directly affect the aggregate demand in this market. However, as a result of this increase, banks find themselves with excess reserves. Hence their demand for bonds (supply of loans) increases, with a consequent downward pressure on the rate of interest. This, in turn, causes the investment curve to rise and thus disrupts the equilibrium of the commodity market. And now the argument proceeds unchanged along the groove already cut by our discussion of Figure 19.

It is, however, worth emphasizing—since this is the crucial point emphasized by classical monetary theory—that in the final equilibrium position banks no longer have to offer a lower interest rate in order to entice additional borrowers. For with costs twice what they originally were, any given project requires the borrowing of twice as much money. At the same time, any project that was worth financing before is worth financing now too. For the anticipated money returns from the project have also doubled, so that the rate of return upon it remains unchanged

---

8 In terms of Figure 14 (p. 143), when the price level has finally doubled, real balances are back to their original value; hence the demand curve again occupies exactly the same position it originally did; hence its intersection with the vertical axis again corresponds to r_0.

9 David Ricardo, *The High Price of Bullion* (1810), *Works*, ed. Sraffa (Cambridge, 1951–52), Vol. III, p. 91. In the original, "issues" appears, and not "issue."

Similar passages from many other classical—and neoclassical—economists will be cited in Chapter XV:1.

10 The reason for "gratuitously" will become clear in Chapter XII:4.

and equal to the original equilibrium rate of interest. Hence, after the additional amount of money has, through the price increase, been "absorbed in the general circulation," individuals increase their demand for loans to the same extent that banks originally increased their supply —so that the equilibrium rate of interest is ultimately unaffected.

From this discussion it can immediately be seen that the invariance of the rate of interest and doubling of the price level holds even under the extreme Keynesian assumption that changes in the amount of money directly affect only the bond, and not the commodity, market; that, in other words, the latter market is completely free of the real-balance effect.[11] Here, too, the effects of a monetary increase work themselves out through an initial reduction in the rate of interest and subsequent dynamic interactions between price movements in the commodity market and interest movements in the bond market. More formally, we can readily see that the comparative-statics argument of this section's opening paragraph is equally valid for the case in which the term M_0/p is omitted from equation (2) above, and this equation is accordingly replaced by

$$(5) \qquad\qquad \psi(Y_0, r) = Y_0,$$

where $E = \psi(Y, r)$ is our new aggregate demand function for commodities. Nor does this omission affect the stability of the system. In particular, equation (5) states that the level of aggregate demand is independent of the price level and that, accordingly—under the assumption of full employment—there is only one possible rate of interest at which the commodity market can be in equilibrium. Hence the curve CC in Figure 18 becomes a straight horizontal line at the height r_0. At any point above this line there exists a deflationary pressure in the commodity market; at any point below, an inflationary one. Hence the directions of the arrows attached to the points a, b, c, and d in Figure 18 are not affected. Hence the system must continue to converge to the equilibrium position.[12]

In this way we have finally and rigorously demonstrated the fact set out at the beginning of this book:[13] that despite our systematic and repeated emphasis on the role of the real-balance effect in the commodity market, such a role is *not* logically necessary for the validity of our conclusions. In particular, these conclusions can be shown to hold even when this effect is completely restricted to the bond market. On

---

[11] For specific references to the *General Theory*, see Note K:1.
[12] For a more rigorous statement, see the end of Mathematical Appendix 8:*a*.
[13] See p. 22, footnote 13.

the other hand, it is all the more clear that there is no reason to limit our monetary theory to this extreme case.

The general argument of this section can be conveniently summarized in terms of the concepts used in Figure 18.[14] As will be recalled, the curves CC and BB of this diagram are drawn for the quantity of money M_0. Let us see what happens to these curves as a result of increasing this quantity to $2M_0$. Clearly, absence of money illusion implies that, for any given rate of interest, the price level must now be twice as high as before in order to restore equilibrium to any given market: for only then will the real value of the doubled money holdings be equal once again to the real value of the original ones, thereby insuring the disappearance of the inflationary pressures that—at an unchanged rate of interest—would otherwise prevail in the market. Hence the curves corresponding to $2M_0$ must each be twice as far to the right as those of Figure 18. These curves are represented in Figure 20 by C_1C_1 and B_1B_1, respectively. From what has just been said, it is clear that they must intersect at the point m, corresponding to the rate of interest r_0 and price level $2p_0$. This is accordingly the new equilibrium position of the economy as a whole.

As in Figure 18, these two curves divide our diagram into four sectors Clearly, the directions of the dynamic market forces in each of the sectors of Figure 20 are related to the equilibrium point m as the directions in the corresponding sectors of Figure 18 are related to its equilibrium point g. In particular, we see from Figure 20 that this original equilibrium point g is now a point of disequilibrium and that its movement toward the new equilibrium position m is described by the dotted path between them. This path is the resultant first of the dynamic forces of sector *III*, and then of those of sector *IV*. It shows with graphic clarity the initial decline in interest and the subsequent return to the original level r_0 as the price level continues to rise toward $2p_0$ It emphasizes that throughout this period of price increase, the actually prevailing market rate of the dynamic process lies below the natural rate, r_0, of the equilibrium situation. It thus provides a mnemonic distillation of the essential price and interest interactions of classical and neoclassical interest theory, in general, and of Wicksell's "cumulative process," in particular.[15]

4. Let us now apply the techniques of the preceding section to an analysis of shifts in liquidity preference. In carrying this analysis out we shall merely be giving graphical expression to the argument already

---

14 I am indebted to Mr. Tsvi Goldberger for suggesting this additional use of Figure 18.
15 These doctrinal implications will be discussed further in Chapter XV:1.

presented in Chapter VIII:5. In particular, once again our fundamental point of departure is that, by the budget restraint, shifts in
liquidity preference manifest themselves as appropriate changes in the
demand conditions of the commodity and bond markets. Thus, for
example, an increase in liquidity preference reflects itself in part by a
downward shift in the commodity demand curve (out of the same real

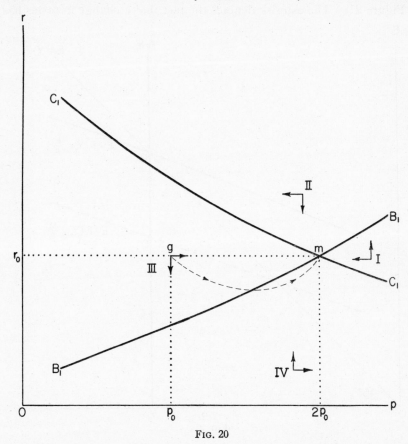

FIG. 20

balances individuals wish to spend less than previously)[16] and in part
by a leftward shift in the demand for bonds and a rightward one in the
supply (individuals feel an increased need for liquidity and therefore
move out of bonds and into money: they are less willing to lend and
more inclined to borrow).

This situation can be described graphically in the following way.

---

16 I.e., there is an increase in K—or, alternatively, a decrease in V.

Assume that we begin from an equilibrium position in which the aggregate demand curve is represented by $E = F\left(Y, r_0, \dfrac{M_0}{p_0}\right)$ in Figure 12 (page 136). As a result of the increase in liquidity preference, this curve now shifts downwards to, say, $E = F^*\left(Y, r_0, \dfrac{M_0}{p_0}\right)$ in Figure 21. The asterisk denotes the fact that a change in tastes has

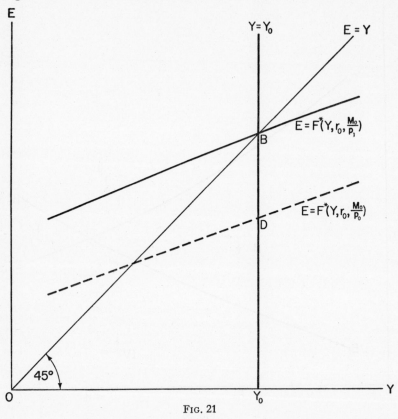

FIG. 21

taken place: at the same rate of interest and price level, individuals wish now to spend less than they did before. Thus the curves in Figures 21 and 12 are cross-sections of two different demand functions. Similarly, the bond market is represented in the initial equilibrium position by the curves of Figure 13 (page 139—not reproduced in the following diagram), and, as a result of the increase in liquidity preference, these then assume the form of the dashed curves in Figure 22.

Clearly, the initial effect of this shift is to generate a downward pressure on the price level, reflected by the deflationary gap BD in Figure 21, and an upward pressure on the rate of interest, reflected by the excess supply RT in Figure 22. Now, as the price level falls, the real-balance effect pushes the commodity demand curve upwards. At the same time, it pushes the bond supply curve further leftwards than the demand curve. In this way the price decrease must ultimately more than eliminate the

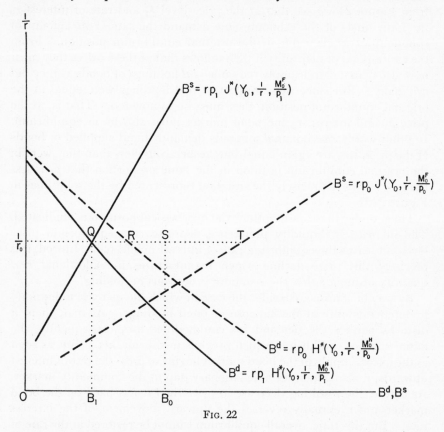

$$B^s = rp_1 \, J^*(Y_0, \tfrac{1}{r}, \tfrac{M_0^F}{P_1})$$

$$B^s = rp_0 \, J^*(Y_0, \tfrac{1}{r}, \tfrac{M_0^F}{P_0})$$

$$B^d = rp_0 \, H^*(Y_0, \tfrac{1}{r}, \tfrac{M_0^H}{P_0})$$

$$B^d = rp_1 \, H^*(Y_0, \tfrac{1}{r}, \tfrac{M_0^H}{P_1})$$

Fig. 22

excess supply in the bond market and thus reverse the initial upward movement of the rate of interest.

Assume that this eventual downward movement of the rate of interest continues until it returns again to r_0. Assume also that, at the same time, prices fall to p_1 and that at this level the stimulation of the real-balance effect is sufficiently strong to close the initial deflationary gap in the commodity market. The demand curve corresponding to the new equilibrium position in this market is then represented by the solid line in

Figure 21. It remains to examine the concurrent situation in the bond market.

We must first be a little more specific about the nature of the shift in liquidity preference. In particular, we assume that the shift in liquidity preference has been a "neutral" one—that it has affected only the desirability of bonds-and-commodities relative to money, not the desirability of bonds and commodities relative to each other. Now, from Figure 21 we see that at the price level p_1 and rate of interest r_0 the individuals of the economy now demand the same *real* amount of commodities as they did in the original equilibrium position. From the assumption of neutrality it then follows that at these prices they must now also demand and supply the same *real* holdings of bonds as they did originally. But since these respective real holdings were equal in the original equilibrium position, they must be so now too. That is, at the price p_1 and interest r_0 the bond market must also be in equilibrium. In other words, the nominal amounts demanded and supplied of bonds at the price $1/r_0$ are again equal but, respectively, less than they were in the original equilibrium position in the same proportion that p_1 is less than p_0. This is precisely the situation represented by the solid lines in Figure 22.[17]

Thus, under these assumptions the neoclassical position is vindicated. The increase in liquidity preference depresses the equilibrium price level but leaves the equilibrium rate of interest unaffected. Indeed, it is precisely this price decline which manufactures the additional *real* quantity of money that the economy is desirous of holding.

By way of contrast, consider the case in which the increase in liquidity preference is only at the expense of bond holdings. At first, then, it disturbs neither the demand for commodities nor, consequently, the initial state of equilibrium which prevails in this market. But as soon as the excess supply in the bond market begins to press the rate of interest upwards, it also generates a deflationary gap in the commodity market. As before, the resulting decrease in price then reacts back on the bond market and eventually reverses the upward movement of the interest rate. But this time, overall equilibrium cannot be restored at the rate of interest r_0. For due to the price decrease and unchanged tastes in the commodity market, this level now corresponds to an inflationary gap. Hence, in order to remove this gap, the new equilibrium position

---

17 Actually, the explanation is more restrictive than the diagram. The latter requires only that, at the price $1/r_0$, the amounts demanded and supplied decrease equi-proportionately, but not necessarily in the same proportion as the price decline. However, only the case considered in the text has economic meaning, for only in this case are the *real* demand and supply for bonds the same as they originally were.

must be marked by an interest rate which is higher than the original one.

It must be emphasized that this effect on the rate of interest is not a consequence of the change in the relative desirability of bonds and money per se. For such a change in desirability occurs in the case of a neutral shift too. Furthermore, as the reader can readily establish for himself, a shift in liquidity preference which is entirely at the expense of commodities and does not at all affect the relative desirability of bonds and money also affects the rate of interest—though in a downward direction. In brief, an increase in liquidity preference which raises the rate of interest must be one which—in some sense—is at the expense of bond holdings *more than* at the expense of commodities.

Once again the argument can be conveniently summarized in terms of Figure 18. An increase in liquidity preference at the expense of both commodities and bonds shifts both CC and BB to the left: at any rate of interest, a lower price level is needed in each market in order to generate the stimulatory real-balance effect necessary to eliminate the initial excess supply created by the shift in liquidity preference. If the relative desirability of commodities and bonds is not affected by this shift, then, by the argument just presented, the new curves—represented by C_2C_2 and B_2B_2 in Figure 23—must intersect at the point n, corresponding to the price p_1 and the rate of interest r_0. The original equilibrium point g is now one of disequilibrium, and the dashed path between g and n shows the movement toward the new equilibrium position. Clearly, this path reflects the directions of the dynamic market forces at work in sectors I and II. It shows the initial rise in interest and the subsequent decline generated by the continuously falling price level.

Consider now the case in which the increase in liquidity preference is only at the expense of bonds. In this case the curve CC remains unaffected, so that we obtain Figure 24. The intersection of the unchanged CC with the leftward-shifted B_2B_2 must clearly be at a lower price level and higher rate of interest than the original equilibrium point g. As the path gw indicates, the movement to this new equilibrium position, w, can be a direct one. On the other hand, as the path gtw indicates, it too may involve an initial rise in the rate of interest above its new equilibrium value and a subsequent decline. Thus, in this case too, the price level may exert a moderating influence on a temporarily overreacting interest rate.

The case of an increase in liquidity preference at the sole expense of commodities is equally clear. Here BB remains constant, while CC shifts to the left. Hence the new equilibrium price and interest levels must both be lower than the original ones.

It is left as an exercise for the reader to show how the foregoing analysis can, *mutatis mutandis*, be applied to the case of a decrease in liquidity preference.   A neutral shift of this type can clearly be represented by Figure 20.   Of particular interest to us, however, is the case in which the shift in liquidity preference is entirely in favor of bonds and does not at all affect the demand for commodities.   As will be recalled from Chapter VI:4, such a change in tastes is analytically equivalent to a technical change in the nature of the bond which in some way makes it more liquid—more readily convertible into money   Both of these

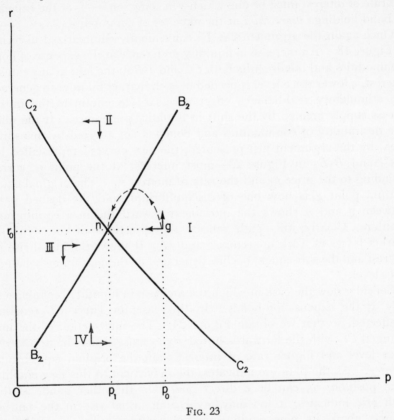

Fig. 23

changes express themselves in Figure 18 as a downward shift in *BB*, with *CC* remaining constant: for both leave demand in the commodity market unchanged, while increasing demand in the bond market, and thereby—for any given price level—lowering the rate of interest that must prevail in order to maintain equilibrium in this market.   Hence the new intersection of *BB* and *CC*—and thus the new equilibrium

170

position—is at a rate of interest below r_0 and a price level above p_0. The more we make bonds liquid, the more BB shifts to the right, the more, therefore, the rate of interest falls and the price level rises, and the smaller, therefore, the *real* quantity of money in the economy becomes

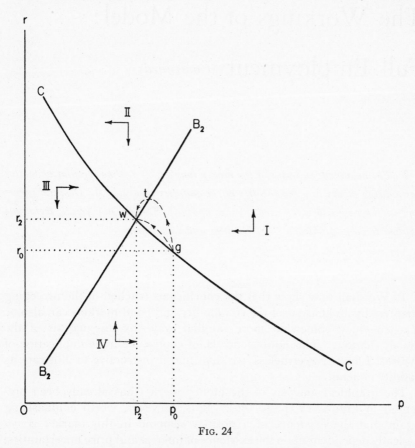

FIG. 24

But even if we were to make bonds completely liquid, there would be no necessity for the equilibrium rate of interest to be driven down thereby to zero. As already emphasized in Chapter VI:4, all that would necessarily happen in this extreme case is that bonds would replace money as the medium of exchange.[18]

---

[18] For an analytical treatment of the argument of this section, see Mathematical Appendix 8:*c*.

CHAPTER XI

The Workings of the Model:

Full Employment (*Continued*)

1-2. *The argument in terms of the money market.* 3. *The speculative motive for holding money and the validity of the quantity theory.* 4. *Demand curves and market-equilibrium curves once again.* 5. *The analytical technique applied to other problems.* 6. *Savings and investment.*

1. We shall now show that the conclusions reached in the preceding chapters by an analysis of the commodity and bond markets can also be reached—in a somewhat more familiar way—by an analysis of the money market. This equivalence is, of course, a simple implication of Walras' Law. Nevertheless, we shall find it instructive to illustrate its validity in detail.

The graphical analysis of the money market has already been presented in Figure 15 (page 146). It is, however, worth emphasizing again that the existence of a positive demand in this market is *not* logically dependent upon the existence of interest and price uncertainties; that—as demonstrated in Chapter VII—an internally consistent theory of money can be constructed even on the assumption that perfect certainty exists with respect to the future values of these variables and that money balances are held only in order to provide a reserve against discrepancies between the inflow and outflow of money. Correspondingly, it is also worth reëmphasizing that the negative slope of the demand curve for money in Figure 15 need *not* depend on the existence of speculation with respect to the future course of an uncertain rate of interest, but can instead be explained by the transactions and precautionary motives just described In particular, as stressed in Chapter

172

VI:2, the higher the rate of interest, the greater the cost in earnings foregone of holding sterile cash balances to satisfy these motives, and the smaller, therefore, the amount of these balances demanded.

Nevertheless, in order to maximize the relevance of the following analysis for contemporary monetary theory, let us now drop the assumption of perfect certainty and follow Keynes in attributing the negative slope of the demand curve for money to the operation of the speculative motive—that is, to the fact that a decrease in the rate of interest increases the probability of a subsequent rise, hence increases the risks of capital losses in holding bonds, and hence causes individuals to shift out of bonds and into money. Let us also follow Keynes in decomposing the equilibrium condition of the money market—equation (4) on page 152—into the special form

$$(1) \qquad p \cdot L_1(Y_0) + p \cdot L_2\left(r, \frac{M_0}{p}\right) = M_0,$$

where $L_1(Y)$ represents the demand for *real* transactions-and-precautionary balances, and $L_2\left(r, \frac{M_0}{p}\right)$, the demand for *real* speculative balances.[1]

Despite our desire to be Keynesians, the argument of Part One has compelled us to write the preceding equation in a form which deviates in two significant ways from the liquidity equation of the *General Theory*. As is shown in Note K:2, this equation has—in our notation—the form

$$(2) \qquad p \cdot L_1(Y_0) + L_2(r) = M_0.$$

Thus, first of all, we have introduced into equation (1) the influence of real balances, M_0/p. Had we not done so, this equation would have described the total demand for money as varying in direct proportion to the price level—that is, as being of uniform unitary elasticity with respect to changes in this level; and, as Chapter II:5 has demonstrated, such an elasticity does not generally exist even at a single point, let alone uniformly. On the other hand, we have introduced this modification in as Keynesian a way as possible. For we have restricted the real-balance effect to the speculative demand—which for Keynes is a reflection of the bond market—and omitted it from the transactions-precautionary demand—which is a reflection of the commodity market.

---

[1] *General Theory*, pp. 168–69, 199–202. In his subsequent later writings Keynes did, however, permit the rate of interest to affect $L_1(\ )$ as well as $L_2(\ )$; see his "Theory of the Rate of Interest" (1937), as reprinted in *Readings in the Theory of Income Distribution*, ed. W. Fellner and B. F. Haley (Philadelphia, 1946), p. 422.

Thus our equation (1) accords with the implicit assumption of the *General Theory* that the real-balance effect influences the former market only.[2]

In the present context, however, this modification of Keynes' equation (2) is relatively unimportant. The really fundamental modification lies instead in the seemingly insignificant p by which equation (1) premultiplies $L_2(\ )$. It is this p which reflects the absence of money illusion in the demand for nominal speculative balances; hence it is this p which, as we shall see, assures the classical invariance of the rate of interest.

Since it will prove to be so crucial for an understanding of Keynesian interest theory, it is worth dwelling at somewhat greater length on the meaning of this money illusion. According to equation (1), if individuals are confronted with a doubled price level and a doubled amount of money, they will respond by doubling their demand for *nominal* speculative balances, $p \cdot L_2\left(r, \dfrac{M_0}{p}\right)$; that is, their demand for *real* speculative balances will remain invariant. On the other hand, equation (2) implies that their demand for *nominal* speculative balances, $L_2(r)$, will remain invariant, so that their demand for *real* speculative balances will decrease. In other words, it implies that the demand for *real* speculative balances is at one level when the monetary unit is called the dollar and at quite another level when it is called the peseta. And this is the essence of money illusion.[3]

We can put this in yet another way. Just as the nominal transactions-precautionary demand represents the desire to hold liquid command over a *real* quantity of commodities, so the nominal speculative demand represents the desire to hold liquid command over a *real* quantity of bonds. Hence just as an increase in the price level affects the first of these demands, so must it affect the second. This is the symmetry underlined by equation (1). And this is precisely the symmetry denied by equation (2)—with its insistence that though the demand for nominal transactions-precautionary balances is dependent on the absolute price level, that for nominal speculative balances is not.

2. Deferring the remaining discussion of equation (2) and Keynesian interest theory to the next chapter, let us now return to the task of analyzing the money market from the viewpoint of equation (1).

---

[2] Detailed references in support of this last sentence are provided in Note K:1.

[3] The reader will recall that changing the monetary unit is analytically equivalent to confronting individuals with an equi-proportionate change in prices *and* initial money holdings; cf. p. 114.

Assume, then, that this market is in the equilibrium position D determined by the intersection of the dashed demand and supply curves in Figure 25. Let this state of equilibrium now be disturbed by a doubling

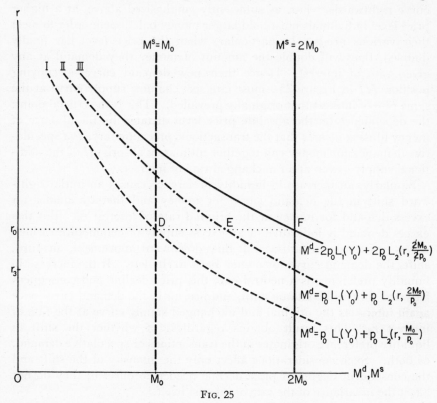

$$M^d = 2p_0 L_1(Y_0) + 2p_0 L_2(r, \frac{2M_0}{2p_0})$$

$$M^d = p_0 L_1(Y_0) + p_0 L_2(r, \frac{2M_0}{p_0})$$

$$M^d = p_0 L_1(Y_0) + p_0 L_2(r, \frac{M_0}{p_0})$$

FIG. 25

of the amount of money. This shifts the supply curve rightwards to $M^s = 2M_0$. It also shifts the demand curve rightwards to position II. For though neither prices nor interest have yet changed, so that the transactions-precautionary demand is unaffected, there is a positive real-balance effect on the speculative demand. However, since this effect operates in other markets as well, this increased speculative demand must be less than the initial increase in the amount of money. Hence an excess supply of money is created at the original equilibrium rate of interest r_0. This is represented in Figure 25 by the line segment EF.

If prices were to remain the same, equilibrium could be reëstablished in this market only at a rate of interest lower than r_0; for only by such a reduction could individuals be induced to hold the additional money now available. But prices cannot and do not remain the same. For

175

the excess supply EF is indicative of an excess demand in the commodity market, and this excess demand must drive prices upwards. This in turn reacts back on the money market and shifts its demand curve rightwards. For, as sufficiently emphasized above, at a higher price level individuals must hold larger money balances in order to meet their various needs. In particular, when the price level has finally doubled, they will double the amount of money they demand at any given rate of interest. Hence their new demand curve—occupying position *III* in Figure 25—must intersect the new supply curve at the same rate of interest that originally prevailed. This is the crucial point: the dependence on the absolute price level dictated by the absence of money illusion insures that the transactions, precautionary, *and* speculative demands for money can together ultimately absorb *all* of the additional supply—even at an unchanged rate of interest.

Similarly, an increase in liquidity preference causes an initial rightward shift in the demand curve for money and thereby creates an excess demand for money at the original rate of interest r_0. But this excess demand is indicative of an excess supply of commodities which drives prices downwards; and this downward movement, in turn, shifts the demand curve for money back to the left. If the increase in liquidity preference is a neutral one, this price decline and consequent leftward shift will continue until, and just until, the demand curve once again intersects the original and unchanged supply curve at the rate of interest r_0. This result obtains regardless of whether the shift in liquidity preference originates in the transactions or speculative demand, or both. Such considerations affect only the intensity of the shift and the consequent degree of price decline needed to offset it; they do not affect the invariance of the rate of interest itself.[4]

Thus when proper attention is paid to the influence of the price level on the demand for money, a study of the money market yields results consistent with those of the preceding chapter. Actually, however, the foregoing demonstration is incomplete. For it provides a partial-equilibrium analysis of the money market alone, instead of a general-equilibrium analysis of this market together with one other market—commodity or bond. It is this general-equilibrium analysis which—by Walras' Law and the assumption[5] that the labor market is always in equilibrium—must be equivalent to our previous general-equilibrium analysis of the commodity and bond markets.

---

4 On these last two sentences, see the end of Mathematical Appendix 7:*b*. These sentences represent a reversal of the view expressed in my "Further Considerations of the General Equilibrium Theory of Money," *Review of Economic Studies*, XIX (1951–52), 194.

5 Cf. Chapter X:2 (beginning).

The reader can, however, readily establish this more rigorous equivalence himself by tracing through the concurrent developments in the second market—whichever it may be. Indeed, for the comparative-statics analysis of a change in the amount of money, this equivalence is obvious from the first paragraph of Chapter X:3, which conducts the analysis from the viewpoint of all four markets simultaneously. More

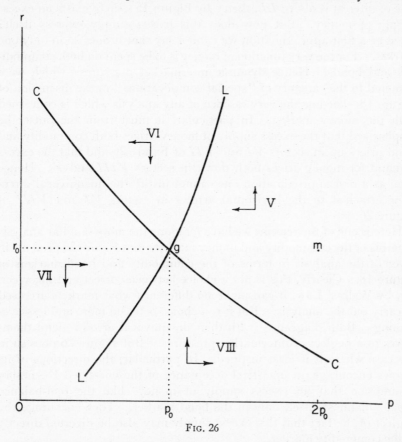

FIG. 26

generally, we can illustrate this equivalence by resorting again to the concepts of Figure 18 (page 155).

Thus consider an analysis from the viewpoint of the commodity and money markets. This shift in viewpoint clearly does not affect the curve *CC* in Figure 18. But it does replace the curve *BB* by a curve which is the locus of all pairs of values of the rate of interest and the price level for which the *money* market is in equilibrium. This new curve is denoted by *LL* in Figure 26. Its positive slope reflects the fact that an increase in the price level shifts the demand curve for money in Figure 15 (page 146) to the right and thus raises the rate of interest necessary to maintain equilibrium in this market.[6]

Let us turn now to the dynamic interpretation of Figure 26. Here we are immediately confronted with the difficulty which we at first succeeded in avoiding in Figure 18. If, for any given price level, the rate of interest is above LL, then—by Figure 15—there exists an excess supply of money. But how does this excess supply express itself? Even as a first approximation we cannot say that it does so in only one market. For the very function of money is to be spent on both commodities and bonds. Hence dynamic intermarket pressures—which were demoted to the category of "special complications" in the discussion of Figure 18—become the very essence of any analysis which is concerned with the money market. In particular, it must from the outset be emphasized that the excess supply of money drives both commodity and bond prices up in sectors VI and VII of Figure 26 and that the excess demand for money drives both down in sectors VIII and V. Hence even as a first approximation one cannot justify the unequivocal directions attached to the horizontal arrows in sectors VI and VIII of Figure 26.

Here is one of the reasons we have foregone the more familiar analysis in terms of the commodity and money markets that Figure 26 presents in favor of the analysis in terms of the commodity and bond markets of Figure 18. Clearly, this is not a choice between correct and incorrect; for, by Walras' Law, it can make no difference what markets are used to carry out the analysis. But it is a choice between more and less misleading. Both diagrams—with their unequivocal arrows—lend themselves to a neglect of intermarket pressures. But Figure 26 does so in the case where it is least justified. In particular, the directions of its arrows encourage an uncritical acceptance of the one-sided Keynesian assumption that an excess supply of money—like the real-balance effect—manifests itself only in the bond market. They encourage the neglect of the fact that this excess supply may also be diverted directly to the commodity market.

Leaving these complications behind, let us assume that the directions of the market forces indicated in the various sectors of Figure 26 are correct. Then, by the same argument used in connection with Figure 18, the system must converge to its equilibrium position: for no matter at what point the economy may be, automatic market forces

---

[6] Except for the fact that the abscissa represents p and not M_0/p—and the consequent reversal of both curves—Figure 26 is identical with Metzler's original graph, *op. cit.*, p. 104.

exist which propel at least one of the variables toward its equilibrium value. It should, however, be emphasized that the dynamic adjustment paths generated by these two diagrams are not identical. In particular, since LL and BB do not coincide, neither do the four sectors of each diagram. (Indeed, it can be shown that LL must lie between CC and BB within sectors II and IV of Figure 18.)[7] Hence there will be some points at which, according to Figure 18, the rate of interest will, say, rise; while, according to Figure 26, it will fall. This reflects the fact that the basic dynamic hypotheses of these two diagrams are different; that, in particular, Figure 18 implies that an excess supply of money directly affects both the interest rate and the price level, whereas Figure 26 presumes that it directly affects only the former.[8]

Figure 26 also enables a rigorous demonstration of the comparative-statics propositions that interest us. As already explained in connection with Figure 20, a doubling of the amount of money shifts CC twice as far to the right; but, by exactly the same reasoning, it also shifts LL twice as far to the right: to repeat, at any given rate of interest, it requires a doubling of the price level to reduce the real value of the doubled money holdings to the real value of the original holdings and thereby restore equilibrium to the market in question. Hence the new curves must intersect at an unchanged rate of interest and a doubled price level. Similarly, an increase in liquidity preference shifts LL to the left. But, if the shift is a neutral one, it shifts CC leftwards to exactly the same extent. Hence the equilibrium rate of interest is not affected.[9] In brief, by relabeling B_1B_1 as L_1L_1 and B_2B_2 as L_2L_2, Figures 20 (page 165) and 23 (page 170) can be used to illustrate the comparative-statics analysis of the aforementioned changes from the viewpoint of the commodity and money markets.[10]

It is left as an exercise for the reader to show that these same results can be achieved by an analysis from the viewpoint of the bond and

---

[7] I am indebted to Mr. Tsvi Goldberger for pointing out and demonstrating this. The argument is as follows: In sector I of Figure 18 there is an excess *supply* of both commodities and bonds; hence, by the budget restraint, there is an excess *demand* for money; hence LL cannot lie within sector I, for, by construction, at any point above LL there exists an excess *supply* of money. Similarly, LL cannot lie within sector III: for here there is an excess *demand* for both commodities and bonds, which implies an excess *supply* of money, whereas at any point below LL there is an excess *demand* for money. Hence LL must lie within sectors II and IV. Here there is an excess demand for one of the goods and an excess supply of the other, permitting the existence now of an excess demand and now of an excess supply of money.

[8] On the discussion of Figure 26—and on the last sentence in particular—see Mathematical Appendix 8:*b*.

[9] For further details, see Mathematical Appendix 8:*d*.

[10] Obviously, this relabeling should not be taken to imply that the curves coincide; see the preceding paragraph.

money markets. The first step of such a demonstration is clearly the replacement of *CC* in Figure 18 by *LL*. As just noted, the latter must lie in sectors *II* and *IV* of this diagram.

3. One advantage of the foregoing explicit analysis in terms of the money market is its underlining of the fact that—Keynes notwithstanding—the classical quantity theory of money does *not* depend on the assumption that the speculative demand "always be zero in equilibrium":[11] at no point in the preceding argument has it been necessary to assume that $L_2(\ ) = 0$. Thus the quantity theory can be valid when money is held also as a store of value for speculative purposes, as well as when it is held only as a medium of exchange for transactions purposes. This illustrates our general contention that no matter why individuals hold money, it can only be the real value of these holdings that concerns them, and that the absence of money illusion which this implies then insures the validity of the classical analysis.

Nevertheless, the assumption that the demand for money is motivated in part by dynamic expectations and interest and price uncertainty can invalidate these classical conclusions. This should certainly not surprise us. For in introducing these elements into the analysis we also introduce many additional "degrees of freedom." Hence, as long as these elements are not in some way tied down, we can—by endowing them with the appropriate properties—obtain any conclusion we might desire Once the Pandora box of expectations and interest and price uncertainty is opened upon the world of economic analysis, anything can happen.

For example, let us drop our usual assumption that the future price level is expected to be the same as the present one. Let us also assume that though the transactions-precautionary demand for money depends on the current price level, p, the speculative demand depends on the anticipated future price level, p^*. Equation (1) then becomes

$$(3) \qquad p \cdot L_1(Y_0) + p^* \cdot L_2\left(r, \frac{M_0}{p^*}\right) = M_0.$$

The classical consequences of a doubling of the quantity of money will now be produced only if p^* increases in the same proportion as p; only, that is, if the elasticity of price expectations is equal to unity. If, on the other hand, we assume it to be greater than unity, the rate of interest will rise; if less than unity, it will fall.

Even this simple example has not been completely analyzed. It is brought in here only to indicate the nature of the considerations from

---

[11] *General Theory*, pp. 208–9. Note that Keynes considers this assumption to be necessary in addition to that of full employment.

which we have abstracted in past chapters and from which we shall—with one exception—continue to abstract in future ones. A full treatment of these considerations would carry us beyond the limited objective of this book. For this objective is to understand the functioning of a money economy under perfect interest and price certainty, before attempting to introduce all the complications of dynamic expectations and interest and price uncertainty.

But—if truth must be told—the neglect of these complications also reflects the prejudiced suspicion that the recent literature on monetary theory has greatly exaggerated their significance for the stability of the system and for its comparative-statics properties. In any event, the preceding paragraphs should suffice to demonstrate the sterility of the anything-can-happen proposition that expectations and uncertainties *can* invalidate the quantity theory. They show the task of expectation economics to lie instead (*a*) in the development of theorems which specify the conditions under which the preceding system of equations will not describe the behavior of individuals in the economy and (*b*) in the determination of the extent to which the corresponding changes will significantly affect the implications of classical monetary theory for the real world.[12]

4. The preceding argument has shown that though the amount of money demanded depends upon the rate of interest, the rate of interest does not depend upon the amount of money. Superficially, there seems to be a paradox here. But it is one that is immediately resolved by noting that the word "depend" is being used in two different senses to describe the outcomes of two distinct conceptual experiments. More specifically, the solution to this paradox lies in distinguishing once again between individual-experiments and demand curves, on the one hand, and market-experiments and market-equilibrium curves, on the other.[13]

Consider first the following individual-experiment. We confront the individual with a lowered rate of interest, holding other things constant, and observe the variation in the amount of money he demands. Alternatively, adopting a Marshallian approach,[14] we force the individual to increase his planned money holdings and then record the reduction in interest upon which he insists, *ceteris paribus*, in order to be

---

12 This section gives further expression to the viewpoint already presented on pp. 84–85, 87, and 95. Some further doubts as to the real importance of expectations in an inflationary process will be presented in Chapter XII:5.

13 On the meaning of this distinction, cf. Chapter III:6.

In what follows we abstract from the real-indebtedness effect.

14 *Principles* (eighth ed.), pp. 94–95.

just willing to maintain these increased holdings. Either of these experiments yields the familiar negatively sloped individual demand curve for money from which the market demand curves of Figures 15 and 25 are aggregated. It is the slope of these curves that we have in mind when we say that the demand for money depends on the rate of interest.

These individual-experiments can be contrasted with another, less familiar one. Once again we force the individual to, say, double his planned money holdings; but this time we simultaneously confront him with a doubling in the price level *and* in his initial money holdings. It follows from the absence of money illusion that in these circumstances the individual will indicate his willingness to maintain these larger holdings without any reduction whatsoever in the interest rate. A corresponding result will hold for the aggregate of individuals in the economy should they all be simultaneously confronted with the change just described. This is represented graphically by the movement from the point *D* to the point *F* in Figure 25.

So much for individual-experiments. Consider now the following market-experiment. Into an economy in equilibrium we introduce a disturbance in the form of a doubling of the quantity of money. We then let this disturbance work itself out in all its manifestations until the economy returns once again to an equilibrium position. Finally, we compare the rate of interest in the new market equilibrium position with that of the original one. As we have seen in our analysis of Figure 25, this rate is unchanged.

This result is completely consistent, as it must be, with those of the preceding individual-experiments. At the close of the market-experiment each individual finds himself confronted with a doubling of the price level and his initial money holdings. Hence the first individual-experiment—in which both these factors are held constant—can be of no relevance for the market-experiment. On the other hand, these increases are precisely those with which the individual is confronted in the second individual-experiment. Indeed, the willingness of the individuals in the economy to double their planned holdings of money without any decrease in the interest rate, as revealed in this experiment, is the explanation of the invariance of the equilibrium interest rate, as revealed by the market-experiment.

Let us now consider *D*, *F*, and all other possible supply-and-demand intersection points that can be generated in Figure 25 by market-experiments of the foregoing type. From what has just been said, it is clear that the locus of these points must be the horizontal line of Figure 27. Each point on this line thus associates a quantity of money with its corresponding, unchanged equilibrium level of interest. Obviously, then, this line is a special case of what we have called a market-equilibrium curve.   It is also clear that, regardless of the slopes of the demand curves in Figure 25, this market-equilibrium curve must have the linear horizontal form specified in Figure 27.   It is this horizontality that we have in mind when we say that the rate of interest does not depend on the quantity of money.

It is tempting to replace these complicated distinctions with the simple statement that just as the *real* quantity of money demanded depends on the rate of interest, so the equilibrium rate of interest depends on the *real* quantity of money; and that in the case at hand this

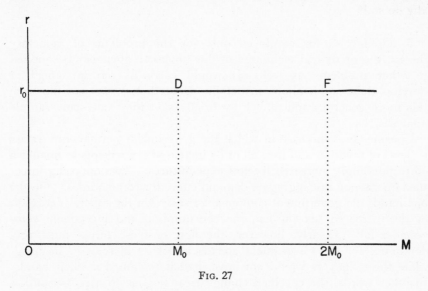

FIG. 27

rate remains constant because this real quantity does also.   Tempting— but, strictly speaking, meaningless.   For both the rate of interest and the real quantity of money in the economy are dependent variables of the analysis; hence their equilibrium values cannot be dependent on each other, but only on the independent variables.[15]

This might tempt us alternatively to say that any change in these independent variables which leaves the equilibrium real quantity of money unaffected must also leave the equilibrium rate of interest

---

[15] This is the same distinction between dependent and independent variables already drawn on pp. 15 and 32.   The reader will also recall the argument of p. 105 that, since one moves in inverse proportion to the other, the price level and the real quantity of money are analytically equivalent, so that either one can be considered as the dependent variable of the analysis.

unaffected, and conversely. This is a meaningful proposition; but, though it happens to hold for the case of a change in the nominal quantity of money, it is generally an invalid one. This is evident from Chapter X:4—where, as we have seen, a neutral shift in liquidity preference changes the price level and hence the real quantity of money in the economy, though not the equilibrium rate of interest. It will also be evident from the two additional cases discussed at the end of the next section, which show that the equilibrium rate of interest can change though the real quantity of money does not. Nevertheless, whenever valid, it is very suggestive to speak in these terms. Hence, though keeping in mind the pitfall that lies inherent in them, we shall occasionally do so.[16]

5. Though so far employed only for the problems of monetary theory, the analytical technique of this book can obviously be applied to other problems as well. It would carry us too far afield to develop these applications in detail. Nevertheless, we can illustrate this more general applicability by briefly sketching out some sample analyses.

Consider first the case in which the government permanently raises its level of taxation and uses all of its increased tax receipts to finance a correspondingly increased level of expenditures. Two opposing forces then operate on the aggregate demand curve for commodities. On the one hand, the government component rises. On the other, as a result of the increased tax burden, the consumption and investment components fall. Clearly, however, the first of these forces must predominate: for the government spends all of its increased "income," while the taxpayers would not have, had it remained in their hands. In other words, the specified change is analogous to a redistribution of income at the expense of those whose marginal propensity to spend is less than unity (the private sector) and in favor of those for whom it equals unity (the government).[17]

Once we have determined that the effect of the specified change is to raise the aggregate demand curve for commodities, the analysis proceeds along familiar channels. As a result of the upward shift in this curve, an inflationary gap is created. The resulting price rise then

---

16 Actually, use has already been made of these terms on p. 162. See, on all of this section, Mathematical Appendix 4:*d*.

17 Note the clear parallelism to the analysis—under conditions of unemployment—of the multiplier effect of a balanced budget. Cf., e.g., P. A. Samuelson, "The Simple Mathematics of Income Determination," in *Income, Employment and Public Policy: Essays in Honor of Alvin H. Hansen* (New York, 1948), pp. 140–42.

generates a negative real-balance effect which pushes the demand curve down again. At the same time, the price rise also disturbs the equilibrium of the bond market and causes the rate of interest to rise. This too helps close the inflationary gap in the commodity market. Equilibrium will finally be reëstablished at a higher price level and higher rate of interest. Once again, this result can alternatively be derived from Figure 18 (page 155): the stated change shifts CC to the right without affecting BB; hence the intersection point must move northeast.

Consider next the case in which a wave of technological inventions increases the productivity of capital. Let us restrict the analysis to a period of time too short for the resulting increase in commodity output to affect the market. Then this technological change has two initial effects. First, it increases the desire of firms to undertake investment projects. This raises the investment component of the aggregate demand curve and thus generates an inflationary gap in the commodity market. Secondly, and concurrently, it increases the need of firms for loan capital with which to finance these new projects. This shifts the supply curve of bonds to the right.

Now, to the extent that the inflationary gap expresses itself in a price rise, it reinforces the upward pressure on the interest rate in the bond market. But to the extent that this rate rises, it decreases the inflationary pressures in the commodity market and thus makes it possible for the gap there to be closed at an unchanged or even lower price level. Thus the new equilibrium position must involve a higher rate of interest; but it need not involve a higher price level. In terms of Figure 18, the technological change shifts CC to the right and BB to the left. Hence the new equilibrium point must definitely be above the old one; but it can be either to its left, right, or even directly above.

Consider finally the case of an increase in savings—or, in our terminology, a decrease in the demand for consumption commodities. If this is accompanied by a corresponding increase in the demand for money holdings, then we have an increase in liquidity preference at the sole expense of commodities. The depressing effect of this change on both interest and the price level has already been analyzed in Chapter X:4. If, instead, this increase in savings is accompanied by a corresponding increase in the demand for bonds (i.e., in lending), the depressing effect on interest is reinforced, but the effect on the price level is rendered indeterminate. In terms of Figure 18, the specified change shifts CC to the left and BB to the right. Hence the new intersection point must definitely be below the old one; but it can be either to its left, right, or even directly below.

185

The reader can work out additional cases for himself. We might, however, note that the foregoing analysis of changes in investment and savings yields results completely in accordance with those of the classical and neoclassical theory of interest.[18]

6. With the immediately preceding exception, we have throughout this book deliberately avoided the concept "savings" and its familiar accompaniment, the "savings = investment" condition. This decision has been based on the fact that such a concept is out of place in an analytical framework which views the economy as consisting of a number of goods, each with a price, and each with a market. For savings are clearly not a good, they have no price, and they are not themselves transacted on a market.[19]

This need not, however, prevent us from defining gross real savings, S, as the difference between gross income after taxes and consumption. We can then write the savings function

$$(4) \qquad S = f\left(Y, r, \frac{M_0^H}{p}\right),$$

where

$$(5) \qquad f\left(Y, r, \frac{M_0^H}{p}\right) \equiv Y - G_0 - g\left(Y, r, \frac{M_0^H}{p}\right).$$

As the reader can see from equations (6) and (8) on page 130, $g(\ )$ is the consumption function and G_0 is the fixed real level of government expenditures, assumed to be financed entirely by taxes. The savings-investment equality can then be written as

$$(6) \qquad f\left(Y, r, \frac{M_0^H}{p}\right) = h\left(Y, r, \frac{M_0^F}{p}\right),$$

where $h(\ )$ is the investment function presented in equation (7) on page 130.

---

18 Cf. Mathematical Appendix 8:*e*.

Note that the last two cases analyzed here (excluding that cited from Chapter X:4) show the possibility of moving to a new equilibrium position in which the price level and hence the real quantity of money is unchanged, but the rate of interest is different. See the discussion at the end of the preceding section.

19 Cf. B. Ohlin, "Alternative Theories of the Rate of Interest," *Economic Journal*, XLVII (1937), 424.

By substituting from identity (5) and rearranging terms, equation (6) becomes

$$(7) \qquad g\left(Y, r, \frac{M_0^H}{p}\right) + h\left(Y, r, \frac{M_0^F}{p}\right) + G_0 = Y.$$

But, by equation (10) on page 131, this is precisely the equilibrium condition for the commodity market described by equation (2) on page 152. In graphical terms, if the savings and investment functions were to be superimposed on Figure 12 (page 136), they would necessarily intersect at the level of real income Y_0. In brief, the level of real income at which the aggregate amount of commodities the economy demands is equal to the amount it supplies is necessarily the same level at which the amount the economy wishes to save is equal to the amount it wishes to invest. Similarly, a level of income at which the amount of commodities demanded is greater than the amount supplied is necessarily one in which the propensity to invest is greater than the propensity to save, and conversely. A corresponding statement holds for a level of real income at which an excess supply of commodities exists.

Thus the savings-investment equality is an alternative statement of the equilibrium condition in the commodity market. As such, it is best replaced by the direct statement of this condition itself. This, of course, has been the procedure followed in the preceding argument.

Clearly, however, any statement involving savings can readily be translated into terms of our model. Consider, for example, the Austrian "monetary over-investment" school's familiar classification of the three alternative ways an increase in investment can be financed.[20] First, there is the case of "financing out of savings." Here the upward shift in the investment function is accompanied by an offsetting downward shift in the consumption function; hence the aggregate demand curve does not rise, so that no upward pressure on prices is created. Then there is the opposite case in which no initial offsetting shift in the consumption function takes place. This must be further subclassified as follows. First, the investment may be "financed out of hoards"; that is, the increased demand for investment commodities may be financed by a decrease in liquidity preference. In this case—to use the shorthand device of Figure 18 (page 155)—CC shifts to the right, while BB remains constant. Second, the investment may be "financed out of inflationary bank credit"; that is, by an increased willingness of

---

[20] Cf., e.g., G. Haberler, *Prosperity and Depression* (third ed.; Geneva, 1941), Chapters 3A and 10A.

banks to buy the bonds of firms.   In this case, both *CC* and *BB* shift
to the right.   The common feature of both these cases—and the one
which distinguishes them from the case of "financing out of savings"—
is the inflationary price development which marks the movement toward
the new equilibrium position.[21]

It must finally be emphasized that the savings-investment condition is
not an alternative statement of the equilibrium condition in the bond
market.   In particular, an act of saving is not necessarily an act of
demanding bonds; for the funds withdrawn from consumption might be
added instead to cash balances.   Conversely, the demand for bonds
might be at the expense of cash balances, instead of at the expense of
consumption.   Similarly, an act of investment is not necessarily an act
of supplying bonds; for the funds for the investment program might
be forthcoming instead from cash balances.   Conversely, the supply of
bonds might be for the purpose of adding to cash balances and not for
financing investment.

Indeed, the very existence of a money economy precludes the simultaneous identity of savings with the demand for bonds, and investment
with their supply.   For we have already seen that the excess of investment over savings is necessarily equal to the excess of commodities
demanded over supply.   Hence if this simultaneous identity were to
hold, the excess demand for commodities would then necessarily equal
the excess supply of bonds.   That is, individuals would always plan to
finance the additional purchase of commodities by the sale of bonds, and
vice versa.   Accordingly, they would never plan to change the level of
their cash balances; that is, their excess demand for these balances
would be identically zero; or, in still other words, Say's Identity would
hold.   But then—to repeat the argument of Chapter VIII:7—this
would mean that any arbitrary departure of prices from their equilibrium level would not create any excess demand or supply of money,
and hence would not generate any corrective market forces to return
the economy to its original equilibrium position.   Hence the equilibrium
level of money prices would be indeterminate—a contradiction in terms
for a money economy.

This indeterminacy can be demonstrated alternatively in terms of
Figure 18.   Since the savings = investment condition is equivalent to
the equilibrium condition for the commodity market, it too is represented by the curve *CC* in this diagram.   Now, if in addition the

---

[21] Note that the increase in investment analyzed in the preceding section falls in none of
these three categories.

Cf. on this paragraph Mathematical Appendix 8:*e*.

savings = investment condition were also equivalent to the equilibrium condition for the bond market (as is implied by the simultaneous identity above), then *CC* and *BB* would necessarily coincide. That is, there would be only one curve in Figure 18. Hence, if the system is stable, any accidental departure from an equilibrium position on this curve would generate market forces which would bring the economy back to another equilibrium position on the same curve; but these forces could not assure a return to the initial equilibrium position itself. That is, there would be no market forces which would stabilize the economy at a determinate level of prices.[22]

---

[22] Actually, by making use of the argument of Chapter VIII:7, we can be even more specific. As shown in the preceding paragraph, the simultaneous identity of savings with the demand for bonds, and investment with their supply, implies the indeterminacy of money prices. In economically meaningful terms, this means that it implies the existence of a barter economy. But in such an economy there are, by definition, no real balances, hence no real-balance effect, and hence no dependence on the absolute price level, p. It follows that the coincidence of *CC* and *BB* just described in the text must take place in a straight horizontal line in Figure 18 at a level corresponding to that of the equilibrium rate of interest. By Walras' Law (since there is no money market and the labor market is always in equilibrium), this rate can be determined equivalently either from the commodity market or from the bond market.

CHAPTER XII

The Nature of the Assumptions

1. *The presence of wage and price flexibility. The absence of money illusion in the bond market. The nature of Keynes' interest theory.* 2. *The absence of money illusion in the labor market.* 3. *The absence of distribution effects. "Forced savings."* 4. *The homogeneity of bonds.* 5. *The absence of government debt and open-market operations.* 6. *The influence of expectations. The money supply as an independent variable.*

1. The argument of the preceding chapters depends for its validity on certain basic assumptions. Some of these assumptions—for example, constancy of tastes, stability of the system, and so forth—are of a general nature made in practically every type of economic analysis. But others are specific to the analysis at hand. It is only with the latter assumptions that this chapter is concerned. It will bring out their nature and significance by investigating the analytical consequences of dropping them. In order to avoid any possible misunderstanding, it should be emphasized that this dropping of assumptions will not be cumulative; instead, each section of this chapter will start anew from the basic model developed above and will show how this model is affected by dropping one, and only one, of its assumptions. The discussion will be carried out only for changes in the quantity of money; the reader can readily establish that it holds also for shifts in liquidity preference.[1]

There is, first of all, the assumption of wage and price flexibility. If this is absent, the dynamic process of Chapter X:3 by which an increasing price level causes a negative real-balance effect in both the commodity

---

[1] Because it drops their simplifying assumptions, this chapter is considerably more complicated than preceding ones. The more general reader might, therefore, find it convenient to restrict himself initially to its first and last sections.

and bond markets—and thus ultimately eliminates the inflationary pressures created there by the initial monetary increase—clearly cannot operate. Hence the economy cannot be brought to a new equilibrium position. Thus, for example, assume that the government accompanies its printing of new money by the institution of a system of absolute wage and price controls. Under these circumstances no

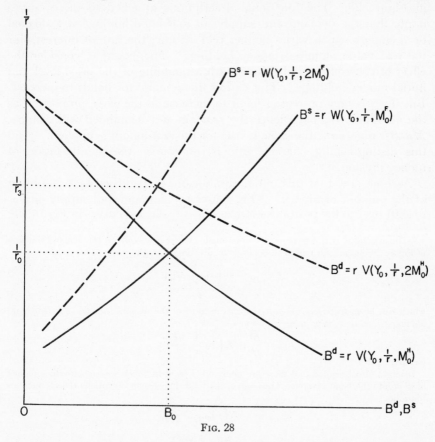

Fig. 28

real-balance effect can be generated, and hence no force can operate to press the aggregate demand curve down again from the level E_1 in Figure 12 (page 136). Accordingly, the inflationary gap AB continues undiminished. In brief, the commodity market is marked by the state of "permanent disequilibrium" so familiar from recent years of suppressed inflation. Similarly, if, in the face of a monetary decrease, wages and prices do not fall, no force can be at work to raise the aggregate demand curve again. We shall discuss this case further in Chapter XIII:4.

We turn next to the fundamental assumption concerning money illusion. Let us for once assume that such an illusion does manifest itself in our system. For example, assume that the bond demand and supply curves are not affected by changes in the price level but are affected by changes in nominal money balances. Then the original equilibrium position of this market is represented by the solid curves in Figure 28. The functional descriptions attached to these curves imply that the demand and supply for *real* bond holdings *are* affected by a change which varies neither real income, the rate of interest, nor the real value of initial money holdings. For example, consider the effect of confronting individuals with a doubling of the price level and initial money holdings. This causes the demand for bonds to increase. But there is now no reason for it to increase in the same proportion as the amount of money; hence the *real* amount demanded will change. *Mutatis mutandis*, the same is true for the *real* amount supplied. And this distinguishing characteristic is, of course, the manifestation of money illusion.[2]

Assume now that this initial equilibrium is disturbed by a doubling of the amount of money. This causes the demand and supply curves to shift over to the positions indicated by the dashed curves in Figure 28:

---

[2] The argument of this paragraph can be made clearer if we convert the demand function of Figure 28 into one for real bond holdings by dividing through by rp. This yields

$$\frac{B^d}{rp} = \frac{W\left(Y_0, \frac{1}{r}, M_0^H\right)}{p},$$

which can be instructively contrasted with the form of the demand function for real bond holdings when there is no money illusion—

$$\frac{B^d}{rp} = H\left(Y_0, \frac{1}{r}, \frac{M_0^H}{p}\right)$$

(see page 138).

It might also be noted that there are many other ways in which we can introduce money illusion into the bond market. Thus any of the following demand functions reflects such an illusion:

$$\frac{B^d}{rp} = H\left(pY_0, \frac{1}{r}, \frac{M_0^H}{p}\right),$$

$$B^d = H\left(Y_0, \frac{1}{r}, \frac{M_0^H}{p}\right),$$

$$\frac{B^d}{r} = H\left(Y_0, \frac{1}{r}, \frac{M_0^H}{p}\right).$$

The first of these functions states that the demand for real bond holdings depends on *nominal*, and not *real*, income. The second function states that the demand for *nominal* bond holdings depends on the *real* economic variables. The third function states the same thing for the money value of the demand for bond holdings.

Note, however, that if, in the last two cases, the bond supply function is of exactly the same form, then the two illusions "cancel out." That is, the *excess*-demand function for bonds is free of money illusion.

in view of their increased balances, individuals wish to lend more and borrow less. Hence at the original rate of interest there now exists an excess demand for bonds, and this begins to press the rate of interest downwards. But this time—unlike Chapter X:3—no force operates to bring about an eventual reversal of this movement. For, due to the fact that it depends only on the *nominal* level of money holdings (our money-illusion assumption), the bond market does not react to the reduction in the *real* value of these holdings caused by the price rise in the commodity market. Hence the rate of interest continues to decline undisturbed to the new equilibrium level r_3 in Figure 28. At the same time, in order to achieve equilibrium in the commodity market, prices must more than double in order to offset the stimulatory effects of a lower rate of interest on aggregate demand in this market. Thus the new equilibrium position is marked by a rate of interest less than r_0 and a price level greater than $2p_0$.

By now presenting this argument in terms of the commodity and money markets instead of the commodity and bond markets, we can at one and the same time illustrate the validity of Walras' Law and uncover the crucial assumption of Keynes' interest theory. In this way we shall be able to complete the discussion of this theory begun in the first section of the preceding chapter.

As will be recalled from that discussion, Keynes' liquidity equation has the form

$$(1) \qquad p \cdot L_1(Y_0) + L_2(r) = M_0.$$

Now, as already emphasized (page 173), Keynes' speculative demand for money, $L_2(r)$, is a reflection of the bond market: it represents the amount of money held as an immediate alternative to holding bonds. Hence the assumption of the preceding equation that this demand is independent of the absolute price level is the obverse side of the assumption that the demand for bonds is so independent. That is, Keynes' conscious or unconscious assumption that there is money illusion in the speculative demand for money (which, as shown on page 174, is what its independence of the price level implies) is the obverse side of the foregoing assumption that there is money illusion in the bond market.[3]

Once we accept the money illusion of his liquidity equation, all of

---

[3] That the foregoing equation reflects money illusion in the speculative demand for money can be made clearer by writing this demand in real terms as $\dfrac{L_2(r)}{p}$. This shows that, say, a doubling of the amount of money and the level of prices decreases the real demand for these speculative balances.

Keynes' conclusions follow as a matter of course. A doubling of the amount of money cannot merely double the price level and leave the equilibrium rate of interest unaffected. For—as equation (1) shows— the price rise generated by such a doubling affects only the transactions-precautionary demand for money and *not* the speculative demand. This is the crucial point. From it, it follows that—unlike the situation described by the illusion-free equation

$$(2) \qquad p \cdot L_1(Y_0) + p \cdot L_2\left(r, \frac{M_0}{p}\right) = M_0$$

of the preceding chapter (page 173)—the doubling of the amount of money and the price level doubles only the demand for nominal transactions balances and leaves unaffected that for nominal speculative balances; hence it can *not* double the *total* demand for nominal money holdings. In terms of Figure 25 (though disregarding the functional descriptions attached to its curves), such a change shifts the demand curve for money from position *I* to *II*; it cannot shift it to position *III*. In other words—and in sharp contrast to the basic property of equation (2) (see page 176)—such a change cannot bring about the absorption of the doubled money supply *at an unchanged rate of interest*; it leaves instead an excess supply equal to *EF*. Hence—to paraphrase the *General Theory*—some proportion of the increased money supply will seek an outlet in the purchase of securities. And this will continue until these purchases have depressed the rate of interest to such an extent that the resulting increase in the speculative demand, together with the increase in the transactions demand brought about by the price rise, suffices to absorb all of the new money. The new equilibrium position is represented in Figure 25 by the intersection of demand curve *II* with the supply curve $M^s = 2M_0$ at the rate of interest r_3.[4]

Nor can the invariance of the rate of interest be preserved by a sufficiently more-than-proportionate price increase which causes the transactions demand alone to absorb all of the increased money supply. For under these assumptions equilibrium could not prevail in the commodity market. In particular, the aggregate demand for commodities is still represented by $E = F\left(Y, r, \frac{M_0}{p}\right)$. Hence, at an unchanged rate of interest r_0, amount of money $2M_0$, and price level

---

[4] *General Theory*, pp. 200–201. I have taken the passage out of its less-than-full-employ-ment context and represented it as talking about a price level which is not explicitly mentioned. For proof that the interpretation in the text nevertheless identifies the crucial element of Keynes' argument—whether he recognized it as such or not—see the detailed evidence in Note K:2. All this will be discussed further in Chapter XV.

greater than $2p_0$, the demand curve in Figure 12 (page 136) will—because of the real-balance effect—be at a level like that of E_2. Hence a deflationary gap will prevail, forcing the price level down again. This will react back on the money market, force interest down too, and thus force the price level up again. In this way we are again brought to the conclusion that interest must fall.

Once again the foregoing analysis can be summarized in terms of Figure 18 (page 155). The curve CC in this diagram remains the same. But, under the conditions described by Figure 28, the bond market

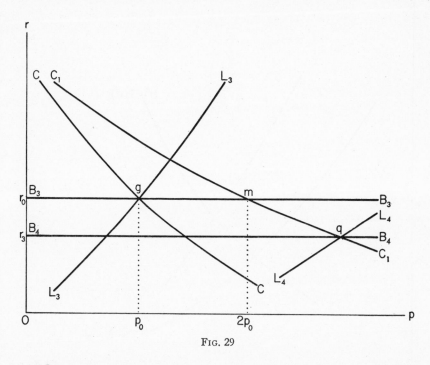

FIG. 29

is unaffected by the price level and can therefore be in equilibrium at only one rate of interest. Hence BB is initially a horizontal line at r_0 and is accordingly represented by B_3B_3 in Figure 29. As in Figure 20 (page 165), a doubling in the amount of money then shifts the curve CC twice as far to the right to C_1C_1. By Figure 28, it also shifts the curve B_3B_3 downwards to B_4B_4, at the height corresponding to the new equilibrium rate, r_3. Hence the equilibrium point moves from g to q—at which point the price level is more than twice as high as it originally was, but the rate of interest is lower.

Alternatively, we can make use of Figure 26 (page 177) and present the argument in terms of the money and commodity markets. The curve B_3B_3 in Figure 29 is then replaced by L_3L_3—this curve being the locus of equilibrium points for Keynes' liquidity equation (1). Consider now the effects of a doubling of the quantity of money. As already emphasized, the distinguishing characteristic of equation (1) is that a doubling of the amount of money and the price level will *not* affect the speculative demand and hence will *not* double the *total*

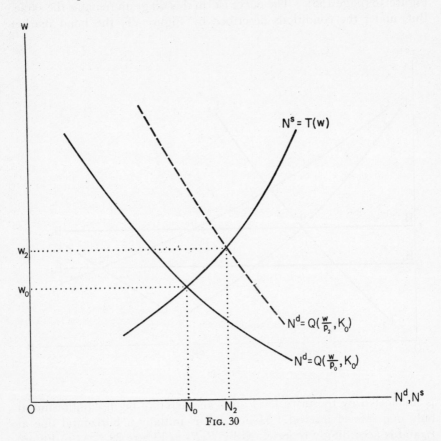

FIG. 30

nominal demand for money. This means that, at the unchanged rate of interest r_0, the price level will have to more than double in order to increase total demand sufficiently to maintain equilibrium in the money market. Hence at this rate of interest the curve L_3L_3 must shift over further to the right than the point m, which corresponds to the price level $2p_0$. The curve corresponding to the amount of money $2M_0$ is accordingly represented by L_4L_4 in Figure 29. Clearly, the intersection

196

of this curve with C_1C_1 must be at a rate of interest less than r_0 and a price level greater than $2p_0$.[5]

2. In a similar way the neutrality of money can be destroyed by the presence of money illusion in the labor market, instead of the bond or money market. Assume, in particular, that though the demand for labor continues to depend on the real wage rate, the supply depends only on the nominal one. The original equilibrium position is now described by the solid curves in Figure 30. Since the vertical axis now represents the nominal wage rate, the demand curve must be drawn as of a given price level. Obviously, money illusion would exist even if the supply curve depended on the price level as well as on the money wage rate—so long as it did not depend on the ratio between them. For simplicity, however, we have drawn the supply curve as dependent solely on the latter.

Assume again that the economy's equilibrium position is disturbed by a doubling of the amount of money. The resulting pressures in the commodity and bond markets start upward movements in the prices of both these goods. As the price level rises, the demand curve in Figure 30 shifts over to the right; for the same money wage rate now corresponds to a lower real one. Thus for the price level p_2, greater than p_0, the equilibrium money wage rate and level of employment are w_2 and N_2, respectively. Clearly, the real wage rate w_2/p_2 must be less than w_0/p_0; for otherwise the amount of labor demanded could not be greater than N_0.

As a result of this decrease in the real wage rate and consequent increase in employment, the supply curve of commodities also shifts to the right. Let the new equilibrium position in this market now be represented by the solid curves in Figure 31. The output Y_2 corresponds, of course, to the input of labor N_2. Thus the increase in the amount of money changes the bench mark of full employment itself.[6]

It remains to determine the relationship between the new equilibrium values—w_2, p_2, and r_2—and the original ones. Consider first the situation in the bond market. By the assumptions made above (pages 138 and 141-42), the increase in real national output to Y_2 shifts both the demand and supply curves for bonds to the right. Assume that these shifts always exactly offset each other. Then—in the absence of any other change—the situation in the bond market is as indicated in

---

[5] The analytical derivation of these results is left as an exercise for the mathematically inclined reader.

[6] The variability of this bench mark will be discussed further in Chapter XIII:1.

Figure 32. That is, the increase in real income does not affect the equilibrium rate of interest. But now we must take account of the fact which is inherent in the initial assumption of our present analysis: namely, that the original doubling of the amount of money has generated a real-balance effect in the bond market which has shifted the

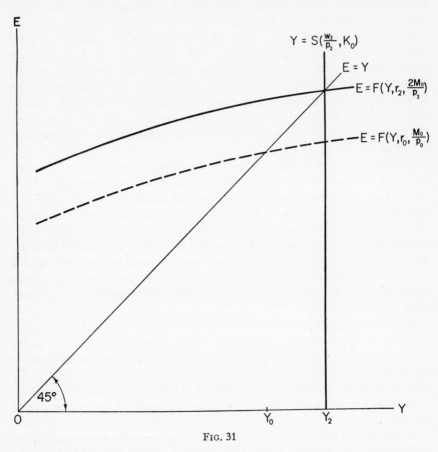

FIG. 31

demand curve to the right and the supply curve to the left. Hence the interest rate must decrease.

Let us now return to the commodity market. At first sight it appears from Figure 31 as if the increased supply creates a downward pressure on the price level which might ultimately offset the initial upward pressure generated by the monetary increase. But a moment's reflection shows that equilibrium could not exist at such a lowered price level. For if the price level were to fall, the real wage rate would rise;

and this would replace the increase in the input of labor and consequent increase in the supply of commodities by a decrease in both these items. On the other hand, the lowered price level would reinforce the initial downward pressure on interest in the bond market, and hence raise the aggregate demand curve for commodities. Hence an inflationary gap would exist in the commodity market. It follows that the new equilibrium price level must lie above p_0.

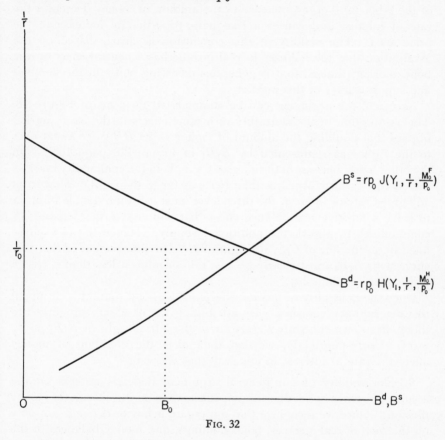

$$B^s = rp_0 \, J(Y_1, \tfrac{1}{r}, \tfrac{M_0^F}{P_0})$$

$$B^d = rp_0 \, H(Y_1, \tfrac{1}{r}, \tfrac{M_0^H}{P_0})$$

FIG. 32

Assume now that the price level has doubled. Then, since there is no money illusion there, the bond market is once again in equilibrium at the original rate of interest r_0. But the commodity market cannot be in equilibrium. For the real value of cash balances is now once again equal to its original value; hence the aggregate demand curve must now coincide with the original dashed one in Figure 31. At the same time, the doubling of the price level and consequent reduction of the real wage rate has increased the input of labor and thus shifted the commodity supply curve to the right. Hence a deflationary gap exists in this market. This would be so *a fortiori* if the price level had more than doubled and the rate of interest had accordingly risen in the bond market.

Thus consideration of all the markets in our economy brings us to the following conclusion: If there is money illusion on the supply side of the labor market, an increase in the amount of money decreases the rate of interest and causes a less-than-proportionate increase in the price level. The validity of this conclusion is clearly based on the assumption that the increase in real income has a neutral effect on the bond market; that is, that it generates offsetting shifts in the demand and supply curves of this market.

As usual, the argument can be summarized in terms of Figure 18. The assumption of the neutrality of income effects in the bond market implies that doubling the amount of money shifts BB twice as far over to the right—as represented by B_1B_1 in Figure 20 (page 165). On the other hand, because of the increased supply in the commodity market, the curve CC shifts over less than twice as far to the right. That is, at any given rate of interest, the price level must less than double in order to leave a positive real-balance effect that will enable the demand for commodities to absorb the additional supply. Hence the new curve must lie to the left of C_1C_1 in Figure 20. The intersection of this new curve with B_1B_1 must clearly be at a rate of interest less than r_0 and a price level less than $2p_0$.

Once the neutrality of income effects in the bond market is dropped, this determinacy vanishes. By attributing the necessary properties to these effects, we can shift BB as far to the left or right of B_1B_1 as we want. Correspondingly, we can then have the doubling of money affect the rate of interest in any way that we want.[7]

3. The validity of our general argument depends no less on the assumed absence of net distribution effects than on the absence of money illusion. Once we recognize that aggregate behavior depends not only on the *total* of real incomes, bond holdings, and money balances in the economy but on their distribution among the individuals of the economy as well, and once we also realistically assume that the monetary increase is not uniformly introduced among these individuals, then the analysis loses all semblance of precision. By specifying the proper effects, we can obtain any desired result.

Assume, for example, that the redistribution of real incomes generated

---

[7] For an analytical treatment, see Mathematical Appendix 9:*a*.

by a price increase is such as to decrease the demand for consumption commodities and increase the demand for bonds. That is, the individuals whose real incomes are increased by the price change have a higher propensity to save and lend than those whose real incomes are decreased. Then a doubling of the amount of money will no longer leave the rate of interest invariant For the "forced savings" created

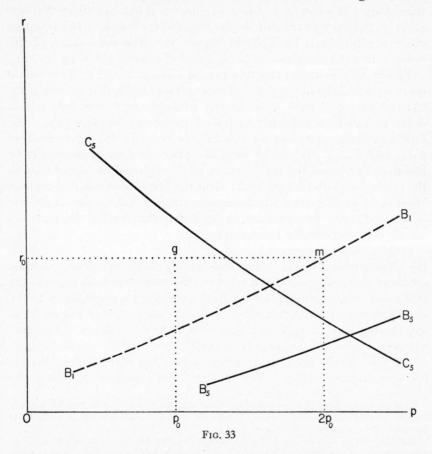

FIG. 33

by the price rise will cause the rate of interest to decline. The level of national income will remain the same, but its composition will change in favor of investment, as against consumption, commodities. This possibility was duly recognized and emphasized by classical and neoclassical economists.[8]

In terms of the concepts of Figure 18, the specified change shifts *CC*

---

[8] These doctrinal issues will be discussed further in Chapter XV.

over to the right; but, because of the initial downward shift in the propensity to consume (upward shift in the propensity to save), not twice as far to the right. That is, it must lie to the left of C_1C_1 in Figure 20 (page 165). The resulting curve is represented by the curve C_5C_5 in Figure 33. By the same reasoning, BB shifts further to the right than B_1B_1; for, at any given rate of interest, the price level must more than double in order to create a negative real-balance effect that will offset the initial upward shift in the demand for bonds. The resulting curve is represented by B_5B_5 in Figure 33. The intersection of this curve with C_5C_5 must clearly be at a rate of interest below r_0.

Figure 33 also shows that the rate of interest would decline even if there were no shift in the demand function for bonds, that is, even if the "forced savings" were used entirely to augment money balances in order to satisfy a suddenly increased preference for liquidity. The final equilibrium position for this case is given by the intersection of C_5C_5 and B_1B_1. As can be seen, the price level must necessarily be less than $2p_0$; hence the real quantity of money must be higher than in the original equilibrium position. It is the pressure of this real-balance effect in the bond market which explains the fact that the rate of interest is reduced, even though there is no initial shift in the demand and supply conditions of the bond market.[9]

Clearly, similar arguments hold for the effects of a price change on the distribution of real bond and money holdings. For example, creditors and debtors need not react in offsetting ways to changes in the real value of outstanding debt. Hence varying assumptions as to the nature of these distribution effects can shift the curves of Figure 33 in any desired way, to yield any desired equilibrium position. This fact has been sufficiently emphasized above.[10]

We note finally that, in a certain sense, the real-balance effect is itself a distribution effect. For our fiat paper money is the debt of the

---

[9] The reader will recall that this type of argument in terms of an alleged relationship between the real quantity of money and the rate of interest is beset with analytical pitfalls and so must be used with care; see the end of Chapter XI:4.

The discussion of this and the preceding paragraphs slurs over a certain difficulty. Once distribution effects are introduced, the slope of BB might become negative. If this should cut CC from above, an increase in the amount of money would then lead to an increase in the rate of interest. It can, however, be shown that, under certain simple dynamic assumptions, the stability of the system precludes this possibility. For a full discussion, see Mathematical Appendix 9:c.

It is left as an exercise for the reader to show that the argument of the text here can be presented alternatively in terms of the commodity and money markets. For an analytical treatment, see Mathematical Appendix 9:d.

[10] Pp. 41 and 58. Note that this indeterminacy holds even if the monetary increase is uniformly introduced. For, by assumption, the resulting price increase generates real-indebtedness effects which do not cancel out.

government; and if the government were to react to changes in the real value of this debt as do households and firms to theirs, there could be no net real-balance effect in the economy as a whole. Any, say, decrease in the price level would generate a positive real-balance effect for households and firms and an exactly offsetting negative one for the government. Thus the preceding analysis has been based on the tacit—though realistic—assumption that the government, alone of all economic units, is unconcerned with the real value of its outstanding (non-interest-bearing) debt, and plans its demand for commodities accordingly.[11]

4. Throughout this book we have assumed that bonds are a homogeneous good, so that no distinction exists between one type of debt and another. This assumption is, to begin with, unrealistic. But once we leave the very simple model with which we have been dealing, it becomes completely unacceptable.

In particular, assume that we extend our model to provide for the existence of a fractional-reserve commercial banking system. The relation of these banks to the rest of the economy is described by the following schematic arrangement, where "Currency in circulation" is the fiat paper money of our previous discussion:

Economic Unit	Liquid Assets	Liquid Liabilities
Households	Currency Demand deposits Bonds of other households Bonds of firms (Government bonds)	Bonds sold to other households Bonds sold to banks
Firms	Currency Demand deposits	Bonds sold to households Bonds sold to banks
Banks	Currency Bonds of households Bonds of firms (Government bonds)	Demand deposits
Government		Currency in circulation (Government bonds)
	Total Liquid Assets	*Total Liquid Liabilities*

Let us defer discussion of the parenthetical entries until the next section. From inspection of the foregoing table we see that every item appears once as an asset and once as a liability. Hence the two grand totals of this table must be equal. Define now the "net liquid-asset

---

[11] The nature of this assumption can be most easily appreciated from a consideration of the table in the following section—after eliminating from it all items related to banks.

position" of the private sector as being equal to the total liquid assets of households and firms *minus* their total liquid liabilities. From the equality of the two grand totals, it follows that this must be positive and equal to the total amount of currency in circulation. Now, our assumption that the stimulating effect of a price decline on a creditor—no matter what the nature of his asset—is always exactly offset by its depressing effect on the corresponding debtor—no matter what the nature of his liability—implies that the effect of this price decline on the economy as a whole can be measured by its effect on the real value of the net liquid-asset position of the private sector; or, what is the same thing, by its effect on the real value of currency in circulation. In particular, we can disregard its effect in increasing the real value of individuals' demand deposits, for this is largely offset by the corresponding increase in the real value of individuals' debts to banks.[12]

More generally, the foregoing assumptions imply that the total amount of demand deposits is of no relevance for the functioning of the economy. Specifically, a parallel expansion of bank loans and deposits changes neither the net asset position of households and firms, nor, consequently, their demand for commodities. This *reductio ad absurdum* merely points up the necessity of distinguishing between the degrees of liquidity and illiquidity of various types of assets and liabilities. Thus, for example, an individual who borrows from a bank must obviously consider the restrictive effect of the increased debt, payable at some future date, to be considerably less powerful than the stimulatory effect of the increased demand deposits, now made available.

In order to take into account these and related considerations, we should actually write the aggregate demand functions as dependent upon the *arrays* of real bond holdings (classified according to their respective degrees of liquidity) and the *arrays* of real money holdings (inclusive of demand deposits). For a complete analysis we should also take account of the influence on demand of the mere availability of lines of credit. But we cannot go into these complications here.[13]

5. Let us now return to our simple model economy without a banking system and investigate the implications of dropping the assumption that the government has always balanced its budget (page 127). Accordingly, we now assume that the government has at various times

---

[12] This was first pointed out by M. Kalecki, "Professor Pigou on the 'Classical Stationary State'—A Comment," *Economic Journal*, LIV (1944), 131–32.

[13] These observations are based on the stimulating discussion of Hart, *op. cit.*, pp. 77–79, 129–30. See also R. N. McKean, "Liquidity and a National Balance Sheet," *Journal of Political Economy*, LVII (1949), as reprinted in *Readings in Monetary Theory*, ed. F. A. Lutz and L. W. Mints (Philadelphia, 1951), pp. 63–88.

in the past incurred budgetary deficits which it has financed by the issue of bonds. These bonds are assumed identical with those issued by firms and, like the latter, are held only by households. We also permit the government to engage in open-market operations.[14]

As can be seen from the table in the preceding section, the net liquid assets of households and firms are now equal to the total of their money and government-bond holdings. This, of course, is identical with the net liability of the government to the private sector. In particular, the total initial bond holdings of firms and households are no longer zero; for after canceling off "positive" creditors with "negative" debtors, we are still left with a positive net indebtedness equal to the nominal value of government bonds held by individuals. Accordingly, even if we neglect distribution effects, we can no longer—as heretofore in Part Two[15]—ignore the influence of total initial bond holdings on aggregate economic behavior. Instead, we must reactivate the assumptions of Part One[16] that the greater the real value of individuals' initial bond holdings, the greater their demand for both commodities and bonds: in brief, the increased wealth of individuals in the form of government-bond holdings is assumed to make them willing both to buy more and to lend more.

These assumptions are reflected in the following system of equations, which must accordingly replace that of Chapter X:1:

Condition for Equilibrium	Market

(3)
$$Q\left(\frac{w}{p}, K_0\right) = \bar{R}\left(\frac{w}{p}\right)$$
Labor

(4)
$$F\left(Y_0, r, \frac{V_0}{rp}, \frac{M_0}{p}\right) = Y_0$$
Commodities

(5)
$$rp \cdot \bar{H}\left(Y_0, \frac{1}{r}, \frac{V_0}{rp}, \frac{M_0^H}{p}\right) = rp \cdot \bar{J}\left(Y_0, \frac{1}{r}, \frac{M_0^F}{p}\right) + V_0$$
Bonds

(6)
$$p \cdot L\left(Y_0, r, \frac{V_0}{rp}, \frac{M_0}{p}\right) = M_0$$
Money

Here V_0 represents the number of government bonds outstanding, and the bars over the functional symbols indicate that these functions differ from those of Chapters IX and X. Since firms are assumed not

---

[14] Alternatively, we might assume that there exists a central bank which carries out these operations. But it seems to me inconsistent to assume, on the one hand, the existence of a banking system and to ignore, on the other, the complications discussed in the preceding section.

[15] Cf. p. 132.

[16] Cf. pp. 50 and 53–54.

to hold government bonds, the real value of these bonds—V_0/rp—does not influence their supply function for bonds. On the other hand, this function now describes only part of the supply side of the bond market; it must clearly be supplemented, as it has been in equation (5), by the total of government bonds outstanding, V_0.[17]

It should be noted that the foregoing model introduces a new way in which an increase in the rate of interest affects economic behavior. For now that net bond holdings are positive, we can no longer assume—as we did on page 132—that the capital losses and gains created by such an increase will cancel out. Instead, there is a net capital loss—represented by the decrease in V_0/rp—which makes its depressing influence felt throughout the economy. In the commodity and money markets, this reinforces the effect already attributed to an increase in interest; in the bond market, however, it opposes it. Indeed, if the capital-loss effect is sufficiently strong, the slope of the demand curve for bonds in Figure 13 (page 139) might become positive.

Even in this case, however, the *excess*-demand curve implicit in Figure 13—which is the excess-demand curve explicit in Figure 14—must retain a negative slope. This can be seen most easily by dividing equation (5) through by rp, and thereby converting it into real terms:

$$(7) \qquad \bar{H}\left(Y_0, \frac{1}{r}, \frac{V_0}{rp}, \frac{M_0^H}{p}\right) = \bar{J}\left(Y_0, \frac{1}{r}, \frac{M_0^F}{p}\right) + \frac{V_0}{rp}.$$

Now, an increase in the rate of interest decreases V_0/rp by a certain amount. As can be seen from the right-hand side of equation (7), this decreases the real supply of bonds by exactly the same amount. At the same time, however—as can be seen from the left-hand side of (7)—the decrease in V_0/rp also exerts a depressing effect on the real demand for bonds. But if we assume that the marginal propensity to spend out of real bond holdings, V_0/rp, is less than unity, this decrease in

---

17 If the analysis of this section were to be extended to an economy with a banking system, it would be more realistic to distinguish on the demand sides of the various markets between government bonds held by households and those held by banks. The former can be treated as have the government bonds in the preceding model; that is, as the source of an independent effect on demand. The latter are best treated as the source, together with the currency in circulation, of the real-balance effect; for they represent demand deposits which do not have an offset in private debt to banks. Cf. the discussion in the preceding section.

Similarly, in a more complicated economy, we should broaden the base of the real-balance effect by adding demand deposits which have an offset in net central-bank debt to the member banks; i.e., an offset in net member-bank reserves held in the central bank. On the other hand, we should deduct government deposits held in the member banks. For further details, see my revised "Price Flexibility and Full Employment," *Readings in Monetary Theory*, Table 1, p. 275. It should, however, be emphasized that this table lumps together the whole of net government debt to the private sector—a procedure whose modification has just been advocated.

real demand must be less than the aforementioned decrease in real supply. Hence the excess supply of real bond holdings must decrease—which means that the amount of excess demand in Figure 14 must increase.

Assume now that the equilibrium of this system is disturbed by the government's printing money to finance increased expenditures. It can readily be seen that, say, a doubling of the amount of money in this way will not merely double equilibrium wages and prices, while leaving the rate of interest unaffected. For under such circumstances the real value of government-bond holdings, V_0/rp, would be less than in the original equilibrium position, whereas other influences on commodity demand would be the same. Hence, by equation (4), there would exist a deflationary gap in the commodity market. Nor would the bond market be in equilibrium: for the decrease in the real value of government bonds must reduce both demand and supply, but, as argued in the preceding paragraph, the latter decrease must be greater than the former. Hence at the original rate of interest there would exist a state of excess demand in the bond market. It follows that the new equilibrium rate of interest must be lower than the original one.

This failure of interest to remain invariant is really implicit in the earlier argument of this chapter. For the assumption that there are government bonds introduces into the analysis elements which are analogous to the presence of both money illusion and distribution effects. The former is reflected on the supply side of the bond market—which shows that the government wishes to maintain V_0 bonds outstanding regardless of the price level. The latter is reflected on the demand sides of the commodity and bond markets—which show that indebtedness effects do not in the aggregate cancel out and are, indeed, represented by the term V_0/rp.

This interpretation suggests that if government bonds could be introduced without violating either of these basic assumptions, then the invariance of the interest rate would be preserved. Assume, then, that the government bond carries a constant-purchasing-power guarantee; that is, each holder of a government bond has the privilege of converting it into a larger number of bonds in accordance with the rise of the price level. Then, everywhere that the symbol for government bonds, V_0, appears in the preceding equations, it must be replaced by pV_0. In this way, both of the previously noted disturbing elements are removed. Correspondingly—as can be verified by direct substitution into this modified system of equations—a doubling of the amount of money brings the economy to a new equilibrium position in which prices and wages have doubled, while the rate of interest has remained invariant.

However, even with a government bond of this type there are certain monetary changes which do affect the rate of interest. In particular, assume that the government uses the new money it prints, not to finance additional expenditures, but to carry out open-market purchases from households. Then the *increase* in the amount of money is necessarily accompanied by a corresponding *decrease* in the number of government bonds outstanding. This is the crucial point. For by the same argument used above, it can then be established that if prices and wages were to double, while interest remained invariant, there would exist an excess supply in the commodity market and an excess demand in the bond market. Once again, the resulting decrease in the equilibrium rate of interest can be interpreted as the consequence of effectively introducing a net indebtedness effect into the analysis.

Clearly, open-market purchases exert a downward pressure on the equilibrium interest rate even when government bonds do not carry a constant-purchasing-power guarantee. Indeed, it can readily be seen that in this case the new equilibrium rate of interest must be lower than in the case where the same increase in the amount of money is used to finance additional government expenditure. For consider the equilibrium price level and rate of interest established in this latter case. They clearly cannot correspond to the equilibrium position established by an equivalent open-market purchase. For at these values the amount of bonds supplied is less than in the first case by the extent of the open-market purchase, while the amount demanded is less by a smaller amount. Hence there exists a state of excess demand in the bond market which drives the rate of interest further downwards.

Thus the lack of invariance of the interest rate in the presence of government debt is completely analogous to its lack of invariance in the presence of the distribution effects analyzed in Section 3. The force of this analogy can best be appreciated by noting that both these propositions can be demonstrated by exactly the same graphical analysis presented there in Figure 33.[18]

6. We turn finally to the assumption that the system is not rendered unstable by elastic expectations. Clearly, it is always possible to specify a set of expectations that will convert an otherwise convergent system into a divergent one. As already emphasized in Chapter XI:3, we are not interested in sterile "existence theorems" of this sort. Instead,

---

18 Here again we have slurred over the difficulties referred to in footnote 9, p. 202, above. For a full discussion, see Mathematical Appendix 9:*e–f*.

This emphasis on the distinction between a monetary increase used to finance additional expenditures and one used to finance open-market purchases follows Metzler, *op. cit.* Metzler's analytical approach, however, differs from the one presented here, and is effectively restricted to the case of a constant-purchasing-power bond.

our question is simply the following one: The analysis of Chapter X:3 depends in a crucial way on a rising price level to create a negative real-balance effect that will gradually eliminate the original inflationary pressure and thus enable the ultimate stabilization of prices at a higher level. Is it reasonable to assume that this price rise can take place without generating such strong expectations of its uninterrupted continuation that the speculative element in the aggregate demand for commodities will predominate and thus drive prices indefinitely upwards?

In judging the reasonableness of our assumption that such expectations will not prevent the ultimate stabilization of prices, we must emphasize that the analysis of preceding chapters deals with the effects of a once-and-for-all increase in the amount of money. The significance of this remark can best be appreciated by noting that most of the traditionally cited cases of runaway inflations with explosive expectations have been marked by continuously increasing injections of new money into the system.[19] In the absence of such renewed injections, it does seem reasonable to assume that the negative real-balance effects of a rising price level must ultimately become strong enough to more than offset the possible expansionary effects of expectations. Individuals may anticipate further price increases; but, in the absence of adequate real money balances, they just do not have the means by which they can indefinitely increase their demands in accordance with their expectations. Hence, after a certain point, these expectations will cease to be self-justifying; and, after a still further point, they will accordingly be replaced by more stable ones which will reflect the leveling-off of prices. In brief, the presence of inflationary expectations may well make the price level rise above its new equilibrium level at some stage of the dynamic process; but the real-balance effect will ultimately push it downwards again.

What is, however, unrealistic about the preceding argument is its naive supposition that the money supply remains absolutely constant after the initial expansion. This constancy reflects the hitherto unmodified assumption that the amount of money is a purely exogenous variable—one that cannot be affected by the economic forces of the system. Actually, of course, the real world offers no justification for such an assumption. On the contrary, it shows that a rising price level itself generates a continuing upward pressure on the money supply and

---

19 Cf. F. D. Graham, *Exchange, Prices, and Production in Hyper-Inflation: Germany 1920–23* (Princeton, 1930), pp. 104–7; P. Cagan, "The Monetary Dynamics of Hyperinflations," *Econometrica*, XXII (1954), 519; Brown, *op. cit.*, p. 179. But this is not to deny that an outstanding characteristic of hyper-inflations—particularly in their final stages—is that the real quantity of money declines continuously.

that, accordingly, the money supply must—to some extent at least—be considered a dependent variable of the analysis.[20]

Thus, for example, firms which have become accustomed to the easy profits of inflationary times will object to the "disinflationary" reduction in real balances caused by the price increase; they will point to the resulting slackening of demand as conclusive evidence that the money supply is no longer adequate for the "needs of the economy"; and they will insist that the government must accordingly expand this supply even further. Similarly, they will strongly resist any attempt to stabilize the volume of bank credit, with the claim that the increased price level has increased the money value of their normal volume of transactions and has therefore created a corresponding increase in the "legitimate credit needs of business." The "real bills doctrine" inherent in these claims may not constitute good monetary theory, but this in no way diminishes its influence in the determination of monetary policy.[21]

Needless to say, in this battle for an ever expanding money supply, business will not stand alone. It will be joined wholeheartedly by labor unions interested in preventing any possible "disinflationary" threat to the continued existence of full employment. And, under certain circumstances, it might even be joined by the Treasury itself. For the price rise may increase the Treasury's expenditures more than its tax receipts, so that it will be faced with the necessity of financing a budgetary deficit.

Thus just at that point of the dynamic process where the price increase generates a real-balance effect strong enough to exert a significant downward pressure on demand—just at that point it may instead generate a further expansion of the monetary supply. In this way, the eventual leveling-off of prices at a higher equilibrium level—as described in Chapter X:3—may be continuously postponed.[22, 23]

---

20 On dependent and exogenous variables, see above, Chapter I:4.

21 For a theoretical and historical discussion of the "real bills doctrine," see L. W. Mints, *A History of Banking Theory* (Chicago, 1945), Chapter III; J. Viner, *Studies in the Theory of International Trade* (New York, 1937), pp. 148–54, 234–43.

22 The viewpoint of this section has been strongly colored by the personal experience of an inflationary process which—by all the rules of expectational economics—should have exploded, but which—because, I believe, of the real-balance effect—did not. I have attempted to analyze this experience in "Monetary and Price Developments in Israel: 1949–1953," *Scripta Hierosolymitana*, Vol. III (1955), especially pp. 30, 40–41.

23 Another example of the way in which the money supply may be a dependent variable of the analysis is provided by an economy whose government adopts as its declared policy the continuous, absolute maintenance of full employment. Assume that the unions disturb the initial equilibrium of such an economy by imposing a higher money wage rate. The resulting threat of unemployment will then cause the government to undertake deficit spending and thereby generate the higher money supply needed to maintain full employment at the increased wage and price levels. Thus the rise in the money wage rate causes a proportionate rise in the amount of money in circulation.

CHAPTER XIII

The Workings of the Model:

Involuntary Unemployment

1. The concept of involuntary unemployment.   2–3. A theory of involuntary unemployment.   4. Monetary theory under conditions of involuntary unemployment.

1. Throughout the static and dynamic analysis of this part, one assumption has remained untouched: namely, that the economy is and remains at a position of full employment.   It is high time to investigate the meaning of this assumption and the implications of dropping it.

We approach the concept "full employment" through its opposite, "involuntary unemployment."   The crucial attribute of this concept is its relativity.   In the absolute sense, the whole notion of "involuntariness" must disappear: for everyone "wants" to do whatever he is doing at the moment; otherwise he would not do it.[1]   It is only by comparing an individual's reactions under given circumstances with his corresponding reactions under arbitrarily designated "ideal" circumstances that we are able to define the element of "involuntariness" which may be involved.   Thus our first task in defining "involuntary unemployment" is to define that behavior which is to be taken as the norm of voluntariness.

Unfortunately, a precise description of this norm is, by its very nature, an impossibility.   In the present context, however, it suffices to

---

[1] I cannot help citing here the Talmudic dictum that—in certain cases of private law where the formal consent of an individual is required—the court is permitted "to coerce him until he says 'I am willing.'"

211

define it in general terms as the economic behavior of an individual maximizing utility in the "normal" environment of a free, peacetime, democratic society, subject to the restraints imposed by the given market prices and his budget. An individual subjected to any additional restraints will be said to be acting involuntarily. Voluntariness, however, is not to be equated with either happiness or justice. For example, an individual acting in accordance with a severe budget restriction may be both poor and unhappy. Thus no moral approbation is necessarily attached to the maintenance of voluntariness in the sense here defined.[2]

The reader will immediately recognize that the behavior corresponding to the "normal" restraints of the preceding paragraph is precisely that behavior described by the ordinary demand and supply curves of economic analysis. Hence, as long as an economic unit is "on" such a curve, it will be said to be acting voluntarily. It follows that the individuals of a given economy cannot all be acting voluntarily at one and the same time unless the economy is in a position of general equilibrium. For, by definition, only in such a position can all the demand and supply curves of the economy simultaneously be satisfied. Conversely, in such a position no one will be acting involuntarily. Indeed, for classical and neoclassical economists, this was precisely the beauty of the equilibrating process of a free market economy. This was the harmony of interests and compatibility of desires achieved by the "invisible hand" which guided it.[3]

The application of this general definition to the specific problem at hand is immediate: The norm of reference to be used in defining involuntary unemployment is the supply curve of labor; for this curve shows the amount of employment which the workers of the economy want to obtain in the light of the money wage, price level, and budget restraints with which they are confronted. Hence as long as workers are "on their supply curve"—that is, as long as they succeed in selling all the labor they want to at the prevailing real wage rate—a state of full employment will be said to exist in the economy. It follows that a state of general equilibrium in the economy as a whole, or even a state of partial equilibrium in the labor market by itself, is *ipso facto* a state of full employment. It also follows that the bench mark of full employment is not an absolute constant, but something which itself varies with every change in the real wage rate or in the subjective or objective

---

2 Cf. F. H. Knight, *The Ethics of Competition* (New York, 1935), pp. 45–58.

3 In the present context, of course, this is nothing but an emotive tautology. See the end of the preceding paragraph and the footnote attached to it.

The notion of involuntariness will be discussed further at the end of Section 3.

determinants of the labor supply curve.   Chapter XII:2 has already
provided us with an example of this variability.

Conversely, if workers are not on this curve, they are acting involun-
tarily.   Thus, if they are at the point A in Figure 34 (a reproduction of
Figure 10), involuntary unemployment to the extent $N_3 - N_1$ exists.
On the other hand, if they are at the point E, there exists involuntary

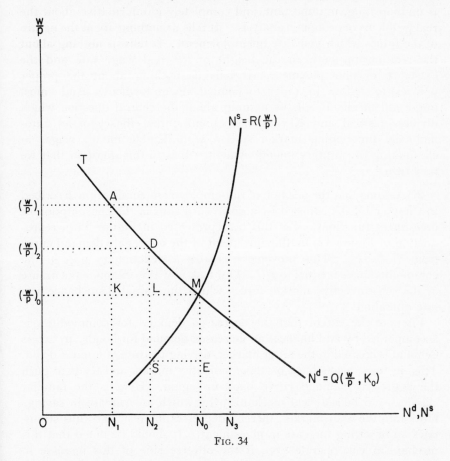

FIG. 34

*over*employment to the extent $N_0 - N_2$.   Such a situation prevails
when, for example, wartime workers are exhorted by appeals to their
patriotism to work longer hours than they would normally choose.

Thus, by definition, the extent of involuntary unemployment is
identical with the extent of the excess supply of labor which exists at
the prevailing real wage rate.   It follows that if the terms are
understood in their usual, strict sense, the coexistence of involuntary

unemployment and flexible money wages precludes the existence of equilibrium. For "flexibility" means that the money wage rate tends to fall with excess supply, and "equilibrium" means that nothing tends to change in the system. Hence, by definition, the foregoing "coexistence theorem" must be true.

But like any other theorem which is tautologically true, this one too is uninteresting, unimportant, and completely uninformative about the real problems of economic analysis. It tells us nothing about the nature of the forces which generate unemployment. It tells us nothing about the relationship between the height of the real wage rate and the existence of unemployment. It tells us nothing about the proper policies to follow in order to combat unemployment. And—most important of all—it tells us nothing about the central question which divides classical and Keynesian economics: the efficacy of an automatically functioning market system with flexible money wages in eliminating involuntary unemployment. It is to this question that we now turn.[4]

2. Assume that the position of full-employment equilibrium described in Chapter IX is disturbed by a downward shift in the consumption or investment functions. Let this be represented in Figure 35 (a reproduction of Figure 12) by the movement of the aggregate demand curve from E to E_2. This movement creates a deflationary gap in the commodity market equal to BC. Our task now is to examine the nature of the self-corrective market forces which this initial disturbance sets into operation.

First, to the extent that the decreased demand for commodities is accompanied by and finances an increased demand for bonds, an excess demand is created in the latter market, driving the rate of interest down. This, in turn, reacts back on the commodity market and tends to push the aggregate demand curve back up again. Here is the familiar classical and neoclassical mechanism by which an increase in savings flows into the loan market, thereby depresses interest, and thus stimulates an offsetting increase in investment. It should be noted that this mechanism will operate even if the obverse side of this increase in savings should consist initially of an increase in the demand for money, without any shift whatsoever in the demand for bonds. In this case,

---

4 For textual proof that Keynes' references to "unemployment equilibrium" were not intended as denials of this innocuous tautology, but were simply based on a usage of "equilibrium" which differs from the usual one—see Note K:3.

From this we can see that much of the heated and still continuing debate on whether there can or cannot be a state of "unemployment equilibrium" is a sterile terminological debate which never would have started had either side bothered to define its terms precisely.

however, the decline in interest must await the impact on the bond market of the positive real-balance effect generated by the downward pressure on prices of the initial deflationary gap. Clearly, in addition to providing this indirect stimulus through the bond market, the real-balance effect also stimulates the commodity market directly.

Thus the downward shift in the commodity demand function auto-

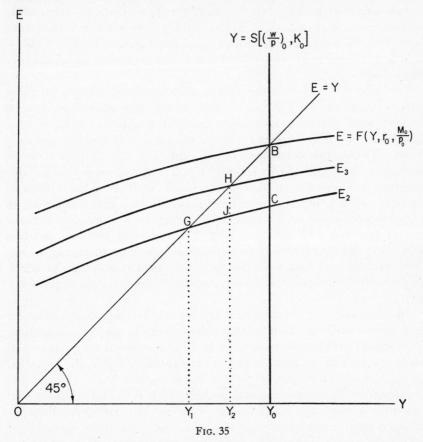

$$Y = S\left[\left(\tfrac{w}{p}\right)_0, K_0\right]$$

$E = Y$

$E = F(Y, r_0, \tfrac{M_0}{p_0})$

E_3

E_2

45°

Y_1 Y_2 Y_0

FIG. 35

matically creates market forces which tend to offset it. If this demand is sufficiently sensitive to these forces, it will quickly return to a full-employment position at a lower level of wages, prices, and interest. Throughout this period of adjustment there will exist a state of excess supply in the commodity market. But due to the assumed shortness of this period, producers will react to their temporary inability to sell by simply permitting their inventories to build up. That is, they will leave their level of production unchanged at Y_0. This, of course, is the

215

tacit assumption on which we have heretofore analyzed the effects of a downward shift in commodity demand.[5]

Once this assumption is dropped, the whole argument must be drastically modified. In the absence of sufficient interest- and price-elasticity, the adjustment process becomes a long, drawn-out one. It cannot then realistically be assumed that firms will continue producing at an unchanged level, for this would require them to accumulate inventories at ever increasing levels. Hence they must eventually take some step to bring current output—and consequently current input—into line with current sales. And this is the beginning of involuntary unemployment.

We must now translate this common-sense conclusion into the more precise terms of our model. Unfortunately, this translation can be neither simple nor immediate. For though it is obvious that there must be some connection between the firms' output of commodities and their input of labor, this connection is not explicit in our demand function for labor in Figure 34.[6] Indeed, to all outward appearances this function depends only on the real wage rate, and not on the volume of output. Furthermore, it must be emphasized that this absence of an express dependence on the volume of output is not a property peculiar to our function, but one that holds for any labor demand function derived in the standard way from the principle of profit maximization. Nevertheless, if we look more closely into the tacit assumptions on which this standard derivation is based, we shall find the vital dependence that we seek.

In particular, our demand function for labor describes the behavior of firms maximizing profits within a framework of perfect competition. This means that the planned labor input it specifies for any given real wage rate reflects the firms' assumptions *that they will be able to sell all of their resulting output at the prevailing market price*. Hence any development in the commodity market which invalidates this crucial assumption must also invalidate these plans. In particular, the continued forced accumulation of unsold outputs described above must eventually make firms drop both their assumption of an unlimited market and, consequently, their plans for labor inputs as described by the demand curve in Figure 34. In other words, the accumulation of these unsold inventories must in some sense eventually cause a leftward

---

[5] Namely, in the case of an increase in liquidity preference in Chapter X:4 and in the case of an increase in the propensity to save on p. 185.

[6] But it is explicit in the commodity supply function when written in the form $Y = \phi[Q(w/p, K_0)]$, where $\phi(\ )$ is the production function, and $Q(\ )$ is the demand function for labor; cf. equation (12) on p. 135.

shift of this demand curve.   Thus the influence of commodity output on labor input reflects itself, not in the *variables* on which the labor demand function is dependent, but in its *form*.

More specifically, the influence of commodity output on labor input expresses itself in our model through the dynamic intermarket pressures discussed at the end of Chapter X:2.   As will be recalled from that discussion, if individuals do not succeed in buying all they want of a given good, they will use part of the unspent funds that accumulate in their hands to bid up the prices of other goods as well.   Similarly, if firms do not succeed in selling all they want of a given good, they will attempt to alleviate their resulting shortage of funds by reducing the prices of other goods as well.   The application of this principle to the case at hand is immediate.   As a result of the initial decrease in demand, a "glut" is created on the commodity market.   In particular, we see from Figure 35 that firms' sales fall short of their Y_0 output by BC units. The pressure of this excess output then causes firms to bid down not only the prices of commodities, but also the price of labor.   Indeed, this pressure manifests itself in a most concrete way.   For when firms planned the inputs of labor described by the demand curve in Figure 34, they assumed that they would be able to pay for these inputs with the sales proceeds of the resulting outputs.   Therefore, when these sales fail to materialize, firms find themselves with their funds tied up in illiquid inventories and hence financially unable to carry out their original plans.[7]   Accordingly, for the input of labor N_0 they now offer a real wage rate below that indicated by the demand curve of Figure 34; or, alternatively, at the real wage rate $(w/p)_0$ they now demand a smaller input.

Thus the initial decrease in commodity demand causes a corresponding decrease in the input of labor.   Clearly, the magnitudes of these decreases must be related.   In particular, assume that as a result of the market pressures just described, firms find themselves at the point L in Figure 34.   That is, at an unchanged real wage rate their labor input consists of N_2 units instead of N_0.   Let the corresponding commodity output [as given by the production function $Y = \phi(N, K_0)$ of page 128] be Y_2 in Figure 35.   Then we can see from this diagram that the firms' output will still exceed their sales by HJ units.   Hence the same market pressures of excess output and accumulating inventories which pushed labor input down from N_0 to N_2 will continue to push this input even further downwards.   Only when this input has been reduced to N_1, with a corresponding reduction in output to Y_1, will

---

7 I am indebted for this observation to Mr. Nissan Liviatan.

these pressures cease; for only then will firms finally succeed in selling all that they produce.

In this way the economy is brought to a position described by the point K in Figure 34 and its corresponding point G in Figure 35. But what must now be emphasized is that this position is *not* one of equilibrium: for at point K there is an excess supply of labor, $N_0 - N_1$, which continues to press down on the money wage rate, and at point G there is an excess supply of commodities, $Y_0 - Y_1$, which continues to press down on the price level.

The nature of both these dynamic pressures requires further clarification. Consider first the point G. Even though this point is not marked by an excess of *output*—firms are selling all they are producing —it is marked by an excess of *supply*. That is, despite the fact that firms have decreased their *actual* output to Y_1, the fact remains that the *optimum* output they *desire* to supply at the real wage rate $(w/p)_0$— *should the market be willing to absorb this output*—is still Y_0. In other words, since the real wage rate has, by assumption, remained unchanged, so has the vertical commodity supply curve. Hence at the point G there is an excess of desired over actual supply equal to $Y_0 - Y_1$ units of commodities. This manifests itself as an excess in the productive capacity of firms. And this idle capacity continues to induce firms to lower their prices in an attempt to increase their volume of sales and thereby return to the optimum output designated by their commodity supply curve.[8]

Consider now the point K in Figure 34. At first sight, $N_0 - N_1$ would seem to represent an excess demand for labor as well as an excess supply, for K is just as much to the left of the demand curve as to the supply curve. Accordingly, the point K would seem to be associated just as much with an upward pressure on the money wage rate as a downward one! But this absurdity is removed as soon as we recall that at the present stage of the analysis the demand curve in Figure 34 does *not* describe the actual behavior of firms; hence the input of labor which this curve specifies—N_0—is *not* really that which firms now attempt to purchase. On the other hand, nothing has happened

---

[8] Once again, I am indebted to Mr. Liviatan for calling my attention to the possible role of excess productive capacity in the dynamic process.

It might be useful at this point to remind the reader about the dual meaning of "Y" in Figure 35. As related to the demand side of the commodity market, it represents the alternative levels of real national *income* which may *actually prevail* in the economy. As related to the supply side, it represents the alternative optimum levels of real national *product* which firms *desire* to produce at different real wage rates. Accordingly, the numbers Y_0, Y_1, $Y_2, \ldots$ on the abscissa of Figure 35 represent now the former, now the latter—and now simply the output of firms, whether optimum or not.

to invalidate the supply curve of Figure 34 as a description of the actual behavior of workers.   Hence the point K is effectively marked only by an excess supply of labor.

Nevertheless, this simultaneous departure of K from both the demand and supply curves does seem unduly bizarre.   But a moment's reflection shows that it really expresses another simple—though usually neglected —fact.   Specifically, it expresses the involuntariness with which firms, no less than workers, must act during periods of unemployment.   For just as the latter are then not receiving as much employment as they would normally like at the prevailing real wage rate, so the former are not providing as much as they would normally like.   Both firms and workers are being coerced by the same *force majeure* of insufficient demand in the commodity market.   Both are thereby being prevented from achieving their optimum mode of behavior.   In particular, the involuntary departure of firms from their labor demand curve as revealed by point K in Figure 34 is the simple counterpart of their involuntary departure from their commodity supply curve as revealed by point G in Figure 35.   Not being able to sell all they want, they cannot employ all they want.   This is the neglected obverse side of involuntary unemployment.

We might, however, note that at the point K there no longer exist the unsold inventories and resulting illiquidity which we used above to explain why the input of labor is pushed leftwards from the points M and L of Figure 34.   Nevertheless, the pressures of these unsold inventories continue to exist in potentiality.   For should firms attempt to increase their input beyond N_1, they will immediately re-create these inventories and hence will be pushed back again to point K.

It might help to represent these ideas graphically by saying that as long as the demand conditions in the commodity market continue to be described by the curve E_2 in Figure 35, the corresponding "demand" conditions in the labor market are described by the kinked curve TAN_1 in Figure 34.   Though this is not a demand curve in the strict sense of the term, it does make clear that the input of labor is—under these conditions—effectively limited to N_1 units.   Correspondingly, it under-lines the fact already noted that the solid demand curve of Figure 34 no longer describes the behavior of firms and that, accordingly, no effective excess demand for labor exists at the point K.

Alternatively, such a kinked demand curve underlines the fact that at the point K the marginal product of labor is *not* represented by N_1A and hence does *not* exceed the real wage rate N_1K.   In brief, the kink at point A emphasizes that should firms increase their input beyond

N_1, they will not be able to sell the resulting additional output. Hence the marginal product of labor at this point is indeterminate.[9] We can now return to our main discussion and emphasize that it is within the foregoing framework of dynamic disequilibrium—and resulting downward pressures on both the price level and the money wage rate—that we must study the problem of involuntary unemployment. This is the real import of the innocuous tautology of the preceding section: not that involuntary unemployment can be defined away, but that it can have no meaning within the confines of static equilibrium analysis. Conversely, the essence of dynamic analysis is involuntariness: its domain consists only of positions *off* the demand or supply curves. Indeed, it is this very departure from these curves, and the resulting striving of individuals to return to the optimum behavior which they represent, which provides the motive power of the dynamic process itself.

Thus our first task in studying involuntary unemployment is to free ourselves of the mental habit—long ingrained by the methods of static analysis—of seeing only the points *on* the demand or supply curve. Once we do this, we find ourselves able to give precise expression to many intuitive, common-sense ideas which have all too frequently been unjustifiably rejected as violating the precepts of rigorous economic analysis. First we see that involuntary unemployment can exist even in a system of perfect competition and wage and price flexibility. In particular, the departure of K from the labor supply curve reflects the existence of involuntary unemployment to the extent $N_0 - N_1$. Second, we see that a deficiency in commodity demand can generate a decrease in labor input without requiring a prior increase in the real

---

[9] There is, nevertheless, a basic analytical problem here whose full solution is still not clear to me: The kink in the curve TAN_1 is one that exists from the viewpoint of the economy as a whole; but, by definition of perfect competition, this kink cannot be taken into account by any individual firm. Now, as already emphasized, at the point K there no longer exist the liquidity pressures of unsold inventories. What, then, keeps each individual firm from expanding its input until it reaches its demand curve for labor?

The answer may be that already implied in the text: each firm does indeed attempt to do this, but some of them then find themselves with unsold inventories which force them to contract input again. Thus K does not represent a static situation, but one in which there are always some firms expanding input and output, and others contracting—though, as long as commodity demand conditions remain unchanged, never in the aggregate succeeding in moving to the right of K.

Another possibility is that these repeated frustrating experiences lead firms to disregard completely their ordinary demand curves as guides to optimum behavior. But this then leaves the question as to how they do determine their behavior. It may be that, as Mr. Liviatan has suggested, a complete answer to this question depends on the development of a theory of the firm operating under conditions of uncertainty with respect to the size of its market.

wage rate. For since the point K is not on the demand curve for labor either, it is not bound by the standard inverse relation between labor input and the real wage rate which this curve specifies.[10] Both of these implications will be discussed further in the next chapter.

3. As just emphasized, the position represented by point K in Figure 34 and point G in Figure 35 is not an equilibrium one. In particular, the excess supplies of the two markets described by these diagrams reinforce each other in exerting a downward pressure on both wages and prices. Let us assume for the moment that these decline in the same proportion (so that the real wage rate is not affected) and examine the implications of this movement for the magnitude of involuntary unemployment.

As explained at the beginning of the preceding section, this price decline creates a positive real-balance effect which exerts both a direct and (through its depressing effect on interest in the bond market) indirect upward pressure on the aggregate demand curve for commodities. Assume that as a result of these pressures this curve rises to, say, E_3 in Figure 35. If firms continued with their output of Y_1, they would find their inventories being drawn down below the desirable level. Hence, by the reverse of the argument of the preceding section, they will increase their labor input above N_1 and, accordingly, their commodity output above Y_1. Clearly, this process will continue until employment has risen to N_2 and output to Y_2. At these levels there will once again be neither a deficiency nor an excess of actual output—though, as we shall emphasize in a moment, this output is still less than that which firms would like to produce.

This possibility of an automatic decrease in the extent of involuntary unemployment is what is denied by the usual oversimplified statement of the Keynesian position. According to it, any attempt of firms to increase their labor input to N_2 would result in an output Y_2, which could not be sold. Indeed, at such an output there would, in Figure 35, be a deflationary gap of HJ which would compel firms to reduce output and, accordingly, input until they had once again returned to Y_1 and N_1, respectively.[11] This argument is clearly based on the tacit assumption that the aggregate commodity demand curve remains unchanged at E_2. In brief, here, as elsewhere, Keynesian economics overlooks the direct influence of the real-balance effect on this demand.[12] Similarly,

---

[10] It might be noted that this inverse relation characterizes the Keynesian theory of employment no less than the classical. Cf. the *General Theory*, pp. 17–18.

[11] Cf. *General Theory*, pp. 261–62.

[12] See Note K:1. On the overlooking of the supply side, see Note M.

it overlooks the supply side of the commodity market which, by its excess over the demand, generates this effect.

Leaving this doctrinal issue behind, we now apply the argument of the preceding section to show that the dynamic process cannot stop at the stage represented by the output Y_2 and input N_2. For with the real wage rate unchanged at $(w/p)_0$, there is still at the point L in Figure 34 an excess supply of labor exerting a downward pressure on wages. Similarly, there is still at the point H in Figure 35 an excess of desired over actual supply of commodities; for since the real wage rate has remained unchanged, so too has the vertical supply curve at Y_0. Hence there remains an excess supply of $Y_0 - Y_2$ (which manifests itself once again in the form of excess productive capacity) exerting a downward pressure on the price level.

Let us continue with our assumption that wages and prices always decline in exactly the same proportion. Then the dynamic process in its entirety can be summarized in the following terms: The initial decrease in commodity demand creates a state of involuntary unemployment. But it also generates a price decline and a consequent real-balance effect which—both directly and indirectly—tends to force this demand up again. As the demand curve rises, it pulls commodity output up after it. And this pulls labor input up concurrently. In particular, as output is pulled diagonally upwards along the 45° radius vector in Figure 35, input is pulled correspondingly rightwards along the horizontal dotted line corresponding to the unchanged real wage rate $(w/p)_0$ in Figure 34. In this way the extent of involuntary unemployment is continuously diminished.

If this process is successful, it will continue until the aggregate demand curve is raised sufficiently to be able once again to absorb the output Y_0. That is, it will bring the economy once again to point B in Figure 35. The resulting disappearance of the excess supply of commodities will have two simultaneous effects. First, it will eliminate the downward pressure on the price level which previously emanated from this market. Second, it will eliminate the dynamic cross-pressure on the labor market which prevented firms from being on their demand curve there. That is, since firms will be able to sell Y_0 units of commodities, they will be willing once again to employ the N_0 workers represented by the point M on the demand curve in Figure 34. Hence involuntary unemployment will disappear from this market and with it the downward pressure on the wage level. Thus both activating forces of the preceding dynamic process will be removed. Correspondingly, the economy will have been brought to a new equilibrium position. By definition[13]—and like any other overall equilibrium position—this position is one of full employment. It differs from the original one only in having lower levels of wages, prices, and interest.

The essential nature of this equilibrating process is not changed if wages and prices do not initially fall in the same proportion. The major difference will be that the real wage rate, and hence the commodity supply curve, will no longer remain constant during the period of adjustment. Thus consider the special case in which the price decline that raises the demand curve in Figure 35 to E_3 is accompanied by a wage decline which lags behind just sufficiently to raise the real wage rate to $(w/p)_2$. At this rate nothing prevents firms from employing the N_2 units specified by the demand curve in Figure 34. For, as can be seen from Figure 35, the conditions of demand in the commodity market are such that firms will be able to sell the full output of Y_2 corresponding to the input of N_2.

In brief, under these assumptions the economy will reach the position described by the point D in Figure 34 and the point H in Figure 35. What distinguishes this position from the one described in the preceding section is that the commodity market is no longer in disequilibrium. For, as already indicated, the rise in the real wage rate has decreased the optimum output of firms. In particular, it has shifted the vertical supply curve as a whole from Y_0 leftwards to Y_2 (a movement *not* shown in Figure 35).[14] Hence there is no excess of either actual or desired output in the commodity market. In other words, there is neither excess output nor excess capacity: firms are producing and selling exactly the optimum output corresponding to the real wage rate $(w/p)_2$. Hence no downward pressure on prices emanates from this market.

On the other hand, the labor market is obviously *not* in equilibrium. In particular, the involuntary unemployment (excess supply of labor) which exists at the real wage rate $(w/p)_2$ will continue pressing the money wage rate downwards. This will reduce the real wage rate, thereby push the optimum labor input and hence the commodity supply curve rightwards again, and thereby renew the downward pressure of excess capacity on the price level. The real-balance effect resulting from the price decline will then renew the upward push on the aggregate demand curve. In this way the economy will once again be propelled back toward the same full-employment equilibrium position of the preceding case. The primary effect of the initial "stickiness" in money wages

---

[13] Cf. p. 212.
[14] For further details on such shifts, see p. 135.

will thus be a prolongation of the dynamic adjustment process into which the economy is thrown by the initial decrease in demand.

Consider now the opposite case in which the wage rate falls faster than the price level, so that the labor market is brought, say, to the point S in Figure 34. Here, by definition, full employment prevails. But this reduction in the real wage rate has shifted the vertical supply curve in Figure 35 to the right of Y_0 (again, not shown in the diagram) and has thereby increased the pressures of excess capacity in the commodity market. Hence the price level will continue to fall, the real wage rate will accordingly rise, and involuntary unemployment will accordingly be re-created. In this way the economy will continue moving toward its overall equilibrium position.

If, however, either the wage rate or the price level is absolutely rigid, this dynamic process cannot work itself through to a successful culmination. In particular, if there were absolute wage rigidity, the process described two paragraphs above would be arrested at the point D in Figure 34 and its related point H in Figure 35. Because of the failure of the real wage rate to fall below $(w/p)_2$, firms would have no inducement to expand input and hence output. Correspondingly, the commodity supply curves would not shift rightwards again. Similarly, if the price level were absolutely rigid, there could be no real-balance effect to stimulate aggregate demand either directly or indirectly. Hence there would be no force to pull output and input back to their full-employment levels. Thus as long as either of these rigidities prevails, the system must remain in a state of unemployment disequilibrium.

The argument of this chapter can now be summarized in the following terms: Equilibrium means full employment, or, equivalently, unemployment means disequilibrium. Hence our study of the corrective market forces automatically generated by the presence of involuntary unemployment is a study of the dynamic workings of an economy in disequilibrium. And the assumption made until now, that, granted flexibility, these forces will restore the economy to a state of full employment, is an assumption that the economy is consistent and stable; that, in other words, an equilibrium position always exists and that the economy will always converge to it. More specifically, it is an assumption that just as the market can "solve" the system of excess-demand equations in Chapter X:1 when the level of real income is held constant during the *tâtonnement*, so can it solve it when the level of real income (and hence employment) is also permitted to vary. This is the conceptual framework within which we must analyze the problem of involuntary unemployment.

4. Deferring further examination of the case of flexible wages and prices to the next chapter, let us now analyze a case of absolute rigidity which has special importance for monetary theory.   Assume that such a rigidity has persisted from the very inception of the dynamic process. Then after the downward shift in demand from E to E_2 in Figure 35 has brought the economy to the position described by point G in this diagram and its related point K in Figure 34, no corrective force will operate to move it back to a full-employment position again.   More specifically, whatever reduction in interest has been directly caused by the increased demand for bonds which may have accompanied the decreased demand for commodities is already reflected in the curve E_2. And, in the absence of a price decline, there will be no real-balance effect to exert any further influence—direct or indirect—upon it.[15]

Into an economy in this position let us now introduce an increase in the amount of money or a neutral decrease in liquidity preference. Either of these changes generates an upward shift in the commodity demand curve and rightward and leftward shifts, respectively, in the bond demand and supply curves.   This causes a fall in the rate of interest, which pushes the aggregate demand curve even further upwards.   Assume that as a result of both of these pressures the demand curve is raised to the position represented by E_3 in Figure 35.   Accordingly, just as in the preceding section, firms will increase their commodity output to Y_2 and hence their labor input to N_2.   That is, the economy will move to—and remain at—the position described by point L in Figure 34 and point H in Figure 35.

Thus we have here a form of comparative-statics analysis—with the difference that neither the initial nor final position is one of general equilibrium.   In particular, our "comparative-statics" theorem states that if we begin from a situation of involuntary unemployment, and if wages and prices are absolutely rigid, then an increase in the amount of money causes an increase in real national product and employment and a decrease in the rate of interest.   Clearly, this result holds for a neutral decrease in liquidity preference as well.[16]

The argument can, of course, be presented alternatively in terms of the money market.   As in Chapter XI:1, write the equilibrium condition of this market in the special form

(1) $$p \cdot L_1(Y) + p \cdot L_2\left(r, \frac{M_0}{p}\right) = M_0,$$

---

15 Cf. beginning of Section 2 above.
16 Note the tacit assumption that the increase in real income increases demand and supply equally in the bond market; cf. pp. 197–98.   Note also that a change in the amount of money affects interest whether used to finance budgetary expenditures or open-market operations; cf. Chapter XII:5.

where p is now assumed constant. A doubling of the amount of money will cause the speculative demand to increase somewhat because of the real-balance effect. It will also cause an increase in the transactions demand through its effect in increasing real income, Y. But—to paraphrase Keynes—there is clearly no reason to expect these increases to absorb all of the increase in the amount of money. In terms of Figure 25 (though disregarding the functional descriptions attached to its curves) they will shift the demand curve over from position I to II and the supply curve over from $M^s = M_0$ to $M^s = 2M_0$, leaving the excess supply EF. Hence part of the monetary increase will find an outlet in the purchase of securities. And these purchases will continue until they have depressed the rate of interest sufficiently to bring about such an increase in the speculative demand that it, together with the increase in the transactions demand brought about by the increase in real income, suffices to absorb all the new money. This new equilibrium position is represented in Figure 25 by the intersection of demand curve II with the supply curve $M^s = 2M_0$ at the rate of interest r_3.[17]

The analysis of this section can be instructively summarized in terms of a diagram which is conceptually analogous to Figure 18.[18] Let us first construct the general-equilibrium system of equations which corresponds to our present set of assumptions. This can be set out as follows:

	Condition for Equilibrium	Market
(2)	$F\left(Y, r, \dfrac{M_0}{p_0}\right) = Y$	Commodities
(3)	$H\left(Y, \dfrac{1}{r}, \dfrac{M_0^H}{p_0}\right) = J\left(Y, \dfrac{1}{r}, \dfrac{M_0^F}{p_0}\right)$	Real bond holdings
(4)	$L\left(Y, r, \dfrac{M_0}{p_0}\right) = \dfrac{M_0}{p_0}$	Real money holdings

Here we have dropped the special form of the demand function specified in (1) and returned to the more general one of Chapter IX:5. The

---

17 I have deliberately phrased the discussion here to parallel that on p. 194 above in order to bring out the similarities and differences of the two interpretations of the same passage in the *General Theory* (p. 200) which they respectively offer. This passage by itself is sufficiently ambiguous to admit of either interpretation. But, as implied on p. 194 above, the evidence of cognate passages makes it clear that the interpretation presented there is the one which really identifies the crucial element in Keynesian interest theory. For further discussion, see Chapter XV below.

18 The following diagrammatic analysis is adapted from the well-known one which Hicks first presented in his "Mr. Keynes and the 'Classics': A Suggested Interpretation," *Econometrica*, V (1937), as reprinted in *Readings in the Theory of Income Distribution*, ed. W. Fellner and B. F. Haley (Philadelphia, 1946), p. 469. Cf. also Modigliani, *op. cit.*, pp. 198–204.

basic differentia of the foregoing system—as contrasted with that of Chapter X:1—is that Y and p have reversed their roles: the former is now a variable and the latter a constant. Because of this assumed absolute price—and wage—rigidity, we also ignore the labor market, which, as already noted, is assumed to remain unchanged in a state of disequilibrium. Similarly, we ignore the aggregate supply function in the commodity market, which no longer can cause the price level to vary. Correspondingly, the "equilibrium" in the commodity market is one of *output*, not of *supply* (page 218). For simplicity, we have also re-written the bond and money equations of Chapter X:1 in real terms.

Consider now the commodity market and assume it to be in a state of equilibrium of the type just described. Let real national product, Y, now increase. Because of the assumed less-than-unity marginal propensity to spend, this increases the demand for commodities by a smaller amount. Hence an excess output is created in the commodity market. In order to restore equilibrium to this market, demand must therefore be stimulated by a decrease in interest. We can in this way generate the curve GG in Figure 36. This curve is the diagrammatic representation of equilibrium condition (2): it is the locus of all pairs of r and Y at which the commodity market can be in equilibrium. By the argument just presented, it must have a negative slope throughout.[19]

At any point to the right of GG, there is an excess of output, hence an accumulation of unwanted inventories, and hence a pressure on firms to decrease their output. Conversely, at any point to the left of GG, there is an excess of demand, hence a drawing down of inventories below their optimum level, and hence a pressure on firms to increase their output. These dynamic pressures are represented by the horizontal arrows of Figure 36.

Let us now turn to the bond market and assume it also to be in an initial state of equilibrium at the rate of interest r_0. Let Y now increase. Under the assumption that this increases the demand and supply for bonds equally, the state of equilibrium in this market continues undisturbed at the unchanged rate of interest r_0. Hence the curve PP— which represents the locus of all equilibrium points in the bond market —is a straight horizontal line at the corresponding height. This line is, of course, the diagrammatic representation of equilibrium condition (3) under our stated assumption. At any point above PP, there is an excess demand for bonds, driving the rate of interest down again; at

---

[19] This is Hicks' *IS* curve; for, as emphasized in Chapter XI:6, the savings = investment condition (from which Hicks derives his curve) is equivalent to the equilibrium condition in the commodity market.

any point below, an excess supply, driving it up. These dynamic pressures are represented by the vertical arrows of Figure 36.

The intersection of GG and PP at point s indicates the rate of interest and level of real national income—r_0 and Y_1—which can simultaneously equilibrate the commodity and bond markets. The arrows of Figure 36 then show us that there always exist automatic

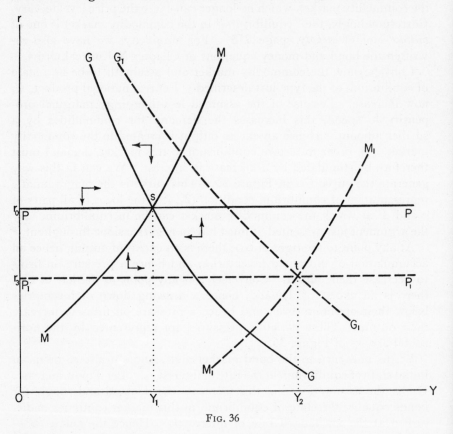

FIG. 36

market forces to drive at least one of the variables in the direction of its equilibrium value. Hence the system is stable and converges to the equilibrium point s.[20]

The curves GG and PP correspond to the initial amount of money M_0. Let this now be increased to $2M_0$. Then GG shifts upwards to, say, G_1G_1: at any given level of real income the rate of interest must be higher in order to eliminate the inflationary gap otherwise created by

[20] For a more rigorous demonstration, see Mathematical Appendix 10:*a.*

the positive real-balance effect of the monetary increase. Similarly, this real-balance effect shifts PP downwards to, say, P_1P_1. The intersection of G_1G_1 and P_1P_1 at point t then indicates the new equilibrium position corresponding to the lower rate of interest, r_3, and the higher level of real national income, Y_2.

If, instead, the analysis is carried out in terms of the commodity and money markets, PP in Figure 36 is replaced by MM. The latter is the diagrammatic representation of equation (4): it is the locus of all points at which the money market can be in equilibrium. Its positive slope represents the fact that an increase in Y increases the amount of money demanded for transactions purposes; hence, in order to maintain equilibrium in this market, this increase must be offset by an increase in interest. The curve MM must, of course, also pass through the point s.[21]

An increase in the amount of money now shifts MM downwards to, say, M_1M_1. In the Keynesian case, where there is no real-balance effect in the commodity market, GG remains unchanged. Hence the new intersection point must obviously be at a rate of interest below r_0 and level of real national income above Y_1. But even in the more general case, where GG also shifts rightwards, it can be shown[22] that it does so less than MM, so that it continues to intersect the latter at a lower rate of interest. This is the implicit assumption of Figure 36.

We might now note that the variability of the equilibrium rate of interest in the analysis of the present section, as compared to its invariance in the case of flexible prices, has a heuristic explanation. In the latter case, an increase in the nominal quantity of money does not in the long run affect its real quantity; hence it does not permanently affect the rate of interest. In the present case, however, because of the price rigidity, the real quantity does permanently increase; hence the rate of interest must generally be affected. From this we can see that to the extent that the price level rises instead of remaining fixed, the effect of a monetary increase on interest and employment is accordingly diminished. In any event, it is clear that the assumptions of the present section carry us into a Keynesian world of unemployment

---

[21] This curve is identical in conception with Hicks' LL. But, unlike his curve, ours does not have a horizontal section near the ordinate. This is a direct consequence of the fact that—in contrast to Hicks'—our demand curve for money does not become a straight horizontal line at a minimum rate of interest, but instead retains its negative slope throughout. Cf. Chapter X:5. But the form of PP may be restricted; see p. 248.

[22] This is essentially what is done in equations (10.11)–(10.19) of Mathematical Appendix 10:*a*.

in which monetary changes express themselves primarily in changes in the level of real national income and the rate of interest, and only secondarily—if at all—in changes in the level of prices.[23]

There is, however, one special case in which—even under the assumption of absolute price rigidity—an increase in the amount of money will affect neither employment nor interest. For generality, assume now that there are government bonds outstanding. Accordingly, let the

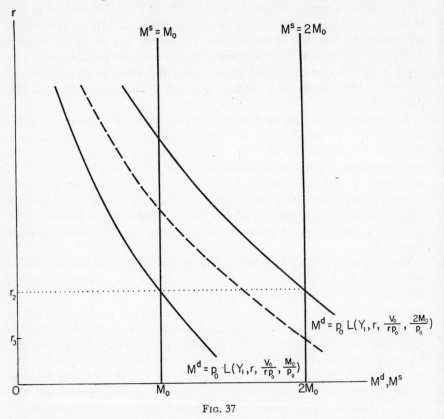

FIG. 37

left-hand curve in Figure 37 represent the demand for money corresponding to the fixed price level, p_0; the less-than-full-employment level

---

[23] The merely heuristic nature of this argument is evident from the immediately following discussion of a case in which the rate of interest remains invariant even though the real quantity of money increases. The reader will also recall the warnings on p. 184 about the pitfalls inherent in reasoning from the real quantity of money to the equilibrium rate of interest. In connection with that discussion, however, note that in the present case the real quantity of money is actually an independent variable of the system; for both the nominal quantity of money and the absolute price level are assumed to be exogenously determined.

of national income, Y_1; the amount of government-bond holdings out-standing, V_0; and initial money holdings, M_0. Let the government now double these holdings by printing new money which it distributes as unemployment compensation. Assume now that such a state of uncertainty exists in the economy that individuals do not use these increased holdings for purchasing either more commodities or more bonds, but merely for augmenting their cash balances. That is, assume that the real-balance effect operates only in the money market. Then, as shown in Figure 37, the demand curve for money will shift over to the right in such a way that at the original rate of interest r_2 and price level p_0 twice as much money will now be demanded as before. Hence monetary expansion in this case does not reduce the rate of interest. Nor, by assumption, does it affect aggregate demand and thereby the level of real national income.[24]

Once, however, we permit the government to use its newly printed money to finance open-market purchases, this invariance disappears. Even if we make the same assumptions as in the preceding paragraph, the demand curve will not shift over twice as far to the right. For the government purchases have reduced the bond holdings of individuals below V_0. This reduction in the wealth of individuals causes them, *ceteris paribus*, to economize on their holdings of money as well as on their consumption of other goods. Hence this creates a leftward shift in the demand curve for money which tends to offset the rightward shift created by the increase in real balances. That is, the open-market purchase sets into operation two opposing forces in the money market. Correspondingly, the demand curve in this market will not shift over in the way described in the preceding paragraph, but will instead occupy the midway position represented, say, by the dashed curve in Figure 37. It follows that there is now an excess supply of money at the original rate r_2, driving interest down. This, in turn, causes the aggregate demand curve for commodities to rise. Final equilibrium is accordingly established at a rate of interest below r_2 and a level of national income above Y_1.

Viewed within the framework of the bond market, the preceding argument acquires a straightforward interpretation. No matter what the individuals of the economy do with the new money they have received, the open-market purchase has decreased the number of government bonds outstanding and has thus shifted the supply curve

---

24 Strictly speaking, this is *not* a case of an increase in the amount of money completely offset by an increase in liquidity preference; for the latter implies a change in the demand *function* for money, and no such change has taken place here.

for bonds leftwards.   Hence the price of bonds must rise—which means that interest must decline.[25]

_____

[25] The analysis of this special case should be considered against the background of Chapter XII:5.

Mathematical Appendix 10:*b* points out a certain inaccuracy in Figure 37.   It also describes certain unlikely circumstances in which even open-market operations will not affect interest.

CHAPTER XIV

Keynesian Versus Classical Theories of Employment: An Interpretation

1. *Keynesian and classical theories of involuntary unemployment.* 2. *The multiplier.* 3. *True and false limits on monetary policy.* 4. *Say's Identity again.* 5. *The problem of secular stagnation.*

1. Let us now develop the argument of the preceding chapter into an analytical framework for interpreting the current debate between Keynesian and classical theories of employment.

As the reader has undoubtedly noticed, the stable dynamic process assumed to operate in Chapter XIII:3 is, in a significant sense, the reverse image of the dynamic process described in Chapter X:3. Just as this earlier process relies upon the inflationary price movement itself to remove the inflationary pressures which initiated it, so our present one relies upon the deflationary price movement itself to remove the deflationary pressures which initiated it. It is precisely this necessity for a major price decline which makes this process unacceptable as a primary ingredient of a modern full-employment policy.[1]

Let us, then, temper this process by supplementing it with the traditional discretionary open-market and rediscounting operations of a central bank. The immediate implication of such operations is that a decline in the rate of interest need no longer wait, as it did in Chapter XIII:2, for a decline in prices. Instead, open-market purchases replace the real-balance effect as the source of increased demand in the bond

---

[1] This will be discussed further below.

233

market.   In this way, by primary reliance on a manipulated lowering of the rate of interest, aggregate demand might be raised to its full-employment level without any prior decline in prices.   Indeed, in this Wicksellian world, such a decline would itself be taken as evidence that the rate of interest had not been lowered sufficiently.[2]

It is the belief in the efficacy of this monetary policy which will be identified here with the neoclassical position.   Correspondingly, it is the denial of this efficacy which will be identified with the Keynesian one.   According to this position, the great degree of uncertainty which surrounds any investment plan makes it unlikely that interest variations of a practical magnitude can be depended upon to stimulate such activity significantly.[3]   Hence, though working in the proper direction, interest reductions are too weak to justify the reliance placed upon them by monetary policy.   For this reason such a policy will not be able to close a deflationary gap with the speed necessary to prevent a protracted price decline.

Thus the success of monetary policy depends ultimately on the stability of the dynamic process initiated by this decline.   This brings us right back to the analysis of Chapter XIII:3.   But now—in order to present the Keynesian position in its entirety—we shall have to introduce into this analysis two hitherto neglected factors.[4]

There is, first of all, the question of distribution effects.   As emphasized in Chapter XII:3, we cannot assume that the negative indebtedness effects of debtors are simply canceled out by the positive effects of creditors.   More specifically—and in Keynes' words—"if the fall of wages and prices goes far, the embarrassment of those entrepreneurs who are heavily indebted may soon reach the point of insolvency,—with severely adverse effects on investment."   In brief, a protracted price decline will cause a wave of bankruptcies which will eliminate both the firms' liabilities and the households' assets, and leave only a seriously impaired state of business confidence.

Second, there is the influence of expectations.   To the extent that the monetary authorities reduce interest only by slow stages, potential investors may delay carrying out their plans in anticipation of benefiting from still lower rates.   Similarly, and more important, the protracted

---

[2] *Interest and Prices*, pp. 189 *et passim*.

[3] On this insensitivity, see Oscar Lange, *Price Flexibility and Employment* (Bloomington, Ind., 1945), p. 85, and the references to empirical studies there cited.   For an excellent theoretical discussion, see G. L. S. Shackle, "Interest Rates and the Pace of Investment," *Economic Journal*, LVI (1946), 1–17.   See also Hicks, *Value and Capital*, pp. 225–26.

[4] The following interpretation of Keynes takes as its point of departure the stimulating discussion of L. R. Klein, *The Keynesian Revolution* (New York, 1947), pp. 80–90, 206–13.

decline in prices and wages will create the expectation of still further declines, and thus lead both households and firms to postpone their purchases. In particular, the anticipation of a lower future price level has the same effects on the amount of labor demanded as a rise in the current real wage rate. For, in making their plans, firms will compare the wage paid for current input with the lower price that will subsequently be received for its resulting output. Due to these factors, the stimulating real-balance effect of a price decline may be more than offset by its depressing expectation effects.[5]

Lest the reader think that this present emphasis on expectations after their deëmphasis above is a piece of rank opportunism, we should point out that this distinction can be rationally justified. In Chapter XII:6 we were concerned with an inflationary process. Hence there was reason to believe that the continuous contraction in the real quantity of money held by individuals would ultimately make it impossible for them to finance the increased demand for goods called for by their expectations, and would thus eventually compel them to modify these expectations themselves. No such restrictive—and hence corrective—influence operates in the case of deflationary expectations; for the passive postponement of expenditures encouraged by them does not have to be financed. This asymmetry is analogous to the one frequently emphasized in connection with the activities of a central bank: the attempts of such a bank to combat inflation by contracting member-bank reserves are more likely to succeed than its attempts to combat deflation by expanding them.

Thus Keynesian economics is the economics of unemployment *dis*equilibrium. It argues that as a result of interest-inelasticity, on the one hand, and distribution and expectation effects, on the other, the dynamic process of Chapter XIII:3—even when aided by monetary policy—is unlikely to converge either smoothly or rapidly to the full-employment equilibrium position. Indeed, if these influences are sufficiently strong, they may even render this process unstable. In such a case the return to full employment would have to await the

---

[5] This and the preceding paragraph are largely adapted from Keynes' discussion in the *General Theory* of the effects to be expected from a protracted decline in money wages and prices. See, in particular, *ibid.*, pp. 205–8, 232–34, and 260–69. The quotation in the preceding paragraph is from p. 264.

It should be clear that we are referring here to the real-balance effect in the broad sense described on p. 206, footnote 17, and not in the proper sense which restricts it to hand-to-hand currency in circulation. For evidence which suggests that even in this broad sense the real-balance effect was of little help in overcoming the unemployment of the 1930's, see the data in the source there cited. These show that over the period 1929–32, real balances *increased* by 46 per cent, while real national product *decreased* by 40 per cent.

fortunate advent of some exogenous force that would expand aggregate demand sufficiently.

A more extreme possibility is that, even without taking into account the discouraging effects of adverse expectations, the stimulating effects of interest and price declines may be too weak ever to generate an aggregate demand strong enough to absorb the output of full employment. That is, these effects may succeed only in raising the aggregate demand curve asymptotically to a less-than-full-employment level. This will be true if the indefinitely increasing real balances generated by the decreasing price level are dissipated to an ever increasing extent in the money market—until, indeed (by the budget restraint), the real demand in this market becomes infinite.[6] Such a possibility involves a denial of the hitherto unquestioned assumption that our basic system of excess-demand equations in Chapter X:1 is consistent. In other words, it contends that, apart from all dynamic considerations, there may exist no set of wages, prices, and interest that can simultaneously equilibrate all the markets of this system. Without committing ourselves as to the reasonableness of this possibility within a static-expectation framework, we note that the inconsistency which it proposes is operationally equivalent to the instability of a consistent system: in neither case do the dynamic forces of the economy succeed in bringing it to an equilibrium position; but in the former case this failure is inherent in the simple fact that no such position exists.[7]

But it is not necessary to go to either of these analytical extremes. As already indicated, even if monetary policy could definitely restore the economy to full employment, there would still remain the crucial question of the length of time it would need. There would still remain the very real possibility that it would necessitate subjecting the economy to an intolerably long period of dynamic adjustment: a period during which wages, prices, and interest would continue to fall, and—what is most important—a period during which varying numbers of workers would continue to suffer from involuntary unemployment. Though I am not aware that he expressed himself in this way, this is the essence

---

6 Cf. pp. 230–31 above. The reason the increase in real balances cannot alternatively find an infinite outlet in the bond market will become clear in Section 3 below.

The reader interested in further details of this asymptotic case is referred to my "Price Flexibility and Full Employment," *op. cit.*, pp. 266–68.

7 Note the economic interpretation this paragraph gives to an inconsistent system. Such a system can be described by any one of the following three equivalent statements: It is impossible for everyone simultaneously to be on his demand and/or supply curve. It is impossible for everyone simultaneously to act voluntarily. It is impossible for the system ever to be in equilibrium; for there must always exist excess demands or supplies to propel it away from whatever position at which it happens to be.

of Keynes' position. This is all that need be established in order to justify his fundamental policy conclusion that the "self-adjusting quality of the economic system"—even when reinforced by central-bank policy—is not enough.[8]

This interpretation forces upon Keynesian economics the abandonment of the once-revolutionary "diagonal-cross" diagram with which it swept its way into the textbooks. It compels it to recognize that this diagram takes account neither of the supply side of the commodity market nor of the real-balance effect which its excess over the demand side generates. It therefore compels it to concede that (in terms of Figure 35) the intersection of the aggregate demand curve, E_2, with the 45° diagonal at G does not imply that there exist no automatic market forces to push real income up from the unemployment level Y_1. Indeed, it compels it to accept the classical contention that such forces not only exist, but even succeed eventually in raising income to the full-employment level Y_0.[9]

But this narrowing of the analytical distance between Keynesian and classical economics does not generate a corresponding narrowing of the policy distance. It still leaves Keynes insisting that the inefficacy of the automatic adjusting process is so great as to be remediable only by a program of direct government investment in public works.[10] And it still leaves modern-day adherents of the classical view conceding the inefficacy of monetary policy by itself, but insisting that it need only be supplemented by an automatic system of contracyclical tax remissions and transfer payments.[11] In brief, our interpretation takes the debate on the degree of government intervention necessary for a practicable full-employment policy out of the realm of those questions that can be decided by a priori considerations of internal consistency and logical validity, and into the realm of those questions that can be decided only by empirical consideration of the actual magnitudes of the relevant economic parameters.

While our interpretation takes off the analytical edge of Keynesian economics in one direction, it sharpens it in another, more vital one. It makes unmistakably clear—what should always have been clear[12]— that the involuntary unemployment of the *General Theory* need *not*

---

[8] *General Theory*, pp. 266–67 and 378.   These passages are cited in full in Note K:3.

[9] These limitations of the standard Keynesian diagram have already been noted on pp. 221–22.   On its overlooking of the supply side, see again Note M.

[10] *General Theory*, p. 378.

[11] Cf., e.g., the members of the "Chicago school"—H. C. Simons, *Economic Policy for a Free Society* (Chicago, 1948), pp. 40–77, 160–83; L. W. Mints, *Monetary Policy for a Competitive Society* (New York, 1950); Milton Friedman, *op. cit.*, pp. 133–56.

[12] For supporting references, see Note K:3.

have its origin in wage rigidities.   Indeed, in this respect we are more Keynesian than Keynes.   For by unequivocally placing the center of emphasis on the inadequacy of aggregate demand in the commodity market, and by recognizing the resulting involuntary unemployment to be a phenomenon of economic dynamics, we have freed ourselves from the static necessity of connecting decreases in employment with increases in the real wage rate.   We have been able to explain the existence of involuntary unemployment without placing any restrictions whatsoever on the movement of the real wage rate.[13]   Conversely, we have shown that reductions in this rate are neither a necessary nor a sufficient condition for the rapid reëstablishment of full-employment equilibrium in the economy.

Correspondingly, our interpretation does not tie the Keynesian theory of unemployment down to any special form of the supply function for labor.   In particular, it is independent of the all-too-frequent assumption that this theory presupposes a supply curve for labor as represented in Figure 38.   The crucial characteristic of this curve is that it remains infinitely elastic at the prevailing—and presumed rigid—money wage rate w_0 until the point N_0.   Accordingly, writers who make use of this curve identify this maximum amount of employment workers are willing to offer at the rate w_0 with the level of "full employment" and define involuntary unemployment as the difference between this level and the one actually existing in the economy, say N_1.[14]

In fact, one cannot escape the impression that Figure 38 is another reflection of the ingrained habit already mentioned (page 220) of seeing only the points *on* the supply curve.   More specifically, the line of reasoning which brought writers to posit a supply curve of the shape specified in Figure 38 seems to have been the following: If the curve did not have this shape, but instead always rose (no matter how slowly), and if at every wage rate workers were always at the uniquely corresponding point upon the curve, then, by definition, no involuntary unemployment could ever exist in the system: workers would always be receiving just exactly as much employment as they desired at the prevailing wage rate.   Hence in order to be able to speak of such unemployment and yet retain the assumption that workers are on their curve, it is necessary to drop the habitual assumption that the supply curve is single-valued and to represent it, instead, as specifying more than

[13] As pointed out on p. 221, Keynes does accept this restriction; cf. *General Theory*, pp. 17–18.
[14] Cf., e.g., Modigliani, *op. cit.*, p. 189.   This also seems to be Keynes' view in the *General Theory*, pp. 8–9, 295, 301–3, and 336.   In any event, it is definitely the way Lange interprets him (*Price Flexibility and Employment*, p. 6, footnote 4).

238

one amount supplied at a given wage rate.   Involuntary unemployment can then be defined as the difference between two points—both of which lie on the same supply curve and correspond to the same wage rate. This is clearly the significance of the horizontal line segment $N_1 N_0$ in Figure 38.

Correspondingly, once we free ourselves of this inhibition against seeing points *off* the supply curve, and once we recognize that the essence of involuntary unemployment is, indeed, being off this curve,

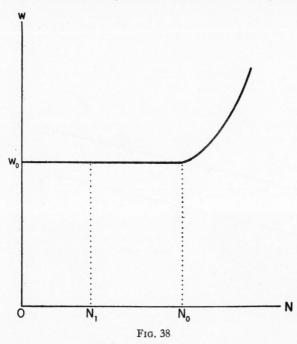

FIG. 38

the necessity for positing any special shape of the labor supply curve in order to be able to speak of involuntary unemployment disappears. This should be clear from the whole argument of Chapter XIII:1–3.

This is not to say that money wage rigidities do not aggravate the depth and duration of involuntary unemployment.   Clearly—as the analysis at the end of Chapter XIII:3 shows—they do.   But it is to deny that such rigidities are logically necessary for the genesis or even persistence of involuntary unemployment.   And it is to deny that even the complete absence of such rigidities would assure the elimination of this unemployment within a socially acceptable period of time.

Nevertheless, our theory does depend on rigidities.   For, by definition, any system which fails to respond quickly and smoothly to equilibrating market forces is suffering from rigidities. But the offending rigidities are not those of extraneous monopolistic elements interfering with the otherwise smooth functioning of a capitalist economy, but those inherent in the very fact that the level of aggregate commodity demand in such an economy is the resultant of individual decisions to consume and to invest, and that these decisions respond

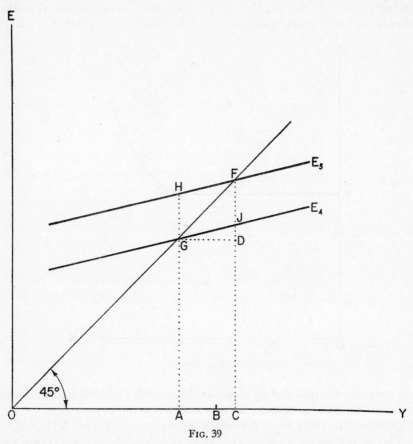

FIG. 39

only "stickily" to market changes in interest and prices. They are the rigidities of sovereign consumers and investors unwilling to modify their expenditure habits on short notice.

2. The preceding interpretation omits two familiar elements of Keynesian economics: the multiplier and the minimum level below which interest cannot fall. With the aid of some modifications, the first of these, as we shall now see, can be introduced into the argument;

but the second, as we shall see in the next section, is based on certain misunderstandings.

We must first distinguish between the "instantaneous" multiplier of comparative-statics analysis and the "successive-period" multiplier of dynamic analysis.[15] The former describes the outcome of a conceptual experiment in which we take an economy at rest in an initial position of unemployment; exogenously inject into it a *permanent* increase in, say, annual government expenditure (that is, one that will continue to remain in force for every future year too); permit this change to work itself out in all its manifestations until the economy once again reaches a position of rest; and then compare the increase in the level of annual national income as between the new and original positions (denoted by ΔY) with the exogenous increase in annual government expenditures (denoted by ΔG).[16]

The graphical technique by which the formula for this multiplier can be derived is quite familiar. Consider the description of the commodity market in Figure 39, where, for simplicity, the aggregate demand curves are assumed to be straight lines. Let the initial position of this curve be represented by E_4. The intersection of this curve with the 45° radius vector determines the initial level of real income in this economy, OA. Assume now that the government component of aggregate demand is suddenly increased by GH units. This pushes up the aggregate demand curve to E_5, generates accordingly the new intersection point F, and thereby determines the new level of real income OC, which is AC units greater than the preceding level.

The comparative-statics multiplier is the ratio of these two increases. Specifically, it is

$$(1) \qquad \frac{\Delta Y}{\Delta G} = \frac{AC}{GH} = \frac{1}{\dfrac{GH}{AC}} = \frac{1}{\dfrac{JF}{AC}} = \frac{1}{\dfrac{DF - DJ}{AC}} = \frac{1}{1 - \dfrac{DJ}{AC}},$$

or

$$(2) \qquad \frac{\Delta Y}{\Delta G} = \frac{1}{1 - \text{the marginal propensity to spend}}.$$

Here we have made use of the parallelism of E_4 and E_5 to equate GH and JF, and of the 45° angle of the radius vector to equate AC and DF. In this way we obtain the standard formula expressed by (2). This

---

[15] For a clear discussion of this distinction, see Haberler, *op. cit.*, pp. 456–58, and the references to J. M. Clark and F. Machlup there cited.

[16] It should be obvious that here and in all that follows the term "year" merely denotes an arbitrary period of time.

shows the traditional greater-than-unity multiplier that is a direct consequence of the equally traditional less-than-unity marginal propensity to spend.

Strictly speaking, however, this multiplier has no place in our model. It is part and parcel of the Keynesian "diagonal-cross" analysis that we have already rejected (page 237). Specifically, by ignoring the supply side of the market, it overlooks the fact that neither point G nor point F is one of equilibrium. Thus it applies the concepts and techniques of comparative statics to a case where they are not really valid. More specifically, it fails to show that even without the assistance of an adventitious increase in government expenditures, automatic market forces will continuously be pushing the level of real income upwards from its original OA level.[17]

To diagnose this difficulty is to suggest the cure. A valid framework for this multiplier within our model can be created by resorting to the pseudo comparative statics of Chapter XIII:4. In particular, if we assume that both wages and prices are absolutely rigid, then the economy will have no automatic tendency to move away from either of its unemployment positions, G or F. Hence comparisons such as those conceived by the instantaneous multiplier can be made.

It should, however, be emphasized that even under these assumptions the preceding formula will usually prove to be oversimplified. Thus, for example, it does not take into account that changes in government expenditure might also affect the rate of interest and hence the level of aggregate demand. Nor does it allow for the possible direct—and discouraging—effect of increased government expenditures on the private propensity to spend—and the propensity to invest in particular. More generally, there is no such thing as "the" multiplier. Every model has its own multiplier. And this can be greater or less than unity—or even negative—in accordance with the assumptions of the model.

Consider now the dynamic successive-period multiplier. This is based on a completely different conceptual experiment. Once again we begin with an exogenous increase in government expenditures; but this time it is assumed to be a once-and-for-all increase during one year only, and not a permanent one continued year after year. We then trace through the expansionary effect of this initial once-and-for-all increase on the real incomes of all subsequent years. Finally, the multiplier is defined as the ratio between the aggregate value of the latter increase and the value of the initial one.

---

[17] Yet another misleading aspect of this multiplier will be discussed in Section 4 below.

The standard derivation of the formula for this multiplier starts from the assumption that individuals' expenditures during one year are determined by their incomes of the preceding one. Indeed, the expenditure function is assumed for simplicity to have the linear form

(3) $$E_t = a + bY_{t-1},$$

where E_t represents real expenditures in year t, Y_{t-1} represents real national income in year $t - 1$, and a and b are constants. Assume now that the government makes a once-and-for-all increase of R dollars (of constant purchasing power) in its expenditures on goods and services. This causes the real income of the initial year to grow by R dollars. By (3), it also causes an increase of bR in real expenditures—and hence real income—in the next year. And this in turn causes an increase in real expenditures of $b(bR) = b^2R$ in the following year. And so on. Hence the final result of the initial increase of R dollars is to increase real national income over all years by

$$R + bR + b^2R + b^3R + \cdots + b^nR + \cdots$$

(4) $$= R(1 + b + b^2 + b^3 + \cdots + b^n + \cdots)$$

$$= R \cdot \frac{1}{1 - b}.$$

By definition, the formula for the dynamic multiplier is then obtained by dividing this through by R to yield

(5) $$\frac{R \cdot \dfrac{1}{1 - b}}{R} = \frac{1}{1 - b} = \frac{1}{1 - \text{the marginal propensity to spend}},$$

which is seen to be identical with the formula for the comparative-statics multiplier in equation (2) above.

There is, of course, nothing coincidental about this identity. For consider our comparative-statics experiment. As already emphasized, this assumes that the government increases its expenditures relative to those of the original equilibrium position, not only in the first year, but in each and every subsequent one as well. Hence, in the year when equilibrium is finally reëstablished, real income is at a higher level, first, because of the increase of R dollars in government expenditures during that year; second, because of the increase of R dollars in government expenditures during the preceding year—which causes income in the final equilibrium year to be higher by bR; third, because of the increase of R dollars in government expenditures two years earlier—which causes income in the final equilibrium year to be higher by $b(bR) = b^2R$; and so on. Thus the total increase in real income between the two equilibrium positions can be decomposed into precisely the same geometric series presented in equation (4). Hence the comparative-statics multiplier, like the dynamic one, must be the sum of this series divided by R.

From this it is also clear that formula (5) is subject to the same reservations already voiced in connection with formula (2). What interests us now, however, is not the exact magnitude of the dynamic

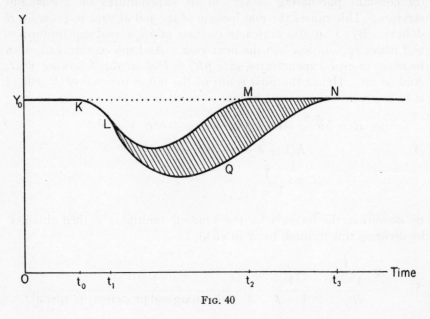

FIG. 40

multiplier, but its general conceptual validity for our model. We therefore emphasize that since the dynamic multiplier is not dependent on the assumption of equilibrium, it can be introduced into our model with much less difficulty than the comparative-statics one. All that must be remembered is that part of the increase in income which occurs after the once-and-for-all increase in government expenditures cannot be ascribed to this increase, but to the automatic equilibrating process of the economy, which would in any case operate to push the level of income upwards. Thus the dynamic multiplier can be credited only with those income increases which would not have occurred in the absence of the government's "pump-priming."

Graphically, we can conceive of this multiplier in our model in the following terms: The curve $KLQN$ in Figure 40 shows what would have happened to the level of real national income over time had the economy been subjected to a sudden decrease in demand at time t_0, and had it then been required to work this deflationary pressure off through the automatic equilibrating process. By way of contrast, the curve KLM shows the corresponding time path of real national income had the government "primed the pump" by a once-and-for-all expenditure at time t_1. It shows how this expenditure speeds up the equilibrating process and brings the economy to full employment at time t_2 instead of t_3. The real national income whose potential loss this government expenditure has prevented is thus represented by the shaded area in Figure 40, and the multiplier is accordingly measured by the ratio between this income and the original once-and-for-all expenditure.[18]

3. Noticeable by its omission from the preceding interpretation of Keynesian economics is the contention that there is a minimum level below which the rate of interest cannot fall. If this were true, then—completely aside from the question of interest-inelasticity which we have emphasized—monetary policy would be confronted with an absolute limitation on its powers to stimulate economic activity. Keynes himself did not seem to attach much importance to this possibility.[19] But later critics—both sympathetic and adverse—have raised it to a key position in the Keynesian argument.[20]

All of these critics—and Keynes too—rationalized this limitation by ascribing a special form to the demand curve for money. In particular, they assumed this curve to become an indefinitely extending horizontal line at that minimum level at which "almost everyone prefers cash to holding a debt which yields so low a rate of interest."[21] Accordingly, they represented this curve as in Figure 41 and argued that it demonstrated the impossibility of driving interest down below r_7.

Now, as has been sufficiently emphasized in Chapter IX:5, this representation of the demand curve for money is incorrect. For when due account is taken of the individuals' planned behavior in all markets, this curve must retain its negative slope throughout. In particular, the budget restraint—together with the assumed impossibility of borrowing infinite amounts—makes it correspondingly impossible for the amount

---

[18] This diagram abstracts from the fact that by time t_2 or t_3 the full-employment level of income will have risen.

[19] *General Theory*, pp. 203 and 207.

[20] Cf., e.g., J. R. Hicks, "Mr. Keynes and the 'Classics,'" *op. cit.*, p. 470; Modigliani, *op. cit.*, p. 199; A. H. Hansen, *A Guide to Keynes* (New York, 1953), pp. 132–33.

[21] *General Theory*, p. 207.

of money demanded to become infinite at any rate of interest. Nevertheless, as we shall now see, there is a very real limitation on the downward influence that monetary policy—in its usual sense—can exert on the rate of interest. But it is a limitation that flows from the significance of the minimum rate r_7 in the bond market, not from any alleged significance in the money market.[22]

Let us assume that there exists in the economy either money illusion in the speculative demand for money, or wage and price rigidities, or both. Then, as shown in Chapters XII:1 and XIII:4, an increase in the amount of money will permanently shift the demand curve for bonds rightwards and the supply curve leftwards and thus reduce the equi-

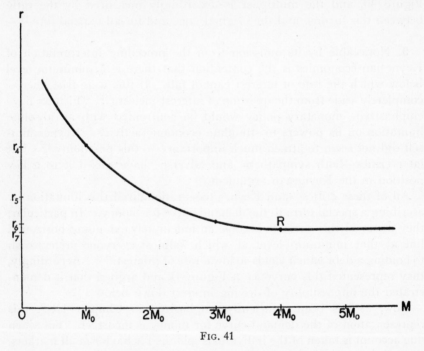

FIG. 41

librium rate of interest.[23] In terms of Figure 42, the successive increases in the amount of money from M_0 to $2M_0$, $3M_0$, and $4M_0$ shift the demand and supply curves from position *I* to *II*, *III*, and *IV*, respectively, and thus cause the point of equilibrium to move from *A* to *B*, *C*, and *D*, respectively.

---

22 Cf. Chapter IX:4, particularly Figure 13.

23 The term "equilibrium" is applied to the case of rigidities subject to the reservations already noted in the pseudo "comparative-statics" analysis of Chapter XIII:4.

Figure 42 also reflects the crucial additional assumption that as the demand curve for bonds shifts upwards, its intersection point with the vertical axis approaches the price $1/r_7$ as a limit.   That is, no matter how large the value of their initial money holdings, individuals will never agree to hold any bonds at a rate of interest below r_7.   At such

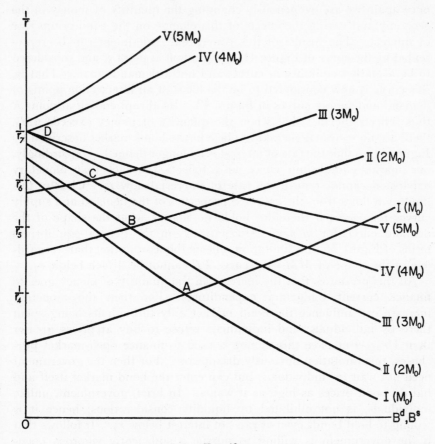

Fig. 42

low rates they will always prefer to hold money instead.[24]   At the same time, the higher the initial money holdings of firms, the less pressed they are to borrow, and the lower, accordingly, the maximum rate of interest they are willing to pay.   It follows that after the monetary expansion has reached a certain point—$4M_0$ in our diagram—the bond market will become inactive: no borrower will be willing to pay the minimum rate

---

[24] Cf. p. 138.

of interest on which lenders insist. This situation is represented by the demand and supply curves of position V

As the reader has undoubtedly realized, the two preceding paragraphs describe a market-experiment identical in general conception with that of Chapter XI:4, though differing in details. In particular, once again we are exogenously changing the quantity of money in the economy and noting the effects of this change on the equilibrium rate of interest. The results of this conceptual experiment can be represented by the curve of Figure 41—now cut off at point R and considered to be a market-equilibrium curve, and not a demand curve. That is, this curve is now considered to be the locus of all intersection points of demand and supply curves in Figure 42. Its abrupt ending at point R thus reflects the fact that when the quantity of money exceeds $4M_0$, there are no transactions taking place in the bond market described by Figure 42, so that the rate of interest is no longer defined. Accordingly, our market-equilibrium curve also reflects the fact that monetary expansion cannot reduce the rate of interest below r_7. Clearly, this limitation flows from the assumed properties of the demand and supply curves for *bonds*; it therefore holds no matter what the shape of the demand curve for *money*. Alternatively, in the general-equilibrium terms of Figure 36, this limitation reflects the assumption that—regardless of the shape of MM—the curve PP cannot be driven below r_7.

All this presumes that the increase in the quantity of money goes to finance current budgetary expenditures. For then the monetary increase can influence the bond market only through its being spent there by individuals; and individuals refuse to buy at prices greater than $1/r_7$. But once this money is used to finance open-market purchases, this limitation obviously disappears. For then the government need not wait for individuals, but can enter the bond market itself and bid up bond prices as high as it wants. In brief, government, unlike individuals, is not inhibited by liquidity considerations; hence it is willing to hold bonds even at rates of interest below r_7. It follows that if the government is willing to pursue a sufficiently vigorous open-market policy—one that encompasses private as well as government bonds—there is no reason why it should not be able to drive interest down as low as it wants.

But things are not quite so simple. By driving interest down below the "minimum" rate, the government also drives all private individuals out of the bond market. In brief, it succeeds in pushing interest down below the level at which "almost everyone prefers cash to holding a debt" only by itself becoming the sole debt-holder—and, by that very fact, the sole lender—in the economy. It thus negates the whole meaning of a policy designed to enable government to influence the overall level of activity in the economy with a minimum of direct intervention.

Thus there is a limitation on the ability of monetary policy to reduce interest. But it is a limitation which originates in political, and not economic, factors. Furthermore, it is highly unlikely that this limitation has ever yet endangered the efficacy of monetary policy. These conclusions hold even in the special case of the kinked demand curve for money described in Figure 16 (page 148). Here, too, only political limitations would prevent the government from choosing (if necessary) any desired rate of interest between r_1 and zero and then offering loans at this rate to firms desirous of undertaking investment.

4. Just as there are some familiar elements missing from our interpretation of Keynes, so are there some missing from our interpretation of the classics. In particular, Section 1 above has presented the classical position without even a mention of Say's Identity.

The usual macroeconomic interpretation of this identity is that, regardless of the rate of interest and level of prices, the total demand of households and firms for commodities is always equal to the total income of the economy.[25] Graphically this means that the aggregate demand curve must coincide with the 45° radius vector. Figure 35 on page 215 is accordingly replaced by Figure 43. As this diagram shows, the special form which Say's Identity imposes upon the aggregate demand curve requires it to intersect the aggregate supply curve at, and only at, the full-employment point B. Furthermore, as long as this identity holds, there can never be any shift in the aggregate demand curve to disturb this equilibrium position even momentarily.

This is a statement of the classical position—as seen with Keynesian eyes.[26] It is another by-product of the oversimplified "diagonal-cross" approach (page 237). For if one starts from the Keynesian assumption that there is neither a real-balance effect nor an aggregate supply curve in the commodity market—and hence no automatic tendency for a state of involuntary unemployment to generate corrective equilibrating forces—then the only way one can conceive of an economy which must necessarily be brought to a position of full employment is in terms of an aggregate demand curve of the special shape depicted by Figure 43. Conversely, once one recognizes the existence of these equilibrating forces, one can also recognize that the classical position is logically dependent, not on any special form of the aggregate demand

---

[25] This is actually stricter than the statement of Say's Identity on pp. 119 and 188 above; for it requires receipts from commodities *alone* always to be spent on commodities *alone*.

[26] *General Theory*, pp. 18–21, 25–26.

function, but only on the assumption that this function—whatever its form—is sufficiently sensitive to price and interest variations to assure the rapid convergence to full employment of the equilibrating process described by Chapter XIII:3. Though there is no evidence that classical economists ever expressed themselves in these terms—and though there is a little evidence that they may sometimes actually have thought in

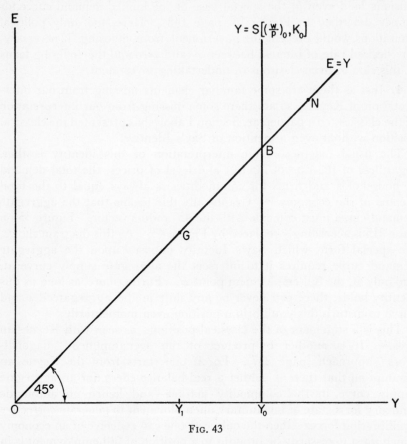

$$Y = S\left[\left(\tfrac{w}{p}\right)_0, K_0\right]$$

E = Y

N

B

G

45°

O Y_1 Y_0 Y

FIG. 43

the Say's Identity terms ascribed to them by Keynes[27]—this is all that need logically be said in order to rationalize their policy conclusions.

The foregoing discussion of Say's Identity also serves to clarify a frequent misunderstanding of its true nature. It is evident from Figure 43 that this identity necessarily involves a marginal propensity

---

[27] See the discussion of the literature in Note L.

to spend equal to one. This has sometimes led to the mechanical cranking of the standard

$$\frac{1}{1 - \text{the marginal propensity to spend}}$$

formula to produce the conclusion that Say's Identity makes the multiplier infinite and thus renders the system unstable. Additional support for this conclusion seems to come from the vision of a "diagonal-cross" diagram in which only the 45° diagonal appears; and in which, therefore, there seems to be no force pinning national income down to one specific level.

It can readily be shown that this line of reasoning is yet another fallacious by-product of the usual Keynesian neglect of the supply side of the commodity market. In particular, once the standard "diagonal-cross" diagram is supplemented by a supply curve—as it is in Figure 43—the nature of the automatic stabilizing forces which bring the economy to the full-employment position B becomes fully evident. Thus, if the economy were at point G in Figure 43, firms would be operating with an excess capacity measured by $Y_0 - Y_1$. Hence they would be under pressure to expand their output. But now—unlike the situation that exists in the case of a normal aggregate demand curve with a marginal propensity to spend of less than unity—this normal tendency would not be aborted by a deficiency in the demand necessary to absorb this additional output.[28] Hence firms would continue to expand production until they brought the economy to the full-employment position B. Conversely, if the economy were at N, firms would be producing more than the optimum output indicated by their supply curve.[29] Hence they would contract production and thereby return the economy once again to B. Thus equilibrium position B is a stable one. Figure 43 also shows how, under the assumption of Say's Identity, the only limit on the ability of the economy to produce is that imposed by the technological and subjective conditions of supply; never that of an inadequacy of demand.

Similarly, the supply side of the commodity market is overlooked in the standard derivation of the multiplier formula. Thus the graphical analysis of Figure 39 takes no account of the possibility that the vertical supply curve may intersect the abscissa at point B and therefore

---

28 Cf. especially p. 221.

29 The reader will recall that the aggregate supply curve is not a technological curve describing physically possible outputs, but a behavior curve describing economically optimum ones. Hence it is quite possible that firms may sometimes inadvertently find themselves to the right of their supply curve.

prevent the multiplier from carrying real income beyond this point. This suffices to demonstrate the general inapplicability of the standard multiplier formula to any case in which the expansionary effects of an exogenous increase in expenditures may be brought up short against the ceiling of full employment. In particular, it is clear that once we take account of this ceiling, the multiplier in the case of Say's Identity will (if it is defined) not be infinite.

Nevertheless, Say's Identity is connected with instability; but it is an instability of money wages and prices, not of real income. Specifically, let us assume—in a minor variation on the argument of Chapter VIII:7—that with the economy at the equilibrium position *B* in Figure 43, a sudden disturbance causes the price level to rise. By assumption, this has no effect on the aggregate demand curve and hence none on the equilibrium of the commodity market. But it reduces the real wage rate and thus creates an excess demand in the labor market. This in turn pushes the money wage rate upwards until the original real wage is restored. In this way the economy is brought to a new equilibrium position in which wages and prices are proportionately higher than they originally were, while real national income remains the same.

But as indicated in Chapter VIII:7, this is a somewhat misleading description. For Say's Identity implies the existence of a barter economy. Hence what manifests itself here as "instability" of the money wage and price levels is actually the reflection of the simple fact that in such an economy these magnitudes are not even defined. From this we can also see that, within its appropriate framework of a barter economy, Say's Identity does not generate any instability whatsoever.

5. The discussion of the preceding section takes place in what is most conveniently described as a cyclical framework: one in which an excess supply of commodities is generated by a downward shift on the demand side of the market. Actually, however, the excess supply which really absorbed the attention of classical economists is that generated by an upward shift on the supply side. Specifically, their primary interest lay in the long-run capability of a capitalist economy to absorb the output of a constantly expanding productive capacity. In modern terms, their main concern was secular stagnation, not cyclical unemployment. Accordingly, they argued the impossibility of a "general glut on the market," not under the chapter heading "Commercial Crises," but under the heading "Effects of Accumulation."[30]

---

[30] On this and all that follows, see discussion of the literature in Note L.

Let us, then, complete the discussion of the preceding section by interpreting the classical position within this secular framework. Assume that due to the growth of population the supply curve for labor shifts to the right; or that due to capital accumulation or technological progress there is a corresponding shift in the demand curve for labor. Either of these changes causes firms to increase their labor inputs and, consequently, their commodity outputs. That is, either of them shifts the commodity supply curve over to the right and thereby disturbs whatever equilibrium situation previously existed in the commodity market.

If, now, the situation of Figure 43 obtains, this disturbance is immediately eliminated; for due to the unitary marginal propensity to spend, the increase in supply is accompanied by an exactly equal increase in the amount demanded. Thus a "general glut" on the commodity market cannot even momentarily exist. Supply always and instantaneously creates its own demand.

This is one interpretation of the classical position; but, as can be surmised from the preceding section, not a necessary one. In particular, this position can be rationalized without resorting to Say's Identity. It suffices instead to assume that the aggregate demand curve has the ordinary shape of those of Figure 35; that, therefore, the increase in supply first creates a deflationary gap; that this, in turn, initiates the dynamic adjustment process of Chapter XIII:3; and that this process ultimately raises aggregate demand to the level necessary to absorb any possible expansion in supply. In brief, a permanent glut is an impossibility because of the corrective market forces set into operation by the existence of temporary ones.

Thus, in a secular as well as cyclical context, the validity of the classical position need not depend on any alleged special shape of the aggregate demand curve, but only on its assumed sensitivity to price and interest variations. Indeed, it is reasonable to assume that this sensitivity is greater in the former context than in the latter. For from the secular viewpoint we can abstract from the adverse expectations generated by *falling* prices and interest and concentrate on the stimulus generated by the fact that they are *low*.

Now, even under these circumstances it is quite likely that interest reductions by themselves may have too weak an influence always to insure the raising of aggregate demand to its full-employment level. But it is quite unlikely that there is a corresponding limitation on the stimulating effect of a price decline. For if this decline continues for a sufficient period of time, the real quantity of money in the economy can be made as large as desired. And, in the absence of adverse expectations, there is little reason to assume that this increased quantity will simply be dissipated on an indefinite augmentation of the real demand for money.[31]   In other words, it is almost certain that—no matter how large the supply of commodities, and even without the assistance of a reduction in interest—the direct real-balance effect in the commodity market can be made strong enough to raise aggregate demand to its full-employment level.   Correspondingly, the foregoing dynamic adjustment process is almost certain to be brought to its equilibrium goal.   In brief, no matter what the level of supply, the system always possesses a full-employment, equilibrium solution to which it is automatically brought by the workings of market forces.   It can never remain in a state of permanent overproduction.[32]

It is this secular context which brings out the ultimate significance of the real-balance effect for the theory of employment.   It is this which underscores the role this effect can play in lending strong—if not decisive—analytical support to the classical side of the Great Debate on the internal consistency of an ever expanding capitalist economy.[33]

We must, however, emphasize that here, as in the preceding section, our concern has been not with what classical economists "really" said but with what is logically sufficient to validate their conclusions.   As usual, it is much more difficult to give a definitive answer to the first of these questions than to the second.   As already noted, there is a little evidence that classical economists may actually have thought in terms of Say's Identity; but there is more evidence that they did not.   On the other hand, there is absolutely no evidence that they thought in the precise terms of the dynamic adjustment process with which we have rationalized their position here.   Indeed, it seems quite likely that they

---

[31] Cf. p. 236.

[32] Cf. p. 224 (bottom).

[33] The word "analytical" should be emphasized.   For the main way demand has *historically* absorbed an expanding supply has been through the development of new products, new tastes, and new and unremitting demands for higher standards of living—and surely not through the real-balance effect.   Similarly, the fact that the classical position is *analytically* consistent does not mean that one must adopt its *policy* attitude toward the problem of secular expansion.   This should be clear from the argument of the preceding section.

The emphasis here on the secular aspect of the real-balance effect follows that of the well-known articles by A. C. Pigou on "The Classical Stationary State," *Economic Journal*, LIII (1943), 343–51, and "Economic Progress in a Stable Environment," *Economica*, XIV (1947), as reprinted in *Readings in Monetary Theory*, pp. 241–51.   See also the emphasis on this role in the *Journal of Political Economy* articles by G. Ackley, "The Wealth-Saving Relationship," LIX (1951), 155; A. Hansen, "The Pigouvian Effect," the same volume, pp. 535–36; and G. Haberler, "The Pigou Effect Once More," LX (1952), 240–46.

The present discussion is, of course, concerned with the theory of employment; the significance of the real-balance effect for monetary theory is much more immediate.   Cf. Chapters II:3 and VIII:3.

never faced up to this problem at all. It seems as if their valid and vigorous insistence that increased production generates increased "means of purchasing" and hence increased demand, coupled with their absolute faith in the "wants and tastes of mankind as unlimited," blinded classical economists to the need for analyzing the exact details of the automatic market mechanism by which demand supposedly keeps pace with supply. What is worse, they transferred this neglect of detail to the short-run cyclical problem as well. And for this analytical lacuna they were rightly and forcefully criticized by Malthus and Sismondi, in their times, and by Keynes, in ours.[34]

---

[34] The first quotation is from J. B. Say, *A Treatise on Political Economy*, trans. C. R. Prinsep (fourth ed.; Philadelphia, 1834), p. 137, first paragraph. See also Say's *Letters to Malthus* (1821, reprinted London, 1936), p. 4. The theme of this quotation is most explicit in Mill, *op. cit.*, pp. 557–58; this passage is discussed in detail in Note L below.

The second quotation is from a letter by Ricardo to Malthus in *Works and Correspondence of David Ricardo*, ed. Sraffa, Vol. VI, p. 134, bottom. See also *Notes on Malthus, Works*, Vol. II, p. 311, and Malthus' letter to Ricardo, *Works*, Vol. VII, p. 122; this last passage is cited in full on p. 474, footnote 18, below.

Further background material for this paragraph is provided by Note L.

CHAPTER XV

A Critique of Classical and

Keynesian Interest Theory

1. The nature of classical and neoclassical interest theory. *2. Keynesian interest theory.* *3. Loanable-funds versus liquidity-preference theories of interest.* *The real and the monetary in the rate of interest.*

1. On various occasions in this book—and in Part Two in particular —we have digressed briefly on the implications of the argument for classical or Keynesian interest theory. The task of this final chapter is to pick up the loose ends of these digressions and—at the risk of some repetition—integrate them into a systematic critique of these two theories.

Let us begin with the classical and neoclassical theory. In modern terms this is best described as a loanable-funds theory. Its point of departure is that "the rate of interest . . . depends essentially and permanently on the comparative amount of real capital offered and demanded in the way of loan." Accordingly, "fluctuations in the rate of interest arise from variations either in the demand for loans or in the supply." These words happen to be those of J. S. Mill. But they represent the thinking of such writers as Hume, Thornton, and Ricardo, before him, and Sidgwick, Marshall, Pigou, Wicksell, and Fisher, after.[1]

At first sight this bears little resemblance to Keynes' picture of a

---

[1] Mill, *Principles*, pp. 647 and 641, respectively; the reader is strongly urged to study for himself the whole of Book III, Chapter XXIII, from which these passages are taken. For specific references to the other writers, see Note J below.

classical theory which in some mysterious way determines the rate of interest at that level which equates savings and investment.[2]　　But it would be unfair to press this criticism of Keynes too far.　For there was no precise attempt in the classical literature to distinguish between savings and the supply of loans, on the one hand, and between investment and the demand for loans, on the other.　There was no recognition of the fact that this distinction is logically inherent in the assumption that a money economy exists; that, more specifically, the existence of a simultaneous identity between savings and lending, and investing and borrowing, implies Say's Identity and hence a barter economy.[3]

　　Though determining the rate of interest in the loan market—which is obviously identical with what we have called the bond market—classical and neoclassical theory always emphasized the crucial interdependence that exists between this market and the commodity market.　This, indeed, is the real significance of its celebrated distinction between the "money rate" and the "natural rate."　These terms are, of course, Wicksell's.　But, as he himself was the first to concede,[4] the theory in back of them had already been sketched out by Ricardo.　And much the same sketch can be found in Thornton and Mill as well.[5]

　　The essence of this theory—and of the interdependence which it stresses—can be set out briefly.　By the "money rate" is meant the rate of interest actually prevailing in the loan market.　By the "natural rate" is meant not a rate quoted upon a market, but the investors' rate of return on capital in the commodity market.　Equilibrium can exist only when these two rates are equal; conversely, any discrepancy between these two rates automatically generates equilibrating forces which bring them to equality.　In particular, if the money rate happens to lie below the natural rate, then individuals can profit by expanding their borrowings and using the proceeds to increase their demand for

---

[2] *General Theory*, Chapter XIV

[3] See end of Chapter XI:6.

This distinction is, of course, a basic point of the *General Theory* (cf., e.g., p. 166), though there is no indication that Keynes saw it as logically inherent in a money economy.

It might also be noted that this distinction is explicit in the modern versions of the loanable-funds theory as presented by Bertil Ohlin, *op. cit.*, pp. 424–26; Robertson, *Essays in Monetary Theory*, p. 3; and Haberler, *Prosperity and Depression*, Part II, especially pp. 292–96.

[4] *Lectures on Political Economy*, trans. E. Classen (London, 1935), Vol. II, p. 200.

[5] Wicksell's concession was made to David Davidson, who had brought his attention to the passage which appears in Ricardo's *Principles of Political Economy*, ed. Sraffa, pp. 363–64. To this can be added the passage from *The High Price of Bullion* cited in full on p. 162 above.

On Henry Thornton, see his *Enquiry into the Nature and Effects of the Paper Credit of Great Britain* (London, 1802), pp. 261–62 and, especially, pp. 287–91 (pp. 237–38, 253–56 of the 1939 reprint).　On Mill, cf. his *Principles*, pp. 645–47, especially p. 647, lines 10–15.

investment goods; assuming full employment, this generates an inflationary gap in the commodity market which drives prices upwards; and this in turn reacts back on the bond market and causes the rate of interest to rise.

Nowhere is this stated more precisely and with fuller appreciation of its deeper significance than in the striking words with which Wicksell defined the major problem to which he addressed himself and indicated the nature of the famed "cumulative process" by which he proposed to solve it: "The money rate of interest depends in the first instance on the excess or scarcity of *money*. How then does it come about that it is eventually determined by the excess or scarcity of *real capital*? . . . The only possible explanation lies in the influence which is exerted on *prices* by the difference between the two rates of interest. When the money rate of interest is relatively too low all prices rise. The demand for money loans is consequently increased, and as a result of a greater need for cash holdings, the supply is diminished. The consequence is that the rate of interest is soon restored to its normal level, so that it again coincides with the natural rate."[6]

Thus Wicksell's "cumulative process" is not the unstable explosive process that almost all later commentators have tried to make of it, but a stable equilibrating process whose function it is to achieve the long-run equality of the money and natural rates of interest. This is not a quibble. For the commonly accepted interpretation of Wicksell completely overlooks the central problem with which he was concerned. And it thereby also overlooks the vital key which he provides to an understanding of one of the central themes of classical interest theory.[7]

It was within the foregoing framework that classical economists carried out their analysis of the effects of an increase in the amount of money. Such an increase could influence the rate of interest only through its prior effect on the demand or supply function in the loan market. Hence if this increase were not expended in this market at

---

6 *Interest and Prices*, pp. 108–11, italics in the original. From the context it is clear that the first sentence refers to "excess or scarcity of money *loans*." For an explanation of why "the greater need for cash holdings" causes the supply of loans to diminish, see bottom of next page.

For other examples of this theme in Wicksell's work, see *ibid.*, pp. xxvi–xxvii and p. 75; *Lectures in Political Economy*, Vol. II, pp. 194, 200, and, especially, 206.

7 For examples of this misinterpretation of Wicksell, see Hicks, *Value and Capital*, pp. 251–54; L. A. Metzler, "Business Cycles and the Modern Theory of Employment," *American Economic Review*, XXXVI (1946), 280, footnote 4; and the additional references cited in my "Wicksell's 'Cumulative Process,'" *Economic Journal*, LXII (1952), 835, footnote 2.

For a detailed discussion of Wicksell's "cumulative process," see Note E:4 below. This also explains what Wicksell meant by the term "cumulative" and shows that he had almost no interest in the unstable case.

all—if, that is, it were directed entirely to the commodity market—interest would not be affected.[8]   But in the classical scheme this was generally not the case.   For the increased money supply was usually assumed to be injected into the economy through the banking system and thus to result in an increased supply of loans.   Hence the rate of interest declined.   But even in this case the decline was only a transitory one.   In the long run, interest would generally return to its original equilibrium level.

This distinction between the short-run variability of interest in the face of a monetary increase and its long-run invariability in no way represents the "unbridged conflict" in classical theorizing that Keynes made it out to be.[9]   It represents instead the well-reasoned conclusion of the analysis which has already been described above: the analysis which takes account of the effect of a rising price level in the commodity market on the rate of interest in the loan market.   For Hume, Thornton, Ricardo, Mill, and Fisher, this effect works its way through the demand side of the latter market: the monetary increase causes a rise in the price of investment goods and thereby increases the volume of borrowing necessary to finance their purchase.   In this way the demand for loans begins to overtake the initially expanded supply.   For Marshall, with his characteristic imprecision, this increased demand for loans results instead from the "confident spirit in the business world" which the price increase generates.   For Giffen and Wicksell, the reaction works its way instead through the supply side of the market: the price increase generates an internal drain which draws bank reserves down and hence forces them to raise their rates again—or, what is the same thing, to decrease again their supply of loans.   This, indeed, is what Wicksell relies upon for the stability of his "cumulative process." The common theme of all these writers is that at the same time that the monetary increase pushes interest down, it also pushes prices up; and that the latter movement must ultimately cause a reversal of the former one.[10]

---

[8] See the discussion of Wicksell on p. 426 below.

[9] *General Theory*, pp. 182–83.

[10] See the specific references in Note J.

It might be worth while to make explicit the hint of the text and to note that, say, Mill's exposition is decidedly more precise and systematic than Marshall's.   More generally, it is difficult to understand why, in its analysis of a monetary increase, the Cambridge school as a whole failed to make use of the specific interrelationship between price and interest movements that Mill and his predecessors had consistently employed.

One cannot also help wondering how Keynes' chapter on "The Classical Theory of the Rate of Interest"—and how, accordingly, the views of a generation which has learned its classical economics from this chapter—would have been affected if Keynes had taken his basic texts from Mill, instead of Marshall and Pigou.

It was this interaction between the commodity and loan markets—in any one of the three preceding forms—which provided the explicit rationale of the classical argument that in the long run, as distinct from the short run, a monetary increase will have a symmetrical effect on the demand and supply of loans, and will therefore leave interest invariant. Or, alternatively, approaching the problem from the viewpoint of the commodity market, classical economists argued that the monetary increase does not change any of the real characteristics of the economy; that, in particular, it does not change the marginal productivity of capital; and that, therefore, it does not change the natural rate of interest. More specifically, the monetary increase causes an equiproportionate increase in the money cost of any investment project and in the money value of its anticipated returns; hence it leaves the rate of profit—and hence the long-run equilibrium rate of interest—unchanged.[11]

It is clear from this discussion that the invariance of interest was not the dogmatic First Principle of Faith of the classical school that its latter-day critics—and defenders—have made of it. It was instead the rational conclusion which emerged from the application of ordinary supply-and-demand analysis to the loan and commodity markets. Furthermore, what strikes one immediately in reading the classical literature is the flexibility with which this conclusion was modified whenever there was reason to believe that, even in the long run, a monetary increase might have an asymmetrical influence on the demand and supply of loans, and might therefore permanently affect the rate of interest.[12]

As a case in point, consider the celebrated classical and neoclassical doctrine of "forced savings." The essence of this doctrine is that an exogenous increase in the quantity of money which accrues initially to entrepreneurs, or to those who lend to them, will increase the proportion of an economy's expenditures going into investment, and that the necessary corresponding increase in savings will be forced upon workers and fixed-income recipients by the inflationary price movement which the monetary expansion generates. In this way such an expansion can increase the amount of real capital in the economy. But if it can do this, it can also lower the marginal productivity of capital and thereby the long-run equilibrium rate of interest. This conclusion was explicitly drawn—without a trace of self-consciousness—by such writers as Mill,

---

11 Cf. the references to Thornton and Mill in footnote 5, p. 257. Cf. also J. S. Nicholson, *Principles of Political Economy* (London, 1897), Vol. II, p. 231; and—in a somewhat different context—W. S. Jevons, *Investigations in Currency and Finance* (London, 1884), p. 22.

12 Cf., e.g., Mill, *op. cit.*, p. 642.

Wicksell, Nicholson, and Pigou. It is but a special case of the general awareness of classical economists that a monetary increase cannot be neutral in its effects unless it is initially distributed among all members of the economy in a uniform way.[13]

On the other hand, classical and neoclassical monetary theorists did not see that shifts in liquidity preference could affect the long-run equilibrium rate of interest. Nor did they see that such an effect might also be directly generated by open-market operations. But it should be clear that these propositions do not strike at any vital foundations of the classical theory. More specifically, if classical economists could recognize the permanent effect on interest of a monetary change in the case of "forced savings," there is no reason why they should not have been equally willing to recognize the corresponding effects of shifts in liquidity preference and open-market operations. We shall return to this question in what follows.[14]

2. To a certain extent we have by-passed the main current of Keynesian interest theory. For this emphasizes the speculative motive and liquidity differentials—two topics which we have largely ignored. But—as already implied by Chapter XI:1—though differing in this way in its microeconomic rationale, our demand function for money is macroeconomically equivalent to Keynes' in its assumed inverse dependence on the rate of interest. Accordingly, our model can properly be used— as it now will be—to criticize the macroeconomic aspects of Keynes' theory.

The basic proposition of Keynes' interest theory is that the rate of interest must operate on the margin of liquidity decisions as well as on those of savings and investment, and that accordingly there is an inverse dependence between the amount of money demanded and this rate. It is true that references to such a dependence can be found earlier in the monetary writings of Walras, Wicksell, Fisher, and Lavington.[15] But these writers essentially ascribed it to the precautionary motive; whereas Keynes, though recognizing this influence, ascribed it primarily to the speculative motive.[16] Furthermore, and more important, each of the above writers—with the exception of Walras—made only passing

---

[13] The passages referred to in the preceding sentence are cited in full in Note J. On the last sentence, see pp. 41 and 98.

[14] This section presupposes as its background the analysis of Chapters X:3, X:4, XII:3, and XII:5.

[15] For specific references, see pp. 389, 399, 418–19.

An even more explicit anticipator of Keynes is the almost completely forgotten Karl Schlesinger. In 1914 this writer presented a two-component demand function for money which bears striking similarity to Keynes' $L_1(\ \ )+L_2(\ \ )$. See pp. 416–17 below.

[16] Cf. above, p. 173, footnote 1.

reference to this dependence; it was left for Keynes to bring it to the fore of monetary theory.

Unfortunately, Keynes' analysis of the implications of this dependence was permeated by a conceptual confusion which has continued to bedevil the subsequent literature as well. In particular, Keynes never distinguished between his basic proposition that the amount of money demanded is inversely dependent upon the rate of interest and the completely different proposition that the equilibrium rate of interest is inversely dependent upon the amount of money. His discussion of liquidity preference in the *General Theory*[17] shifts uninhibitedly from one proposition to the other with never an indication that they are in any way not identical. More specifically, there is never a recognition that, in our terminology, the first of these propositions describes an individual-experiment and the second a market-experiment, and that the truth of the first need not imply the truth of the second.[18]

This confusion shows up with striking clarity in the demand curve for money which characterizes both the Keynesian and non-Keynesian literature of today. As will be recalled, this curve is represented as becoming a straight horizontal line at a certain minimum rate of interest; and this horizontality is rationalized as expressing the proposition that there is a certain minimum rate below which monetary expansion cannot drive interest.[19] There is no recognition of the fact that this proposition should really be described by what we have called a market-equilibrium curve and that, accordingly, its truth is in no way preconditioned on any special shape of the demand curve.[20]

All this is highly ironical. For it means that Keynesian monetary theorists have reproduced in their universe precisely the same confusion of thought of which neoclassical theorists were guilty in theirs. Specifically, the confusion between market-equilibrium and demand curves which marks the neoclassical description of a demand curve for money which is dependent on the reciprocal of the price level also marks the Keynesian description of a demand curve which is dependent on the rate of interest.[21]

Leaving this behind, let us now examine the reason why a change in the amount of money affects interest in the Keynesian system. Two

---

[17] Chapters XIII and XV; see especially the passage from pp. 171–72 cited in full on pp. 466–67 below.

[18] Cf. Chapter XI:4 above.

[19] Cf., e.g., J. R. Hicks, *Trade Cycle* (Oxford, 1950), pp. 141–42.

[20] See the detailed discussion in Chapter XIV:3.

[21] Cf. the discussion of the neoclassical rectangular-hyperbola demand curve for money in Chapter VIII:2. Cf. also p. 145.

interpretations have been presented in this book: Chapter XII:1 attributes this variability to the assumption of money illusion in the speculative demand for money, and Chapter XIII:4—in accordance with more standard interpretations—to the assumption of price and wage rigidities under conditions of unemployment. Clearly, these two interpretations are not mutually exclusive. Correspondingly, most cases in which the *General Theory* analyzes the depressing effect on interest of a monetary increase reflect the joint and reinforcing influence of both money illusion and rigidity. On the other hand, I find it difficult to believe that all Keynes wants to say is that the quantity of money can affect interest under conditions of wage and price rigidity—for classical and neoclassical economists would never have disagreed with such a proposition. This is clearly implied by their repeated emphasis that—under conditions of price flexibility—the injection of new money into the economy will depress interest as long as prices have not yet risen in proportion to the quantity of money.[22]

It should, however, be emphasized that neither of the foregoing assumptions was systematically set out by Keynes in his monetary theory. Nor is there even evidence that he was consciously aware of their presence in his argument. This is particularly true for the assumption of money illusion. But against our failure to find this assumption explicitly recognized, we must place the evidence of the crucial passages in the *General Theory* in which it is all too unconsciously exploited to help derive the major conclusions of Keynesian monetary theory. More specifically, this theory never permits the speculative demand to absorb an increased supply of money except at a lower rate of interest. It never allows for the fact that, provided the price level rises, such an absorption may take place even at an unchanged rate. Nor can this omission be explained as itself proving that the analysis of the *General Theory* proceeds on the assumption of absolute price rigidity. For there are passages in this work in which Keynes explicitly assumes the wage or price level to rise, in which he explains how this rise affects the transactions and precautionary demands, and in which he completely overlooks the fact that it may also affect the speculative demand. And, to the best of my knowledge, this significant omission

---

[22] See the preceding section and, especially, p. 259.

For an example of the interpretation of Keynes in terms of rigidities, see W. Leontief, "Postulates: Keynes' *General Theory* and the Classicists," *The New Economics*, ed. S. E. Harris (New York, 1948), pp. 238–39. See also Leontief's earlier "Fundamental Assumption of Mr. Keynes' Monetary Theory of Unemployment," *op. cit.* This is also the well-known interpretation of Modigliani, *op. cit.*, especially p. 223.

has continued to characterize the later Keynesian—and non-Keynesian —literature as well.[23]

This same omission also mars Keynes' analysis of a shift in liquidity preference. In particular, his failure to see the full impact of the interaction between price and interest variations prevented Keynes from recognizing that a shift in liquidity preference need not always cause a permanent change in the rate of interest.[24] And this error, too, has continued to manifest itself in the later literature. On the other hand, as emphasized at the end of the preceding section, the fact that shifts in liquidity preference can frequently exert a permanent effect on interest is not the vital blow to classical monetary theory that Keynes imagined it to be.

To summarize: The overall tone of the *General Theory* leaves little doubt that Keynes intended his liquidity-preference theory to be a fundamental challenge to classical and neoclassical monetary theory But if this challenge is to meet the latter theory on its own grounds— those of full employment and price flexibility[25]—then Keynes' position cannot be vindicated except by attributing to him the assumption of money illusion in the speculative demand for money. In particular, his extended demonstration that the demand for money depends on the rate of interest does not itself constitute sufficient proof that the equilibrium rate of interest depends on the amount of money.

But since Keynes never explicitly pointed out that his speculative demand was independent of the price level, and since he never undertook to explain why this demand should be involved in such a money illusion, it is difficult to believe that what has turned out here to be the crucial assumption of the liquidity-preference theory has its origin in anything more than a simple—but vital—error. Correspondingly, once this error is corrected, Keynesian theory must give up its claim to have demonstrated the existence of a basic logical fallacy in classical and neoclassical monetary theory. What it has instead demonstrated is the existence in this theory of several significant lacunae. Accordingly, the

---

[23] The significance of the speculative motive's insensitivity to price changes—and the reason this implies the presence of money illusion—can best be appreciated from a comparison of Chapters XI:1 and XII:1. See especially pp. 174 and 194.

The passages from the *General Theory* referred to in the preceding sentence are cited in full and analyzed in Note K:2.

[24] Cf. Chapters X:4 and XI:2.

[25] For evidence that Keynes did offer such a challenge, see *General Theory*, pp. 208–9; this is discussed at the beginning of Chapter XI:3 above. Unfortunately, however, there is also the contradictory evidence of p. 191 where Keynes concedes that "assuming flexible money-wages, the quantity of money as such is, indeed, nugatory in the long period." This contradiction and a suggestion for resolving it are discussed in detail in Note K:2, pp. 469–70.

Keynesian contribution lies in filling these lacunae by analyzing the speculative motive and interest differentials, by emphasizing the dependence of the demand for money on the rate of interest, and by stressing that shifts in liquidity preference can permanently affect this rate.

It should finally be emphasized that the foregoing criticism of Keynes' liquidity-preference theory in no way affects the basic validity of his theory of unemployment. This should be clear from the interpretation of the latter theory in Chapter XIV:1. It is even clearer from Keynes' own statement that "the initial novelty [of the *General Theory*] lies in my maintaining that it is not the rate of interest, but the level of incomes which ensures equality between saving and investment. The arguments which lead up to this initial conclusion are independent of my subsequent theory of the rate of interest, and in fact I reached it before I had reached the latter theory."[26]

3. One question which we have so far deliberately avoided in this book is that which has been hotly and prolongedly debated under the heading "loanable-funds versus liquidity-preference theories." The first of these theories, of course, maintains that the rate of interest is determined in the loan market, while the second maintains that it is determined in the money market. Despite the demonstration over fifteen years ago that these theories are logically equivalent, this pointless debate has continued to recrudesce sporadically in the literature.[27]

The best way of approaching this debate is to try to pin down the meaning of "determined in the loan (money) market." Clearly, this cannot mean that the rate of interest influences only one of the markets. Nor can it mean that the demand and supply functions of one of these markets are solely dependent on the rate of interest, so that a *tâtonnement* in this market alone can determine its equilibrium value. For, as we saw in Chapter IX:4–5, the functions of both markets depend on both the rate of interest and the price level, not to speak of the level of real national income. In brief, the very conception of general-equilibrium analysis requires us to recognize that each market is influenced by all the prices of the system, and each price influences all markets.

A more sophisticated approach would have the phrase "determined in the loan (money) market" mean that the dynamic movement of interest is determined by the excess demand which exists in the loan (money) market. But as has been repeatedly emphasized above, this, too, is a

---

26 "Alternative Theories of the Rate of Interest," *Economic Journal*, XLVII (1937), 250.
27 For a good critical survey of this debate, see B. F. Haley, "Value and Distribution," *Survey of Contemporary Economics*, ed. H. S. Ellis (Philadelphia, 1948), pp. 39–44. See also the discussion by L. R. Klein, W. Fellner, H. M. Somers, and K. Brunner on "Stock and Flow Analysis in Economics," *Econometrica*, XVIII (1950), 236–52.

vestige of partial-equilibrium analysis. In a general-equilibrium framework we cannot logically justify any argument which is based on the assumption that the dynamic pressures for changing a given price can emanate from one, and only one, market.[28] Conversely, we cannot justify any argument which restricts the dynamic influence of excess demand in a given market to one, and only one, price. And, in particular, we cannot possibly justify such a restriction in the case of the money market. For it is the essential nature of money to be spent on all goods—and not just on one.[29]

There still remains the possibility of having the phrase in question refer, not to the actual processes of the market, but to the analytical procedure of the theorist. Specifically, it might refer to the freedom given him by Walras' Law to "drop" one of the market excess-demand equations. If, then, he "drops" the money equation, he has a "loanable-funds" theory; and if the bond equation, a "liquidity-preference" theory. But how shall we classify his theory if he "drops" neither of these equations, but a commodity equation instead?[30] More fundamentally, what can be the entire point of such a distinction if, by the very nature of Walras' Law, it can make no difference which equation he "drops"?[31] And, even more fundamentally, how shall we classify his theory if he "drops" no equation at all, but carries out his analysis in terms of the complete system of equations—with one of them written in a form which makes explicit the equational dependence?[32]

The irrelevance of this whole classificatory scheme is, indeed, one of the conclusions that emerges most explicitly from the argument of this book. If a system is stable—or has certain comparative-statics properties—when analyzed from the viewpoint of the commodity and bond markets, then it must also be stable—or have these properties—when analyzed from the viewpoint of the commodity and money markets. Every set of assumptions in the former framework has its exact counterpart in the latter. And if this counterpart is correctly specified, then— as we have repeatedly seen[33]—an analysis which concentrates on the

---

28 Cf. end of Chapter X:2.

29 Cf. p. 178.

30 In the familiar words of Abba P. Lerner, what happens if he drops the equation for peanuts?

31 Cf. the classic demonstration by Hicks, *Value and Capital*, pp. 158–62. Cf. also above, p. 35, and Mathematical Appendix 3:*a*.

32 This is the procedure advocated in Chapter III:2 and adopted on pp. 40 and 158.

33 In Chapters XI:2 and XII:1.

Note, in particular, that the different dynamic paths we have obtained from the commodity-bond and commodity-money analyses on p. 179 are not the result of the analyses' being carried out in two different markets, but of the fact that we have changed our dynamic assumptions. That is, if in moving over from one market to the other we had instead retained the

bond market must always reach identically the same conclusions as one which concentrates on the money market.   Correspondingly, no logical significance can be attached to any distinction between these two analytical frameworks.

From much the same viewpoint we can approach the frequent discussions as to whether interest is a "real" or "monetary" phenomenon. There are certain tautological ways of settling this debate.   Thus if "monetary" means being matched with the bond or money markets in the same sense that the price of shoes is matched with the shoe market, then the rate of interest—or rather its reciprocal—is clearly matched with the bond market and is therefore a monetary phenomenon.   On the other hand, if "real" means having the dimensions of a relative price and "monetary" the dimensions of a money price, then the rate of interest is obviously a real phenomenon: it is the quotient of two amounts, each of which has the dimensions of a money price.[34]

This is classification by definition, and hence classification without analytical importance.   Let us turn, then, to operationally significant classifications, which are of importance.   Thus, for example, we might say interest is a "real" phenomenon if it influences only the commodity markets; and a "monetary" one if it influences only the bond and/or money markets.   But the general-equilibrium considerations already noted force most contemporary theories to reject such extreme positions and to recognize that interest exerts its influence in all markets and that, in particular, it operates simultaneously on the "threefold margin" of time preference (consumption decisions), marginal productivity of capital (investment decisions), and liquidity preference (decisions as to the relative sizes of bond and money holdings).[35]   Similarly, we should not try to classify the rate of interest as "real" or "monetary" according to the excess demand which determines its dynamic movements; for, from the general-equilibrium viewpoint, these are determined by the excess demands of all markets.[36]

This leaves the familiar criterion that the rate of interest is a "real" phenomenon if it is determined in the commodity markets and a "monetary" phenomenon if it is determined in the bond or money market.[37]   Its continued wide acceptance notwithstanding, this

---

same (explicit and implicit) assumptions as to the effects of the various excess demands on the dynamic movements of the variables, we would have obtained exactly the same dynamic path in both cases.   All this is brought out in detail in Mathematical Appendix 8:*b*.

[34] Cf. p. 51.

[35] Cf. p. 79.

[36] Cf. top of preceding page.

[37] The best-known presentation of this view is that of Modigliani, *op. cit.*

classificatory scheme is entirely unacceptable. It is too suspiciously reminiscent of the invalid dichotomy which we have already criticized and unequivocally rejected above.[38]   More generally, our analysis of this dichotomy has shown us that the equilibrium values of relative prices, the rate of interest, and the absolute price level are simultaneously determined by *all* the markets of the economy; that it is generally impossible to break off a subset of markets which can by itself—that is, by a self-contained *tâtonnement*[39]—determine a subset of variables. And the rate of interest is no exception.

Nevertheless, we can distinguish between the real and the monetary in the rate of interest.   But, once again,[40] this distinction cannot proceed along market lines.   Instead we shall say that interest is a real phenomenon if it behaves like a relative price, and a monetary phenomenon if it behaves like the absolute price level.   More specifically, it is a real phenomenon if its long-run equilibrium value is not affected by exogenous changes which do not affect relative prices, and is affected by those that do.   And it is a monetary phenomenon if its long-run value is affected by exogenous changes which affect only the absolute price level.   From this viewpoint, one of the obvious conclusions of this book is that interest is a real phenomenon: changes in the quantity of money and shifts in liquidity preference which leave relative prices invariant also leave it invariant;[41] while changes in tastes and in technological conditions of production, whose nature it is to cause relative prices to vary, also cause it to vary.[42]

Clearly, this is not a hard and fast criterion.   As has been sufficiently emphasized above, changes in the amount of money and shifts in liquidity preference can affect interest;[43] but so can they sometimes affect relative prices.[44]   Thus our distinction must remain a matter of degree.   Nevertheless, it does enable us to formulate the classical view on the "realness" of interest in terms of the following meaningful hypothesis: Variations in the long-term rate of interest—in time and space—

[38] In particular, one can validly say that the rate of interest is determined in the commodity markets only in the special case where the bond equation, but not the commodity equations, is dependent on real balances (see above, p. 109).   But there is no indication that Modigliani and those who accept his view are aware of the crucial necessity for this assumption.   Indeed, as already pointed out, Modigliani himself explicitly reaffirms the invalid dichotomy (above, pp. 107–8).

[39] Cf. pp. 111–12.
[40] Cf. p. 110.
[41] Cf. Chapters IV:4, VIII:5, X:3–4, and their related Mathematical Appendixes.
[42] Cf. Chapter XI:5–6.   Note in particular the analysis of shifts in the savings and investment functions.
[43] Cf. Chapters X:4 and XII:1–5.
[44] Cf. pp. 41 and 58 above.

have originated primarily in technological changes which have affected the marginal productivity of capital, and in time-preference changes which have affected the desire to save; they have not originated primarily —or even significantly—in changes in the amount of money or shifts in liquidity preference. Keynes thought that he had found a logical error in classical reasoning which justified the immediate rejection of this hypothesis; but, as has been emphasized in the preceding section, it was Keynes' reasoning itself which was in error. Correspondingly, the acceptability of this hypothesis cannot be determined except by detailed historical studies. Thus we have reached the limits of what can be done within the purely theoretical framework of this book. But we might be permitted to express the prejudgment that such studies would give more support to the classical view than to the Keynesian.

MATHEMATICAL APPENDIX

INTRODUCTION

As emphasized in the Preface, this Appendix is not intended to be read independently of the text. Indeed, the reader is specifically warned that it rarely draws the economic implications of the mathematical argument which it presents. Thus in order to obtain these intended implications the reader must in each case study the Appendix together with the sections of the text to which it is explicitly attached. Appendix 1, however, is something of an exception. Though it too is directly related—and, indeed, basic—to the text, it can be read independently of it. It deals with a subject of much wider significance, but one which has not been adequately treated in the standard textbooks on mathematics for economists. This is the reason for its inclusion here.

The main purposes of this Mathematical Appendix are two in number. First, it proves conclusions that the reader of the text is asked to take on faith. Second—and quantitatively more important—it develops the argument with a rigor and precision which the reader has the right to demand, but which the literary and graphical presentations of the text cannot achieve. In particular, it makes clear the full meaning and significance of the crucial distinction between demand curves and market-equilibrium curves, as well as of the fine, though fundamental, distinctions among the various dichotomies of Chapter VIII:3.

It might also be noted that the somewhat extended treatment of Appendixes 8–10 is intended to serve the additional purpose of illustrating the modern mathematical technique of comparative-statics and dynamic analysis by applying it to specific problems of Part Two of the text. In particular, they illustrate and elaborate upon the application—and limitations—of Samuelson's "correspondence principle" in analyzing these problems. It has also been considered desirable to use Appendixes 8–10 to illustrate the detailed workings of Walras' Law in assuring that neither the comparative-statics nor the dynamic analysis of any problem can be affected by the choice of the markets in which this analysis is carried out. This, of course, is a fundamental and recurrent theme of the text.

1. Derivatives in Economic Analysis[1]

a. The purpose of the discussion now to be presented is to make precise the basic conceptual framework which frequently lies behind the argument of the text and of the Mathematical Appendix. Though this framework is implicit in any of the standard expositions of comparative-statics analysis,[2] it has nevertheless remained the center of much confusion in the literature. The following exposition makes no pretense at full mathematical rigor. Nevertheless, it does clarify the nature of this confusion and shows how it can be avoided.[3]

Our primary concern is with the fundamental distinction made in the text between individual-experiments and market-experiments.[4] Mathematically speaking, this is a distinction between derivatives. More generally, it is a reflection of the fact that, by definition, a derivative measures the effect on a dependent variable of a change in an independent variable which is functionally related to it. Hence no derivative has any meaning until this functional relationship is first specified and its variables classified as dependent or independent. The remainder of this discussion is essentially an elaboration of these last two sentences.[5]

Consider, for example, the demand function

$$(1.1) \qquad\qquad q^D = \phi(p),$$

where q^D represents the amount demanded of a certain commodity, and p, its price. Here p is taken as the independent variable, and q^D as the dependent. That is, this function describes the outcome of a conceptual individual-experiment in which an individual (or group of individuals)

---

[1] I am indebted to my colleague Dr. Shmuel Agmon (Department of Mathematics) for reading over Appendix 1. Needless to say, he is in no way responsible for its style or lack of rigor.

[2] See, in particular, P. A. Samuelson, *Foundations of Economic Analysis*, pp. 258–60, 276–78.

[3] My own understanding of these points began with the lucid explanation I heard several years ago from Trygve Haavelmo. I should like to take this opportunity to express again my indebtedness to him.

[4] Cf. Chapters I:4 and III:6.

[5] Cf. on this whole discussion W. F. Osgood, *Advanced Calculus* (New York, 1925), Chapter V, especially pp. 140–41.

is confronted with a price over which he has no control and is asked to indicate the amount of the commodity he demands at that price. Correspondingly, the derivative

$$(1.2) \qquad\qquad \frac{dq^D}{dp} = \phi'(p)$$

describes the change in this amount demanded resulting from an arbitrarily imposed unitary change in the price with which the individual is confronted. By assumption, this derivative is negative.

Alternatively, we can write the demand function in the form

$$(1.3) \qquad\qquad p^D = \psi(q),$$

where $\psi(\ )$ is the inverse function of $\phi(\ )$. This function describes a conceptual experiment in which an individual is arbitrarily confronted with a certain amount of a commodity, q, and asked to indicate the highest per-unit price he is willing to pay for that amount. That is, p^D is Marshall's "demand price."[6] Correspondingly, the derivative

$$(1.4) \qquad\qquad \frac{dp^D}{dq} = \psi'(q)$$

describes the change in this demand price resulting from an arbitrarily imposed unitary change in the quantity of the commodity with which the individual is confronted. This derivative, too, is assumed to be negative.

Thus the derivatives $\phi'(p)$ and $\psi'(q)$ describe, respectively, the outcomes of two conceptually distinct individual-experiments. Indeed, by their very nature these two experiments cannot be conducted simultaneously. It is, of course, true that

$$(1.5) \qquad\qquad \psi'(q) = \frac{1}{\phi'(p)};$$

but this "inverse function rule"[7] should be understood as stating that the effect of an arbitrary variation in price on the quantity demanded also gives us information about the outcome of an alternative experiment which measures the effect of an arbitrary variation in quantity on the demand price.

So much for individual-experiments; let us now turn to market-experiments. Let $q^S = g(p)$ represent the supply function of the market, and equation (1.1) the corresponding demand function. Then

---

6 *Principles*, p. 95.
7 Cf. R. G. D. Allen, *Mathematical Analysis for Economists* (London, 1938), pp. 171–72.

the equilibrium position of this market is described by the following system of equations:

$$q^D = \phi(p),$$

(1.6)
$$q^S = g(p),$$

$$q^D = q^S = q.$$

From the viewpoint of the system as a whole, neither $\dfrac{dq}{dp}$ nor $\dfrac{dp}{dq}$ has any meaning. For, by assumption, this system describes one point—the equilibrium point (q_0, p_0) in Figure 44—and the derivative of a point is

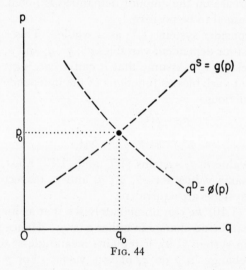

p

$q^S = g(p)$

p_0

$q^D = \varnothing(p)$

O q_0 q

FIG. 44

not defined. In other words, system (1.6) fixes a unique, constant value for p and a unique, constant value for q. Hence it is meaningless to inquire as to the effect of a change in one of these variables on the other. But this, after all, is what is meant by a derivative.

Let us now assume that demand depends also on population, which is assumed to be uninfluenced by the economic forces of our market. Denote this variable by t. Then the foregoing system is replaced by

$$q^D = f(p, t),$$

(1.7)
$$q^S = g(p),$$

$$q^D = q^S = q.$$

277

Instead of (1.2), we now have the partial derivatives denoted by

$$(1.8) \qquad \frac{\partial q^D}{\partial p} = \frac{\partial f(p, t)}{\partial p} \equiv f_1(p, t)$$

and

$$(1.9) \qquad \frac{\partial q^D}{\partial t} = \frac{\partial f(p, t)}{\partial t} \equiv f_2(p, t),$$

where the numbers 1 and 2 denote, respectively, the first and second arguments of $f(p, t)$. The derivative (1.8) measures the same individual-experiment as (1.2); hence it too is negative. The derivative (1.9) measures an individual-experiment in which the population of the economy is suddenly increased, the price being kept constant, and the effect of this increase on the amount demanded is noted. This partial derivative is assumed to be positive.

Let us now consider system (1.7) as a whole. This consists of four equations in the four dependent variables q^D, q^S, q, and p, and the single independent variable t. Assume that it can accordingly be solved out for the dependent variables as functions of the independent one to yield the system of functions

$$(1.10) \qquad \begin{aligned} p &= J(t), \\ q^D = q^S &= q = K(t). \end{aligned}$$

For any given value of t, systems (1.7) and (1.10) must, by definition, both yield the same values for q^D, q^S, q, and p, respectively. In this sense these two systems are equivalent.

From system (1.10) we can immediately see that as long as t remains constant there can be no change in either p or q. Hence in system (1.7) as a whole, as in system (1.6), it remains meaningless[8] to inquire as to the effect of a change in p on q, or vice versa. For p and q are the dependent variables of the system: they cannot change unless the independent variable, t, changes first. All that we can meaningfully ask for is the effects of a change in t on p or on q. These effects are described, respectively, by the following derivatives:

$$(1.11) \qquad \frac{dp}{dt} = J'(t),$$

$$(1.12) \qquad \frac{dq}{dt} = K'(t).$$

---

[8] Meaningless, that is, as long as the dependent and independent variables are defined as they are above. Mathematically, however, there is no reason why p or q could not be designated as an independent variable and t as a dependent one. But this possibility has been excluded by our economic assumption about the exogenous nature of population growth.

278

Though, as just emphasized, systems (1.7) and (1.10) as a whole are equivalent, their individual functions are obviously quite distinct. In particular, those of (1.7) are demand and supply functions, conceptually generated by individual-experiments whose purpose it is to relate amounts demanded and supplied to arbitrarily given price and population levels; while those of (1.10) are market-equilibrium functions, conceptually generated by market-experiments whose purpose it is to relate equilibrium levels of price and quantity to arbitrarily given levels of population.[9] Correspondingly, the derivative of (1.9) is completely distinct from that of (1.12). The former describes the outcome of the individual-experiment already sketched out above.[10] The latter describes the outcome of a market-experiment which begins with the market in a position of equilibrium, disturbs this position by an arbitrary change in population, and then measures the effect of this change on the equilibrium quantity of the market. Clearly, there is no necessity for these two derivatives to be equal.

It is precisely its failure to underline this fundamental distinction that makes the usual notation of differential calculus so undesirable for economic analysis. Thus the symbol $\frac{dq}{dt}$ leaves it dangerously ambiguous as to whether the reference is to $f_2(p, t)$ of equation (1.9) or to $K'(t)$ of equation (1.12). Indeed, it fails to draw the reader's—and writer's—attention to the fact that such a distinction even exists. The discussions of Chapters VIII:2 and XV:2 afford sufficient examples of the analytical errors to which this imprecision can lead.

Correspondingly, it is this ambiguity which has led to the adoption in this Appendix of the notation which denotes the derivative of a function of a single variable by adding a prime to the function [see, e.g., equations (1.2) and (1.11)], and the partial derivative of a function of several variables by adding a subscript to the function to designate the argument with respect to which the partial derivative is being taken [see, e.g., equations (1.8) and (1.9)]. This notation has the additional advantage of emphasizing that the derivative itself is a function—though, of course, a different one—of the same variables on which the originally derived function depends.

This is admittedly a cumbersome notation. But against this disadvantage we must place the advantage of its lack of ambiguity. And, for our present purposes, this is what matters.

b. Before continuing with the foregoing discussion, let us briefly consider another example which illustrates the importance of the

---

9 Cf. Chapter III:6.
10 P. 278.

distinction just made.   This example is drawn from the familiar field
of multiplier analysis.

Let C, I, and Y represent consumption, investment, and national
income, respectively.   Assume the equilibrium position of the economy
to be described by the following simple equations:

(1.13) $C = H(Y)$,

(1.14) $C + I = Y$,

where $H(Y)$ is the consumption function and I is assumed to be exogenous.   That is,

(1.15) $I = I_0$,

where the level I_0 is determined by forces outside the economic system.
The well-known formula for the multiplier, in its usual notation, is then

(1.16) $$\frac{dY}{dI} = \frac{1}{1 - \dfrac{dC}{dY}}.$$

At first sight this is somewhat puzzling.   For, by (1.15), $\dfrac{dI}{dY}$ is

obviously zero; yet by the formula of (1.16), its apparent reciprocal, $\dfrac{dY}{dI}$,

is just as obviously not infinite.   One cannot dismiss this seeming inconsistency by merely saying that derivatives cannot be treated as fractions.
For with respect to the issue at stake, the inverse function rule[11] seems
to imply that they can be so treated and that one can validly write

(1.17) $$\frac{dI}{dY} = \frac{1}{\dfrac{dY}{dI}}.$$

We can, however, readily solve this puzzle by resorting to the notation
advocated at the end of the preceding section.   Consider (1.13)–(1.14).
These are two equations in the two dependent variables—C and Y—
and the one independent variable—I.   Solving out for the dependent
variables as functions of the independent one, we obtain

(1.18) $Y = M(I)$,

(1.19) $C = N(I)$.

---

[11] Cf. above, equation (1.5).

These functions relate a given level of investment to the corresponding equilibrium levels of income and consumption. They are, in our terminology, market-equilibrium functions, in contradistinction to the aggregate demand function represented in (1.13).

Now, by definition, the multiplier is the derivative of (1.18) with respect to I: it describes the outcome of a market-experiment in which the level of investment is arbitrarily changed, and the effect of this change on the equilibrium level of national income is noted. Clearly, this derivative need bear no relationship to the derivative of (1.15) with respect to Y: this describes the outcome of an individual-experiment in which the level of national income is arbitrarily changed, and the effect of this change on the planned level of investment is noted. By the assumption that investment is exogenous, this effect must, of course, be identically zero.

Let us now substitute from (1.13) into (1.14) to yield

$$(1.20) \qquad H(Y) + I = Y.$$

Substituting from (1.18), we then have, by definition of a solution,

$$(1.21) \qquad H[M(I)] + I \equiv M(I).$$

Making use of the "function of a function" rule,[12] and differentiating both sides of this identity with respect to I, we obtain

$$(1.22) \qquad H'(Y)M'(I) + 1 = M'(I).$$

This yields

$$(1.23) \qquad M'(I) = \frac{1}{1 - H'(Y)},$$

where $H'(Y)$ is evaluated at the point of equilibrium.

This is the formula for the multiplier in its most explicit form. It makes unmistakably clear that the derivative on the left-hand side of (1.16) is related to the function (1.18), and not to the investment function (1.15). Thus it also makes clear that our original "puzzle" is merely the result of the failure to distinguish between the derivatives of these two completely different functions.

c. Let us now return to our discussion in Section *a* above. This assumes that the derivatives of the market-equilibrium functions in (1.11)–(1.12) are computed directly from these functions after they have been explicitly solved out from the system of demand and supply

---

[12] Allen, *op. cit.*, p. 169.

equations (1.7). Actually, however, we can obtain these derivatives without first working out this solution. In brief, we can instead make use of the technique of implicit differentiation.[13]

In order to understand this technique—which is used throughout the Appendix—we shall first define the "total differential." Consider, for example, the function $u = H(x, y)$. Let there now be arbitrary incremental changes in the independent variables. Denote these changes by the differentials dx and dy, respectively. These changes must clearly cause a corresponding incremental change in the value of the dependent variable, u. Denote this by du or $dH(\ )$, where $H(\ )$ represents the function $H(x, y)$. Then it can be shown—and this is the fundamental theorem—that

(1.24) $$du = H_1(x, y)dx + H_2(x, y)dy,$$

where, as already noted, the subscripts indicate the argument with respect to which partial differentiation is being carried out.

Assume now that x and y are themselves the functions of other variables,

(1.25) $$x = \phi(v, w) \quad \text{and} \quad y = \psi(v, w).$$

Then, by the fundamental theorem,

(1.26) $$dx = \phi_1(v, w)dv + \phi_2(v, w)dw,$$
$$dy = \psi_1(v, w)dv + \psi_2(v, w)dw.$$

Substituting in (1.24), we then obtain

(1.27) $$du = H_1(\ )[\phi_1(\ )dv + \phi_2(\ )dw] + H_2(\ )[\psi_1(\ )dv + \psi_2(\ )dw].$$

This is the "function of a function" rule for differentials. It should be emphasized that it holds no matter what the nature of the transformation (1.25). In particular, it holds also when we use the transformation $x = x$ and $y = f(x)$. In this case (1.27) becomes

(1.28) $$du = H_1[x, f(x)]dx + H_2[x, f(x)]f'(x)dx.$$

Before applying these equations to the example of the first section, let us make this discussion somewhat more general by assuming that

---

[13] The following is a somewhat amateurish version of the relevant parts of Osgood, *op. cit.*, Chapter V. See also Allen, *op. cit.*, Chapter XIII, and R. Courant, *Differential and Integral Calculus* (second ed.; London, 1937), Vol. I, pp. 457–85; Vol. II, pp. 59–69, 72–73.

Actually, the end of the preceding section has already made use of the technique of implicit differentiation.

just as there is an exogenous variable influencing the demand side, so is there one on the supply side.   In particular, let m be an index of climatic factors, and let an increase in m increase the amount supplied.   System (1.7) is thus replaced by

$$q^D = f(p, t),$$
(1.29) $$\quad q^S = h(p, m),$$
$$q^D = q^S = q.$$

By assumption, the partial derivatives of these functions have the signs $f_1(p, t)<0$, $f_2(p, t)>0$, $h_1(p, m)>0$, and $h_2(p, m)>0$.

Now, system (1.29) is one of four equations in the four dependent variables—q^D, q^S, q, and p—and the two independent variables—t and m.   Assume, then, that it can be solved out for the dependent variables in terms of the independent ones to yield the market-equilibrium functions

$$p = F(t, m),$$
(1.30)
$$q^D = q^S = q = G(t, m).$$

It is desired to determine the signs and magnitudes of the partial derivatives of these functions with respect to t and m without explicitly solving out for the functions $F(\ )$ and $G(\ )$ themselves.

The first step is to substitute the unspecified solutions (1.30) into (1.29) to yield—by definition of a solution—

$$G(t, m) \equiv f[F(t, m), t],$$
(1.31)
$$G(t, m) \equiv h[F(t, m), m].$$

We next apply the fundamental theorem (1.24) in order to take the total differential of both sides of these identities and to obtain

$$dG(t, m) = f_1(p, t)dF(t, m) + f_2(p, t)dt,$$
(1.32)
$$dG(t, m) = h_1(p, m)dF(t, m) + h_2(p, m)dm,$$

where the partial derivatives of $f(\ )$ and $h(\ )$ are evaluated at the point of equilibrium.   Upon expansion, this yields

$$G_1(t, m)dt + G_2(t, m)dm = f_1(p, t)[F_1(t, m)dt + F_2(t, m)dm]$$
$$+ f_2(p, t)dt,$$
(1.33)
$$G_1(t, m)dt + G_2(t, m)dm = h_1(p, m)[F_1(t, m)dt + F_2(t, m)dm]$$
$$+ h_2(p, m)dm.$$

In this system of equations, $f_i(\ )$ and $h_i(\ )$ $(i = 1, 2)$ are the known partial derivatives of the specified functions $f(\ )$ and $h(\ )$; while $F_i(\ )$ and $G_i(\ )$ are the unknown partial derivatives of the unspecified functions $F(\ )$ and $G(\ )$.

Let us first assume that only t varies, while m remains constant. That is, $dm = 0$. Substituting this into (1.33) and dividing through by dt, we obtain

(1.34)
$$G_1(t, m) = f_1(p, t)F_1(t, m) + f_2(p, t),$$
$$G_1(t, m) = h_1(p, m)F_1(t, m).$$

Rewrite this as

(1.35)
$$f_1(p, t)F_1(t, m) - G_1(t, m) = -f_2(p, t),$$
$$h_1(p, m)F_1(t, m) - G_1(t, m) = 0.$$

This can be considered as a system of two equations in the two unknowns, $F_1(t, m)$ and $G_1(t, m)$. Solving this system by the use of determinants, we obtain

$$(1.36) \quad F_1(t, m) = \frac{\begin{vmatrix} -f_2(p, t) & -1 \\ 0 & -1 \end{vmatrix}}{\begin{vmatrix} f_1(p, t) & -1 \\ h_1(p, m) & -1 \end{vmatrix}} = \frac{f_2(p, t)}{-f_1(p, t) + h_1(p, m)}.$$

According to the assumptions made above as to the signs of $f_i(\ )$ and $h_i(\ )$ $(i = 1, 2)$, we see that $F_1(t, m)$ is always positive. Similarly, we obtain

$$(1.37) \quad G_1(t, m) = \frac{h_1(p, m)f_2(p, t)}{-f_1(p, t) + h_1(p, m)},$$

which must also be positive. That is, a positive shift in tastes increases both the equilibrium price and quantity: a rightward shift of the demand curve intersects the unchanged supply curve at a higher price and quantity.

In a corresponding way, by permitting only m to vary, and setting $dt = 0$, we obtain

$$(1.38) \quad F_2(t, m) = \frac{-h_2(p, m)}{-f_1(p, t) + h_1(p, m)} < 0$$

and

$$(1.39) \quad G_2(t, m) = \frac{-f_1(p, t)h_2(p, m)}{-f_1(p, t) + h_1(p, m)} > 0.$$

That is, favorable climatic conditions increase the equilibrium quantity, but decrease the equilibrium price: a rightward shift of the supply curve intersects the fixed demand curve at a higher quantity, but lower price.

Thus the properties of the unknown derivatives can be specified in terms of the known derivatives—without explicitly solving for the functions $F(\ )$ and $G(\ )$. This, of course, is the meaning of implicit differentiation.

We note finally that equation (1.37) clearly shows the distinction emphasized at the end of Section *a* above. In terms of systems (1.7) and (1.10), discussed there, this equation takes the form

$$(1.40) \qquad K'(t) = \frac{g'(p)f_2(p,\,t)}{-f_1(p,\,t) + g'(p)}.$$

Here we explicitly see that $K'(t)$ and $f_2(p,\,t)$ are two completely distinct derivatives. True, the former does depend upon the latter; but it depends just as well upon $g'(p)$ and $f_1(p,\,t)$.

d. Another important application of the total differential—and one used repeatedly in this Appendix—is that connected with maximization subject to side restraints. For rigorous treatments of this question the reader is referred elsewhere.[14] Our present purpose is to provide an intuitive understanding of the problems involved.

Assume, for example, that it is desired to maximize

$$(1.41) \qquad w = f(x, y).$$

This, of course, is accomplished by choosing those values of x and y which satisfy the system of equations

$$(1.42) \qquad \begin{aligned} f_1(x, y) &= 0, \\ f_2(x, y) &= 0, \end{aligned}$$

where $f_i(\ )$ $(i = 1, 2)$ is the partial derivative of $f(\ )$ with respect to its ith argument.[15] Let us now assume that the maximization of $f(\ )$ is to be carried out subject to the additional restriction

$$(1.43) \qquad y = g(x).$$

Then we are no longer free to choose both x and y as in (1.42); for (1.43) tells us that once the value of x is chosen, that of y is immediately

---

14 Osgood, *op. cit.*, pp. 180–82. A more detailed treatment can be found in T. Chaundy, *Differential Calculus* (Oxford, 1935), pp. 256 ff.

15 We assume throughout this section—and the Mathematical Appendix in general—that the second-order conditions for a maximum are satisfied.

specified. In effect, then, we are no longer maximizing a function of two variables—x and y—but a function of one variable only. In particular, substituting (1.43) into (1.41), our problem reduces to the ordinary maximization of

$$(1.44) \qquad w = f[x, g(x)] \equiv h(x)$$

with respect to x.

It might help to visualize this problem if we think of $w = f(x, y)$ as describing the height of a hill at each of its points.[16] If we wish to find the maximum point of this hill, we obviously choose those values of x and y which correspond to its peak. But our task may be limited instead to finding the highest point on the path on this hill which is cut out by its intersection with the vertical surface described by $y = g(x)$. This is what is involved in the maximization of $w = h(x)$. Clearly, there is no reason why this path should pass through the peak; hence there is also no reason why the value of x yielded by the maximization of $w = h(x)$ should be the same as that yielded by the unrestricted maximization of $w = f(x, y)$.

More generally, assume that we wish to maximize

$$(1.45) \qquad u = \psi(x_1, \ldots, x_n),$$

subject to the m side restraints,

$$(1.46) \qquad \phi^j(x_1, \ldots, x_n) = 0 \qquad (j = 1, \ldots, m < n).$$

Assume that we can solve out the m equations of (1.46) for $x_1, \ldots, x_m$ as explicit functions of the remaining x_i:

$$(1.47) \qquad x_j = F^j(x_{m+1}, \ldots, x_n) \qquad (j = 1, \ldots, m).$$

Then the desired maximization is achieved by substituting from (1.47) into (1.45) to yield

$$u = \psi[F^1(x_{m+1}, \ldots, x_n), \ldots, F^m(x_{m+1}, \ldots, x_n), x_{m+1},$$

$$(1.48) \qquad \ldots, x_n]$$

$$\equiv G(x_{m+1}, \ldots, x_n),$$

and by maximizing $G(\ )$ with respect to all its $n - m$ variables.[17]

---

16 The following illustration is due to Allen, *op. cit.*, p. 365.

17 Note that if $m = n$, the function $G(\ )$ becomes a constant, so that the whole problem of maximization disappears. More specifically, under this assumption, system (1.46) has n equations which suffice to determine specific values for each of the n variables, x_i $(i = 1, \ldots, n)$. Hence no freedom is left to choose values of these variables that enable $G(\ )$ to satisfy some maximization criterion.

As in the case of implicit differentiation, however, it is desirable to find a method by which we can find this maximum position without the necessity of carrying out the foregoing substitution explicitly. This is the method of Lagrange multipliers. Let us first see how it is applied to the simple case discussed in (1.41)–(1.44) above

We form first the sum

$$(1.49) \qquad v = f(x, y) - \lambda[y - g(x)],$$

where λ—the so-called Lagrange multiplier—is a new variable arbitrarily introduced into the analysis. Let us now find the values of x and y which maximize this sum for a given value of λ. Differentiating partially with respect to x and y, we obtain the maximum conditions

$$(1.50) \qquad f_1(x, y) + \lambda g'(x) = 0,$$

$$(1.51) \qquad f_2(x, y) - \lambda = 0.$$

To these we add the side restriction (1.43),

$$(1.52) \qquad y = g(x)$$

Thus (1.50)–(1.52) are three equations in the three variables—x, y, and λ. It now remains to show that the value of x determined by this system of equations is necessarily that value which maximizes $w = h(x)$ in (1.44).

In order for $h(x)$ to be at a maximum, its total differential must be zero. That is, it must be impossible to increase $h(x)$ by any incremental displacement, dx, in the value of x. Using the identity of (1.44), we express this condition as

$$(1.53) \qquad dh(x) \equiv df[x, g(x)] = 0$$

Expanding by (1.28), we then obtain

$$(1.54) \qquad f_1[x, g(x)]dx + f_2[x, g(x)]g'(x)dx = 0.$$

Dividing through by dx this reduces to

$$(1.55) \qquad f_1[x, g(x)] + f_2[x, g(x)]g'(x) = 0.$$

But substituting from (1.51) and (1.52) into (1.50), we see that this is precisely the condition which emerges from the use of the Lagrange multiplier. Thus both methods determine the same value of x, and hence—by (1.43)—the same value of y.

Let us now consider the more general case described in (1.45)–(1.48). We introduce into the analysis the Lagrange multipliers λ_j ($j = 1, \ldots, m$) and form the sum

$$(1.56) \qquad V = \psi(x_1, \ldots, x_n) - \sum_{=1}^{m} \lambda_j[x_j - F^j(x_{m+1}, \ldots, x_n)].$$

287

Let us now find the values of the x_i $(i = 1, \ldots, n)$ which maximize this sum for given values of the λ_j. Differentiating partially with respect to the x_i, we obtain

$$(1.57) \qquad \psi_j(x_1, \ldots, x_n) - \lambda_j = 0 \qquad (j = 1, \ldots, m),$$

$$(1.58) \qquad \psi_r(x_1, \ldots, x_n) + \sum_{j=1}^{m} \lambda_j F_r^j(x_{m+1}, \ldots, x_n) = 0$$
$$(r = m + 1, \ldots, n).$$

Add now the side conditions (1.47):

$$(1.59) \qquad x_j = F^j(x_{m+1}, \ldots, x_n) \qquad (j = 1, \ldots, m).$$

Altogether, then, we have $n + m$ equations in the $n + m$ variables—x_i $(i = 1, \ldots, m, m + 1, \ldots, n)$ and λ_j $(j = 1, \ldots, m)$. It remains to show that the values of the x_r $(r = m + 1, \ldots, n)$ determined by this system of equations are necessarily those which maximize $u = G(x_{m+1}, \ldots, x_n)$ in (1.48).

In order for $G(\ )$ to be at a maximum, its total differential,

$$(1.60) \qquad du = \sum_{r=m+1}^{n} G_r(x_{m+1}, \ldots, x_n) dx_r,$$

must be zero no matter what the nature of the displacements dx_r.[18] In particular, setting all but one of the dx_r equal to zero by turn, we obtain the $n - m$ maximum conditions:

$$(1.61) \qquad G_r(x_{m+1}, \ldots, x_n) dx_r = 0 \qquad (r = m + 1, \ldots, n).$$

By (1.27) and identity (1.48), these can be written as[19]

$$(1.62) \qquad \sum_{j=1}^{m} \psi_j [\ ] F_r^j (\ ) dx_r + \psi_r [\ ] dx_r = 0$$
$$(r = m + 1, \ldots, n).$$

Dividing through by dx_r, we obtain the conditions that must be satisfied by the x_r $(r = m + 1, \ldots, n)$ in order to maximize $G(\ )$. But substituting from (1.57) and (1.59) into (1.58), we see that these are precisely the conditions which emerge from the use of the Lagrange multipliers. Thus both methods determine the same values of the x_r $(r = m + 1, \ldots, n)$, and hence—by (1.47)—the same values of the x_j $(j = 1, \ldots, m)$.

---

[18] Cf. Courant, *op. cit.*, Vol. II, p. 185.

[19] The brackets in the following expression emphasize the fact that we are considering the function ψ after substitution—that is, in the form described by (1.48).

2. Appendix to Chapter II

$a.$[1] Consider an economy with n goods, the nth good being paper money. Let $p_1, \ldots, p_n$ be the prices of these n goods in terms of an abstract unit of account. The corresponding money prices of these goods are, then, $p_1/p_n, \ldots, p_{n-1}/p_n, 1$. Finally, the relative prices of the $n-1$ commodities are $p_1/p_k, \ldots, p_{n-1}/p_k$, where p_k is the price of the kth commodity.

It will be convenient for our purposes to define an average level of commodity prices as

$$(2.1) \qquad p = \sum_{j=1}^{n-1} w_j p_j,$$

where the w_j are known weights whose sum is unity. The relative prices can then be written $p_1/p, \ldots, p_{n-1}/p$. The price index, p, will also be used in deflating money incomes and money balances.

Consider a particular individual, the ath. Let $\bar{Z}_1^a, \ldots, \bar{Z}_{n-1}^a$ represent the respective quantities of his initial holdings of the $n-1$ commodities. Similarly, let $\bar{Z}_n^a$ represent his initial quantity of money. Then, in accordance with the definitions of the text, his real income is represented by $\dfrac{\sum_{j=1}^{n-1} p_j \bar{Z}_j^a}{p}$; and the real value of his money balances, by $p_n \bar{Z}_n^a / p$. Let $Z_1^a, \ldots, Z_{n-1}^a$ represent the respective quantities of his optimum collection of goods. Then the demand functions are assumed to have the forms[2]

$$(2.2) \qquad Z_j^a = F_j^a \left(\frac{p_1}{p}, \ldots, \frac{p_{n-1}}{p}, \frac{\sum_{r=1}^{n-1} p_r \bar{Z}_r^a}{p}, \frac{p_n \bar{Z}_n^a}{p} \right) \qquad (j = 1, \ldots, n-1).$$

Define now the excess demand for a commodity:

$$(2.3) \qquad X_j^a = Z_j^a - \bar{Z}_j^a \qquad (j = 1, \ldots, n-1).$$

---

[1] Attached to Chapter II:3–4.

[2] In view of the comments at the end of Mathematical Appendix 1:a above, it might be well to point out that the $F_j(\ )$ are *not* partial derivatives.

Then the commodity excess-demand functions of the ath individual can be written as

$$(2.4) \qquad X_j^a = F_j^a\left(\frac{p_1}{p}, \ldots, \frac{p_{n-1}}{p}, \frac{\sum_{r=1}^{n-1} p_r Z_r^a}{p}, \frac{p_n Z_n^a}{p}\right) - Z_j^a$$

$$(j = 1, \ldots, n-1).$$

These functions clearly have the properties attributed to them in the text: they depend on relative prices, real income, and the real value of initial money balances. True, the excess-demand functions (2.4)—as distinct from the demand functions (2.2)—also depend on the initial quantity Z_j^a. But, as already indicated in the text,[3] this is assumed to remain constant during the discussion; hence this dependence can, for our purposes, be ignored.

We note in particular that an equi-proportionate change in all account-ing prices, or in all money prices *and* the initial amount of money, leaves each of the arguments in (2.2) and (2.4) unaffected; hence it also leaves unaffected the values of these functions. On the other hand, an equi-proportionate change in money prices alone does affect the last argument of each of these functions; hence, in general, it also affects their values. Clearly, however, this effect is not necessarily in pro-portion to the change in money prices. Similarly, an increase in the initial amount of money also increases the last arguments, and there-fore, for a noninferior commodity, the excess amounts demanded—though, again, not necessarily in proportion to the amount of money.

The demand functions (2.2) treat the p_i $(i = 1, \ldots, n)$ as the inde-pendent variables and the Z_j^a as the dependent ones. Let us now reverse the roles of these variables and form accordingly the inverse functions of (2.2). We first rewrite (2.1) as

$$(2.5) \qquad \sum_{j=1}^{n-1} w_j \frac{p_j}{p} = 1.$$

Consider now equations (2.2) and (2.5) as n equations in the n variables p_j/p $(j = 1, \ldots, n-1)$ and $p_n Z_n^a/p$. Assume that we can solve out these equations for the inverse functions

$$(2.6) \qquad \frac{p_j}{p} = \phi_j^a(Z_1^a, \ldots, Z_{n-1}^a; Z_1^a, \ldots, Z_{n-1}^a)$$

$$(j = 1, \ldots, n-1),$$

---

[3] P. 19, footnote 5. Cf. also p. 13.

(2.7) $$\frac{p_n Z_n^a}{p} = \phi_n^a(Z_1^a, \ldots, Z_{n-1}^a; \bar{Z}_1^a, \ldots, \bar{Z}_{n-1}^a).$$

Dividing (2.6) by (2.7), we then obtain

(2.8) $$\frac{p_j}{p_n} = \frac{\bar{Z}_n^a \phi_j^a(Z_1^a, \ldots, Z_{n-1}^a; \bar{Z}_1^a, \ldots, \bar{Z}_{n-1}^a)}{\phi_n^a(Z_1^a, \ldots, Z_{n-1}^a; \bar{Z}_1^a, \ldots, \bar{Z}_{n-1}^a)}$$

$$(j = 1, \ldots, n-1).$$

These are Marshallian demand functions: they express the money demand prices an individual is willing to pay, p_j/p_n, as functions of the Z_j^a and $\bar{Z}_j^a$ $(j = 1, \ldots, n-1)$.[4] We can see from (2.8) that an increase in $\bar{Z}_n^a$ causes a proportionate increase in these demand prices.   Clearly, this same conclusion would hold if we were to obtain the inverses of the excess-demand functions (2.4).   The only difference would be that these inverse functions would depend on the X_j^a instead of the Z_j^a.

b.[5] Let us now digress for a moment in order to assure ourselves that the term "substitution effect" is being used in the text in the same sense defined by Hicks.   The easiest way of accomplishing this is to work within Hicks' model and show that his substitution effect disappears when all prices change in the same proportion.   Using the notation of Hicks' Mathematical Appendix sections 6–8, we can write his excess-demand function as

(2.9) $$x_s = f^s(p_1, \ldots, p_n, M)   (s = 1, \ldots, n).$$

Taking the differential of this function, holding M constant, we obtain

(2.10)
$$dx_s = \sum_{r=1}^{n} f_r^s(p_1, \ldots, p_n, M)dp_r$$

$$= \sum_{r=1}^{n} f_r^s(p_1, \ldots, p_n, M) \cdot p_r \frac{dp_r}{p_r},$$

where $f_r^s(\ )$ is the partial derivative of $f^s(\ )$ with respect to its rth argument.   Assume that all prices change in the same proportion. Denote this common proportion by $\frac{dp}{p}$.   Then we obtain from (2.10)

(2.11) $$\frac{dx_s}{\frac{dp}{p}}\bigg|_{M \text{ const.}} = \sum_{r=1}^{n} f_r^s(p_1, \ldots, p_n, M) \cdot p_r.$$

---

[4] Cf. above, Mathematical Appendix 1:*a*.
[5] Attached to Chapter II:3.

Using Hicks' notation,[6] this is written as

$$\frac{dx_s}{dp}\bigg|_{\substack{p \\ M \text{ const.}}} = \sum_{r=1}^{n}\frac{\partial x_s}{\partial p_r}\cdot p_r = \sum_{r=1}^{n}\left(-x_r\frac{\partial x_s}{\partial M}+X_{rs}\right)p_r$$

(2.12)

$$= \frac{\partial x_s}{\partial M}\sum_{r=1}^{n}(-p_r x_r)+\sum_{r=1}^{n}p_r X_{rs},$$

where the X_{rs} are Hicks' substitution terms. As will be recalled,[7] these terms must obey the rule $\sum_{r=1}^{n}p_r X_{rs}=0$. Hence, using Hicks' equation (6.1), the preceding equation can be rewritten as

(2.13)
$$\frac{dx_s}{dp}\bigg|_{\substack{p \\ M \text{ const.}}} = -M\frac{\partial x_s}{\partial M}.$$

Thus an equi-proportionate change in prices has only an income, and not a substitution, effect.

Equation (2.13) can actually be obtained more directly by first noting that $f^s(\ )$ is homogeneous of degree zero in the p_r and M, and then making use of Euler's theorem[8] to write

(2.14) $0 \equiv \sum_{r=1}^{n} f_r^s(p_1, \quad ., p_n, M)\cdot p_r + f_{n+1}^s(p_1, \quad , p_n, M)\cdot M.$

This can be substituted into (2.11) to yield (2.13). For our present purposes, however, the indirect demonstration (2.10)–(2.13) is preferable, in that it shows explicitly how Hicks' substitution terms cancel out.

c.[9] Let us now return to our main discussion. Let Z_n^a represent the individual's optimum amount of money. Write the demand function for money as

(2.15) $Z_n^a = F_n^d\left(p_1, \ldots, p_{n-1}, p, \sum_{j=1}^{n-1}p_j Z_j^a, p_n Z_n^a\right).$

Let $X_n^a = Z_n^a - \bar{Z}_n^a$ be the excess demand for money. Then the excess-demand function is

(2.16) $X_n^a = F_n^d\left(p_1, \ldots, p_{n-1}, p, \sum_{j=1}^{n-1}p_j Z_j^a, p_n Z_n^a\right) - \bar{Z}_n^a.$

---

6 *Value and Capital*, p. 309, equation (8.1).
7 *Ibid.*, p. 311, rules (1) and (3).
8 Allen, *op. cit.*, pp. 317–20.
9 Attached to Chapter II:5.

Here the form of the function is only generally indicated. However, as emphasized in the text, the budget restraint enables us to write this function in a more specific way, one which clearly shows its relationship to the corresponding commodity functions.

In particular, this restraint states that the money value of the individual's optimum collection must equal the money value of his initial one. That is,

$$(2.17) \qquad \sum_{j=1}^{n-1} \frac{p_j}{p_n} Z_j^a + Z_n^a = \sum_{j=1}^{n-1} \frac{p_j}{p_n} \bar{Z}_j^a + \bar{Z}_n^a.$$

This can be rewritten as

$$(2.18) \qquad X_n^a = Z_n^a - \bar{Z}_n^a = -\sum_{j=1}^{n-1} \frac{p_j}{p_n}(Z_j^a - \bar{Z}_j^a) = -\sum_{j=1}^{n-1} \frac{p_j}{p_n} X_j^a.$$

Substituting from (2.4) into (2.18), we then see that the excess-demand function for money (2.16) has the specific form

$$(2.19)$$

$$F_n^a\left(p_1, \ldots, p_{n-1}, p, \sum_{j=1}^{n-1} p_j \bar{Z}_j^a, p_n \bar{Z}_n^a\right) - \bar{Z}_n^a$$

$$\equiv -\sum_{j=1}^{n-1} \frac{p_j}{p_n}\left[F_j^a\left(\frac{p_1}{p}, \ldots, \frac{p_{n-1}}{p}, \frac{\sum_{r=1}^{n-1} p_r \bar{Z}_r^a}{p}, \frac{p_n \bar{Z}_n^a}{p}\right) - \bar{Z}_j^a \right]$$

$$(2.20) \qquad \equiv \sum_{j=1}^{n-1} \frac{p_j}{p_n}\left[\bar{Z}_j^a - F_j^a\left(\frac{p_1}{p}, \ldots, \frac{p_{n-1}}{p}, \frac{\sum_{r=1}^{n-1} p_r \bar{Z}_r^a}{p}, \frac{p_n \bar{Z}_n^a}{p}\right) \right].$$

As can readily be seen, this function has the properties attributed to it in the text. An equi-proportionate increase in the money prices of commodities *and* in the initial quantity of money leaves unchanged each of the bracketed terms in the above summation. But these terms are now, respectively, premultiplied by a proportionately higher money price, p_j/p_n. Hence the right-hand side of (2.19)—or (2.20)—must increase in the same proportion. Hence so must the amount of excess demand for money, X_n^a.

On the other hand, if only money prices are increased, then, as we have seen, the X_j^a also change. In particular, if none of the commodities are inferior, each of the $F_j^a(\ )$ must decrease; hence each of the bracketed terms in (2.20) must increase. It follows that X_n^a must increase more than proportionately. That is, the real value of the excess demand for money must increase.

This same result can be obtained from (2.16) and (2.20) by multiplying through by p_n and then dividing by p. This yields the excess-demand function for *real* money holdings,

$$(2.21) \quad \frac{p_n X_n^a}{p} = \sum_{j=1}^{n-1} \frac{p_j}{p} \left[Z_j^a - F_j^a \left(\frac{p_1}{p}, \ldots, \frac{p_{n-1}}{p}, \frac{\sum_{r=1}^{n-1} p_r Z_r^a}{p}, \frac{p_n Z_n^a}{p} \right) \right].$$

This function clearly depends only on relative prices, real income, and the real value of initial money balances. It is also clear that an equi-proportionate increase in the p_j ($j = 1, \ldots, n-1$) and p leaves the premultiplicative factors p_j/p unchanged, and increases each of the bracketed terms on the right-hand side of (2.21). Hence the left-hand side must also increase.

Let us turn now from the excess-demand to the demand functions. From (2.21) we obtain the demand function for *real* money holdings,

$$(2.22) \quad \frac{p_n Z_n^a}{p} = \sum_{j=1}^{n-1} \frac{p_j}{p} [Z_j^a - F_j^a(\quad)] + \frac{p_n Z_n^a}{p}.$$

Assume that the marginal propensity to spend on commodities out of initial real money balances is less than unity. Then an equi-proportionate increase in the p_j and p decreases the real value of initial money balances, $p_n Z_n^a/p$, by more than it decreases the aggregate real value of demand for commodities, $\sum_{j=1}^{n-1} \frac{p_j}{p} F_j^a(\quad)$. Hence, by (2.22), it decreases the amount demanded of real money holdings, $p_n Z_n^a/p$.

This same conclusion can be reached more simply by first noting that (2.22) shows the demand for real money holdings to depend only on relative prices, real income, and the real value of initial money balances. Hence we can rewrite (2.22) as

$$(2.23) \quad \frac{p_n Z_n^a}{p} = \psi^a \left(\frac{p_1}{p}, \ldots, \frac{p_{n-1}}{p}, \frac{\sum_{r=1}^{n-1} p_r Z_r^a}{p}, \frac{p_n Z_n^a}{p} \right).$$

Now, the marginal-propensity assumption of the preceding paragraph implies that an individual uses part of any increase in initial real money balances to increase his demand for real money holdings.[10] That is, it implies that these holdings are not an inferior good. Therefore, since an equi-proportionate change in money prices has only a negative

---

[10] Cf. p. 27.

real-balance effect, it must cause a decrease in the demand for these holdings.

In a similar way we can obtain from (2.20) the demand function for nominal money holdings:

$$(2.24) \qquad Z_n^a = \sum_{j=1}^{n-1} \frac{p_j}{p_n} [Z_j^a - F_j^a(\quad)] + Z_n^a.$$

This function clearly has the property that an equi-proportionate increase in the p_j, p, and Z_n^a causes a proportionate increase in Z_n^a. Consider now an increase in the p_j and p alone. Since Z_n^a is a constant, this obviously increases the right-hand side of (2.24) to exactly the same extent that it increases the right-hand side of (2.20). That is, it increases Z_n^a and X_n^a to the same *absolute* extent. Relatively, however, these increases are quite different. For whereas X_n^a increases more than proportionately to the price increase, Z_n^a does so less than proportionately This can be clearly seen by using (2.23) to rewrite (2.24) as

$$(2.25) \qquad Z_n^a = \frac{p}{p_n} \psi^a(\quad).$$

A doubling of all commodity prices doubles the premultiplicative factor p/p_n; but it causes $\psi^a(\quad)$ to decrease. Hence Z_n^a must less than double.[11]

Let us now drop our assumption that none of the commodities are inferior. By definition, the $F_j^a(\quad)$ of such commodities increase as a result of the price increase. Hence the corresponding bracketed terms in (2.22) decrease. Indeed, if this inferiority is sufficiently pronounced, the whole summation in equation (2.22) might decrease. Insofar as *real* money holdings are concerned, this reinforces our preceding conclusion. For it is obvious from (2.22) that the demand for these holdings must decrease. This is merely an expression of the fact that, by the budget restraint, it is impossible for goods-as-a-whole to be inferior. Hence inferiority of commodities implies normalcy of real money holdings.[12]

On the other hand, a change is called for in our description of the demand for *nominal* money holdings. For it is clear from equation (2.24) that under conditions of pronounced commodity inferiority it is no longer certain that an equi-proportionate increase in the p_j and p will cause Z_n^a to increase. Alternatively, in terms of equation (2.25), commodity inferiority may make the demand for real money holdings, $\psi^a(\quad)$, decline so sharply that Z_n^a will also decline.

---

[11] Note, though, that if $\psi^a(\quad)$ is invariant under changes in p, then Z_n^a must double. But such an invariance is highly unlikely; cf. p. 27, lines 19–24.

[12] Cf. the discussion of equation (2.23).

The argument of this section can be conveniently summarized in the following graphical terms: Consider equi-proportionate changes in the $p_j (j = 1, \ldots, n - 1)$ and p. By inserting such changes into equation (2.24), we generate the demand curve for nominal money holdings in Figure 45 (which is identical with Figure 4 of the text). If there are no inferior commodities, this curve must be negatively sloped. If in addition real money holdings are not an inferior good, the elasticity of this curve must be less than unity. If, however, real money holdings are inferior, then, as can be seen from (2.25), this elasticity becomes greater than unity. Finally, if commodity inferiority is sufficiently widespread, the slope of this curve might become positive.

In a similar way we can generate from (2.22)—or (2.23)—a demand

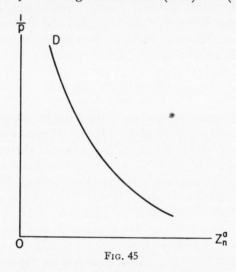

FIG. 45

curve for the good *real* money holdings. The price of this good is nothing but the price level p itself: for if the price of a unit of commodities-in-general is p dollars, the price of a unit of liquid command over a unit of commodities-in-general must also be p dollars. If these holdings are a normal good, the slope of this demand curve in Figure 46 must be negative. If commodities-as-a-whole are also normal, the elasticity of this curve will be less than unity. For from (2.24) we know that, under these circumstances, an increase in the p_j and p increases Z_n^a; hence it follows from (2.23) that $\psi^a(\ )$ must decrease less than in proportion to the increase in p. On the other hand, if commodities-as-a-whole are inferior, $\psi^a(\ )$ may decline more than in proportion to the increase in p. That is, the elasticity of the curve in Figure 46 may be greater than unity. It is clear from equation (2.25) that such an elasticity for the curve in Figure 46 corresponds to a positive slope for the curve in Figure 45, and vice versa.

Similarly, by subjecting (2.21) to equi-proportionate changes in the p_j and p we can generate an *excess*-demand curve for real money holdings. If we relabel the abscissa of Figure 46 to read $p_n X_n^a / p$ instead of $p_n Z_n^a / p$, and if we assume that there are no inferior commodities, such a curve would appear in Figure 46 with a positive slope. The foregoing examination of equation (2.22) shows why the good real money holdings has this peculiar property that the slopes of its demand and excess-demand curves are not the same. In brief, that which distinguishes real money holdings from any other good is the fact that a change in its price necessarily causes a change in its initial quantity.

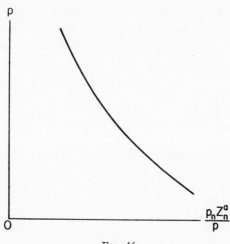

$$p$$

$$\frac{p_n Z_n^a}{p}$$

FIG. 46

We note finally that in Figures 45 and 46—as well as in Figures 3 and 4 of the text—we obtain, strictly speaking, a whole family of curves. Consider, for example, Figure 3. Start with an arbitrarily selected set of prices, $p_1^0, \ldots, p_{n-1}^0$, whose average, by (2.1), is p_0, and with the initial amount of money Z_n^{a0}. Assume that these values, upon insertion into equation (2.24), yield a value for Z_n^a equal to the number M_0. Thus we obtain the point $(M_0, 1/p_0)$ in Figure 3. If we now change the p_j and Z_n^a equi-proportionately, we generate from (2.24) the rectangular hyperbola of that diagram. But consider now another set of values, $p_1^1, \ldots, p_{n-1}^1$, whose average is again p_0. Even if we use the same initial value of money balances, Z_n^{a0}, we will not generally obtain from (2.24) the same value, M_0, for Z_n^a. That is, (2.24) will now yield in Figure 3 a point, $(M_1, 1/p_0)$, where M_1 is generally different from M_0. By subjecting $p_1^1, \ldots, p_{n-1}^1$ and Z_n^{a0} to equi-proportionate changes, we will thus generate from (2.24) a second rectangular hyperbola with as much right as the first one to be considered a demand curve. Continuing in this way, we can generate an infinite number of such rectangular hyperbolas in Figure 3.

This multiplicity of curves is simply a manifestation of the "index-number problem." It reflects the familiar fact that arrays of prices which are the "same" from the viewpoint of their average level are not the "same" from the viewpoint of other attributes. This is a problem from which we have had to abstract in the text[13]—and from which we must continue to abstract here.

d.[14] Assume that there are A individuals in the economy. Let the market demand for any good be represented by $Z_i = \sum_{a=1}^{A} Z_i^a$. Similarly, let the total initial endowment of a good be represented by $\bar{Z}_i = \sum_{a=1}^{A} \bar{Z}_i^a$. Then the market excess-demand function for the jth commodity is

$$
X_j = Z_j - \bar{Z}_j
$$

(2.26)

$$
= \sum_{a=1}^{A} \left[F_j^a \left(\frac{p_1}{p}, \ldots, \frac{p_{n-1}}{p}, \frac{\sum_{r=1}^{n-1} p_r Z_r^a}{p}, \frac{p_n Z_n^a}{p} \right) - \bar{Z}_j^a \right]
$$

For convenience, this will be written as

(2.27)

$$
X_j = F_j \left(\frac{p_1}{p}, \ldots, \frac{p_{n-1}}{p}, \frac{\sum_{r=1}^{n-1} p_r Z_r^1}{p}, \ldots, \frac{\sum_{r=1}^{n-1} p_r Z_r^A}{p}, \frac{p_n Z_n^1}{p}, \right.
$$

$$
\left. \ldots, \frac{p_n Z_n^A}{p} \right) - \bar{Z}_j \qquad (j = 1, \ldots, n-1).
$$

The excess-demand function for money then has the form

(2.28)

$$
X_n = -\sum_{j=1}^{n-1} \frac{p_j}{p_n} \left[F_j \left(\frac{p_1}{p}, \ldots, \frac{p_{n-1}}{p}, \frac{\sum_{r=1}^{n-1} p_r Z_r^1}{p}, \ldots, \frac{\sum_{r=1}^{n-1} p_r Z_r^A}{p}, \right. \right.
$$

$$
\left. \left. \frac{p_n Z_n^1}{p}, \ldots, \frac{p_n Z_n^A}{p} \right) - \bar{Z}_j \right].
$$

---

13 P. 13, footnote 4.
14 Attached to Chapter II:6.

If the marginal propensity to demand out of real income were always equal for any two individuals, and if a corresponding equality were also to hold for real balances, then (2.27) and (2.28) could be rewritten, respectively, as

$$
(2.29) \qquad X_j = F_j\left(\frac{p_1}{p}, \ldots, \frac{p_{n-1}}{p}, \frac{\sum\limits_{r=1}^{n-1} p_r Z_r}{p}, \frac{p_n Z_n}{p}\right) - Z_j
$$

$$
(j = 1, \ldots, n-1)
$$

and

$$
(2.30) \qquad X_n = -\sum_{j=1}^{n-1}\frac{p_j}{p_n}\left[F_j\left(\frac{p_1}{p}, \ldots, \frac{p_{n-1}}{p}, \frac{\sum\limits_{r=1}^{n-1} p_r Z_r}{p}, \frac{p_n Z_n}{p}\right) - Z_j\right].
$$

Thus only under these assumptions are the market excess-demand functions analogous to the individual excess-demand functions.[15]

---

[15] In this and the preceding section, I have denoted the excess demand for nominal money holdings by X_n and X_n^a, respectively. The reader might instead prefer to denote such holdings by $p_n X_n$ and $p_n X_n^a$, respectively. This in no way affects the essentials of the argument. A similar statement holds for Z_n^a and $p_n Z_n^a$.

3. Appendix to Chapter III

a.[1] From (2.27) and (2.28) we obtain the n market excess-demand equations

$$(3.1) \quad F_j\left(\frac{p_1}{p}, \ldots, \frac{p_{n-1}}{p}, \frac{\sum\limits_{r=1}^{n-1} p_r Z_r^1}{p}, \ldots, \frac{\sum\limits_{r=1}^{n-1} p_r Z_r^A}{p}, \frac{p_n Z_n^1}{p}, \right.$$

$$\left. \ldots, \frac{p_n Z_n^A}{p}\right) - Z_j = 0 \quad (j = 1, \ldots, n-1),$$

$$(3.2) \quad \sum_{j=1}^{n-1} \frac{p_j}{p_n}\left[F_j\left(\frac{p_1}{p}, \ldots, \frac{p_{n-1}}{p}, \frac{\sum\limits_{r=1}^{n-1} p_r Z_r^1}{p}, \ldots, \frac{\sum\limits_{r=1}^{n-1} p_r Z_r^A}{p}, \frac{p_n Z_n^1}{p}, \right.\right.$$

$$\left.\left. \ldots, \frac{p_n Z_n^A}{p}\right) - Z_j\right] = 0.$$

To these must be added the definition of the general price level, re-written from (2.1) as

$$(3.3) \quad \sum_{j=1}^{n-1} w_j \frac{p_j}{p} = 1.$$

The dependence which exists among the market equations is clear from the way in which the excess-demand equation for money, (3.2), has been written. There are, thus, a total of n independent equations in the system of $n + 1$ equations (3.1)–(3.3).

The independent variables of this system are the nA initial endowments Z_i^a ($i = 1, \ldots, n$; $a = 1, \ldots, A$) and the $n - 1$ weights w_j ($j = 1, \ldots, n - 1$). We note that the $n + 1$ dependent variables $p_1, \ldots, p_n, p$ appear only in the form of the n ratios $p_1/p, \ldots, p_{n-1}/p$, p_n/p. Hence system (3.1)–(3.3) can at most be solved out for these ratios, in contradistinction to their individual components, the p_i

---

[1] Attached to Chapter III:2.

$(i = 1, \ldots, n)$ and p. Assume now that a solution in terms of these ratios has been determined. Divide through the first $n - 1$ of them by the last one, p_n/p—which is the reciprocal of the average money-price level. This yields the specific money prices $p_1/p_n, \ldots, p_{n-1}/p_n$. It follows that system (3.1)–(3.3) can at most determine money prices. Accounting prices, p_i, must remain indeterminate until the value of one of them is arbitrarily set. This then enables us to determine all of the p_i.[2]

The choice of the dependent equation to be "eliminated" clearly does not affect the solution of the preceding system. Consider, for example, the following two possibilities. First, the equilibrium money prices are solved out from the subset of n equations consisting of (3.1) and (3.3). Second, these prices are, instead, solved out from the subset of n equations consisting of (3.2)–(3.3) and all of equations (3.1) but, say, the first. Let us now multiply each of the $n - 2$ remaining commodity equations by its respective money price, and subtract the sum of these $n - 2$ products from (3.2). Equation (3.2) is then reduced to

$$(3.4) \qquad \frac{p_1}{p_n}[F_1(\quad) - Z_1] = 0.$$

If p_1/p_n is non-zero and finite, this reduces to the excess-demand equation for the first commodity—the equation which was originally eliminated.

Thus no matter which of the commodity equations is eliminated, we can—by the standard operations applicable to sets of simultaneous equations—transform the resulting subset of equations into that obtained by eliminating the money equation. It follows that no matter which of the excess-demand equations is eliminated, the resulting subsets all yield the same solution for the equilibrium set of money prices.

The distinction between accounting and money prices having served its purpose, it can now be dispensed with. Henceforth we shall assume that the good whose accounting price is arbitrarily fixed is money, and that the price so fixed is equal to unity. That is, we set $p_n = 1$. Hence the money and accounting prices of any good must now always be equal.

b.[3] The task of the economist is not complete until he has shown how the market goes about solving the set of equations (3.1)–(3.3). For this purpose Walras formulated his theory of *tâtonnement*, which

---

[2] Note that the indeterminacy of accounting prices is established without making use of the fact that there are $n + 1$ accounting prices and only n independent equations.
[3] Attached to Chapter III:3.

can be represented by the following system of differential equations:[4]

(3.5) $$\frac{dp_j}{dt} = K_j[F_j(\quad) - Z_j] \qquad (j = 1, \ldots, n - 1),$$

(3.6) $$\sum_{j=1}^{n-1} \frac{p_j}{K_j} \frac{dp_j}{dt} = - X_n,$$

(3.7) $$\frac{dp}{dt} = \sum_{j=1}^{n-1} w_j \frac{dp_j}{dt},$$

where t represents time and the K_j are positive constants.

Equations (3.5) state that a positive amount of excess demand in the jth market causes the price of the jth commodity, p_j, to rise over time. The extent of this rise is directly proportionate to the constant K_j, which thus represents the rapidity with which prices react to amounts of excess demand. Equation (3.7) states that the rate of change in the average price level is the weighted average of the rates of change of the individual prices. Equation (3.6) is obtained by substituting from (3.5) into (2.28). It states that, "on the average," an excess supply of money causes the prices p_j to rise. It clearly adds no information to (3.5) and can therefore be ignored.[5]

Starting from any initial set of prices, equations (3.5) and (3.7) describe the movements in prices generated by the resulting excess demands. In this way they trace out the variation over time of each of the price variables. Assume that we can obtain explicit descriptions of these time paths by solving out equations (3.5) and (3.7) for the money prices as functions of time, t:

(3.8) $$p_j = q_j(t) \qquad\qquad (j = 1, \ldots, n - 1),$$

(3.9) $$p = q(t).$$

Clearly, the functions $q_j(\quad)$ and $q(\quad)$ are those whose derivatives are $\frac{dp_j}{dt}$ and $\frac{dp}{dt}$, respectively.

Assume that p_j^0 $(j = 1, \ldots, n - 1)$ and p^0 are the equilibrium values of the system (3.1)–(3.3). Then the system (3.5)–(3.7) is defined as stable if

(3.10) $$\lim_{t = \infty} q_j(t) = p_j^0,$$

(3.11) $$\lim_{t = \infty} q(t) = p^0.$$

---

4 The following is based on the well-known dynamic analysis of Samuelson, *Foundations*, Chapter IX, especially pp. 270–72. On Walras, see Note B, below.

5 For an example in which equation (3.6) is used, see below, Mathematical Appendix 8:*b*.

Thus stability means that the method of successive approximation described by equations (3.5) and (3.7) ultimately succeeds in solving the system of simultaneous equations (3.1)–(3.3).[6]

c.[7] Consider the system (3.1)–(3.3), with p_n now replaced by unity wherever it appears. Assume that for $Z_i^a = Z_i^{a0}$ $(i = 1, \ldots, n;$ $a = 1, \ldots, A)$ this system has the solution $p_j = p_j^0$ $(j = 1, \ldots, n - 1)$ and $p = p^0$. Consider now the solution for $Z_j^a = Z_j^{a0}$ $(j = 1, \ldots, n - 1; a = 1, \ldots, A)$ and $Z_n^a = tZ_n^{a0}$ $(a = 1, \ldots, A)$, where t is a positive constant. That is, consider the effects of an equi-proportionate increase in the initial money holdings of each and every individual. By inspection of (3.1)–(3.3) one can readily see that there must exist a new solution $p_j = tp_j^0$ $(j = 1, \ldots, n - 1)$ and $p = tp_0$.

d.[8] Since the analysis is restricted to changes which do not affect the relative magnitudes of the Z_n^a $(a = 1, \ldots, A)$, we can express each of these initial quantities as a fixed proportion of the total quantity of money in the economy:

$$(3.12) \qquad Z_n^a = k_a Z_n \qquad (a = 1, \ldots, A),$$

where the k_a are given constants. Making use of these equations and of the fact that the Z_j^a $(j = 1, \ldots, n - 1; a = 1, \ldots, A)$ are also constants in the present discussion, and remembering that we have set $p_n = 1$, we can rewrite (3.1) and (3.3) as

$$(3.13) \qquad G_j\left(\frac{p_1}{p}, \ldots, \frac{p_{n-1}}{p}, \frac{Z_n}{p}\right) - Z_j = 0$$
$$(j = 1, \ldots, n - 1),$$

$$(3.14) \qquad \sum_{j=1}^{n-1} w_j \frac{p_j}{p} = 1.$$

Let us now consider (3.13)–(3.14) as constituting a set of n equations in the n variables p_j/p and Z_n/p. Solving out for these variables, we obtain

$$(3.15) \qquad \frac{p_j}{p} = \alpha_j \qquad (j = 1, \ldots, n - 1),$$

$$(3.16) \qquad \frac{Z_n}{p} = \alpha_n,$$

---

6 For the explicit form of functions (3.8)–(3.9) and for the conditions under which they converge as in (3.10)–(3.11), see Samuelson, *Foundations*, pp. 270–72. See also below, Mathematical Appendix 9:b.

7 Attached to Chapter III:4.

8 Attached to Chapter III:6.

where the α_j and α_n are constants for any fixed set of the w_j, Z_j^a, and k_a. Rewriting (3.16) as

(3.17)
$$p = \frac{1}{\alpha_n} Z_n,$$

we see the directly proportionate dependence of the dependent variable, p, on the independent variable, Z_n. Substituting from (3.17) into (3.15), we obtain

(3.18)
$$p_j = \frac{\alpha_j}{\alpha_n} Z_n \qquad (j = 1, \ldots, n - 1)$$

That is, this direct dependence also characterizes each of the individual money prices. In this way we have reaffirmed the conclusion of the preceding section.[9]

The distinction between individual-experiments and demand curves, on the one hand, and market-experiments and market-equilibrium curves, on the other, is now most explicit. The demand curves in Figure 4 of the text are generated from (2.24) in the manner already indicated in our discussion of Figure 45 above. The slopes of these curves are the derivatives of the right-hand side of (2.24) with respect to equi-proportionate changes in the p_j and p. In contrast, the market-equilibrium curve in Figure 5 is a graphical representation of equation (3.16) rewritten as

(3.19)
$$\frac{1}{p} = \frac{\alpha_n}{Z_n}.$$

Obviously, equation (3.19) is completely distinct from equation (2.24). More specifically, the market-equilibrium function will have the form of the rectangular hyperbola described by equation (3.19), regardless of the form of the demand function described by equation (2.24).

This also makes it clear that equation (3.19)—or (3.17)—is *not* a variant of a cash-balance equation. For the latter was intended as an excess-demand equation, and not a market-equilibrium equation—though, as emphasized in the text, it is precisely on this point that there existed a basic confusion among proponents of the cash-balance approach.[10]

---

[9] The present development is obviously related to the derivation of the inverse (Marshallian) demand functions in (2.6)–(2.8) above.

[10] Cf. p. 97 and Chapter VIII:2.

4. Appendix to Chapter IV

a.[1] Consider the ath individual situated in the marketing period of the first week. In that period he decides on his excess demands for the current Monday and for $H - 1$ subsequent Mondays as well. The number H thus represents his economic horizon.

Let Z_{1s}^a $(s = 1, \ldots, n - 2;\ a = 1, \ldots, A)$ represent the ath individual's initial endowment of the sth commodity in this first week. Similarly, let Z_{ks}^a $(k = 2, \ldots, H)$ represent the quantity of the sth commodity with which the individual knows he will be endowed in the kth week in the future. In the same way, Z_{1s}^a represents the amount the individual demands of the sth good in the current week, while Z_{ks}^a $(k = 2, \ldots, H)$ represents the amount he now plans to demand of the sth commodity in the kth week in the future. The amounts of excess demand planned for this and future weeks are then X_{hs}^a, where

$$(4.1) \qquad X_{hs}^a = Z_{hs}^a - Z_{hs}^a$$

$$(a = 1, \ldots, A;\ h = 1, \ldots, H;\ s = 1, \ldots, n - 2).$$

The price of the sth commodity is expected to be exactly the same in each and every week; as before, denote this price by p_s.

The $(n - 1)$th good is assumed to represent bonds. As will be recalled, these are obligations to pay one dollar one week from date of issue. Let Z_{n-1}^a be the given number of matured bonds—each of which will now be redeemed for one dollar—that the individual holds this Monday morning. These are to be contrasted with $Z_{1,\,n-1}^a$, the number of newly issued bonds he demands during the marketing period this Monday afternoon. By definition, these bonds necessarily constitute his initial holdings of the second week. Similarly, $Z_{k,\,n-1}^a$ $(k = 2, \ldots, H)$ represents the number of bonds which he now plans to demand in the kth week; and which, by definition, will constitute his initial, matured bond holdings of the $(k + 1)$th week. In the same way, Z_n^a represents his initial money holdings in the first week; Z_{1n}^a, his amount of money demanded in the first week; and Z_{kn}^a $(k = 2, \ldots, H)$, the

---

[1] Attached to Chapter IV:2–3.

amount he plans to demand in the kth week. Again, by definition, Z_{kn}^a will also constitute the initial money holdings of the $(k + 1)$th week.

By definition, the excess demand for bonds, $X_{h,\,n-1}^a$ $(h = 1, \ldots, H)$, is the same as the demand, $Z_{h,\,n-1}^a$. The excess demand for money now planned for the first week is

$$(4.2) \qquad\qquad X_{1n}^a = Z_{1n}^a - Z_n^a,$$

and for the subsequent weeks,

$$(4.3) \qquad\qquad X_{kn}^a = Z_{kn}^a - Z_{k-1,\,n}^a \qquad\qquad (k = 2, \ldots, H).$$

As shown in the text, the price of a bond, p_{n-1}, is related to the rate of interest, r, in the following way:

$$(4.4) \qquad\qquad \frac{1 - p_{n-1}}{p_{n-1}} = r,$$

or

$$(4.5) \qquad\qquad p_{n-1} = \frac{1}{1 + r}.$$

This price, like any other one, is expected with certainty to be the same in future weeks as in the present one.[2] It follows that an individual who demands $Z_{h,\,n-1}^a$ $(h = 1, \ldots, H)$ bonds is planning to expend $\dfrac{Z_{h,\,n-1}^a}{1 + r}$ dollars on the purchase of new (discounted) bonds in the hth week, and to receive $Z_{h,\,n-1}^a$ dollars from the redemption of these bonds when they mature in the $(h + 1)$th week.

By assumption, the ath individual's excess-demand function for the sth commodity in the hth week can be written as

$$(4.6) \qquad X_{hs}^a = F_{hs}^a\left(\frac{p_1}{p}, \ldots, \frac{p_{n-2}}{p}, r, \frac{Z_{n-1}^a}{p}, \frac{Z_n^a}{p}, \frac{\sum\limits_{s=1}^{n-2} p_s Z_{1s}^a}{p}, \right.$$
$$\left. \frac{\sum\limits_{s=1}^{n-2} p_s Z_{2s}^a}{p}, \ldots, \frac{\sum\limits_{s=1}^{n-2} p_s Z_{Hs}^a}{p}\right) - Z_{hs}^a$$

$$(a = 1, \ldots, A;\ h = 1, \ldots, H;\ s = 1, \ldots, n-2),$$

where the $H - 1$ last arguments of the function $F_{hs}^a(\ \ )$ represent the

2 Cf. p. 49.

anticipated real incomes of future weeks. These anticipations, too, are held with certainty.

The demand—or excess-demand—function for *real* bond holdings in the hth week is

$$(4.7) \qquad \frac{Z^a_{h,\,n-1}}{(1+r)p} = F^a_{h,\,n-1}(\quad) \qquad (h = 1, \ldots, H),$$

where the arguments of this function are the same as those of (4.6). By the budget restraint, the excess-demand function for *real* money holdings in the first week is then

$$(4.8) \qquad \frac{X^a_{1n}}{p} = -\sum_{s=1}^{n-2} \frac{p_s}{p} [F^a_{1s}(\quad) - Z^a_{1s}] - \left[F^a_{1,\,n-1}(\quad) - \frac{Z^a_{n-1}}{p} \right].$$

Similarly, the presently planned excess-demand functions for subsequent weeks are

$$(4.9) \qquad \frac{X^a_{kn}}{p} = -\sum_{s=1}^{n-2} \frac{p_s}{p} [F^a_{ks}(\quad) - Z^a_{ks}]$$
$$- [F^a_{k,\,n-1}(\quad) - (1+r)F^a_{k-1,\,n-1}(\quad)]$$
$$(k = 2, \ldots, H).$$

The last bracketed term on the right-hand side of both (4.8) and (4.9) is the difference between the real value of the individual's planned expenditures on new (discounted) bonds on Monday afternoon of the hth week ($h = 1, \ldots, H$) and the real value of his planned receipts from the matured bonds which he holds on Monday morning of that week.

As can readily be seen, an equi-proportionate increase in the p_s ($s = 1, \ldots, n - 2$), p, and Z^a_n leaves all arguments of (4.6) and (4.7) unaffected, except for Z^a_{n-1}/p. If the individual in question is a creditor, his Z^a_{n-1}/p is positive, and this is reduced by the increase in p; hence he decreases his amounts demanded. If he is a debtor, his Z^a_{n-1}/p is negative, and this is (algebraically) increased by the increase in p; hence he increases his amounts demanded. In brief, we have here the real-indebtedness effect of the text.

The market excess-demand functions can be obtained by aggregating (4.6)–(4.9) over a. To simplify the notation, we shall make use of the fact that the present analysis is concerned with changes which leave the real incomes of all periods constant. Hence, for the purpose of our analysis, the influence of these incomes can be subsumed under the forms of the functions, which can be written as

(4.10)
$$X_{hs} = F_{hs}\left(\frac{p_1}{p}, \ldots, \frac{p_{n-2}}{p}, r, \frac{Z^1_{n-1}}{p}, \ldots, \frac{Z^A_{n-1}}{p}, \frac{Z^1_n}{p},\right.$$
$$\left. \ldots, \frac{Z^A_n}{p}\right) - Z_{hs}$$

$$(h = 1, \ldots, H; s = 1, \ldots, n-2)$$

(4.11)
$$\frac{Z_{h, n-1}}{(1+r)p} = F_{h, n-1}(\ ),$$

(4.12)
$$\frac{X_{1n}}{p} = -\sum_{s=1}^{n-2}\frac{p_s}{p}[F_{1s}(\ ) - Z_{1s}] - F_{1, n-1}(\ ),$$

(4.13)
$$\frac{X_{kn}}{p} = -\sum_{s=1}^{n-2}\frac{p_s}{p}[F_{ks}(\ ) - Z_{ks}]$$
$$- [F_{k, n-1}(\ ) - (1+r)F_{k-1, n-1}(\ )]$$

$$(k = 2, \ldots, H).$$

These equations correspond to (4.6)–(4.9), respectively.

In aggregating (4.12) from (4.8) use has been made of the fact that the economy is a closed one, so that

(4.14)
$$\sum_{a=1}^{A} Z^a_{n-1} = 0.$$

That is, the aggregate amount of matured bonds *actually* held at the beginning of the first week must be zero. On the other hand, there is no reason why

(4.15)
$$F_{h, n-1}(\ ) \equiv \sum_{a=1}^{A} F^a_{h, n-1}(\ ) \qquad (h = 1, \ldots, H)$$

must be zero. That is, there is no reason why the aggregate amount of bonds individuals *plan* to hold at a given set of prices during a given week must be zero. True, it will turn out that the individuals' plans will not be consistent with one another unless this amount is zero; unless, that is, they plan in the aggregate to lend as much as they plan to borrow. But of this the isolated individual formulating his plans is not and cannot be aware.

308

b.[3] From the preceding market excess-demand functions we can construct the corresponding market excess-demand equations for each and every week. However, by the assumption of the text, only those of the current week—that is, only those for $h = 1$—are relevant for the determination of current equilibrium prices and interest. Dropping the now unnecessary time index, h, we write these excess-demand equations as

$$(4.16) \quad F_s\left(\frac{p_1}{p}, \ldots, \frac{p_{n-2}}{p}, r, \frac{Z^1_{n-1}}{p}, \ldots, \frac{Z^A_{n-1}}{p}, \frac{Z^1_n}{p}, \ldots, \frac{Z^A_n}{p}\right) - Z_s = 0$$

$$(s = 1, \ldots, n-2),$$

$$(4.17) \quad F_{n-1}\left(\frac{p_1}{p}, \ldots, \frac{p_{n-2}}{p}, r, \frac{Z^1_{n-1}}{p}, \ldots, \frac{Z^A_{n-1}}{p}, \frac{Z^1_n}{p}, \ldots, \frac{Z^A_n}{p}\right) = 0,$$

$$(4.18) \quad \sum_{s=1}^{n-2} \frac{p_s}{p}[F_s(\ ) - Z_s] + F_{n-1}(\ ) = 0,$$

$$(4.19) \quad \sum_{s=1}^{n-2} w_s \frac{p_s}{p} = 1.$$

Equation (4.19) defines the average price level, p, of the $n - 2$ money prices, p_s; it is analogous to (2.1). Equations (4.16), (4.17), and (4.18) relate, of course, to commodities, bonds, and money, respectively. We have, thus, $n + 1$ equations in the n dependent variables p_s ($s = 1, \ldots, n - 2$), p, and r. It is clear that any set of these variables which satisfies (4.16), (4.17), and (4.19) must also satisfy (4.18). Thus only n of these equations, at most, are independent.

Assume that for $Z^a_{n-1} = Z^{a0}_{n-1}$ and for $Z^a_n = Z^{a0}_n$ ($a = 1, \ldots, A$) the preceding system has the solution $p_s = p^0_s$ ($s = 1, \ldots, n - 2$), $p = p^0$, and $r = r^0$. Consider now the solution for the same values of the Z^{a0}_{n-1}, but for $Z^a_n = tZ^{a0}_n$—where t is a positive constant. That is, consider the effect of an equi-proportionate increase in the initial money holdings of all individuals, their initial bond holdings being kept constant. By inspection of (4.16)–(4.19) one can readily see that at the prices $p_s = tp^0_s$, $p = tp^0$, and $r = r^0$, all arguments of the equations are the same as in the original equilibrium position except for the Z^a_{n-1}/p. These now become Z^{a0}_{n-1}/tp^0 instead of Z^{a0}_{n-1}/p^0. Hence the functions on the left-hand sides of (4.16)–(4.18) need not have the same values as in the original equilibrium position; hence equations (4.16)–(4.18) need no longer be satisfied. That is, the proposed set of values will not generally be the new equilibrium set.

---

[3] Attached to Chapter IV:4.

In contrast, consider the case where both $Z_{n-1}^a = tZ_{n-1}^{a0}$ and $Z_n^a = tZ_n^{a0}$. Here the set of values $p_s = tp_s^0$, $p = tp^0$, and $r = r^0$ clearly constitutes the new equilibrium solution. For with these new values each of the arguments of (4.16)–(4.18) has exactly the same value as in the original equilibrium position. Thus we conclude that an equi-proportionate change in the initial holdings of both bonds and money causes an equi-proportionate change in money prices and leaves the rate of interest unaffected.

c.[4] Alternatively, we can proceed in the same manner as in Mathematical Appendix 3:*d*. In particular, the preceding paragraph deals with a change which does not affect the relative magnitudes of the Z_{n-1}^a and Z_n^a ($a = 1, \ldots, A$). Hence we can express each of these initial quantities as a fixed proportion of, say, the total quantity of money in the economy, Z_n. That is,

$$(4.20) \qquad Z_{n-1}^a = \lambda_a Z_n \qquad (a = 1, \ldots, A),$$

$$(4.21) \qquad Z_n^a = \mu_a Z_n,$$

where the λ_a and μ_a are given constants. Substituting from (4.20)–(4.21) into (4.16)–(4.17), reproducing (4.19), and dropping (4.18) as redundant, we obtain new functions which we write as

$$(4.22) \qquad G_s\left(\frac{p_1}{p}, \ldots, \frac{p_{n-2}}{p}, r, \frac{Z_n}{p}\right) - Z_s = 0$$

$$(s = 1, \ldots, n-2),$$

$$(4.23) \qquad G_{n-1}\left(\frac{p_1}{p}, \ldots, \frac{p_{n-2}}{p}, r, \frac{Z_n}{p}\right) = 0,$$

$$(4.24) \qquad \sum_{s=1}^{n-2} w_s \frac{p_s}{p} = 1.$$

Consider now (4.22)–(4.24) as n equations in the n variables p_s/p, r, and Z_n/p. Solving out the equations for these variables, we obtain

$$(4.25) \qquad \frac{p_s}{p} = \beta_s \qquad (s = 1, \ldots, n-2),$$

$$(4.26) \qquad r = \beta_{n-1},$$

$$(4.27) \qquad \frac{Z_n}{p} = \beta_n,$$

---

[4] Attached to the last paragraph of Chapter IV:4.

where the β_i $(i = 1, \ldots, n)$ are constants for any fixed set of w_s, Z_s^a, λ_a, and μ_a. Revert now to the original designation of dependent variables. Substituting from (4.27) into (4.25) and rewriting, we obtain

(4.28) $$p_s = \frac{\beta_s Z_n}{\beta_n},$$

(4.29) $$r = \beta_{n-1},$$

(4.30) $$p = \frac{1}{\beta_n} Z_n.$$

Equations (4.28) and (4.30)—as equations (3.17)–(3.18) under simpler circumstances—show the directly proportionate dependence of equilibrium money prices on the quantity of money in the economy. In the same way, equation (4.29) shows the rate of interest's complete independence of this quantity. Clearly, the validity of these conclusions is restricted to those cases in which the increase in money is brought about in the manner designated: that is, to cases of equiproportionate changes in the initial bond and money holdings of each individual, with every other independent variable (viz., tastes and the Z_{hs}^a) being held constant.

In connection with the discussion of neutral money in the text, let us see what happens to the solution of equations (4.22)–(4.24) as Z_n approaches zero. Equation (4.28) shows that as this happens each of the individual p_s also approaches zero. But equation (4.25) shows that they do so in a way which preserves their ratios. In particular, we see from (4.25)–(4.26) that the limiting values of p_s/p and r remain β_s and β_{n-1}, respectively. In this sense, money, under the foregoing conditions, is neutral.

d.[5] From equation (4.12) we can obtain the demand function for current nominal money holdings, which we write as

(4.31) $$Z_n = G(p_1, \ldots, p_{n-2}, p, r, Z_{n-1}^1, \ldots, Z_{n-1}^A, Z_n^1, \ldots, Z_n^A).$$

In its aggregate form, this is assumed to have the form of equation (20) in Chapter IX:5:

(4.32) $$M^d = pL\left(Y, r, \frac{M_0}{p}\right).$$

By varying r, keeping all other variables constant, we obtain from

---

[5] Attached to Chapter XI:4.

either of these functions the demand curves in Figure 25 (page 175). Correspondingly, the slope of these curves equals the partial derivative of $G(\ \ )$ or $pL(\ \ )$ with respect to r. Figure 25 reflects the usual assumption that this slope is negative.

On the other hand, equation (4.29) presents a market-equilibrium function: it relates the equilibrium rate of interest to the given amount of money in the economy, and shows it to be independent of this amount. Clearly, this same function can be obtained by solving out the aggregated system (1)–(4) of Chapter X:1 for the rate of interest. The line in Figure 27 is the graphical representation of this function, and hence a market-equilibrium curve. Its horizontality reflects the fact that the derivative of (4.29) with respect to $\bar{Z}_n$ is zero. This must obviously be true regardless of the negative derivatives of (4.31)—or (4.32)—with respect to r. In this way we again explicitly see the fundamental distinction between individual- and market-experiments— and the corresponding necessity of specifying the function whose derivative is being taken.[6]

Assume now that one of the independent variables of the analysis need not remain constant. Let it be represented by the introduction of a parameter α into the functions on the left-hand sides of (4.22)– (4.23). Then, when we solve out (4.22)–(4.24) for the p_s/p, r, and Z_n/p, we no longer obtain constants [as in (4.25)–(4.27)], but instead functions of α, say,

$$(4.33) \qquad\qquad \frac{p_s}{p} = W_s(\alpha) \qquad\qquad (s = 1, \ldots, n-2),$$

$$(4.34) \qquad\qquad r = W_{n-1}(\alpha),$$

$$(4.35) \qquad\qquad \frac{Z_n}{p} = W_n(\alpha).$$

That is, the equilibrium values of our variables now depend on the value of α. Clearly, there is no necessary relation between the derivatives $W_n'(\alpha)$ and $W_{n-1}'(\alpha)$. In particular, there is no reason why a change in α which does not affect the equilibrium value of $\bar{Z}_n/p$ should not nevertheless affect the equilibrium value of r.

---

[6] Cf. above, Mathematical Appendix 1:*a*.

5. Appendix to Chapters V and VI

$a.$[1] Consider the case of an individual operating within a horizon of one week. In the notation of Mathematical Appendixes 1:a and 1:c—with the superscript a dropped for simplicity—such an individual maximizes his total utility,

$$(5.1) \qquad U = u\left(Z_1, Z_2, \ldots, Z_{n-1}, \frac{Z_n}{p}\right),$$

subject to the given prices, p_i, and the budget restraint,

$$(5.2) \qquad \sum_{i=1}^{n} p_i Z_i = \sum_{i=1}^{n} p_i \bar{Z}_i,$$

where, by definition, $p_n = 1$.

Let us carry out this maximization by the Lagrange method.[2] Form the sum

$$(5.3) \qquad u\left(Z_1, \ldots, Z_{n-1}, \frac{Z_n}{p}\right) - \lambda\left[\sum_{i=1}^{n} p_i(Z_i - \bar{Z}_i)\right],$$

where λ is the Lagrange multiplier. Maximizing this sum with respect to the Z_i (λ being considered fixed), we obtain the conditions

$$(5.4) \qquad u_j\left(Z_1, \ldots, Z_{n-1}, \frac{Z_n}{p}\right) - \lambda p_j = 0 \quad (j = 1, \ldots, n-1),$$

$$(5.5) \qquad u_n\left(Z_1, \ldots, Z_{n-1}, \frac{Z_n}{p}\right) - \lambda p = 0,$$

where $u_i(\ )$—the marginal utility of the ith good—is the partial

---

[1] Attached to Chapter V:2–3.

[2] Cf. above, Mathematical Appendix 1:d. In order to bring the following into the exact form presented there, the reader need only rewrite the restraint (5.2) in the explicit form

$$Z_n = -\sum_{i=1}^{n-1} p_i Z_i + \sum_{i=1}^{n} p_i \bar{Z}_i.$$

derivative of $u(\ )$ with respect to its ith argument.   Note that equation (5.5) is completely symmetrical with equations (5.4): for $u_n(\ )$ is the marginal utility of the good real money holdings, and p is its price.[3]

The foregoing equations can be written as

$$(5.6) \qquad \frac{u_1(\ )}{p_1} = \frac{u_2(\ )}{p_2} = \cdots = \frac{u_n(\ )}{p} = \lambda.$$

This is equation (1) of the text.   The parameter λ is clearly what is called there the marginal utility of expenditure.

Eliminating λ from (5.4)–(5.5), we obtain

$$(5.7) \qquad \frac{u_j(\ )}{u_n(\ )} = \frac{p_j}{p} \qquad\qquad (j = 1, \ldots, n-1).$$

To these equations we add the budget restraint, (5.2), which we divide through by p and rewrite as

$$(5.8) \qquad \sum_{j=1}^{n-1} \frac{p_j}{p} Z_j + \frac{Z_n}{p} = \sum_{j=1}^{n-1} \frac{p_j}{p} \bar{Z}_j + \frac{\bar{Z}_n}{p}.$$

Equations (5.7)–(5.8) specify the conditions that must be satisfied by the Z_i ($i = 1, \ldots, n$) in order to maximize $U = u(\ )$ subject to (5.2).

We now consider (5.7)–(5.8) as constituting n equations in the n dependent variables $Z_1, \ldots, Z_{n-1}, Z_n/p$ and the $2n$ independent variables p_j ($j = 1, \ldots, n-1$), p, and $\bar{Z}_i$ ($i = 1, \ldots, n$).   We then note that these independent variables always appear in the form of the ratios $\frac{p_j}{p}$ and $\sum_{j=1}^{n-1} \frac{p_j}{p} \bar{Z}_j + \frac{\bar{Z}_n}{p}$.   Hence, assuming solubility, the dependent variables can be expressed as functions of these ratios.   That is, the preceding maximization procedure yields demand functions of the type posited in equations (2.2) and (2.23) above.   Indeed, the present functions are even more specific; for they depend on the sum of $\sum_{j=1}^{n-1} \frac{p_j}{p} \bar{Z}_j$ and $\frac{\bar{Z}_n}{p}$, and not on their separate influences.

Let us now substitute these demand functions—in this more specific form—into (5.1).[4]   This yields

---

[3] Cf. p. 296.

[4] The following proof is taken from E. B. Wilson, "Notes on Utility Theory and Demand Equations," *Quarterly Journal of Economics*, LX (1945–46), 453–54.

$$U = u\left[F_1\left(\frac{p_1}{p}, \ldots, \frac{p_{n-1}}{p}, \frac{I}{p}\right), \ldots, F_{n-1}\left(\frac{p_1}{p}, \ldots, \frac{p_{n-1}}{p}, \frac{I}{p}\right),\right.$$

(5.9)
$$\left.\psi\left(\frac{p_1}{p}, \ldots, \frac{p_{n-1}}{p}, \frac{I}{p}\right)\right]$$

$$\equiv \phi\left(\frac{p_1}{p}, \ldots, \frac{p_{n-1}}{p}, \frac{I}{p}\right),$$

where

(5.10)
$$I = \sum_{j=1}^{n-1} p_j Z + Z_n.$$

That is, I is the total money value of the initial endowment.

The function $\phi(\ )$ relates the individual's utility from an optimum collection of goods to the independent variables which determine the composition of that collection. Let us now investigate the effect on this level of utility of an increase in I. That is, let us determine the partial derivative of $\phi(\ )$ with respect to I.

Making use of (1.28), we differentiate both sides of identity (5.9) to obtain

(5.11)
$$\frac{\partial \phi(\ )}{\partial I} \equiv u_1(\ )\frac{\partial F_1(\ )}{\partial I} + \cdots + u_{n-1}(\ )\frac{\partial F_{n-1}(\ )}{\partial I}$$
$$+ u_n(\ )\frac{\partial \psi(\ )}{\partial I}.$$

Substituting from (5.4)–(5.5), this becomes

(5.12)
$$\frac{\partial \phi(\ )}{\partial I} = \lambda p_1 \frac{\partial F_1(\ )}{\partial I} + \cdots + \lambda p_{n-1}\frac{\partial F_{n-1}(\ )}{\partial I} + \lambda p \frac{\partial \psi(\ )}{\partial I}$$
$$= \lambda\left[p_1 \frac{\partial F_1(\ )}{\partial I} + \cdots + p_{n-1}\frac{\partial F_{n-1}(\ )}{\partial I} + p\frac{\partial \psi(\ )}{\partial I}\right].$$

We note now that this bracketed expression is the increase in money value of total expenditures caused by a unit increase in the value of the initial endowment, I. Since, by assumption, all of this increase must be used up, the bracketed expression must also equal unity. Alternatively, we can obtain this result by replacing the right-hand side of (5.2) by I, substituting from (2.2) and (2.23) into the left-hand side, and then

315

partially differentiating both sides of the resulting identity with respect to
I.[5]   In any event, we replace the bracketed expression in (5.12) by unity
and thereby obtain

(5.13) $$\frac{\partial \phi(\ \ )}{\partial I} = \lambda.$$

This development shows most clearly the basic conceptual distinction
emphasized in the text between the marginal utility of cash balances,
$u_n(Z_1, \ldots, Z_{n-1}, Z_n/p)$, and the marginal utility of expenditure,
$\dfrac{\partial \phi(p_1/p, \ldots, p_{n-1}/p, I/p)}{\partial I}$. Thus once again we see the importance—
as brought out in Mathematical Appendix 1:a—of specifying the func-
tion being derived.

b.[6] Consider now an individual whose economic horizon extends
over the present week and two successive ones. (As the reader can
verify, the following argument can be readily generalized to the case of
any number of weeks.)   Using the notation of Mathematical Appendix
4:a, we assume that the individual maximizes his utility,

(5.14)
$$U = w\left(Z_{11}, \ldots, Z_{1,\, n-2}, \frac{Z_{1n}}{p}, Z_{21}, \ldots, Z_{2,\, n-2}, \frac{Z_{2n}}{p}, Z_{31}, \right.$$
$$\left. \ldots, Z_{3,\, n-2}\right),$$

subject to his budget restraints.   The omission of bonds from this
function reflects their assumed absolute illiquidity; for this means that
no utility attaches to the holding of bonds per se.   The omission of an
argument Z_{3n}/p reflects the fact that the economic horizon is limited to
a three-week period; hence no utility can be derived from planning to
hold money at the end of this period.   That is, we now drop the
implicit assumption of the preceding section that the individual derives
utility from maintaining positive cash balances even for a period for
which he makes no definite consumption plans.   As we shall see,
however, this assumption can be retained, and Z_{3n}/p accordingly
inserted in the foregoing utility function, without in any way affecting
the basic conclusions of the argument now to be presented.

---

[5] The reader will recall that we are making use here of the special form of (2.2) and (2.23)
yielded by utility maximization; cf. the discussion immediately preceding equation (5.9).
[6] Attached to Chapter VI:1.

The budget restraints for the three weeks are, respectively,

$$(5.15) \quad \sum_{s=1}^{n-2} p_s(Z_{1s} - \bar{Z}_{1s}) + \frac{Z_{1,\,n-1}}{1+r} - \bar{Z}_{n-1} + Z_{1n} - \bar{Z}_n = 0,$$

$$(5.16) \quad \sum_{s=1}^{n-2} p_s(Z_{2s} - \bar{Z}_{2s}) + \frac{Z_{2,\,n-1}}{1+r} - Z_{1,\,n-1} + Z_{2n} - Z_{1n} = 0,$$

$$(5.17) \quad \sum_{s=1}^{n-2} p_s(Z_{3s} - \bar{Z}_{3s}) \qquad\quad - Z_{2,\,n-1} \qquad - Z_{2n} = 0,$$

where $\dfrac{1}{1+r}$ is the price of bonds. These restraints again[7] reflect the fact that the bond and money holdings acquired one week become the initial holdings of the subsequent one. Thus, for example, the individual buys $Z_{1,\,n-1}$ new bonds in the first week at a cost of $\dfrac{Z_{1,\,n-1}}{1+r}$ dollars, and receives for them their maturity value of $Z_{1,\,n-1}$ dollars in the second week. These restraints also reflect the assumption that anticipated prices and interest are always expected to be the same as current ones. We note too that since, by the preceding paragraph, Z_{3n} must always be zero, such a term is omitted from equation (5.17).[8] Similarly, the omission of a term $+\dfrac{Z_{3,\,n-1}}{1+r}$ from this equation reflects the additional restriction that the individual's anticipated net debt position at the end of his economic horizon must be zero, that is, $Z_{3,\,n-1} = 0$.[9]

Form now the expression

$$(5.18) \qquad w(\ ) - \lambda_1[(5.15)] - \lambda_2[(5.16)] - \lambda_3[(5.17)],$$

where the λ_h are Lagrange multipliers. Differentiating with respect to all the Z_{hi} ($h = 1, 2, 3$; $i = 1, \ldots, n$) except $Z_{3,\,n-1}$ and Z_{3n}, we obtain the following conditions for a maximum:

$$(5.19) \qquad \frac{\partial w(\ )}{\partial Z_{1s}} - \lambda_1 p_s = 0 \quad (s = 1, \ldots, n - 2),$$

$$(5.20) \qquad -\frac{\lambda_1}{1+r} + \lambda_2 = 0,$$

---

7 Cf. the beginning of Mathematical Appendix 4:*a*, and particularly the discussion of equations (4.5) and (4.8)–(4.9).

8 For a more rigorous justification of this procedure—if such is needed—see my "Relative Prices, Say's Law, and the Demand for Money," *Econometrica*, XVI (1948), 140–42.

9 See below, penultimate paragraph of this section.

(5.21)
$$\frac{1}{p} \cdot \frac{\partial w(\ )}{\partial \left(\frac{Z_{1n}}{p}\right)} - \lambda_1 \quad + \lambda_2 = 0,$$

(5.22)
$$\frac{\partial w(\ )}{\partial Z_{2s}} - \lambda_2 p_s \qquad = 0 \quad (s = 1, \ldots, n-2),$$

(5.23)
$$-\frac{\lambda_2}{1+r} + \lambda_3 = 0,$$

(5.24)
$$\frac{1}{p} \cdot \frac{\partial w(\ )}{\partial \left(\frac{Z_{2n}}{p}\right)} - \lambda_2 \quad + \lambda_3 = 0,$$

(5.25)
$$\frac{\partial w(\ )}{\partial Z_{3s}} - \lambda_3 p_s \qquad = 0 \quad (s = 1, \ldots, n-2).$$

Clearly, λ_h is the marginal utility of expenditure of the hth week. Thus equation (5.21)—or (5.24)—corresponds to equation (3) of the text. Substituting from (5.24) into (5.21) and rearranging terms, we obtain

(5.26)
$$\lambda_1 = \frac{1}{p} \frac{\partial w(\ )}{\partial \left(\frac{Z_{1n}}{p}\right)} + \frac{1}{p} \frac{\partial w(\ )}{\partial \left(\frac{Z_{2n}}{p}\right)} + \lambda_3,$$

which coincides with equation (4) of the text. Equation (5.20) is clearly the same as equation (6). Equation (5.20) also yields—after multiplying through by $1 + r$ and transposing—

(5.27)
$$- \lambda_1 + \lambda_2 = - \lambda_2 r.$$

Substituting this into (5.21), we obtain equation (7) of the text.

Let us now drop the assumption that the individual plans to hold no money balances at the end of the third week. This means that $w(\ )$ in (5.14) depends also on the argument Z_{3n}/p, and that the budget restraint (5.17) contains also the term $+ Z_{3n}$. Correspondingly, the expression (5.18)—thus modified—would also have to be maximized with respect to Z_{3n} to yield the additional equation

(5.28)
$$\frac{1}{p} \frac{\partial w(\ )}{\partial \left(\frac{Z_{3n}}{p}\right)} - \lambda_3 = 0.$$

Substituting into (5.26), we obtain

(5.29)
$$\lambda_1 = \frac{1}{p} \frac{\partial w(\ )}{\partial \left(\frac{Z_{1n}}{p}\right)} + \frac{1}{p} \frac{\partial w(\ )}{\partial \left(\frac{Z_{2n}}{p}\right)} + \frac{1}{p} \frac{\partial w(\ )}{\partial \left(\frac{Z_{3n}}{p}\right)}.$$

This is the same as equation (5) of the text.

It is also interesting to see what would happen if we were to drop the assumption $Z_{3,\,n-1} = 0$. This would require us to add the term $+\dfrac{Z_{3,\,n-1}}{1+r}$ to the left-hand side of budget restraint (5.17). Correspondingly, we would then have to differentiate (5.18) with respect to $Z_{3,\,n-1}$ as well, and this would yield the additional equation

(5.30)
$$\frac{\lambda_3}{1+r} = 0.$$

Since $1 + r$ is not zero, this implies $\lambda_3 = 0$. Inserted in (5.23), this implies $\lambda_2 = 0$; and this, in turn—upon insertion into (5.20)—implies $\lambda_1 = 0$. In other words, the possibility of borrowing without having to take into account the requirement to make a final repayment enables the individual to plan an unlimited consumption of commodities—one that will carry him to the point where the marginal utility of each and every commodity each and every week is zero. Correspondingly, as we can see from the budget restraints, the individual will plan to sell in each week an unlimited number of bonds in order to cover the costs of his consumption plans for that week—and in order to repay the principal and interest on those bonds he sold the preceding week. It is this program of unlimited consumption, infinite borrowing, and perpetual refunding that the restriction $Z_{3,\,n-1} = 0$ precludes.[10]

We note finally—and leave it as an exercise for the reader to prove—that nothing in the argument of this section is affected by assuming the utility function in (5.14) to have the special form

(5.31)
$$U = w(\ ) \equiv w^1\!\left(Z_{11}, \ldots, Z_{1,\,n-2}, \frac{Z_{1n}}{p}\right)$$
$$+ w^2\!\left(Z_{21}, \ldots, Z_{2,\,n-2}, \frac{Z_{2n}}{p}\right)$$
$$+ w^3\left(Z_{31}, \ldots, Z_{3,\,n-2}\right),$$

where $w^1(\ )$ and $w^2(\ )$ are identical. This function reflects the absence of time preference in the narrow sense of the term.[11] For let

---

10 Cf. p. 53.

The reader should, however, note that this restriction is no longer necessary in Section *e* below, where it is assumed that bonds are liquid and thus enter the utility function. For then the effect of increased negative holdings of bonds in decreasing total utility (because of the illiquidity which they generate) will limit the number of bonds the individual will be willing to have outstanding at any given moment. Cf. the mathematical analysis of the case where bonds are perpetuities possessing some degree of liquidity presented in my "Further Considerations of the General Equilibrium Theory of Money," *op. cit.*, pp. 188–89.

11 Cf. p. 79, footnote 5.

$Z_1^I, \ldots, Z_{n-2}^I, Z_{1n}^I/p$ and $Z_1^{II}, \ldots, Z_{n-2}^{II}, Z_{1n}^{II}/p$ be two different collections of the $n-2$ commodities and of real balances. The foregoing function shows that the level of total utility, U, remains the same whether Collection I is consumed in the first week and Collection II in the second, or whether Collection II is consumed in the first week and Collection I in the second. That is, equation (5.31) shows that the sequence of consumption per se does not affect utility.[12]

c.[13] Returning now to equations (5.19)–(5.25), let us substitute the values for λ_1, λ_2, and λ_3 from (5.19), (5.22), and (5.25), respectively, into the remaining equations to obtain

(5.32)
$$\frac{\dfrac{\partial w(\ )}{\partial Z_{ht}}}{\dfrac{\partial w(\ )}{\partial Z_{h,\,n-2}}} = \frac{p_t}{p_{n-2}}$$

$$(h = 1, 2, 3;\ t = 1, \ldots, n-3),$$

(5.33)
$$\frac{\dfrac{\partial w(\ )}{\partial Z_{k,\,n-2}}}{\dfrac{\partial w(\ )}{\partial Z_{k+1,\,n-2}}} = 1 + r \qquad\qquad (k = 1, 2),$$

(5.34)
$$\frac{\dfrac{\partial w(\ )}{\partial \left(\dfrac{Z_{kn}}{p}\right)}}{\dfrac{\partial w(\ )}{\partial Z_{k+1,\,n-2}}} = \frac{p}{p_{n-2}} \cdot r \qquad\qquad (k = 1, 2).$$

These correspond, respectively, to equations (8), (9), and (11) of the text. In addition, our maximum conditions comprise the budget restraints (5.15)–(5.17) divided through by p; these correspond to equation (13) of the text. We thus have a system of $3n - 2$ equations in the $3n - 2$ dependent variables Z_{hs} ($h = 1, 2, 3;\ s = 1, \ldots, n-2$), $\dfrac{Z_{k,\,n-1}}{(1+r)p}$, and $\dfrac{Z_{kn}}{p}$ ($k = 1, 2$) and in the $4n - 4$ independent variables $p_s, p, r, \bar{Z}_{hs}, \bar{Z}_{n-1}$, and $\bar{Z}_n$. We note now that these independent variables

---

[12] Since the foregoing function assumes that no money is held at the end of the third week, we cannot meaningfully talk about interchanging the collections of this week and, say, the first one. If, however, we were to make the assumption that $w(\ )$ also depends on Z_{3n}/p (see above), such comparisons could be made. Correspondingly, absence of time preference in the narrow sense would then denote the interchangeability of the collections of all three weeks; i.e., that $w^1(\ ) \equiv w^2(\ ) \equiv w^3(\ )$.

[13] Attached to Chapter VI:2.

appear only in the forms of the ratios $\frac{p_s}{p}$ $(s = 1, \ldots, n - 2)$, r, $\sum_{s=1}^{n-2} \frac{p_s}{p} Z_{hs}$ $(h = 1, 2, 3)$, $\frac{Z_{n-1}}{p}$, and $\frac{Z_n}{p}$. Hence, assuming solubility, the dependent variables can be expressed as functions of these ratios. That is, the preceding maximization procedure yields demand functions of the form posited in (4.6)–(4.8) above and, accordingly, excess-demand equations of the form (4.16)–(4.19).

It should be emphasized that we have in this way derived a non-zero demand for bonds even though this good does not enter the utility function.[14] It should also be emphasized that if we were to examine now the planned excess demand for money for the Monday marketing period three weeks hence, we would necessarily discover a state of disequilibrium. For though the supply of money would still be Z_n, the demand would be zero. For, by assumption, individuals do not plan now to hold any money at the end of the third week. But, as emphasized in the text,[15] this potential disequilibrium is not permitted to manifest itself in the *tâtonnement* by which the excess-demand equations for current goods, (4.16)–(4.19), are solved. On the other hand, by the time we reach the "third" week, it will have become the "first" one. Hence individuals will then clearly have positive demands for money balances, so that a state of equilibrium can then be achieved.

d.[16] Alternatively, we can derive the demand functions (4.6)–(4.8) by use of Samuelson's method of revealed preferences.[17] Accept once again the restrictions $Z_{3, n-1} = 0$ and $Z_{3n} = 0$. Assume that at the given prices p_s^0 $(s = 1, \ldots, n - 2)$, p^0, and r^0, and with the given initial endowments Z_{hs}^0 $(h = 1, 2, 3)$, Z_{n-1}^0, and Z_n^0, the individual chooses the collection Z_{hs}^0, $Z_{k, n-1}^0$, and Z_{kn}^0 $(k = 1, 2)$. Since it is more convenient to deal with the goods *real* bond and money holdings, we shall say that this collection consists of Z_{hs}^0, $\frac{Z_{k, n-1}^0}{(1 + r^0)p^0}$, and $\frac{Z_{kn}^0}{p^0}$, and shall denote it by "Collection Zero."

Assume now that we confront the individual with the same rate of interest and commodity endowments, but change other endowments and prices in the proportion t. That is, we confront him with the prices $p_s^* = tp_s^0$, $p^* = tp^0$, and $r^* = r^0$ and with the endowments $Z_{hs}^* = Z_{hs}^0$, $Z_{n-1}^* = tZ_{n-1}^0$, and $Z_n^* = tZ_n^0$. Assume that under these conditions he

---

14 Cf. first paragraph of Chapter VI:3.

15 Cf. pp. 52 and 57–58.

16 Attached to last paragraph of Chapter VI:2.

17 The following argument is adapted from Samuelson, *Foundations*, pp. 111–12. For reasons made clear in the next footnote, it is offered with reservations.

chooses "Collection Star," consisting of Z_{hs}^*, $\dfrac{Z_{k,\,n-1}^*}{(1+r^*)p^*}$, and $\dfrac{Z_{kn}^*}{p^*}$. We desire to show that Collection Zero is identical with Collection Star.

Let us sum up the budget restraints (5.15)–(5.17), transpose terms, and divide through by p to obtain

(5.35)
$$\sum_{h,\,s} \frac{p_s}{p}\, Z_{hs} - r\frac{Z_{1,\,n-1}}{(1+r)p} - r\frac{Z_{2,\,n-1}}{(1+r)p}$$
$$= \sum_{h,\,s} \frac{p_s}{p}\, Z_{hs} + \frac{Z_{n-1}}{p} + \frac{Z_n}{p}.$$

This is the individual's budget restraint for the three-week period as a whole. The change described in the preceding paragraph does not affect the value of the right-hand side of this equation. Hence both of our collections must have the same real value. That is,

(5.36)
$$\sum_{h,\,s} \frac{p_s^0}{p^0}\, Z_{hs}^0 - r^0\frac{Z_{1,\,n-1}^0}{(1+r^0)p^0} - r^0\frac{Z_{2,\,n-1}^0}{(1+r^0)p^0}$$
$$= \sum_{h,\,s} \frac{p_s^*}{p^*}\, Z_{hs}^* - r^*\frac{Z_{1,\,n-1}^*}{(1+r^*)p^*} - r^*\frac{Z_{2,\,n-1}^*}{(1+r^*)p^*}.$$

Now, by assumption,

(5.37)
$$\frac{p_s^0}{p^0} = \frac{p_s^*}{p^*} \quad \text{and} \quad r^* = r^0$$

Substituting this into the right-hand side of (5.36), we see that under the price and endowment conditions that prevailed when Collection Zero was chosen, Collection Star could have been chosen; thus Collection Zero was preferred to Collection Star. But by substituting into the left-hand side of (5.36), we conclude—on the basis of the same reasoning —that Collection Star was preferred to Collection Zero. Hence, if to each set of initial conditions there corresponds one and only one chosen collection, these two collections must be identical. Hence an equi-proportionate change in money prices and in initial bond and money holdings, the rate of interest being held constant, has no effect on the amounts demanded of commodities and *real* bond holdings. By the individual budget restraints (5.15)–(5.17), neither, then, does it have any effect on the amount demanded of *real* money holdings.[18]

---

[18] Though I have not been able to find any fallacy in this argument, I am troubled by the fact that it can apparently be applied to equation (5.15) by itself to show that an equi-proportionate change in the p_s, p, Z_{n-1}, and Z_n—*even when accompanied by changes in the commodity endowments of the second and/or third weeks*—has no effect on the amounts demanded, Z_{1s}, $Z_{1,n-1}/p$, and Z_{1n}/p.

e.[19] Let us now assume that currently issued bonds have a certain degree of liquidity. This assumption is reflected by the insertion of two new arguments, $\dfrac{Z_{1,\,n-1}}{(1+r)p}$ and $\dfrac{Z_{2,\,n-1}}{(1+r)p}$, into the utility function $U = w(\ \ )$ of (5.14). Note that it is these arguments, and not $Z_{1,\,n-1}/p$ and $Z_{2,\,n-1}/p$, that are inserted; for, by assumption, the usefulness of bonds as a secondary reserve manifests itself *only* during the week of issue. Hence only their *discounted* real value is relevant to the analysis.

In accordance with this modification of the utility function, our maximum conditions (5.20) and (5.23) are replaced, respectively, by

$$(5.38) \qquad \frac{1}{(1+r)p}\frac{\partial w(\ )}{\partial\left[\dfrac{Z_{1,\,n-1}}{(1+r)p}\right]} - \frac{\lambda_1}{1+r} + \lambda_2 = 0$$

and

$$(5.39) \qquad \frac{1}{(1+r)p}\frac{\partial w(\ )}{\partial\left[\dfrac{Z_{2,\,n-1}}{(1+r)p}\right]} - \frac{\lambda_2}{1+r} + \lambda_3 = 0.$$

All other maximum conditions of Section *b* above are unaffected. Multiplying (5.38) through by $(1+r)$ and transposing, we obtain

$$(5.40) \qquad \lambda_1 = \frac{1}{p}\frac{\partial w(\ )}{\partial\left[\dfrac{Z_{1,\,n-1}}{(1+r)p}\right]} + (1+r)\lambda_2.$$

Now, $1/p$ is the real purchasing power of a dollar's worth of bonds. Thus equation (5.40) is the same as equation (14) of the text. Multiplying out the second term of (5.40), transposing λ_2 to the left-hand side, and substituting from (5.21), we then obtain

$$(5.41) \qquad \frac{1}{p}\frac{\partial w(\ )}{\partial\left(\dfrac{Z_{1n}}{p}\right)} = \frac{1}{p}\frac{\partial w}{\partial\left[\dfrac{Z_{1,\,n-1}}{(1+r)p}\right]} + r\lambda_2.$$

Upon transposition, this is seen to be the same as equation (15) of the text.

It remains to express these maximum conditions in ordinal terms.

---

[19] Attached to Chapter VI:3.

In order to see that the following results can be obtained for bonds which are perpetuities—and not only for those of one-week maturities considered here—the reader is referred once again to my "Further Considerations of the General Equilibrium Theory of Money," *op. cit.*, p. 188.

Substituting for λ_1 from (5.19), and for λ_2 from (5.22), we rewrite (5.40) as

$$(5.42) \quad \frac{1}{p_{n-2}}\frac{\partial w(\;)}{\partial Z_{1,n-2}} = \frac{1}{p}\frac{\partial w(\;)}{\partial\left[\dfrac{Z_{1,\,n-1}}{(1+r)p}\right]} + (1+r)\frac{1}{p_{n-2}}\frac{\partial w(\;)}{\partial Z_{2,\,n-2}}.$$

Dividing through by $\dfrac{1}{p_{n-2}}\dfrac{\partial w(\;)}{\partial Z_{2,\,n-2}}$ and transposing, we obtain equation (16) of the text. In a similar way we obtain from equation (5.41) equation (17).

f.[20] Finally, let us consider the limiting case in which bonds are perfectly liquid, so that they completely replace money as the medium of exchange. That is, there is no paper money in the economy. Assume, however—for purposes of simplicity—that bonds do *not* also constitute the unit of account. In particular, let this function be fulfilled by the $(n-2)$th commodity, say potatoes. Accordingly, let π_s $(s = 1, \ldots, n-2)$ represent the price of the sth commodity in terms of pounds of potatoes. By definition, $\pi_{n-2} = 1$. Similarly, let the bond now constitute a promise to pay one pound of potatoes (or its value-equivalent) one week hence. The price of this bond, π_{n-1}, is then the value-equivalent in potatoes at which it can now be discounted. Hence once again, as in (4.4)–(4.5), we have

$$(5.43) \qquad\qquad\qquad \pi_{n-1} = \frac{1}{1+r}.$$

Under these assumptions the utility function (5.14) is replaced by

$$(5.44) \quad U = \psi\Big(Z_{11}, \ldots, Z_{1,\,n-2}, \frac{Z_{1,\,n-1}}{1+r}, Z_{21}, \ldots, Z_{2,\,n-2}, \frac{Z_{2,\,n-1}}{1+r},$$
$$Z_{31}, \ldots, Z_{3,\,n-2}\Big),$$

where, as just explained, $\dfrac{Z_{1,\,n-1}}{1+r}$ and $\dfrac{Z_{2,\,n-1}}{1+r}$ represent the real discounted value in potatoes of the bonds which the individual holds. Correspondingly, the budget restraints (5.15)–(5.17) become

$$(5.45) \qquad \sum_{s=1}^{n-2} \pi_s(Z_{1s} - \bar{Z}_{1s}) + \frac{Z_{1,\,n-1}}{1+r} - \bar{Z}_{n-1} = 0,$$

---

20 Attached to Chapter VI:4.

(5.46) $$\sum_{s=1}^{n-2} \pi_s(Z_{2s} - \bar{Z}_{2s}) + \frac{Z_{2,\,n-1}}{1+r} - Z_{1,\,n-1} = 0,$$

(5.47) $$\sum_{s=1}^{n-1} \pi_s(Z_{3s} - \bar{Z}_{3s}) \qquad\quad - Z_{2,\,n-1} = 0.$$

Maximizing

(5.48) $$\psi(\ \ ) - \mu_1[(5.45)] - \mu_2[(5.46)] - \mu_3[(5.47)]$$

with respect to the Z_{hs}, $Z_{1,\,n-1}$, and $Z_{2,\,n-1}$, we obtain

(5.49) $$\frac{\partial\psi(\ \ )}{\partial Z_{hs}} - \mu_h\pi_s = 0$$

$$(h = 1, 2, 3;\ s = 1, \ldots, n - 2),$$

(5.50) $$\frac{1}{1+r}\,\frac{\partial\psi(\ \ )}{\partial\left(\dfrac{Z_{k,\,n-1}}{1+r}\right)} - \frac{\mu_k}{1+r} + \mu_{k+1} = 0 \qquad (k = 1, 2).$$

Like equation (5.39) above, this last equation corresponds to equation (14) of the text.

Remembering that $\pi_{n-2} = 1$, we can rewrite equations (5.49) and (5.50), respectively, in the following ordinal terms:

(5.51) $$\frac{\dfrac{\partial\psi(\ \ )}{\partial Z_{ht}}}{\dfrac{\partial\psi(\ \ )}{\partial Z_{h,\,n-2}}} = \pi_t$$

$$(h = 1, 2, 3;\ t = 1, \ldots, n - 3),$$

(5.52) $$\frac{\dfrac{\partial\psi(\ \ )}{\partial Z_{k,\,n-2}}}{\dfrac{\partial\psi(\ \ )}{\partial Z_{k+1,\,n-2}}} - \frac{\partial\left(\dfrac{Z_{k,\,n-1}}{1+r}\right)}{\dfrac{\partial\psi(\ \ )}{\partial Z_{k+1,\,n-2}}} = 1 + r$$

$$(k = 1, 2).$$

This last equation corresponds to equation (16) of the text. Note that there is no counterpart in the present model for equation (17). This, of course, is implied by the failure of (5.49)–(5.50) to produce a counterpart for equation (15).

We see now that the maximum conditions—(5.45)–(5.47), (5.51)–(5.52)—constitute $3n - 4$ equations in the $3n - 4$ dependent variables —Z_{hs} $(h = 1, 2, 3;\ s = 1, \ldots, n - 2)$, $Z_{k,\,n-1}$ $(k = 1, 2)$—and in the independent variables π_t $(t = 1, \ldots, n - 3)$, r, Z_{hs}, and $Z_{k,\,n-1}$. Assume, then, that we can solve out for the dependent variables as functions of the independent ones. Proceeding in this way, we ultimately obtain the market excess-demand equations for current goods:

(5.53) $\phi_s(\pi_1, \ldots, \pi_{n-3}, r, |Z|) - Z_s = 0$

$$(s = 1, \ldots, n - 2),$$

(5.54) $\displaystyle\sum_{s=1}^{n-2} \pi_s[\phi_s(\pi_1, \ldots, \pi_{n-3}, r, |Z|) - Z_s] = 0,$

where $|Z|$ represents the array of all initial endowments. Equation (5.54) is the demand—or excess-demand—equation for bonds. It is obtained by aggregating (5.45) over all individuals in the economy and remembering that $\sum_a Z^a_{n-1} = 0$.[21]

Clearly, any set of values which satisfies (5.53) must also satisfy (5.54); that is, Walras' Law must still be valid. Hence the foregoing system consists of $n - 2$ equations in the $n - 2$ unknowns—$\pi_1, \ldots,$ π_{n-3} and r. By assumption, then, it can determine the equilibrium values of these unknowns. We note finally that we can transform these equilibrium relative prices in terms of potatoes—denoted, say, by $\pi_1^0, \ldots, \pi_{n-3}^0$—into the corresponding equilibrium prices in terms of the medium of exchange, bonds, by dividing them, respectively, through by $\pi_{n-1}^0 = \dfrac{1}{1 + r^0}$, where r^0 is the equilibrium rate of interest and π_{n-1}^0 is, accordingly, the equilibrium price of bonds in terms of potatoes.

---

21 Cf. equations (4.10)–(4.13) and (4.16)–(4.19), pp. 308–9.

6. Appendix to Chapter VII

by ARYEH DVORETZKY

Problem: In an urn there are N white and N black balls. They are drawn out "at random" one after the other without replacement. Let $w(n)$ and $b(n)$ denote, respectively, the number of white and black balls drawn among the first n. Find the distribution of $\max_{0 \leqslant n \leqslant 2N} [w(n) - b(n)]$; that is, find

$$p_k = Pr\left\{ \max_{0 \leqslant n \leqslant 2N} [w(n) - b(n)] = k \right\}$$

$$(k = 0, 1, \ldots, N).$$

*   *   *   *   *

This problem may be reformulated in the following manner: Let $\omega = (x_1, x_2, \ldots, x_{2N}) = [x_1(\omega), x_2(\omega), \ldots, x_{2N}(\omega)]$ denote a sequence of $2N$ terms, each of the terms being either $+1$ or -1. Consider the sample space formed of all 2^{2N} such sequences and the probability space formed by associating with each such sequence the same probability 2^{-2N}.

Put $S_n(\omega) = \sum_{i=1}^{n} x_i(\omega)$ and $M(\omega) = \max_{0 \leqslant n \leqslant 2N} S_n(\omega)$. Then, in the notation of conditional probability,

(6.1) $$p_k = Pr\{M(\omega) = k \mid S_{2N}(\omega) = 0\}.$$

Putting $P_k = p_k + p_{k+1} + \cdots + p_N = \sum_{\nu=k}^{N} p_\nu$, we have

(6.2) $$P_k = Pr\{M(\omega) \geqslant k \mid S_{2N}(\omega) = 0\} = \frac{Pr\{A_k\}}{Pr\{S_{2N}(\omega) = 0\}},$$

where A_k ($k = 0, 1, \ldots, N$) denotes the set of those sequences ω for which $M(\omega) \geqslant k$ *and* $S_{2N}(\omega) = 0$.

For every sequence ω in A_k there exists a unique integer $m = m(\omega)$, $0 \leqslant m < 2N$, for which $S_\nu(\omega) < k$ for $\nu < m$, $S_m(\omega) = k$, $S_{2N}(\omega) = 0$ [i.e., m is the smallest value for which $S_m(\omega) = k$]. Put now $y_\nu = x_\nu(\omega)$

327

for $1 \leqslant \nu \leqslant m$ and $y_\nu = -x_\nu(\omega)$ for $m < \nu \leqslant 2N$.   Then $(y_1, y_2, \ldots, y_{2N})$ is also a sequence in our sample space, and it satisfies

$$
\begin{aligned}
y_1 + y_2 &+ \cdots + y_{2N} \\
&= \sum_{\nu=1}^{m} y_\nu + \sum_{\nu=m+1}^{2N} y_\nu \\
&= \sum_{\nu=1}^{m} x_\nu(\omega) - \sum_{\nu=m+1}^{2N} x_\nu(\omega) \\
&= \sum_{\nu=1}^{m} x_\nu(\omega) - \sum_{\nu=m+1}^{2N} x_\nu(\omega) + \left(\sum_{\nu=1}^{m} x_\nu(\omega) + \sum_{\nu=m+1}^{2N} x_\nu(\omega) \right) \\
&= 2 \sum_{\nu=1}^{m} x_\nu(\omega) = 2k.
\end{aligned}
$$

We have thus associated with every sequence ω in A_k a sequence ω' for which $S_{2N}(\omega') = 2k$.   Moreover, if B_k denotes the set of sequences for which $S_{2N} = 2k$, we have established a one-to-one correspondence between the sequences in A_k and those in B_k.   Thus both sets contain the same number of sequences, and hence $Pr\{A_k\} = Pr\{B_k\}$.   Hence, by (6.2),

$$
(6.3) \qquad\qquad P_k = \frac{Pr\{S_{2N}(\omega) = 2k\}}{Pr\{S_{2N}(\omega) = 0\}}.
$$

Since $S_{2N}(\omega) = 2k$ means that there are $N + k$ terms in the sequence equal to $+1$ and $N - k$ equal to -1, we have $Pr\{S_{2N}(\omega) = 2k\} = \binom{2N}{N+k} 2^{-2N}$.   Therefore, from (6.3),

$$
(6.4) \qquad\qquad P_k = \frac{\binom{2N}{N+k}}{\binom{2N}{N}} = \frac{N!^2}{(N-k)!\,(N+k)!}
$$

$$
(k = 0, 1, \ldots, N)
$$

and

$$
(6.5) \qquad
\begin{aligned}
p_k = P_k - P_{k+1} &= \frac{N!^2}{(N-k)!\,(N+k)!} \left[1 - \frac{N-k}{N+k+1} \right] \\
&= \frac{(2k+1) \cdot N!^2}{(N-k)!\,(N+k+1)!}.
\end{aligned}
$$

The quantities p_k and P_k above are functions of N as well as of k.

Therefore, we shall denote them by $p_k^{(2N)}$ and $P_k^{(2N)}$, respectively, whenever wishing to study also their dependence on N.

From (6.5) we have

$$\frac{p_{k+1}^{(2N)}}{p_k^{(2N)}} = \frac{2k+3}{2k+1} \cdot \frac{N-k}{N+k+2} = \frac{2kN+3N-2k^2-3k}{2kN+N+2k^2+5k+2}.$$

Thus $p_{k+1} > p_k$ is equivalent to $2N > 4k^2 + 8k + 2$, or $N > 2(k+1)^2 - 1$, that is, to $k+1 < \sqrt{(N+1)/2}$. Therefore $p_k^{(2N)}$ increases steadily as k increases up to the largest integer not exceeding $\sqrt{(N+1)/2}$, and as k increases further, $p_k^{(2N)}$ becomes a monotone decreasing function of k. (If $k_0 = \sqrt{(N+1)/2}$ is an integer, then there are two maxima: at $k = k_0$ and $k = k_0 - 1$.)

Applying Stirling's formula to (6.4), we obtain for $0 \leqslant k < N$

$$\log P_k^{(2N)} = (2N+1) \log N - (N-k+\tfrac{1}{2}) \log (N-k)$$
$$- (N+k+\tfrac{1}{2}) \log (N+k) + R$$
$$= -(N-k+\tfrac{1}{2}) \log \left(1 - \frac{k}{N}\right)$$
$$- (N+k+\tfrac{1}{2}) \log \left(1 + \frac{k}{N}\right) + R,$$

with the remainder term R satisfying $|R| < \dfrac{\text{const.}}{N-k}$. This yields

(6.6) $$\log P_k^{(2N)} \sim -\frac{k^2}{N}$$

as $N \to \infty$ while $\dfrac{k}{N} \to 0$. (The sign $\sim$ signifies that the ratio of the two sides tends to 1; k may also tend to infinity, but less rapidly than N.) If we put

(6.7) $$F_{2N}(\lambda) = Pr\{k \leqslant \lambda\sqrt{2N}\} = Pr\left\{\frac{k}{\sqrt{2N}} \leqslant \lambda\right\},$$

that is, if F_{2N} is the (cumulative) distribution function of $\dfrac{k}{\sqrt{2N}}$, we have from (6.6)

(6.8) $$\lim_{N \to \infty} F_{2N}(\lambda) = 1 - e^{-2\lambda^2}$$

for every $\lambda \geqslant 0$.

From (6.6) and (6.5) we have

(6.9) $$p_k^{(2N)} \sim \frac{2k+1}{N+k+1} e^{-k^2/N}.$$

Thus, if k and N tend to infinity so that $\dfrac{k}{\sqrt{2N}} \to \lambda$, we have

(6.10) $$\lim_{N \to \infty} \sqrt{2N} \cdot p_k^{(2N)} = 4\lambda e^{-2\lambda^2},$$

and the right side of this equation, which is equal to the derivative of the right side of (6.8), may be thought of as the asymptotic density of $k/\sqrt{2N}$. Using an estimate of the remainder in Stirling's formula, it is easy to obtain bounds for the difference of the two sides in (6.6) and (6.9), and hence also estimate the rate of approach to the limit in (6.8) and (6.10).

If for any q, $0 < q < 1$, we denote by $Q_q^{(2N)}$ the q percentile point of k; that is, if $Q_q^{(2N)}$ is the smallest integer m satisfying $p_0^{(2N)} + p_1^{(2N)} + \cdots + p_m^{(2N)} \geqslant q$, then according to (6.7) and (6.8),

(6.11) $$\lim_{N \to \infty} \frac{Q_q^{(2N)}}{\sqrt{2N}} = Q_q,$$

where Q_q is the positive root of $1 - e^{-2\lambda^2} = q$. Thus $Q_q^{(2N)} \sim Q_q\sqrt{2N}$; that is, though it increases with N, its rate of increase is much slower than that of N. Hence as N increases, $Q_q^{(2N)}/N$ generally decreases. Due to the discrete character of the integers, there may, however, occur occasional local exceptions to this rule. Nevertheless, we must always have for every positive integer $\nu > 1$ and $q > p_0^{(2N)} = \dfrac{1}{N+1}$

$$\frac{Q_q^{(2\nu N)}}{\nu N} < \frac{Q_q^{(2N)}}{N}.$$

This is an immediate consequence of the fact that for every positive integer k we have

(6.12) $$P_k^{(2N)} > P_{\nu k}^{(2\nu N)}.$$

To verify (6.12) we rewrite (6.4):

$$P_k^{(2N)} = \frac{N(N-1) \cdots (N-k+1)}{(N+k)(N+k-1) \cdots (N+1)}$$

$$= \prod_{m=1}^{k} \left(1 - \frac{k}{N+m}\right).$$

Then also

$$P_{\nu k}^{(2\nu N)} = \prod_{m=1}^{\nu k} \left(1 - \frac{\nu k}{\nu N + m}\right).$$

All the factors in these products are positive and smaller than 1, while the factors corresponding to $m = \nu, 2\nu, \ldots, k\nu$ of the last product are precisely equal to the factors corresponding to $m = 1, 2, \ldots, k$ (i.e.,

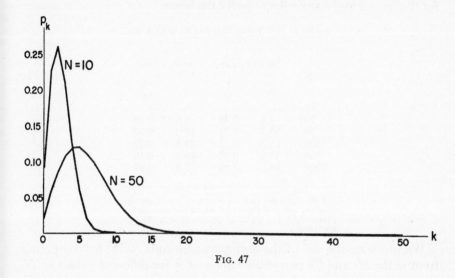

FIG. 47

to all the factors) appearing in the expression for $P_k^{(2N)}$. This proves (6.12).

It may finally be remarked that the asymptotic result expressed by (6.8) remains valid under very general assumptions. Thus it is possible to prove the following:

Let X_n ($n = 1, 2, \ldots$) be an infinite sequence of independent random variables satisfying $|X_n| \leqslant H < \infty$ ($n = 1, 2, \ldots$) having mean zero and variance σ_n^2. Then if $\sum_{n=1}^{\infty} \sigma_n^2 = \infty$, we have, on putting $Y_n = X_1 + X_2 + \cdots + X_n$ and $s_n^2 = \sigma_1^2 + \sigma_2^2 + \cdots + \sigma_n^2$,

$$\lim_{n \to \infty} Pr\left\{ \max_{0 \leqslant m \leqslant n} Y_m \leqslant \lambda s_n \mid Y_n < H \right\} = 1 - e^{-2\lambda^2}$$

for every $\lambda \geqslant 0$.

This, and indeed considerably more general results, follow from the fact that the stochastic process involved here approaches that of the Brownian motion $x(t)$, and the probability we are seeking approaches that of $Pr\left\{ \max_{0 \leqslant t \leqslant 1} x(t) \leqslant \lambda \mid x(1) = 0 \right\}$, which is easily computed to be $1 - e^{-2\lambda^2}$.[1]

Numerical Illustration:[2] Figure 47 shows the exact distributions of k—as given by (6.5)—for $N = 10$ and $N = 50$. The ranges of these distributions are, of course, 0–10 and 0–50, respectively. The reader can verify that the asymptotic formula (6.10) gives a fair approximation for the former and an excellent one for the latter.

TABLE OF PERCENTILE VALUES

N	90 PER CENT		99 PER CENT	
	k	$\dfrac{k}{N}$	k	$\dfrac{k}{N}$
10†	4.8	0.48	6.8	0.68
50	10.7	0.21	15.2	0.30
100	15.2	0.15	21.5	0.21
500	33.9	0.07	48.0	0.10
1000	48.0	0.05	67.9	0.07

† As given by (6.4), $k = 4$ and $k = 6$ are the smallest integral values for which the cumulative probability $1 - P_k$ is at least .90 and .99, respectively.

We illustrate the use of the asymptotic formula (6.11) by computing from it the 90 and 99 percentile values of k for different values of N. The appropriate formulas are $k = 1.07\sqrt{2N}$ and $k = 1.52\sqrt{2N}$, respectively. These yield the values shown in the table above. This table ignores the fact that k, of course, can actually assume integral values only.

---

[1] For a study of Brownian motion, see, e.g., P. Levy, *Processes stochastiques et mouvement Brownian* (Paris, 1948), or J. L. Doob, *Stochastic Processes* (New York, 1953).

[2] Figure 47 and the Table of Percentile Values were prepared by Mr. Tsvi Goldberger.

7. Appendix to Chapter VIII

a.[1] The text distinguishes four types of dichotomies. These can be described in the following terms:

(i) The first dichotomy is implicit in the discussion of Mathematical Appendix 4:*c*. At the first stage of this dichotomy we consider the amount of money, Z_n, to be fixed but unknown, and solve out equations (4.22)–(4.24) for the relative prices, rate of interest, and real value of cash balances, as in (4.25)–(4.27). At the second stage we add the equation specifying the amount of money,

$$(7.1) \qquad\qquad Z_n = Z_n^0,$$

and thereby determine the money prices, as in (4.28)–(4.30).

(ii) The second dichotomy is also implicit in a preceding discussion. In particular, let us consider again our model (4.22)–(4.24) and apply to it the reasoning of Mathematical Appendix 3:*a*. In contradistinction to the preceding paragraph, however, Z_n is now assumed to be a known constant. On the other hand, we now drop the assumption that $p_n = 1$ and, accordingly, replace the argument Z_n/p of these equations by $p_n Z_n/p$. It is then evident that the dependent variables p_i $(i = 1, \ldots, n)$ and p appear in system (4.22)–(4.24) so modified only in the form of the n ratios p_i/p. Hence the n equations of this system can at most be solved out for

$$(7.2) \qquad \frac{p_s}{p} = k_s \qquad\qquad (s = 1, \ldots, n-2),$$

$$r = k_{n-1}, \quad \text{and} \quad \frac{p_n}{p} = k_n,$$

where the k_i are constants. These solutions can then be rewritten as

$$(7.3) \qquad \frac{p_s}{p_n} = \frac{k_s}{k_n}, \quad r = k_{n-1}, \quad \text{and} \quad \frac{p}{p_n} = \frac{1}{k_n}.$$

---

[1] Attached to Chapter VIII:3.

333

Thus at this stage of the dichotomy we have already determined money prices, p_s/p_n; but we have not yet determined accounting prices, p_s. The second stage, then, consists of arbitrarily specifying the accounting price of any one of the commodities or of money. Thus, for example, we can add the equation

(7.4) $$p_n = t,$$

where t is a constant. Substituting this in (7.3), we then obtain the accounting prices of all other goods. The implications of the distinction between (7.4) and (7.1) have already been drawn in the text (pages 106–7).

(iii) The third, and invalid, dichotomy begins by assuming that the excess-demand functions for commodities and bonds are independent of the absolute price level, so that the corresponding excess-demand equations can be written as

(7.5) $$D_s\left(\frac{p_1}{p}, \ldots, \frac{p_{n-2}}{p}, r\right) - Z_s = 0$$

$$(s = 1, \ldots, n-2),$$

(7.6) $$D_{n-1}\left(\frac{p_1}{p}, \ldots, \frac{p_{n-2}}{p}, r\right) = 0,$$

where

(7.7) $$\sum_{s=1}^{n-2} w_s \frac{p_s}{p} = 1$$

To these is added the excess-demand equation for money in, say, its Cambridge form:

(7.8) $$KpT - Z_n = 0,$$

where Z_n and K are constants, and T is a function of the Z_s or $D_s(\ )$, or both.[2]

Choosing (7.6) as the equation to be "eliminated" by virtue of Walras' Law, we then dichotomize the pricing process in the following way: In the first stage we consider the subset of $n-1$ equations (7.5) and (7.7). These depend only on—and therefore can determine—the

---

[2] For generality, the dichotomy is stated here for the case of a model with bonds. If the reader prefers to work with the more familiar case of a model with only commodities and money, he need only consider the $(n-1)$th good to be another commodity, replace r by p_{n-1}/p, and rewrite (7.6) as

$$D_{n-1}(\ ) - Z_{n-1} = 0.$$

This does not affect the following argument in any significant way.

equilibrium values of the $n-1$ variables p_s/p and r. In the second stage we use these values to fix the value of T in (7.8). Since K and Z_n are constants, this equation can then determine the equilibrium value of the remaining variable, p.

It can readily be shown that this dichotomy is internally inconsistent. For by the budget restraint we know that the excess-demand function for money must have the form

$$(7.9) \qquad -p\sum_{s=1}^{n-2}\frac{p_s}{p}[D_s(\ )-Z_s]-pD_{n-1}(\ ).$$

This implies that a doubling of money prices causes a doubling of the amount of excess demand for money. But the excess-demand function $KpT-Z_n$ does not have this property. Thus the form of the monetary function implicit in the left-hand sides of (7.5)–(7.7) is inconsistent with the form explicit in the left-hand side of (7.8).

Nor can this dichotomy be saved by jettisoning the Cambridge equation. For let the excess-demand function for money be changed in such a way as to eliminate the preceding inconsistency. That is, let it explicitly assume the form (7.9). Equation (7.8) is accordingly replaced by

$$(7.10) \qquad \sum_{s=1}^{n-2}\frac{p_s}{p}[D_s(\ )-Z_s]+D_{n-1}(\ )=0.$$

It is immediately seen that the dependent variables of this equation are precisely those of (7.5) and (7.7); in particular, the variable p appears only as the denominator of the price ratios, p_s/p, and never by itself. Hence this equation cannot possibly determine the value of any variable not already determined by (7.5) and (7.7); and these equations, in turn, can at most determine the values of the only variables which appear in them—the p_s/p and r. Thus the assumption that demand depends only on relative prices implies that the value of p is indeterminate.

Our criticism of the foregoing dichotomy can thus be summarized in the following terms: With the quantity theory, its excess-demand *functions* are inconsistent. Without the quantity theory, its system of excess-demand *equations* is indeterminate.

(iv) The fourth dichotomy—the "Keynesian case"—replaces (7.6) by

$$(7.11) \qquad D^*_{n-1}\left(\frac{p_1}{p},\ldots,\frac{p_{n-2}}{p},r,\frac{Z_n}{p}\right)=0.$$

335

The form of the excess-demand function for money then becomes

(7.12)
$$-p \sum_{s=1}^{n-2} \frac{p_s}{p} \left[D_s\left(\frac{p_1}{p}, \ldots, \frac{p_{n-2}}{p}, r\right) - Z_s \right]$$
$$- p D_{n-1}^*\left(\frac{p_1}{p}, \ldots, \frac{p_{n-2}}{p}, r, \frac{Z_n}{p}\right).$$

This no longer implies that a doubling of prices doubles the amount of excess demand for money. On the other hand, it does imply that a doubling of prices *and* Z_n does do so. But this property is precisely that shared by the Cambridge function $KpT - Z_n$.

Similarly, equation (7.10) is replaced by

(7.13)
$$\sum_{s=1}^{n-2} \frac{p_s}{p} [D_s(\ \ ) - Z_s] + D^*\left(\frac{p_1}{p}, \ldots, \frac{p_{n-2}}{p}, r, \frac{Z_n}{p}\right) = 0.$$

Here the variable p does appear by itself. Hence we can say that specification of the commodity equations (7.5) and (7.7) determines relative prices and the rate of interest, while specification of (7.13)—or (7.11)—then determines the absolute price level.

(v) As soon, however, as we leave the very special assumptions of this case, we cannot generally split up the pricing process in this way. To be more specific, consider system (4.16)–(4.19). Use Walras' Law again to "eliminate" the bond equation—(4.17). Let us now assign an arbitrary value, p^0, to the absolute price level. The subset (4.16) and (4.19) then constitutes $n - 1$ equations in the $n - 1$ variables $p_1/p^0, \ldots, p_{n-2}/p^0$, r. Hence it can determine a solution for these variables—say $(p_1/p^0)_0, \ldots, (p_{n-2}/p^0)_0, r_0$. Let us now insert these values into the money equation (4.18). This leaves only a single unknown variable in this equation—p. Hence (4.18) determines a value for this variable—say p^1. Clearly, there is no reason why p^0 and p^1 must be equal. Hence there is no reason why equations (4.16) and (4.19) must be satisfied by the set of values p^1 and $(p_1/p^0)_0, \ldots,$ $(p_{n-2}/p^0)_0, r_0$. That is, there is no reason why $(p_1/p^0)_0, \ldots, (p_{n-2}/p^0)_0,$ r_0 should be the equilibrium relative prices and rate of interest of the system (4.16)–(4.19) as a whole. Or, to put it the other way around, they will necessarily constitute these equilibrium values only if equations (4.16) are not affected by a change in the absolute price level from p^0 to p^1 which leaves relative prices constant—only, that is, if equations (4.16) are not affected by equi-proportionate changes in the p_s and p. But this can be true only if these equations do not depend on the Z_{n-1}/p and Z_n/p. And this, of course, is the "Keynesian case" of the preceding paragraph.

336

b.[3] For the purpose of analyzing a shift in liquidity preference we first define the "liquidity parameter" α^a. This is an index of the amount of liquidity satisfaction the ath individual derives from holding one dollar of real money balances: the higher this satisfaction, the higher α^a. This index can then be used to "deflate" the objective quantity of real balances, Z_n^a/p, in order to obtain its "subjective quantity," $\alpha^a Z_n^a/p$. An increase in α^a thus causes an increase in the subjective quantity of real balances, even though their objective quantity has not changed.

Let us now introduce this parameter into our system by modifying (4.16)–(4.19) in the following way:

(7.14)
$$F_s\left(\frac{p_1}{p}, \ldots, \frac{p_{n-2}}{p}, r, \frac{Z_{n-1}^1}{p}, \ldots, \frac{Z_{n-1}^A}{p}, \frac{\alpha^1 Z_n^1}{p}, \ldots, \frac{\alpha^A Z_n^A}{p}\right)$$
$$- Z_s = 0 \qquad\qquad (s = 1, \ldots, n-2),$$

(7.15)
$$F_{n-1}\left(\frac{p_1}{p}, \ldots, \frac{p_{n-2}}{p}, r, \frac{Z_{n-1}^1}{p}, \ldots, \frac{Z_{n-1}^A}{p}, \frac{\alpha^1 Z_n^1}{p}, \ldots, \frac{\alpha^A Z_n^A}{p}\right) = 0,$$

(7.16)
$$-\sum_{s=1}^{n-2} \frac{p_s}{p} [F_s(\ ) - Z_s] - F_{n-1}(\ ) = 0,$$

(7.17)
$$\sum_{s=1}^{n-2} w_s \frac{p_s}{p} = 1.$$

A decrease in α^a thus decreases the arguments referring to real balances, and hence decreases the amounts demanded of commodities and bonds. From the left-hand side of (7.16)—which is, of course, the excess-demand function for real money holdings (4.12)—we then see that this causes an increase in the amount of money demanded. Thus a decrease in α^a is identified with an increase in liquidity preference.

It must now be emphasized that the α^a have been introduced into the foregoing functions in a very special way. In particular, consider the market for the first commodity. The "intensity" of an individual's increased liquidity preference with respect to this market is defined as being measured by the equi-proportionate decrease in prices necessary to restore his subjective quantity of money to its original level with respect to its influence on this market. The preceding model assumes that this intensity is the same for each and every market. And it is this symmetry which defines a "neutral" shift in liquidity preference.

This case is to be contrasted with the one in which the ath individual

---

[3] Attached to Chapter VIII:5.

is assumed to have a different liquidity parameter, α_j^a ($j = 1, \ldots, n-1$), for each and every market. Then his subjective quantities of money relevant to these markets, $\alpha_j^a \bar{Z}_n^a / p$, are also different. Or, in other words, an increase in liquidity preference does not generally take place with the same intensity in each market. Or, in still other words, the extent of the price decline necessary to offset the effects of the increased liquidity preference on the individual's demand in one market is not generally the same as that necessary for another. Such a case will be analyzed in Mathematical Appendix 8:*c*.

Our neutrality assumption clearly makes the problem of a shift in liquidity preference analytically equivalent to the already familiar problem of a change in the quantity of money. In particular, at the level of individual-experiments, the functions on the left-hand sides of (7.14)–(7.16) show that the excess amounts demanded of commodities, *real* bond holdings, and *real* money holdings are assumed to remain unaffected by an equi-proportionate change in the p_s, p, $\bar{Z}_{n-1}^a$, *and* α^a— all other independent variables being held constant. Correspondingly, at the level of market-experiments, equations (7.14)–(7.17) show that— provided there are neutral real-indebtedness effects—an equi-proportionate change in the α^a causes an equi-proportionate change in the equilibrium values of p_s and p, and leaves the equilibrium value of r invariant. The rigorous proof of this proposition obviously parallels that of Mathematical Appendix 4:*b* for an equi-proportionate change in the $\bar{Z}_n^a$.

Clearly, the validity of this proposition depends on the assumption that each individual's shift in liquidity preference is of the same intensity in each and every market. On the other hand, it does not depend on the assumption that each individual has only one liquidity parameter in a *given* market. In particular, assume that the individual holds money for both the transactions and precautionary motives. Correspondingly, let β^a and γ^a be the respective liquidity parameters of these two motives. That is, a decrease in β^a (γ^a) represents an increased desire to hold transactions (precautionary) balances. Now, no matter why the individual wants to hold, say, 10 per cent larger real money balances, his increased liquidity preference can be satisfied by (approximately) a 9 per cent decline in prices. This symmetry between changes in β^a and γ^a implies that they cannot enter the demand functions as sums, but only as products. In particular, wherever α^a appears in the foregoing equations, it should be replaced by $\beta^a \gamma^a$. Hence the basic argument of this section is not affected by assuming the demand for money to depend on two separate motives.[4]

---

[4] Cf. above, p. 176.

c.[5] From (4.6)–(4.8) write the market excess-demand equations for the current week in the form

$$(7.18) \quad Q_s\left(\frac{p_1}{p}, \ldots, \frac{p_{n-2}}{p}, r, \left|\frac{Z^a_{n-1}}{p}\right|, \left|\frac{Z^a_n}{p}\right|, \left|\frac{\sum\limits_{s=1}^{n-2} p_s Z^a_{hs}}{p}\right|\right) - Z_s = 0$$

$$(s = 1, \ldots, n-2),$$

$$(7.19) \quad Q_{n-1}(\ ) = 0,$$

$$(7.20) \quad Q_n(\ ) - Z_n = 0,$$

$$(7.21) \quad \sum_{s=1}^{n-2} w_s \frac{p_s}{p} = 1,$$

where $\left|\dfrac{Z^a_{n-1}}{p}\right|$, $\left|\dfrac{Z^a_n}{p}\right|$, and $\left|\dfrac{\sum\limits_{s=1}^{n-2} p_s Z^a_{hs}}{p}\right|$ represent the respective arrays of the relevant arguments for all values of a and h. Clearly, (7.20) will be satisfied if the other equations are.

Assume that for $Z^a_{hs} = Z^{a0}_{hs}$ ($s = 1, \ldots, n-2$; $a = 1, \ldots, A$; $h = 1, \ldots, H$) and $Z^a_u = Z^{a0}_u$ ($u = n-1, n$) these equations have the solution $p_s = p^0_s$, $p = p^0$, $r = r^0$. Consider now the system of equations for $Z^a_{hs} = t^0 Z^a_{hs}$ and for $Z^a_u = Z^{a0}_u$ ($u = n-1, n$), where t^0 is a given positive constant. Take a trial solution of the form $p_s = k p^0_s$, $p = k p^0$, and $r = r^0$, where k is an unknown positive constant. Insert this into equation (7.18) for $s = 1$ to yield

$$(7.22) \quad Q_1\left(\frac{p^0_1}{p^0}, \ldots, \frac{p^0_{n-2}}{p^0}, r^0, \left|\frac{Z^{a0}_{n-1}}{kp^0}\right|, \left|\frac{Z^{a0}_n}{kp^0}\right|, \left|\frac{\sum\limits_{s=1}^{n-2} p^0_s t^0 Z^{a0}_{hs}}{p^0}\right|\right) - t^0 Z^0_1 = 0.$$

This is a single equation in one unknown, k. Assume that it has a solution $k = k^0$.

Clearly, just as we obtained an equation in k from (7.18) for $s = 1$, so can we obtain similar equations for $s = 2, \ldots, n-2$, not to speak of the equation that can be obtained from (7.19). There is no reason why these additional equations should also be satisfied by $k = k^0$. In brief, the insertion of this trial solution into (7.18)–(7.19) gives us an overdetermined system of $n-1$ independent equations in

---

[5] Attached to Chapter VIII:6.

the single variable, k. This is clearly true even in the absence of a distribution effect.[6]

We note finally that even if all $n - 1$ equations should yield the same solution for k, there is no reason why this should be $k = 1/t^0$.

d.[7] Let us denote by

$$(7.23) \qquad X_i(p_1, \ldots, p_{n-2}, p, r) = 0 \qquad (i = 1, \ldots, n)$$

the market excess-demand equation for the ith good, where the $(n - 1)$th good is bonds, and the nth, money. According to Lange,[8] Say's Identity states

$$(7.24) \qquad \sum_{j=1}^{n-1} p_j X_j(p_1, \ldots, p_{n-2}, p, r) \equiv 0,$$

or, what is more appropriate for our purposes,

$$(7.25) \qquad \begin{aligned} X_{n-1}&(p_1, \ldots, p_{n-2}, p, r) \\ &\equiv -(1 + r) \sum_{s=1}^{n-2} p_s X_s(p_1, \ldots, p_{n-2}, p, r). \end{aligned}$$

Alternatively, comparing (7.24) with (4.12), we can follow Lange and state Say's Identity as

$$(7.26) \qquad X_n(p_1, \ldots, p_{n-2}, p, r) \equiv 0.$$

Consider now the first $n - 2$ equations of (7.23) together with the definition of p as given by (7.7). Take a specific value of $p = p^0$, and assume that for this value this system of $n - 1$ equations has a unique solution for the $n - 1$ variables p_s ($s = 1, \ldots, n - 2$) and r. By (7.25), this solution together with $p = p^0$ must also satisfy (7.23) for $i = n - 1$. And, as is obvious from (7.26), it must also satisfy (7.23) for $i = n$. Hence this set of values must be an equilibrium one.

Take now any other value, $p = p^1$. In general, the solution of (7.23) and (7.7) corresponding to this new value will differ from the preceding one. But by (7.25) this solution too must be an equilibrium

---

[6] The reader should establish for himself that this line of reasoning does not lead to an overdeterminacy in the preceding section and in Mathematical Appendixes 3:c and 4:b. Cf. p. 118, footnote 53, above.

[7] Attached to Chapter VIII:7.

[8] "Say's Law . . . ," *op. cit.*, pp. 49–53. For generality, I have extended Lange's analysis to the case of an economy with bonds.

one.   Thus Say's Identity implies that money prices are indeterminate.[9]
Hence this identity can meaningfully exist only in a barter economy.

Consider now such an economy.   Its operation is essentially described by the model of Mathematical Appendix 5:*f*.   All that we need
to do is drop the assumption of this model that bonds are liquid.   But,
as the reader can verify, this does not affect the basic properties of its
equations.   In particular, the budget restraint of a barter economy is
described by (5.45).   As can readily be seen, this implies the existence
of Say's Identity.   At the same time, the demand functions of such an
economy are described by (5.53)—where, as will be recalled, $\pi_1, \ldots,$
π_{n-3} are *relative* prices.   That is, these functions satisfy the homogeneity postulate.   Hence relative prices and interest can be determined
in the commodity markets alone.   But this is not a vindication of the
dichotomy in Section *a*(iii) above.   For under these circumstances
money prices are not even defined.

It should finally be noted that our line of reasoning here is that Say's
Identity implies a barter economy and hence the homogeneity postulate.
This is to be contrasted with Lange's accepted procedure of deducing
this postulate directly from Say's Identity.   According to Lange's
argument, Say's Identity "excludes the use of cash balances for
financing purchases of commodities";[10] or, alternatively, it precludes
"the substitution of money for commodities."[11]   Hence Say's Identity
implies that "the quantity demanded of each commodity will depend
only on relative commodity prices."[12]

This, however, is a *non sequitur*.   For the constancy of money
expenditures on commodities does not imply the absence of the real-
balance effect.   Thus, for example, a doubling of all prices might,
through the real-balance effect, cause a halving of all quantities
demanded, so that the total money expenditure on commodities remains
constant.   All we know from Say's Identity per se is that no matter
how the real-balance effect might manifest itself, the functional
dependence described by (7.24) makes it impossible for any change in
prices to cause the amount of excess demand for money to depart from
its zero value in (7.26).

---

[9] In more general terms, the addition of Say's Identity to Walras' Law implies that there are
only $n - 2$ independent equations in (7.23).   Hence these together with the remaining equation (7.7) do not suffice to determine the n variables, p_s $(s = 1, \ldots, n - 2), p$, and r.

[10] Lange, "Say's Law . . . ," *op. cit.*, p. 53; see also pp. 63–64.

[11] G. S. Becker and W. J. Baumol, " The Classical Monetary Theory . . . ," *Economica*,
XIX (1952), 358.

[12] *Ibid.*

8. Appendix to Chapters X and XI

a.[1] According to the assumptions made in the text, our dynamic analysis can be restricted to the bond and commodity markets. The equilibrium conditions for these markets are, respectively,

$$(8.1) \qquad B\left(Y_0, \frac{1}{r}, \frac{M}{p}\right) = 0,$$

$$(8.2) \qquad F\left(Y_0, r, \frac{M}{p}\right) - Y_0 = 0,$$

where M is a constant and

$$(8.3) \qquad B\left(Y_0, \frac{1}{r}, \frac{M}{p}\right) \equiv H\left(Y_0, \frac{1}{r}, \frac{M^H}{p}\right) - J\left(Y_0, \frac{1}{r}, \frac{M^F}{p}\right).$$

This identity makes use of the assumption that the distribution of money balances in the economy does not affect the equilibrium rate of interest. According to the discussion of Chapter IX, the partial derivatives of these functions are $B_1 \gtreqless 0$, $B_2 < 0$, $B_3 > 0$, $F_1 > 0$, $F_2 < 0$, and $F_3 > 0$, where the subscripts indicate the arguments with respect to which differentiation is carried out. Since Y is assumed constant at Y_0, B_1 and F_1 play no role in the following analysis.

Consider now the general case in which the *tâtonnement* of the economy is described by the following dynamic equations:[2]

$$(8.4) \qquad \frac{dr}{dt} = - K_1 B\left(Y_0, \frac{1}{r}, \frac{M}{p}\right) - K_2\left[F\left(Y_0, r, \frac{M}{p}\right) - Y_0\right],$$

$$(8.5) \qquad \frac{dp}{dt} = K_3 B\left(Y_0, \frac{1}{r}, \frac{M}{p}\right) + K_4\left[F\left(Y_0, r, \frac{M}{p}\right) - Y_0\right],$$

where the K_j $(j = 1, \ldots, 4)$ are positive constants. By differentiating

---

1 Attached to Chapter X:2.
2 On the following, cf. Mathematical Appendix 3:*b*.

the functions $B(\ )$ and $F(\ )$, we obtain a linear approximation in the neighborhood of the equilibrium point:

$$
(8.6) \quad
\begin{aligned}
\frac{dr}{dt} &= \left[\frac{K_1 B_2}{r_0^2} - K_2 F_2\right](r - r_0) \\
&\qquad + \left[\frac{K_1 B_3 M}{p_0^2} + \frac{K_2 F_3 M}{p_0^2}\right](p - p_0),
\end{aligned}
$$

$$
(8.7) \quad
\begin{aligned}
\frac{dp}{dt} &= \left[-\frac{K_3 B_2}{r_0^2} + K_4 F_2\right](r - r_0) \\
&\qquad + \left[-\frac{K_3 B_3 M}{p_0^2} - \frac{K_4 F_3 M}{p_0^2}\right](p - p_0).
\end{aligned}
$$

Let

$$
(8.8) \quad
\begin{aligned}
a &= -\frac{B_2}{r_0^2} > 0, & b &= F_2 < 0, \\
c &= -\frac{B_3 M}{p_0^2} < 0, & d &= -\frac{F_3 M}{p_0^2} < 0.
\end{aligned}
$$

Then it can be shown that a method of successive approximation which proceeds according to the rules (8.4)–(8.5) will converge to the solution of equations (8.1)–(8.2) if the following characteristic equation in x,

$$
(8.9) \quad
\begin{vmatrix}
-K_1 a - K_2 b - x & -K_1 c - K_2 d \\
K_3 a + K_4 b & K_3 c + K_4 d - x
\end{vmatrix} = 0,
$$

has roots whose real parts are negative.[3]
   Expanding (8.9), we obtain

$$
(8.10) \quad x^2 + gx + h = 0,
$$

where

$$
(8.11) \quad
\begin{aligned}
g &= K_1 a + K_2 b - K_3 c - K_4 d, \\
h &= -K_1 K_4 ad - K_2 K_3 bc + K_1 K_4 bc + K_2 K_3 ad.
\end{aligned}
$$

It follows that the signs of both g and h are dependent on the relative magnitudes of the K_j and the partial derivatives. Hence the signs of the real parts of the solutions for x cannot be specified. Accordingly, the convergence of the system cannot be generally established.

---

[3] As already indicated, this procedure is based on Samuelson, *Foundations*, pp. 269 ff. Cf. also Metzler, "Wealth, Saving, and the Rate of Interest," *op. cit.*, pp. 115–16.
   Note one property of this system of successive approximation: If it converges, it must converge to a solution. This is a consequence of the assumption that the K_j are constant.

Clearly, the smaller K_2 and K_3, the more likely that the signs of g and h will both be positive. In the extreme case where $K_2 = K_3 = 0$, this must definitely be so. By the quadratic formula for the solution of (8.10),

$$(8.12) \qquad x = \frac{-g \pm \sqrt{g^2 - 4h}}{2},$$

it then follows that the real parts of the roots of x must be negative. Hence in this case—which corresponds to that described by Figure 18 of the text—the dynamic system must definitely converge to the equilibrium solution. Note that this conclusion holds even under the extreme Keynesian assumption $F_3(\quad) \equiv 0$.

b.[4] Assume now that the analysis is carried out instead in terms of the commodity and money markets. Then (8.1) is replaced by

$$(8.13) \qquad L\left(Y_0, r, \frac{M}{p}\right) - \frac{M}{p} = 0,$$

where $L_1 > 0$, $L_2 < 0$, and $1 > L_3 > 0$. Under the Keynesian assumption of Figure 26 that excess demand in the money market affects only the rate of interest, dynamic system (8.4)–(8.5) is then replaced by

$$(8.14) \qquad \frac{dr}{dt} = Q_1\left[L\left(Y_0, r, \frac{M}{p}\right) - \frac{M}{p}\right],$$

$$(8.15) \qquad \frac{dp}{dt} = Q_2\left[F\left(Y_0, r, \frac{M}{p}\right) - Y_0\right],$$

where Q_1 and Q_2 are positive constants. Using the same procedure as in the preceding section, we can show that system (8.14)–(8.15) is stable if the following characteristic equation in x,

$$(8.16) \qquad \begin{vmatrix} Q_1L_2 - x & \dfrac{Q_1M(1 - L_3)}{p^2} \\ Q_2F_2 & \dfrac{-Q_2MF_3}{p^2} - x \end{vmatrix} = 0,$$

has roots whose real parts are negative. Expanding, we obtain

$$(8.17) \qquad \begin{aligned} &x^2 + \left[\frac{Q_2MF_3}{p^2} - Q_1L_2\right]x \\ &+ \left[\frac{-Q_1Q_2ML_2F_3}{p^2} - \frac{Q_1Q_2MF_2(1 - L_3)}{p^2}\right] = 0. \end{aligned}$$

---

[4] Attached to Chapter XI:2 and pp. 266–67.

By assumption as to the signs of the partial derivatives, both the coefficient of x and the constant term in the preceding equation are positive. Hence the real parts of its solutions are negative. Hence system (8.14)–(8.15) is stable. Once again this conclusion holds even in the extreme Keynesian case where $F_3(\ ) \equiv 0$.

It should, however, be emphasized that though system (8.4)–(8.5) with $K_2 = K_3 = 0$ and system (8.14)–(8.15) both converge, they are *not* dynamically equivalent. In particular, under the assumption that the labor market is always in equilibrium, equations (8.1)–(8.2) and the budget restraint imply that the excess-demand function for real money holdings has the form[5]

(8.18)
$$
L\left(Y_0, r, \frac{M}{p}\right) - \frac{M}{p}
$$
$$
\equiv -\left[F\left(Y_0, r, \frac{M}{p}\right) - Y_0\right] - B\left(Y_0, \frac{1}{r}, \frac{M}{p}\right).
$$

Consider now (8.4)–(8.5) for $K_2 = K_3 = 0$. Substituting these into (8.18), we obtain[6]

(8.19)
$$
-\frac{1}{K_4}\frac{dp}{dt} + \frac{1}{K_1}\frac{dr}{dt} = L\left(Y_0, r, \frac{M}{p}\right) - \frac{M}{p}.
$$

That is, an excess demand for money simultaneously causes prices to fall and interest to rise. Thus the dynamic impetuses described by (8.19)—and implicit in (8.4)–(8.5)—are quite different from those described by (8.14). Correspondingly, aside from the fact of their convergence, the time paths of r and p generated by (8.4)–(8.5) bear no necessary relationship to those generated by (8.14)–(8.15). This is the meaning of the discrepancy between Figures 18 and 26 noted in the text.[7]

On the other hand, it is obvious that, for $K_2 = K_3 = 0$, systems (8.4)–(8.5), (8.4) and (8.19), and (8.5) and (8.19) are all dynamically equivalent. In particular, each of the last two can be reduced to the first by appropriate substitutions. Thus our choice of the markets in which to conduct our dynamic analysis cannot per se affect the nature of this analysis. We must, however, take care that in passing over from one pair of markets to another we do not unknowingly modify the nature of our dynamic assumptions.

---

[5] Cf. equation (4.12) above.
[6] This is a direct application of equation (3.6) above
[7] Above, p. 179.

c.[8] The analysis of a shift in liquidity preference follows the approach of Mathematical Appendix 7:b. If, as in the case analyzed there, this shift is neutral as between commodities and bonds, then the arguments M/p in (8.1)–(8.2) are replaced by $\mu M/p$—where μ is the liquidity parameter. It is then obvious by inspection that a change in μ causes the equilibrium price level in (8.1)–(8.2) to change in the same proportion and leaves the equilibrium rate of interest unaffected.

Let us now drop the assumption of neutrality and rewrite (8.1)–(8.2) as

$$(8.20) \qquad F\left(Y_0,\ r,\ \frac{\alpha M}{p}\right) - Y_0 = 0,$$

$$(8.21) \qquad B\left(Y_0,\ \frac{1}{r},\ \frac{\beta M}{p}\right) = 0,$$

where α and β are liquidity parameters. Clearly, an increase in liquidity preference need no longer affect the commodity and bond markets with the same intensity. That is, if we conduct an individual-experiment in which we increase liquidity preference, the price decline that will be found necessary to offset this increase in the commodity market need not be the same as that needed in the bond market. Indeed, we can think of an extreme case in which the increase in liquidity preference takes place only at the expense of commodities, so that no price decrease whatsoever is needed to restore demand in the bond market. Such a case is represented in the left-hand sides of (8.20)–(8.21) by a decrease in α, with β remaining constant. At the other extreme we have the case of an increase in liquidity preference solely at the expense of bonds. This is represented by a decrease in β, with α remaining constant.[9]

From these individual-experiments we can proceed to the corresponding market-experiments. In particular, consider the effect of an increase in liquidity preference on the equilibrium price level and rate of interest when this increase is solely at the expense of commodities. Holding β constant and differentiating (8.20)–(8.21) with respect to α, we obtain[10]

---

[8] Attached to Chapter X:4.

[9] It should be clear that this distinction between α and β has nothing at all to do with the distinction between β^a and γ^a in Mathematical Appendix 7:b above. The latter refers to the insertion of two separate liquidity parameters into a *single* demand function.

[10] I must confess that I am not using here the more cumbersome notation advocated at such length in Mathematical Appendix 1:a. In terms of that discussion, we are assuming here that

$$(8.22) \qquad F_2 \frac{\partial r}{\partial \alpha} - \frac{\alpha F_3 M}{p^2} \frac{\partial p}{\partial \alpha} = -\frac{F_3 M}{p},$$

$$(8.23) \qquad -\frac{B_2}{r^2} \frac{\partial r}{\partial \alpha} - \frac{\beta B_3 M}{p^2} \frac{\partial p}{\partial \alpha} = 0.$$

Let

$$(8.24) \quad |D| = \begin{vmatrix} F_2 & -\dfrac{\alpha F_3 M}{p^2} \\[2ex] -\dfrac{B_2}{r^2} & -\dfrac{\beta B_3 M}{p^2} \end{vmatrix} = -\frac{\beta F_2 B_3 M}{p^2} - \frac{\alpha F_3 B_2 M}{p^2 r^2}.$$

By assumptions as to the signs of the partial derivatives, this must be positive. We now consider (8.22)–(8.23) as constituting a system of two equations in the two variables, $\dfrac{\partial r}{\partial \alpha}$ and $\dfrac{\partial p}{\partial \alpha}$, and solve it out by the use of determinants to yield

$$(8.25) \qquad \frac{\partial r}{\partial \alpha} = \frac{\begin{vmatrix} -\dfrac{F_3 M}{p} & -\dfrac{\alpha F_3 M}{p^2} \\[2ex] 0 & -\dfrac{\beta B_3 M}{p^2} \end{vmatrix}}{|D|} = \frac{\beta F_3 B_3 M^2}{p^3 |D|} > 0$$

and

$$(8.26) \qquad \frac{\partial p}{\partial \alpha} = \frac{\begin{vmatrix} F_2 & -\dfrac{F_3 M}{p} \\[2ex] -\dfrac{B_2}{r^2} & 0 \end{vmatrix}}{|D|} = \frac{-F_3 B_2 M}{r^2 p |D|} > 0.$$

---

system (8.20)–(8.21) can be solved out for the dependent variables, r and p, as (market-equilibrium) functions of the independent ones, α and β, to yield, say,

$$r = \phi(\alpha, \beta),$$
$$p = \psi(\alpha, \beta).$$

The symbols $\dfrac{\partial r}{\partial \alpha}$ and $\dfrac{\partial p}{\partial \alpha}$ then represent the respective partial derivatives of these functions with respect to α. In terms of our advocated notation, they are $\phi_1(\alpha, \beta)$ and $\psi_1(\alpha, \beta)$, respectively. Similarly, in (8.27)–(8.28) below, the symbols $\dfrac{\partial r}{\partial \beta}$ and $\dfrac{\partial p}{\partial \beta}$ represent, respectively, $\phi_2(\alpha, \beta)$ and $\psi_2(\alpha, \beta)$. For further details—and for an explanation of the whole procedure used in (8.22)–(8.28)—see the discussion of implicit differentiation in Mathematical Appendix 1:c.

The foregoing observations should also be applied, *mutatis mutandis*, to all subsequent cases in which we solve out a system of equations for the derivatives of its dependent variables with respect to its independent ones.

347

In a similar way, if only β were to change while α remained constant, we would obtain

(8.27) $$\frac{\partial r}{\partial \beta} = \frac{-\alpha F_3 B_3 M^2}{p^3 |D|} < 0,$$

(8.28) $$\frac{\partial p}{\partial \beta} = \frac{-F_2 B_3 M}{p |D|} > 0.$$

d.[11] These shifts in liquidity preference can be analyzed equivalently in terms of the commodity and money markets. Our equations are then

(8.29) $$F\left(Y_0, r, \frac{M}{p}, \lambda\right) - Y_0 = 0,$$

(8.30) $$L\left(Y_0, r, \frac{M}{p}, \lambda\right) - \frac{M}{p} = 0,$$

where λ is the liquidity parameter. By assumption, $F_4 > 0$ and $L_4 < 0$. That is, a decrease in λ—already identified with an increase in liquidity preference—causes an increase in the amount of money demanded, and a decrease in the amount of commodities demanded.

Differentiating the foregoing system with respect to λ, we obtain

(8.31) $$F_2 \frac{dr}{d\lambda} - \frac{MF_3}{p^2} \frac{dp}{d\lambda} = -F_4,$$

(8.32) $$L_2 \frac{dr}{d\lambda} + \frac{M(1 - L_3)}{p^2} \frac{dp}{d\lambda} = -L_4.$$

Solving out, we obtain

(8.33) $$\frac{dr}{d\lambda} = \frac{\begin{vmatrix} -F_4 & \dfrac{-MF_3}{p^2} \\ -L_4 & \dfrac{M(1 - L_3)}{p^2} \end{vmatrix}}{\Delta} = \frac{-MF_4(1 - L_3) - MF_3 L_4}{p^2 \Delta}$$

and

(8.34) $$\frac{dp}{d\lambda} = \frac{\begin{vmatrix} F_2 & -F_4 \\ L_2 & -L_4 \end{vmatrix}}{\Delta} = \frac{-F_2 L_4 + F_4 L_2}{\Delta},$$

---

[11] Attached to Chapter XI:2.

For an explanation of the procedure used here—and, in particular, for the meaning of the derivatives $\dfrac{dr}{d\lambda}$ and $\dfrac{dp}{d\lambda}$ in (8.31)–(8.34)—see the preceding footnote.

where

$$(8.35) \quad \Delta = \begin{vmatrix} F_2 & \dfrac{-MF_3}{p^2} \\[2ex] L_2 & \dfrac{M(1-L_3)}{p^2} \end{vmatrix} = \frac{MF_2(1-L_3) + ML_2F_3}{p^2}.$$

By our assumptions as to the signs of the partial derivatives, Δ is negative, $\dfrac{dp}{d\lambda}$ is positive, and $\dfrac{dr}{d\lambda}$ is of indeterminate sign.

Let us now assume that the shift in liquidity preference is entirely at the expense of bonds. Then $F_4 = 0$. Hence $\dfrac{dr}{d\lambda}$ is negative—which agrees with (8.27).

Assume next that the shift is entirely at the expense of commodities. We first make use of this assumption and (8.29)–(8.30) to rewrite (8.18) as

$$(8.36) \quad \begin{aligned} & L\left(Y_0, r, \frac{M}{p}, \lambda\right) - \frac{M}{p} \\[1ex] & \equiv -\left[F\left(Y_0, r, \frac{M}{p}, \lambda\right) - Y_0\right] - B\left(Y_0, \frac{1}{r}, \frac{M}{p}\right). \end{aligned}$$

Differentiating both sides of this identity partially with respect to λ, we obtain

$$(8.37) \quad L_4 = -F_4.$$

That is, by the budget restraint, any increase in the demand for real money holdings must be exactly matched by a decrease in the demand for commodities. Substituting in (8.33), we then obtain

$$(8.38) \quad \frac{dr}{d\lambda} = \frac{-MF_4(1 - L_3 - F_3)}{p^2\Delta}.$$

By assumption, the marginal propensities to spend out of real balances on commodities, bonds, and money holdings, respectively, are all positive, and their sum is equal to unity. It follows that

$$(8.39) \quad 0 < F_3 + L_3 < 1$$

Substituting in (8.38), we see that $\dfrac{dr}{d\lambda}$ is positive—which agrees with (8.25).

Consider finally the case in which the shift in liquidity preference is neutral as between commodities and bonds. Then, by Mathematical

Appendix 7:*b*, the excess-demand functions for both commodities and *real* money holdings are not affected by equi-proportionate changes in λ and p. That is, the left-hand sides of (8.29)–(8.30) are both homogeneous of degree zero in these variables. Applying Euler's theorem on homogeneous functions to these left-hand sides, respectively, we then obtain

$$(8.40) \qquad \frac{-MF_3}{p} + \lambda F_4 = 0,$$

$$(8.41) \qquad \frac{M(1 - L_3)}{p} + \lambda L_4 = 0.$$

Substituting in (8.33), we see that under these conditions $\frac{dr}{d\lambda} = 0$.

e.[12] Consider the system

$$(8.42) \qquad F\left(Y_0, r, \frac{M}{p}, \alpha\right) - Y_0 = 0,$$

$$(8.43) \qquad B\left(Y_0, \frac{1}{r}, \frac{M}{p}, \alpha\right) = 0,$$

where α is an as yet unspecified parameter. Differentiating this system with respect to α and solving out by use of determinants, we obtain

$$(8.44) \qquad \frac{dr}{d\alpha} = \frac{M(F_4 B_3 - F_3 B_4)}{p^2 \Delta}$$

and

$$(8.45) \qquad \frac{dp}{d\alpha} = -\frac{B_4 F_2 + \frac{B_2 F_4}{r^2}}{\Delta},$$

where

$$(8.46) \qquad \Delta = -\frac{M}{p^2}\left(F_2 B_3 + \frac{F_3 B_2}{r^2}\right) > 0.$$

Let α represent the marginal productivity of capital. Then an increase in productivity stimulates investment activity; hence $F_4 > 0$. Now, if firms plan to finance this increased activity entirely by increasing their supply of bonds, then $B_4 = -F_4 < 0$. If, instead, the financing comes entirely out of their cash balances, then $B_4 = 0$. In both of

---

12 Attached to Chapter XI:5–6.

these cases (though in the former more so) $\dfrac{dr}{d\alpha}$ is positive. In the latter, $\dfrac{dp}{d\alpha}$ is also positive. But in the former its sign can be positive, negative, or zero, depending on the relative magnitudes of the partial derivatives.

Alternatively, let α be an index of the "tastes" for saving. Specifically, an increase in α represents an increased desire to save. Hence $F_4 < 0$. If all of these savings are directed to the bond market, then $B_4 = -F_4 > 0$; if to cash balances, then $B_4 = 0$. In both of these cases (though in the former more so) $\dfrac{dr}{d\alpha}$ is negative. In the latter, $\dfrac{dp}{d\alpha}$ is also negative. But in the former its sign can be positive, negative, or zero, depending on the relative magnitudes of the partial derivatives. Thus the argument of this paragraph is the exact obverse of that of the preceding one.

9. Appendix to Chapter XII

a.[1] The equilibrium condition in the labor market when there is money illusion on the supply side is represented by

$$(9.1) \qquad Q\left(\frac{w}{p}, K_0\right) - T(w) = 0.$$

In contrast with our preceding models, a change in the quantity of money now changes the real wage rate. Hence we can no longer conduct the analysis of such a change under the assumption that the levels of employment and real income are fixed at N_0 and Y_0, respectively. In particular, we must now write the equilibrium condition for the commodity market in the complete form implied by Chapter IX:2–3:

$$(9.2) \qquad F\left\{\phi\left[Q\left(\frac{w}{p}, K_0\right)\right], r, \frac{M}{p}\right\} - \phi\left[Q\left(\frac{w}{p}, K_0\right)\right] = 0,$$

where $\phi[\ \ ]$ is the production function. Similarly, the bond equation becomes

$$(9.3) \qquad B\left\{\phi\left[Q\left(\frac{w}{p}, K_0\right)\right], \frac{1}{r}, \frac{M}{p}\right\} = 0.$$

By assumption, $Q_1 < 0$, $T' > 0$, $1 > F_1 > 0$, $F_2 < 0$, $F_3 > 0$, $\phi' > 0$, $B_1 = 0$, $B_2 < 0$, $B_3 > 0$. Differentiating (9.1)–(9.3) with respect to M, we then obtain

$$(9.4) \qquad \frac{dr}{dM} = -B_3 \cdot \frac{w}{p^3} T'\phi'Q_1(F_1 - 1) \cdot \frac{1}{|A|}$$

and

$$(9.5) \qquad \frac{dp}{dM} = \left(\frac{Q_1}{p} - T'\right)\left(\frac{F_3}{p}\frac{B_2}{r^2} + \frac{F_2 B_3}{p}\right) \cdot \frac{1}{|A|},$$

---

[1] Attached to Chapter XII:2.

Once again, the reader is referred to p. 346, footnote 10, for an explanation of the technique of differentiation used here.

where

(9.6)
$$|A| = \left(\frac{Q_1}{p} - T'\right)\left(\frac{F_3 M B_2}{p^2 r^2} + \frac{F_2 M B_3}{p^2}\right)$$
$$- \frac{\phi' Q_1(F_1 - 1)}{p} \cdot \frac{w}{p} T' \frac{B_2}{r^2}.$$

By our assumptions as to the signs of the partial derivatives, $|A| > 0$. Hence $\frac{dr}{dM} < 0$ and $\frac{dp}{dM} > 0$. It can also be readily shown that the derivative $\frac{dw}{dM}$ must have the same sign as $\frac{dp}{dM}$. Substituting from (9.6) into (9.5), we can also see that $\frac{M}{p} \frac{dp}{dM} < 1$. All these results clearly depend on the assumption that changes in real national product have a neutral effect on the bond market; that is, $B_1 = 0$.

b. The immediately following sections make repeated use of Samuelson's "correspondence principle."[2] The application of this principle will be simplified by first developing the following proposition:[3]

Assume that the dynamic movements of a model are described by the system of differential equations

(9.7)
$$\frac{dp_i}{dt} = \sum_{j=1}^{n} K_{ij} X_i(p_1, \ldots, p_n) \qquad (i = 1, \ldots, n),$$

where the $X_i(\ )$ are the excess-demand functions and the K_{ij} are constants. Define the matrices

(9.8)
$$K = \begin{pmatrix} K_{11} & K_{12} & \cdots & K_{1n} \\ K_{21} & K_{22} & \cdots & K_{2n} \\ \cdots\cdots\cdots\cdots\cdots \\ K_{n1} & K_{n2} & \cdots & K_{nn} \end{pmatrix}$$

and

(9.9)
$$A = \begin{pmatrix} a_{11} & a_{12} & \cdots & a_{1n} \\ a_{21} & a_{22} & \cdots & a_{2n} \\ \cdots\cdots\cdots\cdots\cdots \\ a_{n1} & a_{n2} & \cdots & a_{nn} \end{pmatrix},$$

---

[2] *Foundations*, Chapter IX.

[3] Due to A. S. Amitsur. See the reference in my "Limitations of Samuelson's 'Correspondence Principle,'" *Metroeconomica*, IV (1952), 39, footnote 3.

where a_{ij} is the partial derivative of $X_i(\ \ )$ with respect to p_j, evaluated at the point of equilibrium. Then system (9.7) is stable if the characteristic equation

$$(9.10) \qquad\qquad |KA - zI| = 0$$

(where I is the identity matrix) yields roots for z whose real parts are all negative.[4]

Denote these roots by z_i. Then it follows from the properties of characteristic equations that

$$(9.11) \qquad\qquad \prod_{i=1}^{n} z_i = |KA|.$$

Assume that m of these roots are complex. These must occur in pairs of the type $x + iy$ and $x - iy$. Hence m must be even. Furthermore, the product of these m roots must be positive. Thus the sign of $|KA|$ must be the same as the sign of the product of the $n - m$ real roots. If the system is stable, this product—and hence $|KA| = |K|\,|A|$—must therefore be positive for an even n, and negative for an odd one.

System (8.4)–(8.5) above provides an example of this proposition. It has been shown that if $K_2 = K_3 = 0$, this system must be stable. Under this assumption $|K|$ is a diagonal determinant equal to the negative quantity $-K_1 K_4$. It follows from the preceding paragraph that $|A| = ad - bc$ must then be negative. From (8.8) we see that this is indeed so.

c.[5] Let us now make use of the foregoing proposition to determine the properties of a system which provides for the influence of distribution effects. Let

$$(9.12) \qquad\qquad h = h(p)$$

be an index of the distribution effect which results from a price change. By the assumptions of the text we have

$$(9.13) \qquad\qquad B\left[Y_0, \frac{1}{r}, \frac{M}{p}, h(p)\right] = 0,$$

$$(9.14) \qquad\qquad F\left[Y_0, r, \frac{M}{p}, h(p)\right] - Y_0 = 0,$$

---

[4] Cf. Samuelson, *Foundations*, pp. 274–75. The discussion in Mathematical Appendix 3:b above deals with the special case in which K is a diagonal matrix.

[5] Attached to Chapter XII:3.

where $h'(\ \ ) > 0$, $B_4 > 0$, and $F_4 < 0$. Differentiating with respect to M, we obtain

(9.15) $\qquad -\dfrac{B_2}{r^2}\dfrac{dr}{dM} + \left(-\dfrac{MB_3}{p^2} + B_4 h'\right)\dfrac{dp}{dM} = -\dfrac{B_3}{p},$

(9.16) $\qquad F_2\dfrac{dr}{dM} + \left(-\dfrac{MF_3}{p^2} + F_4 h'\right)\dfrac{dp}{dM} = -\dfrac{F_3}{p}.$

Let

(9.17) $\qquad |T| = \begin{vmatrix} -\dfrac{B_2}{r^2} & -\dfrac{MB_3}{p^2} + B_4 h' \\[2ex] F_2 & -\dfrac{MF_3}{p^2} + F_4 h' \end{vmatrix}.$

Solving out (9.15)–(9.16), we then obtain

(9.18) $\qquad \dfrac{dr}{dM} = \dfrac{-B_3 F_4 h' + F_3 B_4 h'}{p|T|}$

and

(9.19) $\qquad \dfrac{dp}{dM} = \dfrac{\dfrac{B_2 F_3}{r^2} + B_3 F_2}{p|T|}.$

Knowledge of the signs of the partial derivatives of $B[\ \ ]$ and $F[\ \ ]$ alone does not suffice to determine the sign of $|T|$. Hence, in the absence of any additional information, the signs of our comparative-statics derivatives $\dfrac{dr}{dM}$ and $\dfrac{dp}{dM}$ are also indeterminate.

Let us now form the dynamic counterpart of (9.13)–(9.14):

(9.20) $\qquad \dfrac{dr}{dt} = -K_5 B[\ \ ] - K_6\{F[\ \ ] - Y_0\},$

(9.21) $\qquad \dfrac{dp}{dt} = K_7 B[\ \ ] + K_8\{F[\ \ ] - Y_0\},$

where the K_j are all positive. Assume this system to be stable. The determinant $|K|$ of the preceding section is then equal to $-K_5 K_8 + K_6 K_7$. This can be positive, negative, or zero. Hence the sign of $|T|$—which corresponds to the $|A|$ of the preceding section—remains indeterminate even after we add the condition that the system must be stable. That is, dynamic analysis does not provide the necessary additional information about comparative-statics analysis: the "correspondence principle" does not work. If, however, we simplify our dynamic analysis and assume that excess demand in a given market affects only the price of that market, then $K_6 = K_7 = 0$, $|K| = -K_5 K_8$ is negative, and therefore (since there is an even number of equations) $|T|$ must also be negative. Thus under these assumptions the stability of the system implies that $\dfrac{dr}{dM}$ must be negative and $\dfrac{dp}{dM}$ positive

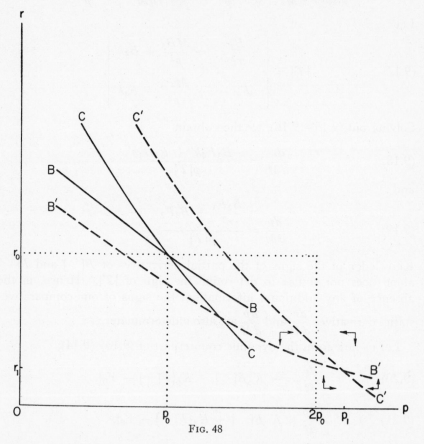

Fig. 48

The graphical analysis of this case in Figure 33 of the text presents *BB* as being negatively sloped. Under our present assumptions, however, this is not necessarily true. In particular, a price increase now generates two opposing forces: on the one hand, it decreases the demand for bonds through the real-balance effect; on the other, it increases demand through the distribution effect. If, then, the latter force is sufficiently strong, the slope of *BB* might become negative.

356

There are now two possibilities: BB might cut CC either from above or from below. Consider first the latter possibility. As shown in Figure 48, the curves intersect initially at the point (p_0, r_0). Let the quantity of money now double. Then, as explained in the text, CC shifts to the right. But, in contrast with the text, BB now shifts to the left: the increase in the quantity of money has created an excess demand in the bond market, and, at any given rate of interest, this excess—under our

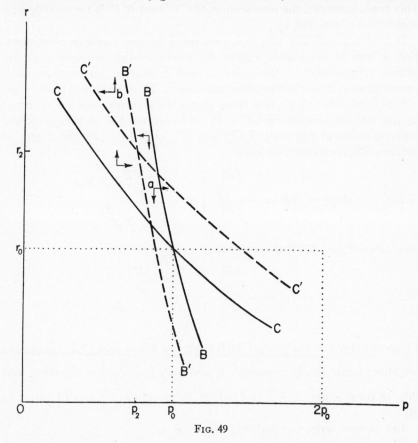

FIG. 49

present assumptions—can be removed only by a price decrease. The intersection of $C'C'$ and $B'B'$ then determines the new equilibrium position (p_1, r_1). By construction, r_1 must be less than r_0.

It can readily be seen that in this case the negative slope of $B'B'$ does not interfere with the stability of the system. It is still true that at any point to the right of $C'C'$ there exists a state of excess supply of commodities driving prices down, while at any point above $B'B'$ there is an

excess demand for bonds driving interest down. The arrows attached
to the four representative points surrounding (p_1, r_1) in Figure 48 show
the operation of these market forces. At each of these points, at least
one of the variables is moving in the direction of equilibrium.

Consider now the case in which BB cuts CC from above. This
situation is represented in Figure 49. Once again the increase in the
quantity of money causes CC to shift to the right and BB to the left.
This time, however, the intersection of $C'C'$ and $B'B'$ is necessarily at a
higher rate of interest, r_2.

It is this possibility which is precluded by our stability conditions.
For, as can be seen from Figure 49, whenever the economy is in the
sectors represented by the points a and b, market forces press both
variables away from their equilibrium values. Thus the system is unstable.

It is instructive to see how these geometrical restrictions are reflected
in the stability condition $|T| < 0$. The curve BB is the graphical
representation of equation (9.13); and CC, of (9.14). By the theory of
implicit differentiation, we have

$$(9.22) \qquad \text{slope of } BB = -\frac{\dfrac{\partial B[\ ]}{\partial p}}{\dfrac{\partial B[\ ]}{\partial r}} = -\frac{-\dfrac{MB_3}{p^2} + B_4 h'}{\dfrac{-B_2}{r^2}}$$

and, since Y_0 in (9.14) is a constant,

$$(9.23) \qquad \text{slope of } CC = -\frac{\dfrac{\partial F[\ ]}{\partial p}}{\dfrac{\partial F[\ ]}{\partial r}} = -\frac{-\dfrac{MF_3}{p^2} + F_4 h'}{F_2}.$$

From the signs of the partial derivatives we know that (9.23) is always
negative; while (9.22) is positive if and only if $\dfrac{\partial B[\ ]}{\partial p}$ is negative, and
this, in turn, is negative if and only if B_4 is sufficiently small relative to
B_3.

Let us now write our stability condition as

$$(9.24) \qquad |T| = \begin{vmatrix} \dfrac{\partial B[\ ]}{\partial r} & \dfrac{\partial B[\ ]}{\partial p} \\ \dfrac{\partial F[\ ]}{\partial r} & \dfrac{\partial F[\ ]}{\partial p} \end{vmatrix}$$

$$= \frac{\partial B[\ ]}{\partial r} \cdot \frac{\partial F[\ ]}{\partial p} - \frac{\partial B[\ ]}{\partial p} \cdot \frac{\partial F[\ ]}{\partial r} < 0,$$

where the partial derivatives are evaluated at the point of equilibrium.
Transposing and dividing through, we then obtain

$$
(9.25) \qquad -\frac{\dfrac{\partial F[\ ]}{\partial p}}{\dfrac{\partial F[\ ]}{\partial r}} < -\frac{\dfrac{\partial B[\ ]}{\partial p}}{\dfrac{\partial B[\ ]}{\partial r}}.
$$

That is, under our simple dynamic assumptions, stability implies that
at the point of equilibrium the slope of CC is less than that of BB.
When the latter slope is positive, this is always satisfied; when negative,
it is satisfied if and only if it cuts CC from below.

It should be emphasized again that these results flow from the oversimplified dynamic assumption that excess demand in one market
affects only the price of that market. In the absence of this assumption,
stability of the system will not necessarily imply that an increase in the
quantity of money reduces interest.

d.[6] These results can be obtained alternatively from the commodity
and money markets. In particular, replace (9.13) by

$$
(9.26) \qquad pL\left[Y_0, r, \frac{M}{p}, h(p)\right] - M = 0,
$$

where $L_2 < 0, 1 > L_3 > 0$, and, by assumption, $L_4 > 0$. Then instead
of (9.15) we have

$$
(9.27) \qquad L_2\frac{dr}{dM} + \left[\frac{M}{p^2}(1 - L_3) + L_4h'\right]\frac{dp}{dM} = -\frac{L_3}{p} + \frac{1}{p}.
$$

Let

$$
(9.28) \qquad |R| = \begin{vmatrix} L_2 & \dfrac{M}{p^2}(1 - L_3) + L_4h' \\ F_2 & -\dfrac{M}{p^2}F_3 + F_4h' \end{vmatrix} > 0.
$$

Solving out (9.16) and (9.27), we obtain

$$
(9.29) \qquad \frac{dr}{dM} = \frac{h'}{p|R|}[(1 - L_3)F_4 + F_3L_4],
$$

$$
(9.30) \qquad \frac{dp}{dM} = -\frac{1}{p|R|}[L_2F_3 + (1 - L_3)F_2].
$$

---

[6] Attached to Chapter XII:3.

Hence $\dfrac{dp}{dM}$ must be positive.   Consider now the sign of $\dfrac{dr}{dM}$.   Assume that

(9.31) $(1 - L_3)F_4 + F_3 L_4 \geqq 0.$

Dividing through both sides of this inequality by $(1 - L_3)L_4$, we obtain

(9.32) $\dfrac{F_4}{L_4} + \dfrac{F_3}{1 - L_3} \geqq 0.$

Now, by assumption, the decreased demand for commodities caused by the distribution effect is used partly to supplement cash balances and partly to increase the demand for bonds.   That is,

(9.33) $- F_4 = L_4 + B_4,$

where $B_4 \geqq 0$.   From this it follows that

(9.34) $- \dfrac{F_4}{L_4} \geqq 1.$

The equality sign holds if the "forced savings" are used exclusively to increase money balances.   Transposing (9.32) and substituting, we then obtain

(9.35) $\dfrac{F_3}{1 - L_3} \geqq - \dfrac{F_4}{L_4} \geqq 1$

or

(9.36) $F_3 + L_3 \geqq 1.$

But this contradicts our assumption that part of any increase in cash balances is also used to increase the demand for bonds.   Hence the assumption that (9.31) is greater than zero leads to a contradiction. Hence $\dfrac{dr}{dM}$ must be negative or zero.   More specifically, if the equality sign holds in both (9.34) and (9.36), then $\dfrac{dr}{dM}$ as computed from (9.29) is zero.   Note, though, that under these assumptions, $B_3 = B_4 = 0$, so that $\dfrac{dr}{dM}$ as computed from (9.18) is also zero.[7]

---

[7] The analysis of this section is actually more restricted than that of the preceding one.   In particular, our assumption here that $0 < L_3 < 1$ implies that $\dfrac{\partial \left[L(\ ) - \dfrac{M}{p} \right]}{\partial p}$ is always positive

e.[8] Let us now examine the influence of government debt and open-market operations. Rewrite equations (7) and (4) of the text as

(9.37)
$$B\left(Y_0, \frac{1}{r}, \frac{V}{rp}, \frac{M}{p}\right) - \frac{V}{rp} = 0,$$

(9.38)
$$F\left(Y_0, r, \frac{V}{rp}, \frac{M}{p}\right) - Y_0 = 0.$$

For convenience, the bars over the functional symbols have been dropped; it must, however, be remembered that the foregoing functions are different from those of the preceding section. By assumption, $0 < F_3 < 1$ and $0 < B_3 < 1$. It is also assumed that in equilibrium $F_3 < F_4$ and $B_3 < B_4$; this represents the greater liquidity of money holdings as compared with bond holdings.

Consider first the case in which the amount of money is increased in order to finance additional budgetary expenditures. Differentiating (9.37)–(9.38) with respect to M, holding V constant, we obtain

(9.39)
$$\left[-\frac{B_2}{r^2} + \frac{(1 - B_3)V}{r^2 p}\right]\frac{dr}{dM}$$
$$+ \left[\frac{V}{rp^2}(1 - B_3) - \frac{B_4 M}{p^2}\right]\frac{dp}{dM} = -\frac{B_4}{p},$$

(9.40)
$$\left(F_2 - \frac{F_3 V}{r^2 p}\right)\frac{dr}{dM}$$
$$+ \left(-\frac{F_3 V}{rp^2} - \frac{F_4 M}{p^2}\right)\frac{dp}{dM} = -\frac{F_4}{p}.$$

Let

(9.41)
$$|W| = \begin{vmatrix} -\dfrac{B_2}{r^2} + \dfrac{(1 - B_3)V}{r^2 p} & \dfrac{V}{rp^2}(1 - B_3) - \dfrac{B_4 M}{p^2} \\[2ex] F_2 - \dfrac{F_3 V}{r^2 p} & -\dfrac{F_3 V}{rp^2} - \dfrac{F_4 M}{p^2} \end{vmatrix}.$$

—as is shown by the element in the first row, second column, of $|R|$ in (9.28); whereas the assumption of the preceding section that $\dfrac{\partial B[\ ]}{\partial p}$ might be positive implies—by the budget restraint (8.18), with the functions suitably modified—that L_3 might become greater than unity, so that $\dfrac{\partial\left[L(\ ) - \dfrac{M}{p}\right]}{\partial p}$ might become negative. This is the reason we can determine the sign of $|R|$ here without resort to the "correspondence principle." Cf. also the discussion of the excess-demand curve for real money holdings on p. 297.

[8] Attached to Chapter XII:5.

We can then write our solutions of (9.39)–(9.40) as

(9.42)
$$\frac{dr}{dM} = \frac{V[B_4 F_3 + (1 - B_3)F_4]}{rp^3|W|}$$

and

(9.43)
$$\frac{dp}{dM} = \frac{F_4\left[\dfrac{B_2}{r^2} - \dfrac{(1 - B_3)V}{r^2 p}\right] + B_4\left[F_2 - \dfrac{F_3 V}{r^2 p}\right]}{p|W|}.$$

Using the same method as in Section *b* above, we can then show that under the simple dynamic hypothesis that an excess demand in a given market affects only the price of that market, stability of the system implies that $|W|$ is negative.   Hence $\dfrac{dr}{dM}$ is negative and $\dfrac{dp}{dM}$ positive.

Once again, these results can be interpreted graphically.   In the commodity market the real-balance and real-indebtedness effects always reinforce each other; hence CC retains its negative slope.   There is no such harmony of forces in the bond market.   An increase in price decreases the demand for real bond holdings through the real-indebtedness and real-balance effects, but at the same time decreases the supply of real bond holdings.   Only if the first effect is stronger than the second will the excess demand for bonds be negatively sloped with respect to the price level.   This indeterminacy corresponds to the indeterminacy in the sign of the coefficient of $\dfrac{dp}{dM}$ in (9.39)—which, of course, equals

$\dfrac{\partial\left[B(\ ) - \dfrac{V}{rp}\right]}{\partial p}$.   On the other hand, $\dfrac{\partial\left[B(\ ) - \dfrac{V}{rp}\right]}{\partial r}$—equal to the

coefficient of $\dfrac{dr}{dM}$ in (9.39)—must always be positive.

Thus a negative slope for BB can eventuate under exactly the same circumstances discussed above in connection with equations (9.22)–(9.23).   Correspondingly, the graphical analysis of Figures 47 and 48 above can be applied directly to the present case too.

For the sake of completeness we might note the case—excluded by our present assumptions—in which $\dfrac{\partial\left[B(\ ) - \dfrac{V}{rp}\right]}{\partial r}$ might be negative.

Then the slope of BB can be negative either because both the numerator and denominator of (9.22) are positive—the only possibility which existed until now—or because both are negative.   In the latter case stability can obtain only when BB cuts CC from above.   Furthermore, an increase in the quantity of money shifts BB to the right; for the excess demand it generates is now eliminated by an increase in interest. There can also be the case in which the numerator of (9.22) is positive, while the denominator is negative, so that BB once again has a positive slope.   Here an increase in the quantity of money shifts BB to the left and CC to the right, thus increasing interest.   But this case is excluded by our stability condition.   The reader can establish this by graphical analysis.   Alternatively, he can readily see that if in (9.41) the elements in the first row of $|W|$ are negative and positive, respectively, then $|W|$ must be positive, violating our stability condition.

One further case which violates our stability condition is that in which any increase in the quantity of money is used entirely to increase money balances. That is, $B_4 = F_4 = 0$. By assumption, this implies $B_3 = F_3 = 0$.   Substituting into (9.41), we see that $|W|$ reduces to the positive quantity, $-F_2V/rp^2$.

Let us now return to (9.37)–(9.38) and consider the case in which the change in M is the result of open-market operations.   Here, by assumption, V is no longer constant.   Specifically, letting dM represent the change in the quantity of money and dV the corresponding change in the number of bonds outstanding, we must have

$$(9.44) \qquad\qquad dM = -\frac{1}{r}dV$$

That is, the increase in the quantity of money in circulation is equal to the amount expended on the purchase of bonds.

Differentiating (9.37)–(9.38) with respect to M again, but this time letting V vary in accordance with (9.44), we obtain a system of equations which is the same as (9.39)–(9.40), except that the right-hand sides of these equations are replaced by $-\dfrac{B_4}{p} - \dfrac{1 - B_3}{p}$ and $-\dfrac{F_4}{p} + \dfrac{F_3}{p}$, respectively.   Solving out, we obtain

$$(9.45) \qquad \frac{dr}{dM} = \frac{\left(\dfrac{V}{r} + M\right)[B_4F_3 + (1 - B_3)F_4]}{p^3|W|} < 0,$$

$$(9.46) \qquad \frac{dp}{dM} = \frac{(F_4 - F_3)\left[\dfrac{B_2}{r^2} - \dfrac{(1 - B_3)V}{r^2p}\right]}{p|W|}$$

$$+ \frac{[B_4 + (1 - B_3)]\left[F_2 - \dfrac{F_3V}{r^2p}\right]}{p|W|} > 0,$$

where once again the negative sign of $|W|$ is implied by the assumption of stability. Note that (9.45) is greater in absolute value than (9.42). Note also that the sign of (9.46) depends on the assumption $F_4 > F_3$. This insures that, in the commodity market, the stimulating effect of the increase in the amount of money holdings more than offsets the discouraging effect of the corresponding decrease in the amount of bond holdings. Graphically, this implies that CC cannot shift to the left and so cannot intersect the new BB at a lower price level.

f.[9] Consider finally the case of a constant-purchasing-power bond. Equations (9.37)–(9.38) are then replaced by

$$(9.47) \qquad B\left(Y_0, \frac{1}{r}, \frac{V}{r}, \frac{M}{p}\right) - \frac{V}{r} = 0,$$

$$(9.48) \qquad F\left(Y_0, r, \frac{V}{r}, \frac{M}{p}\right) - Y_0 = 0.$$

An increase in the quantity of money injected into the system through increased government budgetary expenditures clearly causes a proportionate increase in prices and leaves the rate of interest invariant. Consider now an increase injected through open-market operations. Here we must replace (9.44) by

$$(9.49) \qquad dM = -\frac{p}{r}dV.$$

That is, the amount of money injected into the system by the purchase of a given number of bonds depends on the general price level as well as on the price of bonds. Differentiating (9.47)–(9.48) with respect to M, making use of (9.49), we obtain

$$(9.50) \qquad \left[-\frac{B_2}{r^2} + \frac{V(1-B_3)}{r^2}\right]\frac{dr}{dM} - \frac{B_4 M}{p^2}\frac{dp}{dM}$$
$$= -\frac{B_4}{p} - \frac{(1-B_3)}{p},$$

$$(9.51) \qquad \left(F_2 - \frac{VF_3}{r^2}\right)\frac{dr}{dM} - \frac{F_4 M}{p^2}\frac{dp}{dM}$$
$$= -\frac{F_4}{p} + \frac{F_3}{p}.$$

---

[9] Attached to Chapter XII:5.

Let

$$(9.52) \qquad |X| = \begin{vmatrix} -\dfrac{B_2}{r^2} + \dfrac{V(1-B_3)}{r^2} & -\dfrac{B_4 M}{p^2} \\[2em] F_2 - \dfrac{VF_3}{r^2} & -\dfrac{F_4 M}{p^2} \end{vmatrix} < 0.$$

Solving out, we obtain

$$(9.53) \qquad \frac{dr}{dM} = \frac{M[B_4 F_3 + (1-B_3)F_4]}{p^3 |X|} < 0,$$

$$(9.54) \qquad \begin{aligned} \frac{dp}{dM} &= \frac{(F_4 - F_3)\left[\dfrac{B_2}{r^2} - \dfrac{(1-B_3)V}{r^2}\right]}{p|X|} \\[1.5em] &+ \frac{[B_4 + (1-B_3)]\left[F_2 - \dfrac{F_3 V}{r^2 p}\right]}{p|X|} > 0. \end{aligned}$$

Here we have again used the assumption $F_4 > F_3$.

It should finally be emphasized that we have not been able to determine the signs of our comparative-statics derivatives in Sections *c* and *e* above except by using the information implied by the assumption that the system is stable under highly oversimplified dynamic conditions. Correspondingly, as soon as we consider more complicated—and, presumably, more realistic—conditions, the comparative-statics conclusions of the aforementioned sections need no longer hold. Thus our repeated use of the "correspondence principle" should not blind the reader to the fact that it is really an analytical tool of much narrower applicability than its name would lead us to believe.[10]

---

[10] Cf. the article cited in Section *b* above.

10. Appendix to Chapters XIII and XIV

a.[1] Let our system be represented by

(10.1)
$$F\left(Y, r, \frac{V}{rp}, \frac{M}{p}\right) - Y = 0,$$

(10.2)
$$B\left(Y, \frac{1}{r}, \frac{V}{rp}, \frac{M}{p}\right) - \frac{V}{rp} = 0,$$

where p is now constant and Y variable. By assumption, $0 < F_1 < 1$ and $B_1 = 0$. Let this system operate according to the dynamic principles

(10.3)
$$\frac{dY}{dt} = K_1[F(\ ) - Y],$$

(10.4)
$$\frac{dr}{dt} = -K_2\left[B(\ ) - \frac{V}{rp}\right],$$

where K_1 and K_2 are positive. Let

(10.5)
$$|A| = \begin{vmatrix} F_1 - 1 & F_2 - \dfrac{F_3 V}{r^2 p} \\ 0 & -\dfrac{B_2}{r^2} - \dfrac{(B_3 - 1)V}{r^2 p} \end{vmatrix} < 0.$$

The system is stable if the characteristic equation $|KA - xI| = 0$, or, more specifically,

(10.6)
$$[K_1(F_1 - 1) - x]\left[K_2\left(\frac{B_2}{r^2} + \frac{(B_3 - 1)V}{r^2 p}\right) - x\right] = 0,$$

has roots whose real parts are negative. Inspection of this equation shows that this condition is met.

Consider now the effects of an increase in the quantity of money used

---

1 Attached to Chapter XIII:4.

For an explanation of the technique of differentiation used here, the reader is referred once again to p. 346, footnote 10.

to finance budgetary expenditures.[2]   Differentiating (10.1)–(10.2) with respect to M, the variable V being held constant, we obtain

(10.7) $\quad \dfrac{dY}{dM} = \dfrac{F_4\left[\dfrac{B_2}{r^2} - \dfrac{(1-B_3)V}{r^2 p}\right] + B_4\left[F_2 - \dfrac{F_3 V}{r^2 p}\right]}{p|A|} > 0$

and

(10.8) $\qquad\qquad \dfrac{dr}{dM} = \dfrac{(1-F_1)B_4}{p|A|} < 0,$

where we have once again made use of the assumption $B_1 = 0$.   These results hold also when either $F_3 = 0$ and/or $B_3 = 0$.

In the case where the monetary increase goes to finance open-market purchases, we differentiate (10.1)–(10.2) with respect to M, letting V vary in accordance with (9.44), to obtain

(10.9) $\quad \dfrac{dY}{dM} = \dfrac{(F_4 - F_3)\left[\dfrac{B_2}{r^2} - \dfrac{(1-B_3)V}{r^2 p}\right]}{p|A|}$

$\qquad\qquad + \dfrac{[B_4 + (1 - B_3)]\left(F_2 - \dfrac{F_3 V}{r^2 p}\right)}{p|A|} > 0$

and

(10.10) $\qquad \dfrac{dr}{dM} = \dfrac{(1 - F_1)[B_4 + (1 - B_3)]}{p|A|} < 0.$

The identity of the numerators of (10.7) and (9.43), on the one hand, and (10.9) and (9.46), on the other, is the mathematical counterpart of the familiar observation of "depression economics" that an increase in the quantity of money can expend itself either in increasing real output or in raising prices.

Alternatively, we can obtain these results from an analysis of the commodity and money markets.   Replace (10.2) by

(10.11) $\qquad\qquad L\left(Y, r, \dfrac{V}{rp}, \dfrac{M}{p}\right) - \dfrac{M}{p} = 0,$

where $L_3 > 0$; and (10.4) by

(10.12) $\qquad\qquad \dfrac{dr}{dt} = K_3\left[L(\ \ ) - \dfrac{M}{p}\right],$

_____

[2] The following analysis parallels that of the preceding section.

where K_3 is positive.   Let

(10.13)
$$|B| = \begin{vmatrix} F_1 - 1 & F_2 - \dfrac{F_3 V}{r^2 p} \\[2mm] L_1 & L_2 - \dfrac{L_3 V}{r^2 p} \end{vmatrix} > 0.$$

The reader can then verify that the characteristic equation

(10.14) $|KB - yI| = 0$

has roots for y whose real parts are negative.

Consider now the case of a budgetary increase in the quantity of money.   Here we differentiate (10.1) and (10.11) with respect to M, holding V constant, to obtain

(10.15)
$$\frac{dY}{dM} = \frac{\begin{vmatrix} \dfrac{-F_4}{p} & F_2 - \dfrac{F_3 V}{r^2 p} \\[3mm] \dfrac{-(L_4 - 1)}{p} & L_2 - \dfrac{L_3 V}{r^2 p} \end{vmatrix}}{|B|} > 0$$

and

(10.16)
$$\frac{dr}{dM} = \frac{\begin{vmatrix} F_1 - 1 & \dfrac{-F_4}{p} \\[3mm] L_1 & \dfrac{-(L_4 - 1)}{p} \end{vmatrix}}{|B|}$$
$$= \frac{-(1 - F_1)(1 - L_4) + F_4 L_1}{p|B|}$$

From the budget restraint and the assumption $B_1 = 0$, we have $F_1 + L_1 = 1$ and $F_4 + B_4 + L_4 = 1$, where all the derivatives are positive.   Hence

(10.17) $\dfrac{1 - F_1}{L_1} = 1$ and $\dfrac{1 - L_4}{F_4} > 1.$

Assume now that

(10.18) $-(1 - F_1)(1 - L_4) + F_4 L_1 \geqq 0.$

This implies

(10.19) $-\dfrac{1 - F_1}{L_1} + \dfrac{F_4}{1 - L_4} \geqq 0,$

a contradiction. Hence (10.18) and $\dfrac{dr}{dM}$ must be negative. These results hold also when either $F_3 = 0$ and/or $L_3 = 0$.

Let us now examine the case of open-market operations. Once again we differentiate (10.1) and (10.11) with respect to M, but now we let V vary in accordance with (9.44). This yields

$$(10.20) \quad \frac{dY}{dM} = \frac{\begin{vmatrix} \dfrac{F_3}{p} - \dfrac{F_4}{p} & F_2 - \dfrac{F_3 V}{r^2 p} \\ \dfrac{L_3}{p} - \dfrac{(L_4 - 1)}{p} & L_2 - \dfrac{L_3 V}{r^2 p} \end{vmatrix}}{|B|} > 0$$

and

$$(10.21) \quad \frac{dr}{dM} = \frac{\begin{vmatrix} F_1 - 1 & F_3 - F_4 \\ L_1 & L_3 - (L_4 - 1) \end{vmatrix}}{p|B|}$$

$$= \frac{\begin{vmatrix} F_1 - 1 & -F_4 \\ L_1 & -(L_4 - 1) \end{vmatrix}}{p|B|} + \frac{\begin{vmatrix} F_1 - 1 & F_3 \\ L_1 & L_3 \end{vmatrix}}{p|B|} < 0.$$

Comparing (10.21) to (10.16), we see that the fall in interest must be greater in the former case.

b.[3] Consider now the special case where any increase in the quantity of money is merely added to cash balances. That is, $L_4 = 1$. This implies $B_4 = F_4 = 0$. Since money is assumed more liquid than bonds, we must have in equilibrium $B_3 \leqq B_4$ and $F_3 \leqq F_4$. Hence $B_3 = F_3 = 0$. And this in turn implies $L_3 = 1$. Substituting these values into (10.5) or (10.13), we see that, unlike the situation in Mathematical Appendix 9:*e*,[4] the stability of the system is not thereby affected.

If, now, the quantity of money is increased to finance transfer payments, $\dfrac{dr}{dM} = \dfrac{dY}{dM} = 0$. This can be seen either from equations (10.7)–(10.8) or (10.15)–(10.16). On the other hand, in the case of open-market operations, the signs of the derivatives are not affected, as can be seen from either (10.9)–(10.10) or (10.20)–(10.21).

We now note an inaccuracy in Figure 37 of the text. In the case

---

[3] Attached to Chapter XIII:4.
[4] P. 363.

under discussion, $L_3 = L_4 = 1$. Thus the stimulating effect of the increased money holdings must be exactly offset by the discouraging effect of the decreased bond holdings. Hence the dashed curve in Figure 37 must initially coincide with the original curve! Only as income increases will this shift to the right.

If we now drop the assumption $B_3 < B_4$ in equilibrium, we can conceive of circumstances in which even open-market purchases will not affect the rate of interest. In particular, assume again $L_4 = 1$, so that $B_4 = F_4 = 0$. But now assume $B_3 = 1$, so that $F_3 = L_3 = 0$. These values reduce both (10.9)–(10.10) and (10.20)–(10.21) to zero. The economic interpretation of these results is that in the bond market individuals passively adapt their demand to the reduced supply of bonds left after the government's purchase, and make no attempt to use the money which they receive as a result of this open-market operation to replenish their holdings of bonds. In this way demand and supply in the bond market decrease to exactly the same extent, so that no downward pressure on interest is generated. Alternatively, in terms of the money market, individuals passively adapt their demand to the newly increased supply and remain indifferent to the fact that their bond holdings have decreased. Hence only the increased balances act on the demand for money, and these shift it over to the right-hand demand curve in Figure 37.

This is truly schizophrenia: In the bond market, a decrease in bond holdings affects individuals' demand, but an increase in money holdings does not; in the money market, the opposite holds true. It is difficult to conceive of economic circumstances in which we would have to concern ourselves with such behavior.

SUPPLEMENTARY NOTES

AND

STUDIES IN THE LITERATURE

INTRODUCTION

The purpose of this Supplement is to provide the detailed textual evidence necessary to support the interpretation and criticism of the literature presented in the text. In order to do this, however, it has been necessary to present full-length studies of the monetary theories of Walras, Wicksell, and Cassel. Nevertheless, the reader is again warned that neither these studies nor, *a fortiori*, the less comprehensive notes on the other writers are intended to be read by themselves. Indeed, unless they are read together with the sections of the text to which they are explicitly attached, they are likely to appear as disjointed, captious criticisms of arbitrarily selected passages. The meaning of it all—the reasons for selecting the passages in question and the significance of the criticism leveled against them—can be understood only from the text itself.

To state this in somewhat more positive terms, the detailed studies of Notes B–K, together with their broader implications as developed, interpreted, and summarized in Chapters VIII:1–4 and XV:1–2, are intended to constitute a critical history of the general-equilibrium theory of money from its inception by Walras to its most recent statements by Keynes, Hicks, Leontief, Modigliani, and others. But it is a history largely written from a very special viewpoint. In brief, our main interest is in the degree to which general-equilibrium theorists succeeded in their declared objective of integrating monetary theory with value theory.[1] Our criterion is a twofold one: first, the extent to which these theorists applied the formal apparatus of marginal-utility analysis to the theory of money; second—and far more important—the extent to which they consistently carried over their recognition of the real-balance effect to all phases of monetary and value theory.

As shown in the text, the critical points where we must test for such a recognition—or, rather, for its absence—are in the failure to present a stability analysis of the equilibrium absolute price level, in the assumption of a uniform unitary elasticity of demand for money, and in the

---

[1] It should be emphasized that this objective is one that characterized practically all economic theorists, and not just those of the general-equilibrium school. See the detailed examination of the literature in Marget, *Theory of Prices*, Vol. II, pp. 3–133.

invalid dichotomization of the pricing process. To the extent that it is relevant, each of the writers cited in the following notes will be subjected to this triple test. In many ways, the first of these tests is at once the simplest and the most revealing. And this explains why our history must begin with a thorough appreciation of the vital role of the *tâtonnement* in the general theoretical framework of Walras.

The Mechanism of the Quantity Theory
in the Earlier Literature[1]

Examples of early expositions of the quantity theory which make it clear that an increase in the quantity of money raises prices through its prior effect in increasing demand are provided by Richard Cantillon,[2] Henry Thornton,[3] David Ricardo,[4] and John Stuart Mill.[5] On the other hand, it must be admitted that there were early exponents of the quantity theory who failed to provide any economic explanation of the effect of money on prices. Thus Montesquieu wrote:

If we compare the mass of gold and silver in the whole world with the quantity of merchandise therein contained, it is certain that every commodity or merchandise in particular may be compared to a certain portion of the entire mass of gold and silver. As the total of the one is to the total of the other, so part of the one will be to part of the other. Let us suppose that there is only one commodity or merchandise in the world, or only one to be purchased, and that this is divisible like money; a part of this merchandise will answer to a part of the mass of gold and silver; the half of the total of the one to the half of the total of the other; the tenth, the hundredth, the thousandth, part of the one to the tenth, the hundredth, the thousandth part of the other. . . . the establishment of the price of things fundamentally depends on the proportion of the total of things to the total of signs.[6]

Similar passages appear in David Hume[7] and James Mill.[8] Even here, however, we should hesitate before concluding that these writers failed

---

[1] Attached to Chapter VIII:1, especially p. 98.

[2] *Essay on the Nature of Trade* (1755), trans. and ed. H. Higgs (London, 1931), Part II, Chapters VI–VII, especially pp. 161 and 179.

[3] *An Enquiry into the Nature and Effects of the Paper Credit of Great Britain* (London, 1802), pp. 195 ff., 259–67.

[4] *The High Price of Bullion* (1810), in *The Works and Correspondence of David Ricardo,* ed. P. Sraffa (Cambridge, 1951), Vol. III, p. 91; *Reply to Mr. Bosanquet* (1811), *ibid.,* p. 217; *Notes on the Bullion Report and Evidence* (1810), *ibid.,* pp. 362–63; *Notes on Trotter* (1810), *ibid.,* p. 390, footnote 38.

[5] *Principles of Political Economy,* ed. W. J. Ashley (London, 1909), pp. 491–93, 496, 524. On this last page Mill writes: " Money acts upon prices in no other way than by being tendered in exchange for commodities."

[6] *The Spirit of the Laws,* trans. T. Nugent (New York, 1949), Vol. I, pp. 378–79.

[7] *Essays, Moral, Political, and Literary,* in *Philosophical Works* (Boston, 1854), Vol. III, pp. 313, 318, 334, 341–42.

[8] *Elements of Political Economy* (London, 1821), p. 95.

to see that an increase in the quantity of money raises prices only because it first increases demand.   They may have instead considered this causal relationship to be too obvious for comment.   Thus, for example, James Mill made it clear that he was aware of this relationship when he wrote:

> The man who goes first to market with the augmented quantity of money, either raises the price of the commodities which he purchases, or he does not raise it.[9]

Another case in point is Ricardo.   As against the purely mechanical exposition of the quantity theory in his *Principles*,[10] we have the other passages already cited that show that he fully understood the effect of an increase in the quantity of money in increasing demand.

We might finally observe—in connection with the discussion in Note G:2 below—that since, for the most part, classical value theory did not systematically discuss the problem of stability of equilibrium, no significance can be attached to the corresponding gap in its monetary theory.   There are, however, exceptions.   In particular, J. S. Mill is as open to criticism as any neoclassical economist for failing to include in his chapter on "The Value of Money as Dependent on Demand and Supply" a counterpart of the embryonic stability discussion of his earlier chapter on "Demand and Supply in their Relation to Value."[11]

---

[9] *Ibid.*, p. 123.

[10] *Principles of Political Economy and Taxation*, ed. Sraffa, Chapter XXVII; see in particular p. 352.

[11] *Op. cit.*, Book III, Chapter II, §4, and Chapter VIII.

Walras' Theory of *Tâtonnement*[1]

Walras' theory of *tâtonnement* would seem to be one of his most imaginative and valuable contributions to economic analysis. This makes it all the more difficult to understand why it was neglected, misunderstood, and even disparaged for so many years.

There can be no mistaking the central role of this theory in Walras' argument. At each successive stage of this argument—beginning with an exchange economy, continuing with a simple production economy, and then going on to a production economy in which capital goods are transacted—Walras first shows how the additional complication he has just introduced does not affect the equality between the number of equations and the number of unknown prices. He then goes on to say: "In this way . . . prices are determined mathematically. Now there remains only to show—and this is the essential point—that the problem of exchange for which we have just given a theoretical solution is the selfsame problem that is solved empirically on the market by the mechanism of free competition." At each stage Walras then follows this programmatic declaration with a clear and detailed description of the *tâtonnement* by which the market solves the system of equations relevant to his particular assumptions.[2] Indeed, the only stage of his

---

[1] Attached to Chapter III:3.

Except for its discussion of recontracting, this note was written substantially in its present form before the appearance of J. A. Schumpeter's authoritative critique of Walras in his *History of Economic Analysis* (New York, 1954), pp. 998–1026. On the main points of interpretation, as the reader will see, this note repeats Schumpeter's conclusions. There are, however, some significant differences which are duly pointed out.

Unless otherwise indicated, all references to Walras' *Eléments d'économie politique pure* are to the definitive edition (Paris, 1926) as translated and edited by W. Jaffé under the title *Elements of Pure Economics* (London, 1954). For convenience, this will be referred to henceforth as *Elements*.

[2] The quotation is from *Elements*, pp. 162–63. Variations upon it—corresponding to the various stages of Walras' argument—appear on pp. 169, 241–42, and 282, respectively. The descriptions of the corresponding *tâtonnements* appear, accordingly, on pp. 169–72, 243–54 (which constitute Lesson 21), and 284–95 (which constitute Lesson 25), respectively.

It might be noted that Walras' theory of *tâtonnement* goes back to the very first edition (1874–77) of the *Eléments*; see *ibid.*, pp. 126–31, 251–57.

Goodwin (*op. cit.*, p. 5), basing himself on p. 106 of the *Elements*, says: "Walras disavowed in advance the use of this kind of market adjustment [i.e., the *tâtonnement*] as a practical

argument at which he fails to provide such a detailed description is that which interests us most in this book: the stage at which he introduces the new good, fiat paper money, and the new price, the value of this money in terms of commodities.[3]

One question of importance for the history of doctrine is whether Walras made his theory of *tâtonnement* logically watertight by assuming the presence of recontracting.[4]   If he did not make such an assumption, and if, accordingly, he visualized some purchases as being effected at the provisional prices "cried out," then he could not validly conclude that the *tâtonnement* necessarily brings the economy to that same set of prices yielded by a direct mathematical solution of the system of excess-demand equations.   For, in the absence of recontract, the intermediary purchases which are carried out must affect the nature of the market excess-demand functions which determine the subsequent evolvement of the *tâtonnement*.   In particular, the set of prices which prevails when the market is finally cleared depends on the time path of the *tâtonnement* as a whole and will, therefore, not generally be the same for any two *tâtonnements*.

The general view of the contemporary literature has been that Walras did assume recontracting.   Unfortunately, this view was until recently based on passages in the *Elements* which are—to say the least—not really explicit on the point in question.[5]   Now, however, Jaffé and Schumpeter have independently supported this interpretation by citing the following apparently explicit passage, occurring in Walras' discussion of a production economy:

[During the process of *tâtonnement*] . . . entrepreneurs use *tickets* ["*bons*"] to represent the successive quantities of *products* which are first determined at random and then increased or decreased according as there is an excess of selling price over cost of production or vice versa, until selling price and cost are equal; and, on the other hand, . . . landowners, workers and capitalists also use *tickets* to represent the successive quantities

---

device. . . .   He explicitly states that it is only a mathematical method of solution and not the practical one exemplified in the behavior of real markets."   Actually, the passage on p. 106 says just the opposite—as do all the other passages just cited.   Goodwin's statement must accordingly be rejected as a fundamental misinterpretation of Walras' conceptual framework. Goodwin repeats this interpretation in his "Static and Dynamic Linear General Equilibrium Models" in *Input-Output Relations*, ed. The Netherlands Economic Institute (Leiden, 1953), pp. 59–60.

3 See Note C:4 below.

4 The term is, of course, Edgeworth's.   See his *Mathematical Psychics* (London, 1881; reprinted 1953), pp. 17, 35 ff.; *Papers Relating to Political Economy* (London, 1925), Vol. II, pp. 311–12.

5 Cf. Kaldor, *op. cit.*, p. 126, who bases himself on *Elements*, pp. 169–70; and Hicks, *Value and Capital*, p. 128, who bases himself instead on *Elements*, pp. 83–84.   It is worth noting that Hicks earlier considered this same passage to be "ambiguous," and gives no reason for his change of mind.   ["Léon Walras," *Econometrica*, II (1934), 342, footnote 11.]

of *services* [which they offer] at prices first cried at random and then raised or lowered according as there is an excess of demand over offer or vice versa, until the two become equal.[6]

There can be no question that this passage describes a process of recontracting in which entrepreneurs and sellers of productive services merely note their offers to buy and sell on "tickets" and continuously revise these offers as the *tâtonnement* proceeds toward the equilibrium set of prices.   But what can be questioned is whether Walras wrote this passage with full understanding of the analytical problem that called forth Edgeworth's device of recontracting.   In particular, this problem exists for an exchange economy no less than for a production economy; yet Walras feels it necessary to introduce his tickets only in the latter case.

This distinction is made most clear in the sentences with which Walras precedes the foregoing passage.   Here he writes:

. . . the process of *tâtonnement* in production entails a complication *which was not present* in the case of exchange.   In exchange, [the total existing quantities of] commodities do not undergo any change.   When a price is cried, and the effective demand and offer corresponding to this price are not equal, another price is cried for which there is another corresponding effective demand and offer.   In production, productive services are transformed into products.   After certain prices for services have been cried and certain quantities of products have been manufactured, if these prices and quantities are not the equilibrium prices and quantities, it will be necessary not only to cry new prices but also to manufacture revised quantities of products.   In order to work out as rigorous a description of the process of *tâtonnement* in production as we did in exchange and yet take this additional circumstance into account, we have only to imagine, on the one hand, that entrepreneurs use *tickets* . . .[7]

—and on into the preceding passage.   It is also noteworthy that this passage does *not* make provision for consumers also to make use of tickets.   Similarly, in the Preface to the fourth edition (1900) of the *Eléments*—in which the device of tickets was first used—Walras writes:

In the theory of production, I no longer represented the preliminary *tâtonnement* toward equilibrium as it takes place effectively, but I assumed, instead, that it was done *by means of tickets* ["*sur bons*"] and then carried this fiction through the remainder of the book.[8]

---

[6] *Elements*, ed. Jaffé, p. 242, italics and all but first set of brackets in translation.   See Jaffé's illuminating explanation of the term "*bons*," *ibid.*, pp. 528–29, and note his statement that this device solves the "'problem of the path.'"   On Schumpeter, see *op. cit.*, p. 1002.

[7] *Elements*, p. 242, brackets in translation, but italics added.   The term "groping" has also been replaced by the original "*tâtonnement.*"

[8] *Ibid.*, p. 37.   First set of italics added, other italics and brackets in translation.

In the second and third editions Walras had essentially made use of the method described on p. 37 of the text above; see the relevant passage from these editions cited by Jaffé on pp. 582–83 of his edition.

All these passages make it clear that Walras was not fully aware of the logical necessity for recontracting.   Instead, his reasoning seems to be that the *tâtonnement* in a production economy can affect the quantities of commodities produced for the market and hence their equilibrium prices, whereas in an exchange economy there is no danger of this since these quantities are fixed.   There is no recognition of the fact that even in the latter economy the *tâtonnement* does not reach a unique set of prices unless recontracting takes place.   Or, to put it in other words, Walras seems to forget that the given data of a production economy are not the quantities of commodities, but the quantities of productive services;[9] hence just as the *tâtonnement* does not affect the given data of the exchange economy, so does it not affect those of the production economy.   Hence there can be no difference between these two economies as to the logical necessity for assuming the existence of tickets in analyzing their workings.

Let us now assume recontract and turn to the problem of the convergence of the *tâtonnement*.   Though recognizing the existence of this problem, Walras did not deal with it adequately   He realized that a *tâtonnement* on one price which brings it to equilibrium will generally, because of the general interdependence of the system, disturb the equilibrium of other markets.   But he argued that the direct pressure of excess demand in a given market definitely pushed its price toward its equilibrium level, while the changes in other prices "exerted indirect influences, some in the direction of equality and some in the opposite direction . . . so that up to a certain point they cancelled each other out.   Hence, the new system of prices . . . is closer to equilibrium than the old system . . . ; and it is only necessary to continue this process along the same lines for the system to move closer and closer to equilibrium."[10] The invalidity of this argument is sufficiently demonstrated by any of the divergent dynamic systems described in Mathematical Appendixes 3 and 9 above.

With the exception of Wicksell,[11] none of Walras' immediate successors carried the theory of *tâtonnement* beyond the point to which he himself had brought it.   Writers such as Antonelli, Aupetit, and Osorio simply repeated his exposition.[12]   Pareto, perhaps more than

---

[9] *Ibid.*, p. 238, line 4.

[10] *Ibid.*, p. 172.   For similar passages, see pp. 251–53, 470.

[11] See Note E:1 below for a description of Wicksell's extension of the theory of *tâtonnement* (though without use of this term) to the determination of the absolute price level.

[12] E. Antonelli, *Principes d'économie pure* (Paris, 1914); A. Aupetit, *Essai sur la théorie générale de la monnaie* (Paris, 1901); A. Osorio, *Théorie mathématique de l'échange*, trans. J. D'Almada (Paris, 1913).

the others, realized the power and beauty of the theory.[13]   He was also
the only one who specially mentioned the problem of the convergence of
the *tâtonnement*—though his attempt to show that this must always take
place is actually invalid.[14]   Fisher made no explicit reference to the
process of *tâtonnement*; but he described the process implicitly—under
ideal circumstances—through the hydrostatic mechanism which he
used to illustrate his exposition.[15]   On the other hand, Auspitz and
Lieben,[16] Barone,[17] and Cassel[18] merely repeated Walras' demonstration of the equality between the number of equations and the number of
unknown prices—without in any way indicating that one must also
explain how the market solves these equations.   And in this they set

[13] V. Pareto, *Cours d'économie politique* (Lausanne, 1896), Vol. I, pp. 24–25, 45–47, 61;
Manuel d'économie politique (second ed.; Paris, 1927), pp. 232–34.

[14] This attempt is made in his *Cours*, Vol. I, p. 61, footnote 2.   This footnote, with italics
added, reads:

> It would be desirable to demonstrate that, by these various adjustments, the equilibrium
> position is always approached.   For this it is observed that, *provided a sufficiently close
> value is taken*, these successive approximations approach closer and closer to the solution
> of the [market excess-demand] equations. . . .   We shall not develop this demonstration
> here, which would be useless for anyone not knowing mathematics, and which can be
> established very easily by anyone acquainted with the general theory of equations.

If this footnote refers to the successive approximations described in the text to which it is
attached, then it is obviously wrong.   For in his text Pareto clearly has in mind a Walrasian
dynamic system like the one described in Mathematical Appendix 3:*b* above; and, as already
emphasized, such a system need not necessarily converge to the equilibrium solution.

Pareto's error seems to have originated in the following way: In the note just cited he is
tacitly considering the various systems of successive approximation (e.g., Newton's) which
always converge to the solution of an equation, provided one starts with a value sufficiently
close to this solution.   That this is what Pareto had in mind is suggested by the phrase which
has been italicized above; for this phrase has no relevance for a Walrasian system of *tâtonnement*.   This conjecture is also supported by Pareto's reference to "the general theory of equations" at the end of his note.   Thus Pareto was misled by his over-suggestive terminology into
forgetting that the "successive approximations" provided by the normal operation of market
forces are not those specified by the theory of equations; and that, consequently, the theorems
of the latter are not in the least relevant to the analysis of the former.

I am indebted to my colleague of the Mathematics Department, Dr. Shmuel Agmon, for the
foregoing interpretation of Pareto's footnote.

[15] Irving Fisher, *Mathematical Investigations in the Theory of Value and Prices* (1892;
reprinted by the Yale University Press, 1925).   The circumstances are ideal in that they must
always lead to convergence.   For a somewhat more explicit recognition of the process of
tâtonnement, see *ibid.*, p. 55.

[16] R. Auspitz and R. Lieben, *Recherches sur la théorie du prix*, trans. L. Suret (Paris,
1914), Appendix IV.   The original German work appeared in 1889.

[17] E. Barone, "The Ministry of Production in the Collectivist State," in *Collectivist Economic
Planning*, ed. F. A. Hayek (London, 1935), pp. 247–51, 274.   The original Italian article
appeared in 1908.

[18] G. Cassel, *Theory of Social Economy*, trans. S. L. Barron (new revised ed.; New York,
1932), Chapter IV.   But in his *Nature and Necessity of Interest* (London, 1903), pp. 79–80,
Cassel shows a full appreciation of the theory of *tâtonnement*—though without using this term,
and without referring to Walras.

the pattern for the almost complete neglect of this fundamental question in the general-equilibrium literature of the interwar period.[19]

There can be no doubt that this neglect was abetted by the severe criticism to which the theory of *tâtonnement* was subjected by both economists and mathematicians. But in neither case have I succeeded in finding an understanding of the very real problem which Walras was trying to solve. Thus Edgeworth, in his oft-cited review of the second edition of Walras' *Eléments*, writes:

> He diffuses over some thirty-five pages an idea which might have been adequately presented in a few paragraphs. For it is, after all, not a very good idea. What the author professes to demonstrate is the course which the higgling of the market takes— the path, as it were, by which the economic system works down to equilibrium. Now, as Jevons points out, the equations of exchange are of a statical, not a dynamical, character. They define a position of equilibrium, but they afford no information as to the path by which that point is reached. Prof. Walras' laboured lessons indicate *a* way, not *the* way of descent to equilibrium.[20]

Clearly, the third sentence of this citation is involved in a basic misconception; for Walras was primarily interested in describing, not the actual path to equilibrium, but the nature of the automatic forces which propel the economy along this path—be what it may. Again, the penultimate sentence reveals a failure to realize that the *differences* between "statical" demand and supply functions can be used, as Walras did use them, to explain the motivating force of this movement. Finally, as Pareto pointed out, Walras' way may only be *a* way; but it is *the* way which represents the workings of economic phenomena.[21]

---

[19] Thus F. Divisia merely counts equations and unknowns [*Economique rationelle* (Paris, 1927), Titre VI], and Hicks does the same (*Value and Capital*, Chapters IV, VIII, and XII, and their mathematical appendixes). The same is true for such standard works of the period as A. L. Bowley, *Mathematical Groundwork of Economics* (Oxford, 1924), pp. 20–22, 47–54; G. C. Evans, *Mathematical Introduction to Economics* (New York, 1930); and O. Weinberger, *Mathematische Volkswirtschaftslehre* (Leipzig, 1930), pp. 94–106. H. L. Moore's *Synthetic Economics* (New York, 1929) is in a somewhat ambiguous position. When counting equations, Moore makes no reference to the theory of *tâtonnement* (pp. 53, 100–106); but in other contexts he does (p. 152). The reader will also find it instructive to compare what E. H. Phelps Brown writes under the heading "The Solution of Equations and the Workings of the Market" with what Walras writes in similar contexts [*The Framework of the Pricing System* (London, 1936), pp. 83–90, 128–32].

A notable exception to this neglect is provided by O. Lange's stimulating use of the theory of *tâtonnement* to establish the feasibility of a socialist economy. See his *Economic Theory of Socialism* (Minneapolis, 1938), pp. 70–72, 89–90.

[20] *Nature*, XL (1889), 435, italics in original; cited by G. J. Stigler, *Production and Distribution Theories* (New York, 1941), p. 245. For Walras' reaction to the first sentence of the passage cited here, see *Elements*, p. 470.

See also Edgeworth's *Papers Relating to Political Economy*, Vol. II, p. 311.

[21] *Cours*, Vol. I, pp. 24–25.

It should also be clear that the attempts sometimes made to *contrast* Edgeworth's theory of recontracting with Walras' theory of *tâtonnement* are based on a fundamental misunderstanding. As emphasized above, the latter must be supplemented by the former in order to make it rigorous.

The mathematicians first criticized the easy assumption of many general-equilibrium economists[22] that equality between the number of equations and variables implies the existence of a unique solution, and then went on to demonstrate rigorously the conditions necessary for such uniqueness. Unfortunately, the foremost among them—Wald— implied that this demonstration with the "recondite methods of modern mathematics" was an *alternative* to Walras' theory of *tâtonnement*.[23] Neither Wald nor any of the other writers who proved the existence of a unique solution recognized that this theory dealt with a fundamental problem which they in their work completely ignored: namely, how did the *market* reach this solution?[24]

The reader may feel that the foregoing charge of neglect is too formalistic in its conception, and that discussions of the theory of *tâtonnement* can be found in the literature—though without use of this term and without reference to Walras.[25]   In particular, he might claim that every discussion of the stability of equilibrium is *ipso facto* a discussion of the dynamics of a *tâtonnement*.   But this is not so.   First of all, there are certain stability discussions which are not even based on a dynamic analysis of the market; this, after all, is what Samuelson has so significantly and revealingly taught us about Hicks' discussion.[26] Second, even when these discussions are implicitly or explicitly based on such an analysis, it is not at all clear that the writers in question saw the analytical equivalence between the existence of stability, on the one

---

[22] But—as Jaffé has emphasized—not of Walras.   Cf. *Elements*, pp. 108–9, 142, 200.   In the last of these references Walras does, however, argue that multiple equilibria "are, in general, not possible" in the case of an economy with many commodities.

[23] A. Wald, "On Some Systems of Equations of Mathematical Economics," *Econometrica*, XIX (1951), 384–85 (trans. by O. Eckstein from the 1936 article).   This is not to deny the validity of Wald's refutation of Walras' proof that the *tâtonnement* must converge; cf. above.

For an example of a writer who considers the possible existence of multiple solutions as constituting a refutation of the theory of *tâtonnement* itself, see G. Demaria, "Pareto," reprinted in *The Development of Economic Thought*, ed. H. W. Spiegel (New York, 1952), p. 639.

[24] In addition to the article by Wald just cited, see J. von Neumann, "A Model of General Economic Equilibrium," *Review of Economic Studies*, XIII (1945–46), pp. 1–9 (trans. by O. Morgenstern from the 1938 article).   See also the papers by K. Schlesinger and A. Wald in *Ergebnisse eines mathematischen Kolloquiums*, VI (1933–34), 10–20.   Note in particular the concluding comment by K. Menger.

See also K. J. Arrow and G. Debreu, "Existence of an Equilibrium for a Competitive Economy," *Econometrica*, XXII (1954), 265–90.   It should, however, be emphasized that this article explicitly eschews any discussion of the stability of the equilibrium position (*ibid.*, p. 266).

[25] Cf. in this connection Pareto's comment that the "germ" of Walras' theory existed already in the familiar theoretical distinction between market and normal prices (*Cours*, Vol. I, p. 46, footnote).

[26] Samuelson, *Foundations*, p. 270.   For Hicks' recognition of this criticism, see the second edition of *Value and Capital*, pp. 335–37.

hand, and the dynamic convergence of the *tâtonnement*, on the other. That is, it is not at all clear that they saw the equivalence between the statement "if the system is at its equilibrium position, then any arbitrary departure from this position generates dynamic market forces which bring it back," and the statement "no matter what the initial position from which the system starts, the dynamic workings of market forces bring it to its equilibrium position."

Only the slightest of nuances separates these two statements. Yet I would conjecture that an exhaustive study of the literature would show that this nuance generally blocked their full identification—and hence their full understanding. Before the reader rejects this conjecture as far-fetched, let him pause to consider the following thought-provoking facts: First, there is no evidence that Walras himself made this identification. He discusses stable and unstable equilibrium positions before he brings in his theory of *tâtonnement*;[27] conversely, once he brings this theory in, he never refers to this earlier discussion or even uses the term "stability."[28]   Second, even Schumpeter, who at one point explicitly identifies these two statements,[29] at other points implicitly distinguishes between them;[30] and—what is far more significant—at still other points mistakenly presents Hicks' nondynamic stability analysis as if it were relevant to Walras' dynamic theory of *tâtonnement*.[31]   Finally, Samuelson himself—despite the fact that his path-breaking stability analysis is marked throughout by generous references to Walras—does not make explicit what seems to me to be the fundamental relation between his work and Walras': that his work ends the seventy-year analytical exile of Walras' theory of *tâtonnement*;

---

27 *Elements*, pp. 108–12. The first detailed presentation of the theory of *tâtonnement* appears on pp. 162 ff.; cf. above, footnote 2.   True, on p. 106 there is a brief anticipation of this theory; but this makes it all the more significant that in his stability discussion a few pages later Walras does not refer back to it.

28 This accords with yet another analytical characteristic of the *Elements*. Walras—like Marshall—never seems to have discussed unstable equilibrium except in a context of multiple equilibrium positions.   In particular, the unstable position is almost always an intermediary one between two stable positions.   There is no reference to the possibility that there may exist only one equilibrium position and that this may be unstable. Now, Walras recognizes the possibility of multiple equilibrium positions only for the case of a two-commodity economy; he explicitly assumes it away for the case of a multi-commodity one (*ibid.*, p. 200).   At the same time, he develops his theory of *tâtonnement* only after he has already generalized the argument to such an economy.   It is thus easy to imagine that this assumed impossibility of multiple equilibrium could have prevented Walras from thinking about his *tâtonnement* within the conceptual framework of his earlier discussion of stable and unstable equilibrium positions.

29 *Op. cit.*, p. 1002, footnote 8; p. 1007, footnote 22, first sentence. Note also that—as Schumpeter himself emphasizes—the distinction he later attempts to make is not relevant for our present discussion (*op. cit.*, p. 1007, footnote 25).

30 *Ibid.*, p. 1006, lines 7–10; p. 1008, bottom; p. 1014, lines 5–6.

31 *Ibid.*, p. 1009, footnote 28; p. 1014, footnote 42.

that it constitutes the first significant development of this theory beyond Walras' pioneering presentation; that, in brief, it is the long-delayed, critical, and rigorous analysis of the conditions under which Walras' *tâtonnement* will bring the economy to its equilibrium solution.[32]

---

[32] Samuelson, *Foundations*, Chapter IX—a slightly revised version of Samuelson's well-known 1941 *Econometrica* article. Cf. also above, Chapter III:3 and Mathematical Appendix 3:*b*.

Walras' Theory of Money[1]

1. INTRODUCTION

"But it is above all the theory of money which was entirely revised as a result of the studies on this question which I pursued from 1876 to 1899." With this prefatory remark to the definitive edition of his *Eléments*, Walras identified the major development that had taken place between the first and last editions of his basic work.[2]

---

[1] Attached to Chapters V:1 and VIII:1–3.

I am indebted to Professor William Jaffé for reading this study and giving me the benefit of his criticisms. These criticisms have convinced me that at least on one point I was not interpreting Walras properly (see p. 400, footnote 52). I have also noted some of the points of interpretation on which we have not been able to reach agreement.

This study is concerned primarily with Walras' pure theory of a fiat paper money. It makes only passing mention of his theory of a commodity-money, and completely leaves aside his theory of bimetallism. In brief, it attempts primarily to understand Lesson 29 and the first two sections of Lesson 30 in the definitive edition of the *Eléments*.

The following bibliographical review provides the necessary background for this study: The first edition of Walras' *Eléments d'économie politique pure* appeared in two parts, in 1874 and 1877, respectively—with the first part including the chapters on monetary theory. This was followed by the *Théorie de la monnaie*, published originally in the *Revue scientifique* of April 10 and 17, 1886, and separately reprinted in that same year. The second and third editions of the *Eléments*—which are equivalent for our present purposes—then appeared in 1889 and 1896, respectively. In 1898 Walras revised and expanded his *Théorie de la monnaie*, added to it a "Note sur la 'Théorie de la quantité,'" and published it in his *Etudes d'économie politique appliquée*. On May 3, 1899, he read his memoir on "Equations de la circulation" before the Société Vaudoise des Sciences Naturelles. This was published that same year in the *Bulletin* of the Société (XXXV, 85–103). The new approach to monetary theory developed in this memoir was then presented without significant change in the fourth and definitive editions of the *Eléments*, published in 1900 and 1926, respectively. For our purposes, these two editions are equivalent.

[2] *Eléments d'économie politique pure* (*édition définitive*), p. ix.

In the 1952 reprint of this edition (which is what I have used) the text reads "*qui a été entière-/ment modifiée*" (where the solidus indicates the end of a line). Professor Jaffé has pointed out to me the very interesting fact that in the fourth edition of the *Eléments* this clause appears in the much weaker form "*qui a été sensible-/ment modifiée*" and that in the definitive 1926 edition the space originally occupied by "*qui a été sensible-*" is just a blank. Accordingly, Jaffé followed the fourth edition in his own translation.

Upon closer inspection, one can also see that the words "*été entière-*" have been inserted separately in the 1952 reprint of the definitive edition. Whether this change is one that was authorized by Walras or whether it was put in by a strange hand is something that we shall probably never know. But I cannot help feeling that it was authorized by Walras himself, correctly reëvaluating the extent of the changes which he had made.

Marget's well-known study makes it unnecessary to describe one phase of this development: the change from the transactions equation of the first edition to the cash-balance equation of the *Théorie de la monnaie* and later editions of the *Eléments*.[3]   It is, however, clear that Walras considered as of at least equal importance the change that he introduced only in the last edition.   In the words of the Preface to this edition:

In the first edition, this solution [of the problem of the value of money] was based on the concept of the "circulation to be cleared" ["*circulation à desservir*"][4] which I had borrowed from the economists.   Beginning with the second edition it was based on the concept of the "desired cash balance" ["*l'encaisse désirée*"],[5] of which I made use in my *Théorie de la monnaie*.   However, in this second edition and in the third, as in the first, the equation of the equality between the supply and the demand for money was always presented separately and empirically.   In the present edition, it is deduced rationally from the budget restraint and from the equations of maximum utility [i.e., the marginal-utility conditions] at the same time as the equations of the equality between the supply and demand for circulating capital.   In this way the *theory of circulation and of money*, like the *theories of exchange, of production, and of capitalization and credit*, comprises the positing and solving of a corresponding system of equations.[6]

The nature of Walras' distinction can be most easily appreciated by going back to the earlier works to which he refers.   In the original version of the *Théorie de la monnaie* there had been no attempt to deduce the money equation from the principle of utility maximization.   Instead, Walras had arbitrarily stated:

Without investigating the natural circumstances which may require landowners, workers, capitalists, and entrepreneurs to hold, at a given moment, a cash-balance of varying size in order to carry out purchases of varying sizes, we posit that, for simplicity,

---

3 A. W. Marget, "Léon Walras and the 'Cash-Balance Approach' to the Problem of the Value of Money," *Journal of Political Economy*, XXXIX (1931), 573–86.
However, for reasons made clear in the next section, I think it incorrect to identify Walras with the cash-balance *approach* in the accepted Cambridge sense of the term; for this reason I have referred here in the text only to the cash-balance *equation*.
4 This is Jaffé's translation of the term (*op. cit.*, p. 38).   Schumpeter translates it as "monetary requirements" of the economy (*op. cit.*, p. 1020).   Cf. also, Marget, "Léon Walras . . . ," *op. cit.*, p. 575, footnote 14.
5 This is again Jaffé's translation.
6 *Eléments d'économie politique pure* (*édition définitive*), pp. ix–x, my own translation; Jaffé's translation of the last two sentences of this passage is incorrect.
I have translated Walras' "*équation d'échange*" as "budget restraint."   This is the sense in which the term is used, *ibid.*, on pp. 251, 254, and 303.   Note in particular the last reference, in which we find the same juxtaposition as in the Preface of "*l'équation de l'échange*" and "*les équations de satisfaction maxima.*"   This parallelism is particularly significant in view of the fact that both the Preface and the material on p. 303 were newly written for the fourth edition.   It explains why the term "*l'équation de l'échange*" is not used to describe the budget restraint in parts of the book carried over from earlier editions; cf., e.g., pp. 123 and 209–10.

the value of this cash-balance and of these purchases depends not only on the [objective] situation, but also on the character and habits of each individual. . . . What must now be understood is that when a consumer or a producer requires to have in his possession a certain store [*provision*] of . . . money, he is concerned not with the [nominal] quantity of this money—which as such is a matter of indifference to him— but solely with the quantity of other goods, commodities or services, that he will be able to obtain in exchange for his money. Let . . . (A) then represent a commodity which is also the unit of account and the medium of exchange; let Q'_a be the existing quantity of this commodity; let α, β, γ, δ, . . . represent the respective quantities of the commodities (A), (B), (C), (D), . . . whose money value individuals require, at any given moment, to hold in the form of cash. The quantity of money Q''_a needed to satisfy these requirements is then

$$\alpha + \beta p_b + \gamma p_c + \delta p_d + \cdots$$

[where p_b, p_c, p_d, . . . are the respective prices of (B), (C), (D), . . . in terms of (A)].[7]

As Marget has emphasized,[8] this demand function for money has precisely the same form as that presented in Keynes' familiar cash-balance equation, $n = pk$.

It is readily seen that this passage deals only with the case of a money which also has normal commodity uses.[9] Correspondingly, the term "marginal utility of money" in the *Théorie de la monnaie* refers only to the utility of money as a commodity.[10] It must also be emphasized that Walras uses marginal-utility analysis in this work only *after* the preceding cash-balance equation is developed, and only for the purpose of demonstrating the validity of the quantity theory for a money which is also a commodity. Furthermore, this demonstration is restricted to the case where (1) the marginal utility of the money-commodity is inversely proportional to its quantity, and (2) the money value of the *encaisse désirée* is directly proportionate to the prices of other commodities.[11] We shall return to this point again below.

The preceding passage is reproduced in the second and third editions of the *Éléments*—with one important change. Instead of referring to a commodity-money, it now refers to a fiat paper money [12] Correspond-

---

7 *Théorie de la monnaie* (Paris, 1886), p. 13.

8 "Léon Walras . . . ," *op. cit.*, pp. 580 ff.

9 Walras does, however, later discuss an economy in which both metallic and paper money exist (*Théorie de la monnaie*, p. 14). But note that in the version which appears in *Etudes d'économie politique appliquée* (Paris, 1898), this paper money becomes one against which a metallic reserve is held (pp. 98–100).

10 Cf. also *ibid.*, p. 7, for a similar statement in an article written by Walras in 1884.

11 *Théorie de la monnaie*, p. 13.
This second assumption actually contradicts Walras' cash-balance equation at the end of the preceding passage. In particular, it ignores the existence of the term α. Cf. footnote 14 below.

12 The passage appears on pp. 377–78 of both editions. Another change in it—though one not significant for our present purposes—is that it generalizes the preceding demand function to include the *encaisse désirée* of producers and sellers of productive services, as well as of consumers.

ingly, there is no resort to marginal-utility analysis at any point. In particular, the validity of the quantity theory is established directly from the cash-balance equation itself.[13] This absence of marginal-utility analysis also marks Walras' subsequent discussion of a commodity-money.[14]

Perhaps the most significant point added to these editions of the *Eléments* is the explicit relation between the *encaisse désirée* and the rate of interest. In Walras' own words:

> In a society where one holds money in cash from the moment when one receives it until the day when one gives it out in payment or lends it out, money renders few services, and those who hold it, producers or consumers, fruitlessly lose [*perdent inutilement*] the interest on the capital which it represents.[15]

Furthermore, the cash-balance equation is solved in the market by a *tâtonnement* on the rate of interest.[16] We shall return to this question again below.

There is no definite indication of the date on which Walras revised his *Théorie de la monnaie* for inclusion in his *Etudes d'économie politique appliquée* (1898). But it would seem to be sometime after the appearance of the third edition of the *Eléments* (1896). For the passage cited above from the original *Théorie de la monnaie*—which, as just pointed out, appears with few changes in this edition—is now extensively reformulated. In particular, considering again the case of a commodity (*A*) which also serves as money, Walras writes:

> When a landowner, worker, capitalist or entrepreneur desires to have in his possession, at a given moment, a certain store [*provision*] of . . . money, it is evident that he is not concerned with the [nominal] quantity of this money, but only with the quantity of goods, commodities or services, *that he wants to buy with it.* In other words, the need one has for money is nothing but the need that one has for goods *that one will buy with this money.* This need is the need for storage [*besoin d'approvisionnement*];[17] it is satisfied at the cost of interest, and that is why the effective demand for money is a decreasing function of the rate of interest. . . . Let α, β, γ, δ, . . . be the respective quantities of (*A*), (*B*), (*C*), (*D*), . . . that consumers and

---

13 *Eléments* (second and third editions), p. 379.

14 *Ibid.*, pp. 383–86.

Note that here Walras points out that the presence of the term *a* (which corresponds to the α of the *Théorie de la monnaie*) makes the monetary demand for money only *approximately* a rectangular hyperbola (p. 384). Cf. footnote 11 above.

15 *Ibid.*, p. 382. Cf. also p. 380, lines 11–14.

16 *Ibid.*, p. 381.

17 This is Lange's translation. See his "Rate of Interest and the Optimum Propensity to Consume," *Economica*, V (1938), as reprinted in *Readings in Business Cycle Theory*, ed. G. Haberler (Philadelphia, 1944), p. 179, footnote 1.

The meaning of this phrase will be discussed in the next section.

producers *would like to buy at a given moment* in order to maintain their fixed and circulating capital at [a given interest] . . . rate. Then the quantity of money

$$H_a = \alpha + \beta p_b + \gamma p_c + \delta p_d + \cdots$$

would be the *encaisse désirée*.[18]

Finally, we point out that in the " Note sur la ' Théorie de la quantité' " appended to the revised version of the *Théorie de la monnaie*, Walras returns to the procedure of his original version and uses marginal-utility analysis to validate the quantity theory in the case of a money which is also a commodity.[19]

To summarize: In all his work before the fourth edition of the *Eléments*,[20] Walras merely posited his cash-balance equation on the basis of considerations which were extraneous to the main body of his argument. More specifically, in contrast with his analysis of every other good, Walras did not derive the demand function for money from utility maximization. Indeed, he made no use of marginal-utility analysis in his monetary theory except to deal with the case of a money which was also a commodity—and even here only *after* he had first posited the monetary equation. And in the second and third editions of the *Eléments* he did not even use it then.

2. THE CONCEPTUAL FRAMEWORK

Let us now see how all this was changed in the fourth edition. Here again Walras starts with the case of a fiat paper money. Now, however, for the first time, he analyzes the demand for such a money in terms of marginal utility. In particular, he speaks of the "service of storage" (*"service d'approvisionnement"*)[21] which is provided by this money; describes the utility of these services in terms of ordinary utility functions; and derives the cash-balance equation from the maximization of these functions subject to the budget restraint.[22] This was the newly achieved integration of monetary theory and value theory which Walras acclaimed with such evident satisfaction in his Preface to this edition.[23]

Deferring the details of this derivation to the next section, let us first

---

18 *Etudes d'économie politique appliquée*, pp. 94–95, italics added. Cf. also p. 154, line 5.

19 *Ibid.*, pp. 153–58. This "Note" was definitely written between 1896 and 1898; see the reference to the former date in its first paragraph.

20 Except, of course, for the memoir of 1899 referred to in footnote 1, p. 386 above.

21 As noted above, this is Lange's translation ("Optimum Propensity to Consume," *op. cit.*, p. 179, footnote 1).

22 I was quite rightly taken to task a few years ago by W. Jaffé for carelessly failing to see this in one of my earlier articles on this question. See his discussion in *Econometrica*, XIX (1951), 327.

23 See the passages cited on pp. 386–87 above.

examine the crucial phrase "*service d'approvisionnement.*" What Walras seems to have had in mind—though we cannot be sure—is the following: The theories of exchange, production, and capital formation —Parts II–V of the *Elements*—are based on the provisional assumption that the economy is one of barter. Accordingly, its prices are all expressed in terms of one of the commodities, arbitrarily selected as the *numéraire*.[24] The equilibrium prices of this economy are then determined at the beginning of the period through a *tâtonnement* which makes use of tickets to enable recontract.[25] The production of the period is then carried out in accordance with these prices. At the end of the period entrepreneurs use the resulting produce to pay landowners, workers, and capitalists for the productive services they provided during the period. By the assumption of equilibrium, the total value of what entrepreneurs must pay is equal, and just equal, to the total value of what they have produced.

In Part VI of the *Elements* Walras drops the assumption that consumers—who are, of course, the sellers of productive services—must wait until the end of the production period to acquire commodities. Instead, once the *tâtonnement* is completed, he requires the sale of commodities to begin immediately. And this is what creates the need for consumers and producers to hold at the beginning of the period inventories of raw materials, finished commodities—and money. In Walras' own words:

> Once equilibrium has been achieved in principle, upon completion of the preliminary *tâtonnement* by means of tickets, the actual transfer of services will begin immediately and will continue *in a given manner* during the whole period of time considered. The payment for these services, evaluated in *numéraire*, will be made in money *at fixed dates*. The delivery of the products will also begin immediately and will continue *in a given manner* during the same period. And the payments for these products, evaluated in *numéraire*, will also be made in money *at fixed dates*. It is readily seen that the introduction of these conditions makes it necessary, first, so far as consumers are concerned, that they have on hand a fund of circulating or working capital consisting of: (1) certain quantities of final products . . .; and (2) a certain quantity of cash on hand. . . .
>
> In a real operating economy, every consumer, whether landowner, labourer, or capitalist, has at every moment a fairly exact idea of: (1) what stocks of [final] products he ought to have for his convenience and (2) what cash balances he ought to have . . . in order to replenish these stocks and make current purchases of consumers' goods and services for daily consumption while waiting to receive rents, wages, and interest payable *at fixed future dates.* . . . There may be a small element of uncertainty

---

24 The reader is reminded here of Marget's conclusive demonstration that Walras' "*numéraire*" is a concrete commodity and *not* an abstract unit of account ["Monetary Aspects of the Walrasian System," *Journal of Political Economy*, XLIII (1935), 172–79].

25 Cf. Note B above, pp. 378–79 in particular.

which is due solely to the difficulty of foreseeing possible changes in the data of the problem.   If, however, we suppose these data constant for a given period of time and if we suppose the prices of goods and services and also the dates of their purchase and sale to be known for the whole period, *there will be no occasion for uncertainty.*[26]

We note first that Walras has not really succeeded in providing a rationale for the holding of money.   For, as the italicized phrases of the preceding passage show, the individuals of his economy know with certainty the exact amounts they must make and receive in payments, and the exact dates on which these payments must take place.   Hence there is no reason why they should hold sterile cash balances during the intervening dates when they can instead hold interest-yielding assets. This, of course, is Hicks' well-known criticism of Walras.[27]   But, as the argument of Chapter VII above shows, it is not at all a vital one. In particular, the deficiency which Hicks emphasizes can be remedied— without calling for a change in any other part of Walras' logical struc- ture—by simply dropping the assumption that the dates of payment are fixed and certain.[28]

What is, however, of far greater significance is the clear evidence of the preceding passages that Walras was *not* an exponent of the cash- balance approach to monetary theory in the accepted sense of the term. For the essence of this approach is that the individual chooses to hold money as a *reserve* against possible discrepancies between payments and receipts, and against all sorts of other contingencies.[29]   For Walras, however, the individual holds money, not out of choice, but out of

---

[26] *Elements*, ed. Jaffé, pp. 316–17, with a few minor modifications and italics added.   Cf. also *ibid.*, p. 242.

The foregoing interpretation of these paragraphs follows Schumpeter, *op. cit.*, p. 1021.   It is also supported by A. Aupetit's exposition of Walras' monetary theory in his *Essai sur la théorie générale de la monnaie* (Paris, 1901), pp. 121–26.

[27] "Gleichgewicht und Konjunctur," *Zeitschrift für Nationalökonomie*, IV (1933), 446–48. Cf. also R. E. Kuenne, "Walras, Leontief, and the Interdependence of Economic Activities," *Quarterly Journal of Economics*, LXVIII (1954), 327–29.

[28] Marget answers Hicks' criticism by saying that "even in a world in which everything were perfectly foreseen, a lack of synchronization between the receipt of income and its outlay would give rise to a need for cash-balances so long as there are not perfect facilities for the borrowing of money in anticipation of receipts and the investment of money during the period elapsing between receipt and outlay" ("Monetary Aspects of the Walrasian System," *op. cit.*, pp. 160–61).

I have not followed Marget's approach here because "imperfect facilities" cannot be introduced into Walras' theory of money without *ipso facto* introducing them into his theory of capital formation; and this cannot be done without requiring changes in the latter theory. The device of Chapter VII, on the other hand, need not in any way affect the other parts of Walras' theory.

Cf. also Kuenne, *op. cit.*, pp. 329, 332.

[29] Cf., e.g., the references to Marshall, Pigou, Lavington, Robertson, and Mises in Note D below, and to Wicksell in Note E:1.

necessity: he plans to buy a given quantity of goods; for some reason, though, he cannot buy it now but only at a fixed date in the future; consequently, he is compelled by the force of circumstances to hold his money in "storage" until then.   At no point in the protracted development of his theory of the *encaisse désirée*—not in its first formulation in the *Théorie de la monnaie* in 1886, nor in its revision in the *Etudes d'économie politique appliquée* in 1898, nor in its definitive statement in the *Eléments* of 1900—does Walras even hint that he is thinking in terms of a monetary reserve.[30]   Thus, although Walras must definitely be credited with having presented a cash-balance *equation*, he cannot be credited with having presented a cash-balance *theory*.[31]

An immediate corollary of the two preceding paragraphs is the conclusion that Walras does not succeed in providing a conceptual framework which logically entitles him to introduce the *service d'approvisionnement* of money into the utility function.   Or, to put it the other way around, the conceptual framework which Walras does provide can actually explain the holding of money without such a procedure—just as the conceptual framework of Chapter VI above explains the holding of bonds without introducing them into the utility function.   In both cases the very structure of the economy makes the individual willing to maintain these holdings even though he derives no utility from them as such.   For in both cases these holdings are necessary if the individual is to acquire an optimum collection of commodities.[32]

In sum, Walras was so desirous of impressing his monetary theory into the formal apparatus of utility analysis that he paid insufficient attention to the details necessary to make this apparatus economically meaningful.   This impression can only be strengthened by his even more mechanical application of this apparatus to the theory of saving. Here, as in the case of money, Walras announced in the Preface to the fourth edition of the *Eléments* that he would no longer simply posit behavior functions "empirically," but would instead derive them "rationally" from utility analysis.   But he then proceeded to do this by

---

[30] See the phrases italicized in the preceding passage and in the passage from *Etudes d'économie politique appliquée* cited on pp. 389–90.

This is the reason I find Lange's rendition of "*service d'approvisionnement*" as "service of storage" preferable to Jaffé's rendition as "service of availability" (*Elements*, p. 315).   The latter carries with it too much of a connotation of "available as a reserve."

[31] This would seem to disagree with Marget's interpretation in his "Léon Walras and the 'Cash-Balance Approach' to the Problem of the Value of Money," *op. cit.*   Note, however, that Marget does not discuss the question just emphasized in the text and concentrates primarily on the cash-balance equation as such.   On the nature of this equation, see the passages from the *Théorie de la monnaie* cited in the preceding section.

[32] Cf. the first paragraph of Chapter VI:3, and Mathematical Appendix 5:*e*.   Cf. also Kuenne, *op. cit.*, p. 332, who makes much the same criticism of Walras.

defining a new good, the perpetuity; mechanically inserting this good into the utility function; and then maximizing the resulting function subject to the budget restraint. Once again there is not even an attempt to explain the economic meaning of such a utility function.[33, 34]

3. THE UTILITY ANALYSIS

Leaving these problems behind, let us—for the sake of argument—accept Walras' insertion of the *service d'approvisionnement* into the utility function and see how his analysis proceeds from that point on. Let us also adapt this analysis to the case of an exchange economy. This does not affect the essentials of Walras' argument, yet does enable us to examine its validity under simplified circumstances. Clearly, whatever analytical difficulties we shall uncover under these circumstances will exist *a fortiori* in the more complicated ones actually considered by Walras.

Walras' point of departure is that an individual's demand for cash balances is a special case of his demand to hold inventories of goods, and that the *services d'approvisionnement* of these inventories are related to the goods themselves just as productive services are related to the capital goods which generate them. That is, inventories are circulating capital, to be analyzed in a manner completely analogous to that used for fixed capital. Hence if (A), (B), (C), ... are commodities and 1, p_b, p_c, ... their prices in terms of the *numéraire* (A), and if (A'), (B'), (C'), ... are

---

[33] Clearly, it is possible to provide such an explanation. Thus, for example, perpetuities might be taken as representing the future commodities for which they can be exchanged [cf. Jaffé's "Léon Walras' Theory of Capital Accumulation," *Studies in Mathematical Economics and Econometrics* (Chicago, 1942), p. 44]. Indeed, in the second and third editions of *Eléments* (p. 271) Walras does say that in order to derive the savings function mathematically, it is necessary "to distinguish between *present* utility and *future* utility"; but this sentence disappears in the fourth edition. Jaffé tries to rationalize this by arguing that since Walras' theoretical structure is "a cross-section in time of the processes involving exchange, production, capital accumulation, and circulating media, it would have been irrelevant for Walras to include any function of a lapse of time explicitly" ("Léon Walras' Theory of Capital Accumulation," *op. cit.*, p. 43). But all this is irrelevant to our main point that in the fourth edition Walras does not feel it necessary to offer *any* economic explanation of his utility function and proceeds in a completely mechanical way.

Cf. *Elements*, ed. Jaffé, p. 45, footnote 2, and p. 275. Jaffé quotes the relevant passages from the second and third editions, *ibid.*, p. 587, and also cites some interesting correspondence on this point between Walras, on the one hand, and Bortkiewicz and Böhm-Bawerk, on the other.

[34] The deficiency in Walras' conceptual framework set forth in this section makes clear the dangers of relating Walras' H_α to the Cambridge K. In particular, it calls for a reëxamination of Marget's view that Walras' *encaisse désirée* H_α indicates a full appreciation on his part of the problem of the velocity of circulation. ("Léon Walras . . . ," *op. cit.*, pp. 590 ff.)

these same commodities considered as circulating capital rendering a *service d'approvisionnement* "in the larders and cupboards of consumers," then the prices of these services are $p_{a'} = i$, $p_{b'} = p_b i$, $p_{c'} = p_c i$, ... (where i is the rate of interest) just as the net prices of ordinary productive services are equal to the value of the capital good rendering this service multiplied by the rate of interest.[35] Similarly, (U) is fiat paper money "having a price of its own [in terms of (A)] p_u, and a price for its *service d'approvisionnement* $p_{u'} = p_u i$."[36] Finally, there are the perpetuities (E), whose price in terms of (A) is $p_e = 1/i$. Walras also makes use of the symbol (E'), but does *not* define $p_{e'}$, which, by analogy, should equal $p_e i = 1$.

For simplicity we shall omit Walras' analysis of the demand for (A'), (B'), ... and concentrate exclusively on his analysis of the demand for (U). Consider, then, an individual with certain initial endowments of goods, and, in particular, with the initial endowment of money q_u. Let his excess demands for the goods (A), (B), ... , (E) be represented by d_a, d_b, ... , d_e, respectively; and his excess supplies of productive services by o_l, o_p, o_k, ... The respective prices of these services are p_l, p_p, p_k, ... The individual's budget restraint is then

(1) $\quad o_l p_l + o_p p_p + o_k p_k + \cdots + o_u p_{u'} = d_a + d_b p_b + \cdots + d_e p_e,$

where the left-hand side gives us the income of the individual, and the right-hand side his expenditure.[37]

The individual's optimum values for o_l, o_p, o_k, ... , d_a, d_b, ... , d_e are assumed to be determined as in the earlier chapters on the theory of exchange, production, and capitalization. Walras turns, then, to the remaining variable, o_u, and states:

Finally, as regards money, let $r = \phi_\alpha(q)$, $r = \phi_\beta(q)$, ... , $r = \phi_\epsilon(q)$ be our individual's utility or want equations for the *services d'approvisionnement* of products (A'), (B'), ... and perpetual net income (E'), not *in kind*, but *in money*. The quantities α, β, ... , ϵ, positive or negative, of these services which he desires at the

---

[35] *Elements*, ed. Jaffé, p. 319. This should be read against the background of *ibid.*, pp. 267–72. See also pp. 42–43.

[36] *Ibid.*, p. 320. This distinction between the two prices of money is another point on which I erred grievously some years ago, and for which I was rightly criticized by Jaffé. Cf. above, p. 390, footnote 22.

It should be clear that p_u is analogous to the reciprocal of the absolute price level.

[37] This is the first equation on p. 320 of the *Elements* (ed. Jaffé) with the terms representing circulating capital other than money omitted for simplicity. The term $o_u p_{u'}$ will be explained below.

This, and what follows, must be read against the background of Walras' earlier argument on pp. 237 ff., 274 ff., and 278 ff. of the *Elements*.

prices $p_{a'}$, $p_{b'}$, ... will be determined at one and the same time by the budget restraint and by the following equations of maximum satisfaction:

$$\phi_\alpha(\alpha) = p_{a'}\phi_a(d_a),$$
(2) $$\phi_\beta(\beta) = p_{b'}\phi_a(d_a),$$
$$\cdots\cdots\cdots\cdots\cdots$$
$$\phi_\epsilon(\epsilon) = p_{a'}\phi_a(d_a),$$

from which we obtain first, the quantities desired of the services (A'), (B'), ..., (E') [in the form of money][38]

$$\alpha = f_\alpha(p_t,\, p_p,\, p_k \cdots p_b,\, p_c,\, p_d \cdots p_{a'},\, p_{b'} \cdots p_{u'},\, p_e),$$
(3) $$\beta = f_\beta(p_t,\, p_p,\, p_k \cdots p_b,\, p_c,\, p_d \cdots p_{a'},\, p_{b'} \cdots p_{u'},\, p_e),$$
$$\cdots\cdots\cdots\cdots\cdots\cdots\cdots\cdots\cdots\cdots\cdots\cdots$$
$$\epsilon = f_\epsilon(p_t,\, p_p,\, p_k \cdots p_b,\, p_c,\, p_d \cdots p_{a'},\, p_{b'} \cdots p_{u'},\, p_e),$$

secondly, the value of these quantities expressed in terms of *numéraire*

(4) $$\alpha p_{a'} + \beta p_{b'} + \cdots + \epsilon p_{a'},$$

and finally the quantity of money effectively offered

(5) $$o_u = q_u - \frac{\alpha p_{a'} + \beta p_{b'} + \cdots + \epsilon p_{a'}}{p_{u'}}.$$

In a similar manner we could derive the quantities effectively offered by the other individuals and, consequently, the total effective offer of money

(6) $$O_u = Q_u - \frac{d_\alpha\, p_{a'} + d_\beta p_{b'} + \cdots + d_\epsilon p_{a'}}{p_{u'}}$$

[where O_u, Q_u, d_α, d_β, ..., d_ϵ are the respective aggregates over all individuals of o_u, q_u, α, β, ..., ϵ].

The value of all or part of the final products and perpetual net income *which individuals wish to purchase*, and which they desire to keep in their possession in the form of money [earmarked] for transactions or investment [purposes],[39] constitutes their *encaisse désirée*.[40]

---

[38] The argument $p_{m'}$ related to circulating capital has been omitted from the following equations. See the preceding footnote.

[39] "*Monnaie de circulation ou d'épargne.*" I have followed Schumpeter's translation (*op. cit.*, p. 1000, footnote 5, and p. 1023, lines 6–8). Jaffé renders this expression as "cash or money savings."

[40] *Elements*, ed. Jaffé, pp. 320–21, with equation numbers and last set of italics added, and with the change in translation noted in the preceding footnote. I have also added all the bracketed expressions except the first, which is Jaffé's.

In the original version of this passage in the memoir on "Equations de la circulation" (*op. cit.*, pp. 90–91), Walras does not mention (E') and ϵ in the first paragraph, omits accordingly the last equations of (2) and (3) and the last term of (4), but nevertheless writes (5) and (6) in the form presented here, with the following additional explanation:

[In equations (5) and (6)] $\epsilon p_{a'}$ and $d_\epsilon p_{a'}$ are the value in *numéraire* of the service of the money [earmarked] *for investment* [*purposes*] [*épargne*], individual or total, just as $\alpha p_{a'} + \beta p_{b'} + \cdots$ and $d_\alpha p_{a'} + d_\beta p_{b'} + \cdots$ are the value in *numéraire* of the service of the money [earmarked] *for transactions* [*purposes*], individual or total, and $\dfrac{\epsilon p_{a'}}{p_{u'}}$ and

The phrase *"which individuals wish to purchase"*—which should be read together with the corresponding phrases of the revised *Théorie de la monnaie*[41]—reminds us that Walras conceives of the demand for money as being broken up into a differentiated mass whose component parts are conceptually earmarked for the respective quantities of commodities which the individual plans to buy.[42] Accordingly, Walras represents the utility of the *service d'approvisionnement* of money, not by a single function, but by a sequence of functions of these respective quantities. Note that in this way he also effectively expresses utility as a function of

---

$\dfrac{d_\epsilon p_{a'}}{p_{u'}}$ are the equivalents in money (U) of the quantities ϵ and d_ϵ of *numéraire* (A), just as $\dfrac{\alpha p_{a'} + \beta p_{b'} + \cdots}{p_{u'}}$ and $\dfrac{d_\alpha p_{a'} + d_\beta p_{b'} + \cdots}{p_{u'}}$ are the equivalents in money (U) of the quantities $\alpha, \beta, \ldots$ and $d_\alpha, d_\beta, \ldots$ of $(A'), (B'), \ldots$. In effect, individuals wish to have in their possession the value of all or part of the new capital [goods that they want to buy], fixed or circulating, just like the value of all or part of the consumers' goods that they want to buy, the sum total constituting their *encaisse désirée*.

It might also be noted that in this memoir the last argument in the functions on the right-hand side of (3) is written as i, instead of its reciprocal, p_e, which appears here in the *Elements*.

41 Cf. above, pp. 389–90.

42 Note, however, a curious asymmetry in Walras' procedure. Whereas $\alpha, \beta, \ldots$ are conceived as quantities of $(A'), (B'), \ldots$, ϵ is conceived not as a quantity of (E'), but of (A). This is clear from the passage of "Equations de la circulation" cited in footnote 40. Walras may have adopted this asymmetry in order to achieve a symmetrical form for his equations (2) and (4)–(6); for if ϵ is a quantity of (E'), the last equation of (2) must be written as

$$\phi_\epsilon(\epsilon) = \phi_a(d_a),$$

the last term of (4) as $+ \epsilon$, and, accordingly, the last terms in the numerators of the fractions in (5) and (6) as $+ \epsilon$ and $+ d_\epsilon$, respectively. That is, in each case the factor $p_{a'}$ which Walras now uses must be replaced by $p_{e'} = p_e i = 1$. See also the two paragraphs which follow now in the text.

I must, however, admit that as a result of Professor Jaffé's criticisms (see above, p. 386, footnote 1), I am not as sure as I originally was that Walras is guilty here of an asymmetry. Basing his argument especially on pp. 289–90 of the *Elements*, Jaffé has—in a personal letter— emphasized that Walras considers perpetuities, (E), only as an "imaginary" analytical construct (*ibid.*, p. 274) without "real" existence in his system. Correspondingly, individuals are assumed to use their savings to buy capital goods directly, and not perpetuities. (This is also borne out by the end of the passage from "Equations de la circulation" cited in footnote 40 above.) Hence, Jaffé argues, "(E') cannot properly be conceived as a quantity of money held available for the eventual purchase of such securities. This money is held in lieu of and available for the eventual purchase of real capital goods only; and all we can say is that the purchase of such real capital goods is tantamount to, but does not consist in, the purchase of as many units of the *imaginary* commodity (E) as there are units of the *numéraire* (A) which the capital goods will yield net of depreciation, etc."

The reason that I am not fully satisfied with this explanation is that if (E) is "real" enough to be treated like any other commodity with respect to having its own marginal-utility function and appearing in the budget restraint (*ibid.*, pp. 274–75), why should it not also be "real" enough to be treated like any other commodity with respect to having its own conceptual *service d'approvisionnement*? Why does Walras draw the line where he does?

It is hard to see how this question can be definitively settled. Fortunately, it is not important for the problems which interest us in this study.

the *real*—as distinct from *nominal*—amount of money the individual holds. This is in keeping with his repeated emphasis that it is only with the former that the individual is concerned.[43]

Clearly, the whole purpose of Walras' rather complicated procedure is to reduce the problem of monetary theory to that of simply introducing into the ordinary theory of consumers' behavior some additional "commodities," (A'), (B'), ..., with their respective prices, $p_{a'}$, $p_{b'}$, ... Correspondingly, the optimum amounts of these "commodities" are determined by equations of exactly the same form as those presented for this theory in the earlier parts of the *Elements*. In particular, the "equations of maximum satisfaction" (2) show that the marginal utilities of the optimum quantities α, β, ...—like those of the optimum quantities of all other commodities—are proportionate to their respective prices, and that the factor of proportionality is the marginal utility of the *numéraire*, (A).[44]

In fact, it seems to me that had not Walras adhered so unswervingly to the exact equational forms of his earlier exposition, he could have presented the optimum conditions of his monetary theory in a more persuasive and meaningful way. Specifically, let us rewrite (2) as

$$(7) \qquad \phi_\alpha(\alpha) = \frac{\phi_\beta(\beta)}{p_b} = \frac{\phi_\gamma(\gamma)}{p_c} = \cdots = i\phi_a(d_a).$$

Since all prices are in terms of (A), the reciprocal of p_b is the number of units of (B) that can be obtained for one unit of (A). The preceding equations thus state that a necessary condition for the maximization of utility is that the marginal utility of one unit of real balances held for purchasing power over (A) *equal* the marginal utility of one unit of real balances held for purchasing power over (B), etc., *equal* the common term $i\phi_a(d_a)$. Considering, first, all but the last of these equations, we see that, in the individual's optimum position, we can disregard all conceptual earmarkings and speak unambiguously of *the* marginal utility of real money balances. If we now note that $\phi_a(d_a)$ can be regarded as the marginal utility of one unit-of-(A)'s worth of expenditure, we then see that the last of equations (7) reduces to the simple statement that, in the individual's optimum position, the marginal utility of one unit-of-(A)'s worth of real balances must equal the marginal utility of i units-of-(A)'s worth of expenditure.[45] In this way Walras could

---

[43] See the passages from the first and second editions of the *Théorie de la monnaie* cited on pp. 387–88 and 389–90 above.

[44] More generally, compare equations (1)–(3) here with the corresponding equations on p. 165, or pp. 238–39, or pp. 278–79 of the *Elements*.

[45] Note that, except for its neglect of the time element, this is identical with equation (7) above, p. 75.

have rigorously and precisely derived the general relationship between the demand for money and the rate of interest which he had emphasized in the second and third editions of the *Eléments* and in the revised version of the *Théorie de la monnaie*.[46]

Indeed, it is possible that Walras' failure to emphasize this relationship in the definitive edition of the *Elements*—it is adverted to only once, and even then not in his discussion of monetary theory proper[47] —may be connected with his failure to present his "equations of maximum satisfaction" in the form (7). On the other hand, Walras may have considered this relationship to be already expressed in his definition of the price of the *service d'approvisionnement* of money as $p_{u'} = p_u i$, and in his observation that, for money also the *numéraire*, this reduces to $p_{u'} = i$.[48]

Be that as it may, we note now that by dividing Walras' equation (4) through by i we obtain

$$(8) \qquad\qquad \alpha + \beta p_b + \cdots + \epsilon.$$

This measures the total demand for real money balances in terms of the *numéraire* (A). Clearly, function (8) is the same cash-balance function which Walras first posited in his *Théorie de la monnaie* and then repeated in earlier editions of the *Eléments*.[49] And so Walras makes good his claim to have succeeded in deriving this function from the same utility analysis that he applies to all other problems in the theory of consumers' behavior.[50]

The real demand, (8), can be transformed into the nominal demand for units of paper money by dividing through by p_u—which is analogous, in the more familiar version of the cash-balance equation, to multiplying KT by the absolute price level, P. This is essentially what Walras does in his equation (5).[51] In particular, substituting $p_a i = p_{a'}, p_b i = p_{b'}, \ldots, p_u i = p_{u'}$, this reduces to

$$(9) \qquad\qquad o_u = q_u - \frac{\alpha + \beta p_b + \cdots + \epsilon}{p_u}.$$

That is, o_u is the difference between the initial and optimum values of nominal money holdings. From the budget restraint (1) we can then

---

[46] Cf. the passages cited on pp. 389–90 above.

[47] *Elements*, ed. Jaffé, p. 242, lines 7 to 5 from bottom.

[48] *Ibid.*, p. 320 (top).

[49] Cf. pp. 388 and 390 above.

[50] Cf. the passages from the Preface to the fourth edition of the *Elements* cited on p. 387 above.

[51] That this is his intention is even clearer from the passage in "Equations de la circulation" cited on p. 396, footnote 40, above.

infer that Walras conceives this difference as being invested in new capital goods to provide a yield equal to the rate of interest i, and, therefore, as contributing (in terms of *numéraire*) $o_u p_{u'}$ to the individual's income.[52]

Walras concludes this phase of his analysis by deriving from (6) the market excess-supply equation for money

$$(10) \qquad Q_u - \frac{d_\alpha p_{a'} + d_\beta p_{b'} + \cdots + d_\epsilon p_{a'}}{p_{u'}} = 0,$$

and demonstrating that the introduction of money into his model has not affected the equality between the number of equations and variables. Hence the problem is mathematically determinate.[53]

4. The *Tâtonnement*

"Our next step is to pass from the theoretical solution which was formulated mathematically to the practical solution which is reached in the market."[54] With this standard formula[55] Walras opens his

---

[52] This is also the way I understand the terms in the budget restraint on p. 320 of the *Elements* which deal with circulating capital. These terms—which have for simplicity been omitted from our discussion (above, p. 395, footnote 37)—are $o_{a'} p_{a'} + o_{b'} p_{b'} + \cdots + q_m p_{m'}$. They would seem to represent the interest (in terms of *numéraire*) that can be earned by investing the value of the excess circulating capital $o_{a'}, o_{b'}, \ldots$ in new capital goods.

The sentence in the text to which this footnote is attached has also been changed as a result of the criticism by Professor Jaffé already noted above (p. 397, footnote 42). In its original version this sentence assumed the entire excess supply of money, o_u, to be invested—in Keynesian-like fashion—in the purchase of perpetuities. I am indebted to Jaffé for bringing this misinterpretation to my attention.

Professor Jaffé informs me that he would now prefer to omit all mention of "securities" in his note 7 on pp. 542–43 of the *Elements*. Similarly, in the next to the last line of that note, he would now prefer to consider the source of the net income to be "new capital goods," and not "loans."

At the same time, I am unable to accept Jaffé's interpretation of $o_{b'} p_{b'}$ and, by implication, $o_u p_{u'}$, as given in his note 7; for Jaffé treats this as an income item even when this excess supply is used to acquire consumption goods.

It might also be pointed out that equations (8) and (9) in the text here are presented in Jaffé's (*ibid.*, pp. 543–44) and Kuenne's (*op. cit.*, p. 335) interpretations of Walras' monetary theory as well.

[53] *Elements*, pp. 323–24.

The reader should recall that we are adapting Walras' analysis to an exchange economy. The foregoing equation is accordingly obtained from Walras' equation (10) (*ibid.*, p. 323) by setting the left-hand side identically equal to zero, and by substituting into the right-hand side from Walras' equation (9) on p. 321.

Clearly, just as equation (5) can be transformed into (9), so equation (10) can be transformed into

$$Q_u - \frac{d_\alpha p_a + d_\beta p_b + \cdots + d_\epsilon p_a}{p_u} = 0.$$

[54] *Ibid.*, p. 325.

[55] See the beginning of Note B above.

discussion of the *tâtonnement* by which an economy with paper money reaches the equilibrium solution of its system of market excess-demand equations—among which now appears (10). This is for us the most crucial—and, at the same time, most obscure—part of Walras' monetary theory.

Walras conducts this whole discussion against the explicit background of the detailed description of the *tâtonnement* presented in his earlier chapter on production and capital formation. He shows how, except for equation (10) above, all of the new equations introduced by his theory of circulation and money can be fitted into the various subsets of this earlier system of equations and solved together with them. In Walras' own words:

Only . . . equation (10) expressing the equality between the demand and offer of (U) remain[s] outside [this solution].[56] Consequently, if a price $p'_{u'}$ is cried at random and is held fixed during the process of *tâtonnement* in production and capital formation, we come to the last equation from which the equality between the price of the *numéraire* and unity is deduced at the same time as the equality between the demand and offer of the *numéraire*,[57] so that there remains only to solve . . . [equation (10) above].[58] If we set[59]

(11) $$d_\alpha p_{a'} + d_\beta p_{b'} + \cdots + d_\epsilon p_{a'} = H_\alpha,$$

then [equation (10)][60] becomes

(12) $$Q_u = \frac{H_\alpha}{p_{u'}}.$$

. . . if perchance

(13) $$Q_u p'_{u'} = H_\alpha,$$

the question [of the *tâtonnement*][60] would be completely settled. Generally, however, we find that

(14) $$Q_u p'_{u'} \gtrless H_\alpha,$$

and the problem is to determine how equality between the demand and offer of money is reached by a *tâtonnement* [involving an adjustment][60] in $p'_{u'}$.

On referring back to the various terms that enter into the composition of H_α, we perceive that they are not absolutely independent of $p_{u'}$, in view of the fact that $p_{u'}$ figures in the term $o_u p_{u'}$ of the budget restraint [(1)][60] which, together with the equations of maximum satisfaction [(2)],[60] enables us to deduce the quantities α,

---

56 Jaffé's brackets.
57 This is essentially a statement of Walras' Law; the full meaning of this passage can be grasped only by reading it against the background of p. 294 of the *Elements*, section 259.
    The reader must also remember that the *numéraire* referred to here is commodity (*A*), and *not* paper money (*U*).
58 My own brackets.
59 Once again, I am modifying this passage in a nonessential way in order to adapt it to an exchange economy.
60 My own brackets.
    The reader will recall that $p_{u'}$ is the value of $p_{u'}$ arbitrarily chosen at the beginning of this passage and held fixed until now.

$\beta, \ldots, \epsilon$ for any one individual, and, consequently, the aggregate quantities d_α, $d_\beta, \ldots, d_\epsilon$ for all individuals together; but [we perceive][60] that, nevertheless, they do not depend upon it $[p_{u'}]$ except very indirectly and very weakly.[61] That being the case, the equation of monetary circulation, when money is not a commodity, comes very close, in reality, to falling outside the system of equations of [general][62] economic equilibrium. If we first suppose [general][62] economic equilibrium to be established, then the equation of monetary circulation would be solved almost without any *tâtonnement*, simply by raising or lowering $p_{u'}$ according as[63] $Q_u \gtrless \dfrac{H_\alpha}{p'_{u'}}$ at the price $p'_{u'}$ which had been cried at random. If, however,[64] this increase or decrease in $p_{u'}$ were to change H_α ever so slightly, it would only be necessary to continue the general process of *tâtonnement* in order to be sure of reaching equilibrium. This is what actually takes place in the money market.

Thus: *The price of the service of money is established through its rise or fall according as the* encaisse désirée *is greater or less than the quantity of money*.

There is, then, an equilibrium price $p_{u'}$; and if i is the equilibrium rate of net income, the unit quantity of money will be worth $p_u = \dfrac{p_{u'}}{i} \ldots$. Setting $H_\alpha = H_\alpha i$, we have

$$(15) \qquad\qquad\qquad\qquad Q_u = \frac{H_\alpha}{p_u}.[65]$$

This is the sum total of Walras' discussion of the *tâtonnement* by which the level of $p_{u'}$, and hence p_u, is determined. It shows that Walras

---

61 This clause—which, as we shall see below, is crucial for a proper interpretation of Walras —appears in the original as "*mais que, toutefois, ils n'en dépendent que très indirectement et très faiblement.*" Jaffé renders this as a separate sentence which reads: "We must admit, however, that the dependence of these items on $p_{u'}$ is very indirect and very weak." This creates the misleading impression that Walras regards a "*strong* dependence" on $p_{u'}$ as the most favorable circumstance for the establishment of his theory, and that, therefore, a "*weak* dependence" is something that has to be somewhat grudgingly "admitted"—whereas, in point of fact, as the continuation of the passage shows, Walras regards this "weak dependence" as a most useful circumstance that enables him to simplify his analysis greatly. Indeed, he is happiest when he can assume that this dependence does not exist at all.

62 Jaffé's brackets.

63 Walras' inequality signs here should be reversed; for, say, an excess supply of money causes both bond and commodity prices in terms of (U) to rise, hence i and p_u to fall, and hence $p_{u'} = p_u i$ to fall *a fortiori*. (That Walras reads "$\gtrless$" as "greater than or less than" —and not "less than or greater than"—can be seen from p. 172, line 7, and p. 245, lines 6–8—and the corresponding passages in the original.)

64 As I understand it, in the preceding sentence Walras describes the *tâtonnement* as it would take place if H_α were completely independent of $p_{u'}$; whereas in the present sentence he relaxes this assumption to permit some degree of dependence.

65 *Elements*, ed. Jaffé, pp. 325–27, with some minor changes to make the terminology of this translation consistent with that used elsewhere in this book—and with the major change in translation described in footnote 61. The equation numbers have again been added for convenience of reference. Italics in original.

It might be noted that Walras does not then deduce the quantity theory directly from equation (15)—as in the second and third editions of the *Eléments*—but reverts to the practice of his *Théorie de la monnaie* and deduces it from the application of a type of marginal-utility analysis to (15). (Cf. pp. 389–90 above and *Elements*, pp. 327–29.)

I do not understand the reason for Walras' reversion; nor do I fully understand the analysis itself. But it would take us too far from our main interests to pursue this question in detail.

is quite willing to assume that, with $p_{u'}$ arbitrarily fixed at the level $p'_{u'}$, a *tâtonnement* in the commodity markets first achieves equilibrium there; that, once this is accomplished, a *tâtonnement* in the money market then determines the equilibrium level of $p_{u'}$; *and that this latter* tâtonnement *can be carried out without reacting back and disturbing the equilibrium initially achieved in the commodity markets.* It fails to indicate any realization on the part of Walras that such a dichotomization of the pricing process contradicts the very conditions necessary for the existence of a monetary economy.

More specifically, assume that the economy as a whole is in equilibrium at a certain level of money prices. Let there now be an arbitrary change in $p_{u'}$, and let us assume that this does not react back on the commodity markets. Then these markets are still in equilibrium. Hence, by Walras' Law, so is the money market. Thus no market forces are created anywhere in the system to force $p_{u'}$ back to its original level. It follows that the equilibrium level of $p_{u'}$ is indeterminate. By the last paragraph of the passage just cited above, so, then, is the level of p_u. Thus if Walras' assumptions are carried to their extreme—and he certainly shows no objection in principle to having this done—they imply the indeterminacy of money prices, and hence the impossibility of all monetary theory.[66]

This basic inconsistency is itself the product of minor ones. Thus the crucial—though tacit—assumption of the third paragraph of the preceding passage is that the insensitivity of H_α to changes in $p_{u'}$ implies a corresponding absence of repercussions elsewhere in the system. But this cannot be true. In particular, substituting equation (11) into (6), we obtain

$$(16) \qquad\qquad O_u = Q_u - \frac{H_\alpha}{p_{u'}}.$$

---

[66] On this and the preceding paragraph, see pp. 111–12 and 108–9 above, respectively.

The statement in the preceding passage most revealing of Walras' state of mind is the one which reads: "... the equation of monetary circulation, when money is not a commodity, comes very close, in reality, to falling outside the system of equations of [general] economic equilibrium." I first cited this statement as evidence that Walras had dichotomized the pricing process invalidly in my "Indeterminacy of Absolute Prices in Classical Economic Theory," *Econometrica*, XVII (1949), 12. Unfortunately, I obscured the issue by confusing $p_{u'}$ and p_u (cf. above, p. 395, footnote 36). At the same time, however, the exclusive concentration of my critics—and Walras' defenders—on this confusion has prevented them from seeing the real issue involved. Accordingly, their argument does not meet the criticism of Walras just explained in the text. Cf. Jaffé, *Elements*, p. 547, and Kuenne, *op. cit.*, p. 330.

Schumpeter, on the other hand, attempts to explain away Walras' foregoing statement as "an approximation to which the standards of rigorous analysis do not apply," made for the purpose of achieving "a simple form of the 'quantity theory'" (*op. cit.*, p. 1025). But this would seem to indicate that Schumpeter himself did not realize that, as just shown in the text, this "approximation" implies a denial of all monetary theory, and of the quantity theory in particular.

Clearly, the invariance of H_α with respect to changes in $p_{u'}$ does *not* imply any corresponding invariance of $O_u p_{u'}$. Hence a change in $p_{u'}$ will affect this term in budget restraint (1)—aggregated over all individuals—and thereby the state of demand in all markets of the economy.

There is, furthermore, a striking contrast between Walras' discussion of the *tâtonnement* here and in all preceding cases. In particular, his usual detailed and extended examination of the workings of the *tâtonnement* is significantly absent. Thus nowhere in the preceding passage does Walras describe the specific market mechanism through which any discrepancy between the supply and demand for money generates self-eliminating variations in $p_{u'}$. All he has to say on this crucial question is summed up in the noncommittal formula that "the equation of monetary circulation would be solved . . . simply by raising or lowering $p_{u'}$ according as $Q_u \gtrless H_\alpha/p'_{u'}$ at the price $p'_{u'}$ which has been cried out at random."[67]

Similarly, though Walras normally uses the device of arbitrarily holding one variable constant while completing a *tâtonnement* on the others, and then releasing the variable in question and completing a *tâtonnement* upon it, he always emphasizes that the variations generated by this second *tâtonnement* disturb the equilibrium initially achieved by the first one and require it to be recommenced; accordingly, he always proceeds next to describe in detail this recommenced *tâtonnement* and to prove that by continuing in this way the system will ultimately converge to its equilibrium position. Only in the preceding passage does he depart from this customary attempt at rigorous precision and rest with the vague, general assurance that if variations "in $p_{u'}$ were to change H_α ever so slightly, it would only be necessary to continue the general process of *tâtonnement* in order to be sure of reaching equilibrium."[68]

At first sight, it seems possible to mitigate the force of the immediately foregoing criticisms[69] by assuming that by variations in $p_{u'}$ Walras has in mind variations in i; and that, accordingly, he restricts himself in the preceding passage to a bare reference to the *tâtonnement* because he has already presented a detailed description of it in his theory of capital formation (Lesson 25). Support for this contention comes from the fact that in the second and third editions of the *Eléments*—which also deal

---

67 I have left the inequality signs uncorrected; cf. above, p. 402, footnote 63.

68 In order to appreciate the full force of the contrast drawn in the two preceding paragraphs, the reader must compare for himself the extended discussions of Lessons 21 and 25 with the cryptic generalities of the preceding passage. Cf. also Note B above.

Of course, as shown above (p. 380), Walras' general attempt to prove the convergence of the *tâtonnement* is invalid. But this is an irrelevant consideration here.

69 But not—it should be emphasized—that on the preceding page. This fundamental criticism of Walras is unaffected by the contention now to be presented.

with the case of a paper money[70]—Walras explicitly identifies "*le marché du capital monnaie et le marché de la monnaie*" and states that "it is thus natural that the price cried out [during the *tâtonnement*] on the market for money be the rate of interest on money-capital."[71] Additional support seems to come implicitly from a later discussion in the definitive edition of the *Elements* itself in which Walras deals with the case of a commodity-money—(*A*)—that is also *numéraire*. Since the price of (*A*) is thus by definition unity, the price of its *service d'approvisionnement* reduces to *i*. Correspondingly, Walras writes equation (12) above in the special form

$$(17) \qquad\qquad Q''_{a'} = \frac{H_\alpha}{i},$$

where $Q''_{a'}$ is the quantity of (*A*) used as money. If, now, there is an increase or decrease in $Q''_{a'}$,

---

[70] Cf. above, p. 388.

[71] *Eléments* (second and third editions), p. 381. Cf. the whole discussion there on pp. 379–83.

It should be emphasized—as Professor Jaffé has emphasized to me—that Walras is referring here to the market for *money-capital* (i.e., the market on which money is lent and borrowed for investment purposes) and *not* to the market for the sale and purchase of *capital goods*. But though conceptually distinct, these two markets are closely related in the Walrasian system: for the "rate of interest" determined in the former must always "tend to equality" with the uniform "rate of net income" determined in the latter. (This "rate of net income" is the ratio between the price of the service of a capital good—net of depreciation and insurance charges—and the price of the capital good itself; in equilibrium, this rate must obviously be the same for any capital good.) (*Ibid.*, p. 381; cf. also *ibid.*, pp. 288–89, and *Elements*, ed. Jaffé, pp. 268–69 and 289–90.)

At the same time, it should also be emphasized that—in sharp contrast to Wicksell and Keynes of the *Treatise*—Walras makes little, if any, analytical use of the distinction between these two markets—and these two rates. Indeed, in the second and third editions of the *Eléments* he makes it clear that the market for money-capital "is only of practical and not theoretical interest" and that, accordingly, the analysis can concentrate exclusively on the market for capital goods (p. 289); and in the definitive edition he refers to the market for money-capital as a "superfoetation in theory" (ed. Jaffé, p. 290). Similarly, he uses the same symbol "*i*" to refer now to the rate of net income (*ibid.*, throughout Lessons 24 and 25) and now to the rate of interest (*ibid.*, p. 333, in the passage cited immediately below; cf. also the substitution on the bottom of p. 332 and the reference to "interest charges" on the bottom of p. 242). Accordingly, I have sometimes used "*i*" in this double sense in the present discussion too.

I might finally add the opinion that Walras' whole attempt to identify the markets for money and money-capital in the second and third editions of the *Eléments* seems to be based on a serious confusion between the demand and supply for money *balances* and the demand and supply for money *loans*; or, in our terminology, on a confusion between the market for *money* and the market for *bonds*. Nor do I feel that there is an adequate analysis in these editions of the relationship between the *tâtonnement* on the rate of interest in the market for money-capital and the *tâtonnement* on the rate of net income in the market for capital goods. Similarly, the role of the absolute price level and the way in which the equilibrium value of this level is determined on the market are not at all clear in the second and third editions— and in the definitive one too, if by variations in $p_{u'}$ Walras means variations in *i*. All this requires much more discussion than can be undertaken here.

... the rate of interest i will fall or rise in the money market, with the result that consumers will increase or decrease their *encaisse désirée*, since this is made up of quantities d_α, d_β, ... of (A'), (B'), ... which are decreasing functions of $p_{a'} = i$, $p_{b'} = p_b i$, ... and consequently of i. But, so long as the quantity of products does not increase, these movements can only result in a rise or fall in the prices p_b, ...[72] Entrepreneurs, on seeing this rise or fall in the prices of their products, will want to expand or contract their output, all the more so because the fall or rise in the rate of interest constitutes an additional cause of profit or loss to them. In the end, however, all they will succeed in doing is to raise or lower the prices of the productive services the quantity of which has remained fixed [*ex hypothesi*]. This rise or this fall will induce capitalists having more or less savings at their disposal to increase or decrease their demand for new capital goods; but since the aggregate quantity of capital goods still remains constant, the prices of these goods will merely rise or fall. Once the rise or fall in prices has permeated the entire system, the rate of interest will return to what it was [before the change in Q''].[73]

As persuasive as it might at first seem, this contention cannot stand up to a critical examination. First of all, if $p_{u'}$ denotes i, why does Walras say in the third paragraph of the first passage above[74] that the dependence of α, β, ... on $p_{u'}$ results only from the term $o_u p_{u'}$ in the budget restraint? Do not equations (3) show us that, completely aside from this term, α, β, ... depend on p_e, which is the reciprocal of the rate of interest? Indeed, do not these equations in their original form depend explicitly on *both* $p_{u'}$ *and* i?[75] Secondly, the last paragraph cited in the first passage definitely gives the impression that i has been determined independently of the *tâtonnement* on $p_{u'}$, and that therefore, once the equilibrium level of the latter is determined, the equilibrium value of p_u can be determined by dividing $p_{u'}$ by i.[76] Thirdly,

---

[72] I do not understand Walras' reasoning here. True, an increase in the amount of money depresses interest, thereby stimulates demand for (B), ..., and thereby causes p_b, ... to rise. But does it do so *because* the decrease in i causes the *encaisse désirée* to increase, or *in spite* of this? Would not the upward pressure on p_b be greater, the smaller the tendency to divert the increased quantity of money into cash balances?

A similarly puzzling passage appears in the second and third editions of the *Eléments* (p. 383) where a rise in interest is presented as decreasing the *encaisse désirée* and *thereby* the money prices of goods.

[73] *Elements*, p. 333; Jaffé's brackets.

It might be noted that this description of the way in which the rate of interest ultimately returns to its original level is an improvement over the unsupported statement of the second and third editions of the *Eléments* (p. 383) that it will do so. But, as compared with the analyses of other writers, it still leaves much to be desired. Cf. Note J below.

[74] For convenience I shall refer to the passage from the *Elements* cited on pp. 401–2 above as "the first passage" and to that just cited as "the second passage."

[75] "Equations de la circulation," *op. cit.*, p. 90; cf. above, p. 396, footnote 40.

[76] This impression emerges even more strongly from the exposition of Aupetit—who wrote under the immediate impact of Walras, and who adheres with only minor variations to the latter's presentation. After developing an equation which corresponds to (13) above, Aupetit writes:

This equation, in which all terms but one are predetermined, determines $p_{u'}$—that is,

if $p_{u'}$ denotes i, how can we reconcile the crucial dependence of $d_\alpha, d_\beta, \ldots$ on i in the second passage with Walras' desire to assume in the first passage that "the aggregate quantities $d_\alpha, d_\beta, \ldots$ do not depend upon it $[p_{u'}]$ except very indirectly and very weakly"? Finally, if the first passage is also concerned with a *tâtonnement* on i, why is not the argument of the second passage introduced initially there? For, as Walras' own presentation in the second and third editions of the *Eléments* shows, this argument is not restricted to the case of commodity-money, but is also applicable to that of fiat paper money.[77, 78]

All these considerations lead to the conclusion that by "*tâtonnement* on $p_{u'}$" in the first passage above, Walras could not have meant "*tâtonnement* on i." Instead, either he conceived of the *tâtonnement* as taking place on $p_{u'}$ as a whole; or, what seems more likely, he conceived of the *tâtonnement* as taking place on p_u, the reciprocal of the absolute price level, and—since he assumed the rate of interest to be already determined in the capital market[79]—represented the movements of this variable by the directly proportionate $p_{u'}$. In either case, the money market introduces a new variable into the analysis which, in accordance with the general Walrasian scheme, must be accorded a separate *tâtonnement*. It is also clear that this variable influences α, $\beta, \ldots$ only through the term $o_u p_{u'}$ in the budget restraint. Finally, it is clear that the argument of the second passage deals with a problem that does not exist for Walras in the first one, and that he therefore has no reason to introduce this argument there. In particular, under the

---

the price of the service of money in terms of the *numéraire* [commodity (A)]. Knowing $p_{u'}$, we can then obtain the price of every commodity in terms of [paper money] (U) by multiplying their respective prices in (A) by the price of (A) in terms of (U), that is by $\dfrac{i}{p_{u'}}$ [to yield]

$$p_{a,u} = \frac{i}{p_{u'}}, \quad p_{b,u} = p_b \frac{i}{p_{u'}}, \quad p_{c,u} = p_c \frac{i}{p_{u'}}, \ldots.$$

From equation (13) and the preceding equations Aupetit then deduces the validity of the quantity theory of money. [*Essai sur la théorie générale de la monnaie* (Paris, 1901), p. 126 with notation changed to accord with Walras'.]

[77] Another point that might be mentioned here is that, for an exchange economy, the variable i does not appear explicitly in Walras' excess-demand equation for money; cf. p. 400, footnote 53, above. Note, however, that this is not so for the excess-demand equation which Walras actually analyzes on p. 326 of the *Elements*. Here, because of the assumption of a production economy, there is a term p_k which prevents all the i's from canceling out. For this reason I do not think that this point is relevant to the present discussion.

[78] The outstanding interpreter of the first passage as dealing with a *tâtonnement* on i is Schumpeter (*op. cit.*, p. 1024), who has been followed on this by Kuenne (*op. cit.*, p. 330, footnote 9). But neither one of these writers offers any textual evidence in support of this interpretation. And neither one sees any of the exegetical difficulties, just listed, which make such an interpretation untenable.

[79] Cf. the preceding and next paragraph of the text.

assumption of a commodity-money which is also *numéraire*, the analogue of p_u is identically unity. Hence, unlike the situation in the first passage, there can be no *tâtonnement* upon it. Hence the entire *tâtonnement* in this case must take place on i. And this is what Walras finds "remarkable": that even though the *tâtonnement* is so different from that of the first passage, the conclusion that an increase in the quantity of money decreases its value remains the same.[80]

Further, and perhaps conclusive, evidence that Walras thought of the *tâtonnement* in the first passage as proceeding on p_u is afforded by the case which Walras analyzes immediately after the second passage. Here he continues to consider a commodity-money, (A); but now he assumes that the *numéraire* is another commodity, (B). He then writes:

> The curve representing the price of the monetized (A) in terms of another commodity (B) as a function of the quantity of (A) monetized closely approximates[81] a rectangular hyperbola. . . . The equation of this curve is
>
> (18) $$q = \frac{H}{p},$$
>
> [where q is the quantity of (A) in monetary use and p is its price in terms of (B) and] H is the *encaisse désirée* reckoned in terms of (B), *which*[82] *is assumed to be predetermined*.[83]

Now, H is the analogue of H_α in equation (15), and p is the analogue of p_u.[84] Thus the italicized phrase in the preceding passage would seem to imply that Walras considers H_α "to be predetermined"—that is, to remain unaffected by the *tâtonnement* in the money market.[85] But in the first passage Walras is also willing to assume that H_α remains unaffected by this *tâtonnement*.[86]   Since $H_\alpha = H_\alpha i$, so that

(19) $$i = \frac{H_\alpha}{H_\alpha},$$

---

80 "What is most remarkable, in the case of a commodity which serves both as money and as *numéraire*, is the manner in which all prices rise and fall in terms of (A) in response to an increase or decrease in the *rareté* or value of this commodity in its monetary use when there is a decrease or increase in its quantity" (*Elements*, p. 333). After another sentence, this is followed by the second passage cited above.

81 Walras does not refer again to this reservation and proceeds to present the curve as an *exact* rectangular hyperbola. The reservation itself is a carry-over from the parallel passage of the second and third editions of the *Eléments* (p. 384) which has already been discussed on p. 389, footnote 14, above.

82 From the context it is clear that this refers to H.

83 *Elements*, ed. Jaffé, p. 334, italics added.

84 This is particularly clear from Walras' footnote on p. 334.

85 For further support of this contention, see the discussion of Schlesinger on p. 410, footnote 94, below.

86 See above, p. 402.

this means that i is also predetermined. Hence the *tâtonnement* must proceed on p_u. Alternatively, since

(20) $$\frac{H_\alpha}{p_{u'}} = \frac{1}{p_u}\left(\frac{H_\alpha}{i}\right) = \frac{1}{p_u}H_\alpha,$$

and since H_α is predetermined, the *tâtonnement* on $p_{u'}$ in

(21) $$Q_u = \frac{H_\alpha}{p_{u'}}$$

must be a *tâtonnement* on p_u.

At this point the reader may well ask: Why, then, does not Walras explicitly carry out the *tâtonnement* of the first passage on p_u? He must, however, remember that the presentation of the argument in terms of $p_{u'}$ is dictated by Walras' basic conception of the theory of money as a special case of the theory of circulating capital. This has been sufficiently emphasized in the preceding section.[87]

We might also digress for a moment to suggest that in the preceding passage Walras seems to regard the invariance of H with respect to p as a necessary condition for the validity of the quantity theory. A corresponding impression holds for his willingness—in the first passage cited above—to assume the invariance of H_α with respect to changes in $p_{u'}$.[88] Clearly, however, all that need be assumed for the validity of the theory is that H be invariant with respect to an equi-proportionate change in p *and* in initial holdings of money. In brief, Walras seems to be guilty here of a confusion between a demand curve and a market-equilibrium curve.[89] More specifically, Walras' interpretation of his rectangular hyperbola seems to slip back and forth between these two completely different contexts. First, this hyperbola is a demand curve—it is a graphical representation of the excess-demand function (18),[90] and shifts to the right or left according as there is an increase or decrease in the *encaisse désirée*.[91] But then it is also a market-equilibrium curve—for it shows that, were it not for its nonmonetary use, the purchasing power of money would vary inversely with its quantity. Similarly, I cannot escape the impression that when Walras concludes the summary of his Preface with the statement that "the price of money,

---

[87] See pp. 394–95 and 398. Walras' discussion in the Preface to the *Elements*, ed. Jaffé, pp. 42–43, is particularly illuminating on this point.

[88] This is definitely Schumpeter's view: "The main motive [of this assumed invariance] seems to have been a wish to gain possession of a simple form of 'quantity theory'" (*op. cit.*, p. 1025, footnote 71).

[89] Cf. above, Chapter VIII:2.

[90] Observe the notational symmetry between (18) and the excess-demand function (12).

[91] *Elements*, ed. Jaffé, p. 336 (bottom).

qua money [is] established as an inverse function of its quantity,"[92] it is equation (15) above he has in mind—and this despite the fact that it is developed as an excess-demand equation.

To return now to our main problem, we note that if Walras' first passage on the money market deals with a *tâtonnement* on p_u, the more serious the criticism to which it is open. For his willingness to assume that this *tâtonnement* can proceed "outside the system of equations of [general] economic equilibrium"[93] then constitutes a willingness to ignore the influence of variations in the absolute price level on the commodity markets. That is, it constitutes an overlooking of the real-balance effect. Correspondingly, it then follows that in the Walrasian scheme equilibrium relative prices—that is, prices of commodities in terms of commodity (*A*)—can be determined within the commodity markets by themselves; and the equilibrium absolute price level—that is, the reciprocal of the price of paper money in terms of (*A*)—can then be determined within the money market without in any way disturbing the equilibrium relative prices already determined in the commodity markets. And so we are led to the highly probable conclusion that the invalid dichotomy was born together with general-equilibrium analysis—and had the same father.[94]

---

[92] *Ibid.*, p. 43.

[93] Above, p. 402.

[94] Cf. Chapter VIII:3 above.

Once again, the credibility of this conclusion can only be strengthened when we see how those who wrote under Walras' shadow approached the problem. Thus in his monograph on the *Theorie der Geld- und Kreditwirtschaft* (Munich, 1914), Karl Schlesinger analyzes the details of various payment procedures all of which yield an excess-demand equation for money that is essentially Walras'

$$Q_u = \frac{H\alpha}{p_u}$$

[cf. equation (15) above]. In each case he presents as a necessary precondition of his analysis the assumption that

... purchases and sales [of goods] ... are independent of the price of money [p_u] and are determined solely by the other data of the economy ... , so that the real value of the liquid purchasing power [$H\alpha$] which must be held in order to carry out transactions can be determined without regard to p_u. [*Ibid.*, p. 91; cf. also the similar statements on pp. 85–86, 87, 90, and 99. Footnote 1 on p. 97 is also revealing.]

Since $H\alpha$ is thus predetermined, and since Q_u is given to begin with, the foregoing equation depends upon only one unknown, p_u, and can therefore determine its equilibrium value.

Thus Schlesinger presents a perfect statement of the invalid dichotomy. It might also be noted that he rationalizes the assumption just quoted by saying that "no one will hesitate to sell at a lower price in view of his certainty that he will be able to buy at the same low prices" (*ibid.*, p. 85). The familiar ring of the "homogeneity postulate" is unmistakable.

All this is the more significant in view of Schlesinger's unusually explicit use of the real-balance effect in explaining how an excess demand for money generates an increased supply of—and a decreased demand for—commodities, and hence a downward pressure on the price level; while an excess supply of money generates just the opposite pressures (*ibid.*,

5. Conclusions

Our study has shown that Walras' monetary theory was based on a mechanical application of the marginal-utility apparatus.   At no point did Walras ever attempt to explain why money has utility.   Nor did he ever recognize the fundamental nature of money in providing a reserve against contingencies.   Correspondingly, he failed to clothe his elaborate mathematical framework with adequate economic meaning.

Furthermore, even in the definitive edition of the *Elements* Walras did not succeed in his proclaimed objective of presenting a finished and integrated theory of money.   At a lower level of criticism, his theory has the minor inaccuracies[95] and rough edges[96] of an argument that has not been thought through to its logical end.   At a higher level of criticism, his theory of money is not fully integrated with his theory of production and capital formation.   This manifests itself in his failure to follow the basic pattern of this earlier theory in presenting a detailed and precise description of the *tâtonnement* in the money market.   More important, the meager description that Walras does provide shows no recognition of the vital necessity—if money prices are to be determinate—for the existence of a mutual interdependence between this *tâtonnement* and that taking place in the commodity markets.[97]   And this fundamental criticism holds even if it should be true that Walras was not guilty of the invalid dichotomy in the fullest sense of the term.   Similarly, whether or not this dichotomy exists in Walras' theory, the fact remains that at no point does Walras even advert to the real-balance effect in his analysis of the determination of the absolute price level.[98]

Nevertheless, our evaluation of Walras' pioneering development of a general-equilibrium theory of money can only be enhanced when we see how little his immediate followers did to remedy these deficiencies in his analysis.   Indeed, only two of them advanced this analysis beyond Walras' own formulation—though neither one of them did so with

---

pp. 84–87).   Thus Schlesinger provides a vivid example of the mental block which prevented a full understanding of the real-balance effect (cf. end of Chapter VIII:3).

(I have made use here—and in Note D—of a Hebrew translation of Chapter III of Schlesinger's work prepared at my request by Mr. Tsvi Goldberger.   I am greatly indebted to him for this assistance.)

[95] Cf. p. 402, footnote 63; pp. 403–4; and p. 406, footnote 72.

[96] Cf. p. 392, pp. 398–99, and p. 406, footnote 73.

[97] Cf. pp. 403–4 above.

[98] All this should make clear why I find it impossible to accept Schumpeter's presentation of Walras' monetary theory as one fully integrated with his theory of production and capital formation (*op. cit.*, pp. 1020–21, 1025).   A similar statement holds for Jaffé [*Econometrica*, XIX (1951), 327], Kuenne (*op. cit.*, p. 336), and Marget (*Theory of Prices*, Vol. II, p. 284, footnote 132).

explicit reference to his work.   The first was Wicksell, whose analysis of the *tâtonnement* in the money market will be discussed in Note E below. The second was Schlesinger, whose analysis of the conceptual framework which endows money holdings with utility will be discussed in Note D.[99]   But for the rest, they had nothing to say.   Pareto, Walras' intellectual successor, almost completely ignored his monetary theory.[100] Aupetit, though writing a monograph on the question, added but minor glosses to Walras' analysis.   While popularizers of Walras— such as Antonelli[101]—barely departed from the text he had set for them. All this was part of the uninterrupted neglect and distortion which Walras' monetary theory suffered at the hands of later writers.[102]

---

[99] But, as just emphasized, Schlesinger was even more clearly in error than Walras in his analysis of the determination of the absolute price level.

[100] V. Pareto, *Cours d'économie politique* (Lausanne, 1896), Vol. I, pp. 163–299.   Schumpeter considers Pareto to have "slid back rather than advanced in this particular field" (*op. cit.*, p. 1082).   Marget is even more critical ("Léon Walras . . . ," *op. cit.*, pp. 596–97; "Monetary Aspects . . . ," *op. cit.*, pp. 152–54).

[101] E. Antonelli, *Principes d'économie pure* (Paris, 1914), Chapter VI.

[102] The details of this neglect have, of course, been fully chronicled by Marget in his well-known "Léon Walras . . . ," *op. cit.*, especially pp. 595 ff.

The Marginal-Utility Theory of Money after Walras[1]

The marginal-utility theory of money after Walras was the paralyzed victim of the "circularity" bogey. This bogey achieved its most imposing form at the hands of Helfferich.[2] Its intimidatory powers were further increased by Divisia's mathematical proof that the utility function could not depend upon the amount of money.[3] And despite Marget's deft puncturing of its facade many years ago,[4] it has continued to be accorded respectable consideration in the most recent literature.[5]

It seems quite likely that this bogey was also in back of the tendency —already noted by Marget[6]—of many writers formally to deny the applicability of marginal-utility analysis to money, while at the same time presenting a cash-balance approach, which by its very nature involves a comparison of choices and hence an analysis of utilities. Of particular interest are such writers as Wicksell,[7] Fisher,[8] and Keynes in his neo-

---

[1] Attached to Chapter V, Sections 1 and 5.
This note is intended only to highlight certain points. For a more general discussion of the literature on this question—including the circularity charge—cf. Marget, *The Theory of Prices*, Vols. I and II, consulting Subject Index under "Utility analysis and the cash-balance approach"; see, in particular, Vol. I, pp. 450 ff., 480 ff.; Vol. II, pp. 84 ff. See also H. S. Ellis, *German Monetary Theory: 1905–1933* (Cambridge, Mass., 1934), Chapters IV–V; and—for a defense of the charge—B. M. Anderson, *The Value of Money* (New York, 1917), Chapter V.
Ellis also refers to a monograph on this question by W. Hirsch entitled *Grenznutzentheorie und Geldwerttheorie unter besonderer Berücksichtigung der "österreichischen" Schule* (Jena, 1928). This monograph concludes that the circularity charge is valid and that marginal-utility analysis is therefore inapplicable to money (Ellis, *op. cit.*, p. 89).
[2] K. Helfferich, *Money*, trans. L. Infield (London, 1927), pp. 526–27.
[3] F. Divisia, *Economique rationelle* (Paris, 1927), pp. 423–33. This proof falls to the ground as soon as we drop its basic assumption that "utility of money" means the utility of the commodities which money can buy.
[4] *Theory of Prices*, Vol. I, p. 445, footnote 86.
[5] Cf., e.g., Schumpeter, *op. cit.*, pp. 1089–90.
[6] *Theory of Prices*, Vol. II, pp. 84–86, 92–93.
[7] *Lectures in Political Economy*, Vol. II, *Money*, trans. E. Classen (London, 1935), pp. 20, 130; *Interest and Prices*, pp. 18 and 29.
[8] *Purchasing Power of Money*, p. 32. Needless to say, Fisher was not a cash-balance theorist in the sense of determining the value of money by its demand and supply; but he implicitly explained the holding of money in the same terms used by this theory. Cf. *ibid*. pp. 153–54. This is cited in full and discussed in Note F:1 below.

classical days[9]—each of whom was at pains to state that "money as such has no utility except what is derived from its exchange-value, that is to say from the utility of the things which it can buy"—and each of whom then proceeded to base his analysis precisely on the advantage and convenience (utility) of holding money *as such*.[10] One cannot help being struck by the irony of the fact that these writers, who actually provided a conceptual framework which could have justified the formal application of utility analysis to money, did not do so; while Walras, who actually lacked this framework, did.[11]

It is even more ironical that Mises—who is known in the literature as *the* advocate of the application of marginal-utility analysis to money— should have made this application solely in terms of "the marginal utility of the goods for which the money can be exchanged,"[12] and not in terms of the liquidity advantages of holding money that he described so clearly in other parts of his work.[13] As a result, Mises was forced to base his attempted escape from the circularity charge on a historical regression to the time when "the value of money is nothing other than the value of an object that is useful in some other way than as money."[14] Without going into the merits of this analytical construct, we need merely note that the argument of Chapter V:5 frees the marginal-utility theory of money from any logical dependence upon it. We might further note that this argument[15] also shows the incorrectness of Mises' contention that the quantity theory presupposes an inverse relationship between the quantity of money and its marginal utility.[16]

Walras' immediate followers made no mention of the circularity charge; but, for the most part—and as emphasized at the end of Note

---

9 J. M. Keynes, *A Tract on Monetary Reform* (London, 1923), p. 75. The following quotation in the text is from this reference. For a similar statement by an older member of Cambridge, see H. Sidgwick, *The Principles of Political Economy* (London, 1883), pp. 267–68. Cf. also M. Pantaleoni, *Pure Economics*, trans. T. B. Bruce (London, 1898), pp. 228–29; D. Kinley, *Money* (New York, 1904), p. 143. The latter, though, is somewhat ambiguous.

10 On Wicksell and Fisher, see Notes E:1 and F:1 below, respectively. On Keynes, see *Tract on Monetary Reform*, p. 78.

11 Cf. Note C:2 above, especially p. 393.

12 L. von Mises, *The Theory of Money and Credit*, trans. H. E. Batson (New York, 1935), p. 109.

13 *Ibid.*, pp. 134–35, 147–48.

14 *Ibid.*, p. 121. Hicks aptly describes Mises' theory as leading to the conclusion that "money is a ghost of gold." ["A Suggestion for Simplifying the Theory of Money," *Economica*, II (1935), as reprinted in *Readings in Monetary Theory*, p. 14.]

15 Chapter V:3, especially the penultimate paragraph.

16 Mises, *op. cit.*, pp. 141–42. It will be recalled that this contention also manifests itself at certain phases of Walras' work, and possibly even in the definitive edition of the *Elements* (cf. above, p. 388, and p. 402, footnote 65). Pareto, on the other hand, is definitely free of this confusion (*Cours*, Vol. I, p. 178, footnote).

C above—neither did they develop his marginal-utility theory of money any further. Indeed, Pareto retrogressed on this point. For he used "marginal utility of money" to denote only "the utility of the money-commodity in its non-monetary uses or the utility of the money-income";[17] never the utility of the *service d'approvisionnement* of money. As already noted, the only one to improve on Walras' theory was Karl Schlesinger. And he suffered even more neglect than his predecessor.[18]

Unfortunately, space does not permit us to present the full-length study of Schlesinger's work that its highly stimulating originality clearly warrants. From the viewpoint of our present interests, this work is best regarded as dealing with the deficiencies in the conceptual framework of Walras' monetary theory. In particular, it remedies these deficiencies by providing a precise specification of the payment procedure that generates a demand for money.[19]

Schlesinger proceeds by a series of successively more complicated stages. In the final one he distinguishes between payments whose magnitudes and future due-dates are *fixed*, and those which are *uncertain*. The monetary demand generated by the first type of payments is determined without recourse to utility analysis. It is simply the maximum cumulative discrepancy between daily cash outflow and inflow that will be generated during the period in question by the *given* payment stream with which the individual is confronted. In other words, the very nature of this stream compels the individual to hold this

---

[17] Marget, "Monetary Aspects . . . ," *op. cit.*, pp. 152–54.

We might in this connection note that when Pareto deals with the case of a money which may not have utility for some individual, he becomes involved in an error. Thus he writes: "It may be that the possessor of a good . . . derives no satisfaction from it; then we can say that he will *offer the entire quantity* at his disposal." But in the very next paragraph he fails to apply this principle correctly. For he states that for some individual money may have no utility, and therefore "he will use *the entire quantity that he receives* to procure [other] goods." If Pareto had applied his first statement correctly, he should have concluded: "and therefore he will use the entire quantity that he receives *plus his original stock* to procure other goods" (*Manuel*, p. 593, only first set of italics in original).

Even if we accept Pareto's second statement, this does not provide a determinate monetary theory. For to assume that every individual always holds on to his initial holdings of money is to become involved in the indeterminacy of Say's Identity. See above, Chapter VIII:7; see also Divisia, *op. cit.*, pp. 402–13 for an elaboration of Pareto's second statement, and a pointing out of this same indeterminacy.

[18] Marget, "Léon Walras . . . ," *op. cit.*, p. 594.

In what follows, I have once again made use of the translation of Schlesinger's work referred to on p. 411, footnote 94, above.

[19] Cf. Note C:2 above.

Because Schlesinger does not refer to Walras in the main part of his analysis, Marget surmises that he "did not derive his inspiration directly from Walras at all" (*ibid.*, p. 595). This conclusion seems to me unjustified. Though it would have been better if Schlesinger had defined the precise relation of his work to Walras', the fact remains that he deals with a problem that Walras neglected. Hence the absence of explicit citations.

amount of money at the beginning of the period if he is to avoid certain default. There is no room for the weighing of alternatives on his part.[20]

The element of alternative choices—and hence of utility analysis—enters only with respect to the uncertain payments.[21] If the individual did not hold a cash reserve against these payments, he would have to meet them by the forced sale of assets. And since future asset prices are uncertain, this involves the risk of loss. Hence it is rational for the individual to hold money instead of income-yielding assets; for the interest foregone on these holdings "is like an insurance premium paid to avoid this risk."[22] Denoting the real value of cash balances by r_w, Schlesinger represents the marginal utility of the insurance service which they thus provide by $f(r_w)$. He then states that the individual will not be in his optimum position unless $i = f(r_w)$, where i is the rate of interest.[23]

It can readily be seen that this optimum condition is incorrectly stated. The rate of interest does not have the dimensions of utility, and so cannot be equal to $f(r_w)$, which does. Instead of "i" Schlesinger should have written "the marginal utility of i dollars' worth of expenditure."[24]

Leaving this behind, we note that Schlesinger's analysis brings him finally to an excess-demand equation for money which he writes in the form

$$pF(Y) + p\Phi(r, Y) = M_0.$$

Here $F(Y)$ is the demand generated by the fixed payments, and $\Phi(r, Y)$ is that generated by the uncertain payments.[25] Schlesinger emphasizes that, because of the "law of large numbers," an increase in Y causes a less-than-proportionate increase in both of these functions.[26] Thus an expansion in his volume of transactions enables the individual to economize on the relative size of his cash balances. This, however, is true only if the increase in Y represents an increase in the *number* of trans-

---

20 Schlesinger, *Theorie*, pp. 91–96. Cf. pp. 392–93 above.

21 Unfortunately, this distinction is not the absolute one that it should be in Schlesinger's work. Thus on pp. 93–94 he indicates that even the "fixed" payment stream may be modified by the individual's investing money in times of cash surplus, and disinvesting in times of deficit.

22 *Ibid.*, pp. 96–97.

23 *Ibid.*, pp. 98–99.

24 Cf. equation (7), p. 75 above.

25 This is Schlesinger's equation IV (p. 100) with Q_u replaced by M_0, $1/p_u$ by p, i by r, and W—the real volume of transactions—by Y. The subscripts attached to the original functions have been dropped.

We might note here that Schlesinger indicates that the rate of interest also influences $F(\ )$, though he never introduces this rate explicitly into the function (*ibid.*, p. 93).

26 *Ibid.*, pp. 95–96, 99.

actions and not solely in their individual *magnitudes*. In the latter case the relative size of cash balances would remain the same.[27]

As the reader has undoubtedly noted, there is a remarkable similarity between the preceding excess-demand equation and Keynes'

$$L_1(Y) + L_2(r) = M_0.$$

Surely we do not read meaning into Schlesinger's analysis by saying that the first term in his equation reflects the transactions demand and the second term the speculative demand. In particular, Schlesinger's $\Phi(r, Y)$—which reflects the risk entailed in holding assets—can properly be taken as a generalization of Keynes' speculative demand—which reflects the risk entailed in holding the specific asset, bonds. Indeed, the only fundamental difference between the two foregoing equations lies in the fact that Schlesinger premultiplies both of his demand components by p and thus frees his equation from the money illusion which is so significantly present in Keynes' equation.[28]

After Schlesinger, formal mathematical developments of a marginal-utility theory of money seem to have been restricted to Leser[29] and Samuelson.[30] The latter's analysis is presented as a modified version of Walras'. Actually, though, it improves the conceptual framework of Walras' analysis by presupposing the existence of certain unspecified "contingencies" and by then explaining the utility of money in terms of its availability to meet them.[31] Leser, on the other hand, makes no reference to Walras. But his work is similar to Walras' in its failure to explain what endows money with utility and in its conceptual earmarking of the money balance for the various commodities.[32] In one fundamental respect, however, Leser's development differs from—and is inferior to—Walras'. For it is effectively restricted to the unrealistic one-week-horizon case described in Chapter V:2 above. In particular, the equilibrium condition on whose properties Leser concentrates exclusively[33] corresponds to equation (1) of this discussion—which is the same as equation (5.6) of the Mathematical Appendix. Accordingly, Leser's monetary theory is one in which the rate of interest plays no role whatsoever.

---

[27] *Ibid.*, p. 88. Cf. p. 93 above.

[28] Cf. Chapter XII:1.

[29] C. E. V. Leser, "The Consumer's Demand for Money," *Econometrica*, XI (1943), 123–40.

[30] *Foundations*, pp. 117–22.

[31] *Ibid.*, p. 118. Cf. above, pp. 392–93. This distinction between Samuelson and Walras was first emphasized by Kuenne, *op. cit.*, p. 332, footnote 3.

[32] Leser, *op. cit.*, p. 124. Cf. above, p. 397.

[33] *Ibid.*, p. 125.

So much for the mathematical economists.   We might now return to our ordinary cash-balance theorists and note that though—as emphasized above—most of them were inhibited by fears of "circularity" from applying marginal-utility analysis to money, there were nevertheless some who spoke explicitly of the marginal utility of money balances and who attempted to describe the optimum condition that it must satisfy.   Thus, for example, Lavington is well known for his statement that:

Resources devoted to consumption supply an income of immediate satisfaction; those held as a stock of currency yield a return of convenience and security; those devoted to investment in the narrower sense of the term yield a return in the form of interest. In so far therefore as his judgment gives effect to his self-interest, the quantity of resources which he holds in the form of money will be such that the unit of resources which is just and only just worth while holding in this form yields him a return of convenience and security equal to the yield of satisfaction derived from the marginal unit spent on consumables, and equal also to the net rate of interest.[34]

Here, again, we have the same confusion already noted in the case of Schlesinger: "satisfaction" and "interest" do not have the same dimensions, and so cannot be compared.   As Robertson has implied, this may be a mere slip of the pen.[35]   But Robertson fails to see that the correction of this slip reveals an even more basic misconception.   For Lavington's last sentence would then state that an optimum position obtains when the marginal utility of a dollar held in cash balances is equal at one and the same time to the marginal utility of *one* and *r* dollars' worth of commodities—where 100*r* per cent is the rate of interest.   The nature of this misconception can best be seen against the background of Chapter VI:1 above.   In brief, Lavington confuses the subjective sacrifice of *permanently* adding a dollar to cash balances[36] with that of adding it for only *one period*.[37]

A statement in the same vein as Lavington's—though without his error—can be found in Fisher:

The most salable of all properties is, of course, money; and as Karl Menger pointed out, it is precisely this salability which makes it money.   The *convenience* of surely

---

34 F. Lavington, *The English Capital Market* (London, 1921), p. 30.   This statement goes back to much less precise ones by A. Marshall, *Official Papers* (London, 1926), p. 268 (evidence before the Committee on Indian Currency, 1899, answer to question 11,759); and *Money Credit and Commerce* (London, 1923), p. 44.   See also Pigou, *Essays in Applied Economics*, pp. 179–80, noting the reference to T. N. Carver.

35 D. H. Robertson, *Essays in Monetary Theory* (London, 1940), p. 17, footnote 2.   This reads: "Lavington had better, I think, have written 'measured also by.'"

36 Cf. equation (5), p. 75 above.

37 Cf. p. 75 above, equation (7).

There is also an uncomfortable vagueness on this point in Robertson's *Money* (revised ed.: London, 1948), p. 36.

being able, without any previous preparation, to dispose of it for any exchange, in other words, its *liquidity*, is itself a sufficient return upon the capital which a man seems to keep idle in money form.   This liquidity of our cash balance takes the place of any rate of interest in the ordinary sense of the word.   A man who keeps an average cash balance of $100, rather than put his money in a savings bank to yield him $5 a year, does so because of its liquidity.   Its readiness for use at a moment's notice is, to him, worth at least $5 a year.[38]

The reader himself will have to explain how this striking passage can be made consistent with Fisher's observation referred to at the beginning of this note about "the fundamental peculiarity which money alone of all goods possesses,—the fact that it has no power to satisfy human wants except a power *to purchase* things which do have such power."[39]

---

[38] *The Theory of Interest* (New York, 1930), p. 216, italics in original.   All but the last two sentences of this passage appear in a similar form in Fisher's earlier *Rate of Interest* (New York, 1907), p. 212.   Cf. also the reference to the "waste of interest" in the *Purchasing Power of Money*, p. 152.

For a similar recognition by Wicksell of the dependence of the demand for money on the rate of interest, see *Interest and Prices*, p. 119; *Lectures*, Vol. II, p. 197.

[39] *Purchasing Power of Money*, p. 32, italics in original.

Wicksell's Monetary Theory

1. The Determination of the Absolute Price Level[1]

As already noted,[2] Wicksell denied the relevance of utility analysis for monetary theory. But despite this formal methodological declaration, he developed a cash-balance approach based implicitly on the services that money holdings as such provide. The striking passage in *Interest and Prices*[3] in which this is made clear is also the one which provides a description, unique in the literature, of the *tâtonnement* by which the absolute price level is determined. It reads:

Now let us suppose that for some reason or other commodity prices rise while the stock of money remains unchanged, or that the stock of money is diminished while prices remain temporarily unchanged. The cash balances will gradually appear to be *too small in relation to the new level of prices* (though in the first case they have not on the average altered in absolute amount. It is true that in this case I can rely on a higher level of receipts in the future. But meanwhile I run the risk of being unable to meet my obligations punctually, and at best I may easily be forced by shortage of ready money to forgo some purchase that would otherwise have been profitable.) I therefore seek to enlarge my balance. This can only be done—neglecting for the present the possibility of borrowing, etc.—through a *reduction* in my *demand* for goods and services, or through an *increase* in the *supply* of my own commodity (forthcoming either earlier or at a lower price than would otherwise have been the case), or through both together. The same is true of all other owners and consumers of commodities. But in fact nobody will succeed in realizing the object at which each is aiming—to increase his cash balance; for the sum of individual cash balances is limited by the amount of the available stock of money, or rather is identical with it. On the other hand, the universal reduction in demand and increase in supply of commodities will necessarily bring about a continuous fall in all prices. This can only cease when prices have fallen to the level at which the cash balances are regarded as *adequate*. (In the first case prices will now have fallen to their original level.)[4]

Despite the vividness with which the real-balance effect is here

---

[1] Attached to Chapter VIII:1.
[2] See beginning of Note D.
[3] London, 1936. Trans. R. F. Kahn from the original German of *Geldzins und Güter-preise* (1898).
[4] *Ibid.*, pp. 39–40, italics and parentheses in original.
See also in this context Wicksell's *Lectures on Political Economy*, Vol. II, *Money*, trans. E. Classen (London, 1935; the original Swedish edition appeared in 1906), pp. 142–43, 160–61. This will be referred to henceforth in this study as *Lectures II*.

described, there is another passage in Wicksell which indicates that even he might not have appreciated its full significance. This occurs in his defense of the quantity theory against Marx's criticism that the validity of the theory depends

... on the absurd hypothesis that commodities are without a price, and money without a value, when they first enter into circulation, and that, once in the circulation, an aliquot part of the medley of commodities is exchanged for an aliquot part of the heap of precious metals.[5]

The obvious answer to this criticism is that it is based on a fundamental misunderstanding of the equilibrating process: that commodities are always "with" a price and money always "with" a value, but that the dynamic workings of the real-balance effect assure that this price level—or this value—will not continue to prevail unless it is proportionate to the quantity of money. But Wicksell rests instead with the lame retort that Marx's cost-of-production theory must also start from the same "hypothesis" which he criticizes.[6]

2. THE DEMAND CURVE FOR MONEY [7]

On the basis of the rectangular hyperbola which he draws in his *Lectures II*,[8] Wicksell is usually lumped together with Walras and economists of the Cambridge school as having maintained that the demand for money has uniform unitary elasticity.[9] Nevertheless, closer examination of Wicksell's discussion makes it quite clear that he was not guilty of this error, and that he intended his rectangular hyperbola to represent the market-equilibrium curve of Figure 5 of the text, and not the demand curve of Figure 4.[10]

In particular, a reading of this discussion shows that Wicksell is not concerned with the "demand for money"—he does not even mention this term—but with the relationship between the quantity of money and its equilibrium exchange value. Wicksell emphasizes that money is like other goods in that an increase in its given supply decreases its value, but that it has the "special peculiarity" that this inverse dependence is necessarily a proportionate one. This is what he illustrates by the rectangular hyperbola mentioned above. The diagram in which this hyperbola is drawn—and in which it is contrasted with the correspond-

---

5 K. Marx, *Capital*, trans. S. Moore and E. Aveling (Chicago, 1906), Vol. I, p. 139. Marx is referring here to Montesquieu's discussion cited in Note A above.
6 *Lectures II*, pp. 147–48.
7 Attached to Chapter VIII:2.
8 P. 142. See Figure 50 below.
9 Cf., e.g., Marget, *Theory of Prices*, Vol. II, p. 648.
10 Cf. above, pp. 42–44.

ing curves for commodities—is reproduced here as Figure 50. It is significant that the term "demand" does not appear in this diagram at all. It is also significant—and again just what our interpretation leads us to expect—that though the discussion on which this diagram is based makes use of "elasticity of demand" in the Marshallian sense,[11] Wicksell does *not* use this term to describe the properties of the rectangular hyperbola which he presents.

Further evidence in support of our interpretation is provided by a

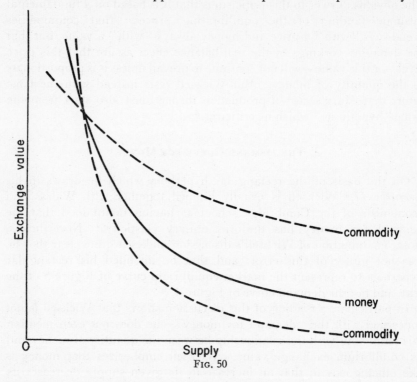

Fig. 50

comparison of the foregoing diagram with the one presented by Wicksell in his theory of value. Here he analyzes the market for commodity *B* in terms of the diagram reproduced in Figure 51, where *D* is expressly designated as the demand curve, and *S* as the supply.[12] In sharp distinction to Figure 50, the price variable now appears on the horizontal axis. But this apparently mysterious reversal of axes is precisely what the logic of Wicksell's argument—as it has been inter-

---

[11] *Lectures II*, p. 141, line 9 from bottom.
[12] This is Wicksell's diagram in *Lectures I*, p. 56, with some minor changes. Cf. also his earlier *Value Capital and Rent*, trans. S. H. Frowein (London, 1954), pp. 87–88.

preted here—requires. For the demand and supply curves of Figure 51 describe the outcome of a conceptual *individual*-experiment which takes the price of the commodity as the *independent* variable; hence, in accordance with mathematical custom, this variable appears on the horizontal axis. But the market-equilibrium curves of Figure 50 describe the outcome of a conceptual *market*-experiment which takes the price as the *dependent* variable; hence, in accordance with this same custom, it now appears on the vertical axis. Thus the difference

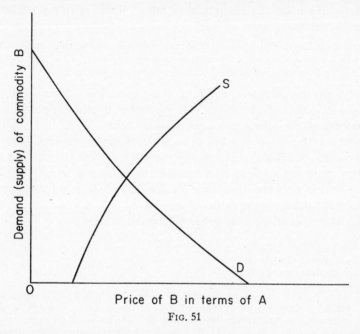

Price of B in terms of A

FIG. 51

between these two diagrams is not a chance one, but the systematic reflection of their differing conceptual frameworks![13]

We might finally note that though we can thus be sure that Wicksell does not intend the rectangular hyperbola of Figure 50 as a demand curve for money, he at no point indicates what he does consider the form of this curve to be. On this very crucial question our information is sadly deficient.

---

[13] It should be emphasized that, as Mr. Bent Hansen has kindly verified for me, this distinction between the two diagrams characterizes all the Swedish editions of Wicksell's *Lectures* as well.

In this connection we should note that the rectangular hyperbola which Walras draws in his monetary theory appears in a diagram in which—just as in his earlier theory of exchange—price appears on the horizontal axis. See *Elements*, ed. Jaffé, comparing pp. 94–103 with p. 335. Cf. also above, p. 409.

3. The Relationship Between Relative Prices and Money Prices[14]

Despite the fact that Wicksell devotes a complete chapter of his *Interest and Prices* to the question of "Relative Prices and Money Prices,"[15] he fails to make his view on this question completely clear. For one thing, he retains the same term "money prices" both when he considers money which is an abstract unit of account and when he considers money which is a concrete medium of exchange. This alone suffices to create serious exegetical pitfalls. Thus at one point in the chapter he writes:

The exchange of commodities in itself, and the conditions of production and consumption on which it depends, affect only exchange values or *relative* prices: they can exert *no direct influence whatever on the absolute level of money prices.*[16]

Similarly, in the *Lectures* we find: The quantities demanded "are expressed in [terms of] the $n - 1$ ratios between the money prices of the n commodities."[17] Both passages provide what seems to be a clear statement of the invalid proposition that demand depends only on relative prices.[18] But this is actually not the case; for in both passages it is clear from the context that Wicksell is assuming money to be an abstract unit of account; hence the "price ratios" he is referring to are —in our terminology—the ratios of *accounting*, and not *money*, prices.[19] Thus his statements are completely unobjectionable.[20]

---

14 Attached to Chapter VIII:3.
15 This is the title of Chapter III.
16 *Ibid.*, p. 23, italics in original.
17 *Lectures I*, p. 66.
18 And this is the way I superficially interpreted these passages in my "Indeterminacy of Absolute Prices...," *op. cit.*, p. 12, footnote 5, and "Invalidity of Classical Monetary Theory," *Econometrica*, XIX (1951), 149, footnote 30. The nature of my error was made clear to me by a letter from Professor D. H. Robertson in the summer of 1951. It was also pointed out by G. S. Becker and W. J. Baumol, in their "Classical Monetary Theory: The Outcome of the Discussion," *Economica*, XIX (1952), 370.
It might be noted that this same error has been repeated more recently in G. L. S. Shackle's Foreword to Wicksell's *Value Capital and Rent*, p. 8. Here Shackle cites a passage from *Interest and Prices*, p. 39, which actually assumes that money does *not* function as a store of value—and uses it in an attempted interpretation of Wicksell's theory for a money which *is* a store of value. See the next footnote.
19 "... we shall now leave on one side the function that money fulfills as a store of value" (*Interest and Prices*, p. 23). From the context—and particularly from the discussion when this assumption is dropped later on p. 39—it is clear that by this assumption Wicksell meant that money is equivalent to an abstract unit of account. See also *ibid.*, p. 24.
"These prices may also be regarded as expressed ... in terms of a measure of value, such as money, which takes no part in the real exchange" (*Lectures I*, p. 66). "... goods are only exchanged for goods (so that money, if it is used at all, functions in a merely formal manner)" (*ibid.*, p. 67). In his discussion on these pages Wicksell clearly demonstrates—to use our terminology—the determinacy of money prices and indeterminacy of accounting prices.
20 See p. 23 above.

424

A little later in this chapter Wicksell does, however, refer to the case of a money which has concrete existence and which can therefore act as a "store of value." But even here he leaves his position uncomfortably obscure. In particular, he writes:

... one thing is certain: money prices, as opposed to relative prices, can never be governed by the conditions of the commodity market itself (or of the production of goods); it is rather in the relations of this market to the *money market*, in the widest sense of the term, that it is necessary to search for the causes that regulate money prices.[21]

The implication here is unmistakable that relative prices *can be* "governed by the conditions of the commodity market itself." But there is no way of knowing if this ambiguous phrase refers to the "conditions" of equilibrium in the commodity market itself—in which case it is an expression of the invalid dichotomy—or to the "conditions" of the initial given quantities in this market—in which case it is not.[22]

4. THE "CUMULATIVE PROCESS"[23]

A correct appreciation of the place of the "cumulative process" in Wicksell's monetary theory must start from the understanding that Wicksell always regarded himself as an adherent of the quantity theory and as one of its loyal defenders against critics.[24] At the same time, however, he consistently opposed mechanical formulations of this theory and emphasized the importance of rationalizing it in economic terms. This, indeed, was his explicit purpose in writing the vivid passage cited in full on page 420 above. It must also be stressed that the "money" which Wicksell associated with the quantity theory was the metallic currency which served as legal tender and as the ultimate reserves of the banking system. In particular, he did *not* include in it demand deposits. Instead, he regarded the expansion of demand deposits as an increase in the "virtual velocity" of the metallic bank reserves, enabling them to carry out a larger volume of payments.[25]

---

[21] *Interest and Prices*, p. 24, italics in original. See also the equally obscure observation on p. 94 that "relative prices are the only things that really matter so far as production and consumption are concerned."

[22] In this case it is an expression of the first—and valid—dichotomy described in Chapter VIII:3 above.

[23] Attached to Chapter X:3 (end), and XV:1.

In addition to the references to *Interest and Prices* and *Lectures II* given in this section, the reader might also find it profitable to consult Wicksell's "Influence of the Rate of Interest on Prices," *Economic Journal*, XVII (1907), 213–19.

[24] *Interest and Prices*, Chapters IV–V; *Lectures II*, pp. 141–75.

[25] *Interest and Prices*, pp. 59–62; *Lectures II*, pp. 67–70, 168–69.

It is against this background that Wicksell defined his major analytical task: One of the "weakness[es] of the Quantity Theory . . . [is that it] assumes an almost completely individualistic system of holding cash balances," whereas such balances have been "replaced in practice by a kind of collective holding of balances, arising out of the acceptance by banks of deposits."[26]   In particular, an increase in the quantity of metallic money in a modern economy goes primarily to supplement bank reserves, and not private cash balances.   Hence there exists no direct real-balance effect to drive prices upwards.   It is therefore necessary to supplement the traditional quantity theory with an explanation of how an increase in bank reserves ultimately brings about an increase in prices.   And this is the role of the "cumulative process."[27, 28]

The details of this process can best be seen by following through Wicksell's analysis of what is in many ways his "standard case." Assume a gold-standard world, and consider one particular economy, A, which does not produce gold.   Start off from a position of equilibrium. Assume now that this equilibrium is disturbed by the discovery of new gold fields in economy B.   Wicksell now distinguishes between two effects of the discovery of gold, both of which tend to increase prices in the non-gold-producing country, A.   First, there is a direct effect due to the increased demand of B for the goods of A.   This causes a price increase in A without any change in the interest rate.[29]   If the gold were to be kept entirely within the hands of private individuals in A, there would be no further effects.   If, however, some of the gold is transferred directly to A's banks by foreign capitalists, or is deposited there by the public of A, then there is an additional effect.

---

26 *Interest and Prices*, p. 41.

27 In addition to the references in the three preceding footnotes, see *Interest and Prices*, pp. viii, xxiii–xxiv, 79–80, 101; *Lectures II*, p. 160.

That Wicksell was an advocate of the quantity theory has been duly emphasized by Marget in his *Theory of Prices*, Vol. I, Chapters VI–X.   In particular, Marget takes Ohlin to task for implying the contrary in his Introduction to the English translation of *Interest and Prices* (p. xiv; cf. Marget, *Theory of Prices*, p. 184, footnote 73, and p. 221, footnote 43).

In this connection Wicksell seems to have suffered more from his "introducers" than from his critics.   Thus in his Foreword to Wicksell's *Value Capital and Rent*, Shackle returns to Ohlin's implication that Wicksell was an opponent of the quantity theory (*ibid.*, pp. 8–9). Shackle bases himself primarily on Wicksell's statement that the validity of the quantity theory depends on the "flimsy" assumption that the "velocity of circulation of money" remains unchanged (*Interest and Prices*, p. 42).   But, as is clear from what has just been explained in the text, this is simply a misunderstanding of Wicksell's usage of "velocity."   In particular, Wicksell meant nothing more damaging to the quantity theory by this statement than did Fisher in his making the equation of exchange depend on M' as well as M.   Cf. also *Interest and Prices*, pp. 61–62.

28 The remainder of the present study reproduces with minor changes the contents of my "Wicksell's 'Cumulative Process,'" *op. cit.*, pp. 836–44.

29 *Lectures II*, pp. 197–98, 215–16.

The banks, finding themselves with excess reserves, will desire to expand their loans. In order to attract borrowers, they will reduce the bank rate. This will have two consequences: "in the first place saving will be discouraged and for that reason there will be an increased demand for goods and services for present consumption. In the second place [since the real rate—the marginal efficiency of capital—depends only on real factors,[30] which have not changed] the profit opportunities of entrepreneurs will thus be increased." Hence they will increase their bank borrowings. The new demand deposits that will thus be placed at their disposal[31] will enable them to increase their "demand for goods and services, as well as for raw materials already in the market for future production. . . . Owing to the increased income thus accruing to the workers, land-owners, and the owners of raw materials, etc., the prices of consumption goods will begin to rise, the more so as the factors of production previously available are now withdrawn for the purposes of future production. Equilibrium in the market for goods and services will therefore be disturbed. As against an increased demand in two directions there will be an unchanged or even diminished supply [since we are assuming full employment], which must result in an increase in wages (rent) and, directly or indirectly, in prices."[32] Again, it must be emphasized that "only in so far as new gold is deposited in the banks in the form of 'capital', i.e., without being drawn out in cheques and notes soon after, can it give rise to a lowering of interest rates and in that way affect prices."[33]

---

[30] *Lectures II*, pp. 190–91, 199; *Interest and Prices*, pp. xxvi, 106, Chapter IX.

[31] Throughout his analysis it is clear that Wicksell assumes an expansion in bank credit to be a fundamental intermediate step of the process. For detailed textual evidence, see Marget, *Theory of Prices*, Vol. I, pp. 183 ff. Marget refers to *Interest and Prices*, pp. xxiv, 27, 76, 82 (footnote), 83 f., 85, 101, 105, 110, 135, 144, 152, 190; and to *Lectures II*, p. 197. Wicksell's failure to make this assumption even more explicit is another reflection of the already emphasized fact that he did *not* consider demand deposits as constituting part of the money supply proper.

[32] *Lectures II*, pp. 194–95; cf. also *Interest and Prices*, pp. 87 ff. The assumption of full employment is explicitly made on p. 195 of the former reference.

In his *Interest and Prices* Wicksell considers only the indirect effect, and so insists that no change in prices can take place without a prior change in the interest rate. In *Lectures II* Wicksell not only modifies this stand by introducing the direct effect, but goes as far as to relegate the indirect effect to secondary importance, stating that "contrary to Ricardo's view, [it] does not happen as a rule" (*Lectures II*, p. 215). (Cf. also the passage from Wicksell's Preface to the first Swedish edition of *Lectures II* cited by Ohlin in his Introduction to *Interest and Prices*, pp. xv–xvi. This Preface is omitted from the English translation.)

In the light of Viner's study of the treatment accorded to the direct and indirect effects in the classical literature, it is interesting to note that Wicksell attributes his earlier view to the classical school [*ibid.*; Jacob Viner, *Studies in the Theory of International Trade* (New York, 1937), pp. 394–403].

[33] *Lectures II*, p. 215.

The resulting price increase is, to use Wicksell's term, "cumulative"; that is, a *given* discrepancy between the bank rate[34] and the real rate will, *if maintained indefinitely*, bring about a *continuous*, and not merely a *given*, increase in prices. In other words, after the initial increase in prices, "a further rise in prices [does not] require a further fall in the rate of interest." It must be emphasized that by "cumulative process" Wicksell does *not* mean a self-generating one, that is, one which carries within itself all the elements necessary for its own perpetuation. Specifically, as we have just seen, even if the discrepancy between real and market rates were to be maintained during subsequent periods, prices could not continue to rise unless bank credit continued to expand. Nor does Wicksell mean that the process continues because it generates expectations of further price rises. For he assumes that entrepreneurs generally anticipate future prices to be the same as present ones. He does recognize that this assumption is not always true. But, as we shall soon see, he makes it clear that he considers the case of elastic price expectations to be a special one, outside his main field of investigation.[35]

The question then arises: Are there any forces which bring the cumulative process to an end? Do there exist any "limits . . . which restrict the power of the banks" to maintain a rate lower than the real one indefinitely?[36] Taking account of the effect of higher prices on the reserves of the banks, Wicksell answers this question in the affirmative. First of all, the high prices will cause an external drain, forcing the banks to raise their rate. But this is not a sufficient answer; for if other countries are expanding at the same rate, this influence will not be operative.[37]

Wicksell then introduces the fundamental restrictive element in this process: If the banks maintain their rate below the real one, the resulting expansion of bank loans will ultimately bring about an internal drain. For "when there are no [bank] notes of small denomination and where metallic money is used in business, then on this assumption [of a continuous rise in commodity prices] the increased demand for gold for internal business would soon empty the bank's vaults." Hence, in order to protect their reserves, the banks must raise their rates. In this

---

[34] In what follows, this term is used interchangeably with "market rate," since, in Wicksell's system, this is initially set by the banks.

[35] The quotation in this paragraph is from *Interest and Prices*, pp. 93–94.

Supporting evidence for the second half of this paragraph will be found in the references cited in footnote 32 above; *Interest and Prices*, p. 95; and *Lectures II*, pp. 185 and 196. Cf. also the discussion below of the "divergent case."

[36] *Interest and Prices*, pp. 111 ff.

[37] *Lectures II*, p. 189; *Interest and Prices*, pp. 78, 113.

way, "the two rates of interest . . . reach *ultimate* equality, but only after, and as a result of, a previous movement of prices."[38, 39] When this equality is reached, there will be no further incentive for entrepreneurs to increase their borrowings from the banks. Throughout this process of adjustment the marginal efficiency of capital—that is, the real rate of interest—remains unchanged: for the prices of productive services and investment goods rise in the same proportion as the anticipated prices of the goods they produce. Thus the system is brought to a new equilibrium position: one in which the market rate of interest is the same as it was before the disturbance, but prices are, and remain, at a higher level.[40]

Thus the operation of a cumulative process does not imply that the system is unstable, and that, after the initial disturbance, it continuously moves away from an equilibrium position. On the contrary, through its effects on bank reserves, the cumulative process in Wicksell's analysis plays the role of the fundamental equilibrating mechanism forcing the banks to eliminate any discrepancy between the rate they set and the real rate, and thus restoring equilibrium to the loan market.

Underlying the preceding analysis is a simple hypothesis about the dynamic behavior of the market rate. Wicksell assumes that "banks never alter their interest rates unless they are induced to do so by the force of outside circumstances. They raise the rate when their gold stocks are threatened with depletion, or their current obligations are so great that their disparity in relation to their gold holdings is regarded as dangerous, or, still more, where both of these things occur together, as is often the case."[41] This passage makes it clear that Wicksell considers a decrease in absolute reserves and an increase in deposits as being two distinct phenomena, even though each causes a decline in the reserve ratio. In fact, the general tenor of Wicksell's presentation is that banks are much more sensitive to the former than they are to the latter.

---

[38] An implicit assumption of the analysis is that there is no rationing of credit. Cf. Marget, *Theory of Prices*, Vol. I, pp. 223 ff.

[39] The two citations in the text are from *Lectures II*, p. 189, and *Interest and Prices*, p. 135, respectively. Italics in original. There will also be an internal drain into industrial use; cf. *Interest and Prices*, p. 113; *Lectures II*, pp. 124–25.

For other passages dealing with the process described in the text, cf. the following: *Lectures II*, pp. 90, 124–26, 164, 179, 186, 194, 196, 198, 201–2, 204; *Interest and Prices*, pp. xxvi–xxvii, 113–17. Cf. also the passage from *Interest and Prices*, pp. 108–11, cited on p. 258 above.

[40] *Lectures II*, pp. 198–99. Cf. also *Interest and Prices*, p. 95.

In the first reference Wicksell discusses the possibility that the process of adjustment will also affect the real rate through "forced savings." This will be discussed further in Note J.

[41] *Lectures II*, p. 204.

This interpretation is supported by some explicit passages.[42] But, most important of all, it is a necessary dynamic assumption of Wicksell's system as presented above. For if bankers were guided, not by their *absolute* reserves, but solely by their reserve *ratio*, then they would raise their rates and slow up the expansion of their loans as soon as their reserve ratio declined. In this way the cumulative process could *conceivably* be brought to an end without an internal drain; correspondingly, the movement of prices would not be the *necessary* intermediate step of the argument that it is in Wicksell's presentation.

This exclusive concentration on the level of absolute reserves also explains why Wicksell does not incorporate into his analysis another equilibrating mechanism: namely, as prices rise, the demand for loans at any given rate of interest increases, since entrepreneurs need more money to carry out their projects. Ordinarily, one would say that this would tend to raise the rate of interest. But if we accept Wicksell's assumption that bankers change the rate only in response to changes in their absolute reserves, this increase in demand cannot directly affect the rate. Consequently, this influence is never even mentioned in Wicksell's analysis.[43]

Wicksell emphasizes that it takes time for this equilibrating process to work. In fact, it is the lag in the adjustment of the market rate to the real rate which enables him to explain the fact that historically rising prices and rising interest rates go together. Wicksell stresses that it is not the level of the market rate which counts, but its relation to the real rate. If the market rate is only slowly moving up toward equality with the real rate, then throughout the period of adjustment the expansion of bank loans is continuing, and with it the increase of prices. Hence the data do not contradict his theory.[44]

Wicksell also recognizes that if the price increase continues for some

---

[42] Thus the second passage referred to in footnote 39 above goes on to say: "Prices constitute, so to speak, a spiral spring which serves to transmit the power between the natural and the money rates of interest; but the spring must first be sufficiently stretched or compressed. In a pure cash economy, the spring is short and rigid; it becomes longer and more elastic in accordance with the stage of development of the system of credit and banking." (*Interest and Prices*, pp. 135–36.)

There is a similar passage some twenty-five pages before: "... it is clear that in an elastic monetary system where there is only a small reaction against an alteration in prices [i.e., a small internal drain], a fairly constant difference between the two rates of interest could be maintained for a long time, and the effect on prices might be considerable." (*Ibid.*, p. 110.)

Unless Wicksell is assuming the difference in sensitivity just described, it is hard to see why there should be the difference he indicates between a cash and credit economy.

[43] Compare this with the passages from Hume, Thornton, Ricardo, and Mill cited in Note J below.

[44] *Interest and Prices*, pp. 107, 167–68; *Lectures II*, pp. 205–7.

time, the assumption that anticipated prices are the same as present ones may have to be dropped. "The upward movement of prices will in some measure 'create its own draught.' When prices have been rising steadily for some time, entrepreneurs will begin to reckon on the basis not merely of the prices already attained, but of a further rise in prices." In such an event, "to put an immediate stop to any further rise in prices, it would not be sufficient for the banks to restore the rate of interest to its original level." Wicksell's position here seems to be that even in this case the system will return to equilibrium, but that the return will be a spiraling one. That is, the market rate will first rise above the real rate, and then, as the anticipated price rises fail to materialize, it will fall back to equality with it. He does admit that in the case of a speculative fever there may be "no limit to the rise in prices." But he gives scant attention to this possibility, and explicitly declares that it is outside his main field of interest.[45]

On the basis of the preceding exposition it is also quite easy to see the conditions under which the divergent case—in which prices continue to rise indefinitely—can occur. Two situations must be distinguished: If there is a banking system operating with required gold reserves, "the condition on which the banks could maintain a rate of interest permanently below the real rate would therefore be an incessant flow to them of new gold, and under such circumstances commodity prices would also rise continuously."[46]

If, however, there is a Wicksellian "ideal bank" or "pure credit" system,[47] no such condition is necessary. In this system no one desires to use gold; all money is in the form of demand deposits and bank notes. Hence banks have no need to maintain any gold reserves, are never in any danger of an internal drain, and are thus completely free to set and maintain indefinitely any market rate they choose. If this rate is less than the real one, bank credit and demand deposits will expand. By increasing the quantity of money in this way, the banks can bring about any specified price level by maintaining a discrepancy between the market and real rates until the desired price level is reached, and then equalizing the rates at that point.[48]

---

[45] *Interest and Prices*, pp. 96–98. In his *Lectures II*, Wicksell devotes only five lines to this subject (p. 207).

[46] *Lectures II*, p. 198.

[47] Described in *Lectures II*, pp. 84–91; *Interest and Prices*, pp. 68 ff.

[48] Cf. the references on p. 427, footnote 31, and p. 429, footnote 39. It might also be noted that in his Preface to *Interest and Prices* (p. xxvi), Wicksell restricts the conclusion that the market and real rates must be equalized to the "monetary system of actual fact." Cf. also *ibid.*, p. 80, and especially pp. 110–11. Cf. also the discussion which now follows on Wicksell's passage, *ibid.*, pp. 100–101.

It is within the preceding context that we must understand the frequently quoted passage in which Wicksell writes:

> It should now be clear that, in so far as our hypothetical conclusions are in accordance with reality, the movement and equilibrium of actual money prices represent a fundamentally different phenomenon, *above all in a fully developed credit system*, from those of *relative* prices. The latter might perhaps be compared with a mechanical system which satisfies the conditions of *stable* equilibrium, for instance a pendulum. Every movement away from the position of equilibrium sets forces into operation— on a scale that increases with the extent of the movement—which tend to restore the system to its original position, and actually succeed in doing so, though some oscillations may intervene.
>
> The analogous picture for *money* prices should rather be some easily movable object, such as a cylinder, which rests on a horizontal plane in so-called *neutral* equilibrium. The plane is somewhat rough, and a certain force is required to set the price-cylinder in motion and to keep it in motion. But so long as this force—the raising or lowering of the rate of interest—remains in operation, the cylinder continues to move in the same direction. Indeed, it will, after a time, start "rolling": the motion is an accelerated one up to a certain point, and it continues for a time even when the force has ceased to operate. Once the cylinder has come to rest, there is no tendency for it to be restored to its original position. It simply remains where it is so long as no opposite forces come into operation to push it back.
>
> It is, of course, clear that such forces can never be entirely absent, no matter how developed the credit system may be, if a precious metal or some other material substance serves as a monetary basis. The simple quantity theory is no longer adequate to deal with the nature of these reactions and with the manner of their operation. It is this question which we shall shortly be considering.[49]

It would be a serious misunderstanding of Wicksell's analysis to interpret this passage as making an absolute distinction between the two types of equilibria.[50] Such an interpretation is directly refuted by the demonstration above that Wicksell uses the cumulative process as an equilibrating mechanism bringing the system to *one definite level of money prices*. But even aside from this fundamental objection, the internal evidence of this passage, as well as of its counterpart in *Lectures II*, shows that Wicksell is not making a general distinction, but is restricting his analysis (as he must, to be consistent) to the case of a pure credit economy.

This evidence is unmistakable. There is, in the first place, the first italicized phrase of the passage.[51] Secondly, in the corresponding passage in *Lectures II*[52] the statement that the equilibrium of money

---

49 *Interest and Prices*, pp. 100–101. All but the first italics are in the original.

50 This is the interpretation given by G. Myrdal [*Monetary Equilibrium* (London, 1939), pp. 35–36] and P. N. Rosenstein-Rodan ["The Coördination of the General Theories of Money and Price," *Economica*, III (1936), 275–76].

51 Not italicized in the original.

52 *Lectures II*, p. 197.

prices is only a neutral one is explicitly restricted to the case of "a monetary system of unlimited elasticity"—an alternative term Wicksell uses to describe his pure credit system.[53] Finally, the concluding paragraph of the above-quoted passage removes any doubt that might remain. In fact, this concluding paragraph (which is the last one of Chapter VII) clearly sets the stage—and gives the cue—for the analysis of the equilibrating cumulative process which Wicksell goes on to describe in Chapter VIII.[54]

Thus, when read with the qualification upon which he himself insists, Wicksell's dramatic contrast reduces to a commonplace. When, in addition, we recall that throughout this process of moving from one point of "neutral" equilibrium to another the volume of demand deposits is continuously changing,[55] it is immediately apparent that, under corresponding conditions, even relative prices would be in "neutral equilibrium"! For what Wicksell is essentially saying is that the level of money prices is indeterminate as long as the quantity of money is not fixed, and that continuous changes in the quantity of money will cause continuous changes in the "price" (value) of money relative to other commodities. But the same statement can be made for the relative price of potatoes—if the quantity of potatoes in the market is continuously changing. Conversely, the equilibrium of money prices can be just as stable as that of relative prices—provided that in each case the initial quantities remain unchanged.

Indeed, one cannot read the foregoing passage without feeling that the emphasis which Wicksell places upon it is simply a reflection of his failure to include demand deposits in his definition of the money supply. Accordingly, one cannot help feeling that had he worked with a modern definition of "money," he would never have written this passage in the first place.[56]

---

[53] In support of this interpretation of "unlimited elasticity," cf. *Lectures II*, p. 194, lines 6–15; *Interest and Prices*, pp. 110, 135.

[54] On this whole discussion, cf. the references in footnote 48 on p. 431.

Though Rosenstein-Rodan quotes from the passage cited here in support of his interpretation, he significantly omits both the first italicized phrase and the final paragraph (*op. cit.*, p. 275, footnote 2).

Note how the last paragraph of this passage bears out the interpretation of Wicksell's relation to the quantity theory emphasized at the beginning of this section.

[55] Cf. above, p. 427, footnote 31.

[56] For the broader implications of the cumulative process as a simultaneous *tâtonnement* in the commodity and bond (bank-loan) markets, see Chapter XV:1 above.

N O T E **F**

Newcomb, Fisher, and the Transactions
Approach to the Quantity Theory

1. The Real-Balance Effect[1]

Newcomb's work is of particular interest to us because of his clear emphasis on the fact that changes in the quantity of money affect prices only through their prior effect on the demand for commodities.[2] Indeed, he explicitly writes this demand as a function of the quantity of money. Furthermore, the form of his function is such that it is unaffected by an equi-proportionate change in the price level *and* in the quantity of money![3] Nevertheless, it would be a mistake to accept all this as definite recognition of the real-balance effect. For nowhere in his argument does Newcomb bring in that crucial intermediary stage where the monetary increase makes individuals feel that their cash balances are larger than needed so that they can expand their purchases accordingly.[4] That is, Newcomb fails to distinguish sufficiently, if at all, between money considered as an income or expenditure flow, and money considered as a reserve balance.[5]

Though drawing his inspiration from Newcomb,[6] Fisher greatly improved the latter's exposition on this point. In particular, the following passage clearly reveals Fisher's understanding of each component of the tripartite quantity-theory thesis,[7] and of the real-balance effect in particular:

---

1 Attached to Chapter VIII:1.

2 S. Newcomb, *Principles of Political Economy* (New York, 1885), pp. 315–58 (especially pp. 342–44 and 351–55) and pp. 380–84.

3 *Ibid.*, equation (b) on p. 354, and the discussion leading up to it. The equation is $D = N \cdot \frac{F}{P}$—where D is the amount of commodities demanded, N a constant, F the "flow of currency," and P the price level. On p. 323 we find F defined as $V \cdot R$—where V is the volume of currency and R its velocity of circulation.

4 Contrast this with the corresponding passages from Wicksell (Note E:1 above) and Fisher (next paragraph).

5 Cf. Newcomb, *op. cit.*, pp. 218–19, 351–55, 380–87. Note also that the formula in footnote 3 above depends on the "flow of currency." Cf. also the beginning of Note A above.

6 See the dedication page in the *Purchasing Power of Money* (New York, 1911).

7 Above, p. 97.

434

Suppose, for a moment, that a doubling in the currency in circulation should not at once raise prices, but should halve the velocities instead; such a result would evidently upset for each individual the adjustment which he had made of cash on hand. Prices being unchanged, he now has double the amount of money and deposits which his convenience had taught him to keep on hand. He will then try to get rid of the surplus money and deposits by buying goods. But as somebody else must be found to take the money off his hands, its mere transfer will not diminish the amount in the community. It will simply increase somebody else's surplus. Everybody has money on his hands beyond what experience and convenience have shown to be necessary. Everybody will want to exchange this relatively useless extra money for goods, and the desire so to do must surely drive up the price of goods. No one can deny that the effect of every one's desiring to spend more money will be to raise prices. Obviously this tendency will continue until there is found another adjustment of quantities [of money] to expenditures, and the V's are the same as originally. That is, if there is no change in the quantities sold (the Q's), the only possible effect of doubling M and M' will be a doubling of the p's; for we have just seen that the V's cannot be permanently reduced without causing people to have surplus money and deposits, and there cannot be surplus money and deposits without a desire to spend it, and there cannot be a desire to spend it without a rise in prices. In short, the only way to get rid of a plethora of money is to raise prices to correspond.[8, 9]

2. The Question of Stability Analysis [10]

Clearly, there is a type of stability analysis in the preceding passage. But I am troubled by the fact that Fisher presents it within a comparative-statics framework, and not (as in the stability analysis of his value theory[11]) within a static one. Consequently, I wonder if Fisher would have applied the foregoing argument to show (like Wicksell) that if the p's fall while M remains constant, the p's will be forced up again. This would be an unjustified quibble—were it not for the evidence of the literature that just such an incomplete recognition of the real-balance effect has repeatedly existed.[12]

3. The Relationship Between the Monetary Equation and the Commodity Equations [13]

The contention of Chapter VIII:4 that Fisher failed to understand the proper relationship between the monetary equation and the commodity

---

[8] *Ibid.*, pp. 153–54. The bracketed expression "of money" is inserted on the basis of the following passage two pages earlier: "He adjusts this time of turnover [i.e., V] by adjusting his average quantity of pocket money, or till money, to suit his expenditures [*ibid.*, p. 152]."

[9] For a similar passage, see Fisher's *Elementary Principles of Economics* (New York, 1912), pp. 242–47.

[10] Attached to Chapter VIII:1.

[11] *Elementary Principles*, pp. 266–67.

[12] Cf. Notes G:2 and I:3 below. Cf. also pp. 383–84 above.

[13] Attached to Chapter VIII:3–4.

equations is based primarily on the following passage from the *Purchasing Power of Money*, reproduced together with its crucial footnote:

[It is a] . . . fallacious idea that the price level cannot be determined by other factors in the equation of exchange because it is already determined by other causes, usually alluded to as "supply and demand." This vague phrase has covered multitudes of sins of slothful analysts in economics. Those who place such implicit reliance on the competency of supply and demand to fix prices, irrespective of the quantity of money, deposits, velocity, and trade, will have their confidence rudely shaken if they will follow the reasoning as to price causation of separate articles. They will find that there are always just one *too few equations* to determine the unknown quantities [i.e., money prices] involved.* The equation of exchange is needed in each case to supplement the equations of supply and demand.

It would take us too far afield to insert here a complete statement of price-determining principles. But the compatibility of the equation of exchange with the equations which have to deal with prices individually may be brought home to the reader sufficiently for our present purposes by emphasizing the distinction between (1) individual prices relatively to each other and (2) the price *level*. The equation of exchange determines the latter (the price level) only, and the latter only is the subject of this book. It will not help, but only hinder the reader to mix with the discussion of price levels the principles determining individual prices relatively to each other.

* Cf. Irving Fisher, "Mathematical Investigations in the Theory of Value and Prices," *Transactions of the Connecticut Academy of Arts and Sciences*, Vol. IX, 1892, p. 62.[14]

Admittedly, this passage does not *explicitly* say that the commodity demand and supply equations by themselves determine relative prices. But it certainly is hard to see what other meaning it could have. At any rate, it is clear that Fisher conceived the special role of the equation of exchange to be the determination of the absolute price level. It is also unmistakably clear—and this is what has already been noted in the text—that Fisher was confused as to the nature of the various prices. For if we check the reference he cites in the footnote we will see that the equation added there is the definitional $p_n = 1$, serving to determine *accounting* prices, and not the equation of exchange, serving to determine *money* prices![15] In other words, Fisher confused the valid dichotomy between money and accounting prices with the invalid one between relative and money prices.

At first sight, the following passage offers corroborating evidence for this contention:

The demand for sugar is not only relative to the price of sugar, but also to the general level of other things. Not only is the demand for sugar at ten cents a pound greater

---

[14] Pp. 174–75, italics in original. Part of this passage has already been cited in the text, p. 114. The work cited in Fisher's footnote was reprinted in New Haven, 1925. All references are to this reprint.

[15] Cf. also the equation added on p. 59 of the *Mathematical Investigations in the Theory of Value and Prices*.

than the demand at twenty cents a pound (at a given level of prices of other things), but the demand at twenty cents *at a high level of prices* is greater than the demand at twenty cents *at a low level of prices.* In fact if the price level is doubled, the demand at twenty cents a pound will be as great as the demand was before at ten cents a pound, assuming that the doubling applies likewise to wages and incomes generally.[16]

Here is a seemingly unambiguous statement that demand is unaffected by a doubling of all prices.[17] Nevertheless, the evidence is not conclusive; for Fisher may tacitly be assuming that this doubling of prices is accompanied by a doubling of money holdings, so that there is no real-balance effect. That this is not a far-fetched possibility is suggested by the parallel discussion in his *Elementary Principles of Economics,* which begins with the explicit assumption "that we change our monetary unit so that what is now fifty cents should be called a dollar."[18] On the other hand, this discussion in no way indicates that Fisher was aware of the crucial importance of this accompanying increase in the amount of money. This is particularly noticeable in his subsequent statement that "if previously people were willing to take [a certain quantity of sugar] . . . at one price, they are now willing to take it at double that price, because this double price means in purchasing power exactly the same thing as the original price."[19] The equally necessary "and because their initial nominal money holdings have also doubled" is significantly absent.

Actually, the *Elementary Principles of Economics* provides just as convincing proof as the *Purchasing Power of Money* that Fisher was guilty of the invalid dichotomy. Chapter XV of the former—in which the passages just cited appear—is essentially an elaboration of the two passages from the latter cited earlier in this section. The reader must study this Chapter XV for himself and see if he can leave it with any other impression than that of the invalid dichotomy. It should particularly be emphasized that the final, summarizing paragraph of this chapter is the source of the very revealing passage cited in full at the end of Chapter VIII:4 above.[20]

---

16 *Purchasing Power of Money,* pp. 176–77, italics in original.

17 Indeed, this is the way I understood it until W. J. Baumol (in a letter written in the spring of 1953) suggested the possibility set out in the next sentence.

18 *Elementary Principles,* p. 274.

19 *Ibid.,* p. 275.

20 Note also how this chapter constantly develops the theme that "individual prices, such, for instance, as the price of sugar, presuppose a price level" (*ibid.,* p. 258).

It might finally be noted that A. G. Hart also interprets Fisher's *Elementary Principles* this way—though without realizing that the dichotomy is invalid. Cf. his *Money, Debt, and Economic Activity* (second ed.; New York, 1953), p. 144, footnote 4.

Marshall, Pigou, and the Cambridge Cash-Balance Approach to the Quantity Theory

1. THE REAL-BALANCE EFFECT [1]

The Cambridge cash-balance tradition begins, of course, with Marshall[2] and continues with Pigou,[3] Keynes,[4] and Robertson.[5] None of these writers provides as vivid or systematic a picture of the real-balance effect as do Wicksell[6] and Fisher.[7] Nevertheless, they do at various points indicate their recognition of this effect.[8]

2. THE ABSENCE OF STABILITY ANALYSIS [9]

One of the central motivations of the Cambridge cash-balance

---

[1] Attached to Chapter VIII:1.

[2] A. Marshall, *Money Credit and Commerce* (London, 1923), pp. 43–50, 282–84. As Marshall emphasized, the crucial parts of this analysis are reproduced from his testimony before the Gold and Silver Commission (1887–88) and Indian Currency Committee (1899). This is reprinted in *Official Papers by Alfred Marshall* (London, 1926), pp. 34–38, 51–52, 267–69. For the dating of Marshall's development of monetary theory even further back, to the 1870's, see J. M. Keynes, "Alfred Marshall, 1842–1924," in *Memorials of Alfred Marshall*, ed. A. C. Pigou (London, 1925), pp. 27–30.

For the real-balance effect, see *Money Credit and Commerce*, bottom of p. 43; *Official Papers*, p. 52. On the other hand, it might be noted that in his *Economics of Industry* (London, 1881), Marshall analyzes the consequences of a general decline of prices without making any mention of this effect [Book III, Chapter I, §5; as reprinted in *Readings in Business Cycles and National Income*, ed. A. H. Hansen and R. V. Clemence (New York, 1953), p. 102].

[3] A. C. Pigou, "The Value of Money," *Quarterly Journal of Economics*, XXXII (1917–18), reprinted in *Readings in Monetary Theory*, ed. F. A. Lutz and L. W. Mints (Philadelphia, 1951), pp. 162–83. This appears in a revised form under the title "The Exchange Value of Legal Tender Money," *Essays in Applied Economics* (London, 1923), pp. 174–98. For the real-balance effect, see "Value of Money," *op. cit.*, pp. 166–67.

[4] J. M. Keynes, *Tract on Monetary Reform* (London, 1923), pp. 74–79. For the real-balance effect, see bottom of p. 75. For the terming of Fisher's theory as "artificial," see bottom of p. 78. Cf. also Keynes' review of Fisher's *Purchasing Power of Money*, in *Economic Journal*, XXI (1911), 394–96.

[5] D. H. Robertson, *Money* (revised ed.; London, 1948), pp. 27–40, 180–81. For the real-balance effect, see the reference to "the alternative attractions of increased consumption" on p. 36.

[6] Above, Note E:1.

[7] Above, Note F:1.

[8] See the specific references in the preceding footnotes.

[9] Attached to Chapter VIII:1.

approach is the desire to integrate monetary theory and value theory. Thus Marshall goes out of his way to show how the value of money can be determined by the use of ordinary demand and supply curves.[10] Pigou systematically organizes his analysis of the "Value of Money"[11] under the successive section headings "The Demand for Legal Tender Money," "The Supply of Legal Tender Money," and "Demand and Supply." And Robertson stresses that his book on *Money* is "the second volume of a series [namely, Cambridge Economic Handbooks]. Its connection with its predecessor—Mr. Henderson's *Supply and Demand*—is to be found in the emphasis laid on the theory of money as a special case of the general theory of value."[12]

It is the contrast it affords with this obvious desire that lends crucial significance to the complete failure of Cambridge economists to carry over to their monetary theory the stability analysis of their value theory. Thus Marshall's graphical analysis of international trade in Appendix J of *Money Credit and Commerce* has a detailed discussion of stability conditions,[13] but his graphical analysis of the determination of the value of money in Appendix C is void of even an allusion to such a discussion. This omission must also be contrasted with Marshall's well-known discussions of stability conditions in his ordinary theory of value.[14] The same asymmetry characterizes Pigou—who refers to the latter discussions in their appropriate contexts,[15] but who makes no attempt to apply them to monetary theory. Similarly instructive is the absence of stability analysis in Robertson's *Money*[16] as compared with its presence in Henderson's *Supply and Demand*.[17]

It is particularly interesting to see how this asymmetry is perpetuated in the early textbooks which drew their inspiration from Marshall. Thus both J. S. Nicholson[18] and S. Chapman[19] present simple stability

---

10 *Money Credit and Commerce*, Appendix C. Note too how Keynes emphasizes that Marshall taught "the quantity theory of money as a part of the general theory of value" ("Alfred Marshall, 1842–1924," *op. cit.*, p. 29).

11 *Op. cit.*

12 *Money*, p. xii. Robertson returns to this theme on p. 30.

13 See especially p. 341. Cf. also his *Pure Theory of Foreign Trade* (reprinted London, 1930), Chapter II.

14 *Principles*, pp. 345–46, 806–7. Cf. also his *Pure Theory of Domestic Values* (reprinted London, 1930), pp. 11–14.

15 *Economics of Welfare* (fourth ed.; London, 1932), pp. 794–801; *Economics of Stationary States* (London, 1935), p. 39.

16 Pp. 27–38.

17 (Revised ed.; London, 1932), Chapter II, especially bottom of p. 23.

18 *Principles of Political Economy* (London: Vol. I, 1893; Vol. II, 1897; Vol. III, 1901). On the debt to Marshall, see the Preface to Vol. I.

19 *Outlines of Political Economy* (second ed.; London, 1917). On Marshall, see once again the Preface.

discussions in their value-theory chapters[20] and omit such discussions in their monetary-theory ones.[21] But at the same time, Chapman concludes his discussion of the quantity theory by emphasizing that "the reader will now perceive that the theory of money fits into the ordinary theory of the determination of the value of things by demand and supply"![22]

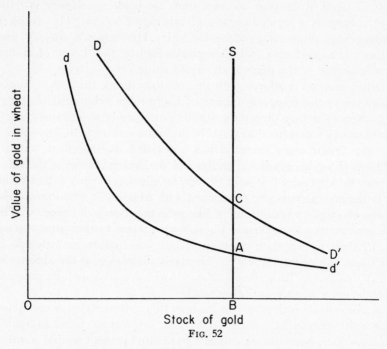

Fig. 52

3. The Unitary Elasticity of Demand for Money[23]

In the well-known Appendix C to his *Money Credit and Commerce*, Marshall presents a diagram, reproduced here as Figure 52, in which

---

[20] Nicholson, in Vol. II, pp. 38–39; Chapman, on pp. 168–72.

[21] Nicholson, in Vol. II, pp. 118–22; Chapman, on pp. 211–17. It might be noted that neither does any such discussion appear in Nicholson's *Treatise on Money* (London, 1888).

[22] *Op. cit.*, p. 215. Among modern cash-balance expositions, Chandler's (*op. cit.*, pp. 549–50) seems to be the only one with a stability analysis.

We might note that David Barbour does present the beginnings of a stability analysis when he asks what happens if "all prices and wages . . . are increased five-fold." His argument —which is not very complete—is, however, carried out entirely in terms of the effect of such a price rise in generating an internal drain and thereby reducing bank reserves; the effect on the real value of individual cash reserves is completely ignored. It should also be emphasized that Barbour's thinking on monetary theory does not show any Marshallian influence. [*The Standard of Value* (London, 1912), p. 37; see also pp. 38–40, 44.]

[23] Attached to Chapter VIII:2.

the demand curve for gold in its monetary use is represented by the rectangular hyperbola *dd'*. Similarly, "supply is . . . shown by a vertical straight line [*BS*] representing a given aggregate stock of gold."[24] If gold has only monetary uses, its equilibrium value is then determined by the intersection of *dd'* and *BS* at *A*. If, however, it also has nonmonetary uses, its equilibrium value is determined by the intersection of *DD'* with *BS*—where *DD'* represents the composite demand curve for both types of uses. In his classic essay on the "Value of Money," Pigou essentially restricts himself to the monetary demand, refines and elaborates Marshall's discussion considerably, but also emphasizes that the demand curve for money has the form of a rectangular hyperbola and is therefore of uniform unitary elasticity.[25]

It must be emphasized that, unlike Wicksell,[26] Marshall and Pigou are definitely—and incorrectly—referring to the ordinary Marshallian demand curve of Figure 4, and *not* to the market-equilibrium curve of Figure 5.[27] Correspondingly, they are definitely—and incorrectly— using "unitary elasticity of demand for money" in the ordinary Marshallian sense of elasticity. That this is the intended usage can be seen from the fact that the only distinction Marshall draws in Appendix C between his rectangular hyperbola and any other demand curve is that the former refers to a stock and not a flow.[28] It can be seen even more explicitly from the footnote at the end of the Appendix, in which Marshall refers the reader to the specific demand and supply curves of the *Principles* for an extension of his analysis to more complicated cases. This footnote concludes with the observation that even in these cases "the representative currency-demand curve for gold would be a rectangular hyperbola."

The case of Pigou is also clear. In what other than the usual Marshallian sense can we understand the passage in which he writes that "when the supply of legal-tender money varies in a given measure, the resultant change in the value of money will be less, the more elastic is the demand. Since, however, the demand for money always has an elasticity equal to unity, this proposition has no practical implications."[29] To this can be added the equally revealing passage cited at the beginning of Chapter VIII:2 above.

There still remains the nominal possibility that Marshall and Pigou

---

24 *Money Credit and Commerce*, p. 283.
25 "Value of Money," *op. cit.*, p. 165; "The Exchange Value of Legal Tender Money," *op. cit.*, p. 176, lines 16–18; p. 190.
26 Above, Note E:2.
27 Cf. pp. 42–44 above.
28 *Money Credit and Commerce*, p. 282.
29 "The Exchange Value of Legal Tender Money," *op. cit.*, p. 190.

are tacitly assuming that the amount of money is changed with the price level, so that they have in mind the demand curve of Figure 3 (page 28) and not that of Figure 4. But this too must be ruled out. For Marshallian demand theory is based on a *ceteris paribus* demand curve in which only the price varies;[30] hence if this standard assumption is dropped to permit significant variations of another variable too— as is required by Figure 3—surely some explicit comment to that effect should be forthcoming.

Furthermore, the whole point of Marshallian value theory is to organize the separate forces which determine the equilibrium price into two categories—demand and supply—which, ideally, are mutually exclusive. Now, the distinguishing feature of the demand curve in Figure 3 is that it depends on the *supply* of money. Surely this interdependence of demand and supply—so unusual for Marshall—would have been explicitly pointed out by him. This consideration is even more telling with reference to Pigou. For though he does point out that "the demand schedule and the supply schedule for money are not strictly independent of one another," he does not base this observation on the grounds described by Figure 3.[31]

Marshall and Pigou made the phrase "unitary elasticity of demand for money" a standard fixture of monetary theory.[32] In its use in the later literature we can clearly see the continued confusion with which this term is used to refer now (incorrectly) to the demand curve of Figure 4, now (correctly) to the market-equilibrium curve of Figure 5, and now indiscriminately to both at the same time. Thus Chapman writes:

. . . if the quantity of commodities remains fixed, an increase of money causes depreciation of money and a decrease of money appreciation of money. The latter proposition is sometimes expressed quantitatively in technical language by saying that the *elasticity of demand for money is unity* (see pp. 42–44).[33]

This by itself is a perfect description of the market-equilibrium rectangular hyperbola in Figure 5; but the pages to which Chapman refers at the end of the passage provide an explanation of the elasticity of demand of a Marshallian demand curve! Similarly, Taussig writes:

Hence when there is twice as much money, the same number of commodities will be offered for the money, and prices will be twice as high as before. In other words, using a phrase already explained, the elasticity of demand for money is unity.[34]

---

30 This is a slight oversimplification, permissible in the present context.

31 "Value of Money," *op. cit.*, p. 181.

32 But, as Marget has emphasized, Walras had earlier presented a graphical analysis in all essentials identical with Marshall's Figure J. See "Léon Walras . . . ," *op. cit.*, pp. 578–79. Cf. also above, p. 408.

33 *Op. cit.*, pp. 217–18, italics and page references in original.

34 F. W. Taussig, *Principles of Economics* (fourth ed., revised; New York, 1939), Vol. I, p. 252.

Once again, though the first sentence describes a market-equilibrium curve, the only context in which Taussig has "already explained" the phrase "elasticity of demand" is in connection with a Marshallian demand curve.[35] Finally, we can consider the example of Cannan, who, for the most part, uses "unitary elasticity of demand" in the Marshallian sense,[36] but who also argues in the market-equilibrium sense that this elasticity may be less than unity because the expectations generated by a rising price level might cause it to rise more than in proportion to the quantity of money.[37, 38]

It might finally be noted that incorrect descriptions of the demand curve for money as having unitary elasticity in the Marshallian sense have continued to characterize the more recent literature too—as the examples of Samuelson,[39] Chandler,[40] and Hart [41] show.

4. THE RELATIONSHIP BETWEEN MONETARY THEORY AND VALUE THEORY [42]

To the best of my knowledge, the only discussion by Cambridge economists on the relationship between monetary theory and value theory that is relevant to our present inquiry occurs at the beginning of Pigou's essay on the "Value of Money." Here Pigou writes:

For the present purpose [of determining the value of money] it is convenient to adopt a plan similar to that employed by Dr. Marshall in his unpublished paper on the "Pure Theory of Foreign Trade," which has been reproduced in Professor Pantaleoni's *Pure Economics*, and to assume that the value of all commodities other than money in

---

[35] *Ibid.*, pp. 126–30.
Note also that later on, on p. 252, Taussig writes:

Herein the position of money is unique. As regards the immense majority of commodities, demand is elastic in some cases, inelastic in others, but rarely so balanced that the same sum is always spent on any one.

Here again he seems to be using elasticity in the Marshallian sense.
[36] E. Cannan, "The Application of the Theoretical Apparatus of Supply and Demand to Units of Currency," *Economic Journal*, XXXI (1921), reprinted in *Readings in Monetary Theory*, p. 10. See also his *Money: Its Connexion with Rising and Falling Prices* (fourth ed., revised; London, 1923), pp. 66–70.
[37] *Ibid.*, pp. 69–71; "The Application . . . ," *op. cit.*, pp. 10–12.
[38] Though not as explicit as Chapman and Taussig, Keynes' discussion in his *Tract on Monetary Reform* (pp. 75–77) seems to me to be involved in their same confusion between demand curves and market-equilibrium curves. There is also some hint of this confusion in Marshall's *Money Credit and Commerce*, p. 45.
[39] *Foundations of Economic Analysis*, p. 121. Cf. also his *Economics: An Introductory Analysis* (second ed.; New York, 1951), p. 346 (bottom).
[40] *Op. cit.*, pp. 549–50.
[41] *Op. cit.*, p. 197.
[42] Attached to Chapter VIII:3.

terms of one another *is determined independently of the value of money*. On this assumption, the value of any combination of commodities in general can be cited in terms of any single commodity. The aggregate of all commodities is represented by so many bushels of wheat; and the value of money by the number of bushels of wheat which a unit of it will purchase. This value is governed, like the value of everything else, by the general conditions of demand and supply. An investigation of the causes upon which the value of money depends means, therefore, just as it would do if we were concerned with lead or tobacco, a detailed analysis of these two groups of forces. To this analysis, therefore, we may at once proceed.[43]

The crucial question is the meaning of the phrase which has been italicized. If this means "determined independently *by value theory*," then Pigou is clearly involved in the false dichotomy discussed at length in Chapter VIII:3. But what else can the phrase mean? It cannot refer to the determination of relative prices that takes place in the first stage of the first dichotomy of Chapter VIII:3.[44] For in this stage the forms of the demand functions are already known, and, in particular, their dependence on the amount of real balances already specified; hence one of the major tasks Pigou sets out for himself (viz., the determination of the demand for money) is already fully accomplished. Furthermore, as emphasized in the text, this first stage constitutes all of economic analysis; all that remains is the arbitrary specification of the quantity of money. This is hardly the fitting point of departure for an essay whose whole purpose is to show how demand-and-supply analysis can be applied to the problem of money.

Further light on this question is cast by the passage in Marshall to which Pigou seems to be referring. This passage reads as follows:

The pure theory of foreign trade . . . is based upon the hypothesis that two countries, say England and Germany, carry on trade with each other but only with each other. . . . *It is assumed that the pure theory of domestic values has provided the means of measuring the value in England of all the various wares exported by England in terms of any one of them.* Suppose cloth of a definite quality to be one of them; then the value, in England, of all the wares which England exports may be expressed as that of a certain number of yards of cloth. So the value in Germany of all the wares which Germany exports may be expressed as that of, say, a certain number of yards of linen.[45]

The parallelisms between this passage and Pigou's are quite clear. Hence, if Pigou is "adopting" Marshall's plan, he is assuming that "the value of all commodities other than money in terms of one another" has been "independently determined" by the "pure theory of domestic values." But this is the essence of the invalid dichotomy.[46]

---

[43] "Value of Money," *op. cit.*, pp. 163–64, italics added.
[44] Cf. p. 106.
[45] A. Marshall, *The Pure Theory of Foreign Trade*, p. 1, italics added.
[46] Cf. p. 112 above.

Monetary Aspects of the Casselian System

Cassel's familiar version of the Walrasian system[1] is of particular interest to us because of its oft-quoted conclusion that the system of equations can determine prices "only up to a multiplicative factor" and that it is the function of monetary theory to provide this missing factor.[2]   In order to understand the meaning of this conclusion in Cassel's system, we must first unravel the implicit assumptions on which the system is based.   This is the purpose of the present study. As with Walras above, we can restrict the discussion to the case of a simple exchange economy.

Cassel presents his system in Book I of his work.   This location is of critical significance.   For Cassel repeatedly emphasizes that the prevailing assumption of Book I is that money exists only as an abstract unit of account.[3]   Correspondingly, the prices to which he refers throughout this book—and throughout the well-known Chapter IV, in particular—are, in our terminology, accounting prices.

---

[1] G. Cassel, *The Theory of Social Economy*, trans. S. L. Barron (new revised ed.; New York, 1932), Chapter IV.   As Wicksell has emphasized, despite the obvious indebtedness of his work to Walras', Cassel does not cite him even once (*Lectures I*, p. 225).

[2] *Theory of Social Economy*, p. 155.

[3] Cf. the following two passages, occurring in Book I: "In the following theoretical inquiries into the exchange economy in general, we shall regard money merely in its use as a common scale of reckoning in all economic valuations.   This does not mean that the eventual actual use of a material commodity as a medium of exchange has no special economic significance.   Such a significance there is, but the study of it belongs to the special theory of money, and must be deferred to Book III." (*Ibid.*, pp. 46–47.)

"Money shall, as we said, be introduced only as a scale of reckoning. . . .   We may assume money calculations to be merely bookkeeping, and payments in money as so many book entries. For the moment we will ignore the existence of a material commodity used as money.   The question of how the scale of reckoning is itself decided upon—how prices are fixed in concrete figures—must be left open until we consider it in the special theory of money." (*Ibid.*, p. 50.)

For similar passages, see p. 383, last paragraph before new section (for the meaning of "price-scale" in this paragraph, see *ibid.*, p. 374); and p. 440, lines 3–4.

These passages make it quite clear that on this one point Wicksell's criticism of Cassel in his *Lectures I* (p. 224) is not valid.   For Wicksell interprets Cassel as dealing with a unit of account which is also a commodity.   Note, however, that Wicksell later grudgingly indicates that Cassel may have had in mind an abstract unit of account and seems to concede that in such a case Cassel's argument is logically intact (*ibid.*, p. 225, lines 5–7).

Similarly, the fact that Bent Hansen disregards the preceding passages suffices to invalidate the interpretation of Cassel which he presents in his " Role of Money in the Classical Economic

Let us now examine Cassel's system in detail. For convenience we shall denote his abstract unit of account by the "guinea." Assume that there is a simple exchange economy[4] with n commodities, the respective accounting—that is, guinea—prices of which are denoted by $p_1, \ldots, p_n$. Each consumer in this economy is given an initial credit of a fixed number of guineas which he is free to spend as he chooses during the period.[5] Let the demand functions of this economy be represented by[6]

$$
\begin{aligned}
D_1 &= F_1(p_1, \ldots, p_n), \\
D_2 &= F_2(p_1, \ldots, p_n), \\
&\ \cdots\cdots\cdots\cdots\cdots \\
D_n &= F_n(p_1, \ldots, p_n).
\end{aligned}
$$

(1)

Let "the [given] quantities of goods available to consumers in a particular period"[7] be represented by S_i. Our equilibrium conditions are then[8]

$$
\begin{aligned}
F_1(p_1, \ldots, p_n) &= S_1, \\
F_2(p_1, \ldots, p_n) &= S_2, \\
&\ \cdots\cdots\cdots\cdots\cdots \\
F_n(p_1, \ldots, p_n) &= S_n.
\end{aligned}
$$

(2)

Interdependence System—Patinkin vs. Cassel [in Danish]," *Ekonomisk Tidskrift*, LIV (1952), 100–120. These passages are also ignored in H. Dickson's criticism in the same volume (pp. 152–59) and Hansen's reply to him (pp. 226–27). See also footnote 5 below.

I am indebted to Hansen for providing me with a typescript of R. S. Stedman's English translation of his article.

4 In order to avoid possible confusion, it might be noted that our use of this term does not correspond to Cassel's. He uses it to describe an economy in which production may also take place (*Theory of Social Economy*, pp. 42 ff.).

5 "We first assume that the quantity of money which every consumer expends on the satisfaction of his wants in the period under consideration is fixed in advance." (*Ibid.*, p. 138.)

Lest we think that the phrase "quantity of money" refers to a money which physically exists as a medium of exchange, and thus indicates a dropping of the general assumption of Book I that money is only an abstract unit of account, we should note how Cassel describes this assumption at every later point: " In the present case, where the money expenditure of consumers is given beforehand . . ." (*ibid.*, p. 140); "Our main assumptions were that the sums of money to be spent by consumers are fixed beforehand, . . ." (pp. 148–49); "We first assumed, as we said, that the sum of money which every consumer expends for the satisfaction of his wants in the unit period is fixed in advance" (p. 150); ". . . on the assumption that the aggregate payments of consumers were given" (p. 151); "This condition was fulfilled so long as the total expenditure of the consumer, reckoned in money terms, was taken for granted" (p. 155).

Each of these passages bears out the interpretation presented here in the text. Each also shows us how we should understand the parallel passages in the nonmathematical version of Cassel's argument on pp. 64 (lines 1–6), 73 (lines 8–6 from bottom), and 76 (lines 18–22).

It is on the passage from p. 140 that Hansen—mistakenly, in my judgment—justifies his procedure of ignoring Cassel's general proclamation of the role of money in his Book I (Hansen, *op. cit.*, p. 108).

6 The following reproduces Cassel's system (1), *Theory of Social Economy*, p. 139.

7 *Ibid.*, p. 138. See also p. 141, lines 4–7.

8 The following reproduces Cassel's system (2), *ibid.*, p. 140.

Cassel then concludes: "This series of equations contains n equations for determining the n unknown prices; which is, in general, sufficient for determining the n unknown quantities. In the present case, where the money expenditure of consumers is given beforehand, prices, too, are obviously fixed at their absolute level."[9]

The first thing that strikes our attention in this passage is the apparent failure to take account of the equational dependence dictated by Walras' Law. But a closer investigation of Cassel's system shows that actually no such dependence exists! This is a consequence of the crucial assumption that the amounts individuals can spend are fixed beforehand and are therefore independent of the amounts of commodities supplied on the market. That is, these supplies appear, as it were, from some exogenous source, so that their sale does not generate income for consumers. It is the severing of this customary link which invalidates Walras' Law and thereby validates Cassel's otherwise unacceptable procedure.

We can see this most clearly through the following reformulation of Cassel's argument: Let each individual maximize his utility, subject to the restraint of the fixed number of guineas he can spend. Let I_0 represent the total amount of guinea-credits made available in the economy as a whole. Then it can be readily shown that, in the absence of distribution effects, the demand functions in (1) above have the form

$$D_1 = G_1\left(\frac{p_1}{p_n}, \ldots , \frac{p_{n-1}}{p_n}, \frac{I_0}{p_n}\right),$$

$$\cdots\cdots\cdots\cdots\cdots\cdots\cdots\cdots\cdots\cdots$$

$$(3) \quad D_{n-1} = G_{n-1}\left(\frac{p_1}{p_n}, \ldots , \frac{p_{n-1}}{p_n}, \frac{I_0}{p_n}\right),$$

$$D_n = G_n\left(\frac{p_1}{p_n}, \ldots , \frac{p_{n-1}}{p_n}, \frac{I_0}{p_n}\right) \equiv I_0 - \sum_{j=1}^{n-1} p_j G_j\left(\frac{p_1}{p_n}, \ldots , \frac{p_{n-1}}{p_n}, \frac{I_0}{p_n}\right).$$

For simplicity, we have deflated all prices by p_n; we could just as well have taken any other price. We have also made use of the budget restraint

$$(4) \qquad\qquad \sum_{i=1}^{n} p_i D_i = I_0$$

to rewrite the demand function for the nth commodity as indicated.[10]

---

[9] *Ibid.*, p. 140.
[10] That Cassel was aware that his demand functions depended on I_0, but that he omitted this because of its constancy, is indicated by his statement on p. 152, lines 8–9.

Our equilibrium conditions (2) then become

$$G_1\left(\frac{p_1}{p_n}, \ldots, \frac{p_{n-1}}{p_n}, \frac{I_0}{p_n}\right) = S_1,$$

. . . .

(5)

$$G_{n-1}\left(\frac{p_1}{p_n}, \ldots, \frac{p_{n-1}}{p_n}, \frac{I_0}{p_n}\right) = S_{n-1},$$

$$I_0 - \sum_{j=1}^{n-1} p_j G_j\left(\frac{p_1}{p_n}, \ldots, \frac{p_{n-1}}{p_n}, \frac{I_0}{p_n}\right) = S_n,$$

where the S_i are constants. Because of the argument I_0/p_n, the p_i do *not* appear solely as ratios. Hence, as Cassel states, the preceding system is one of n equations in the n individual prices, p_i.

Let us now see if this system possesses the usual equational dependence of general-equilibrium systems. Assume that the set of prices $p_1^0, \ldots, p_n^0$ satisfy the first $n - 1$ of these equilibrium equations. This set will also satisfy the last equation if and only if

(6)
$$I_0 - \sum_{j=1}^{n-1} p_j^0 S_j = S_n.$$

But, in general, there is no reason to suppose that this will be the case. That is, the last equation of (5) also adds a restriction on the prices. Walras' Law does not hold![11]

There can be no doubt that Cassel was fully aware of the nature of his assumptions. Thus, after completing his discussion of the preceding case, and in the way of passing on to more complicated ones, he wrote:

> The assumption that the money expenditure of consumers on the purchase of finished goods for satisfying their wants is fixed in advance must now be dropped. The money payments of a consumer are clearly determined by his income. . . .
>
> The income of the individual is, however, determined by the prices of the factors of production which he sells in the course of the productive process. The various incomes of the members of the exchange economy are thus determined by the pricing process, and neither these incomes nor the payments made with them should therefore be regarded as magnitudes, fixed in advance, in the pricing problem. Not until we regard income, too, as one of the unknowns in the pricing problem are we in a position to deal

---

11 For a simple numerical example of the preceding system, see E. H. Phelps Brown, *The Framework of the Pricing System* (London, 1936), pp. 80–83. The assumptions of this example effectively reduce money to a pure unit of account (*ibid.*, pp. 43–45).

with the pricing problem in a way which accurately reflects our exchange economy, shows that consumers are at the same time producers, and indicates how much of the final product the individual producer is in a position to acquire in exchange for his productive labour. The pricing problem, thus given a general application, contains in itself the problem of economic distribution.[12]

Under the new assumption that consumers' incomes are generated by their sales of initial quantities of commodities,[13] the budget restraint (4) is replaced by

(7)
$$\sum_{i=1}^{n} p_i D_i = \sum_{i=1}^{n} p_i S_i;$$

and Cassel's demand equations (1) now assume the familiar form[14]

$$D_1 = H_1\left(\frac{p_1}{p_n}, \ldots, \frac{p_{n-1}}{p_n}\right),$$

. . . .

(8)
$$D_{n-1} = H_{n-1}\left(\frac{p_1}{p_n}, \ldots, \frac{p_{n-1}}{p_n}\right),$$

$$D_n = H_n\left(\frac{p_1}{p_n}, \ldots, \frac{p_{n-1}}{p_n}\right) \equiv S_n + \sum_{j=1}^{n-1} \frac{p_j}{p_n}\left[S_j - H_j\left(\frac{p_1}{p_n}, \ldots, \frac{p_{n-1}}{p_n}\right)\right].$$

In contrast with the demand functions (3), these depend solely on the ratios of the prices. And, just as our interpretation leads us to expect, this is precisely the property which Cassel now—*and for the first time*—ascribes to his demand functions.[15]

---

12 *Theory of Social Economy*, pp. 150–51.

To translate these passages into a form appropriate for an exchange economy in our sense of the term, replace "factors of production" in the first sentence of the second paragraph cited by "initial quantities of commodities." Analytically, nothing is thereby changed.

13 See the preceding footnote.

14 Cf. Mathematical Appendix 2:*d*.

15 As I read it, Cassel's argument proceeds as follows: In the paragraph beginning on the bottom of p. 151 he explains that as a result of the new assumptions set out in the long citation above, "the content of equations [(1)] . . . is now changed" since they "no longer include the total payments which we previously assumed to be given as constants." The argument is then interrupted by the paragraph beginning "So far . . ." on p. 152 and is not taken up again until the paragraph beginning "It is clear . . ." on p. 154. In this paragraph Cassel then says that the demand functions depend only on the ratios of the prices of the productive services. Translated into terms of an exchange economy in our sense of the term, this means that they depend on the ratios of the accounting prices of commodities. This is the basis for the interpretation in the text here.

The equilibrium conditions corresponding to the foregoing demand functions have the form[16]

$$H_1\left(\frac{p_1}{p_n}, \ldots, \frac{p_{n-1}}{p_n}\right) = S_1,$$

$$\cdots\cdots\cdots\cdots\cdots\cdots$$

(9)
$$H_{n-1}\left(\frac{p_1}{p_n}, \ldots, \frac{p_{n-1}}{p_n}\right) = S_{n-1},$$

$$\sum_{j=1}^{n-1}\frac{p_j}{p_n}\left[S_j - H_j\left(\frac{p_1}{p_n}, \ldots, \frac{p_{n-1}}{p_n}\right)\right] = 0.$$

We note, first, that the reintroduction of the supply-income nexus has revalidated Walras' Law: any set of prices satisfying the first $n - 1$ equations must clearly also satisfy the nth. We note second—in the words of the oft-quoted statement with which Cassel concludes his discussion and to which we referred at the beginning of this study—that

... the system of equations is indeterminate, in that it determines the prices in question only up to a multiplicative factor; or, as it is popularly expressed, determines only the relative and not the absolute prices. In order to obtain the absolute prices, a new condition must be introduced; for example, the price of a commodity or of a group of commodities must be given. This condition was fulfilled so long as the total expenditure of the consumer, reckoned in money terms, was taken for granted. In the general pricing problem, a multiplicative factor of all prices remains undetermined. The determination of this factor, and, consequently, the final solution of the pricing problem, belongs to the theory of money.[17]

This brings us to our main point. For if the foregoing interpretation is correct, what Cassel has established is the indeterminacy of *accounting* prices. He is, then, quite right in saying that this indeterminacy can be removed by specifying "the price of a commodity or of a group of commodities." He is, however, quite wrong in implying that this is what is done by "the theory of money." For, on the one hand, the specification of accounting prices is a purely arbitrary act, completely outside the realm of economic analysis; while, on the other, the theory of

---

16 Note that the following system is equivalent to that of Mathematical Appendix 3:*a*.

17 *Ibid.*, p. 155.

Phelps Brown (*op. cit.*, pp. 142–46) overlooks the fact that the introduction of the supply-income nexus renders his system indeterminate. This can be seen most easily by noting that the replacement of the two budget restraints on the bottom of p. 212 by those on the bottom of p. 144 leaves the resulting system on pp. 212–13 dependent only on the ratios of prices.

money is concerned with *money* and not *accounting* prices. Thus Cassel, like Fisher, is guilty of confusing these fundamentally distinct prices.[18]

As a corollary to the preceding confusion, Cassel seems also to have confused the valid dichotomy between money and accounting prices with the invalid one between relative and money prices. In particular, because of his failure to realize the crucial analytical distinction between money which is only an abstract unit of account and money which is also a concrete medium of exchange, Cassel carries over intact his analysis of Book I (which, as already emphasized, assumes an abstract money) to Book III (which assumes a concrete one). Accordingly, he continues to refer in Book III to this earlier analysis and to imply that his commodity equations of Book I are valid also for a money economy; that these equations determine only relative, and not money, prices; and that this indeterminacy is removed by adding to these equations the cash-balance equation, $PTR = M$, where R is the equivalent of the Cambridge K. This interpretation—and its attribution to Cassel of the invalid dichotomy—is borne out by the juxtaposition of the passage from Book I of the *Theory of Social Economy* just cited and the following two passages from Book III:

> For theoretical economics, our analysis of money has a special significance. Just as the fixing of prices is a primary practical need of every system of exchange, so also must the fundamental treatment of the theory of exchange be carried through as an analysis of the determination of prices. It has been shown in the first two Books of this work that such a theory can be worked out as a theory of the determination of prices *without it being necessary for special attention to be devoted to the part played by the existing means of payment*. The analysis of the origin of the monetary system shows that this role, by its very conception, is distinct from the part played by the price-scale. For the purposes of theoretical treatment, it is natural that the part played by the means of payment, and especially its significance for the price-scale, should be made the object of a special inquiry. This gives us the task of Book III.[19]
>
> When the demand for money is given, equilibrium requires the demand for money

---

[18] The reader will find it convenient to read this paragraph against the background of Chapters III:2–3 and VIII:3. See especially pp. 106–7. On Fisher, see beginning of Note F:3.

It should be clear that my criticism of Cassel is not the fruitless terminological one that the foregoing statement uses "absolute prices" to denote what I call "accounting prices," but the substantive one that the last sentence of this statement describes the determination of accounting prices—be they called what one wishes—in an incorrect way.

[19] *Theory of Social Economy*, p. 383, with italics added. Much the same passage appears in the earlier edition of Cassel's work translated by J. McCabe (New York, 1924), p. 356. Indeed, I suspect that the original German versions are identical.

Note that Cassel uses "theory of the determination of prices" to mean "theory of the determination *of relative commodity prices.*" This is important for an understanding of some of the passages quoted below.

to be equal to the total quantity of money present M—that is, that $PTR = M$. This equation suffices to determine the unknown—the general price-level.[20]

Further support for this interpretation comes from Cassel's discussion in his *Fundamental Thoughts in Economics*,[21] in which he refers back to the discussion in his *Theory of Social Economy*[22] and writes:

True, there remains the important question: How is the unit of money fixed, what determines its purchasing power, and how can the stability of this unit be guaranteed? These questions cannot be answered at the outset of our study of economics. They must necessarily be deferred to a later exposition of the theory of money. However, our discussion has already shown what is the essential task of this theory: the theory of money has to clear up how the purchasing power of an abstract unit of money is determined.

In our first exposition of the general economic theory we must simply postulate a unit of money as fixed and invariable. If we do that we are able to construct a theory of prices, and the result of this theory is that, in a state of equilibrium, the prices of all goods are determined. However, as they are determined in a unit which is itself left undetermined, it is clear that the prices of goods can only be determined, in the general theory, relatively to one another.[23] This means that the prices of goods are determined except for a multiplicative factor which rests undetermined. This degree of undeterminedness can be removed by fixing absolutely one price. As soon as this is done, all prices are fixed at their absolute level. To explain how this absolute fixation of prices is possible is just the special task of the theory of money, and this is, therefore, a question which must be passed by in an exposition of the general economic theory. When we come later to the theory of money, it will show itself to be a great advantage to have the objects of this theory thus definitely fixed beforehand. The exposition here given of the role of the scarcity of the means of payment with regard to fixation of absolute price already determines the main lines on which the whole theory of money has to proceed.[24]

The place of the theory of money in the general economic theory is, according to what I have said, determined by the nature of the solution of the general problem of price-setting outlined in these lectures.[25] We have postulated a monetary unit in which we can reckon all prices, and we have found that prices reckoned in this unit are determined *by our system of equations* except for a multiplicative factor. This degree of undeterminedness can only be removed by fixing the unit in which prices are reckoned. To show how this is done is the task of the theory of money.[26]

---

[20] *Theory of Social Economy*, trans. S. L. Barron, p. 457. Much the same passage appears in the earlier McCabe translation (New York, 1924), p. 432.

For similar passages in the Barron translation, see p. 456, paragraph beginning "If we wish ...," and p. 458, lines 6–8.

[21] London, 1925.

[22] Trans. McCabe.

[23] Note again how by "general economic theory" Cassel means "general theory *of the determination of relative commodity prices*."

Note too how this paragraph up to this point—and particularly its first sentence—fits in with the statement of the invalid dichotomy given on pp. 111–12 above.

[24] *Fundamental Thoughts in Economics*, pp. 61–63.

[25] Once again, by "general economic theory" and "general problem of price-setting" Cassel is referring to relative commodity prices; see footnote 23 above.

[26] *Ibid.*, p. 123, italics added.

The following passage from Cassel's *On Quantitative Thinking in Economics*[27]—which also takes the *Theory of Social Economy* as its frame of reference—is likewise revealing:

In my representation of the equilibrium theory of prices a monetary system is postulated, and the question of how the monetary unit itself is fixed is left to be treated in a separate theory of money. The central task of this theory is to show how the unit of money may be fixed by a suitable restriction of the supply of means of payment. Thus the general price-problem is divided into two problems: first a problem of how *relative* prices are determined; secondly, a problem of how the *general level* of prices is fixed. This separation of the two different sides of the general price-problem is a *first* characteristic of my treatment of this problem. I believe that it is so natural, and has such great scientific and educational advantage, that it is hardly possible to do without it.[28]

We note finally that in his monetary theory Cassel implies the existence of a demand curve for money which is of uniform unitary elasticity. Specifically, he states that "the demand for money, in conditions which otherwise are equal, is proportional to the general price-level."[29] As in the case of Marshall and Pigou,[30] it is clear from the context that Cassel is referring here to a demand curve, and not a market-equilibrium curve.[31]

---

27 Oxford, 1935.

28 *Ibid.*, p. 154, italics in original.

For additional support of the foregoing interpretation, see Cassel's earlier discussion in his *Nature and Necessity of Interest* (London, 1903), pp. 70–71 and 158–60, noting in particular the statement on p. 70 that "it has been thought necessary to make a separate theory of value: such a theory should explain the relative values of commodities, *irrespective of any common measure of value or medium of exchange*" (italics added).

See also the following passage from Cassel's "Rate of Interest, the Bank Rate, and the Stabilization of Prices," *Quarterly Journal of Economics*, XLII (1927–28), as reprinted in *Readings in Monetary Theory*, p. 319, noting again the explicit sense in which Cassel uses the term "general economic theory":

When we postulate an abstract unit in which all prices are reckoned, we are able to study all problems concerning relative prices; that is we can master the whole domain usually comprised under the heading of general economic theory. There remains, however, one essential question to be solved. The question is, how the unit itself is determined, or, in other words, how the absolute height of prices is fixed. This question forms the object of the theory of money, and its solution is in fact the only essential task of this theory.

In the paragraph before this passage, Cassel refers to his *Theory of Social Economy*.

On the other hand, it should be pointed out that at another point in his writing Cassel provides what might be taken to be an expression of the valid first dichotomy of Chapter VIII:3. In particular, he states that "the equilibrium system of equations can only determine *relative* prices. The *absolute* height of prices is a monetary question, depending as it does on the supply of means of payment." ["Keynes' 'General Theory,'" *International Labour Review*, XXXVI (1937), 439, italics in original.]

29 *Theory of Social Economy*, p. 456.

30 Above, Note G:3.

31 Bent Hansen has informed me that the material referred to in footnotes 20 and 29 above does not appear in the second revised Swedish edition (1938) of Cassel's work. More specifically, all the material in the Barron translation from p. 455 (line 2 from bottom) to the end of §50 on p. 459 is omitted from this Swedish edition. I am unable to judge the significance of this fact.

Dichotomies of the Pricing Process

1. THE FIRST VALID DICHOTOMY[1]

I have not succeeded in finding an example spelled out in detail of the valid dichotomy between money and relative prices. It should, however, be clear from the text that it is implicit in any of the frequent statements in the literature that a change in the quantity of money causes a proportionate change in prices. The reason these statements fall just a shade below being full expressions of the dichotomy is that they usually do not explicitly add the obvious and undoubtedly recognized implication that relative prices remain unaffected. In some cases, however, this is made explicit—as the following passage from McCulloch shows:

> But though the quantity of money in circulation determines the *price* of commodities, or their value estimated in money, it does not exercise the smallest influence over the quantity of other commodities for which any one in particular will exchange.[2]

We have also the following passage from Davenport:

> The level of general prices, therefore, is unimportant to the trader. If what he sells changes in price, this does not matter so long as what he buys correspondingly changes. *The real and essential relations of goods to goods are finally in no wise complicated by the situation of prices in general or by the volume of media.* So elastic is the demand for media that indefinite increases in its volume may be absorbed through a general rise of prices.[3]

This passage is of particular interest in that it illustrates one of the pitfalls of textual interpretation on the point in question. Specifically, the first sentence by itself seems to say that demand must remain unaffected by a proportionate change in prices; but subsequent sentences show that Davenport is here considering a change in prices accompanied by a corresponding change in the amount of money, so that no

---

[1] Attached to Chapter VIII:3, especially pp. 105–6.

The nature of this dichotomy and its misleading similarities to the invalid third dichotomy were described in my "Further Considerations of the General Equilibrium Theory of Money," *op. cit.*, Section 5. See also my "Indeterminacy of Absolute Prices," *op. cit.*, p. 23.

[2] J. R. McCulloch, *The Principles of Political Economy* (fourth ed.; Edinburgh, 1849), p. 217, italics in original.

[3] H. J. Davenport, *The Economics of Enterprise* (New York, 1913), p. 273, italics added.

454

real-balance effect exists. But, as in the case of Fisher,[4] there is no evidence that Davenport was aware of the critical importance of this additional assumption.

Passages similar to McCulloch's can be found in James Mill,[5] Barbour,[6] Hawtrey,[7] and Cassel.[8]

2. THE SECOND VALID DICHOTOMY[9]

There are many examples of the valid dichotomy between money and accounting prices.[10] In all of them the presentation is like that of Mathematical Appendix 8:*a*(ii) above. Thus see, for example, Wicksell,[11] Fisher,[12] Bowley,[13] and Cassel.[14] The last of these inspired similar statements by other members of the Swedish school such as Ohlin,[15] Lindahl,[16] and Lundberg.[17]

3. THE THIRD AND INVALID DICHOTOMY[18]

The preceding notes have presented the varying degrees of evidence that leads one to suspect that the original exponents of general-equilibrium analysis—Walras,[19] Fisher,[20] and Cassel[21]—were themselves already involved in the invalid dichotomy. Regardless of the conclusiveness of this evidence, this much is clear: none of these writers—

---

[4] See the penultimate paragraph of Note F:3 above.

[5] *Op. cit.*, p. 121.

[6] *Op. cit.*, pp. 41, 44.

[7] *Currency and Credit*, pp. 35–36. Note that Hawtrey's assumed "unit of value" is not an abstract one in our sense of the term, but corresponds instead to a fiat paper money. Its "abstractness" for Hawtrey lies in its existence only as an account in the bank. But since these accounts constitute hoards of purchasing power, they "exist" in exactly the same sense that paper money does [*ibid.*, pp. 3, 5, 7, 14 ("In the first place . . ."), and 33].

[8] Cf. p. 453, footnote 28, above. As emphasized there, however, Cassel was confused on this point.

[9] Attached to Chapter VIII:3, especially pp. 106-7.

[10] For an early example of a precisely drawn distinction between accounting and money prices, see A. Cournot, *Mathematical Principles of the Theory of Wealth* (1838), trans. N. T. Bacon (New York, 1929), p. 27. Cournot, however, has no discussion of the dichotomy.

[11] *Lectures I*, pp. 66–67; cf. above, Note E:3. See also his *Value Capital and Rent*, pp. 79–80, 91–92.

[12] *Mathematical Investigations in the Theory of Value and Prices*, pp. 58–62.

[13] A. L. Bowley, *The Mathematical Groundwork of Economics* (Oxford, 1924), p. 52.

[14] As interpreted in Note H above, especially pp. 450–51.

[15] B. Ohlin, *Interregional and International Trade* (Cambridge, Mass., 1933), p. 556.

[16] E. Lindahl, *Studies in the Theory of Money and Capital* (London, 1939), pp. 282–83.

[17] E. Lundberg, *Studies in the Theory of Economic Expansion* (Stockholm, 1937), pp. 6–7

[18] Attached to Chapter VIII:3, especially p. 108, footnote 33, and p. 112.

[19] Note C:4 (end). See also the discussion there of Schlesinger.

[20] Note F:3.

[21] Note H, pp. 451–53.

nor Wicksell either[22]—explicitly and precisely defined the correct relationship that exists between the commodity equations and the money equation. Thus if they were not the advocates of the invalid dichotomy, they were certainly not its opponents.

When we turn to later writers, all doubts disappear. Here we find explicit presentations of the invalid dichotomy in all its details. The first such presentation—to my knowledge—was due to Divisia. This writer considered an economy consisting of only commodities and money. He then took it upon himself to fill the monetary "lacuna" in Pareto's theory (he ignored Walras) and did so by clearly stating that the commodity equations, which independently determine relative prices, must be "complemented" by the monetary equation, which then determines the absolute price level.[23] This invalid description of the relationship between monetary and value theory acquired the status of undisputed, received doctrine in its repeated endorsements and restatements at the hands of such writers as Marget,[24] Rosenstein-Rodan,[25] Myrdal,[26] Lange,[27] Modigliani,[28] Schneider,[29] Hickman,[30] and

---

[22] Note E:3. Cf. also the discussion of Pigou in Note G:4.

[23] F. Divisia, *Economique rationelle* (Paris, 1927), pp. 413–15. His argument is essentially the one presented in Mathematical Appendix 7:a(iii)—with the $(n - 1)$th good treated as a commodity (see *ibid.*, p. 334, footnote 2).

[24] *Theory of Prices*, Vol. II, p. 284, footnote 132, where Marget endorses Divisia's treatment as "superior to that of Pareto" and "in all essentials identical" with that of Walras.

[25] *Op. cit.*, pp. 257–58.

[26] *Op. cit.*, pp. 11–12.

[27] " Say's Law . . . ," *op. cit.*, pp. 64–65. True, Lange does object here to the dichotomy—but only because he adds to it the assumption of Say's Identity. When, however, he drops this assumption, he explicitly concedes to Modigliani that the dichotomy is valid (Modigliani, *op. cit.*, p. 217, footnote 35).

It might also be noted that in Appendix 4 to his *Price Flexibility and Employment* (Bloomington, Ind., 1945), Lange presents a model which, despite the fact that it includes bonds, is involved in exactly the same type of indeterminacy as that shown to hold for the invalid dichotomy. The reason for this is that Lange effectively applies the homogeneity postulate to the bond equation as well as to the commodity equations. That is, his explicit assumptions imply that the former too is independent of real balances. Hence an equi-proportionate departure of prices from an initial set of equilibrium values does not disturb equilibrium in the bond market either. Hence the absolute level of money prices is indeterminate. (For the details of this argument, cf. above, p. 110.)

The puzzling thing is that even though Lange himself proves this indeterminacy in the Appendix to his book (p. 102), he makes no mention of it in the text proper! This leads to all sorts of internal inconsistencies in his argument. Thus on p. 14 of the text he argues that an equi-proportionate decrease in prices may well cause a decrease in the *real* excess demand for money; while on p. 100 of the Appendix he proves that the excess-demand function for *nominal* money holdings is homogeneous of degree one in the prices—so that an equi-proportionate change in prices can *never* affect the real value of these holdings.

[28] *Op. cit.*, Section 13. The title of this section is "The Logical Consistency of the Quantity Theory of Money and the Dichotomy of Monetary and Real Economics." In the penultimate paragraph of this section Modigliani writes: "The necessary condition for money to be neutral

---

[*Footnotes 29 and 30 on next page.*]

Hart.[31, 32]   This status was reinforced by the acceptance of the invalid dichotomy's central proposition by Leontief,[33] Haberler,[34] Marschak,[35]

is that the $n - 1$ 'real' demand and supply equations be homogeneous of order zero. . . ." This is the mathematical term for dependence solely on relative prices. It should also be noted that money is "neutral" for Modigliani if and only if the quantity theory holds. (Cf. above, p. 108, footnote 34.)

29 E. Schneider, *Pricing and Equilibrium*, trans. T. W. Hutchison (London, 1952), pp. 290–307, especially pp. 304–6; cited in F. H. Hahn's review of the book in *Economic Journal*, LXIII (1953), 409.

The following passage from Schneider is particularly instructive:

We have introduced money as a means of payment *after* the equilibrium price relations were determined, simply for the purpose of giving an absolute level to the prices, and in order to determine the multiplicative factor left indeterminate in equations (10), (11), and (12). [These are essentially the excess-demand equations for commodities.] The quantity equation was, as it were, fitted on subsequently as an appendix to the "essential" equations (10), (11), and (12). It is important to emphasize that the equilibrium relative prices are completely independent of the monetary resources of the system. They result from equations (10), (11), and (12), which have nothing to do with monetary factors. [*Op. cit.*, p. 306, italics in original.]

30 W. Braddock Hickman, "The Determinacy of Absolute Prices in Classical Economic Theory," *Econometrica*, XVIII (1950), 9–20.

31 *Op. cit.*, p. 144, especially footnote 4.

32 In my "Dichotomies of the Pricing Process in Economic Theory" [*Economica*, XXI (1954), 124], I also referred to Hicks' *Value and Capital* as providing a statement of the invalid dichotomy. This has been changed here because his case is not as absolutely clear-cut as those of the other writers just listed. In particular, Hicks provides the only instance that I have been able to find of a writer who presents the dichotomy for an economy in which there are bonds as well as commodities (*ibid.*, pp. 158–59). On the other hand, it should be emphasized that there is nothing to indicate that Hicks had in mind the valid form of the dichotomy presented on p. 109 above. Indeed, by his failure to point out the crucial role that the bond market can play in his dichotomy, and by his entitling his discussion "The traditional dichotomy between 'real' and 'monetary' economics" (*ibid.*, p. ix, heading for Section 5 of Chapter XII), Hicks clearly implies that he draws no significant distinction between his version of the dichotomy and the more familiar one presented by the other writers just listed. Similarly, his failure to offer any criticism of this more familiar dichotomy would seem to indicate that he sees no basic objection to it.

33 W. W. Leontief, "The Fundamental Assumption of Mr. Keynes' Monetary Theory of Unemployment," *Quarterly Journal of Economics*, LI (1936–37), 192. Here he italicizes the "homogeneity postulate": "*The quantity of any service or any commodity demanded or supplied by a firm or an individual remains unchanged if all the prices upon which it (directly) depends increase or decrease exactly in the same proportion.*"

Leontief then states:

The significance of this theorem for the analysis of monetary influences within the framework of our economic system has been mentioned often enough. It is best expressed by the well-known hypothetical "experiment" of doubling overnight the cash holdings of all business enterprises and households. Ricardo used this device to show that the prices of all commodities and services will undergo under this condition a proportionally equal change, and the quantities produced, traded and consumed by all individual firms and households will remain exactly the same as before. *His conclusion is obviously based upon the homogeneity postulate.* [*Ibid.*, p. 193, italics added.]

The italicized sentence shows that Leontief considers the homogeneity postulate to be a necessary condition for the quantity theory (cf. above, p. 108, footnote 34). Leontief then argues

[*Footnotes 34 and 35 on next page.*]

Samuelson,[36] Tinbergen,[37] and Boulding[38]—all of whom stated or implied that the commodity equations depend only on relative, and not

---

that the distinguishing feature of Keynes' *General Theory of Employment, Interest, and Money* is the repudiation of this postulate. This context thus makes it clear that Leontief is talking about a money economy and is referring to money prices.

The passage from Leontief cited in Chapter VIII:4 of the text occurs in his "Interrelation of Prices, Output, Savings, and Investment," *Review of Economic Statistics*, XIX (1937), 116. To this passage is appended a footnote referring the reader to the *Q. J. E.* article just cited. This footnote refers to the article as a whole; but there can be no doubt from the context that it is specifically related to the homogeneity postulate—and this is the way I have interpreted it in the text (p. 114).

This postulate has continued to appear in Leontief's writings. See in particular his reaffirmation of it in his comment on my 1949 *Econometrica* article in the same journal, XVIII (1950), 21–24. Indeed, this postulate still forms one of the basic ones on which Leontief develops the "theoretical scheme" in back of his input-output analysis in the second edition of his *Structure of American Economy, 1919–1939* (second ed., enlarged; New York, 1951), Part II, p. 46 in particular. This fact lends even greater strength to T. C. Koopman's observation—made on other grounds—that the "designation 'general equilibrium analysis' for [Leontief's] ... model ... is inappropriate." This, however, does not affect the validity of Leontief's statistical analysis as such. See "Papers and Proceedings," *American Economic Review*, XXXIX (1949), 234.

34 G. Haberler, *Prosperity and Depression* (third ed.; Geneva, 1941), p. 460, footnote 1, where Haberler reproduces Leontief's homogeneity postulate and identifies it with absence of "money illusion." It is particularly interesting to contrast this with the central role Haberler assigns to the real-balance effect elsewhere in his book; see *ibid.*, pp. 242, 389, 403, 491–503.

35 J. Marschak, "Money Illusion and Demand Analysis," *Review of Economic Statistics*, XXV (1943), 40.

36 In his analysis of the demand functions of a money economy Samuelson writes: "These equations are homogeneous of order zero in all prices and income just as in the usual case of demand" (*Foundations*, p. 121). Earlier Samuelson indicates that prices are not necessarily measured in terms of an abstract unit of account (p. 119, lines 8–7 from bottom; p. 120, lines 3–8). Note also Samuelson's reference to Marschak's article mentioned above.

The specific passage from Samuelson cited in Chapter VIII:4 of the text occurs in his "Note on the Pure Theory of Consumer's Behavior," *Economica*, V (1938), 63. It is reproduced here in full—again, with one of those revealing footnotes:

> *Postulate II.* We further assume that the consumer's behavior is independent of the units in which prices are expressed. More specifically, if we multiply all prices and income by the same positive quantity, the amounts taken will remain the same.*
>
> ---
> * This homogeneity assumption has been challenged by Mr. Keynes with respect to a different problem. For the pure theory of consumer's behavior it is probably without objection. In any case it is always implicitly made.

From the context of Postulate II it is clear that Samuelson has accounting prices in mind. This is implied by the fact that the prices of his n goods are written $p_1, \ldots, p_n$, and we never find one of these prices set equal to unity. Now, the footnote is obviously an implicit reference to Leontief's article on Keynes cited in footnote 33 above. Thus Samuelson identifies his postulate, which can be true only for *accounting* prices, with Leontief's homogeneity postulate, which is stated for *money* prices.

37 J. Tinbergen, *Econometrics* (Philadelphia, 1951), p. 20. The crucial passage here reads: "... the so-called 'money-illusion,' through which the absolute value of the prices have an independent significance for ... [the buyer]."

38 K. E. Boulding, "Welfare Economics," in *Survey of Contemporary Economics: Vol. II*, ed. B. F. Haley (Homewood, Ill., 1952), pp. 28–29.

absolute, prices. Indeed, as emphasized in the text (pages 112–13), the willingness of most of these writers to denote the absence of this special type of dependence by the term "money illusion"[39] is itself conclusive evidence of the failure to fully understand the real-balance effect.

[39] This term seems first to have been used by Irving Fisher, though in a completely different sense. For him it denoted "the failure to perceive that the dollar, or any other unit of money, expands or shrinks in value," and the corollary tendency to speak as if the prices of commodities all happened to rise or fall at the same time by coincidence. See his *Money Illusion* (New York, 1928), p. 4.

The Classical and Neoclassical Theory of Money and Interest[1]

The passages on which the interpretation of the text is based—and to whose authors specific references are made—are to be found in Hume,[2] Thornton,[3] Ricardo,[4] Mill,[5] Sidgwick,[6] Marshall,[7] Pigou,[8] Giffen,[9] Wicksell,[10] and Fisher.[11] The reader will also find it instructive to consult Cantillon,[12] Jevons,[13] Bagehot,[14] Palgrave,[15] Walras,[16] Keynes,[17] and Hawtrey.[18]

---

[1] Attached to Chapter XV:1.
On this note, cf. J. W. Angell, *The Theory of International Prices* (Cambridge, Mass., 1926), Chapter V; F. A. Hayek, *Prices and Production* (second ed.; London, 1935), Lecture I.
[2] *Op. cit.*, p. 336.
[3] *Op. cit.*, pp. 261–62, 287–91.
[4] *Principles*, pp. 363–64; *High Price of Bullion, Works and Correspondence*, ed. Sraffa, Vol. III, p. 91.
[5] *Principles*, Book III, Chapter XXIII.
[6] *Op. cit.*, pp. 265, 279–94.
[7] *Principles*, pp. 520–21, 533–34. *Money Credit and Commerce*, pp. 73, 255–57. See also Marshall's testimony before the Gold and Silver Commission (1887) and the Indian Currency Committee (1899) as reprinted in *Official Papers by Alfred Marshall*, pp. 40–52, 127–31, 158, 270, 274, 307.
[8] A. C. Pigou, *Industrial Fluctuations* (second ed.; London, 1929), pp. 275–77.
[9] R. Giffen, *Essays in Finance*, second series (New York, 1886), pp. 37–88, especially pp. 47–51.
[10] See the detailed discussion in Note E:4 above.
[11] *The Rate of Interest*, pp. 8–9; *Elementary Principles of Economics*, 356–57; *The Theory of Interest*, p. 47.
[12] *Op. cit.*, pp. 199, 215. Cantillon emphasizes that the rate of interest is determined by "the proportionate number of Lenders and Borrowers."
[13] W. S. Jevons, *Investigations in Currency and Finance* (London, 1884), pp. 31–32.
[14] W. Bagehot, *Lombard Street* [originally published 1873 (new ed.; London, 1915), pp. 112–13].
[15] R. H. Inglis Palgrave, *Bank Rate in England, France, and Germany, 1844–78* (London, 1880), pp. 139–41. Cf. also the article on "Interest, Theory of," in *Palgrave's Dictionary of Political Economy* (new ed.; London, 1923), Vol. II, p. 428.
[16] *Elements*, ed. Jaffé, p. 333; cf. p. 406, footnote 73, above.
[17] In his review of Fisher's *Purchasing Power of Money, Economic Journal*, XXI (1911), 395.
[18] Independently of Wicksell, and in a somewhat different context, Hawtrey emphasizes the effect of the internal drain caused by a price increase on the discount policy of banks. Indeed, this is the crucial element of his monetary theory of the trade cycle. See, for example, his "Trade Cycle" (1926), reprinted in *Readings in Business Cycle Theory*, ed. G. Haberler (Philadelphia, 1944), especially pp. 341–45.

The following passages show the readiness of classical and neo-classical economists to recognize the permanent influence of a monetary change on the rate of interest in the case of "forced savings."[19]   Thus Mill concludes his analysis of this case with the observation:

> In any supposable case, however, the issue of paper money by bankers increases the proportion of the whole capital of the country which is destined to be lent.   The rate of interest must therefore fall, until some of the lenders give over lending, or until the increase of borrowers absorbs the whole.[20]

In the same vein, Nicholson, after arguing that the rate of interest remains invariant under a change in the monetary unit, writes:

> But although this general position with the assumptions made is theoretically sound, it is easy to show that the transition from one level of prices to another may have an effect on the rate of interest.
>
> In the example just taken the real burden of all fixed charges would be exactly one-twentieth of what it was before the depreciation of the standard. . . . And generally, so far as all old debts with fixed charges are concerned, the proportion of the national income absorbed by them would be so much less, and as a consequence there would be so much more available for fresh investment.   In other words, the extinction of so much debt would leave more to be lent, and if the demand did not increase proportionately, the rate of interest must fall.[21]

Similarly, Wicksell, after describing how an inflow of gold temporarily lowers the market rate but ultimately brings about higher prices at an unchanged rate of interest, writes:

> The objection has been raised to the whole of the above reasoning that a lowering of the loan rate must also depress the real rate. . . . This possibility certainly cannot be entirely rejected.   *Ceteris paribus* a lowering of the real rate unconditionally demands new real capital, i.e., increased saving.   But this would certainly occur, even if involuntarily, owing to the fact that higher prices would compel a restriction of consumption on the part of those people who had fixed money incomes. . . .[22]

As a final example we have the following citation from Pigou:

> When bankers create more credit for business men, they make, in their interest, subject to the explanations given in that chapter, a forced levy of real things from the public, thus increasing the stream of new capital available for them, and causing a fall in the

---

[19] For the history of this doctrine, see Hayek, *op. cit.*, pp. 18–22, and in particular the citation from Malthus on p. 32; "A Note on the Development of the Doctrine of 'Forced Saving,'" *Quarterly Journal of Economics*, XLVII (1932–33), 123–33; Jacob Viner, *Studies in the Theory of International Trade* (New York, 1937), pp. 187–97.

[20] *Essays on Some Unsettled Questions of Political Economy* (reprinted London, 1948), p. 118.

[21] *Principles of Political Economy*, Vol. II, p. 232.

[22] Wicksell, *Lectures II*, pp. 198–99; cf. Note E:4 above, especially p. 429, footnote 40.

Wicksell does not identify the source of the "objection" with which he begins this passage. He might have been thinking of Cassel, who states just this in his *Theory of Social Economy*, trans. J. McCabe (London, 1923), p. 479, footnote.   Unfortunately, I have not been able to check the earlier editions of Wicksell's *Lectures* in order to determine when this passage first appears.   (Cassel's statement was cited by Robertson; see footnote 25 below.)

real rate of interest on long and short loans alike. It is true, in short, that the bankers' rate for money is bound by a mechanical tie to the real rate of interest on long loans: but it is not true that this real rate is determined by conditions wholly outside bankers' control.[23], [24]

As an indication of the unjustified rigidity with which the classical theory of interest is today interpreted, we might finally note that both Metzler, the critic of this theory, and Robertson, its defender, are at one in regarding the proposition that the rate of interest can be permanently affected by forced savings as constituting a significant deviation from the classical view.[25]

---

[23] *Industrial Fluctuations*, p. 277. (Cited by Metzler; see footnote 25 below.)

[24] For another example similar to the preceding ones, see Mises, *op. cit.*, Part III, Chapter V, especially pp. 347–48.

[25] In particular, Metzler cites the foregoing passage from Pigou as evidence that "his ideas concerning the interest rate were somewhat nonclassical even before . . . his *Employment and Equilibrium*" ("Wealth, Saving, and the Rate of Interest," *op. cit.*, p. 95, footnote 7); while Robertson cites Cassel's criticism of Wicksell's earlier position that the real rate remains unchanged throughout the cumulative process as "an exception" to the view of "classical or neo-classical writers" that "the rate of interest can sensibly be regarded as in the long run invariant to changes in the supply of money." Robertson also adds that "Keynes in his *Treatise* days (Vol. I, p. 198) rather unexpectedly sided on this issue with Wicksell's [original view]." ["More Notes on the Rate of Interest," *Review of Economic Studies*, XXI (1953–54), 137.]

NOTE K

Keynes' *General Theory*

1. THE REAL-BALANCE EFFECT [1]

There are several passages in the *General Theory* which clearly reflect Keynes' implicit assumption that the real-balance effect does not directly influence the commodity market.   In particular, when Keynes, in his Chapter XIX, turns to a detailed analysis of the "repercussions" of a wage and price decline on the propensity to consume and on the marginal efficiency of capital, he completely ignores the real-balance effect this decline generates.[2]   Instead he concludes:

> It is, therefore, on the effect of a falling wage- and price-level *on the demand for money* that those who believe in the self-adjusting quality of the economic system must rest the weight of their argument; though I am not aware that they have done so.   If the quantity of money is itself a function of the wage- and price-level, there is indeed, nothing to hope in this direction.   But if the quantity of money is virtually fixed, it is evident that its quantity in terms of wage-units can be indefinitely increased by a sufficient reduction in money wages. . . .[3]

Thus a wage and price decline is analytically equivalent to an increase in the quantity of money; hence, argues Keynes, it is like the latter in influencing effective demand only through its prior influence on the rate of interest.[4]

   In our terminology, then, Keynes restricts the direct influence of the real-balance effect to the money market.   But, as already indicated in the text, this is for him the obverse side of the bond market.   In particular, he repeatedly emphasizes that the alternative to holding

---

[1] Attached to pp. 109–10, 113 (footnote 44), 163, and 173–74.

[2] *General Theory*, pp. 261–66.   Similarly, at an earlier point Keynes observes that "no reason has been given why a change in the quantity of money should affect either the investment demand-schedule or the readiness to save out of a given income" (*ibid.*, p. 182).   True, this comment occurs when Keynes is projecting himself into the classical position, and so may be cited out of context; on the other hand, it clearly implies that Keynes himself has "no reason" to give for such an effect.

[3] *Ibid.*, p. 266, italics added.

[4] *Ibid.*, p. 266.   Note also Keynes' later statement that "the primary effect of a change in the quantity of money on the quantity of effective demand is through its influence on the rate of interest" (*ibid.*, p. 298).

money is to hold bonds, and that any excess supply of the former is diverted to purchasing the latter.[5] There is never any indication that it may also be diverted to purchasing commodities.

It is interesting to speculate on the train of reasoning which misled Keynes into this one-sided view. It seems likely that he did recognize the general influence of assets on the demand for consumption commodities, but that he thought of this influence only in terms of physical assets. This was his initial error. From it, it immediately followed that in his main discussion of the short-run consumption function—where, by assumption, the stock of physical assets is fixed[6]—he did not even consider the possible influence of assets.[7] On the other hand—and this is precisely what our interpretation leads us to expect—as soon as Keynes discussed a period long enough for noticeable capital growth, he immediately recognized that the resulting increase in wealth causes a decrease in the propensity to save.[8] But this, unfortunately, did not bring him to realize that an analogous influence could exist even in the short run, provided one took account of *monetary* assets as well as *physical* ones.

The intellectual atmosphere which characterized the advent of Keynesian economics was hardly conducive to correcting this error. For in those first exciting days of analyzing aggregate demand in terms of the *flows* of consumption and investment, it was distinctly old-fashioned to explore the influence on this demand of the *stock* of money Thus despite the fact that Haberler in 1939 had already begun to draw the implications of the real-balance effect for Keynesian economics,[9] and that Pigou in 1943 had devoted to it a major article,[10] the formulators of Keynesian models continued to ignore this effect in their consumption functions until the obvious pressures of postwar excess liquidity made it impossible to do so any longer. And even then they

[5] *General Theory*, pp. 84, 168–69, 171–72, 199–202, 205–6
[6] *Ibid.*, p. 245.
[7] *Ibid.*, Chapter VIII, especially pp. 91–95.
[8] *Ibid.*, p. 218, second paragraph.
[9] *Prosperity and Depression* (third ed., 1941), pp. 242, 389, and 403. These pages appear unchanged from the 1939 edition. In the 1941 edition Haberler enlarged and elaborated on this earlier discussion (*ibid.*, pp. 491–503). Note also the reference on p. 499 to T. de Scitovsky, "Capital Accumulation, Employment and Price Rigidity," *Review of Economic Studies*, VIII (1940–41), 71–72.
It should, however, be recalled that even Haberler failed to see the full implications of this effect; cf. Note I:3.
[10] A. C. Pigou, "The Classical Stationary State," *Economic Journal*, LIII (1943), 343–51. See also his earlier *Employment and Equilibrium* (London, 1941), pp. 126–29 [cited by G. Ackley, "The Wealth-Saving Relationship," *Journal of Political Economy*, LIX (1951), 154, footnote 1]; and his later "Economic Progress in a Stable Environment," *Economica*, XIV (1947), reprinted in *Readings in Monetary Theory*, pp. 241–51.

did not always see the equilibrating role of this effect in curbing demand during the course of an inflationary price movement.[11]

It should be clear that this criticism can be no cause for comfort in the classical camp, for, as has been sufficiently emphasized in the text,[12] the neoclassical economists were themselves the progenitors of the mental block which prevented the full recognition of the real-balance effect. Indeed, on this point their position is even weaker than Keynes'. For in all probability the neoclassical economists were involved in the invalid dichotomy, whereas Keynes need not have been. In particular, since he recognized the real-balance effect in the bond market, his model can be rationalized along the lines of the system of equations (1), (5), (3), (4) in Chapter X above.[13] On the other hand, it should be emphasized that this is purely a rationalization on our part; there is no intention of implying here that Keynes' procedure on this matter was motivated by any awareness of the invalid dichotomy.

2. The Theory of Interest [14]

On page 199 of the *General Theory*, Keynes writes his liquidity-preference equation in the by-now familiar form

$$M = M_1 + M_2 = L_1(Y) + L_2(r).$$

The proper interpretation of this equation turns on the crucial question as to the units in which M and Y are measured. If they are real units, the equation is free of money illusion, and the interpretation of Chapter XIII:4 applies.[15] If they are nominal units, the equation reflects

---

[11] Cf. Chapter X:3, especially p. 160.

See, for example, the distinctly Keynesian analysis of the report on *Inflationary and Deflationary Tendencies, 1946–48*, prepared by the United Nations Department of Economic Affairs (New York, 1949). Here the damping effect of a price rise is restricted to its effect on the distribution of income (*ibid.*, p. 7). Similarly, Bent Hansen's monograph on the *Theory of Inflation* (London, 1951) completely overlooks this effect; cf. especially pp. 133–35.

To the best of my knowledge, the first explicit account of the role of the real-balance effect in slowing down an inflationary process was given by E. M. Bernstein, "Latent Inflation: Problems and Policies," *International Monetary Fund: Staff Papers*, I (1950), 1–16. It is, of course, implicit in the passage from Wicksell cited in full in Note E:1 above; but see the next paragraph.

[12] Chapter VIII:1–4.

[13] See pp. 152 and 163; cf. also p. 109.

[14] Attached to Chapter XV:2, and to Chapters XII:1 and XIII:4.

[15] Note that in this event Keynes would be involved in the error of attributing uniform unitary elasticity to the demand function for money; cf. Chapter XI:1.

money illusion in the speculative demand, and the interpretation of Chapter XII:1 applies.[16]

Unfortunately, the discussion in which the foregoing equation is imbedded is completely ambiguous on this point. But if we go on a few pages we find the following revealing passage:

> In a static society or in a society in which for any other reason no one feels any uncertainty about the future rates of interest, the Liquidity Function L_2, or the propensity to hoard (as we might term it), will always be zero in equilibrium. Hence in equilibrium $M_2 = 0$ and $M = M_1$; so that any change in M will cause the rate of interest to fluctuate until income reaches a level at which the change in M_1 is equal to, the supposed change in M. Now $M_1 V = Y$, where V is the income-velocity of money as defined above and Y is the aggregate income. Thus if it is practicable to measure the quantity, O, and the price, P, of current output, we have $Y = OP$, and therefore, $MV = OP$; which is much the same as the Quantity Theory of Money in its traditional form.[17]

The equating of Y to OP in this passage clearly implies that the former is measured in nominal units. The equating of $M_1 V$ to Y then implies that M_1, too, is measured in these units. Hence, if this usage is extended to the earlier discussion on page 199, the liquidity-preference equation there is clearly involved in a money illusion.

Further evidence that Keynes conceived of his liquidity-preference equation in nominal terms is provided by the following passage:

> It may illustrate the argument to point out that, if the liquidity-preferences due to the transactions-motive and the precautionary-motive are assumed to absorb a quantity of cash which is not very sensitive to changes in the rate of interest as such and apart from its reactions on the level of income, so that the total quantity of money, less this quantity, is available for satisfying liquidity-preferences due to the speculative-motive, the rate of interest and the price of bonds have to be fixed at the level at which the desire on the part of certain individuals to hold cash (because at that level they feel "bearish" of the future of bonds) is exactly equal to the amount of cash available for the specula-

---

[16] We are assuming here that an increase in Y causes a proportionate increase in the transactions-precautionary demand, so that *this* demand is not affected by money illusion. That this assumption accords with Keynes' is indicated by the passage from the *General Theory*, pp. 171–72, cited below. Cf. also the following passage from a later article: "So far as the active circulation [i.e., transactions and precautionary balances] is concerned, it is sufficiently correct as a first approximation to regard the demand for money as proportionate to the effective demand, i.e., to the level of money income." This is a first approximation only because the active demand "is also to some extent a function of the rate of interest"—a factor obviously ignored in the liquidity-preference equation cited here. This passage would also seem to indicate that Y in this equation should be understood as money income. ["The Theory of the Rate of Interest," in *Lessons of Monetary Experience: Essays in Honor of Irving Fisher* (1937), reprinted in *Readings in the Theory of Income Distribution*, ed. W. Fellner and B. F. Haley (Philadelphia, 1946), pp. 421–22.]

[17] *General Theory*, pp. 208–9.

It might be incidentally noted that Keynes' argument here is incorrect. For, as the analysis of Chapter XI:3 above shows, the condition $L_2 = 0$ is *not* necessary for the validity of the quantity theory.

tive-motive. Thus each increase in the quantity of money must raise the price of bonds sufficiently to exceed the expectations of some "bull" and so influence him to sell his bond for cash and join the "bear" brigade. If, however, there is a negligible demand for cash from the speculative-motive except for a short transitional interval, an increase in the quantity of money will have to lower the rate of interest almost forthwith, in whatever degree is necessary to raise employment *and the wage-unit* sufficiently to cause the additional cash to be absorbed by the transactions-motive and the precautionary-motive.

As a rule, we can suppose that the schedule of liquidity-preference relating the quantity of money to the rate of interest is given by a smooth curve which shows the rate of interest falling as the quantity of money is increased. For there are several different causes all leading towards this result.

In the first place, as the rate of interest falls, it is likely, *cet. par.*, that more money will be absorbed by liquidity-preferences due to the transactions-motive. For if the fall in the rate of interest increases the national income, the amount of money which it is convenient to keep for transactions will be increased more or less proportionately to the increase in income; whilst, at the same time, the cost of the convenience of plenty of ready cash in terms of loss of interest will be diminished. *Unless we measure liquidity-preference in terms of wage-units rather than of money* (which is convenient in some contexts), similar results follow if the increased employment ensuing on a fall in the rate of interest leads to *an increase of wages, i.e. to an increase in the money value of the wage-unit.* In the second place, every fall in the rate of interest may, as we have just seen, increase the quantity of cash which certain individuals will wish to hold because their views as to the future of the rate of interest differ from the market views.[18]

The first italicized clause of the last paragraph clearly indicates that in general Keynes does *not* measure liquidity preference in the real terms of wage-units.[19]

As noted in the text, the money-illusion interpretation receives convincing support from Keynes' significant failure to ever indicate that the nominal speculative demand is sensitive to changes in the price level.[20] In particular, Keynes' discussion of the foregoing equation on pages 200–201 is void of any such recognition. Nor is it likely that this merely

---

[18] *General Theory*, pp. 171–72, italics added.

It might also be noted that this passage clearly reveals Keynes' basic confusion between a demand curve and a market-equilibrium curve (cf. above, p. 262). In particular, in the second paragraph of this passage Keynes sets himself the task of establishing the negative slope of the demand curve for money with respect to the rate of interest. Yet he attempts to do so—in the beginning of the third paragraph—by analyzing the results of a *market-experiment* in which the quantity of money is increased. (That Keynes is considering such an increase in the third paragraph is clear both from the first paragraph and from the sentence which immediately follows the passage just cited: "Nevertheless, circumstances can develop in which even a large increase in the quantity of money may exert a comparatively small influence on the rate of interest.")

[19] Note, however, the ambivalent passage earlier in his discussion in which Keynes states that "an individual's liquidity-preference is given by a schedule of the amounts of his resources, valued in terms of money or of wage-units, which he will wish to retain in the form of money in different sets of circumstances" (*ibid.*, p. 166).

[20] Above, p. 263.

indicates the assumed presence of absolute wage and price rigidity.   For in this discussion Keynes assumes Y to increase as a result of an increase in M; and in general—and even under the assumption of unemployment—Keynes assumes that increases in the level of employment (and hence real income) generate increases in the wage-unit.[21]

Any remaining doubts about the validity of this interpretation are removed by the structure of Keynes' argument in the passage just quoted—a passage which closely parallels that of pages 200–201.   The phrases italicized in the first and last paragraphs of this passage show that Keynes is taking into consideration a possible rise in the wage-unit. Yet though Keynes indicates the implications of this rise for the transactions and precautionary demands, he does not do so for the speculative demand.   This omission is particularly significant in the last paragraph, where—as shown by the last sentence—Keynes is assuming the existence of a speculative demand which is not negligible.

This same significant omission also characterizes Keynes' observation at a later point that "a reduction of the wage-unit will release cash from its other uses for the satisfaction of the liquidity-motive."   It is clear from the context that by "liquidity-motive" Keynes means "speculative motive."   Yet there is no recognition of the fact that just as a reduction of the wage-unit can reduce the demand for cash for "other uses," so too can it reduce the demand for speculative uses.[22]

Consider finally the passage in which Keynes writes:

> If the reader still finds himself perplexed [by the proposition that an increase in the desire to save will not reduce interest], let him ask himself why, the quantity of money being unchanged, a fresh act of saving should diminish the sum which it is desired to keep in liquid form at the existing rate of interest.[23]

It is clear from the context that by "the sum . . ." Keynes is referring to

---

[21] *General Theory*, pp. 249, 251, 301.

[22] *Ibid.*, p. 232 (top).   For a similar passage, see p. 298, lines 11–5 from bottom, noting that by "schedule of liquidity-preference" Keynes has in mind only the schedule of the speculative demand.   For another instance in which this term is used in this narrow sense, see p. 168. This is one of the pitfalls in interpreting Keynes' monetary theory: "liquidity-preference" can mean either the total, $L_1(Y) + L_2(r)$, or just $L_2(r)$ by itself.   The reader must in each case determine the intended meaning from the context.

All of the foregoing passages show us how we should understand the less specific passages in the *General Theory* in which Keynes merely indicates that a fall in the wage-unit increases the real value of money balances and thereby decreases interest (cf., e.g., pp. 253, 266–67).   Here, too, the intention is that the decrease in the wage-unit decreases the amount of money needed for transactions and precautionary motives, and hence increases the residual amount available for the speculative motive.   That is, there is no intention in these passages that the speculative demand is also decreased by the fall in the wage-unit.

[23] *Ibid.*, p. 213.

the speculative demand. The answer, then, to Keynes' confident conundrum is that this "sum" will diminish as a result of the effect of "the fresh act of saving" in decreasing aggregate demand for commodities and hence prices.[24] But this is an answer which Keynes— significantly enough—does not give.

The only passage seemingly at variance with the foregoing interpretation of Keynes occurs in his Appendix to Chapter XIV. Here Keynes cites in full Ricardo's discussion of the rate of interest[25] and then states:

(1) If Ricardo had been content to present his argument solely as applying to any given quantity of money created by the monetary authority, it would still have been correct on the assumption of flexible money-wages. (2) If, that is to say, Ricardo had argued that it would make no permanent alteration to the rate of interest whether the quantity of money was fixed by the monetary authority at ten millions or at a hundred millions, his conclusion would hold. (3) But if by the policy of the monetary authority we mean the terms on which it will increase or decrease the quantity of money, i.e., the rate of interest at which it will, either by a change in the volume of discounts or by open-market operations, increase or decrease its assets—which is what Ricardo expressly does mean in the above quotation—then it is not the case either that the policy of the monetary authority is nugatory or that only one policy is compatible with long-period equilibrium; (4) though in the extreme case where money-wages are assumed to fall without limit in face of involuntary unemployment through a futile competition for employment between the unemployed labourers, there will, it is true, be only two possible long-period positions—full employment and the level of employment corresponding to the rate of interest at which liquidity-preference becomes absolute (in the event of this being less than full employment). (5) Assuming flexible money-wages, the quantity of money as such is, indeed, nugatory in the long period; (6) but the terms on which the monetary authority will change the quantity of money enters as a real determinant into the economic scheme.[26]

At first sight, Keynes' concession to Ricardo in the second sentence seems to contradict the assumption of money illusion in the speculative demand, for under this assumption changes in the quantity of money can permanently alter the rate of interest, even with perfectly flexible money wages.[27] But we must note that this passage as it now stands also contradicts Keynes' own later insistence that the validity of the quantity theory depends on the assumption that the speculative demand is zero.[28] This leads me to suspect that in the preceding passage

---

24 Cf. above, pp. 174 and 185.

25 *Principles*, ed. Sraffa, *op. cit.*, p. 363.

26 *General Theory*, p. 191. The statements have been numbered for convenience of reference. The fifth one has already been cited on p. 264, footnote 25.

27 Cf. Chapter XII:1.

28 See the passage from pp. 208–9 cited at the beginning of this section. Note that Keynes again emphasizes the importance of this assumption for classical theory in his "Theory of the Rate of Interest," *op. cit.*, pp. 423–24.

Keynes is tacitly assuming the absence of any speculative demand. If this is true, both contradictions disappear simultaneously.[29]

We might finally note that Keynes' agreement with Leontief that his differences with classical monetary theory flow from a denial of the homogeneity postulate[30] cannot be taken as evidence that Keynes was aware of his money-illusion assumption in our sense of the term. For, as has been sufficiently emphasized in the text, the denial of Leontief's homogeneity postulate does not imply money illusion in this sense; furthermore, any theory of money must be based on such a denial.[31] Even aside from this, it is not at all clear what Keynes had in mind when he agreed with Leontief. For he supports this agreement with an immediate reference to his paper on the "Theory of the Rate of Interest"[32] where—as far as I can see—this postulate plays no role.

3. The Theory of Unemployment [33]

Clearly, Keynes recognized the importance of wage rigidities in the real world.[34] Nevertheless, as emphasized in the text, these rigidities do not constitute a logically necessary part of his theory of unemployment. Indeed, such an interpretation stands in direct contradiction to Keynes' Chapter XIX, the very title of which is "Changes in Money-Wages." This chapter—which forms the climax of Keynes' argument—applies the analytical apparatus of the *General Theory* to a detailed examination of the implications of downward wage flexibility and concludes that:

There is, therefore, no ground for the belief that a flexible wage policy is capable of maintaining a state of continuous full employment;—any more than for the belief that an open-market monetary policy is capable, unaided, of achieving this result. The economic system cannot be made self-adjusting along these lines.[35]

---

[29] Another obscure point in this passage is the nature of the distinction which Keynes has in mind in his second and third—and fifth and sixth—statements. Without at all being sure, I think it is related to the distinction made in the text between an increase in the quantity of money generated by a gratuitous distribution of new money by the government, and one generated by open-market purchases (Chapter XII:5).

[30] "General Theory of Employment," *Quarterly Journal of Economics*, LI (1936–37), 209.

[31] Chapter VIII:3.

[32] *Op. cit.*

[33] Attached to Chapter XIII:1 (especially p. 214) and Chapter XIV:1 (especially p. 237).

[34] Cf., e.g., *General Theory*, pp. 232–33, 303.

[35] *Ibid.*, p. 267.

In this context one might also cite in full the passage from p. 378 referred to on p. 237 above:

Furthermore, it seems unlikely that the influence of banking policy on the rate of interest will be sufficient by itself to determine an optimum rate of investment. I conceive,

Thus wage rigidities in this chapter are not an *assumption* of the analysis, but the *policy conclusion* which Keynes reaches after investigating the results to be expected from wage flexibility.[36]

All, then, that Keynes means by the statement that the system may settle down to a position of "unemployment equilibrium" is that the automatic workings of the system will *not* restore the system to a position of *full employment equilibrium*.   He does *not* mean "equilibrium" in the usual sense of the term that nothing tends to change in the system. All that is strictly in equilibrium is the level—or, possibly, only the fact— of unemployment; but there is no equilibrium of the money wage rate.[37]

This is admittedly loose—and hence undesirable—usage of a term which has a precise, accepted meaning.   We should recognize it as such and criticize it as such.   But we should not permit it to involve us in a futile and irrelevant debate on whether there can or cannot be a coexistence of "unemployment equilibrium" and "flexible wages." For, as emphasized in the text, if these terms are understood in their usual sense, such a coexistence is by definition impossible.   But, as also emphasized in the text, this has no bearing whatsoever on Keynes' central thesis: namely, that a full-employment policy based on the downward flexibility of money wages is not a practicable one.[38]

> therefore, that a somewhat comprehensive socialisation of investment will prove the only means of securing an approximation to full employment; though this need not exclude all manner of compromises and of devices by which public authority will co-operate with private initiative.

[36] See the final section of this chapter, *ibid.*, pp. 269–71.

[37] Evidence of this usage is provided by the long passage from the *General Theory*, p. 191, cited at the end of the preceding section.   Here, in the fourth statement, Keynes speaks of a "long-period position" of less-than-full employment—even though in this position "money-wages are assumed to fall without limit in face of involuntary unemployment."
Cf. also the following passage from p. 253:

> . . . if competition between unemployed workers always led to a very great reduction of the money-wage, there would be a violent instability in the price-level.   Moreover, there might be no position of stable equilibrium except in conditions consistent with full employment; since the wage-unit might have to fall without limit until it reached a point where the effect of the abundance of money in terms of the wage-unit on the rate of interest was sufficient to restore a level of full employment.   At no other point could there be a resting-place.

Here Keynes is using "equilibrium" in the strict sense of the term.   For a similar passage see pp. 303–4.

[38] Above, pp. 213–14 and 236–37.

NOTE L

On Say's Law[1]

Though the text has shown that Say's Identity is not a logically necessary component of the classical position,[2] there still remains the question as to whether Say, Ricardo, Mill—both senior and junior—and other deniers of the possibility of a "general glut" did or did not think in terms of this identity.

In support of Keynes'[3] and Lange's[4] contention that they did so think, one can cite the following passage from Say:

It is worth while to remark, that a product is no sooner created, than it, *from that instant*, affords a market for other products to the full extent of its own value. When the producer has put the finishing hand to his product, he is most anxious to sell it immediately, lest its value should diminish in his hands. Nor is he less anxious to dispose of the money he may get for it; for the value of money is also perishable. But the only way of getting rid of money is in the purchase of some product or other. Thus the mere circumstance of the creation of one product immediately opens a vent for other products.[5]

Similarly, Ricardo observes:

Whoever is possessed of a commodity is necessarily a demander, either he wishes to consume the commodity himself, and then no purchaser is wanted; or he wishes to sell it, and purchase some other thing with the money, which shall either be consumed by him, or be made instrumental to future production.[6]

And in the same vein James Mill writes:

. . . no man wants money but in order to lay it out, either in articles of productive, or articles of unproductive consumption.[7]

---

[1] Attached to Chapter XIV:4–5.

[2] For an earlier exposition and emphasis on this proposition, see my " Involuntary Unemployment and the Keynesian Supply Function," *Economic Journal*, LIX (1949), 378.

[3] *General Theory*, pp. 18–21, 25–26.

[4] "Say's Law: A Restatement and Criticism," *op. cit.*, pp. 52–53.

[5] J. B. Say, *A Treatise on Political Economy*, trans. C. R. Prinsep from the fourth French edition (Philadelphia, 1834), pp. 138–39; italics added from original French of third edition, *Traité d'économie politique* (Paris, 1817), p. 145.

The force of this evidence is, however, diminished by the fact that one page earlier Say presents the weaker statement that "even when money is obtained with a view to hoard or bury it, the *ultimate* object is always to employ it in a purchase of some kind" (*Treatise*, p. 137, footnote, italics added).

[6] *Notes on Malthus*, *Works*, ed. Sraffa, Vol. II, p. 305.

[7] *Elements of Political Economy* (London, 1821), pp. 191–92.

On the other hand, the standard passage from J. S. Mill which Keynes cites in support of his identity interpretation definitely does *not* carry the meaning that Keynes—and later writers—have attached to it. This passage reads:

> ... what it is which constitutes the means of payment for commodities ... is simply commodities. Each person's means of paying for the productions of other people consists of those which he himself possesses. All sellers are inevitably and *ex vi termini* buyers. Could we suddenly double the productive powers of the country, we should double the supply of commodities in every market; but we should, by the same stroke, double the purchasing power. Everybody would bring a double demand as well as supply: everybody would be able to buy twice as much, because everyone would have twice as much to offer in exchange.[8]

In order to see how this passage has been torn out of context, we must first note its place in the chapter in which it appears. In the first section of this chapter Mill refers to the overproduction thesis of Malthus, Chalmers, and Sismondi. He then begins the second section with the following paragraph:

> When these writers speak of the supply of commodities as outrunning the demand, it is not clear which of the two elements of demand they have in view—the desire to possess, or the means of purchase; whether their meaning is that there are, in such cases, more consumable products in existence than the public desires to consume, or merely more than it is able to pay for. In this uncertainty, it is necessary to examine both suppositions.[9]

Mill then devotes the remainder of this second section to the second "supposition" and shows that the "supply of commodities in general cannot exceed the power of purchase."[10] Finally he returns in the third section to the first "supposition" and argues that "the supply of commodities in general never does exceed the inclination to consume."[11]

Now, the passage which Keynes cites occurs in the second section of Mill's chapter. Hence it cannot refer to the *willingness* to consume—as Keynes would have it—but to the *power* to consume. Indeed, when read within the context that Mill specifies, this passage expresses

---

[8] J. S. Mill, *Principles*, Book III, Chapter XIV, Section 2, pp. 557–58. Cited in full—with minor modifications—by Keynes as an example of the "classical doctrine" that "the whole of the costs of production must necessarily be spent in the aggregate, directly or indirectly, on purchasing the product" (*General Theory*, p. 18).

I hasten to add that on an occasion when I cited this passage myself, I "clarified" its meaning by adding the words "and, presumably, would" in brackets after the "everybody would be able to" of its last sentence. ("Involuntary Unemployment and the Keynesian Supply Function," *op. cit.*, p. 377.) The distortion thereby introduced is clear from what follows immediately.

[9] *Principles*, p. 557.

[10] This is the heading of Section 2 as listed in the Table of Contents, *ibid.*, p. xliii.

[11] Heading for Section 3, *ibid.*, p. xliv.

nothing more objectionable than the innocuous "national income equals national product" identity of contemporary social accounting!

As against the foregoing interpretation of Keynes and Lange, we have the recent interpretation of Becker and Baumol[12] and Schumpeter[13]—all of whom maintain that Say's Law was not intended as an identity; that classical economists had reference only to the long-run ability of the economy to absorb any increase in output; and that this is attested by their explicit recognition of the possibility of short-run oversupply in the market.[14]

Evidence for this long-run interpretation of Say's Law—and, consequently, for viewing it as dealing with the question of secular stagnation as contrasted with that of cyclical depression—is provided by the fact that Ricardo, for example, discusses it in his Chapter XXI, entitled "Effects of Accumulation on Profits and Interest."[15] Similarly, Malthus criticizes this law in Chapter VII of his *Principles* ("On the Immediate Causes of the Progress of Wealth") under the subheading "Of Accumulation, or the Saving from Revenue to add to Capital, considered as a Stimulus to the Increase of Wealth."[16] On the other hand, Ricardo clearly recognizes the short-run "distress" that can be generated by "Sudden Changes in the Channels of Trade."[17] We might also note Ricardo's observation to Malthus:

> It appears to me that one great cause of our difference in opinion, on the subjects which we have so often discussed, is that you have always in your mind the immediate and temporary effects of particular changes—whereas I put these immediate and temporary effects quite aside, and fix my whole attention on the permanent state of things which will result from them.[18]

This distinction between the temporary "excess of all commodities above the money demand" which characterizes a "commercial crisis"

---

12 *Op. cit.*, pp. 360–61, 371–74.

13 *Op. cit.*, pp. 615–25.

See also G. J. Stigler, "Sraffa's *Ricardo*," *American Economic Review*, XLIII (1953), 591–99.

14 Indeed, Schumpeter—following A. P. Lerner—argues that Say's Law simply states that an increase in production generates a corresponding increase in income and hence an increase in aggregate demand (*op. cit.*, pp. 617, 623–24).

15 *Principles, Works*.

16 T. R. Malthus, *Principles of Political Economy* (first ed.) as abridged in Ricardo, *Works*, ed. Sraffa, Vol. II, pp. 300–301. The same is true of the second edition (Tokyo, 1936 reprint), pp. 309, 314.

17 *Principles*, title of Chapter XIX.

18 Letter to Malthus, *Works*, Vol. VII, p. 120.

Note that though Malthus begins his reply to this letter by stating his agreement with this observation, he goes on to say that

> ... a still more specific and fundamental cause of our difference [is that] ... you seem to think that the wants and tastes of mankind are always ready for the supply; while I am most decidedly of opinion that few things are more difficult, than to inspire new tastes and wants, particularly out of old materials. [*Ibid.*, p. 122.]

and the "permanent decline in the circumstances of producers, for want of markets" contemplated by opponents of Say's Law is made most explicitly by J. S. Mill.[19]   It should also be noted that Mill returns to the problem of Say's Law in Book IV (entitled "Influence of the Progress of Society on Production and Distribution"), Chapter IV (entitled "Of the Tendency of Profits to a Minimum"), and emphasizes that the real difficulty generated by an increasing amount of capital "would not consist in any want of a market," but in the fact that it is "impossible . . . to employ this capital without submitting to a rapid reduction of the rate of profit."[20]   All this emphasizes the long-run context in which Mill viewed the problem of overproduction.

It is also significant that in his famous Chapter XV "On Markets," Say adduces evidence in support of his thesis from the fact "that there should now be bought and sold in France five or six times as many commodities, as in the miserable reign of Charles VI [1380–1422]."[21] Again, in his *Letters to Malthus*, Say argues that the enactment of the Elizabethan Poor Laws proves that "*there was* no employ in a country which since then has been able to furnish enough for a double and triple number of laborers."[22]   Here is the same line of reasoning with which modern-day opponents of the "stagnation thesis" attempt to refute it by, say, citing Kuznets' data on the growth in per capita national product of the United States by more than three and a half times during the eighty-year period ending in 1948.[23]

Even if we accept this secular interpretation of Say's Law—and the evidence in favor of it is convincing—we must again emphasize that classical economists failed to specify the market mechanism which makes this law valid.[24]   In particular, they did not think in terms of the automatic price and interest variations analyzed in Chapter XIV:5.   There

---

19 *Principles*, p. 561.

20 *Ibid.*, p. 732.   Mill had already made this clear on pp. 561–62.

21 *Treatise*, p. 137.

22 (London, 1821; reprinted 1936), pp. 4–5, italics in original.

23 S. Kuznets, "Long-Term Changes in the National Income of the United States of America since 1870," *Income & Wealth of the United States: Trends and Structure*, ed. S. Kuznets, Income and Wealth Series II (Cambridge, 1952), p. 55.

24 Cf. end of Chapter XIV:5 above.
There are, indeed, hints here and there of an equilibrating mechanism, but these are never developed into a systematic theory.   Thus Say writes that "excessive saving . . . carries its remedy along with it.   Where the capitals become too abundant, the interest which the capitalists derive from them become too low to balance the privations they impose upon themselves by their savings" (*Letters to Malthus*, p. 37).   For a similar statement, see also Ricardo, *Notes on Malthus*, *Works*, ed. Sraffa, Vol. II, p. 309, note (199).   Ricardo also emphasizes his view that low profits can only mean high wages so that laborers will consume whatever capitalists do not (*ibid.*, pp. 308, 311).   For a similar statement, see J. S. Mill, *Principles*, pp. 66–68, 732.

would be no need to stress this here had not the contrary recently been implied.[25, 26]

---

[25] See Becker and Baumol, *op. cit.*, pp. 360–61, 374. These authors denote the process described in Chapter XIV:5 by the term "Say's Equality" and claim to find it presented in J. S. Mill, *Essays on Some Unsettled Questions of Political Economy*, pp. 67–74.

In these pages Mill does clearly provide a vivid picture of the temporary stagnation that would be generated if, for some reason, people "liked better to possess money than any other commodity" (p. 72). But he does not explain why the stagnation is only temporary, and he certainly does not say—or even imply—that the positive real-balance effect of a declining price level plays any role in the recovery. All he does say on this subject is contained in the following cryptic paragraph:

> It is true that this state [of stagnation] can be only temporary, and must even be succeeded by a reaction of corresponding violence, since those who have sold without buying will certainly buy at last, and there will then be more buyers than sellers. But although the general over-supply is of necessity only temporary, this is no more than may be said of every partial over-supply. An overstocked state of the market is always temporary, and is generally followed by a more than common briskness of demand [p. 71].

The present discussion should thus make it clear that "Say's Equality" is a completely misleading term. More specifically, though passages can be—and have been—cited to show that classical economists might have thought in terms of the "Identity," none have been cited that would justify the attempt to associate them with the "Equality."

[26] At first sight it seems tempting to describe the statement that the system must always be brought to a condition of full-employment equilibrium by

(a) $$\sum_{j=1}^{n-1} p_j D_j = \sum_{j=1}^{n-1} p_j S_j,$$

to be contrasted with the statement of Say's Identity (cf. Mathematical Appendix 7:*d*)

(b) $$\sum_{=1}^{n-1} p_j D_j \equiv \sum_{j=1}^{n-1} p_j S_j,$$

where p_j is the price of the *j*th commodity, D_j its quantity demanded, and S_j its quantity supplied. And this, indeed, is what Schumpeter does (*op. cit.*, p. 619). Actually, however, condition (a) says much less than what is said by Chapter XIV:4–5 and by the earlier article cited above (p. 472, footnote 2). The point of departure of these latter interpretations is that equilibrium means full employment, so that the essence of the classical position is that the system of equilibrium conditions

(c) $D_j(p_1, \ldots, p_{n-1}) = S_j(p_1, \ldots, p_{n-1})$ $(j = 1, \ldots, n-1)$

always has a solution. An immediate implication of this statement is then the much weaker statement (a).

References for the Preface

The critical articles referred to in the Preface are, in chronological order:

Herbert Stein, "Price Flexibility and Full Employment: Comment," *American Economic Review*, XXXIX (1949), 725–26.

This was a criticism of my "Price Flexibility and Full Employment" in the same journal, XXXVIII (1948), 543–64. I commented upon it in *ibid.*, XXXIX (1949), 726–28.

W. Braddock Hickman, "The Determinacy of Absolute Prices in Classical Economic Theory," *Econometrica*, XVIII (1950), 9–20.

Wassily Leontief, "The Consistency of the Classical Theory of Money and Prices," *Econometrica*, XVIII (1950), 21–24.

Cecil G. Phipps, "A Note on Patinkin's 'Relative Prices,'" *Econometrica*, XVIII (1950), 25–26.

These three articles were criticisms of my "Relative Prices, Say's Law, and the Demand for Money," *Econometrica*, XVI (1948), 135–54, and "The Indeterminacy of Absolute Prices in Classical Economic Theory," *ibid.*, XVII (1949), 1–27. They were replied to in my "Invalidity of Classical Monetary Theory," *ibid.*, XIX (1951), 134–51. They were also discussed in Karl Brunner, "Inconsistency and Indeterminacy in Classical Economics," in the same volume, pp. 152–73, and in Yukichi Kurimura, "On the Dichotomy in the Theory of Price," *Metroeconomica*, III (1951), 117–34.

F. H. Hahn, "The General Equilibrium Theory of Money—A Comment," *Review of Economic Studies*, XIX (1951–52), 179–85.

This was a criticism of my "Reconsideration of the General Equilibrium Theory of Money," *Review of Economic Studies*, XVIII (1950–51), 42–61. It was replied to in my "Further Considerations of the General Equilibrium Theory of Money," *ibid.*, XIX (1951–52), 186–95.

Gary S. Becker and William J. Baumol, "The Classical Monetary Theory: The Outcome of the Discussion," *Economica*, XIX (1952), 355–76.

Replied to in my "Dichotomies of the Pricing Process in Economic Theory," *Economica*, XXI (1954), 113–28.   This reply also provides a systematic survey of the entire preceding debate.   I should also add that at the time of writing it I had not yet seen the significance of the absence of stability analysis in neoclassical monetary theory, nor had I completed my study of Walras and his immediate successors.   This is the reason the refutation of Becker and Baumol's position implicit in Chapter VIII:1–4 (and particularly in pp. 112–13) is so much more categorical than in my original reply.

*   *   *   *   *

I might also take advantage of this note to refer briefly to F. J. de Jong's "Supply Functions in Keynesian Economics," *Economic Journal*, LXIV (1954), 3–24.   This is partly given over to a criticism of my "Involuntary Unemployment and the Keynesian Supply Function" in the same journal, LIX (1949), 360–83.   However, as I hope to show in greater detail elsewhere, de Jong's criticisms on p. 7 of his article are irrelevant to the general argument presented on pp. 368–70, 378–81 of my article.   (It is, of course, this general argument which is the basis of that in Chapters XIII–XIV above.)   Similarly, de Jong's contention that Keynes uses an aggregate supply function identical in conception with the one presented in my 1949 article cannot be maintained (cf. de Jong, *op. cit.*, Propositions II, XI, XII, and, especially, XIV).   In particular, Keynes' use of an "aggregate supply function" on pp. 26–27 of the *General Theory* (on which de Jong primarily relies) cannot be interpreted in this way.   This is immediately evident from Keynes' statement that under Say's Identity his (Keynes') "aggregate supply function" coincides with his "aggregate demand function"; whereas, as is shown by Figure 8 of my original article (or in Figure 43 above), this is definitely not true for our function.

As a result of other considerations, however, I have in this book modified my original graphical representation of the aggregate supply curve.   In particular, it is no longer represented as being dependent on Y (a point about which I always felt uncomfortable—"Involuntary Unemployment . . . ," *op. cit.*, p. 366); nor is it depicted as being a horizontal line.   Both of these changes are really in accordance with the general model presented in the original article (*ibid.*, pp. 378–81).

BIBLIOGRAPHY AND INDEXES

BIBLIOGRAPHY OF WORKS CITED[1]

Ackley, G., "The Wealth-Saving Relationship," *Journal of Political Economy*, LIX (1951), 154–61.

Allen, R. G. D., *Mathematical Analysis for Economists*, London, 1938.

Anderson, B. M., *The Value of Money*, New York, 1917.

Angell, J. W., *The Theory of International Prices*, Cambridge, Mass., 1926.

Antonelli, E., *Principes d'économie pure*, Paris, 1914.

Arrow, K. J., and Debreu, G., "Existence of an Equilibrium for a Competitive Economy," *Econometrica*, XXII (1954), 265–90.

Aupetit, A., *Essai sur la théorie générale de la monnaie*, Paris, 1901.

Auspitz, R., and Lieben, R., *Recherches sur la théorie du prix*, trans. L. Suret, Paris, 1914.

Bagehot, W., *Lombard Street* (1873), new ed., London, 1915.

Barbour, D., *The Standard of Value*, London, 1912.

Barone, E., "The Ministry of Production in the Collectivist State," *Collectivist Economic Planning*, ed. F A. Hayek, London, 1935, pp. 245–90.

Baumol, W. J., "The Transactions Demand for Cash: An Inventory Theoretic Approach," *Quarterly Journal of Economics*, LXVI (1952), 545–56.

Becker, G. S., and Baumol, W. J., "The Classical Monetary Theory: The Outcome of the Discussion," *Economica*, XIX (1952), 355–76.

Bernstein, E. M., "Latent Inflation: Problems and Policies," *International Monetary Fund: Staff Papers*, I (1950), 1–16.

Boulding, K. E., *Economic Analysis*, revised ed., New York, 1948.

——, "Welfare Economics," *Survey of Contemporary Economics: Vol. II*, ed. B. F. Haley, Homewood, Ill., 1952, pp. 1–38.

Bowley, A. L., *The Mathematical Groundwork of Economics*, Oxford, 1924.

Brown, A. J., *The Great Inflation: 1939–1951*, London, 1955.

Brown, E. H. P., *The Framework of the Pricing System*, London, 1936.

---

[1] Excludes certain works of a purely mathematical nature cited only in the Mathematical Appendix.

Brunner, K., "Inconsistency and Indeterminacy in Classical Economics," *Econometrica*, XIX (1951), 152–73.

Cagan, P., "The Monetary Dynamics of Hyper-inflations," *Econometrica*, XXII (1954), 518–19.

Cannan, E., "The Application of the Theoretical Apparatus of Supply and Demand to Units of Currency," *Economic Journal*, XXXI (1921); reprinted in *Readings in Monetary Theory*, ed. F. A. Lutz and L. W. Mints, Philadelphia, 1951, pp. 3–12.

———, *Money: Its Connexion with Rising and Falling Prices*, fourth ed., revised, London, 1923.

Cantillon, R., *Essay on the Nature of Trade* (1755), trans. and ed. H. Higgs, London, 1931.

Cassel, G., *The Nature and Necessity of Interest*, London, 1903.

———, *Fundamental Thoughts in Economics*, London, 1925.

———, "The Rate of Interest, the Bank Rate, and the Stabilization of Prices," *Quarterly Journal of Economics*, XLII (1927–28); reprinted in *Readings in Monetary Theory*, ed. F. A. Lutz and L. W. Mints, Philadelphia, 1951, pp. 319–33.

———, *The Theory of Social Economy*, new revised ed., trans. S. L. Barron, New York, 1932. (Trans. J. McCabe, New York, 1924.)

———, *On Quantitative Thinking in Economics*, Oxford, 1935.

———, "Keynes' 'General Theory,'" *International Labour Review*, XXXVI (1937), 437–45.

Chandler, L. V., *Economics of Money and Banking*, revised ed., New York, 1953.

Chapman, S., *Outlines of Political Economy*, second ed., London, 1917.

Christ, C., "A Test of an Econometric Model for the United States, 1921–1947," *Conference on Business Cycles*, New York, 1951, pp. 35–107.

Cohen, M., "Liquid Assets and the Consumption Function," *Review of Economics and Statistics*, XXXVI (1954), 202–11.

Cournot, A., *The Mathematical Principles of the Theory of Wealth* (1838), trans. N. T. Bacon, New York, 1929.

Davenport, H. J., *The Economics of Enterprise*, New York, 1913.

Demaria, G., "Pareto," reprinted in *The Development of Economic Thought*, ed. H. W. Spiegel, New York, 1952, pp. 629–51.

Dickson, H., "Remarks on B. Hansen's Essay on Cassel and Patinkin [in Swedish]," *Ekonomisk Tidskrift*, LIV (1952), 152–59.

Divisia, F., *Economique rationelle*, Paris, 1927.

Edgeworth, F. Y., *Mathematical Psychics* (1881), reprinted New York, 1953.

Edgeworth, F. Y., review of L. Walras' *Eléments d'économie politique pure*, second ed., in *Nature*, XL (1889), 434–36.

———, *Papers Relating to Political Economy*, 3 vols., London, 1925.

Ellis, H. S., *German Monetary Theory: 1905–1933*, Cambridge, Mass., 1934.

Evans, G. C., *Mathematical Introduction to Economics*, New York, 1930.

Fisher, I., *Mathematical Investigations in the Theory of Value and Prices* (1892), reprinted Yale University Press, 1925.

———, *The Rate of Interest*, New York, 1907.

———, *The Purchasing Power of Money*, New York, 1911; new and revised ed., 1913.

———, *Elementary Principles of Economics*, New York, 1912

———, *The Money Illusion*, New York, 1928.

———, *The Theory of Interest*, New York, 1930.

Friedman, M., *Essays in Positive Economics*, Chicago, 1953.

Giffen, R., *Essays in Finance*, second series, New York, 1886.

Gilbert, J. C., "The Demand for Money: The Development of an Economic Concept," *Journal of Political Economy*, LXI (1953), 144–59.

Goodwin, R. M., "Iteration, Automatic Computers, and Economic Dynamics," *Metroeconomica*, III (1951), 1–7.

———, "Static and Dynamic Linear General Equilibrium Models," *Input-Output Relations*, ed. The Netherlands Economic Institute, Leiden, 1953, pp. 54–87.

Graham, F. D., *Exchange, Prices, and Production in Hyper-Inflation: Germany 1920–23*, Princeton, 1930.

Gurley, J. G., "Excess Liquidity and European Monetary Reforms, 1944–1952," *American Economic Review*, XLIII (1953), 76–100.

Haberler, G., *Prosperity and Depression*, third ed., Geneva, 1941.

———, "The Pigou Effect Once More," *Journal of Political Economy*, LX (1951), 240–46.

Hahn, F. H., "The General Equilibrium Theory of Money—A Comment," *Review of Economic Studies*, XIX (1951–52), 179–85.

Haley, B. F., "Value and Distribution," *Survey of Contemporary Economics*, ed. H. S. Ellis, Philadelphia, 1948, pp. 1–48.

Hansen, A. H., "The Pigouvian Effect," *Journal of Political Economy*, LIX (1951), 535–36.

———, *A Guide to Keynes*, New York, 1953.

Hansen, B., *A Study in the Theory of Inflation*, London, 1951.

Hansen, B., "The Role of Money in the Classical Economic Interdependence System—Patinkin vs. Cassel [in Danish]," *Ekonomisk Tidskrift*, LIV (1952), 100–120.

Hart, A. G., *Money, Debt, and Economic Activity*, second ed., New York, 1953.

Hawtrey, R. G., "The Trade Cycle," *De Economist* (1926), as reprinted in *Readings in Business Cycle Theory*, ed. G. Haberler, Philadelphia, 1944, pp. 330–49.

———, *Currency and Credit*, third ed., London, 1927.

Hayek, F. A., "A Note on the Development of the Doctrine of 'Forced Saving,'" *Quarterly Journal of Economics*, XLVII (1932–33), 123–33.

———, *Prices and Production*, second ed., London, 1935.

Hegeland, H., *The Quantity Theory of Money*, Göteborg, 1951.

Helfferich, K., *Money*, trans. L. Infield, London, 1927.

Heller, W. W. (ed.), *Savings in the Modern Economy*, Minneapolis, 1953.

Henderson, H. D., *Supply and Demand*, revised ed., London, 1932.

Hickman, W. B., "The Determinacy of Absolute Prices in Classical Economic Theory," *Econometrica*, XVIII (1950), 9–20.

Hicks, J. R., "Gleichgewicht und Konjunctur," *Zeitschrift für Nationalökonomie*, IV (1933), 441–55.

———, "Léon Walras," *Econometrica*, II (1934), 338–48.

———, "A Suggestion for Simplifying the Theory of Money," *Economica*, II (1935), as reprinted in *Readings in Monetary Theory*, ed. F. A. Lutz and L. W. Mints, Philadelphia, 1951, pp. 13–32.

———, "Mr. Keynes and the 'Classics,'" *Econometrica*, V (1937), as reprinted in *Readings in the Theory of Income Distribution*, ed. W. Fellner and B. F. Haley, Philadelphia, 1946, pp. 461–76.

———, *Value and Capital*, Oxford, 1939; second ed., 1946.

———, *A Contribution to the Theory of the Trade Cycle*, Oxford, 1950.

Hume, D., *Philosophical Works*, 4 vols., Boston, 1854.

Jaffé, W., "Léon Walras' Theory of Capital Accumulation," *Studies in Mathematical Economics and Econometrics*, ed. O. Lange *et al.*, Chicago, 1942, pp. 37–48.

———, "Walrasiana: The *Eléments* and its Critics," *Econometrica*, XIX (1951), 327–28.

Jevons, W. S., *Investigations in Currency and Finance*, London, 1884.

Kaldor, N., "A Classificatory Note on the Determinateness of Equilibrium," *Review of Economic Studies*, I (1933–34), 122–36.

Kalecki, M., "Professor Pigou on the 'Classical Stationary State'—A Comment," *Economic Journal*, LIV (1944), 131–32.

Keynes, J. M., review of I. Fisher's *The Purchasing Power of Money*, in *Economic Journal*, XXI (1911), 393–98.

———, *A Tract on Monetary Reform*, London, 1923.

———, "Alfred Marshall, 1842–1924," *Memorials of Alfred Marshall*, ed. A. C. Pigou, London, 1925, pp. 1–65.

———, *A Treatise on Money*, 2 vols., London, 1930.

———, *The General Theory of Employment, Interest and Money*, New York, 1936.

———, "The General Theory of Employment," *Quarterly Journal of Economics*, LI (1936–37), 209–23.

———, "The Theory of the Rate of Interest," in *Lessons of Monetary Experience: Essays in Honor of Irving Fisher* (1937), as reprinted in *Readings in the Theory of Income Distribution*, ed. W. Fellner and B. F. Haley, Philadelphia, 1946, pp. 418–24.

———, "Alternative Theories of the Rate of Interest," *Economic Journal*, XLVII (1937), 241–52.

Kinley, D., *Money*, New York, 1904.

Klein, L. R., *The Keynesian Revolution*, New York, 1947.

———, *et al.*, "Stock and Flow Analysis in Economics," *Econometrica*, XVIII (1950), 236–52.

Knight, F. H., *The Ethics of Competition*, New York, 1935.

Kuenne, R. E., "Walras, Leontief, and the Interdependence of Economic Activities," *Quarterly Journal of Economics*, LXVIII (1954), 323–54.

Kurimura, Y., "On the Dichotomy in the Theory of Price," *Metroeconomica*, III (1951), 117–34.

Kuznets, S., "Long-Term Changes in the National Income of the United States of America since 1870," *Income & Wealth of the United States: Trends and Structure*, ed. S. Kuznets, International Association for Research in Income and Wealth, Income & Wealth Series II, Cambridge, 1952, pp. 29–241.

Lange, O., *On the Economic Theory of Socialism*, Minneapolis, 1938.

———, "Rate of Interest and the Optimum Propensity to Consume," *Economica*, V (1938), as reprinted in *Readings in Business Cycle Theory*, ed. G. Haberler, Philadelphia, 1944, pp. 169–92.

———, "Say's Law: A Restatement and Criticism," *Studies in Mathematical Economics and Econometrics*, ed. O. Lange *et al.*, Chicago, 1942, pp. 49–68.

———, *Price Flexibility and Employment*, Bloomington, Ind., 1945.

Lavington, F., *The English Capital Market*, London, 1921.

Leontief, W. W., "The Fundamental Assumption of Mr. Keynes' Monetary Theory of Unemployment," *Quarterly Journal of Economics*, LI (1936–37), 192–97.

———, "Interrelation of Prices, Output, Savings, and Investment," *Review of Economic Statistics*, XIX (1937), 109–32.

———, "Postulates: Keynes' *General Theory* and the Classicists," *The New Economics*, ed. S. E. Harris, New York, 1948, pp. 232–42.

———, "The Consistency of the Classical Theory of Money and Prices," *Econometrica*, XVIII (1950), 21–24.

———, *The Structure of American Economy, 1919–39*, second ed., enlarged, New York, 1951.

Leser, C. E. V., "The Consumer's Demand for Money," *Econometrica*, XI (1943), 123–40.

Lindahl, E., *Studies in the Theory of Money and Capital*, London, 1939.

Lundberg, E., *Studies in the Theory of Economic Expansion*, Stockholm, 1937.

McCulloch, J. R., *The Principles of Political Economy*, fourth ed., Edinburgh, 1849.

McKean, R. N., "Liquidity and a National Balance Sheet," *Journal of Political Economy*, LVII (1949), as reprinted in *Readings in Monetary Theory*, ed. F. A. Lutz and L. W. Mints, Philadelphia, 1951, pp. 63–88.

Malthus, T. R., *Principles of Political Economy*, first ed., as abridged in Ricardo, *Works*, ed. Sraffa, Vol. II; second ed., reprinted Tokyo, 1936.

Marget, A. W., "Léon Walras and the 'Cash Balance Approach' to the Problem of the Value of Money," *Journal of Political Economy*, XXXIX (1931), 569–600.

———, "Monetary Aspects of the Walrasian System," *Journal of Political Economy*, XLIII (1935), 145–86.

———, *The Theory of Prices*, New York: Vol. I, 1938; Vol. II, 1942.

Marschak, J., "Money Illusion and Demand Analysis," *Review of Economic Statistics*, XXV (1943), 40–48.

Marshall, A., *Pure Theory of Foreign Trade*, reprinted London, 1930.

———, *Pure Theory of Domestic Values*, reprinted London, 1930.

———, *Principles of Economics*, eighth ed., London, 1920.

———, *Money Credit and Commerce*, London, 1923.

———, *Official Papers*, London, 1926

Marshall, A., and M. P., *Economics of Industry* (1881), excerpt as reprinted in *Readings in Business Cycles and National Income*, ed. A. H. Hansen and R. V. Clemence, New York, 1953, pp. 96–103.

Marx, K., *Capital*, trans. S. Moore and E. Aveling, 3 vols., Chicago, 1906–9.

Metzler, L. A., "Business Cycles and the Modern Theory of Employment," *American Economic Review*, XXXVI (1946), 278–91.

———, "Wealth, Saving, and the Rate of Interest," *Journal of Political Economy*, LIX (1951), 93–116.

Mill, J., *Elements of Political Economy*, London, 1821.

Mill, J. S., *Essays on Some Unsettled Questions of Political Economy* (1844), reprinted London, 1948.

———, *Principles of Political Economy*, ed. W. J. Ashley, London, 1909.

Mints, L. W., *A History of Banking Theory*, Chicago, 1945.

———, *Monetary Policy for a Competitive Society*, New York, 1950.

Mises, L. von, *The Theory of Money and Credit*, trans. H. E. Batson, New York, 1935.

Modigliani, F., "Liquidity Preference and the Theory of Interest and Money," *Econometrica*, XII (1944), as reprinted in *Readings in Monetary Theory*, ed. F. A. Lutz and L. W. Mints, Philadelphia, 1951, pp. 186–239.

Montesquieu, de, *The Spirit of the Laws*, trans. T. Nugent, 2 vols. in 1, New York, 1949.

Moore, H L., *Synthetic Economics*, New York, 1929.

Myrdal, G., *Monetary Equilibrium*, London, 1939.

Neumann, J. von, "A Model of General Economic Equilibrium," *Review of Economic Studies*, XIII (1945–46), 1–9.

Newcomb, S., *Principles of Political Economy*, New York, 1885.

Nicholson, J. S., *A Treatise on Money*, London, 1888.

———, *Principles of Political Economy*, London: Vol. I, 1893; Vol. II, 1897; Vol. III, 1901.

Ohlin, B., *Interregional and International Trade*, Cambridge, Mass., 1933.

———, "Alternative Theories of the Rate of Interest," *Economic Journal*, XLVII (1937), 423–27.

Osorio, A., *Théorie mathématique de l'échange*, trans. J. D'Almada, Paris, 1913.

Palgrave, R. H. I., *Bank Rate in England, France, and Germany, 1844–78*, London, 1880.

Palgrave's Dictionary of Political Economy, new ed., London, 1923, article "Interest, Theory of."

Pantaleoni, M., *Pure Economics*, trans. T. B. Bruce, London, 1898.

Pareto, V., *Cours d'économie politique*, 2 vols., Lausanne, 1896–97.

——, *Manuel d'économie politique*, second ed., Paris, 1927.

Patinkin, D., "Relative Prices, Say's Law, and the Demand for Money," *Econometrica*, XVI (1948), 135–54.

——, "Price Flexibility and Full Employment," *American Economic Review*, XXXVIII (1948), 543–64; *ibid.*, XXXIX (1949), 726–28; reprinted with revisions in *Readings in Monetary Theory*, ed. F. A. Lutz and L. W. Mints, Philadelphia, 1951, pp. 252–83.

——, "The Indeterminacy of Absolute Prices in Classical Economic Theory," *Econometrica*, XVII (1949), 1–27.

——, "Involuntary Unemployment and the Keynesian Supply Function," *Economic Journal*, LIX (1949), 360–83.

——, "The Invalidity of Classical Monetary Theory," *Econometrica*, XIX (1951), 134–51.

——, "A Reconsideration of the General Equilibrium Theory of Money," *Review of Economic Studies*, XVIII (1950–51), 42–61.

——, "Further Considerations of the General Equilibrium Theory of Money," *Review of Economic Studies*, XIX (1951–52), 186–95.

——, "The Limitations of Samuelson's 'Correspondence Principle,'" *Metroeconomica*, IV (1952), 37–43.

——, "Wicksell's Cumulative Process," *Economic Journal*, LXII (1952), 835–47.

——, "Dichotomies of the Pricing Process in Economic Theory," *Economica*, XXI (1954), 113–28.

——, "Keynesian Economics and the Quantity Theory," *Post Keynesian Economics*, ed. K. K. Kurihara, New Brunswick, N.J., 1954, pp. 123–52.

——, "Monetary and Price Developments in Israel: 1949–1953," *Scripta Hierosolymitana*, III (1955), 20–52.

Phipps, C. G., "A Note on Patinkin's 'Relative Prices,'" *Econometrica*, XVIII (1950), 25–26.

Pigou, A. C., "The Value of Money," *Quarterly Journal of Economics*, XXXII (1917–18), as reprinted in *Readings in Monetary Theory*, ed. F. A. Lutz and L. W. Mints, Philadelphia, 1951, pp. 162–83.

——, "The Exchange Value of Legal Tender Money," *Essays in Applied Economics*, London, 1923, pp. 174–98.

——, *Industrial Fluctuations*, second ed., London, 1929.

——, *Economics of Welfare*, fourth ed., London, 1932.

——, *Economics of Stationary States*, London, 1935.

——, *Employment and Equilibrium*, London, 1941.

——, "The Classical Stationary State," *Economic Journal*, LIII (1943), 343–51.

Pigou, A. C., "Economic Progress in a Stable Environment," *Economica*, XIV (1947), as reprinted in *Readings in Monetary Theory*, ed. F. A. Lutz and L. W. Mints, Philadelphia, 1951, pp. 241–51.

Ricardo, D., *Works and Correspondence*, ed. P. Sraffa, 9 vols., Cambridge, 1951–52.

Robertson, D. H., *Essays in Monetary Theory*, London, 1940.

———, *Money*, revised ed., London, 1948.

———, "More Notes on the Rate of Interest," *Review of Economic Studies*, XXI (1953–54), 136–41.

Rosenstein-Rodan, P N., "The Coördination of the General Theories of Money and Price," *Economica*, III (1936), 257–80.

Samuelson, P. A., "A Note on the Pure Theory of Consumer's Behavior," *Economica*, V (1938), 61–71.

———, *Foundations of Economic Analysis*, Cambridge, Mass., 1947.

———, "The Simple Mathematics of Income Determination," *Income, Employment and Public Policy: Essays in Honor of Alvin H. Hansen*, New York, 1948, pp. 133–55.

———, *Economics: An Introductory Analysis*, second ed., New York, 1951.

———, "Consumption Theorems in Terms of Overcompensation rather than Indifference Comparisons," *Economica*, XX (1953), 1–9.

Say, J. B., *Traité d'économie politique*, third ed., Paris, 1817.

———, *Letters to Malthus* (1821), reprinted London, 1936.

———, *A Treatise on Political Economy*, trans C. R. Prinsep from the fourth French ed., Philadelphia, 1834.

Schlesinger, K., *Theorie der Geld- und Kreditwirtschaft*, Munich, 1914.

———, "Über die Produktionsgleichungen der ökonomischen Wertlehre," *Ergebnisse eines mathematischen Kolloquiums*, VI (1933–34), 10–11.

Schneider, E., *Pricing and Equilibrium*, trans. T. W. Hutchison, London, 1952.

Schumpeter, J. A., *History of Economic Analysis*, New York, 1954.

Scitovski, T. de, "Capital Accumulation, Employment and Price Rigidity," *Review of Economic Studies*, VIII (1940–41), 69–88.

Shackle, G. L. S., "Interest Rates and the Pace of Investment," *Economic Journal*, LVI (1946), 1–17.

Shaw, E. S., *Money, Income, and Monetary Policy*, Chicago, 1950.

Sidgwick, H., *The Principles of Political Economy*, London, 1883.

Simons, H. C., *Economic Policy for a Free Society*, Chicago, 1948.

Stein, Herbert, "Price Flexibility and Full Employment: Comment," *American Economic Review*, XXXIX (1949), 725–26.

Stigler, G. J., *Production and Distribution Theories*, New York, 1941.

———, *Theory of Price*, revised ed., New York, 1952.

———, "Sraffa's *Ricardo*," *American Economic Review*, XLIII (1953), 586–99.

Taussig, F. W., *Principles of Economics*, 2 vols., fourth ed., revised, New York, 1939.

Thornton, H., *An Enquiry into the Nature and Effects of the Paper Credit of Great Britain*, London, 1802.

Tinbergen, J., *Econometrics*, Philadelphia, 1951.

Tobin, J., "Asset Holdings and Spending Decisions," "Papers and Proceedings," *American Economic Review*, XLII (1952), 109–23.

United Nations Department of Economic Affairs, *Inflationary and Deflationary Tendencies, 1946–48*, New York, 1949.

Viner, J., *Studies in the Theory of International Trade*, New York, 1937.

Wald, A., "Uber die eindeutige positive Lösbarkeit der neuen Produktionsgleichungen," *Ergebnisse eines mathematischen Kolloquiums*, VI (1933–34), 12–20.

———, "On Some Systems of Equations of Mathematical Economics," *Econometrica*, XIX (1951), 368–403.

Walras, L., *Eléments d'économie politique pure*, Lausanne: first ed., 1874–77; second ed., 1889; third ed., 1896; fourth ed., 1900; definitive ed., 1926.

———, *Théorie de la monnaie*, Paris, 1886.

———, *Etudes d'économie politique appliquée*, Paris, 1898.

———, "Equations de la circulation," *Bulletin de la Société Vaudoise des Sciences Naturelles*, XXXV (1899), 85–103.

———, *Elements of Pure Economics*, trans. and ed. W. Jaffé, London, 1954.

Weinberger, O., *Mathematische Volkswirtschaftslehre*, Leipzig, 1930.

Wicksell, K., *Value Capital and Rent*, trans. S. H. Frowein, London, 1954.

———, *Interest and Prices*, trans. R. F. Kahn, London, 1936.

———, *Lectures on Political Economy* (Vol. I, *General Theory*; Vol. II, *Money*), trans. E. Classen, London, 1934–35

———, "The Influence of the Rate of Interest on Prices," *Economic Journal*, XVII (1907), 213–19.

Wilson, E. B., "Notes on Utility Theory and Demand Equations," *Quarterly Journal of Economics*, LX (1945–46), 453–60.

INDEX OF NAMES

(The symbol "n." after page numbers refers to the footnotes on those pages.)

INDEX OF SUBJECTS[1]

(The symbol "n." after page numbers refers to the footnotes on those pages.)

---

[1]Discussions in the Mathematical Appendix and Supplementary Notes to which cross-references are given in the text are for the most part not listed again in this Index.

Brownian motion, 331
Budget, balanced; *see* Balanced budget
Budget restraint
in barter economy, 10
and demand curve for money, 146–148
distinct from Walras' Law, 34
in economy with bonds, 55, 78
graphical representation of, 69–70
in money economy, 25–26, 29
and voluntariness, 212
Business cycles, 126

Cambridge equation; *see* $M=KPT$
Cambridge K; *see* K
Capital gains and losses, 84, 132, 173, 206–7
Capital market, imperfections of, 53, 140, 392 n.
Cash-balance approach; *see* Quantity theory, cash-balance approach
CC curve
defined, 155–56
relationship to LL curve, 179
when identical with BB curve, 188–89
Central bank, 205, 206 n., 233, 235
Certainty; *see* Expectations, certain
"*Ceteris paribus* experiment," 15 n.
Characteristic equation, 354, 366
"Circularity charge," 62–63, 71–72
"*Circulation à desservir*," 387
Coercion; *see* Involuntariness
Collection, initial; *see* Endowment, initial
Collection, optimum
defined, 10, 46
Commercial crisis, 252
"Commercial paper" theory, 210

Commodities
aggregate demand function for, 130–34
aggregate supply function for, 134–136
defined, 16
excess-demand function for
in barter economy, 13
deduced from revealed preferences, 71, 79–80
deduced from utility maximization, 66–71, 74–79
in money economy, 19–22
in multi-period economy, 50–52
market for, 130–37
Comparative statics, 32, 58, 158, 177, 179; *see also* "Correspondence principle"
Comparative statics, pseudo, 225, 242, 246
Competition, perfect; *see* Perfect competition
Computor
individual as, 11
market as, 36
Confidence, 259
Consumers' sovereignty, 240
Consumption function
form of, 130
in Keynesian economics, 163
and real balances, 22 n., 163
Consumption loans, 61, 137
Consumption stream, 48, 77, 80
Contracyclical policy, 237
Controls, on wages and prices, 191
"Correspondence principle"
application of, 355–56, 359, 362, 364
graphical meaning of, 358–59
limitations of, 355–56, 359, 365
theorem on, 353–54
Cost effect, 142
Cost-of-production theory, 421

Crisis, commercial, 252
"Cumulative process," Wicksell's, 164, 258–59, 425–33

Default, 17, 20, 88
Deflationary gap, 167, 214
"Degrees of freedom," 180
Demand
  defined, 10
  difference from ordinary usage, 10 n., 14 n.
Demand curve
  relation to excess-demand curve, 12
  and voluntariness, 212
Demand curve, Marshallian, 24 n., 181–82, 276, 291, 304 n., 442
Demand deposits, 203–4
Demand price, Marshallian; *see* Demand curve, Marshallian
Dependent equation, 35, 58, 120
  elimination of, 35, 301
Dependent variables, 15, 32, 183, 275–79, 423
  money supply as, 209–10
  "real" and "monetary," 105
Depression economics, 367
Derivatives
  ambiguity in meaning of, 279, 285
  implicit differentiation, 281–85
  nature of, 275–79
  notation for, 279, 346–47
"Diagonal-cross" diagram, 221–22, 237
  and multiplier, 237
  and Say's Identity, 249–50
Dichotomization
  of effects, 110
  of markets, 107, 110
Dichotomy of pricing process
  invalid form of; *see* Invalid dichotomy
  valid forms of, 39, 105–6, 109–10

Differential, total, 282, 288
Differentiation, implicit, 281–85
Dimensions, time; *see* Time dimensions
Discounting of future, 76; *see also* Time preference
Disequilibrium
  and dynamic analysis, 157
  and unemployment theory, 220, 224, 235–36
Disinflation, 210
Disposable income, 132
Distribution effects
  assumed absent, 125–26, 132
  and government bonds, 207–8
  implications of, 200–203
  neutral, 58
  and unemployment, 234
Dynamic analysis, 32, 36, 40–41, 152–62, 178–79, 188–89, 208–10, 227–28, 233, 383–84
  and comparative statics, 202 n.
  deficiencies of in classical monetary theory, 376
  deficiencies of in neoclassical monetary theory, 100–102
  oversimplified assumptions of, 157–158
  and unemployment, 220, 222–23, 224, 234–36
  see also "Correspondence principle"

Elasticity of demand
  for money, 28–30
  and money illusion, 24
  see also Unitary elasticity of demand for money
Elimination of dependent equation, 35, 301
Employment policy, Keynesian, 233–234, 236–37

Price level, absolute, *continued*
  and shifts in liquidity preference,
    115–17, 164–71, 176
  and supply of bonds, 142, 192
  and supply of commodities, 135–
    136
  see also Money prices
Prices, "accounting," "money," and
    "relative"
  defined, 18–19
  see also Accounting prices, Money
    prices, Relative prices, *and*
    Price level, absolute
"*Prix criés*," 36
Probability distribution, 90–94
Production economy, defined, 60
Production function
  and commodity supply function,
    134–35, 216 n.
  and labor demand function, 127–28,
    216 n.
Profit maximization, 128, 130, 135,
    216
"Pump-priming," 244
"Pure credit economy," 86, 121, 431

Quantity equations; *see* Monetary
    equations, neoclassical
Quantity theory
  causal mechanism of, 98
  distinct from quantity equations,
    99
  and expectations and uncertainty,
    180–81
  mechanism in earlier literature, 98,
    375–76
  and non-uniform changes in
    quantity of money, 41
  and speculative motive, 180, 466 n.
  tripartite statement of, 97–98
  validity of, 39–41, 56–59, 99–100,
    158–64, 180–81

Quantity theory, cash-balance ap-
    proach, 1, 21, 97, 304
  distinct from cash-balance equation,
    97 n., 392–93
  dynamic (stability) analysis in, 100–
    101, 376
  more mechanical than transactions
    approach, 100–101
  and unitary elasticity of demand for
    money (rectangular hyperbola),
    103–4
  and utility of money, 63, 413
  see also $M=KPT$
Quantity theory, transactions ap-
    proach, 1, 97; *see also* $MV=PT$

Rate of interest; *see* Interest, rate of
Real-balance effect
  analogous to distribution effect,
    202–3
  and destabilizing expectations, 209
  in more realistic economies, 206 n.
Real-balance effect in bond market,
    20 n., 22 n., 53, 109–10, 138,
    140–41, 163, 173–74, 202
Real-balance effect in commodity
    markets
  and absolute price level, 113
  and consumption function, 130, 133
  defined, 21
  equivalence to "Pigou effect," 21 n.
  and investment function, 130, 133
  not fully understood, 102, 104, 112–
    113
  obverse side of, 89
  overlooked in Keynesian theory,
    109–10, 163, 221
  role in monetary theory, 22, 38,
    109 n., 159, 163–64, 465
  secular significance of, 253–54
  and unemployment, 221
  and wage and price rigidities, 191